IMPORTANT:

HERE IS YOUR REGISTRATION CODE TO ACCESS YOUR PREMIUM McGRAW-HILL ONLINE RESOURCES.

MCGRAW-HILL
ONLINE RESOURCES

REGISTRATION CODE

CPD7-FGM4-VEPY-3PT4-834J

For key premium online resources you need THIS CODE to gain access. Once the code is entered, you will be able to use the Web resources for the length of your course.

If your course is using **WebCT** or **Blackboard**, you'll be able to use this code to access the McGraw-Hill content within your instructor's online course.

Access is provided if you have purchased a new book. If the registration code is missing from this book, the registration screen on our Website, and within your WebCT or Blackboard course, will tell you how to obtain your new code.

Registering for McGraw-Hill Online Resources

To gain access to your McGraw-Hill web resources simply follow the steps below:

1. USE YOUR WEB BROWSER TO GO TO: **www.mhhe.com/nelson5e**
2. CLICK ON **FIRST TIME USER**.
3. ENTER THE REGISTRATION CODE* PRINTED ON THE TEAR-OFF BOOKMARK ON THE RIGHT.
4. AFTER YOU HAVE ENTERED YOUR REGISTRATION CODE, CLICK **REGISTER**.
5. FOLLOW THE INSTRUCTIONS TO SET-UP YOUR PERSONAL UserID AND PASSWORD.
6. WRITE YOUR UserID AND PASSWORD DOWN FOR FUTURE REFERENCE. KEEP IT IN A SAFE PLACE.

TO GAIN ACCESS to the McGraw-Hill content in your instructor's **WebCT** or **Blackboard** course simply log in to the course with the UserID and Password provided by your instructor. Enter the registration code exactly as it appears in the box to the right when prompted by the system. You will only need to use the code the first time you click on McGraw-Hill content.

Thank you, and welcome to your McGraw-Hill online Resources!

Mc Graw Hill Higher Education

* YOUR REGISTRATION CODE CAN BE USED ONLY ONCE TO ESTABLISH ACCESS. IT IS NOT TRANSFERABLE.

0-07-292352-0 T/A NELSON: CRITICAL ISSUES IN EDUCATION, 5/E

Critical Issues in Education

Dialogues and Dialectics

FIFTH EDITION

Jack L. Nelson
Rutgers University

Stuart B. Palonsky
University of Missouri

Mary Rose McCarthy
Pace University

FOREWORD BY

Nel Noddings
Stanford University; Teachers College, Columbia University

Boston Burr Ridge, IL Dubuque, IA Madison, WI New York
San Francisco St. Louis Bangkok Bogotá Caracas Kuala Lumpur
Lisbon London Madrid Mexico City Milan Montreal New Delhi
Santiago Seoul Singapore Sydney Taipei Toronto

CRITICAL ISSUES IN EDUCATION: DIALOGUES AND DIALECTICS,
FIFTH EDITION

Published by McGraw-Hill, a business unit of The McGraw-Hill Companies, Inc., 1221 Avenue of the Americas, New York, NY 10020.

This book is printed on acid-free paper.

3 4 5 6 7 8 9 0 DOC/DOC 0 9 8 7 6 5 4

ISBN 0-07-255511-4

Vice president and editor-in-chief: *Thalia Dorwick*
Developmental editor: *Cara Harvey*
Senior marketing manager: *Pamela S. Cooper*
Senior project manager: *Marilyn Rothenberger*
Production supervisor: *Enboge Chong*
Media technology producer: *Lance Gerhart*
Associate designer: *George Kokkonas*
Cover/interior designer: *JoAnne Schopler*
Cover illustration: *Stephen Schildbach Images.com/CORBIS*
Cover image: *Students*
Associate art editor: *Cristin Yancey*
Senior supplement producer: *David A. Welsh*
Compositor: *Precision Graphics*
Typeface: *10/12 Palatino*
Printer: *R. R. Donnelley/Crawfordsville, IN*

Library of Congress Cataloging-in-Publication Data

Nelson, Jack L.
Critical issues in education : dialogues and dialectics / Jack L. Nelson, Stuart B. Palonsky, Mary Rose McCarthy; foreword Nel Noddings.— 5th ed.
p. cm.
Includes bibliographical references and index.
ISBN 0-07-255511-4 (alk. paper)
1. Education—United States. 2. Teaching—United States. 3. Educational evaluation—United States. 4. Critical thinking—United States. I. Palonsky, Stuart B. II. Mary Rose McCarthy. III. Title.
LA217.2N45 2004
370'.973—dc21 2003046397

www.mhhe.com

About the Authors

JACK L. NELSON is Professor of Education Emeritus of Rutgers University, where he served for thirty years achieving Rutgers rank equivalent to Distinguished Professor. He has a doctorate from the University of Southern California, an M.A. from CSU–Los Angeles, and a B.A. from the University of Denver. Jack's teaching experience includes elementary, secondary, undergraduate, and graduate levels; his university experience in addition to Rutgers includes CSU–Los Angeles, San Jose State University, SUNY–Buffalo, and Cambridge University—and he has been a visiting scholar at the University of California–Berkeley, Stanford University, Colgate University, University of Colorado, University of Washington, CUNY, and, in Australia, at Curtin University and Edith Cowan University–Perth, and the University of Sydney. *Critical Issues in Education* is his seventeenth book; he also has published over 175 chapters, articles, and reviews. Jack has received awards from the American Association of University Professors, and was the 2001 recipient of the National Council for Social Studies Academic Freedom Award. He is listed in *Who's Who in America* and *Contemporary Authors.*

STUART B. PALONSKY is professor of education and Director of the Honors College at the University of Missouri–Columbia. A former public school teacher in New York and New Jersey, Palonsky graduated from the State University of New York at Oneonta and Michigan State University. His publications include the book *900 Shows a Year,* an ethnographic account of high school teaching from a classroom teacher's perspective. In addition, Stu has published numerous articles and reviews in education and social science journals, and has presented research papers on education issues at national and state conferences. For ten years, Palonsky and Nelson were colleagues at Rutgers University. Nelson was the more prolific scholar; Palonsky the better tennis player.

MARY ROSE MCCARTHY is Assistant Professor of Education at Pace University. She earned her Ph.D. in the social foundations of education at the State University of New York at Buffalo with a concentration in the history of education. She earned her M.A. at the University of Rochester. Mary Rose has been a secondary school teacher and administrator, and also has worked as the director of a work cooperative for guests at a Catholic Worker House of Hospitality. She served as a family life educator, working with parents whose children were at risk of being placed in foster care. Mary Rose has been an activist for social change for over thirty years and that commitment is reflected in her current research in educational policy issues and the ways teacher education programs address issues of social justice. She has presented at national conferences of scholarly organizations including the American Educational Research Association, American Studies Association, History of Education Society, American Educational Studies Association, and National Women's Studies Association. Mary Rose has written on Catholic high schools for women, gender issues including breast cancer and religion, writing educational history, and urban education. She currently teaches graduate and undergraduate courses in the foundations of education and in instructional methods.

Brief Table of Contents

Part Two
WHAT SHOULD BE TAUGHT? KNOWLEDGE AND LITERACY

Part Three
HOW SHOULD SCHOOLS BE ORGANIZED AND OPERATED? SCHOOL ENVIRONMENT

Contents

Part Two
WHAT SHOULD BE TAUGHT? KNOWLEDGE AND LITERACY

Foreword

This fifth edition of *Critical Issues in Education* is especially welcome in the wake of September 11th and worldwide acts of terrorism. Decent people everywhere recognize something must be done to combat terrorism, but many of us have doubts about the efficacy of violent retaliation. One act of violence seems to lead relentlessly to another. Still more of us worry about the trend toward censuring (or even censoring) speech that raises questions about the actions of our own government. It is alarming, too, that some of our citizens have expressed willingness to sacrifice constitutional rights such as free speech, privacy, and speedy trial by an impartial jury in the interests of safety. We are understandably afraid. But if we voluntarily give up our rights, one great battle against terrorism will be lost. No doubt, strong arguments could be brought against the position I have just taken, and so readers have encountered a critical issue even before starting the actual text.

Critical issues require critical thinking and vice versa. Obviously, critical issues are best addressed by well-informed logical arguments, but it is not always recognized that critical thinking develops best as it is applied to critical issues. Too many educators would like to teach critical-thinking skills without getting involved in critical issues. They assume these skills can be taught in the abstract—perhaps with a focus on the rules of logic. As a teacher of mathematics and philosophy, I believe knowing the rules of logic helps us to make sound arguments, but it cannot obviate the need to grapple with real issues, and it certainly cannot provide the motivation that arises naturally when issues are passionately contested. Thus, it seems illusionary to suppose we can avoid critical issues and still teach critical thinking.

We must learn to talk to one another without descending into violence. This may be the toughest and most important problem facing humankind, and we have not made much progress despite being aware of the problem for centuries. I used to think (and I still do, but to a smaller degree) that violence is largely a problem of masculinity, but I've begun to see that women often have bought peace by a process of repression. We say to husbands and sons, "Now don't bring up politics with Uncle Ed or taxes with Grandpa or religion with Aunt

Lillian or . . ." and we counsel this avoidance in the hope of a "nice visit" or a "quiet dinner." The advice still seems wise, if our main aim is a nice visit or a quiet dinner. But how will we learn to discuss difficult issues with strangers if we cannot do it even with those well known to us?

In my Foreword to the fourth edition, I recommended that people open conversations with opponents by discussing noncontroversial topics. John Dewey also made this recommendation, and I still endorse it. However, we can't stay at that level and hope to resolve our differences. My hope was (and is) that when dialogue has produced at least the beginnings of a caring relation—one in which it is unthinkable to do real harm to the other—it should be safe to address the issues that separate us. But if we cannot broach issues of race, religion, money, or politics with loved ones and classmates, where will we learn the necessary skills?

Nelson, Palonsky, and McCarthy have given us an opportunity to learn these skills through a book filled with controversial issues in education. The issues are real, the topics "hot," and the presentation lively. Both teachers and students should be motivated to go beyond the text to gather the very latest information on each issue. Because the issues presented here are real and timely, their status can change rapidly, and readers should watch for recent developments.

In rereading *Critical Issues in Education,* I was reminded forcefully of a phenomenon in today's education that troubles me greatly. Educators are not engaging in aims-talk; we are not asking the great "why" questions. More than thirty years ago, this same phenomenon worried Charles Silberman when he wrote about the "mindlessness" of schooling. Carefully documenting his claims about curriculum and classroom teaching, he said, "It is rare to find anyone—teacher, principal, supervisor, or superintendent—who has asked why he is teaching what he is teaching" (1970, pp. 172–173). Today one can make an even sadder comment. The "why" question has been answered mindlessly: "Because it's on the standard test." My hope is that readers of this book will learn the habit of asking why and come up with more adequate answers not only to questions about curriculum and teaching but also to those of larger policy issues.

I'll close this brief, but enthusiastic, Foreword by drawing readers' attention to one of the most crucial of the critical issues discussed here—the privatization of schooling. Is education a public good, as many of us have long supposed, or is it better thought of as a consumer good? A consumer good is one valued by, and of benefit to, the one who selects and purchases it. My acquisition of a consumer good yields no direct benefit to the public. Such goods are offered at a range of prices, and the public is not generally concerned about the goods available to particular segments of the population unless something vital (for example, food) is entirely unobtainable for them. Then compassion or self-interest (fear of reprisal or revolution) triggers public concern.

What is a public good? The very definition of "public good" is a controversial issues (Anton, Fisk, & Holmstrom, 2000). If we define it, as some economists do, as a good that cannot be privatized (for example, the light beam from a lighthouse) or as one that can only be provided by government (national defense, for example), then education is not a public good, because it clearly can be provided by private groups and can be restricted (as the light from the lighthouse cannot be) to those who can afford it. But if we define a public good as one that benefits all of society when acquired by any of its members (and the more who acquire it, the greater the collective benefit), then education is clearly a public good (Noddings, 2001). The question then becomes whether a public good, so defined, can best be distributed, managed, and evaluated by private organizations. Thus we have, in the question of privatization, not one but several controversial questions.

As you read this book, be ready to think and speak up, but be gentle with your opponents.

Nel Noddings

References

ANTON, A., FISK, M., AND HOLMSTROM, N., EDS. (2000). *Not for Sale: In Defense of Public Goods.* Boulder: Westview Press.

NODDINGS, N. (2001). "Public Schooling, Democracy, and Religious Dissent." In R. Soder, J. Goodlad, and T. McMannon, eds. *Developing Democratic Character in the Young.* San Francisco: Jossey-Bass.

SILBERMAN, C. (1970). *Crisis in the Classroom.* New York: Random House.

Preface

We are delighted to welcome you to this fifth edition of original essays covering the great debates about schools in society. And it is a special pleasure to introduce our new coauthor, Mary Rose McCarthy, who brings rich and vital perspectives to this edition.

School and Controversies

Persistent school issues reflect basic human disagreements. Ideological differences in politics, economics, and social values undergird the battles over schools. The issues and competing ideologies deserve critical examination. It is informative to study schooling by reading newspaper or magazine reports of test scores, finance, and school activities. But the media often ignore or gloss over basic social or ideological conflicts and can sterilize issues by presenting only one view; few media provide alternative views of an issue. The implication that there is one correct view obscures historical, political, and social contexts surrounding school controversies.

On the one hand, the public views American education as being in deep trouble and getting worse; on the other hand, they view their local schools as remarkably good, with excellent teachers and high-quality programs. If we had a third hand, we could add another view. New views emerge as debates over education stimulate us to rethink our positions.

Schools, at the beginning of the twenty-first century, are still among the most important and most controversial social institutions. For over three hundred years, people on this continent have agreed on the importance of education, but have disagreed over how it should be controlled, financed, organized, conducted, and evaluated. Two centuries ago, a very young United States was debating the establishment of free and compulsory education, arguing over who should be educated, who should pay, and what should be taught. We have mass education now, but some of these same arguments continue about schools. Of course, controversies about important issues are inevitable and, we argue, healthy in a democratic society.

A century ago John Dewey published "My Pedagogic Creed," calling the school the "fundamental" means for progress and reform of society. His book, *School and Society,* published in 1900, laid out some basic social premises for progressive education. Those progressive premises remain under attack in the first decade of the twenty-first century. Social reformer Jane Addams, speaking at the National Education Association meeting of 1897, noted the social purposes of education and the need for schools to provide improved education to "foreign-born children," a precursor to current battles over multicultural education. Susan B. Anthony, cofounder of the National Womans Suffrage Association, argued, also in 1897, that schools then closed to women should open their doors to equality. Race, class, and gender discrimination remain educational issues more than a century later. Many other school controversies have arisen over the course of time, but pervasive issues survive, often different in patterns and details.

Our effort, in this book, is to explore a collection of pervasive and critical school issues by providing divergent views on each. The issues presented are dynamic. By presenting them in the form of opposing essays, we intend to show how provocative and complex they are. That does not mean they are unsolvable problems; it does suggest that good solutions rely on engaged and informed debate. We see the terrain of education as rugged and rocky, with few clear paths and many conflicting road signs.

For this edition, we completely revised and updated all chapters and we have replaced some topics that appeared in older editions with new chapters on current educational issues debates: equity and a gap in academic achievement, standards-based schooling, technology, and religion–church/state and education.

Organization of the Book

The introductory chapter presents a background and a process for examining reform efforts and debates in education.

The three following sections are each devoted to a major question about schooling and are introduced with background material to provide a thematic context:

Part One: Whose Interests Should Schools Serve? Theme: Justice and Equity

Part Two: What Should Be Taught? Theme: Knowledge and Literacy

Part Three: How Should Schools Be Organized and Operated? Theme: School Environment

Each part contains chapters on specific critical issues, and each chapter contains two essays expressing divergent positions on that issue. Obviously, these do not exhaust all the possible positions; they do provide at least two views on the issue, and references are provided in each chapter to encourage further exploration. At the end of each chapter are a few questions to consider and a brief sample of related data.

The three coauthors each took primary responsibility for writing different parts of this volume. For Jack Nelson this includes Introductions to Part One and Part Two and Chapters 1, 8, 9, 12, 13, 16, and 18. For Stu Palonsky it includes Introduction to Part Three and Chapters 6, 10, 11, 14, 15, 17, and 19. And for Mary Rose McCarthy it includes Chapters 2, 3, 4, 5, and 7.

Acknowledgments

We thank Nel Noddings of Stanford University and Teachers College, Columbia, for her provocative and insightful Foreword.

We also want to thank colleagues and reviewers who made many suggestions for this revision. We received particularly valuable suggestions from a variety of faculty members and students who have used this book in one or more of its four previous editions. Thanks to them for their important contributions.

We owe great intellectual debts to a long list of scholars, writers, teachers, and others who examine the relation of education to society, and who express divergent ideas in the extensive literature available. That group includes a variety of educational and social theorists and critics, as well as a corps of school practitioners who live the life of schools. We also are indebted to students, colleagues, and others who provided specific criticism and assistance as we worked through the various topics. In particular, we express appreciation to Terri Wise, our primary editor at McGraw-Hill; Beth Kaufman, the McGraw-Hill education editor; Marilyn Rothenberger, our project manager; Cara Harvey, development editor; and to Gwen, Nancy, and Cornelia for support, enthusiasm, and criticism when needed.

We especially appreciate the contributions of many colleagues who reviewed the manuscript, criticized the work in progress, or provided provocative ideas to challenge us. Among these are John B. Aston, Southwest Texas State University; Pat Benne, Wittenberg University; David Blacker, University of Delaware; Deron R. Boyles, Georgia State University; Wade A. Carpenter, Berry College; Mark Caruana, attorney, Carlsbad, CA; David Cauble, Western Nebraska Community College; Cathryn A. Chappell, University of Akron; Eleanor Cohen, editorial and technological consultant, Vista, California; Diane Crews, Binghamton University; Warren Crown, Rutgers University; James Daly, Seton Hall University; Emily de la Cruz, Portland State University; Russell Dennis, Bucknell University; Xu Di, University of West Florida; Annette Digby, University of Arkansas; Gloria Earl, Indiana Wesleyan University; Herbert Edwards, attorney, Harbor Springs, Michigan; Paul Edwards, attorney, Colorado Springs, Colorado; Dean Kenneth Eltis, University of Sydney, Australia; William and Sheila Fernekes, Hunterdon, New Jersey, Central High School; Mark Garrison, D'Youville College; William Gaudelli III, Central Florida University; Karen Graves, Denison University; Harry D. Hall, Indiana Wesleyan University; Julia O. Harper, Azusa Pacific University; Sharon Hobbs, Montana State University; Tony W. Johnson, West Chester University; Ramon Khalona, Engineer and Technological Consultant, Carlsbad, CA; Kevin Laws, University of Sydney, Australia; Becky Lewis, University of Buffalo; Stephen Earl Lucas, The University of Illinois at Urbana–Champaign; Chogallah

Maroufi, California State University at Los Angeles; Gary E. Martin, Northern Arizona University; Joseph McCarthy, Suffolk University; Barbara Bredefeld Meyer, Illinois State University; Wally Moroz, Edith Cowan University, Perth, Australia; John D. Napier, University of Georgia; Nel Noddings, Stanford University; Julie R. Palmour, Piedmont College; Valerie Pang, San Diego State University; Maike Philipsen, Virginia Commonwealth University; Ken Phillipson, computer programmer, Melbourne, Australia; Bonnie Rose, Riverside City Schools, California; Dawn Shinew, Washington State University; Barbara R. Sjostrom, Rowan University; Leslie Soodak, Pace University; William Stanley, Monmouth University; Susan Talburt, Georgia State Virginia Commonwealth University; Ronald K. Templeton, The Citadel; Doris Terr, City Schools of New York; David Tyack, Stanford University; Atilano Valencia, California State University, Fresno; Dorothy Watson, University of Missouri; and Burt Weltman, William Paterson College.

We dedicate this effort to Megan, Jordan, Jonathan, Barbara, Mark, Steven, Robert, Mary Catherine and others of the generation of students and teachers who will be at the core of critical education debates in this twenty-first century.

Mary Rose McCarthy

Stuart Palonsky

Jack Nelson

SPECIAL PREFACE BY JACK NELSON AND STUART PALONSKY

Introducing Mary Rose McCarthy

Earlier editions of *Critical Issues in Education* included Ken Carlson as our coauthor. Unfortunately, Ken is unable to continue in this work, and we miss his important and insightful contributions as well as his critical judgment. We are especially fortunate, however, that Mary Rose McCarthy, a professor in educational foundations and history at Pace University, has agreed to join us as coauthor for this fifth edition.

Mary Rose has a set of educational and life experiences that differ significantly from ours. She served as a teacher and as an assistant principal in a Catholic girls' school, and was moderator of the Black Students' Union. She was a consultant for several years to a large urban school district on gender issues in the curriculum, and was a director of a cooperative urban program involving a soup kitchen and shelter. Her academic background includes a B.A. in philosophy, summa cum laude, from State University of New York, an M.A. from the University of Rochester, and a Ph.D. from State University of New York at Buffalo, where she was honored as a Presidential Fellow. Her dissertation was on the topic of social justice in Catholic schools for girls.

Mary Rose regularly publishes and presents scholarly papers on a variety of educational and social issues including women's studies, feminist pedagogy, cancer care, religion, and the relation of gender to race, class, and culture. She has deep interests and substantial activity in dealing with pertinent social issues, justice, and schooling. Her similar interests in social issues and critical thinking, coupled with her wealth of experience in different educational settings, complement us well in developing a book incorporating divergent viewpoints on significant educational issues.

Our longtime colleague and friend, Rita Silverman, also at Pace University, recommended Mary Rose very highly. After working on this book, we certainly agree with Rita's positive assessment about the breadth and depth of Mary Rose's intellectual interests and talents. We also can attest to her excellent grasp of educational issues, her dependability in good writing and meeting deadlines, and her good humor.

We are particularly pleased that Mary Rose agreed to join us in writing and revising this edition, providing all new chapters for her sections and offering sound criticism on the rest.

Jack and Stu

CHAPTER 1

Introduction: Critical Issues and Critical Thinking

About This Book: We submit that education is among the most controversial of all social topics and, as a corollary, is one of society's most important topics. Chapter 1 suggests critical-thinking processes that assist in reasoning through issues, and deals with various social contexts surrounding educational controversies. Then each of three thematic sections includes a series of chapters on significant and persistent school issues related to that theme. The three major themes have a short introductory statement:

Part One: Whose Interests Should Schools Serve? Theme: Justice and Equity

Part Two: What Should Be Taught? Theme: Knowledge and Literacy

Part Three: How Should Schools Be Organized and Operated? Theme: School Environment

Since controversy requires at least two views, each chapter contains two opposing position essays on each issue. These position essays are all original, written only for this book, and include data, research, and arguments that support that view of the issue.

About This Chapter: All important educational issues are also social issues, with interconnections to politics, economics, policy questions, ideology, and social practice—and certainly to our lives. These critical issues require critical thinking. Schooling issues arise in a context, not a vacuum, and the context includes historic and philosophic background as well as scholarly research that attempts to illuminate the issue. Chapter 1, along with the introductions to each thematic section, provides our view of the main social contexts for these schooling issues. After a brief overview of some pervasive controversies in schooling, we discuss critical-thinking processes that use dialogue and dialectic reasoning in examining educational issues. Then we describe some contexts for the issues, such as democratic vitality, globalization, politics, and patterns of criticism and reform of schools. We conclude with a brief examination of historic and contemporary efforts to reform schools, and the controversial results.

EDUCATION AND SCHOOLING: EDUCATION AS CONTROVERSY

If you like arguments, you will love the study of education. Few topics elicit more disagreement and have as much at stake for our future, but the arguments seldom challenge the value of education itself. Rare is the person who questions the importance of education. As a rule, we support education and want to be educated, but disagree over the proper nature, form, and process of education, not on its fundamental virtues. So we argue about education, and about schools. Education is far more than just what goes on in school; we are educated in many ways in many locations, often without even realizing it. But schools are usually at the center of public arguments about education, since schools are the social organizations that take on the formalized task of educating.

If anything, school debates are so strident because we have such a pervasive agreement on the importance of education. If school were inconsequential, it would not be worthy of intense, long-lived disputes. Education is not a trivial pursuit, a minor activity that can be avoided with impunity. It is necessary for the survival of each person and society.

People express strong opinions about many controversial topics, but schooling is unusual because few such controversial topics have so many personally experienced experts. School is one social institution that virtually all people have experienced for long periods, and most have an opinion about it. Schooling is just one of the avenues to education. Education actually occurs in many settings, including the home, workplace, religious institutions, media, libraries, friendships, coffee shops, or just sitting and thinking. In Colonial America, most people received their education outside of schools (Bailyn, 1960). Some of today's reluctant students might prefer that alternative to their life in school, but that is not an option available to many. For these students, school may even be an impediment to education—it interferes with their learning about life. They become educated, despite school.

For the vast majority, however, much of the most important learning, certainly most of the formal learning occurs in school. Book learning, and now computer learning, has long been a hallmark of schools, and society expects schools to remain that central learning location. There is some expectation that school also will be a place of intellectual development. Intellectual differs from academic learning in its development of skeptical and questioning attitudes and focus on ideas rather than on information (Gella, 1976; Gouldner, 1979; Barber, 1998). Academic learning includes formal study of typical subjects: English, science, history, arts, math, social sciences, languages, and so on.

Intellectual learning includes raising questions, critical thinking, creative interpretation, and being unlimited by subject-field discipline boundaries in the examination of ideas. Some segments of society become concerned when schools heavily engage in intellectual learning. Intellectual concern with ideas and skepticism can lead to examination of controversial topics—a threat to some members of the public.

In addition to academic and intellectual responsibilities of schools, there are also social expectations that schools will take on a responsibility for the ethical, physical, and emotional development of children, as well as for their safety, health, and civility. Mourad (2001) comments, "Organized education has been viewed as a key component and instrument of the just civil state from the time of Plato" (p. 739). Academic, intellectual, practical, moral, and behavioral responsibilities have long been multiple foci of schools. In addition, schools have accepted some responsibility for addressing such social problems as drugs, sexual mores, and lapses in morality. For several decades, we have had proposals for making schools even more the centers of their communities, open all year, seven days a week, early morning to late night and taking on more social responsibilities (Dryfoos, 2002).

The significance of the kinds of responsibilities schools already have is suggested in the strength and intensity of the great debates over schools. Schooling, as a major player in the process of education, is particularly important to society's vitality and the viability of each person. In today's world, those who can't read, write, or calculate adequately bear a heavy burden in daily existence. Those lacking fundamental knowledge and skills suffer social, economic, political, and personal difficulty. The society that does not pay enough attention to schooling also suffers; it is on a downhill slope.

Disputed Terrain of Education

Education has certainly been the focus—some say target—of monologues, dialogue, and opposing views for the whole of our lives and over our social history. That tradition will continue. Media headlines in 2010 and beyond will highlight the debates about schooling; some stories will report that schools are miserable and others that schools are doing well. Student scores on standarized tests will be used to illustrate schooling's declining quality and, at another time, to show how things are improving. Positive and negative stories on student behavior, school finance, and school reform will draw attention to differences of opinion about education and what should be done. News of school faults and gaffes, as well as innovation and reform, will continue. The basic arguments about school, however, are longer lasting and more fundamental than newspaper or TV coverage indicates.

School battles often appear to be disagreements over such issues as which school activities are important and which are frills, and how test scores should be interpreted. But there is a larger war among ideologies that goes beyond specific examples of school issues to entail more basic questions about society and education. This long-lasting war is the school-level reflection of the "culture wars" between right- and left-wing intellectuals that have raged for over two decades (Hunter, 1991; Nolan, 1996; Saunders, 1999). Culture wars are defined as a struggle between those who think we have lost our traditional moral and social compass and those who think we must change society. Culture wars often are argued out between basic religious and secular views of life and the world, but religious and secular fundamentalism are not the only areas of dispute.

Nolan (1996) notes:

> Of all the issues that are likely to generate controversy, no issue hits closer to home than the education and care of children. A cursory glance at many of the most heated issues in the culture wars reveals just how pivotal education is. Multiculturalism, sex education, condom distribution, guns in school, textbook selection, creationism, values clarification—controversies over these issues demonstrate how educational institutions have become a primary focus of the culture wars . . . the battle over the schools then is nothing less than a struggle for the future of America. (p. 37)

Current examples of the school war debates abound. Educational historian Diane Ravitch (2000), a former official of the U.S. Department of Education and a persistent critic of progressive education, writes her version of a history of "America's seemingly permanent debates about school standards, curricula and methods" (pp. 14, 15). Ravitch concludes with a claim that progressive education is responsible for a "century-long effort to diminish the intellectual purposes of the schools" (p. 459). She also calls for a return to "fundamental, time-tested truths" (p. 453). Educational scholar William Wraga (2001), in a review of the Ravitch book, identifies its traditionalist bias and other shortcomings, claiming that "Ravitch's argument is undermined by logical fallacies of oversimplification, slanting, and false dilemma, and by internal inconsistencies and errors of omission" (p. 34). Concluding that Ravitch "masks progressivism's successes and the traditional curriculum's flaws," Wraga also argues that progressives make a stronger case for intellectual development than do traditionalists. So we have arguments about the arguments about school reform. And we have a continuing set of important practical and theoretical questions, within competing ideologies.

Some of the continuing questions about education, schools, and society

- How should we evaluate schools, teachers, curricula, society's support of schools?
- How should we address problems of inequality, racism, sexism, and violence in schools?
- Who should be going to school, for how long, to study what, and for what purposes?
- How should schools be financed, and how well?
- What is the best approach to religion, values, character, and academic subjects for schools?

- How should schools be organized and operated?
- Why do we seem clueless about the best education, when there are plenty of clues and firm opinions about it?

Criticism and reform in education are not new phenomena. We have had educational reform advocates for so long that it is impossible to identify their beginnings. Perhaps the first educational reformer, a member of some prehistoric group, rose up to protest that children were not learning the basic skills, as he had. Another member may have proposed a radical new plan to improve children's hunting-and-gathering skills. Some of the bashed skulls lying about prehistoric sites are probably the results of arguments over education.

A Lack of Answers Amid Lots of Answers: Critical Thinking

Questions about schooling stimulate a variety of potential and often competing answers, but there is no single set of clear and uncontested resolutions. Life would be easier, although less interesting, if we had singular and simple answers to all our problems. But critical social issues are usually too complex to be adequately resolved by easy or absolute solutions. In fact, simple answers often create new problems, or merely cause the problems they were supposed to solve to rise again.

Quick, easy, and absolute resolutions are readily available in contemporary society—radio talk shows, newspaper editorials and responses, websites and chatrooms, and coffee shops are among the places where we can find clear and forceful answers to most of our problems, including educational issues. These answers may well be simple, clear, and forceful—but often will be contradictory, competing, or inconsistent. Significant debates over complicated human issues such as sex, politics, and religion are engaging partly because they usually are not subject to quick and easy resolution. Slogans, however, do not solve critical issues.

Emphatically worded and precise answers to school and social questions are enticing, but a proper skepticism and critical thinking are the friends of wisdom. Critical thinking, the main process and goal of education, involves at least:

- recognition that an important issue deserves considered judgment,
- thoughtful formulation of good questions,
- a search for possible answers and pertinent evidence,
- consideration of alternative views, and
- drawing of tentative conclusions that are acceptable until another question or a better answer arises.

Critical thinking is far more difficult, and significantly more important, than just finding answers (Emerson, Boes, and Mosteller, 2002). The search for knowledge goes well beyond puzzle pages with answers printed upside down at the bottom, quiz items with answers at the end of a book, or reporting back to a teacher what an encyclopedia says.

Rather than present a single answer to each school question, we offer, in these chapters, divergent answers based on different views of what is good. Because schools and schooling are such critical issues for contemporary society, our goal is to provide a framework for examining a number of contemporary school issues, presenting illustrative arguments and evidence that represent some diverse opinions on educational issues.

Dialogue and the Case for Dialectic Reasoning

Arguments easily can dissolve into shouting matches, "Says who?" and "Me, that's who!" levels of dialogue, or even fistfights. Whether arguments are trivial or significant, they can be heated and unthinking. It is easy to recognize the merits of our own position, and we are not always eager to admit the virtues of others. Arguments about important topics, however, should not devolve into shouting, shoving, and personal attack. Knowledge and social improvement depend on rational and civil argument; "Disagreement is a key element of communal deliberations" (Makau and Marty, 2001, p. 7). Active democracy requires it (Gutman and Thompson, 1996; Hess, 2002). Good arguments can be thoughtful and reasoned, a dialogue between two different points of view—or dialectic reasoning with opposing views.

Reasoned dialogue calls for understanding the evidence, the quality of sources, and persuasiveness of the argument for divergent views. This is one way to come to understand competing positions (Audi, 2001; McCabe, 2000). Dialectic reasoning, the examination of opposing ideas to develop a creative and superior idea, is a level beyond dialogue (Sim, 1999; Farrar, 2000; Sciabarra, 2000). These are both practices of critical thinking. Critical issues—issues arising about topics with social importance—are worthy of critical thinking. Education is such a topic; critical issues about education abound and deserve reasoned dialogue, dialectic reasoning, and critical thinking—approaches that we support.

Arguments are not the only way to reason. Intuition, for example, is perfectly suitable, as is reading and contemplation. Some arguments lead nowhere: "Says who?" is part of an argument pattern that actually denigrates reason. But topics of most importance are often good places where argument can help open and examine ideas. School is important enough to merit examination of, by, and with argument. Dialogue and dialectic, used in this way, are intended to be dynamic, interactive, and optimistic. They are optimistic since they take the stance that things can and should be improved.

Dialogue merely calls for two persons or two ideas—we can have dialogue with ourselves, but we need two ideas to meet the condition of duality. Monologues, like lectures to others or ourselves, also can be valuable for gaining ideas; most textbooks operate as monologues, presenting one view with evidence to support it. But dialogue is more dynamic and more challenging. Not all dialogue, however, is civil and productive. Dialogue can operate at the lowest level and can be used to browbeat others into agreement, as in a kind of Socratic attack—Noddings (1995b) notes: "Socrates himself taught by engaging others in dialogue . . . he dominates the dialogue and leads the listeners . . . forcing his listeners gently and not so gently to see the errors in their thinking" (pp. 6, 7). But reasoned dialogue involves active consideration of a different view and interest in interaction in discussion. We advocate informed skepticism, using reasoned dialogue in examining educational issues—but we go further, encouraging development of a dialectic approach for some issues in the search for improvement in education.

Dialogue does not expect much beyond civil discussion used to gain understanding. Dialectic reasoning uses disputes and divergent opinions to arrive at a better idea. The dialectic occurs when you pit one argument (thesis) against another (antithesis) in an effort to develop a synthesis superior to either (see Figure 1.1). It is an inquiry into important issues that identifies the main points, important evidence, and logical arguments used by each of at least two divergent views on an issue. This requires critical examination of the evidence and arguments on each side of a dispute, granting each side some credibility to understand and criticize. A dialectic approach is dynamic. A synthesis from one level of dialectic reasoning can become a new thesis at a more sophisticated level, and the process of inquiry continues to spiral (Adler, 1927; Cooper, 1967; Rychlak, 1976; Noddings, 1995b).

The purpose for dialectic reasoning between competing ideas is not to defeat one and accept the other, but to search for an improved idea. Dialectic

FIGURE 1.1 Dialectic Reasoning: A Simplified Diagram

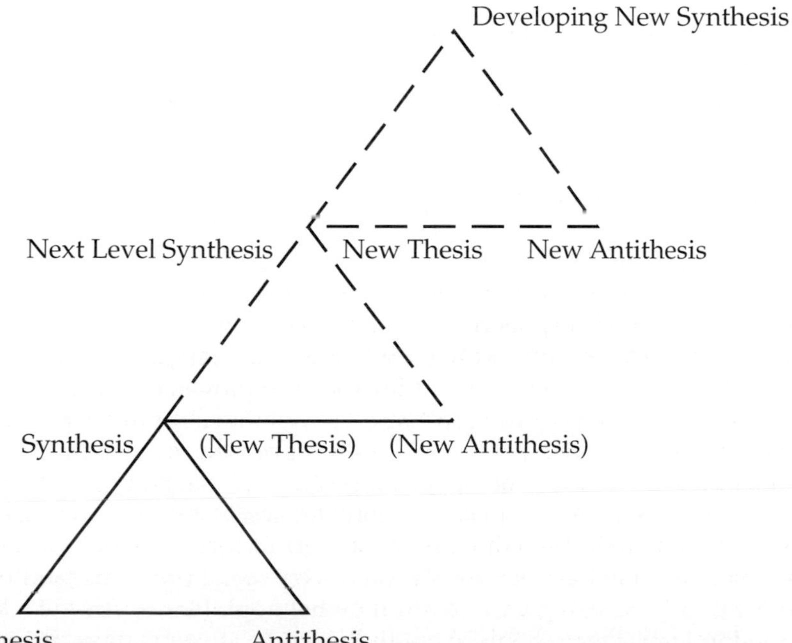

reasoning is not merely the search to identify one side as a winner nor to find a political compromise, especially a compromise that pleases neither side very well. It is a search for a higher level of idea that accommodates or incorporates the most important points in the thesis and antithesis. Sciabarra (2000) describes the dialectic process as:

> Dialectical method is neither dualistic nor monistic. A thinker who employs a dialectic method embraces neither a pole nor the middle of a duality of extremes. Rather, the dialectical method anchors the thinker to both camps. The dialectic thinker refuses to recognize these camps as mutually exclusive or apparent opposites. . . . He or she strives to uncover the common roots of apparent opposites . . . [and] presents an integrated alternative. . . . (p. 16)

For a simple example on a complicated topic: As Marcuse (1960) notes, many early philosophers considered individual freedom and social freedom as opposites. One could enjoy individual freedom only by trampling on social freedoms, and a society could exert its freedom only by limiting the freedom of individuals. One was a thesis, the other its antithesis; apparently opposite views. A synthesis develops as both freedoms are considered necessary to modern civilization and to individuals, using the view that individual freedoms are best maintained in a free society. Without society, humans have no freedom in practice; there is no freedom in mere survival. Without individual freedoms, society cannot be free in practice; the range of individual freedom depends on agreement with other individuals in a social contract requiring essential equality, a system of laws, and rational thinking.

Philosophers have used the idea of dialectics in many different ways; it has justified opposite radical conclusions like absolute social control, as in forms of Marxism, or absolute individualism and against society, as in some of the libertarian ideas of Ayn Rand (Sciabarra, 1999). But Aristotle, the moderate and reasoning philosopher who initiated Western political philosophy, could be considered the father of dialectic reasoning. He saw dialectic and rhetoric as mutually supportive arts, with dialectic the logical means for developing arguments and rhetoric the means of persuasion, speaking or writing, that uses the results of dialectic reasoning. Aristotle favored the dialectic because it required examining serious questions from many different positions.

The dialectic approach is fundamentally optimistic: It assumes there are better ideas for improving society and that examining diverse ideas is a productive way to develop them. Roth (1989) notes that dialectical study of educational issues can offer enlightenment for social improvement and support for reflective teachers. Many issues can't resolve well into a synthesis at any given time, but that does not denigrate the dialectic approach as a good way to comprehend and critically examine opposing positions. Note that dialectic reasoning may require more energy than you think for some of the educational issues in this book, and dialogue will be perfectly satisfactory. The dialectic process, though, is a valuable tool for considering knotty social problems, and offers a means for depersonalizing various strongly held opinions to strive for a common good in improving schools. As with most educative practices, it is not the finding of predetermined right answers, but the process of thinking that is most important. A right answer is good for solving a single problem, but a good process is useful for many problems.

As in any form of human discourse, dialogues and dialectic don't necessarily lead to truth; they can merely repeat errors and bias. Thus, we advocate a healthy, informed skepticism in examining these disputes. In the ancient Greek tradition, exercising skepticism meant to examine or to consider—to raise questions about reasons, evidence, and arguments (Sim, 1999; Wright, 2001). Skepticism is not simply doubt, despair, or cynicism; it is intelligent inquiry. Without skepticism, we easily can fall into "complacent self-deception and dogmatism"; with it, we can "effectively advance the frontiers of inquiry and knowledge," applying this knowledge to "practical life, ethics, and politics" (Kurtz, 1992, p. 9). Dialogues and dialectics on educational issues, with prudent skepticism, are a thoughtful form of inquiry.

DEMOCRATIC VITALITY AND EDUCATIONAL CRITICISM

Critics of schools are easy to find. People are not bashful about noting school problems, but disagree over what is wrong, who is responsible, and what should be done to change schools. Criticism of schools is fully consistent with open democracy. Of all social institutions in a democracy, the school should be the most ready for examination; education rests upon critical assessment and reassessment. That does not mean that all criticism is justified, or even useful. Some of it is simplistic, mean-spirited, or wrong-headedly arrogant. But much of it is thoughtful and cogent. Although some unjustified criticism can be detrimental to education in a democracy, open debate can permit the best ideas to percolate, to be developed and revised, and to be evaluated (DeWiel, 2000).

Over the long haul, schooling has improved and civilization has been served by the debates over education. More people get more education of a better quality across the world now than in previous generations. Despite periodic lapses and declines, the global movement toward increased and improved schooling for more students continues. The debates force us to reconsider ideas about schooling and increase our sophistication about schools and society.

Democratic vitality and educational criticism are good companions. Democracy, as Thomas Jefferson so wisely noted, requires an enlightened public and free dissent. Education is the primary means to enlightenment and to thoughtful dissent. It follows that schools would be among those fundamental social institutions under continuing public criticism in a society striving to improve its democracy.

- Alexis de Tocqueville (1848/1969) introduced his classic study of democracy in the very young United States by stating:

  > The first duty imposed on those who now direct society is to educate democracy; to put, if possible, new life into its beliefs. . . . (p. 12)

- Bertrand Russell (1928) noted that education is basic to democracy:

  > . . . it is in itself desirable to be able to read and write . . . an ignorant population is a disgrace to a civilized country, and . . . democracy is impossible without education. (p. 128)

- And John Dewey (1916) put schools at the center of democracy:

  > The devotion of democracy to education is a familiar fact. . . . a democratic society repudiates the principle of external authority, it must find a substitute in voluntary disposition and interest; these can only be created by education. (p. 87)

Democratic vitality and educational criticism both require open expression of diverse ideas, yet both are based on an optimistic sense of unity of purpose. Diverse ideas and criticism provide necessary tests of our ideas. Criticism easily can appear to be negative, pessimistic, or cynical, but these are not its only forms. Informed skepticism, the purpose for this book, offers a more optimistic view without becoming like Pollyanna. Diverse ideas are sought because we think, optimistically, that education can be improved. Unity of purpose suggests there is a bedrock of agreement on basic values, the criteria against which to judge diverse ideas. Without diverse ideas, there is no vitality and opportunity for progress; without unity of purpose, diverse ideas can be chaotic and irrational.

Global Democratization and Purposes of Education

In this first decade of the twenty-first century, school remains the most common approach to education around the world. Schools for children of the elite classes have existed since ancient times, but mass education in schools is a relatively recent global phenomenon. Though it is essentially a twentieth-century development, mass schooling has become a dominant social institution worldwide as democracy has become the dominant global trend in governments. Brzezinski (2000) comments, "we now seem to be enjoying the global triumph of the idea of democracy" (p. 150). But democratization is not always positive and progressive. Shapiro and Macedo (2000) pose the kind of problems that confront societies and their schools in developing democratic life:

> The principles and practices of democracy continue to spread even more widely, and it is hard to imagine that there is a corner of the globe into which they will not penetrate. But the euphoria of democratic revolutions is typically short-lived, and its attainment seems typically to be followed by disgruntlement and even cynicism about the actual operation of democratic institutions. . . . Of course, it is far easier to perceive the need for reform than to prescribe specific proposals. (p. 1).

In commenting on John Stuart Mill's concepts of the role of education in a democratic society, Garforth (1980) points out that "Undoubtedly, democracy at its best is a great educative force, but . . . it is not immune from dishonesty, corruption, and the betrayal of truth" (p. 20). Democratization brings the need for mass schooling and critical literacy (Torres, 2002). Dictatorship seems to work better with less education for the general public; but miseducation of the public in a democracy is dysfunctional. A strong democracy requires a critical citizenry, a public capable of engaging in critical thinking. Critical citizens depend upon critical education (Norris, 1999; Winthrop, 2000). This is a significant concern for the United States, where democracy and mass education are well developed and supported; it is even more significant for nations where these traditions are weaker.

Global Dimensions of Education

Public and private schools are the social institutions organized to provide formal education in modern nations, involving nearly all the student-age populations. Wealthier nations provide and require schooling for the largest proportion of children for the longest period, but less wealthy nations have rapidly increased primary school education and are moving to expand secondary and higher education opportunities for more students. In 1950, only 16 percent of the world's students of high school age were in secondary schools, and 3 percent of age-related students were in colleges. By 2000, over 34 percent of high-school-age students around the world were in secondary schools and 8 percent of the age-related students were in college. Figure 1.2 shows the global effort to educate.

The schools of the world now employ over 60 million teachers, who comprise the world's largest professional occupation. Finding adequate resources to support these teachers and operate schools is a major global issue. The United Nations has undertaken a significant role in improving education and treatment of children. During the 1990s, over fifteen major sponsored international meetings on education were held, more than one per year. Many international treaties and conventions on education have emerged to indicate the importance of schooling worldwide. Still, schools in

FIGURE 1.2 World Population, School Enrollments, Teachers, and Expenditures, 1980–2000

	1980	1990	2000
Population	4.4 billion	5.3 billion	6.2 billion
Enrollment	856 million	1.1 billion	1.2 billion
Teachers	38 million	47 million	60 million
School Expenditures in U.S. Dollars	$516 billion	$986 billion	$1.8 trillion

the poorest nations face serious shortages of basic requirements, from adequate buildings to textbooks. Some schools in all parts of the world are in poor physical condition and are getting worse, but poorer nations suffer more in lack of school facilities and support. This will further increase separation between rich and poor nations since schooling is future-oriented (*UNESCO World Education Report, 2000*).

The world's population has now surpassed 6 billion, doubling since 1960. Developing nations have about 80 percent of the people, up from 70 percent in 1960. The growth rate has slowed, to about 1.2 percent annually, which, along with better education and health, means the population is aging. The median age in developing nations is now about 24 years old, up from about 19 years a quarter-century ago. The median age in more developed nations is 37, up from 29 years in 1975. Illiteracy not addressed when many of these people were younger is an increasing problem, along with the extensive current global effort to provide literacy to youth. That suggests global needs for educational programs for older citizens in addition to the well-known needs for schooling for the under-18-year-olds of the world.

Educational spending, however, differs significantly between wealthier and poorer nations. In 1980, developed nations spent $408 billion on schools, about 5 percent of their Gross Domestic Product (GDP); less developed nations spent $98 billion, about 4 percent of their GDP, and the least developed spent $3.8 billion, or not quite 3 percent of GDP. In 2000 the more developed nations spent $1,000 billion, still 5 percent of GDP, and the least developed spent $7 billion, now just 2 percent of GDP (*UNESCO World Education Report, 2000*). The gap widens (see Figure 1.3).

Global democratization, population growth and distribution in the world, globalization of trade and industry, economic disparities among nations, and increasing age medians are reasons for an increasing interest in education as a primary means for national development and international interchange. The *United Nations Economic and Social Council Report on the World Social Condition, 2000* (2000) states,

> Education opens doors and facilitates social and economic mobility. . . . Education has assumed a central role in the life of societies, and their general progress has become intimately bound up with the vitality and reach of the educational enterprise. . . . At the global level, it has become the biggest industry, absorbing 5% of the world GDP and generating or helping to generate much more. (p. 16)

In the United States, schooling also involves large numbers—of people, dollars, and locations. The number of U.S. school districts approaches 15,000, and the number of teachers is almost 3.5 million, with school expenditures about $300 billion annually. Table 1.1 summarizes U.S. school enrollments for public and private schools and public school expenditures. Clearly schooling involves significant numbers of people and costs. But school has many payoffs. Unemployment rates are highest for people with less than a high school education, and lowest for those with at least a bachelor's degree; the median income

FIGURE 1.3 School Expenditure, as Percentage of Gross Domestic Product, Selected Nations, Beginning of 21st Century.

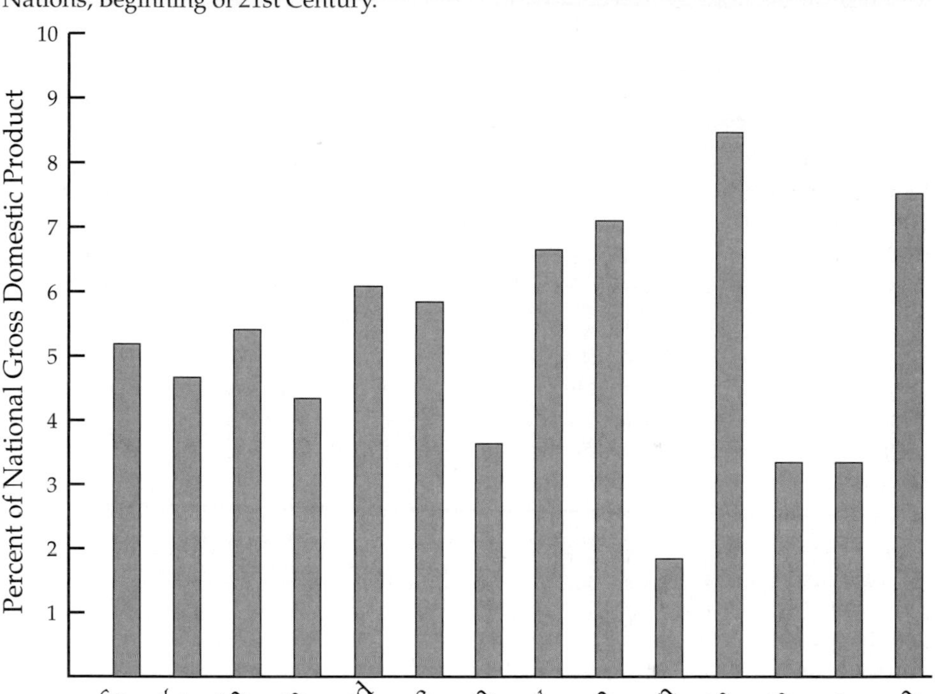

Source: Education at a Glance, 2000. *Paris: Organization for Economic Cooperation and Development; World Statistics Pocketbook 2001. New York: United Nations Department of Economic and Social Affairs.*

of people 25 years and older increases consistent with education level attained (see Figure 1.4).

Schools are a focus of criticism and reform efforts because schools are among the most public of institutions, are one of the most common experiences people have, and are immensely important to the lifeblood and future of societies. Virtually every person spends long periods of life in schools; teachers may spend a lifetime. Schools carry significant social trust for transmitting cultural heritage, developing economic and political competence, and providing inspiration and knowledge to improve the future society. The nature and form of that heritage, competence, and knowledge form constant battlegrounds for different views of what schools ought to be and ought to be doing.

Table 1.1 Enrollment and Expenditures in Public and Private Schools, United States 1900–2010 (Projected; in thousands)

	Elementary and Secondary School Enrollees				*Expenditures (in millions)*	
	Public	%	Private	%	Public	Private
1900	15,500	92	1,350	8	$ 215	n/a
1910	17,800	92	1,550	8	426	n/a
1920	21,500	93	1,690	7	1,036	n/a
1930	25,600	91	2,650	9	2,317	n/a
1940	25,400	91	2,611	9	2,344	n/a
1950	25,111	88	3,380	12	5,838	$ 411
1960	35,150	86	6,300	14	16,700	1,100
1970	45,850	89	5,360	11	43,183	2,500
1980	40,850	88	5,300	12	103,162	7,200
1990	41,200	89	5,230	11	248,900	19,500
2000	47,000	89	5,950	11	389,000	28,400
2010	47,000	89	5,950	11		

Source: Digest of Educational Statistics, 2002. Washington, DC: U.S. Department of Education.
Data for private education are estimated. Private schools include religion-affiliated institutions, some of which include teachers and other staff who are not paid salaries.

THE POLITICAL CONTEXT OF SCHOOLING

The public has lofty expectations for education, giving schools the responsibility for much of their children's welfare, values, skills, and knowledge. One expectation is that schools can correct such social ills as crime, teenage pregnancy, and adolescent rudeness. There is also the expectation that schools will provide self-fulfillment education, ranging from employment skills to personal happiness. Schools, then, are seen as a source of both problems and solutions.

Education has emerged again as one of the most highly charged areas in political contests. Candidates tend to offer clean, neat, and simple answers to long-term school problems. Most candidates for president, state governor, or the U.S. Congress have high-profile, but often inconsistent, messages about schools:

- Cut class size, but also cut school expenses.
- Repair buildings, but also lower taxes.
- Allow more local control, but impose more national standards and support.
- Have schools educate against violence and drug abuse, but also have schools teach only the basics.
- Improve sex education, but do not teach values in school.
- Make teachers more accountable, but give teachers more freedom and responsibility.

FIGURE 1.4 Relation of Education to Income; Workers 18 Years and Older, Period 1975–2000

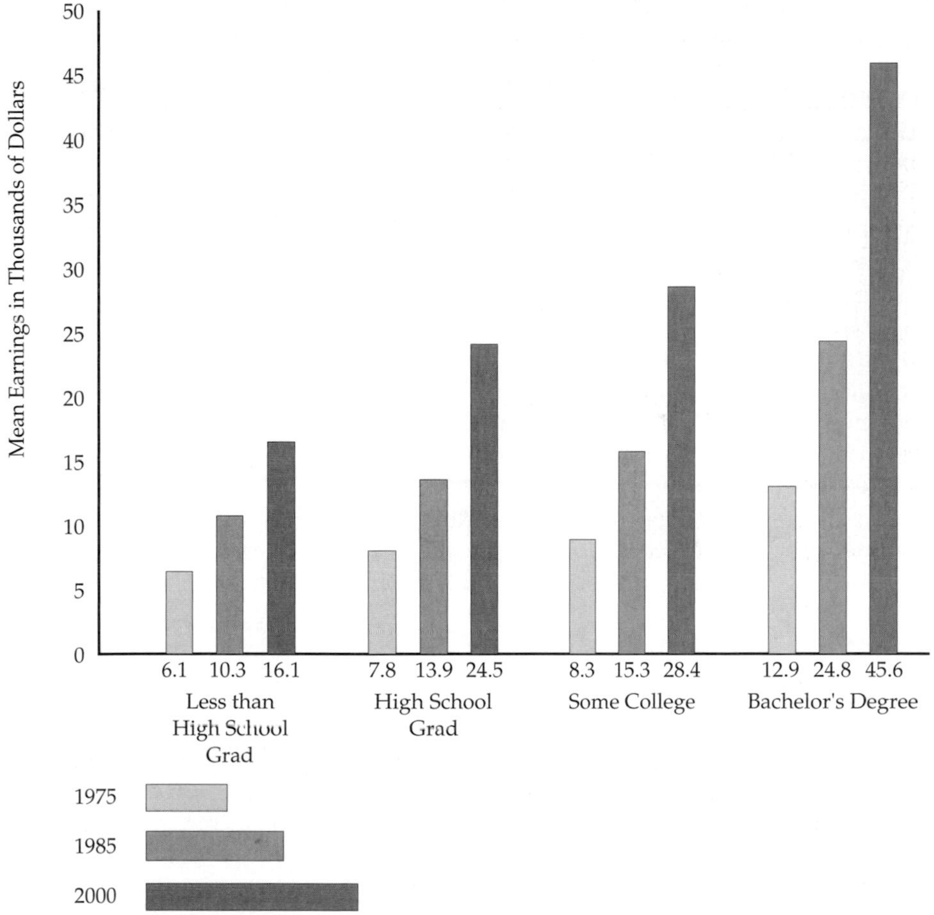

Mean Earnings in Thousands of Dollars

	Less than High School Grad	High School Grad	Some College	Bachelor's Degree
1975	6.1	7.8	8.3	12.9
1985	10.3	13.9	15.3	24.8
2000	16.1	24.5	28.4	45.6

Source: *Gauguin, D. A., and DeBrandt, K. A. (2001).* Education Statistics of the United States. *3rd Ed. Lanham, MD: Bernan.*

- Increase distance learning by computers, but also increase daily school time and the school year.
- Increase school competition for grades and awards, but make schools more collaborative, inclusive, and supportive.

There are reasons for the often schizophrenic quality of school debates. As Theodore Sizer said, "Everybody is for high test scores till their kids get low test scores" (Bronner, 1998). Also, it is easy to claim that our own education was vastly superior to what students now get in school, and to advocate a return to the good old days. But how many would actually want their children to return to the reality and limitations of yesterday's schools?

The political nature of educational debates is illustrated by actions surrounding the Sandia Report on schools just a decade ago. The government suppressed for two years a major government-sponsored study showing U.S. schools were better than the first Bush administration wanted to divulge (Tanner, 1993). The Sandia Report showed U.S. schools were far better than government and influential media were reporting.

The main findings include: (1) scores on SAT tests for comparable students have remained the same or increased over time, but many more students from the lower half of a class now take the test, causing the average score to decline; (2) nonwhite ethnic and racial groups have maintained or improved their SAT test scores since the late 1970s; (3) scores on National Assessment of Educational Progress tests have improved; (4) the United States has the highest college enrollment rates in the world, and the highest percentage of women and minorities who earn degrees; at the same time, scores on the Graduate Record Exam have actually risen significantly; (5) high school dropout rates for all groups except Hispanics have decreased, and the Hispanic group included a high proportion of immigrants who had dropped out of school before they came to the United States; (6) teachers' beginning salaries, after adjusting for inflation, were essentially the same in 1990 as they were in the 1970s; and (7) school expenditures for all except special education students have stagnated, in constant dollars, for over two decades (Huelskamp, 1993; Tanner, 1993, p. 293).

Among its conclusions, the Sandia Report notes: "Much of the 'crisis' commentary today claims total system-wide failure in education. Our research shows that this is simply not true" (Carson, Huelskamp, and Woodall, 1992, p. 99). Delays and revisions, however, effectively suppressed the Report from public view for over two years (Tanner, 1993, p. 292), placing it among the ten most censored news media stories of 1994 (Jensen, 1994).

Not surprisingly, schools are not only the subject of public dispute but also of partisan political interest. Schools are both political agencies and handy targets from every side of party politics. Schools consume more local budget money than any other social agency, and are among the top consumers of state funds. Schools are a major responsibility under state legislation and local control, subjecting them to political pressures both from those in office and those vying to be.

The national level has seen a rekindling of political interest in education since 1975. The Department of Education became a pulpit for strong views on schools when William Bennett was Secretary, even though one of the goals of President Reagan's party was the abolition of the Department. The much-heralded No Child Left Behind Act of 2001 puts the federal government into major school affairs—though it may never be properly funded. Few politicians accept blame for inadequate school funding, building decline, or low test scores, but most have a plan to reform schools, add no cost and guarantee high test scores—the education silver bullet and fantasy.

A TRADITION OF SCHOOL CRITICISM AND REFORM

From the intensity and vigor of public debate over schooling, a debate that has continued in Western society at least since the time of Socrates, one would expect either dramatic changes in schools or their abolition in favor of an alternative structure. At least one critic has argued to abolish schools (Illich, 1971), and some have proposed very significant changes in schooling (Sinclair, 1924; Rafferty, 1968; Apple, 1990). Most changes have been moderate, however, and no serious abolition attempts have occurred. Ideas about education can be very controversial. One of the two accusations leveled against Socrates in the indictment that brought him to trial, and brought on his suicide by taking hemlock, was "corruption of the young." Socrates may have paid the ultimate price for being an educational reformer in a political setting that was not ready for his reforms.

Some school purposes are commonly accepted, such as distributing knowledge and providing opportunity, but controversies arise over what knowledge we should distribute, which children should get which opportunities, and who should be making these decisions. For more than 3,000 years, human societies have recognized the value of education—and argued about what the goal of schooling should be and how to achieve it (Ulich, 1954). For about 300 years, Americans have agreed that education is one of the most significant social topics, but have argued over what schools should be.

Shifts in criticism and efforts at reform are common in U.S. educational history (Cremin, 1961; Welter, 1962; Karier, 1967; Tyack, 1967; Katz, 1971; Ravitch, 2000), but schools actually change only modestly. Traditional and progressive agendas differ, but schools seem to respond by moving very gradually in the direction proposed, with a few widely publicized examples of reform, and then to await the next movement. Kaestle (1985) notes, "[The] real school system is more like a huge tanker going down the middle of a channel, rocking a bit from side to side as it attends to one slight current and then to another" (p. 423).

School Reform in Early Twentieth-Century America

The United States has a long tradition of innovation in education, stemming from its pioneer role in providing popular education to large numbers of students at public expense. There are some major failures in this history, most notably the lack of equal educational opportunities for African Americans, Native Americans, women, immigrants, and those of the lower classes. We have, however, expanded our view of education as a major means for developing democracy and for offering some social mobility. We may not realize these ambitions, and our real intentions may be less altruistic (Katz, 1968). But idealization of democratic reform through education is in the traditional American rhetoric.

American schools, from the nineteenth century, were expected to blend immigrants into the American mainstream through compulsory education with an emphasis on such subjects as English, American history, and civics. A history of racism, sexism, and ethnic prejudice was commonly ignored in American social life and schools, while we labored under the myth that everyone shared a happy society made up of people who should all talk, think, and form values the same way. Schools were a primary social agency to meld students from divergent cultural backgrounds into the American ideal, which, not unsurprisingly, exhibited European, white, male characteristics and values. Standard use of English language and belief in the superiority of Western literature, history, politics, and economics dominated the schools. Schools were key institutions in "Americanizing" generations of immigrants.

In the early twentieth century, urbanization and industrialization had created the need for different forms of school services. Large numbers of children from the working classes were now in schools in urban areas, and many criticized the traditional classical curriculum, teaching methods, and leisure-class approach to school. Graham (1967) identifies extensive development of vocational and technical courses as the most dominant change in schooling before World War I, as school activities broadened to include medical exams, health instruction, free lunch programs, schools open during vacation periods for working parents, and other community services. These reforms fit with the evolving sense of social progressivism. The progressive education movement, from about 1920 to World War II, incorporated severe criticisms of traditional schooling ideas and such practices as corporal punishment, rigid discipline, rote memorization and drill, stress on the classics, and high failure rates.

Progressives offered a program involving students in deciding what was to be studied, engaging in practical experiences and projects and in community activities, opening up study of opposing opinions on controversial topics, practicing democracy in the schools, and study of social problems. Schools became more open to students of all classes, and the curriculum moved from more esoteric studies to courses with social applications, such as home economics, business and vocational education, current events, health, sociology, sex education, and consumer math. Sporadic and severe criticisms of progressive thought cropped up throughout that time, but a major reform movement from the right gained more public interest near the end of the Depression and again following World War II. Graham, summarizing the shift, states:

> Sometime between 1919 and 1955 the phrase "progressive education" shifted from a term of praise to one of opprobrium. To the American public of 1919, progressive education meant all that was good in education; thirty-five years later nearly all the ills in American education were blamed on it. (1967, p. 145)

Gurney Chambers (1948) notes that after the 1929 stock market crash, education came under attack: "Teachers were rebuked for their complacency and inertia, and progressive schools, surprisingly enough, were blamed for the increasing crime and divorce rates and political corruption" (pp. 142–143).

Cycles of Educational Reform After World War II

Attacks on schools increased in intensity and frequency during the late 1940s and 1950s. The great school debates of this time involved many issues that extend into the twenty-first century. Church-state issues, including school prayer and use of public funds for religious school busing and other school services, gained significance. Racial issues, with the implications of the landmark Supreme Court decision in *Brown v. Board of Education of Topeka* (1954) and forced busing, became another focus of school controversy. Rapidly increasing tax burdens, to pay for new schools and teachers required by the baby boom, aroused protests from many school critics. Rising expectations for education, driven by the thousands of "non-college-prep" veterans who went to college on the GI Bill, were applied to the lower schools. Curricular issues, including disputes over the most effective way to teach reading and over test scores showing students did not know enough history or math or science or English, filled the popular press.

Politically, the McCarthy period "Red Scare" produced rampant public fear of a creeping communistic influence in American life and created suspicions that schools were breeding grounds for "communal" and progressive thought. These, and other factors, led to renewed criticism of schools. For many, there was simply a lingering sense that schools were not doing their job. Two books illustrate the criticisms of this period: Albert Lynd's *Quackery in the Public Schools* (1950, p. 53) and Arthur Bestor's *Educational Wastelands* (1953). Each attacked progressive education, and the "educationists" who advocated it, for turning schools from traditional discipline and subject knowledge toward the "felt needs" of children. As historian Clarence Karier notes, ". . . the educationist who spoke out for 'progressive education' and 'life adjustment education' appeared increasingly out of place in the postwar, cold war period" (1985, p. 238).

Major foundations examined America's schools. The Ford Foundation made education a focal point. Grants were made to the Educational Testing Service to improve measures of student performance. The Carnegie Foundation asked James Bryant Conant, former president of Harvard and U.S. Ambassador to West Germany, to conduct a series of studies of public education. There was much public criticism of the academic failures of American schools. Then came the Soviet launch of *Sputnik* in 1957, ahead of the United States, and a new focus for educational reform. The *Sputnik* launch was a highly visible catalyst for conservative critics, illustrating a lack of American competitiveness they attributed to progressive reforms in schools during the pre–World War II period. These critics blamed the "permissive" atmosphere in schools for this deficiency.

Excellence and Its Discontents

Post-*Sputnik* reform included a reinstitution of rigor, discipline, traditional subject teaching, and standards. They added up to the theme, to be repeated in the 1980s, of "Excellence." In fact, there are some remarkable similarities in the language and rationales used in the earlier reform movement and those used in the 1980s efforts to return schools to traditional work. International competition, advancing technology, and the needs of business are rationales cited in the literature of both periods.

Excellence, ill-defined and excessively used, is a cue word that shows up in many reports and statements from both periods. John Gardner's prominent document for the Rockefeller Brothers Fund, *The Pursuit of Excellence: Education and the Future of America* (1958), is one illustration. Another term common to both periods is *mediocrity,* a threat suggested in the title of Mortimer Smith's book, *The Diminished Mind: A Study of Planned Mediocrity in Our Public Schools* (1954).

The Conant Report, *The American High School Today* (1958), was a moderate book that proposed a standard secondary school curriculum, tracking by ability group, special courses for gifted students, improvements in English composition, better counseling, and other recommendations. Federal funds for reform were dramatically increased in the late 1950s and early 1960s. The National Defense Education Act (NDEA) responded to pleas that schools were key to providing "national defense," and that *Sputnik* showed the United States was militarily vulnerable. Funds were provided to improve teaching in science and math, foreign languages, social studies, and English. These curricular projects primarily sought to encourage university scholars in each field to determine better ways to convey the subject matter; many projects attempted to make the curriculum "teacherproof" (as in foolproof) to prevent classroom teachers from teaching it incorrectly. Teacher education came in for its share of criticism, with blasts at teachers' colleges, the progressive techniques they advocated, and quality of students going into teaching. This all sounds hauntingly familiar to those who read current educational criticism.

As the trend toward conservative educational ideas gained support and school practice turned back to standards and "rigor," criticism from the left began to emerge. This liberal criticism was a response to the rote memorization, excessive testing, lock-step schooling, and increased school dropout and failure rates that began to characterize schools. Paul Goodman, George Dennison, Edgar Z. Friedenberg, A. S. Neill in England, Nat Hentoff, John Holt, Herbert Kohl, and Jonathan Kozol, attacked schools for their sterility, bureaucracy, boredom, lack of creativity, rigidity, powerlessness of students and teachers, and inadequacy in educating disadvantaged youth. Holt (1964) stated:

> Most children in school fail. . . . They fail because they are afraid, bored, and confused . . . bored because the things they are given and told to do in school are so trivial, so dull, and make such limited and narrow demands on the wide spectrum of their intelligence, capabilities, and talents. . . . Schools should be a place where children learn what they want to know, instead of what we think they ought to know. (pp. xiii, xiv, 174)

This 1960s left-wing reform rebelled against conservative authoritarianism and the dehumanization of schools. Reforms included open education, nongraded schools, more student freedom, more electives, less reliance on standardized tests, abolition of dress codes and rigid rules, and more teacher-student equality. The Vietnam War and demonstrations spurred the politics that stimulated much of the late 1960s educational reform literature.

Multicultural education was not on the educational agenda in early America because the mass schooling was supposed to produce a melting pot where various cultural strands were blended into the "new American." The civil rights movement in the 1950s and 1960s showed the melting pot thesis about American society was a myth. This led to other approaches to the issue of diversity and unity. One was the advocacy of separatism, where each major subcultural group would go its own way with separate social and school structures. Another was an effort to reconstitute a form of the melting pot idea by enforcing integration in such institutions as housing, restaurants, and schools. Integration often led to resegregation by white flight and establishment of private all-white academies. Multicultural education, which aimed to recognize positive contributions of a variety of national, racial, ethnic, gender, and other groups to American life, developed as a way to recognize both diversity and unity.

The multicultural effort was to correct a century of schooling that featured white male American or European heroes from the middle and upper social classes. African American, Latino, and women authors showed up on lists of standard readings in English classes. The societal contributions of Native Americans, blacks, Chicanos, and females were added to history and civics books. Equal physical education opportunities for boys and girls, compensatory education for the disadvantaged, and programs featuring minority and women role models were developed.

Traditionalism Revisited: The 1980s and Beyond

In the early 1980s, reports of falling SAT and ACT scores, drug abuse, vandalism, and chaos in schools increased public receptivity to reform. Nervousness about international competition, resurgence of business and technology as dominant features of society, and questions about shifting morality and values provided a political setting that could blame schools for inadequacies. The presidentially appointed National Commission on Excellence in Education (1983) published a highly political document, *A Nation at Risk,* which claimed there was a "rising tide of mediocrity" in schools. Ensuing public debate produced a flurry of legislation to develop "excellence" by increasing the competitive nature of schooling and testable standards.

Student protests of the 1960s had died and a negative reaction set in. "Yuppies" (young upwardly mobile professionals) emerged as role models for student style in the 1980s, embracing careerism and corporate fashion. There was an increasing perception of disarray in the American family, and a return to religion for many. The recurrence, under President Reagan, of open confrontation with communism subsided as the Iron Curtain collapsed in the late 1980s. Anti-communism, a major influence on conservative educational reform since the 1920s, seemed to be replaced by the War on Drugs and character education. Schools were blamed for social ills and challenges to traditional values, and they were expected to respond to these strains by suddenly becoming academically excellent and moralistic—"Just say NO!"

Foundations and individual critics again undertook the study of schools. These include generally conservative reports from the Twentieth Century Fund (1983), College Entrance Examination Board (1983), and National Science Foundation (1983), as well as Mortimer Adler's *The Paideia Proposal* (1982). The more liberal works included John Goodlad's *A Place Called School* (1983) and Theodore Sizer's *Horace's Compromise* (1984). Ernest Boyer's moderate *High School* (1983) for the Carnegie Foundation also was popular.

States pumped up school financing until the 1990s recession, and state officials, having enacted myriad new regulations governing school matters, began claiming some credit for educational change (*Results in Education 1990; The Education Reform Decade,* 1990; Webster and McMillin, 1991). In the main, jawboning by the federal government and increased regulatory activity in the states produced little in the way of dramatic change, but many adjustments were undertaken. Most underlying social problems—for example, poverty, family disruption, discrimination, and economic imbalance—worsened during the 1980s, and schools suffer the continuing effects. In the 1990s, the focus of educational criticism and reform shifted from state regulation and test score worries to more diverse views of the national influence on local schools, school choice, curriculum control, at-risk students, restructuring schools to lead to more school-based management, teacher empowerment, parental involvement, and shared decision making. These ideas are potentially conflicting, some leading to increased centralization while others lead to increased decentralization. The core disputes remain.

The idea of replacing the traditional canons of literature and social thought with modern multicultural material engendered other battles now accorded the phrase, Culture Wars. Finn (1990a) and Ravitch (1990), former high officials of the U.S. Department of Education argue for teaching traditional content emphasizing unified American views rather than diverse views from segments of society. The Organization of American Historians, however, supports the teaching of non-Western culture and diversity in schools (Winkler, 1991). Camille Paglia, arguing against feminist positions, says her work "accepts the canonical Western tradition and rejects the modernist idea that culture has collapsed into meaningless fragments" (1990, p. xii). This battle also emerged when Stanford University's faculty debated whether to substitute modern literature for traditional in its basic course, when New York State social studies curriculum revision for multicultural content aroused a firestorm, and when English-only resolutions were adopted by state legislatures.

Other arguments over multicultural education linked it with politically correct speech in schools (*National Review,* 1990; Kinsley, 1991; *The Progressive,* 1991; D'Souza, 1991; Winkler, 1991; Banks, 1995). Should schools emphasize positive influences of divergent minority cultures and women, or should they stress traditional unifying themes from a Eurocentric, white, male-dominated curriculum? Should schools restrict racist, sexist, or other bigoted comments, or does that conflict with free speech?

"Politically correct" (PC) speech, defined as speech that does not denigrate any minority group, gender, or sexual preference, attracts protest because it is equivalent to censorship, stifling free expression. The effort to make schools more civil places by controlling statements that could be offensive to some groups was met by a storm of protest. Protecting civil rights to free speech appeared to be at odds with protecting the civility of schools and protecting the "multiculturally diverse" from enduring negative comments. The argument against PC is that the free marketplace of ideas requires free speech, not courteous speech, and the best response to epithets and slurs is reasoned argument and public disapproval. Although few are open advocates of politically correct regulations in schools, many would like to find a way to limit racist and sexist comments and graffiti. School is an obvious battleground for this issue.

Another continuing issue is the use and abuse of technology in schools. Through the search for knowledge, we develop faster and more comprehensive systems of communication, travel, and research—which then require faster and more comprehensive systems of education to comprehend and extend that knowledge. Economics and politics of this change in technology has not been lost in education battles. Doheny-Farina (1996), discussing the coming of virtual society and virtual schools, cites the argument that "Distance education will become the norm, the least expensive way to deliver the educational product, while face-to-face teaching will be only for the well-to-do"(p. 108). He concludes, however, that "most of those [distance learning] materials will be in the form of prescribed packages, which over time will tend to centralize expertise . . ." and that "the virtualization of school removes it from the fabric of the local community" (pp. 110, 116, 117). That scenario is a serious threat to many and deserves debate. Educational theorist Michael Apple (1994) claims that distance learning de-skills teachers, making them switch-turners and simple conduits for other people's ideas and procedures. That will destroy the central characteristic of democratic education: the freedom to learn and to teach.

Obviously, it is not difficult to find an argument about schools. We as a society share an interest in good schools, but hold strongly felt, diverse views of what makes schools good or bad. These views are shaped by differing visions of the good society and how new generations should be prepared for it. In the United States, we are reform-minded about all aspects of society and, as in our views on schools, we hold widely disparate views on what societal changes we need to make. Historian David Tyack (1991), discussing the intertwining of school reform with social reform, says, "For over a century and a half, Americans have translated their cultural anxieties and hopes into demands for educational reform" (p. 1).

Evaluation of Reforms

There is general agreement that results of multiple reform efforts before the end of the twentieth century have been mixed. No clear evidence indicates that the reforms have significantly changed educational practice. Analyses of the well-publicized 1980s school reform show great diversity in view (Giroux, 1989; Finn, 1990b; Darling-Hammond, 1991; *U.S. News & World Report,* 1990; Fiske, 1991; Safire, 1991; Moynihan, 1991; *New York Times,* 1992). Ideological chasms appear among the analysts as they try to explain why the reforms did not seem to work and what should be done now. Stories about drugs, shootings, and gang violence around schools compete with news articles stating that American students can't read, are ignorant in math and science, and fail tests of common knowledge in history and geography (Holt, 1989; *Newsweek,* 1989; *Business Week,* 1990; Hawley, 1990; McEvoy, 1990; Novak, 1990).

Critics (Bastian et al., 1985; Presseisen, 1985; Giroux, 1988b) on the liberal side charge that the 1980s school reform movement was dominated by mainstream conservative thought. This conservative agenda includes standardization, more testing, a return to basics, more implanting of patriotic values, increased regulation, more homework for students, less student freedom, renewed emphasis on dress codes and socially acceptable behavior for students and teachers, stricter discipline, and teacher accountability. This conservative agenda enhanced changes already under way in schools in response to declining student test scores and a sense that the young had lost respect for authority.

From a liberal/progressive view, schools are defective because they are too standardized, excessively competitive, and too factory-like. Students are measured and sorted in an assembly-line atmosphere where social class, gender, and race determine which students get which treatments. Teachers are deprofessionalized and treated as servile workers. Critical thinking is punished; one kind of curriculum or classroom instruction fits all. Creativity and joy are excluded from the school lexicon because education is supposed to be hard, dreary, boring work (McLaren, 1989; Purpel, 1989; Fisher, 1991; Nathan, 1991; Sacks, 2000; Schoenfeld, 2002). Making schools active, pleasant, student-oriented, critical, and sensitive to social problems is the reform they advocate.

Despite traditionalist reforms, conservative economist Thomas Sowell (1993) argues American schools are low quality and deteriorating even further because of educators' deceptive tactics, the "shockingly low" caliber of teachers and professors of education, dogma about student "self-esteem," teacher tenure, multicultural diversity, and "classroom brainwashing" designed to change students' values. Sowell states: "The brutal reality is that the American system of education is bankrupt. . . . That bankruptcy is both in institutions and in attitudes" (pp. 285–286).

But educational researchers David Berliner and Bruce Biddle (1995) present an opposite view. Based on their examination of test scores, international school finance data, and various other indicators of achievement and support, they conclude school critics are mistaken or uninformed. They discount critics' assertions that student achievement and teacher quality have declined and schools are failing society. Berliner and Biddle summarize their analysis with the response that "these assertions are errant nonsense" (p. 13), and they conclude that "American education has recently been subjected to an unwarranted, vigorous, and damaging attack—a Manufactured Crisis . . . the major claims of the attack turn out to have been myths; the Manufactured Crisis was revealed as a Big Lie" (p. 343).

Conservative school reform does appear to have been the main influence on schooling in the United States at the end of the twentieth century. Proposals and action for school change include academically tougher schools, vouchers, charter schools, rigorous standards and more testing, more discipline, privatized management, and training in moral behavior.

Liberal and radical ideas for schools did not disappear (Fullen, 2000; Bracey, 2002b). Teacher empowerment, academic freedom, student rights, limiting testing, providing student choice, and active social criticism and participation are liberal ideas percolating in school reform to come. Reconstructionist ideas placing schools at the center of social change have not been entirely forgotten in the current surge of literature on schools and reform. William Stanley (1992, 2001) presents a rethinking of social reconstructionism and examines key ideas from the critical pedagogy movement to offer educational possibilities for the twenty-first century. His focus is on practical reasoning, which provides critical examination of social issues and stimulates positive social action. His work proposes a liberating role for schools in society.

Continuing Debates Over Schooling

Human groups have long argued about what knowledge children should learn, how they should behave, and who should teach them. Basic subjects like reading and mathematics instruction are often at the eye of the hurricane because of their importance in the ongoing lives of students and their future prospects. Reading has long been the focus of debates over phonics and whole-language instruction, though often it is a more ideological and political issue than merely finding the best way to teach (Coles, 2001; *Phi Delta Kappan,* 2001). Arguments over the best approaches to mathematical literacy have included "civil rights" questions (Moses and Cobb, 2001), as well as competing ideologies in curricular reform, which Schoenfeld (2002) claims "gave rise to the math wars and catalyzed the existence of what is in essence a neo-conservative back-to-basics movement. This way lies madness" (p. 22). Nearly all subject fields have experienced the same problems in finding stability in seas of change dependent on ideological and political contexts. There is no shortage of current school critics and reformers. They present a bewildering array of educational ideas, from left-wing, right-wing, moderate, and radical positions.

The Changing Focus of Debates

As the twentieth century ended and the twenty-first began, much public debate over education changed from a primary focus on crisis, hand-wringing, and derisive blame to arguments over which political candidate offers more financial support, smaller classes, and better facilities and teachers to schools. The 1980s competition to bash schools and teachers has been partially replaced by a public affirmation that the future of schools and of society are intertwined. Serious disagreements, of course, continue on most school topics and we still get serious teacher-bashing on occasion. The general tenor of the debates, however, has shifted from castigation and condemnation to diverse proposals for cash infusions, accountability, standards, and specific corrective action. Finance problems in this first decade may derail most reforms. There are still sharply negative criticisms of the current state of schooling (Ravitch, 2000), but more moderate voices are more common in the schooling debates of the 2000s.

The 1983 claim that schools were floating on a "rising tide of mediocrity," had put the nation at risk, and were responsible for declining American values and economic competitiveness was followed by different analyses of the same kinds of data indicating schools were not as bad as this and subsequent 1980s and 1990s documents and media portrayed to the public (Bracey, 1992, 1994, 1995, 1997, 1998, 2002a; Berliner, 1993; Berliner and Biddle, 1995). The politics of bashing schools and teachers, however, is to the benefit of politicians seeking an issue that reverberates with the public. The 1980s and early 1990s witnessed a wellspring of strong statements critical of public schools and advocating such things as school vouchers, charter schools, increased teacher accountability, more testing, hiring private corporations to run schools, and state takeovers of failing districts (Ravitch and Viteritti, 1997). The politics of school critique and governmental or privatization intervention for reform were attention-getting and politicians found schools an excellent target. This meant more attention was paid to school failures than to school successes.

Public Ratings of Schools

One of the most surprising things about the spate of extremely negative school criticism between 1980 and now is that public rating of public schools has remained consistently high. Even with negative publicity about schools, survey evidence shows that public rating of *local* public schools actually has been positive, and often increasingly so, for over a quarter-century. The annual Phi Delta Kappa/Gallup Poll has surveyed the public since 1974. In 1992, the poll showed the largest one-year increase in the grades people give their local public schools in almost two decades, from 40 percent grading their schools A or B in 1992 to 47 percent rating them that high in 1993 (Elam et al., 1993). In 1998, the annual poll showed 46 percent of all respondents gave their local schools an A or B, and 52 percent of public school parents gave their children's schools an A or B grade (Rose and Gallup, 1998). For the first time in the 33 years the Gallup Poll has sampled the American public on schools, the Gallup Poll of 2001 found that a majority (51 percent) of the public gives public schools an A or B rating, and 62 percent of parents with children in public schools rate them A or B (Rose and Gallup, 2001). This increasing support for public schools is surprising because of the general sense that schools are not doing well. Those closest to the schools seem to rate them much better than media reports would suggest.

Ironically, people rate their own local schools significantly higher than they rate schools across the nation (only 20 percent in 1998 and 23 percent in 2001 give the nation's schools an A or B). For the school their oldest children attended, the rating is very high (about 65 percent rating them A or B). Gallup interpreted these data to suggest that the more the public knows about actual practices in schools, the better they rate them. The data also indicate that negative publicity from political and media treatment of schooling influences the way people grade schools they know the least, not those they know well.

Any decreasing stridency in negative criticism of schools might suggest school reforms in the past fifteen years have been successful, but that would be a misreading. No clear evidence exists about the reforms and their consequences; outcomes are still in dispute. Although many claims surround specific reforms, few comprehensive studies show that any school is significantly better or worse now as a result of reforms. Since recent evidence shows schools were never as bad as government and media reported, one could make the case that some reforms actually hindered school progress by improperly blaming and alienating teachers and by forcing more testing and governmental intervention in school requirements and operations.

Accountability and Standards

The national Goals 2000 campaign presses schools to meet a strange mix of externally determined goals that are vague (students will come to school ready to learn) or unrealistic (American students will score highest in international mathematics tests). This reflects a political view based on unsupported assumptions that schools have failed and government must interfere (Clinchy, 1995; Resnick and Nolan, 1995). Goals 2000 does not meet the concerns of educational thinkers who propose a qualitatively different idea of progress for schools, one where caring, ethics, critical thinking, and creative imagination are worthy conditions for a liberal education (Greene, 1995; Noddings, 1995a). Clearly, society failed to meet Goals 2000; we are well past 2000 and still do not top international math test scores and not every child comes to school ready to learn, and so on. Was Goals 2000 just political hype, inviting failure on its face? Has government failed or were goals too high, too abstract, too silly? Or has Goals 2000 become lost in multiple new laws and regulations that set standards? Instead of redoing goals, state and federal legislators have adopted legislation to impose rigid and precise standards of what students should know in various academic subjects, by grade level. This is the current concept of school accountability and leads to more testing and probably more hand-wringing as test scores do not satisfy the critics. The No Child Left Behind legislation of 2001 exacerbated this.

The political setting of the standards movement, and ideological underpinnings of the schooling culture wars, is illustrated by the furor raised over proposed standards in American history. The federal government provided substantial funds to a center at UCLA, where historians were to establish standards that identified what students in each grade should know about American history. The initial product offered much more contemporary and multicultural information, highlighting contributions of many people from minority groups. Critics attacked the standards as insufficiently patriotic and the Senate voted against them; historians capitulated and changed the standards to reflect the conservative view. Ideology and politics are firmly entrenched in the battles over schooling. It is easy to inflame emotions in this setting. Still, public schools get good ratings from their closest observers, and schools in the United States are rated by the public higher than many other institutions of American society.

Even though local schools are well received, schooling remains one of the most controversial topics in society. Schools benefit from good criticism, but the suppressed evidence should suggest we maintain a level of skepticism about some negative media reports and political statements about schools. The political nature of educational issues suggests the importance of schooling in contemporary society as well as ideological differences over the direction society and its schools should take.

School Improvement Versus Reform

Although polls continue to show general public support of local schools, most of us can identify one or more areas needing correction. Impatient or burned-out teachers, cloddish administrators, frazzled counselors, and outdated textbooks and curricula are examples. Most of us know the virtues as well as warts and blemishes of schools from our direct personal experience. Some critics propose quick and simplistic reforms to improve schools. Fortunately, most people understand that change in schooling is more complex, and that potential consequences of change need more thought.

Schools are controversial. Nearly everyone can find some fault in the way schools are organized and operated. Education, along with sex, religion, and politics, is one of the most debated topics in society. School, in fact, is the focus of much of the public debate over sex, religion, and politics. Sex education, religious study in schools, and "anti-American" teaching materials are among the many issues swirling about schools.

Reformers see schools as either the cause of some problem or part of the cure. We are led to believe that schools can solve major social problems such as racism, sexism, automobile accidents, AIDS, teenage pregnancy, and drugs. Reform has not been especially productive in student achievement, curing social ills, intellectual development, or student and public happiness about schools. Yet the arguments over reform have helped air ideological and political baggage that weighs on the reforms. The battles are democratic actions. Perhaps there is a better word than *reform* to use in discussing school improvement. Reform school was the institution where young social deviants and juvenile criminals were sent; reform schools seems a strange phrasing in that context.

Unity and Diversity: A Dialectic

Among the conditions of human civilization is the tension between unifying and diverse ideas. We want to share a vision of the good life with others, yet recognize human improvement depends on new ideas that may conflict with that vision. Unity provides a focus, but also complacency; diversity provides stimulation, but also dissension. Both comfort and discontent thus reside in unity and diversity. This tension occurs in all parts of life, and is most evident in important matters such as schooling. It is also at the center of the culture wars; do we impose unity or diversity?

Diversity and unity commonly are seen as contradictory. Some diverse ideas are too radical, too preposterous, or too challenging to deeply held beliefs for some people. Fundamental religions expect unity and do not accept diversity; criticism of religious dogma is considered heretical and sacrilegious. For those religions, just as for some people who believe they have the only truth, unity of belief is sacrosanct.

On the other hand, some question unity. One argument is that unity of purpose or values is a myth perpetuated by those in power to stay in power. Hard work, frugality, and acceptance of authority are seen as fictional values that are part of an effort by the powerful class to hide their oppressive actions, maintain the social order, and enslave docile workers.

Thus, diversity and unity can be seen as adversarial positions, bound in opposition. Those on the side of unity believe diverse ideas can be censored, ignored, or disdained; those arguing for diversity consider unity to be a facade hiding the basic conflicts in society. It also is possible to understand diversity and unity as collateral positions, supporting and energizing. There is even diverse opinion about the relation of diversity to unity. This tension between diversity and unity, multiple views and common principles, informs this book about schools. Among current critical issues in education, debates about purposes and practices of schooling, are such matters as school choice, finance, racism, sexism, child welfare, privatization, curriculum, business orientations, academic freedom, unionism, and testing. These issues reflect deeper social and political tensions between unity and diversity, including tensions between liberty and equality, rights and responsibilities, consensus and conflict, and individual and social development. Diverse ideas combined in a unified purpose is an ideal, not easily and perhaps not ever attained. It is a possible synthesis, drawing on two opposing strands as in dialectic reasoning. But what would it look like in practice? How would we define the kind of diversity and unity expressed?

This book presents two differing views on each topic in each chapter. The views expressed aren't always exactly opposing views, but they represent publicly expressed and divergent ideas about how schooling could be improved. Contrasting these views in terms of evidence presented and logic of each argument can stimulate a realistic dialogue, offering an opportunity to examine issues as they occur in human discourse. Divergent essays sometimes will use the same data or same published works to make opposite cases, but they usually will offer evidence from widely separate literatures. The search for improvement in society and in schooling is a unifying purpose; dialogues require diversity.

School is not only the subject of disputes, it is also the logical place for the thoughtful study of disputes. Schools should be settings where reasoned thought and open inquiry are practiced. That would be the most suitable location for examining disputes about important issues—those characterized by diverse opinions. Critical issues, those of the greatest significance, often stimulate the most intense disputes.

This first decade of the twenty-first century may be placid or panic for schools, a period of recuperation from the latest round of reforms or a new set of attacks. Even in placidity, however, educational issues are sure to arise, cause alarm, and inflame passions. Some of the issues raised will spawn elements of new school reforms and some will lead to school improvement; nearly all will be disputed.

Welcome to this exchange of ideas.

References

ADLER, M. (1927). *Dialectic.* New York: Harcourt Brace.

———. (1982). *The Paideia Proposal.* New York: Macmillan.

APPLE, M. (1990). *Ideology and Curriculum.* 2nd Ed. London: Routledge.

———. (1994). "Computers and the Deskilling of Teachers." *CPSR Newsletter* 12(2):3.

APPLE, M., AND WEIS, L., EDS. (1983). *Ideology and Practice in Schooling.* Philadelphia: Temple University Press.

AUDI, R. (2001). *The Architecture of Reason.* Oxford, England: Oxford University Press.

BAILYN, B. (1960). *Education in the Forming of American Society.* Chapel Hill: University of North Carolina Press.

BANKS, J. A. (1995). "The Historical Reconstruction of Knowledge About Race: Implications for Transformative Teaching." *Educational Researcher* 24:15–25.

BARBER, B. (1998). *Intellectual Pursuits.* Lanham, MD: Rowman & Littlefield.

BASTIAN, A., ET AL. (1985). *Choosing Equality: The Case for Democratic Schooling.* San Francisco: New World Foundation.

BERLINER, D. (1993). "Mythology and the American System of Education." *Kappan* 74:632+.

BERLINER, D., AND BIDDLE, B. J. (1995). *The Manufactured Crisis: Myths, Fraud, and the Attack on America's Public Schools.* Reading, MA: Addison-Wesley.

BESAG, F., AND NELSON, J. (1984). *The Foundations of Education: Stasis and Change.* New York: Random House.

BESTOR, A. (1953). *Educational Wastelands.* Urbana: University of Illinois Press. (2nd Ed., 1985)

BOGGS, C. (1993). *Intellectuals and the Crisis of Modernity.* Albany: SUNY Press.

BOYER, E. (1983). *High School.* New York: Harper & Row.

BRACEY, G. (1992). "The Second Bracey Report on the Condition of Public Education." *Kappan* 74:104–108+.

———. (1994). "The Fourth Bracey Report on the Condition of Public Education." *Kappan* 76:115–127.

———. (1995). "Stedman's Myths Miss the Mark." *Educational Leadership* 52:75–78.

———. (1997). *The Truth About America's Schools: The Bracey Reports, 1991–1997.* Bloomington, IN: *Phi Delta Kappan.*

———. (1998). "The Eighth Bracey Report on the Condition of Public Education." *Phi Delta Kappan* 80(2), 112–131.

———. (2002a) "The 12th Bracey Report on the Condition of Public Education." *Phi Delta Kappan* 84 (2) 135–150.

———. (2002b). *The War Against America's Public Schools.* Boston: Allyn & Bacon/Longmans.

BRAMELD, T. (1956). *Toward a Reconstructed Philosophy of Education.* New York: Holt, Rinehart & Winston.

BRONNER, E. (1998). "Candidates Latch onto Education Issue." *San Diego Union-Tribune.* Sept. 20, A10.

Brown v. Board of Education of Topeka, Shawnee County, Kansas, et al. (1954). 74 Sup. Ct. 686.

BRZEZINSKI, Z. (2000). "Epilogue." In M. F. Plattner, and A. Smolar, eds., *Globalization, Power, and Democracy.* Baltimore: Johns Hopkins Press.

Business Week. (1990). "Using Flash Cards and Grit to Defeat a Secret Shame." July 16, pp. 22, 23.

CARSON, C. C., HUELSKAMP, R. M., AND WOODALL, T. D. (1992). "Perspectives on Education in America." Final Draft, April. Albuquerque, NM: Sandia National Laboratories.

CHAMBERS, G. (1948). "Educational Essentialism Thirty Years After." In R. Hahn and D. Bidna, eds., *Secondary Education: Origins and Directions.* New York: Macmillan, 1970.

CLINCHY, B. MC. (1995). "Goals 2000: The Student as Object." *Kappan* 76:383–385.

COLLEGE ENTRANCE EXAMINATION BOARD. (1983). *Academic Preparation for College.* New York: College Board.

CONANT, J. B. (1959). *The American High School Today.* New York: McGraw-Hill.

COOPER, D., ED. (1967). *To Free a Generation: The Dialectics of Liberalism.* New York: Collier.

COUNTS, G. S. (1932). *Dare the Schools Build a New Social Order?* New York: John Day.

CREMIN, L. (1961). *The Transformation of the School.* New York: Random House.

———. (1965). *The Genius of American Education.* New York: Random House.

DAHL, G. (1999). *Radical Conservatism and the Future of Politics.* London: Sage.

DARLING-HAMMOND, L. (1991). "Achieving Our Goals: Superficial or Structural Reforms?" *Kappan* 72:286–295.

DE RUGIERRO, G. (1959). *The History of European Liberalism.* R. G. Collingwood, translator. Boston: Beacon Press.

DE TOCQUEVILLE, A. (1848/1969). *Democracy In America.* J. P. Mayer, ed. Garden City, NY: Doubleday.

DEWEIL, B. (2000). *Democracy: A History of Ideas.* Vancouver: UBC Press.

DENNISON, G. (1969). *The Lives of Children.* New York: Random House.

DEWEY, J. (1916). *Democracy and Education.* New York: Macmillan.

D'SOUZA, D. (1991). *Illiberal Education: The Politics of Race and Sex on Campus.* New York: Free Press.

DOHENY-FARINA, S. (1996). *The Wired Neighborhood.* New Haven: Yale University Press.

DRYFOOS, J. (2002). "Full-Service Community Schools." *Phi Delta Kappan* 83:393–399.

The Education Reform Decade. (1990). Policy Information Report. Princeton: Educational Testing Service.

ELAM, S., ET AL. (1993). "25th Annual PDK/Gallup Poll." *Phi Delta Kappan* 75. September.

EMERSON, J. D., BOES, L., AND MOSTELLER, F. (2002). "Critical Thinking in College Students." In M. A. Fitzgerald et al., eds. *Educational Media and Technology Yearbook.* Englewood, CO: Libraries Unlimited.

FARRAR, R. C. (2000). *Sartrean Dialectics.* Lanham, MD: Lexington Books.

FINN, C. (1990a). "Why Can't our Colleges Convey our Diverse Culture's Unifying Themes?" *The Chronicle of Higher Education* 36, 40, 41.

———. (1990b). "The Biggest Reform of All." *Kappan* 71, 584–593.

FISHER, F. (1991). "What Really Counts in Schools?" *Educational Leadership* 48, 10–15.

FISKE, E. B. (1991). *Smart Schools, Smart Kids.* New York: Simon & Schuster.

FRIEDENBERG, E. Z. (1965). *Coming of Age in America.* New York: Random House.

FREIRE, P. (1973). *Education for Critical Consciousness.* New York: Continuum.

FULLEN, M. (2000). "Three Stories of Education Reform." *Phi Delta Kappan* 83, 581–584.

GARDNER, J. (1958). *The Pursuit of Excellence: Education and the Future of America.* New York: Rockefeller Brothers Fund.

GARFORTH, F. W. (1980) *Educative Democracy: John Stuart Mill on Education in Society.* Oxford: Oxford University Press.

GELLA, A. (1976). *The Intelligentsia and the Intellectuals.* London: Sage.

GIROUX, H. (1988a). *Teachers as Intellectuals: Toward a Critical Pedagogy of Learning.* Granby, MA: Bergin & Garvey.

———. (1988b). *Schooling and the Struggle for Public Life.* Granby, MA: Bergin & Garvey.

———. (1989). "Rethinking Educational Reform in the Age of George Bush." *Kappan* 70, 728–730.

GOLDFARB, J. C. (1998). *Civility and Subversion: The Intellectual in Democratic Society.* Cambridge, England: Cambridge University Press.

GOODLAD, J. I. (1983). *A Place Called School: Prospects for the Future.* New York: McGraw-Hill.

GOODMAN, P. (1964). *Compulsory Miseducation.* New York: Horizon Press.

GOULDNER, A. (1979). *The Future of Intellectuals and the Rise of the New Class.* New York: Seabury Press.

GRAHAM, P. A. (1967). *Progressive Education: From Arcady to Academe.* New York: Teachers College Press.

GREENE, M. (1995). "Art and Imagination: Reclaiming the Sense of Possibility." *Kappan* 76, 378–382.

GUTMAN, A., AND THOMPSON, D. (1996). *Democracy and Disagreement.* Cambridge: Harvard University Press.

HAHN, R., AND BIDNA, D., EDS. (1970). *Secondary Education: Origins and Directions.* New York: Macmillan.

HAWLEY, R. A. (1990). "The Bumpy Road to Drug-Free Schools." *Phi Delta Kappan* 72, 310–314.

HENTOFF, N. (1977). *Does Anybody Give a Damn?* New York: Alfred Knopf.

———. (1998). "God's Place in the Public Schools." *San Diego Union-Tribune.* Aug. 18, B7.

HESS, D. G. (2002). "Discussing Controversial Public Issues in Secondary Social Studies Classrooms." *Theory and Research in Social Education* 30(1), 10–41.

HOLT, J. (1964). *How Children Fail.* New York: Pitman.

HOLT, R. (1989). "Can we Make our Schools Safe?" *NEA Today* 8, 4–6.

HUELSKAMP, R. (1993). "Perspectives on Education in America." *Phi Delta Kappan* 74, 717–720.

HUNTER, J. D. (1991). *Culture Wars: The Struggle to Define America.* New York: Basic Books.

ILLICH, I. (1971). *Deschooling Society.* New York: Harper & Row.

International Education Indicators. (1997). National Center for Educational Statistics. Washington, DC: U.S. Department of Education.

JACOBY, R. (1987). *The Lost Intellectuals.* New York: Basic Books.

JENSEN, C. (1994). *Censored: The News that Didn't Make the News—and Why.* New York: Four Walls Eight Windows Press.

KAESTLE, C. F. (1985). "Education Reform and the Swinging Pendulum." *Kappan* 66, 410–415.

KARIER, C. (1967). *Man, Society and Education.* Chicago: Scott, Foresman.

———. (1985). "Retrospective One." In A. Bestor, *Educational Wastelands.* 2nd Ed. Urbana: University of Illinois Press.

KATZ, M. (1968). *The Irony of Early School Reform.* Cambridge: Harvard University Press.

———. (1971). *Class, Bureaucracy, and Schools: The Illusion of Educational Change in America.* New York: Praeger.

KERLINGER, F. (1984). *Liberalism and Conservatism.* Hillsdale, NJ: Erlbaum.

KOHL, H. (1967). *36 Children.* New York: New American Library.

KOHLBERG, L. (1981). *The Meaning and Measurement of Moral Development.* Worcester, MA: Clark University Press.

KOZOL, J. (1967). *Death at an Early Age.* Boston: Houghton Mifflin.

KURTZ, P. (1992). *The New Skepticism.* Buffalo, NY: Prometheus Books.

LLOYD, T. (1988). *In Defense of Liberalism.* Oxford: Basil Blackwell.

LYND, A. (1950). *Quackery in the Public Schools.* Boston: Little, Brown.

MAKAU, J. M., AND MARTY, D. L. (2001). *Cooperative Argumentation: A Model for a Deliberative Community.* Prospect Heights, IL: Waveland Press.

MARCUSE, H. (1960). *Reason and Revolution.* Boston: Beacon Press.

MARSHALL, C. (1997). *Feminist Critical Policy Analysis I: A Perspective from Primary and Secondary Schooling.* London: Falmer Press.

MARTIN, J. R. (1994). *Changing the Educational Landscape: Philosophy, Women, and Curriculum.* New York: Routledge.

MCCABE, M. M. (2000). *Plato and His Predecessors.* Cambridge, England: Cambridge University Press.

MCLAREN, P. (1989). *Life in Schools.* New York: Longman.

MOSES, R., AND COBB. C. E. (2001). *Radical Equations: Math Literacy and Civil Rights.* Boston: Beacon Press.

MOURAD, R. (2001). "Education after Foucault: The Question of Civility." *Teachers College Record* 103(5), 739–759.

MOYNIHAN, D. P. (1991). "Educational Goals and Political Plans." *The Public Interest* Winter, pp. 32–49.

NATHAN, J. (1991). "Toward Educational Change and Economic Justice: An Interview with Herbert Kohl." *Phi Delta Kappan* 72, 678–681.

NATIONAL COMMISSION ON EXCELLENCE IN EDUCATION. (1983). *A Nation at Risk.* Washington, DC: U.S. Government Printing Office.

National Review. (1990). "Academic Watch." 42, 18.

NATIONAL SCIENCE FOUNDATION. (1983). *Educating Americans for the 21st Century.* Washington, DC: Author.

NEILL, A. S. (1966). *Summerhill: A Radical Approach to Child Rearing.* New York: Hart.

NELSON, J. L., CARLSON, K., AND LINTON, T. L. (1972). *Radical Ideas and the Schools.* New York: Holt, Rinehart & Winston.

Newsweek. (1989). "Kids: Deadly Force." 111, 18–20.

New York Times. (1992). "Education Life." Special supplement. Jan. 5, Sec. 4A, pp. 1–60.

NODDINGS, N. (1984a). *Awakening the Inner Eye: Intuition and Education.* New York: Teachers College Press.

———. (1984b). *Caring: A Feminine Approach to Ethics and Moral Education.* Berkeley: University of California Press.

———. (1995a). "A Morally Defensible Mission for Schools in the 21st Century." *Kappan* 76, 365–368.

———. (1995b). *Philosophy of Education.* Boulder, CO: Westview Press.

NOLAN, J. L. (1996). *The American Culture Wars.* Charlottesville: University of Virginia Press.

NORRIS, P. ED. (1999). *Critical Citizens.* New York: Oxford University Press.

NOVAK, M. (1990). "Scaring our Children." *Forbes* 144, 167.

PAGLIA, C. (1990). *Sexual Personae.* New Haven: Yale Press.

Phi Delta Kappan. "No Quick and Dirty (2001). Editor's Page. *Phi Delta Kappan* 83, 278.

PIAGET, J. (1950). *The Psychology of Intelligence.* London: Routledge & Kegan Paul.

PIERCE, R. K. (1993). *What are We Trying to Teach Them, Anyway?* San Francisco: Center for Self-Governance.

PRESSEISEN, B. (1985). *Unlearned Lessons.* Philadelphia: Falmer Press.

THE PROGRESSIVE. (1991). "The PC Monster." 55, 9.

Projections of Education Statistics to 2008. (1996). National Center for Educational Statistics. Washington, DC: U.S. Department of Education.

PURPEL, D. (1989). *The Moral and Spiritual Crisis in Education: A Curriculum for Justice and Compassion in Education.* Granby, MA: Bergin & Garvey.

RAFFERTY, M. (1968). *Max Rafferty on Education.* New York: Devon Adair.

RASPBERRY, W. (1998). "Public Schools Bad for Education." *San Diego News-Tribune.* Aug. 18, B6.

RAVITCH, D. (1990). "Multiculturalism: E Pluribus Plures." *American Scholar* 59, 337–354.

———. (2000). *Left Back: A Century of Failed School Reforms.* New York: Simon & Schuster.

RAVITCH, D., AND VITERITTI, J. (1997). *New Schools for a New Century.* New Haven: Yale University Press.

RESNICK, L., AND NOLAN, K. (1995). "Where in the World are World Class Standards?" *Educational Leadership* 52, 6–11.

Results in Education: 1990. (1990). The Governors' 1991 Report on Education. Washington, DC: National Governors' Association.

ROSE, L. C., AND GALLUP, A. M. (1998). "The 30th Phi Delta Kappa/Gallup Poll of the Public's Attitudes Toward the Public Schools." *Phi Delta Kappan* 80(1), 41–56.

———. (2001). "The 33rd Annual Phi Delta Kappa/Gallup Poll." *Phi Delta Kappan* 83, 41–47.

ROTH, R. A. (1989). "Preparing Reflective Practitioners." *Journal of Teacher Education* 40, 31–35.

RUSSELL, B. (1928). *Sceptical Essays.* London: George Allen & Unwin.

RYCHLAK, J. F., ED. (1976). *Dialectic.* Basil, Switzerland: Karger.

SACKS, P. (1999). *Standardized Minds.* Cambridge, MA: Perseus Books.

SAFIRE, W. (1991). "Abandon the Pony Express." *New York Times.* April 25, 140, A17.

SAUNDERS, F. S. (1999). *The Cultural Cold War.* New York: New Press.

SCHOENFELD, A. H. (2002). "Making Mathematics Work for All Children." *Educational Researcher* 31:13–25.

SCIABARRA, C. M. (1999). *Ayn Rand: The Russian Radical.* University Park: Pennsylvania State University Press.

———. (2000). *Total Freedom: Toward Dialectical Libertarianism.* University Park: Pennsylvania State University Press.

SHAPIRO, I., AND MACEDO, S. (2000). *Designing Democratic Institutions, Nomos 42.* New York: New York University Press.

SIM, M. (1999). *From Puzzles to Principles.* Lanham, MD: Lexington Books.

SINCLAIR, U. (1924). *The Goslings.* Pasadena: Sinclair.

SIZER, T. (1984). *Horace's Compromise: The Dilemma of the American High School.* Boston: Houghton Mifflin.

SOWELL, T. (1993). *Inside American Education: The Decline, the Deception, the Dogmas.* New York: Free Press.

SMITH, M. (1954). *The Diminished Mind.* New York: Regnery.

STANLEY, W. B. (1981). "Toward a Reconstruction of Social Education." *Theory and Research in Social Education* 9:67–89.

———. (1992). *Education for Utopia: Social Reconstructionism and Critical Pedagogy in the Postmodern Era.* Albany: SUNY Press.

STANLEY, W. B. ED. (2001). *Social Studies Research for the 21st Century.* Greenwich, CT: Information Age Publishers.

TANNER, D. (1993). "A Nation Truly at Risk." *Kappan* 75, 288–297.

TORRES, C. A. (2002). "Globalization, Education, and Citizenship" *American Educational Research Journal* 39(2), 363–378.

TWENTIETH-CENTURY FUND. (1983). *Making the Grade.* New York: Author.

TYACK, D. (1967). *Turning Points in American Educational History.* Waltham, MA: Blaisdell.

———. (1991). "Public School Reform: Policy Talk and Institutional Practice." *American Journal of Education* 100, 1–19.

U.S. News & World Report. (1990). "The Keys to School Reform." Feb. 26, 108, 50+.

ULICH, R. (1954). *Three Thousand Years of Educational Wisdom.* 2nd Ed. Cambridge: Harvard University Press.

UNESCO COUNCIL (2000). Report on the World Social Condition, 2000 New York: United Nations.

UNESCO World Education Report, 2000 (2000). "The Right to Education: Towards Education for All Throughout Life." Paris: UNESCO Publishing.

UNESCO World Education Report, 2000. (2000). Paris: UNESCO.

WEBSTER, W. E., AND MCMILLIN, J. D. (1991). "A Report on Calls for Secondary School Reform in the United States." NASSP Bulletin 75, 77–83.

WEIS, L., AND FINE. M., EDS. (2000). *Construction Sites: Excavating Race, Class, and Gender Among Urban Youth.* New York: Teachers College Press.

WELTER, R. (1962). *Popular Education and Democratic Thought in America.* New York: Columbia University Press.

WILLIAMS, R. H. (1997). *Cultural Wars in American Politics.* New York: Aldine de Gruyter.

WINKLER, K. (1991). "Organization of American Historians Backs Teaching of non Western Culture and Diversity in Schools." *The Chronicle of Higher Education* 37, 5–8.

WINTHROP, N. (2000). *Democratic Theory as Public Philosophy.* Sydney: Ashgate.

WRAGA, W. (2001). "Left Out: The Villainization of Progressive Education in the United States," Review of Left Back. *Educational Researcher* 30, 7.

WRIGHT, L. (2001). *Critical Thinking.* New York: Oxford University Press.

PART ONE

Whose Interests Should Schools Serve?

Justice and Equity

About Part One: Ideas about justice and equity are basic to social relations, formal and informal. From the nature and operation of nations and international interchange to how individuals interact with others, justice and equity questions surround us. In assessing the quality of equity and justice, interests are a major concern. This book is concerned with competing interests in education—interests of individuals and groups with divergent ideas about how schools should serve them and society. Each chapter incorporates disputes between interests, with schooling issues as our focus.

The chapters of Part One are devoted to competing ideological, social, and political interests surrounding the ideas of justice and equity in assessing the school's role in society. Topics covered in Chapters 2 through 8 include divergent interests in family choice and school vouchers, privatization of public schools, equity in school financing, minority and majority equity in education, gender equity, standards and school accountability, and church/state issues in schooling. Each topic involves basic questions regarding application of justice and equity in American society, and involves ideological and political contexts. We use such filters as liberalism and conservatism as well as personal principles to define and evaluate justice and equity. This introduction outlines those contexts.

LIBERALISM, LIBERALS, CONSERVATIVES, AND RADICALS: CONFUSION

Continuing disputes about justice and equity as they apply to individual and social rights are among the grand debates in democratic history and philosophy. These disputes revolve around disparate opinions about the relative rights of individuals and of society, and how equity among those rights should be determined. Although it is a bit confusing to use a similar term to mean different things, note that the current models of "conservatives" and "liberals" follow a Western tradition of liberalism.

Liberalism, a belief in freedom and equality, is the dominant political philosophy among Western democracies (de Ruggiero, 1927, 1959; Noddings, 1995; Klosko, 2000; Richardson, 2001). Shapiro (1958), who traces the history of liberalism through major political literature, states: "What has characterized liberalism at all times is its unshaken belief in the necessity of freedom to achieve every desirable aim. . . . Equality is another fundamental liberal principle . . . the principle of equality for all human beings everywhere" (pp. 10, 11). This dual belief separates the philosophy of modern Western nations from some other political ideas, such as divine right of kings, aristocracy by birth and social class, or theocratic rule. In the United States and other Western democracies, we don't argue seriously for a return to colonial-period theocratic governments, European feudal dictatorships, or politically powerful monarchies. We do argue about the relative weight that should be given to individual freedoms and social constraints (Dahl, 1999; Kramer and Kimball, 1999; Riesman, 1999; Geuss 2001; Henderson, 2001; Newey, 2001). Berlin (1969), points out that

> "Liberty is not the only goal . . . if others are deprived of it . . . then I do not want it for myself. . . . To avoid glaring inequality or widespread misery I am ready to sacrifice some, or all, of my freedom; I may do so willingly and freely: but it is freedom that I am giving up for the sake of justice or equality. . . ." (p. 125)

In the main, both conservatives and liberals in the United States support the basic ideas of democratic freedoms and equality—tenets of traditional liberalism (Dewey, 1930; Lippman, 1934; Russell, 1955; Spitz, 1982; Bellah et al., 1985; Gutman, 1999; Spragens, 1999; Gill, 2001; Tomasi, 2001). The major differences between conservatives and liberals revolve around what are the best definitions/criteria for freedom and equality, what is the best balance between them, how that balance can best be achieved, and how each is served in a specific situation. These differences provide plenty of fuel for political and educational argument.

In addition to possible confusions in the use of the term *liberalism,* another of the intriguing and often confusing trends in contemporary politics and educational politics is the shifting of ideas between conservatives and liberals as they attempt to influence the public's interests and plot potentially successful political positions. The political parties move toward the center to capture votes to get their candidates elected, resulting in some blurring of the conservative and liberal markers we are accustomed to using. Basic ideological differences may remain for the Republican and Democratic parties, but individual candidates don't easily fit on all issues in public life. Each party has a conservative and a liberal wing, and there is a large group of people inside and out of the parties who prefer to be considered independent.

New Democrats, like Bill Clinton, worked to cut the deficit, stimulate the economy and increase corporate wealth, cut welfare, and actively support imposing national standards on schools. These had been Republican and conservative views. New Republicans, like George W. Bush, increase public spending and the deficit, support the U.S. Department of Education, and expand the Peace Corps—previously Democratic and liberal views. Specific political party positions and the views of individual candidates may not correlate well with divergent underlying political ideologies, from conservative to liberal. But within each party there is often a contest among candidates to be identifed as more conservative, if Republican, or more liberal, if Democrat, as a way of attracting core party voters. This suggests the basic ideological orientation of each of the parties, but conservative and liberal labels don't stick on individuals as well as some might like.

We continue, despite the confusions, to use conservative and liberal labels to identify ideas and issues, and to mark various people. For example, Bernard Goldberg (2002), a former CBS executive, publishes an exposé filled with anecdotes from his experiences that he claims show the media has a "liberal" bias. David Brock (2002), a widely read and quoted conservative author, publishes an exposé that confesses to a career of overstatement and falsification of information in his active denigration of "liberal" causes and sanctifying of "conservative" ones. Both books make the best-seller lists and the authors are interviewed across the United States in stories about conservative and liberal politics. The labels still have meaning, despite the confusions and shifting, in politics and education.

Contemporary political disputes between "conservatives" and "liberals" occur over questions of balance and process, and they spill over into our debates on lawmaking, court proceedings, and schooling. Current conservatives, in general, want to limit governmental interference in individual freedom; and current liberals generally want to ensure individual rights by governmental regulation. Conservatives argue for unregulated rights of individuals to own guns; liberals for governmental regulation of gun ownership. There are many areas of muddiness in this separation, giving pause in gross labelling. One of these areas is abortion, where liberals tend to support women's right to choose and conservatives tend to support government policy to restrict abortions. Another is free speech, where liberals tend to support more individual freedom and conservatives tend to want limits imposed on opposing views of sexuality, patriotism, politics, and economics. A third example includes some school topics, where liberals tend to support more individual freedom for students and teachers to examine controversial topics, to protest, and to criticize, and conservatives tend to support standards, school and teacher accountability, socially acceptable student behavior, and restrictions on what topics can be studied.

INTERESTS, POLITICS, AND IDEOLOGY

Our interests are incorporated in and modified by ideas—liberal, conservative, radical, reactionary. Although these labels may not identify each of us or our views on various topics, they represent broad, divergent views of what should be, and can be used to examine social and educational issues. Ideologies enable people to explain and justify the society they would prefer. An ideology includes assumptions about the nature and purpose of society and related nature of individuals (Shils, 1968); it provides criteria against which one can judge human life and society (Lane, 1962); and it provides a means for self-identification (Erikson, 1960). Ideologies are broadly coherent structures of attitudes, values, and beliefs that influence individual perceptions and social policy (Piper, 1997).

Political ideologies are widely known, from radical right to radical left with conservatives and liberals somewhere near the center. The right and left political conflict is easily illustrated, though often starkly presented. Former Supreme Court nominee Robert Bork (1995), for example, argues, "Modern liberalism is . . . a disease of our cultural elites, the people who control the institutions that manufacture or dissseminate ideas, attitudes and symbols . . . the root of egalitarianism lies in envy and insecurity, which are in turn products of self-pity, arguably the most pervasive and powerful emotion known to mankind" (pp. 141, 144). An opposing view is offered by Braun and Scheinberg (1997), who argue from the left side, "Right wing extremism serves as a point of entry for wide-ranging problems of hatred, xenophobia and nationalism that frustrate the healthy functioning of democracy" (p. 33).

Bork obviously sides with individual liberty and against egalitarianism, but his use of "liberalism" as a term to label liberals illustrates one kind of confusion we noted and that often arises in political literature and ideological dispute. Liberalism, we suggest, can be used to include both individual freedom and equality. The balance between them fuels most conservative-liberal debate. Bork's use of liberalism implies that liberals are necessarily egalitarians (striving for equal conditions for all) and are unconcerned with individual freedoms. Notwithstanding the disparaging and unecessarily limiting statement by Bork that the concept of "modern liberalism" is a "disease" of egalitarianism, traditional ideas of liberalism are based on the dual concept of human freedom and equality of opportunity—not on the necessity of equality of condition anticipated by egalitarianism. In a similar broad sweep from the other direction, Braun and Scheinberg (1997) include all right-wing "extremists" in a general statement that implies culpability in supporting or condoning antidemocratic behaviors. Ideological debates can be fiery and passionate, if not always reasonable, realistic, or precise.

Definitions of "conservative" and "liberal" may be slippery, but these terms are commonly applied and widely understood to refer to two distinct groups of ideas and people in any time period. Liberal ideas in one period may be considered conservative in another, and vice versa. Neoconservative and neoliberal views are a rethinking of conservative or liberal ideas (Steinfels, 1979; Rothenberg, 1984; DeMuth and Kristol, 1995; Piper, 1997; Dahl, 1999; Newey, 2001; Richardson, 2001). For example, Simhony and Weinstein (2001) claim the new liberalism goes beyond the stale liberalism-communitarian debates of the 1980s, and aims to reconcile the split between "individuality and sociability," with liberals shifting away from social or government programs as the primary answer to most social and individual problems.

More deeply discordant ideological roots, including a variety of radical positions on what a society and its schools should be, run beyond the mainstream liberal-conservative dialogue. Radical critiques influence the general debate by providing extreme positions, allowing liberals and conservatives to take more popular positions in the center. Radical ideas tend to have limited credibility in mainstream discussions, but liberals and conservatives draw from those ideas in proposing reforms (Dahl, 1999). Critical positions often appear first in the radical literature, then filter into the liberal and conservative rhetoric (Nelson, Carlson, and Linton, 1972; Dahl, 1999; Simhony and Weinstein, 2001). Those mainstream views sound more reasonable as bases for reform, but radical ideas contain the seeds for longer-term and more significant change. In the age when kings and queens were presumed to rule by divine right, democracy was a radical view. In a dictatorship, individual freedom is radical. Even in a democracy, ideological views of individual rights, however, compete with opposing views of equality and common purpose—a battle within liberalism. More radical positions on individualism and communitarianism offer insights into problems and possibilities.

INDIVIDUALISM AND COMMUNITARIANISM

To what extent should we allow individuals to do as they wish, under the notion of individual rights? And to what extent should the community have the right to exert control over individual behavior? Some argue that individuals have rights only in the sense that society grants them, and they can be taken away when society desires. Others pose the idea of individual rights as natural—something like the unalienable rights suggested in the Declaration of Independence. But the Declaration and the U.S. Constitution, with its rights and amendments, is a document produced by an emerging national community. The Constitution has been and can be altered. Yet if the community agrees that individuals have absolute and natural rights, presumably, it could not abrogate those rights without consent of the individuals. This knotty problem has fueled debates in philosophy and political theory through Western history. Battles over limits of free speech and community standards dot the landscape of court decisions based on U.S. constitutional interpretations. One of the major struggles in determining justice in a democracy lies in finding a suitable balance between the interests of individuals and communities. This struggle has many titles, but often is described as an ideological battle between individualism and communitarianism. These ideologies compete in their emphases, and in their more extreme versions offer a dialectic.

More radical factions separate much further than the mainstream conservative-liberal dialogue on issues of individualism and communitarianism. The radical right wing, known as reactionaries or libertarians, advocates individual freedoms with the least restraint possible.

Nozick (1974) phrases it:

> "Individuals have rights, and there are things no person or group may do to them (without violating their rights). So strong and far-reaching are these rights that they raise the question of what, if anything, the state and its officials may do. How much room do individual rights leave for the state? . . . Our main conclusions about the state are that a minimal state, limited to the narrow functions of protection against force, theft, fraud, enforcement of contracts, and so on, is justified; that any more extensive state will violate person's rights not to be forced to do certain things, and is unjustified. (p. ix)

Libertarians and anarchists share a strong concern for individual rights and a distaste for governmental regulation. There are not many anarchists about now, and they often are seen as left-wing extremists. The Libertarian Political Party, usually perceived as one of the far-right groups, has not been very popular in elections, but runs many candidates. Views expressed by many people on the conservative side are that we should get the government off our backs, privatize most public activities, deregulate industries, allow more latitude to entrepreneurs, significantly cut and simplify or eliminate taxes, and initiate a host of other political shifts to emphasize individual rights.

These ideas, carried much further, result in a libertarian or anarchistic view. In addition to an antistate position, libertarians convey a strong procapitalism view. The concept is relatively unfettered entrepreneurship and private enterprise. Excessive governmental control is assumed to kill individual initiative. Government, to libertarians, is an unfortunate development that has grown too large and too encompassing—stifling individual freedoms. Herbert Spencer (1981) wrote, "The great political superstition of the past was the divine right of kings. The great political superstition of the present is the divine right of parliaments" (p. 123).

Strong libertarians want to dismantle the government, abolishing regulation, taxation, and public financing. They would eliminate social security, medicare, welfare, public education, and the right of government to take property under eminent domain; libertarians aim at "nothing short of the privatization of social existence" (Newman, 1984, p. 162). As Thomas Sowell (1999), a commentator on the right, says: "The welfare state, however, has made many of the respectable, self-supporting poor look like chumps, as the government has lavished innumerable programs on those who violate all rules and refuse to take responsibility for themselves" (p. 89). Not all libertarians share the view that all government is harmful; some recognize a need for some governmental role in mediating disputes, regulating commerce in basic human needs, and protecting society.

On the other side are communitarians of various stripes. Their major critique involves greed and social corruption unregulated capitalism can engender, and the selfishness and self-centeredness that accompanies individualism. They believe community, our social glue, is in serious jeopardy from excessive individualism. Some of these critiques take great pains to separate individualism—a belief in oneself above others—from individuality—an expression of the value of recognizing each person's worth. John Dewey (1933) published a significant treatise on that separation, and developed in his writings on democracy and schooling his concept that individual differences and individual learning are consistent with his concept of education as a social process (Dewey, 1916, 1930). Dewey also writes of a broader set of conflicts:

> There can be no conflict between the individual and the social. For both of these terms refer to pure abstractions. What do exist are conflicts between some individuals and some arrangements in social life; between groups and classes of individuals; between nations and races; between old traditions embedded in institutions and new ways of thinking and acting which spring from those few individuals who attack what is socially accepted. (Dewey, in Ratner, 1939, p. 435)

Communitarians don't always ignore or denigrate the value of individuals; they advocate a balance between individual liberty and social needs for common purposes—balancing rights and order. Amitai Etzioni (1996) notes a major shift from "traditional" social order by edict, authoritarian rule, and rigid control to increasing individual rights.

He argues:

> . . . after the forces of modernity rolled back the forces of traditionalism, these [modernity] forces did not come to a halt; instead, in the last generation (roughly from 1960 on), they pushed ahead relentlessly, eroding the much weakened foundations of social virtue and order while seeking to expand liberty ever more. As a result, we shall see that some societies have lost their equilibrium, and are heavily burdened with the antisocial consequences of excessive liberty (not a concept libertarians or liberals often use). (p. xvii)

More radical communitarians argue for egalitarian answers to the excesses of individualism. They see a breakdown of social values, family structures, social responsibilities, shared interests, and collective purposes that constitute a decent society. Among their concerns is the greedy continuation of "me" generation mentality and expansion of "yuppiness," antigovernment attacks that can undermine public confidence and lead to debilitating and discriminatory competitiveness, destruction of environmental protections and other regulatory needs, increased private territoriality, and suspicion of others. Unbridled individualism poses, they contend, clear and negative repercussions in charitable works, public welfare, public services, and public education—those major contributions to our civilization. Excessive individualism also appears in efforts to deregulate utilities and corporations, privatize public services, and maintain a social hierarchy based on birth, wealth, and historical status. Certainly, individualism is not usually advocated by members of the social class at the bottom. A premise of individualists is that those who have had should continue to have. Egalitarian answers, in opposition, include expansion and guarantees of equal opportunities, forms of affirmative action, progressive taxation and redistribution of wealth, and such programs as national health care, Head Start, and safety net welfare. These intend to correct or mitigate inequalities among groups.

Following the Enron debacle in 2002, and a series of similar failures in corporate and accounting self-regulation, there has been an upsurge of interest in increasing public regulation and accountability. As in the antitrust period in the early twentieth century, this has ignited public concern about patterns of deregulation, privatization, and rampant individualism that identified the 1990s.

COMPETING INTERESTS

We all have interests and we are members of groups which have interests. We want good things for ourselves, our families, our friends, our associations, and our society. Our interests may also include wanting negative consequences for our enemies, our competitors, and others who oppose our interests. We like to hear that our nation's writers, scientists, athletes, actors, students, or workers have won awards in international competition. We are dismayed by reports that our children's test scores are lower than some other nations'. There are, of course, times when our personal interests and family or group interests are in opposition, as when arguing about who should get the family car, what kind of career to pursue, or whether to support a war. Varying interests undergird most arguments.

Enlightened self-interest is a pleasant way of describing why we do things that benefit ourselves without hurting others. Novelist and philosopher Ayn Rand (1943, 1957, 1997) became popular as a strong advocate of self-interest, though she included a provision that individuals respect others' rights. She considered selfishness a virtue and argued against altruism and its idea that others are more important than oneself. Rand's views provide excellent examples of rugged individualism and "titanic self-assertion" (Gladstein, 1999, p. 1). An economic theory developed by Anthony Downs (1997) provided similar support for enlightened self-interest in the marketplace.

Greed arises cloaked in unenlightened self-interest. Enron, WorldCom, and other corporation greed illustrated this point in 2002 with major executives making off with millions of dollars in salary, perks, and stock options while workers were underpaid, lost retirement and benefits, and were misinformed, even as the executives knew how badly the company was doing. Graft and corruption in politics, school business, corporate life, and even religious institutions provide further illustration of unenlightened self-interest.

Even enlightened self-interest, where no damage is intended for others, can still create serious conflicts as individual or group interests compete for scarce resources. Who gets to decide whose self-interests are enlightened, and on what criteria?

Group interests also can be competitive. Special interests have become a term of derision in politics—we label the opposition candidate in an election campaign as being in the clutches of special interest groups. Yet we all belong to various special interest groups, by our own or our family's occupations, geographic area, hobbies, charities, travel, religion, shopping, educational pursuits, and nearly all other endeavors. We support environmental, political, consumer, business, trade, town, state, and other associations in their efforts to influence public opinion or politics. Obviously, these interests do not always coincide. We would like lower taxes, but appreciate public benefits such as roads, police, clean parks, and schools. We prefer a healthy environment, but like products that come from chemicals, plastics, and other pollution-producing manufacturers. We join or support groups that advocate those ideas we share, even if at times we act in a manner that is not consistent.

Then there are our societal and national interests. Our stated policy, whether under a Democratic or Republican administration, is to defend national interests in international affairs—trade, borders, war, terrorism, and so on. Can you imagine any nation that did not have the same policy? Not remarkably, each nation has national interest as foremost, though clearly the definition and delineation of national interest is always dependent upon that government's determination of its own interests and persuasive abilities. National interest has been one of the fuels of war, genocide, militarism, border protection, isolation, denial of human rights, trade restriction, and international posturing. It also has been a fuel of peace, international understanding, freedom, trade agreements, charity, economic development, and the protection of human rights (Nelson and Green, 1980). Our use of language shows interests at work: the "Axis of Evil" identifies nations and groups our government considers threatening, "Manifest Destiny" was invoked to cover the invasion of Native American territory in the West, the "war on terrorism" is used as grounds for changing accepted patterns of civil rights and civil liberties.

Societal interests involve such matters as general safety and welfare, the environment, health, education, security, transportation, communication, freedom, and order. These topics concern people across such political boundaries as cities, states, and nations. Not only are residents of cities such as Chicago or Phoenix interested in safe highways and airports or good hospitals and schools—these are public interests, whether the social institutions are privately or publicly operated. The public has a stake in how these quality-of-life areas are handled; many are government controlled and operated, some are government regulated and privately operated, and some are privately controlled and operated, with little governmental oversight.

Schooling is one of the most important of those broad public concerns in the United States. Laws govern nearly all forms of schooling to include required attendance, financing, and operational requirements. Most school-age students in the United States attend public schools, controlled and operated by government. But about 15 percent of all students are enrolled in some form of private schooling, including independent schools, religiously affiliated schools, trade schools, and home schooling. In addition, there are efforts to provide vouchers for funding to parents who want to take their children from public schools to private schools, efforts to establish charter schools in the public districts for relief from some governmental regulation, and efforts to privatize public school operation by contracting with corporations. Each of these topics, covered in Chapters 2 through 8, poses conflicts among interests and raises issues of justice and equity.

Ideas of justice and equity provide rationales for mediating, adjudicating, mitigating, criticizing, and evaluating the various conflicts among interests; but justice and equity are not without debate themselves.

JUSTICE AND EQUITY: SOUNDS GOOD TO ME

Justice sounds simple enough, and is certainly above dispute as a fundamental element in a well-ordered society—or family, organization, school, or relationship with others. We want to live in a society, family, school, or relationship that is just. We rail against situations we consider unjust. The difficulty, of course, is that justice depends on many factors: a set of socially agreed values and principles, legal and moral traditions, the political and economic situation, technical and practical definitions of terms used, the time period and geographic location, social and individual conditions, and the eye of the beholder. Justice, then, is dependent on such things as where you happen to be, when, who you are, how you are represented, and what you think of it.

This is not to suggest that justice is just a fuzzy idea that can never be defined, is constantly changing, and is too nebulous to have much impact on your life. Indeed, justice is the forming idea for nearly all political theory, law, ethics, and human relations. It has a history of very specific definitions in particular situations, yet is still under constant redefinition by a variety of people from parents to legislators. Burning witches at the stake was considered justice at one time; using the rod to physically punish misbehaving students was an accepted schoolmarm's role in the school justice system of the past. The ultimate punishment, death, is considered too uncivilized to be justice in some nations; others use it routinely.

The existing concept of justice has an impact on your life in virtually all settings, and can easily be the most important of influences. Consider being accused of a serious crime you did or did not commit; consider being the victim of a serious crime. Think of the times you got a grade you did not think you deserved; think of the teacher's view of the same grade. Put yourself into the shoes of someone who suffers severe physical or mental disorder, or lives in a dictatorship, or is audited by the IRS. Each of these has a justice component. Even everyday complaints about restaurant food or a department store purchase pose questions of justice, albeit more trivial. Waiters and store clerks usually employ a sense of justice in dealing with or ignoring complaining customers. Justice is both an ideal and a practical matter of significance for individuals and society, but it is a concept fraught with difficulties in definition and interpretation.

Justice incorporates ideas of impartiality and fairness, two concepts as difficult to discern as justice. Was Solomon impartial? Could his decision be fair to all? How do we know that any judge is impartial and fair? Was the Supreme Court impartial and fair in deciding the election between George W. Bush and Al Gore in 2000? Was the Supreme Court impartial and fair in their differing historic decisions on slavery, women's suffrage, segregated schools, abortion? Were those stock market analysts impartial when they recommended buying more Enron stock while it was collapsing? Was your teacher fair and impartial when you got the grade you think you did not deserve? Is school a good place to learn about justice, fairness, and impartiality—and do schools provide good models for how justice, fairness, and impartiality should work?

Stuart Hampshire (2000), arguing that the basis of justice lies in human conflicts, stated ". . . fairness in procedures for resolving conflicts is the fundamental kind of fairness" (p. 4). Conflicts are a continuing and engaging human condition. Dialogue and dialectics can assist in examining conflicting views, but our sense of justice requires a belief in fair procedures for dealing with them (Fishkin, 1992). The procedural fairness Hampshire advocates may result in unequal conditions. Both divorcing parents who fight over child custody are unlikely to believe the result was entirely fair when only one of them wins. Selecting the Teachers of the Year in a school district may incorporate a fair procedure with impartial judging, but some teachers are likely to see the results as unfair. But when we think the procedures were generally fair, unequal results can be better tolerated.

The concept of fairness is essential to our ideas of justice—and fair procedures are a basic condition for justice in a legitimate democracy. Legitimacy, in a democracy, is the granting of authority to government by the people—a form of social contract. This is the idea of the consent of the governed, a concept disputed by some political theorists, but it continues to be widely held (Rawls, 1999). We accept decisions, even if we don't like them, when we feel the procedure is fair. If there is widespread concern that basic procedures are unfair, we have social unrest and the seeds of revolution. Justice is a particularly significant idea in society and in schooling.

EQUITY AND EQUALITY

Equity is a concept directly related to justice, and includes the idea of equal treatment under natural law or rights, without bias or favoritism. Equity and equality are concepts that can differ significantly. Equality can be measured by condition—each person has exactly the same. Or it can be equality of treatment—each one is treated the same based on some principle: "all men are created equal." But often we think that some seem to be more equal than others; and we can suspect gender inequality at work in the preceding quote on the equality of men. These are issues of equity and justice. Is it possible to distribute things in a truly equal manner? Political scientist David Spitz (1982) notes that "Equality drives us into an insoluble moral dilemma, and therefore into practices that contradict what we preach. . . . To impose equality of results . . . is to limit equality of opportunity. We cannot have both equalities simultaneously" (p. 105).

Equity does not require equality; it does expect a process deemed fair. Most of our notions of equality in the United States are procedural—equal treatment under the law, which is similar to the idea of procedural fairness. These ideas provide for opportunity, but do not specify equal results or conditions. The idea of equity provides a concept for judging the procedure of equal treatment. Under equity, exactly equal conditions or results are not required; there is no mandate that good things are distributed to all in an equal manner. Instead, there is an expectation for justice—any unequal distribution must be justified by some significant social/ethical principle (Rawls, 1971, 1999, 2001).

For example, we could justify providing special funds and separate programs for gifted and talented students in school because those students are meritorious and have the potential to give back more to the school and, later, to society. But not everyone would agree this is a democratic or equitable justification or that these students deserve special treatment or make more community contribution. Using Rawlsian theory on distributive justice, McKenzie (1984) studied school programs for gifted and talented students and concluded such programs were undemocratic, unfair in selection and special treatment, and did not provide for having those specially treated students give something back to the school and society. Tracking students into separate curriculums for college preparation, vocational training, general studies, and special education brings up similar issues of justice and equity. Are inclusion or mainstreaming programs more equitable and just? Are separate special education programs more educationally appropriate for individual students? Do these interests conflict?

In the last quarter of the twentieth century, we decided justice is served when we provide special access to public buildings for people who require a wheelchair. That is based on a principle of equity turned into law that equal access requires special treatment for one group. Equity, then, can include inequality if the basic premise is that of justice. Affirmative action programs are predicated on this idea, making up for previous unjust discrimination. Improved funding for programs such as special education, Head Start, and school lunches for poor families is an equity topic. Special school treatment of the children of minority families, whether by ethnic group, nationality, or income, represents another example.

Programs to redress previous inequalities and discrimination based on gender, race, class, or sexual orientation also are equity issues. Inequalities in public financing among local school districts, the subject of several different state supreme court decisions based on equal treatment, is an equity and justice topic of continuing importance. Children, their parents, taxpayers, constitutional lawyers, citizens in neighboring school districts, and most of the rest of society have interests involved in determination of such equity issues. Should new national standards in various subject fields be imposed on all children in every school? Is this equitable and just? Should some public schools be operated by private corporations; should private schools have access to public money; should religion be part of public education and should it be supported by public funds? Each of these examples, of course, has been and continues to be hotly contested social and educational policy and practice. As in political discourse, these issues have ideological dimensions.

IDEOLOGICAL ROOTS OF SCHOOL DISPUTES

Competing ideas with differing expectations for schools include freedom and equality, public and private, individual and society, the masses and the elites, unity and diversity, and the religious and the secular.

There are many dualisms, for example, mind/body, self/others, either/or. That dualisms are false is a truism in that they don't exist in complete isolation from each other and don't usually require a pristine choice. We can't have mind without body, and body without mind may be possible, but we have no certain knowledge of that. So we can't choose either body or mind. That such dualisms are false, of course, is true. Yet we continuously are faced with situations where we must exercise choice among competing interests. Those choices often are between two political ideologies, two opposing sets of interests, or two parts of a dialectic—each side of which entails some potentially good and bad consequences. Dualisms are useful as mental constructions to assist in making that choice or finding a new synthesis; they can assist in reasoned dialogue about competing interests and ideologies. Schooling is one very public activity where such dualisms occur with frequency.

Schools are directly engaged in developing the individuals and society of the future and people care a great deal about what kind of individuals and society will develop. As Apple (1990) states, "the conflicts over what should be taught are sharp and deep. It is not only an educational issue, but one that is inherently ideological and political" (p. vii).

Ideologies also provide basic rationales for divergent educational views that want to either sustain, alter, or overthrow the contemporary school (Christenson et al., 1971). An ideology provides unity around its beliefs. Thus, traditionalists share a general view that schools ought to follow time-honored ideas, practices, and authorities from a previous golden age of education. Progressivists share a different view that schools must be flexible, child-centered, and future-oriented.

Each ideology provides different views of schooling, from advocating abolition of public schools to using public schools for social criticism and the overthrow of oppression. Divergent views of schooling and politics can be understood in terms of an ideological continuum: from elitist positions on the extreme right to egalitarian positions on the extreme left, with mainstream conservative and liberal positions in the center (see Figure 1).

Radical right-wing ideas about schooling are not uniform; they come from different special interest groups. Some promote teaching fundamentalist religious dogma. Some seek to censor teaching materials dealing with sex, socialism, atheism, or anything they think is anti-American. And some want to undercut publicly supported schools in favor of elite schooling for a select group of students. Right-wing groups have attacked secular humanism, feminism, abortion rights, sex education, global education, and values education in schools (Kaplan, 1994).

Radical educational ideologies from the right include the views of:

> libertarians: "get government off our backs and out of our schools,"
>
> abolitionists: "abolish public schooling," and
>
> extreme elitists: "schooling for the best only; the rest into the work pool."

The radical left wing also offers a critical view of schools. Some see education as the way for the masses to uncover the evils of capitalism and the corporate state. Some propose education as the means for revolution, opening all the institutions of society to criticism. And some advocate free schools, where students may study whatever they want and all costs are borne by the public. Left-wing groups have attacked business-sponsored teaching materials, religious dogma in public schools, tracking, discrimination, social control, and education for patriotic obedience.

FIGURE 1 A Spectrum of Political and Educational Views

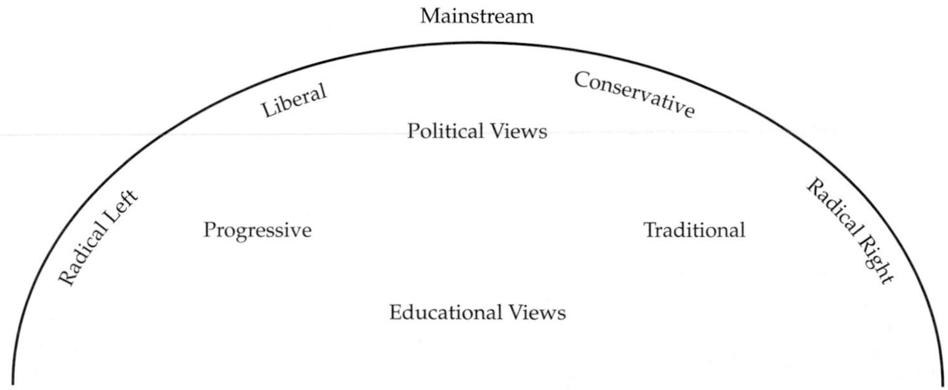

Radical left-wing views include those of:

> liberationists: "liberate students from oppressive forces in school and society,"
>
> reconstructionists: "use schools to criticize and remake society," and
>
> extreme egalitarians: "abolish all privilege or distinction."

Conservative, liberal, and radical views of society and education provide different rationales for criticism of schools and different proposals for reform. They are general frameworks that underlie individual and group discontent with schools. Radical views are important because they present stark and clearly defined differences between egalitarian and elitistic ideologies. However, mainstream conservative and liberal ideas govern most reform movements because of their general popularity and immense influence over media and government. Liberals, conservatives, and radicals differ in their views of which mainstream position has the schools in its grip (Aronowitz and Giroux, 1993).

The importance of education in society is reflected in controversies surrounding divergent ideological positions and the interests they represent. Hunter (1991), writing about the school as a focus of conflicting ideologies, says:

> . . . America is in the midst of a culture war that has and will continue to have reverberations not only within public policy but within the lives of ordinary Americans everywhere." . . .
>
> Because skills, values, and habits of life are passed on to children in school, it was inevitable that the schools would be an arena of cultural conflict. (pp. 34, 37)

Ideologies exist to explain or justify purposes and practices or to challenge them. In education these fundamental goals and general practices have varied during different times and in different locations. Primitive education was dedicated to survival and continuing rituals and life patterns established by elders. Ancient schooling was largely devoted to inculcation of religious learnings. In Athens philosophic and contemplative schooling supplanted religious, while Spartan education was heavily committed to the military life. Roman schooling was more practical than philosophic and intended for developing strong loyalty and citizenship. Spiritual ideas predominated in schools of the Middle Ages, a preparation for the afterlife. The Renaissance brought different goals for schools—enlightenment, development of human capacities, and individual creativity. For most of this time formal schooling was for the elites, usually for families of religious, social, and political leaders. The main schooling arguments concerned how society's leaders should be prepared; strict learning of traditional roles, rituals, and concepts of knowledge—or contemplation of the good—or enlightenment and more flexible learnings.

Mass education arose as democracy developed, fostered especially in schooling of the United States from the mid-nineteenth century, and now spread throughout the industrialized world.

Schooling for all developed some different educational goals, under differing ideologies: basic literacy and numeracy, social control, civic responsibility, loyalty and patriotism, vocational and home training, character and values development, health and safety knowlege, human relationships, self-reliance and realization, and solving problems. Schooling also shifted toward more secular, scientific, and technological goals: understanding our environments and ourselves, improving global political/economic/social interrelations, developing work and life skills and attitudes, using and examining technology, improving society, and critical thinking. Consistent with the evolution in democratic political concepts, ideas about schooling shifted from a focus on basic literacy and social control to broader intellectual development and increasing interest in individuality. Clearly, newer developments in educational ideas challenged established purposes and practices in schools, and posed interesting questions on the relation of individuals to their societies, and important issues of justice and equity.

What dimensions of justice and equity should be expected in schools and classrooms? How should schools address justice and equity regarding individual choice, racism, gender, class, wealth, and religion? What interests are at stake? What ideologies frame the questions and answers? Competing answers to these questions show disparate interests. Chapters 2 through 8 involve schooling issues that raise questions of justice, fairness, and impartiality.

We would like to include in this volume all viewpoints on each educational issue, but that is an obvious impossibility. We have, therefore, limited each chapter to two distinct positions about the topic covered to stress the dialogue or dialectic quality of the issue. These positions draw from liberal-progressive ideas, from conservative-traditional, and from radical critiques from the left or right. Additional references to conservative, liberal, and radical literature are included, and we encourage exploration of these highly divergent views.

References

APPLE, M. (1990). *Ideology and Curriculum.* 2nd Ed. London: Routledge.

ARONOWITZ, S., AND GIROUX, H. (1983). *Education Under Siege.* South Hadley, MA: Bergin & Garvey. (2nd Ed., 1993).

BELLAH, R. N., ET AL., (1985). *Habits of the Heart: Individualism and Commitment in American Life.* Berkeley: University of California Press.

BERLIN, I. (1969). *Four Essays on Liberty.* Oxford: Oxford University Press.

BORK, R. (1995). "Culture and Kristol." In C. DeMuth and W. Kristol, eds., *The Neoconservative Imagination.* Washington, DC: AEI Press.

BRAUN, A., AND SCHEINBERG, S. (1997). *The Extreme Right.* Boulder, CO: Westview Press.

BROCK, D. (2002). *Blinded by the Right: The Conscience of an Ex-Conservative.* New York: Crown Publishers.

CHRISTENSON, R. M., ET AL. (1971). *Ideologies and Modern Politics.* New York: Dodd, Mead.

DAHL, G. (1999). *Radical Conservatism and the Future of Politics.* London: Sage.

DEMUTH, C., AND KRISTOL, W. (1995) *The Neoconservative Imagination.* Washington DC: AEI Press.

DE RUGGERIO, G. (1927). *The History of European Liberalism.* R. G. Collingwood, translator. Boston: Beacon Press. (2nd Ed., 1959).

DEWEY, J. (1916). *Democracy and Education.* New York: Macmillan.

———. (1930). *Individualism Old and New.* New York: Minton, Balch, & Co.

———. (1933). *How We Think.* Boston: D. C. Heath.

DOWNS, A. (1957). *An Economic Theory of Democracy.* New York: Harper/Addison Wesley. (2nd Ed., 1997).

ERIKSON, E. H. (1960). *Childhood and Society.* New York: W. W. Norton.

ETZIONI, A. (1996). *The New Golden Rule.* New York: Basic Books.

FISHKIN, J. S. (1992). *The Dialogue of Justice.* New Haven, CT: Yale University Press.

GEUSS, R. (2001). *History and Illusion in Politics.* Cambridge, England: Cambridge University Press.

GILL, E. R. (2001). *Becoming Free: Autonomy and Diversity in the Liberal Polity.* Lawrence, KS: University of Kansas Press.

GLADSTEIN, M. R. (1999). *The New Ayn Rand Companion.* Westport, CT: Greenwood.

GOLDBERG, B. (2002). *Bias: A CBS Insider Exposes How the Media Distort the News.* Washington, DC: Regnery Publishers.

GUTMAN, A. (1999). *Democratic Education.* Princeton: Princeton University Press.

HAMPSHIRE, S. (2000). *Justice Is Conflict.* Princeton: Princeton University Press.

HENDERSON, D. (2001). *Anti-Liberalism 2000.* London: Institute of Economic Affairs.

HUNTER, J. D. (1991). *Culture Wars: The Struggle to Define America.* New York: Basic Books.

KAPLAN, G. R. (1994). "Shotgun Wedding: Notes on Public Education's Encounter with the New Christian Right." *Kappan* 75:11–12.

KLOSKO, G. (2000). *Democratic Procedures and Liberal Consensus.* New York: Oxford University Press.

KRAMER, H., AND KIMBALL, R. (1999). *The Betrayal of Liberalism.* Chicago: Ivan R. Dee.

LANE, R. E. (1962). *Political Ideology.* New York: The Free Press of Glencoe.

LIPPMAN, W. (1934). *The Method of Freedom.* New York: Macmillan.

MCKENZIE, J. (1984). *A Study of the Relative Democratic Nature of Gifted Education Programs in New Jersey.* Unpublished dissertation, Rutgers University.

NELSON, J., CARLSON, K., AND LINTON, T. (1972). *Radical Ideas and the Schools.* New York: Holt, Rinehart & Winston.

NELSON, J., AND GREEN, V. (1980). *International Human Rights.* Stanfordville, NY: Coleman Publishers.

NEWEY, G. (2001). *After Politics.* New York: Palgrave.

NEWMAN, S. L. (1984). *Liberalism at Wit's End.* Ithaca, NY: Cornell University Press.

NODDINGS, N. (1995). *Philosophy of Education.* Boulder, CO: Westview Press.

NOZICK, R. (1974). *Anarchy, State, and Utopia.* New York: Basic Books.

PIPER, J. R. (1997). *Ideologies and Institutions.* New York: Rowman and Littlefield.

RAND, A. (1943). *The Fountainhead.* New York: New American Library. (2nd Ed., 1957).

———. (1997). *The Journals of Ayn Rand.* D. Harriman, ed. New York: Dutton.

RATNER, J. (1939). *Intelligence in the Modern World: John Dewey's Philosophy.* New York: Random House.

RAWLS, J. (1971). *A Theory of Justice.* Cambridge, MA: Harvard University Press. (2nd Ed., 1999).

———. (1999). *The Law of Peoples.* Cambridge, MA: Harvard University Press.

———. (2001). *Justice as Fairness.* E. Kelly, ed. Cambridge, MA: Harvard University Press.

REISMAN, D. (1999). *Conservative Capitalism.* New York: St. Martins Press.

RICHARDSON, J. L. (2001). *Contending Liberalisms in World Politics.* Boulder, CO: Lynne Rienner Publications.

ROTHENBERG, R. (1984). *The Neoliberals.* New York: Simon & Schuster.

RUSSELL, B. (1955). *Authority and the Individual.* London: Allen and Unwin.

SHAPIRO, J. S. (1958). *Liberalism: Its Meaning and History.* New York: D. Van Nostrand.

SHILS, E. (1968). "The Concept of Ideology." In D. Sills, ed., *The International Encyclopedia of the Social Sciences.* New York: Macmillan.

SIMHONY, A., AND WEINSTEIN, D. (2001). *The New Liberalism.* Cambridge, England: Cambridge University Press.

SPENCER, H. (1981). *The Man Versus the State.* Indianapolis, IN: Liberty Classics.

SPITZ, D. (1982). *The Real World of Liberalism.* Chicago: University of Chicago Press.

SPRAGENS, T. A. (1999). *Civic Liberalism.* Lanham, MD: Rowman and Littlefield.

SOWELL, T. (1999). *The Quest for Cosmic Justice.* New York: Free Press.

STEINFELS, P. (1979). *The Neoconservatives.* New York: Simon & Schuster.

TOMASI, J. (2001). *Liberalism Beyond Justice.* Princeton: Princeton University Press.

CHAPTER 2

School Choice: Family or Public Funding

POSITION 1: FOR FAMILY CHOICE IN EDUCATION

Choice is a self-contained reform with its own rationale and justification. It has the capacity all by itself to bring about the kind of transformation that, for years, reformers have been seeking to engineer in myriad other ways.

—CHUBB AND MOE, 1990, P. 217

Why Educational Choice Is Needed

If your children attended a school in which most students scored below the state average on standardized tests, what could you do? What if they were enrolled in a school with few certified teachers, overcrowded classrooms, few computers, little lab equipment, and not enough books or other supplies? Could you find a way to get them the education they needed? If you were unhappy with your child's school because the curriculum was not rigorous enough or because it violated your beliefs and values, how could you remedy the situation? At the moment, there are very few options and, depending on a family's income, those choices become even more limited.

Dissatisfied families can work to correct problems in their children's public schools. Doing so, however, often involves a long, cumbersome process of political action—meeting with teachers and principals, attending school board meetings, working on committees, and being an active presence in a school. Time and energy commitments usually are more than most parents can make, and risk of failure and frustration is high. Even when these efforts are successful, the resulting changes may come too late for the students whose parents initially tried to make them. Students are in a particular grade for only one year. Schools often cannot modify programs or policies that quickly. Although working for long-term change is an option, it is a choice that doesn't meet the most immediate needs of parents and children.

Families with enough money can make other choices. They can decide to send their children to expensive, nonsectarian private schools. Their budget can absorb the cost of this decision even as the parents continue paying taxes to support public schools. Additionally, because there are only a limited number of such schools, attending them may mean students must live away from their families for long periods. This disruption of family life for the sake of a child's education is not often an attractive option for parents or young people, even when the family can afford it. Instead of increasing parental influence in children's lives, this choice weakens it. No matter where private schools are located, however, they remain options only for the wealthiest families since the tuition costs run into the tens of thousands of dollars per child (U.S. Department of Education, 1999; Galindo, 2002).

Parents with more limited financial resources can choose to send their children to less expensive and more accessible private schools affiliated with religious organizations (U.S. Department of Education, 1999). In fact, of the almost 28,000 private schools in the United States, close to 80 percent have connections to a religious group (Broughman and Colaciello, 2001). Availability of such schools provides parents dissatisfied with public schools with additional choices. Parents often believe these private schools, compared with public schools, provide safer and more academically focused environments. To obtain those benefits for their children, they willingly pay tuition in addition to their school taxes. However, this choice is still of limited help. Many families are not comfortable with the differences between their religious beliefs and those of the organization sponsoring the school. In times of economic distress, tuition may become too much of a burden for the family budget to bear. These schools simply do not provide enough choice for families.

Indeed, if a family has no surplus funds in its budget, the option of any kind of private school is not available. Fewer than 3 percent of students enrolled in private school come from families with "low incomes"—that is, from families whose income is in the bottom 20 percent of all family incomes in this country (U.S. Department of Education, 1999). Most poor children attend urban public schools with woefully inadequate facilities (Kozol, 1991). Their academic achievement lags far behind their counterparts in suburban public schools (Campbell, Hombo, and Mazzeo, 2000). Many parents who live in inner cities and are members of ethnic or racial minority groups are deeply concerned about the quality of their children's education (Black Alliance for Educational Opportunity, 2002). However, without viable family choice programs for all—rich and poor—they cannot translate their concerns into actions. Although the 2001 No Child Left Behind Act attempts to provide more choice by allowing parents to transfer their children from failing schools to other public schools whose students have higher academic achievement levels, the option is not viable unless the new school has room and is willing to accept them. School districts across the country have been slow to provide such options (Schemo, 2002). Indeed, they have little incentive to do so.

Most students still are assigned to public schools based on where they live (U.S. Department of Education, 2002). Because Americans wanted to maintain a high level of local control over schools, districts were established based on geography—meaning cities, towns, villages or any part of those municipalities can become school districts. That way local branches of government, most often school boards, can be elected by and held responsible to residents of the areas the schools serve. In practice, however, these forms of governance have become less responsive to dissatisfied parents. Many critics believe public school bureaucracy has, over time, become elaborate and self-protective (Friedman and Friedman, 1980; Chubb and Moe, 1990; Flake, 1999).

For example, once a district is established, students are assigned to schools based on where they live within and among those districts. The dividing lines are firmly maintained. Moving from school to school within a district often is difficult; moving from district to district (unless the family changes its residence) is almost impossible. Assigning students to schools based on their residence minimizes parents' choice about the school their children can attend. Families' financial situations, not their commitments to their children, determine the amount of educational choice they have. If a family can afford to live where a school matches their hopes and ambitions, then all is well. If a family lives where that match does not exist, and they cannot afford to move to a better district, their relative poverty deprives them of the freedom to choose their children's school.

Others besides parents are concerned about education and have expertise to contribute in deciding what kind of schools and programs will best serve children and our society. Educators have access to research about academic programs that ensure success for children having difficulties with traditional ways of teaching and learning. Health professionals have suggestions about issues affecting children's physical and emotional well-being and how those concerns can be addressed in schools. Businesspeople can offer advice and support to schools in preparing young people for their future in an ever-more demanding job market. However, despite the good will and knowledge these people bring to questions about education, none of them is as concerned about the welfare of an individual child as his or her loving and committed parents. While parental authority with regard to children is not unlimited in this country, we Americans believe that generally it should be the most significant factor in determining most aspects of a child's life. Of those concerned about a child's education, parents have the most long-term relationship with children, giving them insights into what is right for their child that not the most famous educational expert could ever hope to have. Ultimately, parents should be the final decision makers about *their* child's education. As Americans we should work to ensure that all parents have this right, not just those who have achieved a certain level of economic success.

We are, however, coming to recognize that state-sponsored schools have put a stranglehold on parental choice. We need to allow the educational system to operate within a free competitive and competitive market. "Only a truly competitive educational industry can empower the ultimate consumers of educational services—parents and their children" (Friedman, 2000).

Family choice is an issue that is not going to go away. The stakes for individuals are too high. The question before us as a country is not if we should create viable family choice programs, but how we should do so. Although the latest Gallup poll shows concern among Americans about such programs, nearly half the people surveyed (44 percent) said they would favor a proposal in their state to allow parents to send their school-age children to any public, private, or church-related school they chose, with the government paying all or part of the tuition in nonpublic schools. Among those with children in public school, the proportion rose to 52 percent. (Rose and Gallup, 2001). Well-crafted choice programs could ease concerns some have expressed about accountability of private schools receiving taxpayer dollars.

Creating Options for Parents and Children

Charter Schools and Open Enrollment

We could create choice programs in several ways. First, we could do so in a limited fashion by encouraging options within public school systems. Government funds still would be used exclusively for those schools, but under such a system parents would have more options if they were dissatisfied with a particular school. We could introduce a more radical change by directing taxpayer dollars from providers of education, public schools, to consumers of educational services, parents and children. Those consumers would be allowed to make choices about where to spend that money.

The first option has been tried with limited success. Some districts have been giving families choices about their children's schooling since the Civil Rights Movement of the 1960s and 70s. Magnet schools that offer specialized curriculum designed to draw students from all across a district were tools in the desegregation plans of many urban districts. Some of those schools continue to operate. Voluntary transfer programs, sometimes called "open-enrollment," also have been in place on a limited basis. Since 1988 eighteen states have enacted legislation allowing transfer both within and among school districts. Another eleven states have regulations allowing transfer only within the same district. Nearly 4 million students participate in open-enrollment programs (U.S. Department of Education, 2000).

Public schools districts have created schools of choice for reasons other than racial integration. Since the 1970s, qualified teachers have been given state permission (called a charter) to create new, more independent schools in which educational innovations could be explored. Now thirty-seven states and the District of Columbia have laws allowing the establishment of schools that are partially autonomous from the districts in which they are located. Members of these school communities believe freedom from state and local regulations enables them to better meet students' needs. In addition, they see charter schools as places where an "alternative vision of schooling" can be lived out—where such educational values as diversity, inquiry, and community can more fully be realized than in traditional public schools (U.S. Department of Education, 2000).

In the early 1990s researchers concluded that despite positive benefits children who participate in charter schools received, little evidence directly connected these programs with improvement in school performance or student achievement (Cookson and Shroff, 1992). More recent studies, though, conclude that in some cases the presence of even this limited form of competition causes school districts to improve their services (Center for Educational Reform, 2000; Hoxby, 2000, 2001). For example, in New York City, District 4, where parents had choices about the schools their children would attend, math and reading test scores improved more than in any of the other thirty-two community districts (Reese, 1999).

However, magnet and charter schools do not ultimately provide students and their families with a full array of educational choices. They all remain part of the public school system and are, therefore, accountable to special interest groups as well as parents. Two studies confirm that nearly half of all charter schools report experiencing difficulties with school boards, state departments of education, unions or districts (U.S. Department of Education, 2000). Charter schools must contend with collective bargaining agreements already in place, with inadequate funding formulas, unrealistic timetables for improvements, and cumbersome application processes. "Not enough rules were waived. Not enough contractual provisions were set aside. Education code red tape may have been snipped but not the other kinds that schools often encounter: financial rules, personnel rules, retirement system rules, zoning and building rules, health rules, etc." (Finn et al., 1997, p. 8). As long as choices families have remain under control of educational bureaucracy, real change will not take place.

Vouchers

The second option, providing taxpayer dollars directly to families, puts decisions about children's education back where it belongs, in the hands of their parents. "Vouchers" are one mechanism for transferring taxpayer dollars to families. In such a program, families with children receive a check from the government to be used to pay for the educational program of their choice. To work best, a voucher program would give the same amount of money to every child. Additional subsidies would be available for children with handicapping conditions. Most of the money would come from state and local taxes; additional funds for children with special needs would come from the federal government. There would be no restrictions against parents adding their own money to what they receive from the government to pay for schools that cost more than the voucher amount. Similarly, there would be no regulations preventing using these funds at the school of a parent's choice. Private non-sectarian schools, those with religious affiliations, and government-sponsored schools all would be valid choices. Some proponents of voucher plans suggest that to increase the competitive nature of this system, there should be no added subsidies from the government to any of the options. The amount of funding a school received from taxpayers would be determined by enrollment, which itself would be driven by customer satisfaction. (Merrifield, 2001). Others suggest that government could provide additional funds to schools it sponsored. Parents still would use their vouchers at such schools but would do so knowing the schools' budgets exceeded the amount of income from the vouchers (Friedman and Friedman, 1980).

In the early 1990s experiments with vouchers began with privately funded programs. There are at least eight such programs across the country. Two of the largest are Children First America and the Children's Scholarship Fund. Children First America had helped to create tuition scholarship programs for children in over 70 cities. The Children's Scholarship Fund sponsors nearly 40,000 children across the country. However these programs cannot meet the need. For example, over 1.25 million applications for funding were received by Children's Scholarship Fund. Its leaders concluded that philanthropy alone cannot meet American families' desires to have adequate funding to choose their children's schools freely. They believe we need to consider using tax dollars to pay for voucher programs for every child (Garrett, 2001).

Currently, publicly funded voucher programs exist in only a few areas of the country. In 2002 Florida introduced a statewide voucher program for students whose schools fail to meet state standards. Milwaukee and Cleveland have the largest publicly funded voucher programs. Approximately 11,000 students from low-income families receive vouchers to attend private schools in those cities. The schools meet state health and safety standards/regulations, and agree to use random selection processes in admitting voucher students. Neither program provides students with amounts equivalent to the amount of per-pupil state aid for public school attendance. Research on the Milwaukee and Cleveland programs indicate many benefits from the vouchers. Poor children have been freed from attending underperforming schools with unmotivated classmates and teachers. The schools they attend are better integrated than their former public schools. Most of all their academic achievement has improved. (Greene, Peterson, and Du, 1996; Fuller and Mitchell, 1999). There is every reason to believe that, by creating more publicly funded choice programs, we could extend these benefits to many more families. In fact, we should replace the current way of funding education in America with voucher programs in every state in the country. That would give every parent a real choice about their children's education.

Benefits of Voucher Programs

Voucher programs would address concerns about injustices in the American educational system. With adequately funded programs, all parents, regardless of income, would be able to provide their children with an education that meets their needs and interests. What are now privileges of the wealthy would become entitlements of all. For example, many parents feel public schools policies, practices, and teaching violate their religious principles.

Some parents believe schools do not, in fact, take neutral positions but actually teach values that contradict their own (Branch, 1995; Beckwith, 2001). Members of some traditions also find school policies to be problematic as their children attempt to practice their religion. Young Muslims often cannot find space within their schools in which they can meet their obligation to pray; they cannot leave school on Fridays, their holy day, to attend services at their mosques (Schwartz, 1999). Both Muslims and Jews sometimes find it difficult to obtain food that meets their dietary laws in public school cafeterias. In addition, religious holidays and ritual fasting days often are not acknowledged in public schools. The coeducational nature of public schools also violates the religious beliefs of some students and their families whose traditions teach that boys and girls should be educated separately (Speck, 1997; Haynes, 1998). Voucher programs would allow parents to remove their children from public schools they find offensive and place them in schools whose curricula or policies did not violate their religious or moral values. They would be able to choose schools that contributed to their children's growth in the family's religious or spiritual tradition. Doing so would no longer be a privilege of the wealthy few. Since these parents support education through their taxes, they should be able to use their share of tax dollars in schools that do not threaten their children's religious faith (Rosen, 2000).

Voucher programs also could help us address the long-standing problem of segregation in American schools. Even though a family might not have enough money to move out of a neighborhood, parents could use vouchers to choose schools for their children outside of the area in which they live. Families would be able to send their children to schools that did not replicate the racial segregation of their neighborhoods. Vouchers would give private schools the opportunity to accept children whose families are unable to pay tuition and to whom schools could not afford to provide scholarships. In doing so, school populations could become more racially diverse. There is evidence that private schools, especially religiously affiliated private schools, are already less segregated than public schools (U.S. Department of Education, 2002). Under a voucher system we could expect this voluntary and peaceful integration of schools to increase. This result seems to have been verified by the Milwaukee and Cleveland experiments (Fuller and Mitchell, 1999; Greene, 1999).

In a system where schools compete for students, the institutions' survival would be dependent on consumers' decisions about where to spend their vouchers. Therefore, schools would have more motivation to ensure high levels of customer satisfaction than they do under the current system. Obviously, student achievement would directly affect parents' evaluation of a school. Voucher programs would create an educational system in which more children were likely to succeed. The new funding would help existing private schools and create new ones dedicated to increasing student achievement. The competition would force government schools to improve their students' learning outcomes as well (Clark, 1993). Research indicates that public schools have improved in areas where private school voucher programs have been established (Reese, 1999). This set of benefits is one of the reasons so many parents whose children attend schools with high failure rates are so supportive of voucher programs (Witte et al.,1995; Flake, 1999).

Voucher systems and the resultant competitive educational market also would increase the number of schools designed to meet students' special interests and needs. For example, schools for the performing arts and those emphasizing science and technology would be more available. The increased variety of schools could be expected to stimulate students' motivation since there would be a better match between their interests and a school's offerings.

Students who don't fit easily or comfortably in currently designed schools would have a better chance of finding an appropriate place under a voucher system encouraging the creation of innovative programs.

These benefits for parents and students would minimize the amount of social conflict over schools. Because parents could choose their child's educational program and change to another if they were unhappy, their satisfaction with schools could be expected to rise. Research on this seems quite clear. Parents who can choose their children's schools are more satisfied with them than parents who have no choice (Metcalf et al., 1998; Fuller and Mitchell, 1999; Greene, 1999; Peterson, 1999a; Witte et al., 1999). Even though many schools would be privately owned, they would give parents and students a more significant voice in school governance than in public schools where they compete with representatives of special interest groups. (Chubb and Moe, 1990).

Voucher programs will not only help parents and students. Teachers also will benefit under these plans. School survival will depend on parent satisfaction with student achievement, and since such achievement depends on competent instruction, good teachers will be highly in demand. As a result, teachers' salaries will increase as schools compete to attract these skilled professionals. In addition, as the number and variety of schools increase, teachers will be more able to find schools whose values, missions, and methods match their own. Consequently, teacher satisfaction will rise under voucher programs as well.

Concerns About Choice Plans Using Vouchers

Critics of choice plans rightly point out several areas of concern. If voucher plans are implemented, we must be sure they are constitutional, fair, and consistent with American values. All these conditions can be met if voucher plans are carefully designed.

The issue of constitutionality most often is raised when critics question using taxpayer dollars to educate children in schools affiliated with religious groups. This concern is rooted in their understanding of the doctrine of the separation of church and state. The First Amendment states, "Congress shall make no law respecting an establishment of religion." The Supreme Court most often has interpreted that to mean that only the federal government has no authority over religion. For most of our history, state and local government were left to act as they wanted about the matter. However, in the 1940s the court began to look more closely at the issue and created some standards limiting states' and municipalities' relationships to religious institutions. In the process the Court reached some decisions establishing a greater distance between church and state than previously had existed.

However, the Court also has held that many government policies benefiting religious groups *are* constitutional. For example, tax exemption for churches and religious schools, tax deductions for contributions to religious charities, tax credits for tuition paid to religious schools, transportation for children in those schools, and police or fire protection of religious institutions have all been declared legal. Even more closely related to the question of school choice, the G.I. Bill, Pell Grants, federally subsidized student loans, and state tuition assistance programs for college students have not been declared unconstitutional even though some money from those programs has gone to schools directly affiliated with religious groups.

What the Supreme Court seems to have established is a policy of "neutrality" with regard to such funding. If a program provides benefits to individuals according to neutral guidelines, then it can be declared constitutional, even if the individuals choose to use those benefits for a service provided by a religious group. The government is not itself supporting a religious institution; individuals are doing so through private decisions (*Mueller v. Allen*, 1983; *Witters v. Washington Deptartment of Services for the Blind*, 1986; *Widmer v. Vincent et al.*, 1981; *Zobrest v. Catalina Foothills School District*, 1993; *Agostini v. Felton*, 1997). The court has ruled that the issue is not *what* is funded through taxpayer money, but *how* that funding reaches the religious institution. If an individual makes an independent and private decision to spend tax dollars to which he or she is entitled on a service provided by a religious institution, then the wall between church and state has not been breached (Lewin, 1999; Lindsey, 2000; Rosen, 2000). Using this reasoning, in *Zelman v. Doris Simmons-Harris* (2002) the justices ruled the Cleveland voucher program was constitutional. In doing so the Court established that it is constitutional for a state to provide families with public money to use at private schools, even those affiliated with religious organizations.

The admissions policies of private schools to which parents could direct taxpayer dollars is another area of concern to voucher program critics. They are rightly concerned about whether a market system will allow schools to discriminate in their admissions policies. They suggest that religious schools, for example, will be able to admit only those applicants whose parents are members of the religious organization with which the schools are affiliated. They further argue that private schools will be able to refuse students with handicapping conditions that create special educational needs.

While it is certainly justified to worry about unfair admissions policies, current law already protects young people from arbitrary discrimination. In fact, in 2000, these laws were used to correct just such problems in the admissions policies of several high schools participating in the Milwaukee voucher program (People For the American Way Foundation, 2000).

However, the Supreme Court also has ruled that private organizations, even those that benefit from indirect taxpayer support, can refuse to admit members whose inclusion would significantly breach the organization's First Amendment right to express its beliefs (*Roberts v. United States Jaycees*, 1984; *Hurley v. Irish American Gay, Lesbian, Bisexual Group of Boston*, 1995; *Boy Scouts of America v. Dale*, 2000). The court has not yet established if this ruling applies to church-affiliated schools.

A third concern raised about vouchers to fund parental choice in education is that people or organizations whose beliefs violate American ideals will be able to maintain schools teaching those beliefs using taxpayer dollars. For example, critics suggest that groups such as the Ku Klux Klan might use voucher funding to establish schools in which they could teach white supremacy (Center for Educational Reform, 2000). These suggestions raise legitimate concerns about regulation. However, those raising these objections seem to forget that laws already exist to prevent anyone in the United States from advocating illegal activities. Teachers or administrators in private schools are not exempt from these statutes. In addition, just because government no longer would be the exclusive operator of schools under voucher programs, it does not necessarily follow that government could not regulate educational institutions receiving taxpayer dollars indirectly. Many countries in Europe fund private and religious schools with public dollars. They establish "inspectorates" to verify those institutions are indeed providing children with an education and nothing illegal takes place in them. Americans could modify those systems to fit our needs without returning to a governmental monopoly in education (Peterson, 1999b).

Funding schools associated with religious or political minority groups raises some legitimate questions. However, critics seem to forget that tolerance for diverse opinions is at the heart of America's democratic tradition. By suggesting we not fund schools in which opinions or beliefs of a particular group are taught, critics may unwittingly be participating in a form of censorship that in other settings they would find unacceptable. Lack of government funding may prevent these schools from operating and, therefore, prevent them from expressing their beliefs and opinions as they are entitled to do under the First Amendment. The fact that it would be a new task for government to regulate such schools does not mean it would be impossible (Peterson, 1999b).

Concerns about whether prejudice and bigotry will be taught in voucher-funded schools are legitimate. However, these worries appear to be less important to those most likely to be the target of the hatred than their children's current forced attendance at public schools that fail to educate but are their only option under the system we have now. Many urban and minority parents believe that, although it is possible if not probable that there will be problems with a voucher-funded educational system, those difficulties will not be worse than the ones they face now (Black Alliance for Educational Opportunity, 2002). They are right. As a society we need the benefits voucher programs will bring. We must accept the challenge of designing them in ways that are faithful to American law and values.

Conclusion

The goal of those who established the American public school system was to provide education for all American children in a way that all those who benefited from their training would share its financial cost. However, achieving that dream never required that government operate schools, only that we should fund them through our taxes. Vouchers provide a way to fund schools without subjecting them to unresponsive bureaucratic control. We no longer can afford not to make the change. All families deserve to be able to choose education that works for their children. Although some abuses may occur within such programs, they will be no worse than the system we currently have. Many children are in schools where "test scores are abysmal, graduation rates are atrocious and overall performance is so low that many schools have been shut down all together" (Flake, 1999). The poor performance of public schools has affected urban communities across the country. Inability to provide good schools prevents city neighborhoods from attracting strong families; they are unwilling to buy homes in neighborhoods where schools are failing. Our unwillingness to put the power of good education at their disposal fails to give poor and marginalized children the tools they need to change their situations. Voucher programs will give parents of these and all children real options. They no longer will be recipients of choices made by others with less investment in their children's lives. We need to make family choice a reality—publicly funded vouchers will do just that.

POSITION 2: AGAINST VOUCHERS

Many of us seem to have forgotten why America established public schools in the first place, the means we established to make choices about education, and what we have learned not only about the advantages but also about the limitations of choice. . . . As conservatives have framed the debate, the question has been, "Are you for or against choice?" But the question ought to be, "What kind of choice are you for?"

—TYACK, 1999

There are many ways to provide parents and students with choices about schools and education that are not *as* problematic as voucher programs. Proponents of such programs seem to ignore or demean all other possibilities, painting their alternative as the only one with any real hope of reforming American education. However, in their enthusiasm for their position they underestimate the difficulties inherent in publicly funding payments to private schools.

We should oppose voucher programs allowing parents to use public funds in private schools for several reasons. They will undermine an educational system that, for all its flaws, still enables parents, students, teachers, administrators, and other citizens to learn "what a democratic life means and how it might be led" (Dewey, 1916, p. 7). In violation of the Constitution, they break down the barrier between church and state. They pose legal problems by diverting public funds to private coffers. They will have unacceptable financial consequences for schools and taxpayers, impede continuing development of American values such as diversity and tolerance, and lead to more divisiveness based on unequal economic or social condition. Finally, voucher plans simply will not deliver the improvements in academic achievement their supporters promise.

Differing Forms of Choice

Families already do have choices about the educational system. The problem is that we don't currently have the kind of choices that voucher proponents want. That is, we don't give tax dollars to private schools nor do we use taxpayer money raised from the public at large to subsidize private individual parental decisions about schooling. Those who argue for "family choice" forget that parents' and children's concerns are not the only ones to be considered when we decide what kind of education to provide with public funds. Since all taxpayers contribute the funds used for education, they have a right to make choices about schools as well. That is, there are social purposes for schooling that must be considered as significant along with the individual purposes of parents for their children. For over 150 years, Americans have chosen to provide schooling, at taxpayers' expense, for all children. We have done so for some very good reasons, which those who propose vouchers for private schools seem to have forgotten.

Americans accepted the notion of the "common school" in the mid-nineteenth century to provide future generations with knowledge, skills, and values they would need to improve society and create positive social interactions within their communities. Through public education, young people would learn how to behave as responsible, productive citizens of a democratic society, learn the importance of voting, and develop the habits of responsible and honest workers. They also would learn tolerance and respect for diverse peoples and different points of view that make up this country (Good and Braden, 2000).

We were willing to hand over hard-earned money to the government for schools because we believed such schools would return "profits" to every member of society, not just to children attending them and their families. That return on investment is what justified pooling our resources and distributing them through the government (Ascher, Fruchter, and Berne, 1996). Even with their faults and problems, public schools have returned that social profit over a long period. The United States has a remarkable record in educating nearly all children through the high school level through public funding of public schools. Although the United States started with only private schools for the very wealthy or powerful, by the twentieth century public schools had become the American model of democratic education for the rest of the world. Private schools, despite some opinion they are better, actually serve less than 15 percent of all students and have been at that level for more than three-quarters of a century.

Citizens of the United States also decided that choices about education should be made collectively through the electoral and representative processes characteristic of American life. So we established schools managed through elected school boards or other forms of local government. If people disagreed with decisions by elected officials, they could elect others. This process would maintain the right of taxpayers to make choices about schools they supported financially. Voucher plans effectively take away this right.

Voucher proponents want to sidestep this democratic decision-making process and dislike the compromises it demands in such areas as curriculum or policy. Because they *are* compromises, they require everyone to "give in and give up" on some issues. Perhaps dissatisfied parents and other voucher supporters believe they have had to give up too much while others have given too little. Even if they're right, however, that is how the democratic process works. Minority positions, those that cannot mount sufficient public pressure, do not carry the day in our political system. However, democratic institutions also safeguard the rights of minority groups, especially their right to participate, to make the strongest possible case for their position and perhaps, eventually, to sway the majority (Apple and Beane, 1995).

Voucher plans, however, do not really represent an attempt of a minority to gain more influence within the democratic decision-making process regarding education. Instead, they allow parents to bypass it altogether when it comes to school governance and accountability. (Paris, 1995). Using taxpayer money, parents will be able to choose to send their children to private schools that avoid the difficulties of working within "democratic procedures that accept as legitimate views from disparate actors with conflicting agendas and incompatible styles" (Henig, 1994, p. 23).

Religion, Tolerance, and Democratic Ideals

Among the choices parents can make with their vouchers will be schools affiliated with religious institutions. Proponents of voucher programs argue such use of taxpayer money is constitutional; it does not follow that it is good public policy. Determining the constitutionality of a policy means only it "could" be implemented, not that it "should" be.

Voucher plans making it easier for students to attend schools that separate people by their religious beliefs can contribute to isolation from, and misunderstanding of, those whose beliefs are different from their own. In an age where we need citizens who are more, not less, capable of accepting religious differences, sectarian schools do not prepare young people adequately enough to deserve public funding. As we have seen, in a democracy it is within the right of the citizens to determine what return it wants on the investment of its tax dollars. In this case, then, it is not a violation of families' rights if society decides only to fund schools that will be most likely to provide students with experiences of, and contact with, people who are unlike themselves and their families. A collective decision to teach students the democratic values of pluralism and tolerance through school experiences of those realities does not lessen parents' rights to choose to teach their children the family's religious values. It is simply a decision of how best to use tax dollars to achieve society's goals.

Some proponents of voucher plans will argue that research indicates people who attend private schools actually fulfill their civic duties fully and faithfully. They will point to studies suggesting private school graduates are more tolerant than their public school counterparts (Greeley and Rossi, 1966; Gallup and Castelli, 1987; Greeley, 1990). These studies, however, apply only to graduates of Catholic schools, which since World War I have quite deliberately set out to prove their loyalty to the values and laws of the United States.

There is reason from other studies to believe such tolerance is not a universal product of private schools with religious affiliations (Peshkin, 1986; Fleming and Hunt, 1987). For example, a recent study of textbooks used in some conservative Christian schools seems to indicate they could encourage negative, judgmental attitudes toward people not sharing the school community's religious beliefs (Paterson, 2000). This research suggests that to whatever degree these texts represent the school curricula, they are troubling in several ways. Being exposed to such texts may make students less able to tell the difference between essays designed to persuade the reader of a particular point of view and those presenting balanced accounts of political issues. Such curricula may create citizens inclined to be hostile to the federal government. They may encourage students to label other people and to dismiss their arguments on the basis of those stereotypes rather than on their merits. Using government funds to develop such attitudes in students is questionable in light of our historical decision to use public funds for education to create a citizenry committed to democratic ideals of tolerance and compromise. It is not that alternative ideals should not be presented in schools funded by communities whose beliefs they represent. However, they should not be taught at taxpayer expense.

Financial Consequences of Voucher Plans

Whether we consider fully or partially funded voucher plans, they all have negative financial consequences.

Fully funded voucher programs, the kind envisioned by many who want market forces to control education, would mean that parents or guardians of every school-age child in America would receive a check from the government. The basic amount of the check, under most proposals, would be the same for every student. Those with special needs would receive additional funds. Under some plans, the amount a parent received would be equal to the amount currently spent in local public school districts. Under most plans, the amount would be much less, although some proposals include the possibility that government-sponsored schools could continue and those, perhaps, would be funded at their current levels (Friedman and Friedman, 1980).

Fully funded voucher schemes have consequences for taxpayers and for teachers. If these plans are implemented, the total amount spent by government on education will increase dramatically. In the United States, more than 5 million students are in private schools that charge an average tuition of over $3,100 (Broughman and Colaciello, 2001). Parents of these students do not currently receive any government funds for these tuition expenses. If they did and we continued to provide the amount of aid to education that we do now, even if we did it in the form of vouchers, the extra cost would be over $16 billion per year. Legislators and their constituents would have to support the increases in taxes required to provide such additional money.

If we decided to maintain educational spending at its current level and not increase taxes, then the $16 billion for students in private schools would be subtracted from the amount of money available for students who attend public schools now. So even if those students received vouchers, their checks would not equal the amount their school districts currently receive for their education.

Some proponents of voucher programs would argue that the decrease in available money would not be a problem because the amount of money available through vouchers still would pay the tuition at a private school. They point out that those private schools currently educate students at an average cost half the price of a public school education. Presence of vouchers would cause an increase in the number of such cost-efficient private schools and force government-sponsored schools to scale back their expenses to stay competitive. This argument, however, is problematic. It ignores the fact that private schools have lower expenditures primarily because of the dramatically lower salaries they pay teachers, especially in the religiously affiliated schools. Sectarian schools are the ones whose tuitions most often fall in the "average" range of $3,100. More elite, nonsectarian schools have much higher average tuition. Teachers in religious schools may have faith commitments that motivate them to work for low wages. That is not necessarily the case for others in the profession.

Supporters of vouchers often argue that the competitive nature of the educational system under their plans will create a "seller's" market for teachers. That is, because good teachers will be in demand, they will be able to ask for and receive higher salaries. However, the structures of the plans they support do not seem to guarantee any such consequence. In fact, under most plans, unless parents could supplement their vouchers with additional tuition, private schools could not raise teachers' salaries and public schools would have to lower them or significantly increase student to teacher ratios.

Partially funded voucher plans also have financial implications. These plans usually are proposed as alternatives for students in urban schools where the level of academic achievement is below state standards. The families of students in these "underperforming" schools would be given government funds to seek alternative education for their children. In most proposals, these funds would not equal the amount it costs to educate a child in the public schools. The Milwaukee and Cleveland plans are models of this type of program. They were designed to provide educational opportunity for students of low-income families living in those cities. In both cases, the vouchers provided only partial funding—only a part of the amount spent on students who remained in public schools. In Cleveland public schools in school year 1999–2000, the per-pupil cost was $4,910. Voucher student cost was $1,832 and that amount included administrative costs for the program. In Milwaukee, the per-pupil public school expenditure was $6,011. Voucher students' tuition payments averaged $5,106 (U.S. General Accounting Office, 2001).

In Milwaukee, half the voucher funds come from state revenues directed to the city school district; the other half comes from the budgets of school districts in other parts of the state. In Cleveland, the cost of the voucher program is deducted from the city's share of state revenues for students from low-income families. In the 1999–2000 school year, the total cost of the program in Cleveland was $6.2 million. Milwaukee's program cost $38.9 million. In both cases, public school districts received less funding than they would if the state was not subsidizing students' attendance at private schools. The GAO admits the "full impact of these funding methods on the public schools is unknown" (U.S. General Accounting Office, 2001, p. 4).

Supporters of the plans are adamant that they cause school districts no real harm because students for whom the aid was intended left the district. Therefore, they argue, the schools incur no expenses for those children. They ignore the fact, however, that public schools' fixed costs remain the same. Buildings still need heat and electricity. School buses still require fuel and maintenance. Decreased funding leaves districts with less money to pay those bills. When school budgets require adjustments to cover nondiscretionary expenses such as these often require, it often means reduction in staffing or academic programs. Decreases due to voucher programs can be expected to have similar effects.

Other Consequences of School Vouchers

Racial Isolation

Supporters of voucher programs argue their plans could increase racial integration in American schools. They argue that because private schools recruit young people from larger geographic areas than public schools, the private institutions, especially those with religious affiliations, have more diverse student populations than public schools. Availability of vouchers will make it possible for more minority parents, disproportionately represented among the poor, to choose private schools. Thus, they conclude, parental choice through voucher programs will result in more integrated schools.

However, research does not support this belief. Studies in the United States as well as other countries indicate that family choice programs, including voucher programs, do not decrease racial segregation. In fact, the data from those studies suggest that the programs lead to less integrated educational settings (Levin, 1997).

In Milwaukee supporters claim the voucher plan appears to have resulted in more integration in private schools that participate in the program (Fuller and Mitchell, 1999). Ironically, however, the increased racial balance at those schools may have been the result of a form of "white flight." The study's own data show that the number of minorities in private schools accepting vouchers have increased over the life of the program. However, the same data show the number of white students in those schools have decreased even more. So the greater diversity in those private schools may not be the result of a happy and peaceful process of integration. On the contrary, it could represent a trend toward increasing segregation in schools that previously were more integrated than the public schools.

The possibility that educational choice programs such as vouchers could result in increased racial isolation should not be shocking. After all, some of the first attempts in this country to protect families' rights to choose their children's school occurred during periods of racial unrest. In the Jim Crow era in the South, a dual educational system was developed to support white parents' right to choose not to educate their children side by side with black ones. During the early days of court-ordered desegregation in those same states, white parents created networks of segregated private schools to protect that same right and lobbied state officials to provide financial aid to the new schools. In some situations, they successfully pressured governors and state legislatures to shut down public school systems rather than integrate them, leaving black families with few, if any, educational choices. In the North during periods when urban schools were required to integrate by the courts, white parents attempted to remove their children from public schools and enroll them in nearby Catholic ones. Many bishops in northern cities were forced to issue orders preventing schools under their control from registering such "refugees" from integration. Pressure for public taxpayer aid to parochial schools began to reemerge during this same period.

"Racial animosities and fears provided the soil in which many of the earliest proposals for vouchers and school choice took root. It would be comforting to believe that we have severed our ties to the unflattering past, but it would be naïve as well" (Henig, 1994, p. 114). Supporters of voucher programs rarely suggest, for example, that we maintain the public school system but allow students greater choice among districts. They usually do not advocate that students who attend underperforming urban schools, and for whom they claim to be concerned, should be able to use their vouchers to transfer to successful schools in nearby suburban districts.

Supporters of voucher programs seem able to ignore the way racial and class prejudice would affect the educational "marketplace" they are trying to create. Parents most often measure school quality by the quality of the students. In the minds of many, that "quality" is most often found in white, middle-, and upper-class children (Wells and Crain, 1992). There is no reason to believe that a single factor such as vouchers will change consumers' perception of what makes a school "good." There will continue to be greater competition for places in schools where the student body's racial and economic makeup matches families' perceptions of what guarantees a quality school. In a voucher system school, owners and administrators would be competing for students and their money. School officials would be pressured to create student bodies that appeal to families' beliefs about what kind of people attend "good" schools. These pressures easily could result in admissions practices limiting the number of students of color, students with special needs, and students with histories of poor academic performance. It would be highly unlikely that such policies would result in more integrated schools. Voucher programs would require parents to be well informed about educational options available for their children. Already privileged families would be better able to investigate possibilities and advocate for their children, putting them in a better position to compete for admission to schools most in demand.

Selecting a child's kindergarten or elementary school would come to replicate the current competition for admission to colleges with prestigious reputations. There would be winners and losers, and our experience tells us something about the racial, ethnic, and socioeconomic backgrounds of each. In addition, parents who are members of a minority group often have had experiences of discrimination and bigotry that, in some cases, result in feelings of distrust, disillusion, and resentment toward social institutions perceived as being controlled by majority group members. Those feelings could cause parents to remove their children from the competition to attend prestigious schools. The parents might assume, for example, that their children also would have hurtful experiences in such settings. There is nothing in the voucher plans being proposed by educational free marketeers to diminish these social realities. Consequently, there is no reason to believe those same plans will not maintain or increase current social inequalities and isolation.

Questions of School Accountability

Another reason to reject voucher plans is because it is almost impossible to construct them in ways that would guarantee private schools were truly accountable to the public from whom they would be receiving their funding. If we regulate publicly funded private schools, we will have to introduce governmental interference in religious schools in a way that has never before happened in the United States. We would be asking those schools to compromise their independence in areas that many members of those communities would see as crucial to their mission. For example, religious schools currently are able to admit on a preferential basis those students whose families are members of the religious organization with which the school is affiliated. They also can decide to use textbooks supporting the beliefs of their faith communities even in subjects other than religion. They can require all students, regardless of their own traditions, to participate in religious instruction and ceremonies. They control their curriculum, teacher hiring, and most other aspects of school operation. It is questionable whether these practices could continue if governmental regulation was a condition of their receiving vouchers. Taxpayers paying the costs of private schools would have a right to hold such schools accountable and responsible. That is done best through government regulation.

All private schools, religious or nonsectarian, would have to rethink their admissions policies under governmental regulation. Currently, such schools can require test scores, written applications, interviews, and recommendations as part of the admissions process. They can set standards for these criteria as well as for prior academic and behavioral performances. Private schools can refuse to admit students who do not meet these standards. Based on that freedom, private schools are under no obligation to admit or provide services for students with special needs. In addition, private schools currently are able to expel students who fail to follow their policies. Private school deliberations of budget and contracting are private, as are most business items. These rights and privileges are not extended to public schools and, if private schools were to come under governmental regulation, they might lose them as well.

There is evidence that private schools would be unwilling to submit to such accountability to receive government funding. A U.S. Department of Education report indicated that the vast majority of such schools would not sacrifice the freedom to be selective about their student body, their independence from state testing programs, or their ability to require participation in religious instruction or activities to be eligible for vouchers (Williams, 1995). If private schools are unwilling to comply with standards public schools currently have to meet, then governmental oversight of voucher schools seems likely indeed.

Without such accountability, voucher plans will not be acceptable to Americans. For the last four years at least three-quarters of those surveyed in the

Gallup/Phi Delta Kappan Poll have said they believe that "private or church-related schools that accept government tuition payments should be accountable to the state in the way public schools are accountable" (Rose and Gallup, 2001). A more detailed poll, commissioned by the American Federation of Teachers, indicated over 80 percent of those surveyed believed private schools receiving voucher payments should have admissions policies that do not discriminate on the basis of race or religion. Similar percentages believe schools also should meet state health, safety, and curriculum regulations, employ only certified teachers, disclose their budgets, and use the same tests as public schools. More than 75 percent also believed such schools should abide by the Americans with Disabilities Act (American Federation of Teachers, 2001).

Opinions expressed by those taking part in these surveys may indicate Americans are aware of the consequences of a voucher system that was not accountable to the public. In such systems, fraud and theft could become serious problems. We know, for example, that in the relatively unregulated postsecondary trade-school market, in which students can use government funds such as subsidized student loans or Pell grants, dishonesty and profiteering have been ongoing issues. These schools have been guilty of overstating their placement rates and amount of money graduates could expect to earn. In addition, dishonest directors of these schools have enriched themselves by raiding the institutions' budgets. These practices have resulted in financial disasters for some of the schools, putting them out of business and leaving students without the education for which taxpayers had already paid (Winerip, 1994). Without careful oversight, the enormous amounts of money at stake in voucher plans may tempt unscrupulous people to commit similar crimes in the operation of elementary and high schools. Even when no dishonesty is intended, private schools, especially new ones, may have very short lives, especially under plans in which vouchers would be worth less than the amounts being spent in public schools. The difficulty of providing quality education at bargain basement prices would be insurmountable in many cases. Schools would go out of business, perhaps in midyear, leaving young people and their families without options. That is not a responsible choice for parents.

Finally, requiring governmental oversight of voucher schools would result in increased costs that taxpayers would have to absorb. Ironically, it also would result in an educational bureaucracy even larger than the one voucher proponents believe is already too big. The difficulties in creating a system of accountability for publicly funded private schools make voucher programs unworkable.

Vouchers' Impact on Academic Achievement

Proponents of voucher programs claim that a major benefit will be improved academic achievement. Children who can use vouchers to leave schools where students fail to meet achievement standards will be able to find programs in which they can succeed. If supporters of vouchers could prove vouchers guaranteed such success, it might make sense to initiate them across the country. However, claims of increased academic achievement are, at best, overblown and at worst, simply untrue.

Thirty years of research on the differences between private and public schools have demonstrated that private school students have a slightly higher average academic achievement than their public school counterparts. However, that same research indicates that most differences between students can be attributed to factors beyond schools' control such as the amount of education a student's parents completed and income levels of the student's family. The fact that public schools are required to take all legitimate students, while private schools can be selective, also makes one wonder about research that compares the academic achievement of private and public school students. The "private school effect," the amount of the difference in achievement between public and private school students that can actually be attributed to attending private school, is very small indeed (Coleman, Hoffer, and Kilgore, 1982; Alexander and Pallas, 1985; Hoffer, 2000). Despite this research, proponents of voucher programs still insist that providing an opportunity for underachieving students to attend private schools will help them reach higher academic standards.

However, research on the two largest voucher programs, those in Milwaukee and Cleveland, continue to demonstrate that attending a private school does not in and of itself guarantee higher academic achievement. Evaluations by researchers under contract to Wisconsin and Ohio have found "little or no difference in voucher and public school students' performances" in Cleveland and Milwaukee (Witte et al., 1995, 1997; Metcalf et al., 1998; U.S. General Accounting Office, 2001). Other scholars, including some who are strong public supporters of voucher programs, have found only very small gains and then only in certain subject areas (Greene, Peterson, and Du, 1996). These findings are not surprising in light of the earlier research on comparisons between student achievement in private and public schools. Students in both the public and private schools in the Milwaukee and Cleveland studies live in similar economic situations in the same communities. Factors shown to be most significant are just about the same for each group of students. The "private school effect" is minimal. In fact, a researcher in Milwaukee found that making changes in public school settings so the number of students in those classrooms was comparable to the number of students in private school classrooms eliminated the "private school effect" (Rouse, 1998).

Voucher programs allowing students to attend private schools will not by themselves improve children's academic performance. Making reforms we know work—such as decreasing class size and implementing curricula proven successful in a variety of settings—will. Voucher supporters may try other arguments to make their case. Increasing academic achievement should not be one of them.

Conclusion

Voucher programs are not good public policy. They threaten to dismantle a system of education that has provided America's children with schools where they could meet people who were different from them, who had other beliefs, languages, customs, and opinions. In the public schools of this country, young people have learned to get along with one another despite those differences. They have become citizens of this democracy.

Voucher programs would cost taxpayers more money than they currently pay for education. In exchange for that increased expense, they would get schools accountable only to their "customers" and vulnerable to dishonest and scheming profiteers. In addition, by all indications, they would get schools that would not increase the academic achievement of the most needy students. We risk losing our public schools—some of the strongest centers of democratic community life—if we allow vouchers to drain them of funds and students. Vouchers would be a very bad bargain indeed for the American public.

For Discussion

1. The Supreme Court has ruled that providing parents with governmental funds to pay for their children's education is constitutional even if they use the money to pay for tuition at a school sponsored by a religious organization. How can you reconcile that ruling with the constitutional guarantee of the separation of church and state?
2. Sponsors of vouchers have argued that allowing schools to become part of the "free market" competition is the only way to improve the quality of public education in the United States. Do you agree with the idea of allowing market forces to operate on schools? Are there any characteristics of the free market system that would prevent competition among schools from achieving the goal of equality? Does freedom of choice alone guarantee that all consumers have an equal chance in the marketplace? Do other protections need to be in place?
3. Imagine that a voucher program has been created in your state, and you have been asked to create the "accountability" regulations for private schools receiving such payments. Create a set of rules and develop a "white paper" explaining your rationale.
4. Design a proposal for a charter school you'd like to create. Explain the mission of the school, its organizational structure, and the ways it would differ from a traditional public school. Investigate your state and local school district's regulations concerning charter schools and be sure your proposal complies with those rules.

References

Agostini v. Felton. (1997). 522 U.S. 803.

AMERICAN FEDERATION OF TEACHERS. (2001). "Vouchers and the Accountability Dilemma." *AFT on the Issues.* (www.aft.org./vouchers/dilemma/page1.htm)

ALEXANDER, K. L., AND PALLAS, A. M. (1985). "School Sector and Cognitive Performance: When is a Little a Little?" *Sociology of Education.* April, 115–128.

APPLE, M., AND BEANE, J. (1995). *Democratic Schools.* Alexandria, VA: ACSD.

ASCHER, C., FRUCHETER, N., AND BERNE, R. (1996). *Hard Lessons: Public Schools and Privatization.* New York: 20th Century Fund Report.

BECKWITH, F. (2001). "Is Public Education Really Neutral?" (Teachers in Focus Website: www.family.org/cforum/teachersmag/features/a0002814.html)

BLACK ALLIANCE FOR EDUCATIONAL OPPORTUNITY. (2002). (www.schoolchoiceinfo.org/baeo/)

Boy Scouts of America v. Dale. (2000). 530 U.S. 640.

BRANCH, C. (1995). "Public Education or Pagan Indoctrination? A Report on New Age Influence in the Schools." *Christian Research Institute.* Statement D 118. (www.equip.orf/free/DN118.htm)

BROUGHMAN, W., AND COLACIELLO, L. (2001). *Private School Universe Study.* Washington, DC: U.S. Department of Education, National Center for Education Statistics. (http://nces.ed.gov/pubs2002/quarterly/fall)

CAMPBELL, J., HOMBO, C., AND MAZZEO, J. (2000). "NAEP 1999 Trends in Academic Progress: Three Decades of Student Performance." *National Assessment of Educational Progress.* (http://nces.ed.gov/nationsreportcard/pubs/main1999/2000469.asp)

CENTER FOR EDUCATIONAL REFORM. (2000). "Nine Lies About School Choice: Answering the Critics." (www.edreform.com)

CHUBB, J., AND MOE, T. (1990). *Politics, Markets and America's Schools.* Washington, DC: Brookings Institution.

CLARK, J. (1993). "Pro-Choice." *Mother Jones.* Sept., 52–54.

COLEMAN, J., HOFFER, T., AND KILGORE, S. (1982). *High School Achievement.* New York: Basic Books.

COOKSON, P., AND SCHROFF, S. (1992). "School Choice and Urban Education Report." *Teachers College Monograph.* (http://eric-web.tc.columbia.edu/monographs/uds/110)

DEWEY, J. (1916). *Democracy and Education.* New York: Macmillan.

FINN, C., ET AL. (1997). "The Birth-Pains and Life-Cycles of Charter Schools." *Charter Schools in Action Project, Final Report.* Part II. Indianapolis: Hudson Institute.

FLAKE, F. (1999). "No Excuses for Failing Our Children." *Policy Review.* Jan.–Feb., 93. Heritage Foundation. (www.heritage.org/policyreview/jan99/flake.html)

FLEMING, D., AND HUNT, T. "The World as Seen by Students in Accelerated Christian Education Schools." *Phi Delta Kappan.* March, 518–523.

FRIEDMAN, M. (2000). "Why America Needs School Vouchers." *Wall Street Journal,* Sept. 28, p. A22.

FRIEDMAN, M., AND FRIEDMAN, R. (1980). *Free to Choose.* New York: Harcourt Brace Jovanovich.

FULLER, H., AND MITCHELL, G. (1999). "The Impact of School Choice on Racial and Ethnic Enrollment in Milwaukee Public Schools. *Current Educational Issues.* Dec., 99(2).

GALINDO, M. (2002). "Profile of Statistical Indicators 2001–2002." Washington, DC: National Association of Independent Schools. (www.nais.org/docs/docload2.cfm?file_id=1640)

GALLUP, G., AND CASTELLI, J. (1987). *The American Catholic People: Their Beliefs, Practices and Values.* Garden City, NY: Doubleday.

GARRETT, J. (2001). "School Choice 2001: Increasing Opportunities for America's Children to Succeed." Heritage Foundation. (www.heritage.org/schools/background.html)

GOOD, T., AND BRADEN, J. (2000). *The Great School Debate: Choice, Vouchers and Charters.* Mahwah, NJ: Lawrence Erlbaum.

Greeley, A. (1990). *The Catholic Myth: The Behavior and Beliefs of American Catholics.* New York: Scribner.

GREELEY, A., AND ROSSI, P. (1966). *The Education of Catholic Americans.* Chicago: Aldine.

GREENE, J. (1999). "Choice and Community: the Racial, Economic and Religious Content of Parental Choice in Cleveland." Columbus: Buckeye Institute for Public Policy Solutions. (www.buckeyeinstitute.org/greene.pdf)

GREENE, J., PETERSON, P., AND DU, J. (1996). *The Effectiveness of School Choice in Milwaukee.* Cambridge: Harvard University Press.

HAYNES, C. (1998). "Muslim Students' Needs in Public Schools." *Update on Law-Related Education,* 22(1), 17–21.

HENIG, J. (1994). *Rethinking School Choices: Limits of the Market Metaphor.* Princeton: Princeton University Press.

HOFFER, T. (2000). "Catholic School Attendance and Student Achievement: A review and Extension of the Research." In J. Youniss, and J. Convey, eds, *Catholic Schools at the Crossroads.* New York: Teachers College Press.

HOXBY, C. (2000). "Does Competition Among Public Schools Benefit Students and Taxpayers?" *American Economic Review.* Dec. pp. 1209–1238.

———. (2001). "The Difference that Choice Makes." *Economist.* Jan. 27, p. 78.

Hurley v. Irish American Gay, Lesbian, Bisexual Group of Boston. (1995). 515 U.S. 557.

KOZOL, J. (1991). *Savage Inequalities: Children in America's Schools.* New York: Crown.

LEVIN, H. (1997). *Educational Vouchers: Effectiveness, Choice and Costs.* Stanford: Stanford University Press.

LEWIN, N. (1999). "Are Vouchers Constitutional?" *Policy Review.* Heritage Foundation. Jan.–Feb., no. 93. (www.heritage.org/policyreview/jan99/lewin.html)

LINDSEY, D. (2000). "Vouchers and the Law." *Salon.Com.* March 27. (www.salon.com/new/feature/2000/03/27/vouchers)

MERRIFIELD, J. (2001). *The School Choice Wars.* Lanham, MD: Scarecrow Press.

METCALF, K., ET AL. (1998). *A Comprehensive Evaluation of Cleveland Scholarship and Tutoring Program and Evaluation of the Cleveland School Program. Second Year Report, 1997–1998.* Bloomington: University of Indiana.

Mueller v. Allen. (1983). 463 U.S. 388.

PARIS, D. (1995). *Ideology and Educational Reform: Themes and Theories in Public Education.* Boulder: Westview Press.

PATERSON, F. (2000). "Building a Conservative Base: Teaching History and Civics in Voucher-Supported Schools." *Phi Delta Kappan.* Oct., 150–155.

PEOPLE FOR THE AMERICAN WAY FOUNDATION. (2000). "Whose Lies and Distortions?" (www.pfaw.org/issues/education/voucher.whoselies.shtml)

PESHKIN, A. (1986). *God's Choice: The Total World of a Fundamentalist Christian School.* Chicago: University of Chicago Press.

PETERSON, P. (1999a). "The Effects of School Choice in New York City." In S. Mayer, and P. Peterson, eds., *Earning and Learning: How Schools Matter.* Washington, DC: Brookings Institution.

———. (1999b). "Top Ten Questions Asked About School Choice." *Brookings Papers on Education Policy: 1999.* Washington, DC: Brookings Institution.

REESE, N. (1999). "Public School Benefits of Private School Vouchers." *Policy Review.* Heritage Foundation. Jan.–Feb., 93. (www.heritage.org/policyreview/jan99/rees.html)

Roberts v. United States Jaycees. (1984). 468 U.S. 609.

ROSE, L., AND GALLUP, A. (2001). "The 33rd Annual Phi Delta Kappan/Gallup Poll of the Public's Attitudes Toward the Public Schools." *Phi Delta Kappan.* Sept., 41–58.

ROSEN, G. (2000). "Are School Vouchers Un-American?" *Commentary.* February. (www.findarticles.com/cf_0/m1061/2_109/59270719/print.jhtml)

ROUSE, C. (1998). "Private School Vouchers and Student Achievement: An Evaluation of the Milwaukee Parental Choice Program." *Quarterly Journal of Economics.* May, pp. 553–602.

SCHEMO, D. (2002). "Few Exercise New Right to Leave Failing Schools." *The New York Times.* Aug. 28, Sec. A, p. 1

SCHWARTZ, W. (1999). "Arab American Students in Public Schools." ERIC Digest, 142. (http://eric-web.tc.columbia.edu/digests/dig142.html)

SPECK, W. (1997). "Respect for Religious Differences: The Case of Muslim Students." *New Directions for Teaching and Learning* 70, 39–46.

TYACK, D. (1999). "Choice Options." *The American Prospect* 10(42), Jan. 1–Feb. 1. (www.prospect.org/print-friendly/printv10/42/tyack-d.html)

U.S. DEPARTMENT OF EDUCATION. (1999). "The Conditions of Education, 1999." Washington, DC: National Center for Education Statistics. (http://www.nces.ed.gov)

———. (2000). "The Conditions of Education, 2000." Washington, DC: National Center for Education Statistics. (http://www.nces.ed.gov)

———. (2002). "The Conditions of Education, 2002." Washington, DC: National Center for Education Statistics. (http://www.nces.ed.gov)

U.S. GENERAL ACCOUNTING OFFICE. (2001). "Report to the Honorable Judd Gregg, U.S. Senate: School Vouchers—Publicly Funded Programs in Cleveland and Milwaukee." Washington, DC: U.S. Government Printing Office.

WELLS, A., AND CRAIN, R. (1992). "Do Parents Choose School Quality of School Status? A Sociological Theory of Free Market Education." In P. Cookson, ed., *The Choice Controversy.*

Widmar et al. v. Vincent et al. (1981). 454 U.S. 263.

WILLIAMS, L. (1995). *The Regulation of Private Schools in America: A State By State Analysis.* U.S. Department of Education. Office on Non-Public Education. Washington, DC: U.S. Government Printing Office.

WINERIP, M. (1994). "Billions for Education Lost in Fraud, Waste and Abuse" *The New York Times.* Feb. 2, Sec. A, p.1.

WITTE, J. (1999). "The Milwaukee Voucher Experience: The Good, the Bad and the Ugly." *Phi Delta Kappan* 81(1), 59–64.

WITTE, J., ET AL. (1995). *Fifth-Year Report: Milwaukee Parental Choice Program.* Madison: University of Wisconsin.

———. (1997). *Achievement Effects of Milwaukee Voucher Program.* Madison: University of Wisconsin.

Witters v. Washington Department of Services for the Blind. (1986). 474 U.S. 481.

Zelman v. Doris Simmons-Harris. (2002). 536 U.S. 639.

Zobrest v. Catalina Foothills School District. (1993). 509 U.S. 1.

CHAPTER 3

Financing Schools: Equity or Disparity

POSITION 1: FOR JUSTICE IN EDUCATIONAL FINANCE

"I don't wanna feel like we're charity," she snaps back. . . . "But there are things we need like books, new curtains and paper. It's not like we're using it for something stupid. I know they wanna spend on their kids . . . but maybe they could just spare a little."

—GOODMAN, 1999, P. 15

Some Consequences of Inequitable School Funding

In 1991, Jonathan Kozol described the "savage inequalities" American children faced in public school. The shocking disparities among school facilities and resources constitute unequal educational opportunities for our young people. The differences among schools within a state or even a district result from the way we finance public education in the United States since a fundamental injustice is built into that system. Because so much of our school funding comes from local property taxes, rich people pay a smaller share of their income to fund public schools for children in their school districts. Poor people, although making greater sacrifices for their children, have less to spend on their education.

U.S. public schools have long been a beacon of hope for the residents of this country. From the early 1800s education offered the promise of social mobility. Schooling would help to equalize opportunities for all young people to better their lot in life. When reformers encouraged taxpayers to accept the responsibility of paying for schools, they promised that by doing so they would be providing young people with the chance to increase their own wealth and that of the nation as a whole. Tax dollars spent on school would help to eliminate the potential for conflict between rich and poor by decreasing the numbers of the poor. Horace Mann expressed the belief this way: "Education, then, beyond all other devices of human origin, is the great equalizer of the conditions of men—the balance-wheel of the social machinery" (Mann, quoted in Cremin, 1957, p. 87). The way we fund public education, however, robs schools of their potential to act as that equalizer. By looking at some consequences of that injustice we can understand that schools do not provide adequate support for equality of opportunity or achievement. The conditions of underfunded schools make the best argument for why we must change school financing.

For the most part, those children in the United States whom fate has placed in middle- or upper-class families attend schools that are well equipped, safe, and clean. They have science labs and the necessary supplies for conducting experiments. They have access to up-to-date technology, which often is housed in libraries stocked with reference materials. Their textbooks are relatively new and, more importantly, each student has one. The schools of the "lucky" have art rooms and gyms, pools and playing fields, auditoriums and music rooms.

Most American children born into poor families attend schools in which the facilities are run-down and dangerous. The buildings are generally older than the schools of their wealthier counterparts. Science labs have obsolete equipment and lack the supplies students need to perform experiments. They lack computers and their libraries are stocked with out-of-date reference materials. In many cases, there are not enough textbooks for each student to have one of his or her own, not even of the old, hand-me-down books that are characteristic of these schools. Art rooms and gyms suffer from the same lack of resources as the rest of the building. Their urban locations often mean that there is no room for playing fields or basketball courts. Because schools of the poor house more children than they had been designed to do, auditoriums and music rooms often have been converted to classrooms. Paint peels off the walls and roofs leak (Kozol, 1991; Elam, 1993; Chaddock, 1998; Reid and Anchors, 2002).

In the New York metropolitan region, for example, wealthy districts in northern Westchester County spend a third more per pupil than do poorer districts in lower Westchester and New York City (New York State Department of Education, 2001). This disparity results in dramatically different educational experiences for children (Kozol, 1991; New York State Department of Education, 2001). In the poorer districts, class sizes are larger and there are fewer resources, such as books and computers. Teachers' salaries are significantly lower, resulting in greater teacher turnover. School buildings are in need of major repairs and have inadequate labs, gyms, and other facilities (Campaign for Fiscal Equity, 1999; New York State Department of Education, 2001).

Student achievement varies among the districts and is correlated with pupils' need level and amount of money spent on their education. Twice as many students in low-need, highly funded districts score at the highest levels on fourth-grade state exams as in New York City. The ratio was the same for achieving passing grades on the first-level high school mathematics exam (New York State Department of Education, 2001). Although many factors may have contributed to the students' achievement levels, surely the correlation between low spending and low test scores is hard to ignore.

Causes of Inequitable School Funding

The Property Tax

Although many Americans came to believe that education should not be a luxury only the wealthy could afford, they worried about how publicly funded schools would be controlled. As compromises built into the Constitution suggest, having secured their independence from England, Americans in the early Republican period wanted to limit the power of centralized governments. In establishing public schools, they did not want local communities to lose control over what children would learn and who would teach them. States authorized local governments to impose property taxes on their citizens and to use those funds for the support of schools. Because these revenues came from local communities, rather than state or federal governments, primary control of schools remained with municipalities themselves. Through elected boards of education, the community maintained control of curriculum, hiring of teachers, and allocation of funding. Despite the growing oversight of schools by state agencies and centralization of teacher preparation and, sometimes, curriculum, nineteenth-century Americans were reassured local funding guaranteed ultimate control of their schools would remain in their hands (Tyack, 1974; Katz, 1975; Urban and Wagoner, 2000).

The system remained in place, essentially unchanged, until the 1930s. When a local school district ran out of money, they had nowhere to turn for help. Most often they closed their doors until additional revenues were available. During the Depression, cities, towns, and villages faced tremendous financial difficulties. School districts across the country had difficulty meeting payrolls and maintaining their buildings. Many states were able to provide assistance through their income and sales tax collections (Chinni,1996; Mackey, 1998). State-level financial contributions more than doubled for public education between 1930 and 1950, finally averaging approximately 40 percent of school budgets (Mackey, 1998). That percentage has continued to increase slowly. Nationally, states contribute almost half of school districts' revenue. Local funding is slightly less than half. A small contribution from federal tax dollars (roughly 7 percent) makes up the remainder (National Center for Education Statistics, 2001b).

So if states are providing almost half of school districts' resources, why do disparities among districts still exist? Can't states provide enough money to equalize the resources available to each child regardless of his or her parents' income? To a certain extent states' contribution to school funding has helped lessen the differences among schools (Connecticut State Department of Education, 2001; New Jersey Department of Education, 2002). However, continued reliance on local property taxes to fund almost half of a district's budget still leads to large disparities in the amount of money available to educate students. Here's how it happens.

A local school district is authorized to levy property taxes and, through their votes, citizens have some voice in the rate at which they will be taxed.

Let's imagine two districts—one urban and one suburban—that adopt the same property tax rate of 2 percent. In the suburban community, District A, the total value of property that can be taxed averages out to be $250,000 per child enrolled in the district's schools. In the inner-city community, District B, the property tax base is $50,000 per pupil. When taxpayers in each community pay the same rate, 2 percent, District A raises $5,000 to spend on each student in its schools. District B raises only $1,000. To achieve equality with District A in the amount they could spend on their children's education, taxpayers in District B would have to agree to a tax rate of 10 percent. When you consider that most taxpayers in District B have dramatically lower incomes than those in District A, you can see how much of a hardship such a high tax rate would be. People who already are poor would be forced to pay a much higher percentage of their income to fund their schools than their wealthier neighbors do. The higher rates of taxes in District B would make them less attractive to homeowners and business owners.

Despite the sacrifices involved in creating such higher tax rates, that is what many urban and rural school districts have been forced to do. However, political and economic realities put a ceiling on how much they could raise the tax rate and how much of the funds could be allocated to school expenses. As a result, even though residents of those communities pay a higher share of their income to fund their schools, they never raise enough money to equal resources available to schools in wealthier communities (Ladd and Hansen, 1999). This pattern creates fundamental inequalities of educational opportunity in the United States and must be remedied by reforming the way we finance schools. We need to find a way to ensure every U.S. school is guaranteed enough funding to educate the children entrusted to it.

Federal Role in School Finance

Another cause of inequity in educational funding is the extremely limited role the federal government plays in paying for schools. Differences between school district spending are repeated among the states. States like New Jersey, New York, Connecticut and Rhode Island traditionally spend approximately twice as much per student as do Utah, Mississippi, Louisiana and Tennessee (National Center for Education Statistics, 2001b). Even when adjusted for differences in the cost of living among the states, the real disparities between available funds for schools remain.

Many people oppose proposals for creating greater equity among the states regarding school funding. They suggest there is no connection between the amount of money a state or school district spends per pupil and the academic achievement of those students. However, an interesting fact emerges when we begin to compare the average academic achievement of students in a state and the average amount of money districts in that state spend on schooling.

The National Assessment of Educational Progress (NAEP) is a project of the National Center for Education Statistics. Since 1969, it has conducted a series of tests administered nationwide and designed to assess students' achievements in a variety of subject areas. Also known as "The Nation's Report Card," the NAEP is a required assessment for states receiving Title I grants (National Center for Education Statistics, 2002). When we compare student achievement on the NAEP in a given state and per-pupil spending in that state, an interesting fact emerges. Of the forty-three in which the test was taken, eleven states whose test scores were identified in a recent study as being in the lowest quartile (the bottom 25 percent) of achievement provide their students with less than the national average funding ($6,491) for their education (see Figure 3.1). While this fact may not prove a causal relationship between per-pupil spending and academic achievement, it certainly suggests there may be one.

Americans spend a greater percentage of our revenues on education than do most citizens in the other democratic nations with market economies. In most countries, however, most of the funding for grammar and high schools comes from the central government. In the United States, only 7 percent comes from the federal government; the rest of the funding comes from state and local sources. Since those amounts depend on a region's wealth, the quality of children's education is determined by where they live (Halstead, 2000; Organisation for Economic Cooperation and Development, 2001; 2002). While this policy often is justified as a way of maintaining local control over schools, Americans accept other funding practices—such as centralized funded for the interstate highway system—without suggesting that such policies impact on individual freedom (Chinni, 1996). We justify this system of centralized financing for road systems because we believe the safety of drivers and passengers is

FIGURE 3.1 NAEP Results and Per-Pupil Spending for Selected States

State	Rank in NAEP*	Per-Pupil Spending†
Alabama	40	$4,582
Arizona	33	$5,224
Arkansas	38	$4,756
California	41	$5,544
Florida	36	$6,306
Georgia	35	$5,562
Louisiana	42	$5,155
Mississippi	43	$4,156
New Mexico	37	$4,788
South Carolina	39	$5,335
Tennessee	34	$4,719

**Grissmer et al. (2000).* Improving Student Achievement. *Washington, DC: Rand Corp. Average scores for tests taken between 1990–1996 in participating states.*

†National Center for Education Statistics. (2001a). Current expenditure per pupil in constant 1998–1999 dollars, average expenditure 1990–1996.

too important to allow differences in state and local wealth to affect road maintenance. The same logic should apply to the centralization of funding for schools.

Not only do local school districts benefit from having safe, well-functioning schools; we all do. Citizens whose good educations prove to them that society cares about their lives and futures think thoughtfully about public policies and carry out civic duties such as voting and serving on juries. As a nation we benefit from their commitment. They provide the kind of check on government excesses and abuses that the founding fathers envisioned. Well-educated citizens are prepared to contribute to society both economically and culturally. The benefits of their education accrue to all of us at least as much as do the benefits from a well-maintained highway system. Failure to provide equity in school finance reveals how little we put into practice all our talk about the value of children in this society. "No agreement exists in our society that we have an obligation to provide minimal living standards to kids, let alone education." (Orfield, 1994) We can and should make a beginning toward actualizing our care for young people by ensuring there is equity in education funding.

Opposition to Changes in School Financing

States' contributions to school funding often are being distributed in ways designed to reduce differences among districts' resources for education. These limited (and unsuccessful) attempts to improve equity in school funding result from legal challenges to state formulas for distributing money to schools. Since the 1970s court cases in at least forty-four states challenged school funding inequities as violations of their constitutions. Decisions in nineteen of those cases have required school finance reform and most states have made some changes in the way they pay for schools. Due to increases in state contributions to educational funding as a result of these cases, states now contribute almost half of all money available to schools (Odden and Picus, 1992). These changes, however, did not come easily. In some states there was vociferous and politically powerful opposition to them.

In New Jersey, for example, the state fought the court's decision for more than twenty years. Parents, school staff, and elected officials from wealthier districts mounted vigorous campaigns against implementation of the court's order to equalize spending in public schools.

> (There was) stubborn, hard-bitten opposition to distributing public resources equitably. Many individuals and groups fought publicly and zealously to continue to use the public schools and the public purse to maintain advantages for wealthy white communities, families and children at the expense of poor non-white communities, families and children. . . . Many of the participants felt no sense of shame as they argued to maintain an inherently unequal system of public education in which public money was used to confer private privilege to students in their well-appointed suburban schools while basic health and safety standards were routinely violated in their underfinanced urban counterparts. (Firestone, Goertz, and Natriello, 1997, p. 159)

This opposition should not be unexpected. The authors of a comprehensive report on financing American schools found that conflicts involved in providing equity in school financing are rooted in competing values.

> Most Americans believe in equality of opportunity, but they also believe in the right of parents to choose to spend their money for the benefit of their own children. Most Americans believe that every child has a right to a good education in a publicly funded common school but they also believe in freedom of mobility in a way that allows affluent Americans to live together in locales able to easily support good schools and that tends to concentrate poverty and disadvantage, often in urban areas. . . . None of these commitments is unworthy and each has a claim for attention. But given these conflicting values, no model of either the finance system or of the education system as a whole could ever be consistent with all of them. (Ladd and Hansen, 1999, p. 264)

In the last twenty years in their unyielding pursuit of less governmental involvement in our lives, conservative politicians and their supporters have shifted the balance of power in such conflicts in favor of the rights of individuals and away from the common good. For example, in the last twenty years many Americans have come to resent efforts made by the government to achieve equality of opportunity for all citizens. They believe these efforts unfairly penalize hardworking people who have achieved a measure of success through their own labor and sacrifice. They believe these governmental attempts to create a just society are fundamentally unfair and reward those who do not work as hard as they do and who have come to expect handouts. They believe their tax dollars are "theirs" and do not belong to the community at large. They expect returns on those payments that directly benefit them and their families. These attitudes have played out in congressional and local elections (Holmes, 1995), in court cases challenging affirmative action plans in state university systems (Walsh, 2001; Wilgoren, 2001) and in proposals to apply similar plans in college athletic programs (Chavez, 2002).

This attitude plays out in a special way with regard to property taxes. Connected as they are to the value of the homes they have struggled to provide for their families, property taxes represent, for many people, an investment in their children's future. They believe they should be used for their own school districts and not applied to those of children whose parents are unwilling to support education in their locality. They are absolutely opposed to a redistribution of those tax dollars to support the education of children other than their own. Not surprisingly, these attitudes are disproportionately represented among citizens with above-average incomes who live in wealthier school districts (Campbell and Fischel, 1996; Heubert, 1999).

These beliefs, however, are incorrect in several ways. In many localities poor people work hard to provide education for their children, and pay a higher share of their income, often at higher tax rates, than do wealthier people (Ladd and Hansen, 1999). In return they get inadequate schools that provide fewer opportunities and result in lower student achievement levels. Those who adopt the "me-first" attitude also justify it by making claims about their own success that are not completely accurate. They attribute their achievements only to hard work and ignore advantages race and socioeconomic status of their own parents may have given them. Consciously or unconsciously they appear to want to maintain advantages with which their children come into the world even if doing so means other children are seriously disadvantaged. Correct or not, however, these attitudes are translated into powerful political forces when citizens who hold them exercise their right to vote. They result in opposition to proposals that school funding be centralized at the state or federal level.

The genius of the American system of government, however, helps us work through these conflicts of values in unique ways. The system of checks and balances built into our political system protects us from impulses to sacrifice our commitment to equality in the name of individual freedom. In the case of school financing, the courts have provided the much-needed check to legislative and executive policies that unfairly limit the educational opportunity and achievement of poor and/or minority students. By holding states accountable to their constitutional obligations to provide adequate schooling for all their children, the courts prevent "prejudices against discrete and insular minorities" from affecting "political processes ordinarily to be relied upon to protect minorities" (*United States v. Carolene Products*, 1938). In addition they ensure that the Fourteenth Amendment, providing equal protection under the law for all citizens, is safeguarded even from understandable desires of loving parents to care first and foremost for their own children.

The courts have been correct in insisting states create educational finance systems that prevent school districts from having radically different per-pupil budgets. Education is a necessity to assure the continuation of the United States as a working democracy and a prosperous economy. It is a public service whose benefits are shared by all. "Insofar as education produces a more informed and responsible citizenry with a greater appreciation for the diversity of the cultures and traditions of our populace, the entire society benefits" (Ascher, Fruchter, and Berne, 1996, p. 9). As such, combining our resources to provide that service is a democratic and justifiable public policy.

The Future of Equity in School Funding

The kind of equity we have been discussing so far is called *fiscal neutrality*. In a state that accepted this standard, it would be unconstitutional to limit a child's educational opportunities by the taxable wealth of his or her school district; instead the amount of funding provided would have to be based on the taxable wealth of the whole state (Long, 1999). The earliest fiscal equity case established this as the litmus test for the constitutionality of school financing in various states (*Serrano v. Priest*, 1971). It is a fairly straightforward, dollar-for-dollar equality; it is easily measured, if not so easily achieved. However, other court decisions have pointed us toward more complex, and ultimately more just, definitions of equity when the term is applied to school funding.

In cases in New Jersey, West Virginia, Kentucky, Texas, Washington, Massachusetts, Wyoming, Ohio, South Carolina, and New Hampshire judges referred to articles of the state constitutions that established the public education system (Long, 1999). Many of these clauses described the types of education to which the children of the state were entitled. In New Jersey, for example, the constitution promises young people a "thorough and efficient" system of public education (Long, 1999, p. 2). In New York, they are entitled to a "sound basic education"(Campaign for Fiscal Equity, 2001b, p. 2). These cases have brought up the necessity of considering whether school finance formulas provide a kind of equity called *adequacy* to children within a state. That means, in many cases, courts are ruling that states are required to provide enough resources to its school districts to ensure the children under their care have "a level of resources that is sufficient to meet defined or absolute, rather than relative . . . . standards" of educational achievement (Berne and Stiefel, 1999, p. 22).

The shift from fiscal equity to adequacy as the measure of justice in school financing is important. It require states to define what constitutes an acceptable level of academic achievement for their students, determine what resources are needed to see each child meets those standards, and then to create funding formulas providing those resources to every student in the state (Berne and Stiefel, 1999; Ladd and Hansen, 1999; Smith, 2001). The movement to adequacy considerations forces lawmakers to consider the outcomes of educational spending. Instead of just determining whether the "input" into education—the money we spend—is equal in amount, thinking about adequacy allows us to decide whether we are spending enough money to see that all children actually learn. In addition the attention on providing "adequate" education will force school districts to focus on connections between spending and achievement; in doing so they will use our tax dollars more efficiently and more effectively. Finally, the move to adequacy as criteria for justice in school financing will drive the educational system to eliminate disparities in children's educational achievement based on their parents' financial situations (Ladd and Hansen, 1999).

For example, let's assume a state established high academic standards that students would have to meet to demonstrate satisfactory academic achievement—that is, to show they had received an adequate education. If that state determined that disadvantaged students—often clustered in one school district—required more resources to meet those standards than did students with more material privilege, then the state could create a school finance formula providing for those needs. That is, disparities in the dollar amount of aid provided to school districts could exist, if the state could show such differences were necessary in order to provide an adequate education for all (Ladd and Hansen, 1999).

This strategy for achieving justice in educational funding would be a real improvement over the limited success fiscal equity plans have achieved. Real gains have been made through those plans and should not be dismissed. Recent studies indicate disparities in school finance have been reduced in states where the courts have ordered changes in funding formulas. More money has become available for children in the poorest districts. These improvements have been made without reducing the spending in the wealthiest districts by increasing spending in the poorest and middle-level districts. They have weakened the connection between a district or family's resources and the amount spent on children's education. (Evans, Murray, and Schwab, 1999; Mathis, 2000; Jimerson, 2001). "Court mandated reform has therefore changed state school finance systems in the general direction many reformers hoped for." (Evans, Murray, and Schwab, 1999).

However, fiscal equity does not guarantee children in a state will receive adequate education. California and Hawaii have high levels of equality in the amount of resources schools receive; both, however, spend less than the national average on their students (National Center for Education Statistics, 2001a). Schools in both states lack many of the resources to provide well-maintained and adequately staffed schools (Connell, 1998). If we set "broad" or "high" standards of adequacy for our young people *and* are committed to providing the resources to help all children receive that education, such conditions no longer will be allowed to exist in any state in the country.

Money does matter when it comes to education. Despite early studies emphasizing the influence of nonschool factors, such as family background and neighborhood environment (Coleman, 1966; Hanushek, 1996), growing evidence shows student achievement is affected by the amount of money schools spend on their education (Hedges, Laine, and Greenwald, 1994; Hedges and Greenwald, 1996). If schools have enough financial resources to create small classes, employ experienced and well-educated teachers, provide ongoing professional development for those teachers, buy enough textbooks and other curricular materials, repair and maintain their buildings, then student achievement is positively affected (Ferguson and Ladd, 1996; Mosteller, Light, and Sacks, 1996; Finn, 1998).

A commitment to providing high-standard adequacy in education requires we provide all schools with those resources. Of course adequate oversight by federal, state, and local government is needed to ensure resources are being spent appropriately and honestly. Although such accountability may be difficult to achieve, the current lack of accountability for providing adequate resources to guarantee children's academic achievement is intolerable.

Equity in school finance is a matter of justice. We need to decide whether we believe that all children in this country are judged to be deserving of equal treatment. Clearly, they are currently not receiving that protection under the present system of paying for schools. Issues of individual freedom, local control, and overinvolvement by government in our daily lives certainly deserve consideration. They do not, however, automatically outweigh the rights of all children to receive an education that will empower them to be competent to take up their duties as citizens, members of society, and workers.

> A genuinely common public school best reflects our belief in the worth of each individual. . . . This equality can not be only the formal guarantees of legal rights and basic freedoms or merely some "basic" education. It should extend to the commitment that each person potentially has "special capacities for leading a rich life" and deserves through the schools the opportunity to develop those capacities. (Paris, 1995, p. 195)

Working for justice in educational finance is one of the most powerful ways we can help fulfill our national promise to create such schools—to enrich the children who attend them and ourselves. As Jonathan Kozol suggests, if we do not carry out that commitment, we risk sending hundreds of thousands of children living in poverty the message that they do not count, that this society does not value them. By warehousing them in schools with leaky roofs and broken toilets, while we lavish luxuries on their suburban counterparts, we tell them they do not matter to us. By failing to provide textbooks and teachers, we tell them they do not really belong to us. The danger here is that they will begin to believe us. They will have little to lose by rejecting our rules and laws if they think we have already rejected them. By failing to create a just system of financing education, we will be failing to live up to the pledge of allegiance we make to this country—there will be no secure liberty without justice for all of America's children (Kozol, 1991).

POSITION 2: AGAINST CENTRALIZATION IN EDUCATIONAL FINANCING

> *"We've never aspired to be average here," says Becky Graddock. . . . "If our costs are a little high, it reflects the fact that we want our kids to be able to compete."*
>
> —GOODMAN, 1999, PP. 8–9

Those suggesting we centralize funding for American public schools in an attempt to ensure equal opportunity for children are well meaning but misguided. They demonstrate a concern for justice for some but almost completely ignore the rights of others. In the concern to provide what they call equal educational opportunity for children, they forget to consider taxpayers' freedom to exercise the maximum possible control over the use of their money. They deny those footing the bill the opportunity to see their funds are spent efficiently, wisely, and honestly, ignore strong reasons for allowing parents and other taxpayers to support their own children's schools to the full extent of their ability, and dismiss strong arguments in favor of supporting academic achievement for more able students who will be able to make significant returns on public funds spent on their education.

The Missing Connection Between School Finances and Academic Achievement

Those who support centralized educational funding schemes believe we should allow federal or state governments to collect taxes and distribute them equally among all school districts. In doing so, they say, we will provide schools in poorer districts with needed resources to help students improve their academic performance. Sounds as if the plan has possibilities for addressing the persistent problem of underachievement by students from low socioeconomic backgrounds. It would if a link could be made between a school's material resources and its students' academic achievement. However, in over four decades, scholars have been unable to demonstrate conclusively that such a link exists.

The first of these research efforts, the famous "Coleman study," took place in the mid-1960s. It was the era of President Johnson's War on Poverty, and many Americans were convinced schools could be a primary tool in winning that battle. James Coleman and his colleagues conducted a large-scale national survey of thousands of schools. They calculated the resources they assumed would be connected to student achievement—teacher education and experience, number of books in the library, laboratory equipment, and so on. In other words, they counted the things money can buy. The results were surprising, even to them. They concluded that a school's material resources had little effect on student achievement. Instead they found that "family background differences account for much more variance in achievements than do school differences" (Coleman, 1966, p. 73). Other researchers have reached the same conclusion. "There is no strong system relationship between school expenditures and student performance" (Hanushek, 1989, p. 46). Recently some researchers have claimed their studies indicate that a few factors related to funding do affect school performance (Hedges, Laine, and Greenwald, 1994); however, even they cannot definitively show that providing more resources to schools serving children from poor or uncaring family backgrounds will automatically improve those children's academic achievement.

We have come to understand that many factors other than financial resources affect students' academic achievement. We know students who grow up with no educated role models often are unable to see school success as a real possibility. In fact, some young people who are members of minority groups actually have come to reject school success, believing that to achieve good grades they would have to "act white." They decide that the price of separating themselves from their poor communities, troubled parents, or indifferent peers is too high in return for the chance to participate more fully in a capitalist system (Fordham and Ogbu, 1986). We can add resources to such students' schools but doing so will not necessarily result in academic achievement. All the money in the world cannot resolve their ambivalence about academic success; that is up to them and their families.

Even when poor parents want their children to succeed in school and encourage them to do so, their efforts will fall short. Mothers and fathers living in poverty are not able to prepare young people for challenges they will face in schools. They do not have the money to buy them books or computers; they cannot take them to museums or concerts. They have so many other problems and demands on their time that they cannot even give their children the attention they need to grow and develop. So poor children come to school less prepared than those whose parents have more time and money to share with them (Brantlinger, Majd-Jabbari, and Guskin, 1996). No matter how hard we try, no matter how much money we spend on education, we cannot seem to make up for all that was lost in their preschool years.

Let's face it—if more money led to better academic performance, we would have it by now. In the last three decades of the twentieth century, we spent more money for each child's education than most other industrialized countries did (Viadero, 1998; Organisation for Economic Cooperation and Development,

2001). Within that period (controlling for inflation) educational funding rose 60 percent and spending per pupil tripled (National Center for Education Statistics, 2001b). Some children, however, are still less successful than others. Despite all our efforts, for example, children from minority groups still score substantially lower on standardized tests than do white children (Haney, 1993). It may simply be, as some scholars have suggested, that members of some racial and ethnic groups are, on average, less intellectually gifted than those of other groups (Herrnstein and Murray, 1994; D'Souza, 1995). It is not "justice" to spend large sums of other people's money on their education when the return will be smaller than if we invested those same dollars on children who have a better chance of succeeding. Taxpayers have a right to insist their hard-earned money be spent in the most efficient way possible.

Instead of diverting other people's money to schools with large numbers of failing students, it would be a wiser use of public funds to provide poor children and their families with social services they need to create better lives. We need to change the realities of their homes and neighborhoods if children are going to be able to take advantage of what schools have to offer. We should channel tax dollars to fight crime, provide recreational facilities, and create jobs, rather than waste money on schools, and ensure that every child has adequate health care—both physical and mental—and live in safe homes and neighborhoods. Only then will they come to school ready to learn (Hess, 1998; Hunter, 2000). Spending money to solve their economic and social problems directly will be a better choice than putting more money into school districts that are often corrupt and mismanaged.

Historical Misuse of Public Funds in Urban School Districts

Proponents of centralized educational funding claim to be most concerned about children in failing urban schools. Some of their advocates even argue that all the factors we have been discussing mean these students need and deserve more of the public resources than those students whose backgrounds better prepare them for school success (Hansen, 2001). According to these advocates, federal and state government should turn over to poor children's schools even larger sums of taxpayer money than they do now (Halstead, 2000, 2002). It is a strange suggestion—to reward failing schools and punish successful ones.

Increased funding to failing school districts will indeed reward some people; however, it will not necessarily help students. For example, increasing teachers' salaries will further enrich professionals who are already middle class. Requiring more professional development for teachers will increase the income of consultants who provide teacher training (Levin, 1976; Barbanel, 1994; Dillon 1994). Prepackaged instructional programs many districts are encouraged to buy (Slavin, 1997) bring profits to their creators. However, there is no guarantee such expenditures will help children in any way.

Urban schools have long been used to better the lives of some city residents at the expense of children's education. Urban school districts historically have been a source of patronage jobs politicians could hand out in exchange for votes. Members of various ethnic communities have, in their turn, assumed control of the districts and provided salaries to members of their constituencies—sometimes without requiring work in return (Connors, 1971). ". . . (T)he history of patronage is a method by which city residents without access to other political and economic resources have taken care of themselves and their friends" (Anyon, 1997, p. 159). In the 1980s one critic charged that in a city in the Northeast, "The political patronage has been so widespread that those filling district positions of responsibility have no idea of their actual duties. Positions were created to be filled by cronies. Routine hiring, evaluating and record keeping were not only bypassed but not even expected" (Morris, 1989, p. 18). The situation has not dramatically improved. "(T)he patronage system in large cities has been responsible for the appointment of many unskilled, educationally marginal school administrators. The history of patronage has also been partly responsible for those inner-city teachers who are ineffective" (Anyon, 1997, p. 158). The legacy of uncertified and unqualified teachers remains a problem for urban school systems (Holloway, 2000).

In many school districts patronage jobs have resulted in bureaucracies that hamper teachers' abilities to meet students' needs. Employees within these bureaucracies are sometimes involved in corrupt and illegal activities. Administrators in large urban districts have been arrested for taking bribes and diverting public funds for their private use (Berger, 1992; Ainsworth, 1993; Fried, 1994, 1995; Clowes, 2000; Heartland Institute, 2000). Any scheme to increase funding to these districts would have to ensure new monies did not create more ineffective administrative positions. In addition, oversight procedures would need to be in place to prevent misappropriation of new funds.

As part of their legacy of providing patronage jobs, urban schools also employ a large number of paraprofessionals. These jobs are an excellent source of income for local community members. Cafeteria workers, teachers' aides, attendance assistants, special education aides, bus drivers, transportation aides, and sentries are all positions that ordinarily require no education beyond high school. They are jobs members of the neighborhoods around the schools seek out. Getting one's name on "the list" is often a matter of *who,* not *what,* you know. In many cities these paraprofessionals have unionized and command far higher wages in the school system than they would be able to earn in similar private sector jobs. Instead of spending money to put more well-prepared teachers in classrooms, school districts may use their increased state aid to add more "assistants" as has been done in the past (Connell, 1998). The pressure to do so may come from community members who do not have enough education to be teachers. There is nothing in the history of urban school personnel policies to suggest that politicians on school boards or in municipal governments will be able to resist such urgings from their constituents (Anyon, 1997). We should not expect increasing aid to such schools by centralizing or equalizing school funding will be accompanied by a complete reform of the patronage system. The difference is that more money will be spent on jobs instead of education.

Providing services to schools also has been a lucrative business for many. Urban schools notoriously are inefficient at managing their money (Clowes, 2000). The lack of oversight often results in disproportionately high costs. For example, construction costs for the New York City schools recently soared to double the original estimates. The district's bloated bureaucracy made it almost impossible to hold anyone accountable for cost overruns (Ventura, 2002). In addition, contractors who work for urban school districts often are required to pay "kickbacks" or bribes to school officials to secure work (Ave, 2002; Guthrie, 2002). Cities pay more for services and supplies that often are shoddy so that corrupt employees can become wealthy. When such practices come to light, charges and countercharges fly back and forth in the media. The accusations often result in lawsuits that cost school districts large sums of money—none of which goes to improve children's education (Finnie and Guthrie, 2001; Guthrie, 2002). Instead lawyers and contractors get rich.

Those who demand, in the name of justice, that hardworking taxpayers provide more funds to these mismanaged districts need to rethink their priorities. No such increases in funding should take place until appropriate personnel, accounting, and management policies and practices are in place. Fairness to those paying the bills demands no less. No taxpayer should be asked to sacrifice to provide opportunities for "fat cats" to get richer by skimming money from school budgets or providing jobs for those who keep them in power. School finance equalization plans would do just that.

The Consequences of Centralizing School Finance

Those who propose we centralize school funding at the state or federal level in order to fund all schools equally seem oblivious to what happens when such attempts are made. The "equalizers" have been successful in some states, often with disastrous results.

Leveling Down

There are two options for creating equalization plans for school spending. The financing can be "leveled up" or "leveled down." In leveling up, the state funds all schools at the same per-pupil rate as the wealthiest districts. In leveling down, all schools receive a per-pupil amount equivalent to that being spent in middle-class or poorer districts in the state. In most leveling-down schemes, a limit is placed on what a district can spend above the state subsidy. Leveling up is an expensive proposition. It would require an increase in taxes across a state; people pay higher taxes but only a few of them see increased services to their communities as a result of those rate hikes. As a result leveling-up schemes are unpopular and rarely are implemented fully. Ohio has been trying for more than a decade to implement such a plan; New Jersey has been trying for more than three decades to develop a plan that would satisfy the court's insistence on equal spending at a high enough level to ensure student achievement. So far these and most other states where leveling up has been attempted still have unequal per-pupil spending among school districts.

It seems as if the only plans that really result in making per-pupil spending equal across a state are the ones that level the spending downward—that is, only those plans that set the base level of resources per child at the amount being spent in poorer, not richer, districts actually go into effect in states (Hoxby, 1999). In 1971, the California Supreme Court heard the first legal challenge to differences in school financing. In that case, *Serrano v. Priest,* the court held that inequalities in district per-pupil funding violated the equal protection clauses of the state and federal constitution. Those who supported equalization of school spending believed they had won a victory. They assumed the changes resulting from the court order would improve education for all California's students. They were wrong. Taxpayers revolted against any plan to increase state taxes in order to equalize school spending (Fischel, 1989, 1996). They passed Proposition 13, which placed a "cap" on taxes and effectively limited funds for all California districts. As a result of these limits, although their funding levels are almost equal, all California's schools are chronically underfunded (Theobold and Picus, 1991; O'Sullivan, Sexton, and Sheffrin, 1995). "Although in this respect, the plaintiffs won the equity they sought, it is to some extent a victory of losers. Though the state ranks eighth in per-capita income in the nation, the share of its income that now goes to public education is a meager 3.8 percent—placing California forty-sixth among the 50 states. Its average class size is the largest in the nation" (Kozol, 1991, p. 221). The students in poor urban schools did not receive better education. Instead all students in the state suffered.

Decreases in Local Support

Research into other instances of equalization attempts shows the increases in state financial support for schools often were accompanied by decreases in local support. In other words, schools did not experience a real increase in resources (Bahl, Sjoquist, and Williams, 1990). This consequence was likely to take place in districts where the total value of property in the area was relatively low and had to be taxed at a high rate even to raise the limited funds schools were receiving. The municipalities sometimes saw the increased state aid as an opportunity to reduce the local tax burden on residents instead of a chance to provide better schools for their children (Reschovsky, 1994). This decision makes sense politically and economically for those cities and towns. High property taxes encourage neither growth nor re-elections. It is not fair, however, to take other people's money, say you are doing so to improve children's education, and then fail to do so. Centralized school-funding plans encourage such behavior by their very nature and we should not implement them.

It is not only local financial support for schools that suffers as a result of centralizing finance. When equalization plans result in leveling down school spending, many parents fear a resulting decrease in the quality of the schools in their community. Consequently, they choose to send their children to private schools. These decisions result in fewer concerned families in public schools—

fewer parents in PTAs, at school board meetings and school-sponsored extracurricular events (Kenny and Husted, 1996). No school district can afford to lose the parents who are most interested in their children's school success.

Loss of Local Control

One of the most unique aspects of the U.S. school system is the fact that schools historically have been designed to meet the needs of individual areas. In the late nineteenth and early twentieth century, for example, different courses of study were taught in rural schools than in urban ones. Each local school district, working with concerned members of the community, was able to create schools that met their children's needs (Cremin, 1961). Schools were able to hire and fire teachers and could do so based on criteria established locally. A teacher needed to live up to an individual community's standards, not just ones created by some state bureaucrats with little or no sense of the municipality's needs or values.

Even in the late twentieth century, local control of schools remained an important aspect of their governance. Taxpayers could accept or reject school boards' proposed budgets. They could elect or throw out of office school board members. In doing so, they ensured that their ideas for their children's education would be carried out in the schools. In addition, taxpayers could select those elected officials who set property tax rates for funding schools, and thus could work to see their tax burden would not be unduly high. Because most people in a town, city, or village had attended a local school or had children who did, interest in a local school district was high. The added dimension of locally controlling school funding increased taxpayers' involvement in the schools. People are willing to pay if they can see their money is being spent on something of value and that they have something to say about what constitutes that value.

When school funding is substantially centralized—when states take over most of the task of paying for education—taxpayers lose a substantial amount of the control over the schools for which they are paying. For example, in many states where the state's share of school funding has increased, so have rules and regulations. States across the country are establishing standards for student performance. These standards are often innocuous statements of general academic achievement. For example, in New York the standards for academic achievement in languages other than English are Standard 1: students will be able to use a language other than English for communication and Standard 2: students will develop cross-cultural skills and understanding (New York State Department of Education, 1996).

Who could argue with such bland proposals? On the other hand, who can, with a straight face, argue that they represent adequate guidance for schools struggling to measure student performance. Indeed such standards usually are backed up by systems of evaluating students through tests prepared by the states' departments of education. School districts and individual teachers have little say in the curriculum they are expected to deliver and even less input into tests their students will take. While state taxpayers may have a right to see their money is being well spent, the procedure for doing so takes away large amounts of local influence over what young people learn and how they are evaluated.

Standardized curriculum and testing affects schools in unique ways. Teachers whose schools are located in wealthier districts often have developed challenging curriculum for their students. They believe this curriculum and project-based assessments they use are more stringent than standardized tests prepared by states. For example, in Scarsdale, a wealthy district outside New York City, parents kept students home from an eighth-grade test to protest the negative impact exams were having on education in their schools. They believed teachers were being forced to "teach to the test" instead of to students' needs and interests. They did not win their point. State officials pressured school district administrators, claiming they had contributed to the boycott of the tests (West, 2001). Parents, fearful their district leaders would be penalized, allowed their children to take the tests the following year (Hartocollis, 2002).

Many "alternative" schools also have developed programs relying on authentic assessment—performance tasks such as conducting research projects, creating portfolios, and performing experiments. They have joined such groups as the Coalition for Essential Schools. Some of these schools also believe that standardized curriculum and testing mandated by state departments of education are inadequate for their students' needs. However, in some locations where a state provides large amounts of school funding, a school not participating in the curriculum and testing risks losing state accreditation and financial support (Perez-Pena, 2001; Chiles, 2002; Hartocollis, 2002).

These examples are chilling reminders that by centralizing and equalizing school funding by leveling down we will be penalizing schools that already work. We will be jeopardizing the future of those schools that provide models of what schools can be and do. Without those shining examples, it will be even more difficult for other schools to create successful programs of their own. We cannot risk their loss, even in the name of fairness. We must consider what justice really demands and not accept easy "feel-good" plans that put educational excellence in danger.

In centralized funding schemes, local taxpayers also experience diminished authority over how their money will be spent because decisions about school finance are made in a state legislature instead of by a district's school board. When school taxes are collected by the state instead of municipalities, the money from a locality goes into a big pot. Interest groups from all across the state want to use that money for their pet projects. The money must be divided in many more ways than if it were allocated locally. The number of people involved in the process increases when funding is centralized. It takes longer to decide on state budgets, and passing them requires a level of compromise that would be unheard of in a local process. Imagine the chaos if every school in the country was forced to wait for state budgets before the local districts would know how many teachers or administrators they would be able to afford! In New York State, for example, the budget has not been passed on time in nearly two decades (*The New York Times*, 2001). Local control is not only a matter of convenience; it is a matter of efficiency and, therefore, justice. Every taxpayer has the right to expect the funds they provide will be available in a speedy way for the services for which they had been collected.

Good Schools Are a Reward for Hard Work

Whether proponents of centralized educational funding like it or not, we live in a capitalist society. We have an economic system that thrives on full and fair competition among businesses and workers. If you produce a product or provide a service that members of society value, you are more highly rewarded than those who do not. It is a system that has created a standard of living in the United States that is the envy of the rest of the world. We provide safety nets for those who cannot participate in the free market; we do so even for the children of those who *will* not take part.

However, one reason this economy works so well is because people can enjoy the fruits of their labor. Those who "crack the system" and figure out what the public will buy can reap monetary rewards they then can translate into assets, one of the most cherished of which is a home. One of the factors that most influences those homebuyers is the opportunity to provide better schools and safer neighborhoods for their children. In turn, the quality of schools is an important factor in determining the market value of a home. Equalizing funding for schools and ensuring that all students receive the same advantages will remove one of the primary reasons why one house is worth more than another.

The American economic system is based on competition and on the idea that some things are "better" than others. These perceived advantages provide an incentive for most Americans to work hard, to save and spend their money. If we centralize school spending and equalize the education children receive, we remove one of the greatest incentives for adults to make sacrifices of time and money this economy requires. It may not seem "fair" but, in general, the system works and it is foolish to think about making dramatic changes to it.

Of course, as part of the safety net, we can continue to provide schools at public expense, although there clearly is no part of the country's Constitution that requires us to do so. The schools we fund, though, should reflect a community's commitment to education and its ability to provide it for its children. The resultant gradations in school resources are the consequences of the economic system that works well in so many ways. By maintaining the current system of educational funding, we are holding out the promise of something better to all Americans. Kozol (1991) laments the fact that children in poorer school districts perceive the differences between their schools and those in wealthier districts. He suggests this awareness makes young people bitter, and that as a result they eventually drop out of the competition that is at the heart of the American economic system. There is, however, another way of looking at the children's awareness. We can see it as the same kind of knowledge that has propelled so many others in this country to work harder than they ever imagined possible. We can see it as providing the same kind of motivation possessed by the pioneers who crossed this country in search of a better life. Some who currently live in municipalities that provide more resources for their schools started out in neighborhoods such as those that Kozol and others describe. Their hard work, determination, and perseverance enabled them to provide a better life for their children. We should not assume that today's young people are incapable of the same kind of effort and success. We need to hold out the promise of rewards for the kind of behavior that most benefits this society. Centralizing and equalizing school funding takes away one of the primary reasons people choose to act in ways that will build up this great country. We cannot risk the consequences of removing that motivation.

For Discussion

1. Look again at Figure 3.1. Speculate on what factors other than lower than average per-pupil expenditures might account for the poor results on the NAEP exams.
2. Some proposals for reducing school financial inequity rely on a shift from property tax revenue to sales tax revenue. Discuss the pros and cons of such a shift. Remember to consider questions such as the reliability of each revenue source in times of economic difficulty.
3. Consider how increased state contributions to school districts may affect local control of schools. Research your own state's policies with regard to the level of independence school districts have in the areas of curriculum, testing, personnel, and length of the school year.
4. For a moment turn the whole question of school financing on its head and consider whether governments have the right to tax citizens to pay for schools. Discuss whether such taxation violates individual rights of those citizens who do not have children in public schools. In doing so, you might try to support the arguments that only parents have the right and obligation to provide their children with education they deem appropriate and government has no right to interfere in their decisions. What might be some effects on the country of implementing such a school financing policy?

References

AINSWORTH, B. (1993). "The Tragedy of Bill Honig." *California Journal.* 24(3) 7–12.

ANYON, J. (1997). *Ghetto Schooling.* New York: Teachers College Press.

ASCHER, C., FRUCHTER, N., AND BERNE, R. (1996). *Hard Lessons: Public Schools and Privatization.* New York: 20th Century Fund Report.

AVE, M. (2002). "Schools' Minority Adviser Dismissed." *St. Petersburg Times.* Feb. 21, p. 3B.

BAHL, R., SJOQUIST, D., AND WILLIAMS, L. (1990). "School Finance Reform and Impact on Property Taxes." *Proceedings of the Eighty-Third Annual Conference on Taxation.* Columbus: National Tax Association—Tax Institute of America.

BARBANEL, J. (1994) "Some Retired Teachers Evade Income Restrictions." *The New York Times.* March 15, p. B3.

BERGER, J. (1992). "Principal Admits Misusing School Funds." *The New York Times.* Feb. 21, p. B1.

BERNE, R., AND STIEFEL, L. (1999). "Concepts of School Finance Equity 1970–Present." In H. Ladd, and J. Hansen, eds., *Making Money Matter: Financing America's Schools.* Washington, DC: National Academy Press.

BRANTLINGER, E., MAJD-JABBARI, M., AND GUSKIN, S. (1996). "Self-Interest and Liberal Educational Discourse: How Ideology Works for Middle-Class Mothers." *American Educational Research Journal.* 33(3), 571–597.

CAMPAIGN FOR FISCAL EQUITY. (1999). "Running on Empty: High Standards and Missing Resources in New York City's Public Schools." Eric Document ED430063.

———. (2001a). "State of Learning in New York." (www.cfequity.org)

———. (2001b) "In Evidence: Policy Reports from the CFE Trial. Special Report: The Trial's Court Decision." Vol. 3. (www.cfequity.org/decn25.pdf)

CAMPBELL, C., AND FISCHEL, W. (1996). "Preferences for School Finance Systems: Voters Versus Judges." *National Tax Journal.* 49(1), 1–15.

CHADDOCK, G. (1998). "Urban Schools Targeted for Makeover." *The Christian Science Monitor.* Jan. 28, Features Sec., p. 12.

CHAVEZ, L. (2002). "Preferences Hurt Minorities." *USA Today.* Oct. 21, p. 11A.

CHILES, N. (2002). "120 8th Graders Boycott State Test." *Newsday.* March 6, p. A14.

CHINNI, D. (1996). "Today's Landed Gentry: How Our Public Education System Rewards Those Who Start Out Ahead." *Washington Monthly.* 28(10), 24–27.

CLOWES, G. (2000). "'Accountable' Public Schools Squander Funds." *School Reform News.* (Heartland Organization: www.heartland.org)

COLEMAN, J. (1966). *Equality of Educational Opportunity.* Washington, DC: U.S. Department of Health, Education, and Welfare, Office of Education.

CONNECTICUT STATE DEPARTMENT OF EDUCATION. (2001). "1999–2000 Connecticut Public School Expenditures." (www.state.ct.us/sde/dgm/Report1/cpse2000)

CONNELL, N. (1998). "Underfunded Schools: Why Money Matters." *Dollars and Sense.* 216, 14–19.

CONNORS, R. (1971). *A Cycle of Power: The Career of Jersey City Mayor Frank Hague.* Metuchen, NJ: Scarecrow Press.

CREMIN, L. (1961). *The Transformation of the School: Progressivism in American Education 1876–1957.* New York: Random House.

CREMIN, L., ED. (1957). *The Republic and the School: Horace Mann on the Education of Free Men.* New York: Teachers College Press.

DILLON, S. (1994). "School Board Said to Misuse Consultants." *The New York Times.* Aug. 10, pp. B1–B2.

D'SOUZA, D. (1995). *The End of Racism: Principles for a Multiracial Society.* New York: Free Press.

ELAM, S. (1993). *The State of the Nation's Public Schools.* Bloomington, IN: Phi Delta Kappan.

EVANS, W., MURRAY, S., AND SCHWAB, R. (1999). "Impact of Court Mandated School Finance Reform." In H. Ladd, and J. Hansen, eds., *Making Money Matter: Financing America's Schools.* Washington, DC: National Academy Press.

FERGUSON, R., AND LADD, H. (1996). "How and Why Money Matters: An Analysis of Alabama Schools." In H. Ladd, ed., *Holding Schools Accountable: Performance-Based Reform in Education.* Washington, DC: Brookings Institution.

FINN, J. (1998). "Class Size and Students-At-Risk: What Is Known? What Is Next?" Commissioned paper prepared for the National Institution on the Education of At-Risk Students. Washington, DC: Office of Educational Research and Improvement, Department of Education.

FINNIE, C., AND GUTHRIE, J. (2001). "Suit Alleges San Francisco Schools' Kickbacks." *San Francisco Chronicle.* Nov. 17, p. A1.

FIRESTONE, W., GOERTZ, M., AND NATRIELLO, G. (1997). *From Cashbox to Classroom: The Struggle for Fiscal Reform and Educational Change in New Jersey.* New York: Teachers College Press.

FISCHEL, W. (1989). "Did Serrano Cause Proposition 13?" *National Tax Journal.* Dec., pp. 465–474.

———. (1996). "How Serrano Caused Proposition 13." *Journal of Law and Politics.* 12, 607–645.

FORDHAM, S., AND OGBU, J. (1986). "Black Students' School Success: Coping with the 'Burden of Acting White.'" *The Urban Review.* 18(1), 176–206.

FRIED, J. (1994). "Principal Charged with Stealing Funds." *The New York Times.* May 19, p. B3.

———. (1995). "More Corruption Charges Against Former Principal." *The New York Times.* March 1, p. B3.

GOODMAN, D. (1999). "America's Newest Class War." *Mojo Wire Magazine.* (Sept./Oct.). (www.motherjones.com/mother_jones/SO99/goodman.html)

GRISSMER, D., ET AL. (2000). *Improving Student Achievement: What State NAEP Test Scores Tell Us.* Washington, DC: Rand Corp.

GUTHRIE, J. (2002). "San Francisco Schools Sue Heating Contractor." *San Francisco Chronicle.* March 7, p. A16.

HALSTEAD, T. (2000) "The National Debate Over School Funding Needs a Federal Focus." *Los Angeles Times.* Oct. 8, p. M2.

———. (2002). "Rich School, Poor School." *The New York Times.* Sec. A, Jan. 8, p. 19.

HANEY, W. (1993). "Testing and Minorities." In L. Weis, and M. Fine, eds., *Beyond Silenced Voices: Class, Race and Gender in U.S. Schools.* Albany: SUNY Press.

HANSEN, J. (2001). "21st Century School Finance: How is the Context Changing?" Education Commission of the States. ECS Issue Paper. Education Finance in the States: Its Past, Present and Future. (www.ecs.org/clearinghouse/28/04/2804.htm)

HANUSHEK, E. (1989). "The Impact of Differential Expenditures on School Performance." *Educational Researcher.* May, pp. 45–51.

———. (1996) "School Resources and Student Performances." In G. Burtless, ed., *Does Money Matter?: The Effect of School Resources on Student Achievement and Adult Success.* Washington, DC: Brookings Institution.

HARTOCOLLIS, A. (2002). "Boycotts and a Bill Protest Mandatory State Tests." *The New York Times.* March 6, p. B9.

HEARTLAND INSTITUTE. (2000). "State Education Roundup—Focus on Public School Corruption." *School Reform News,* Nov. (www.heartland.org)

HEDGES, L., AND GREENWALD, R. (1996). "Have Times Changed? The Relationship Between School Resources and Student Performance." In G. Burtless, ed., *Does Money Matter?: The Effect of School Resources on Student Achievement and Adult Success.* Washington, DC: Brookings Institution.

HEDGES, L., LAINE, R., AND GREENWALD, R. (1994). "Does Money Matter? A Meta-Analysis of Studies of the Effects of Differential School Inputs on Student Outcomes." *Educational Researcher.* 23(3), 5–14.

HERRNSTEIN, R., AND MURRAY, C. (1994). *The Bell Curve: Intelligence and Class Structure in American Life.* New York: Free Press.

HESS, F. (1998). "Courting Backlash: The Risks of Emphasizing Input Equity over School Performance." *Virginia Journal of Social Policy and the Law.* 6(1), 11–46.

HEUBERT, J., ED. (1999). *Law and School Reform: Six Strategies for Promoting Educational Equity.* New Haven: Yale University Press.

HOLLOWAY, L. (2000). "Deal is Struck on *Placement* of Instructors." *The New York Times.* Aug. 25, Sec. B, p. 1.

HOLMES, S. (1995). "Backlash Against Affirmative Action Troubles Advocates." *The New York Times.* Feb. 7, p. B9.

HOXBY, C. (1999). "All School Finance Equalizations are Not Created Equal." National Bureau of Economic Research Working Papers. Cambridge: National Bureau of Economic Research.

HUNTER, R. (2000). "The Unpopular Issues of Poverty and Isolation." *School Administrator.* 57(4), 54.

JIMERSON, L. (2001). "A Reasonably Equal Share: Educational Equity in Vermont. A Status Report, Year 2000–2001." Rural School and Community Trust, Washington, DC. ERIC Document, ED 451008.

KATZ, M. (1975). *Class, Bureaucracy and Schools: The Illusion of Educational Change in America.* New York: Praeger.

KENNY, L., AND HUSTED, T. (1996). "The Legacy of Serrano: The Impact of Mandated Equal Spending on Private School Enrollment." Working Paper, Economics Department, University of Florida, Gainesville.

KOZOL, J. (1991). *Savage Inequalities: Children in America's Schools.* New York: Crown.

LADD, H., AND HANSEN, J., EDS. (1999). *Making Money Matter: Financing America's Schools.* Washington, DC: National Academy Press.

LEVIN, H. (1976). "Effects of Expenditure Increases on Educational Resource Allocation and Effectiveness." In M. Carnoy, and H. Levin, eds., *The Limits of Educational Reform.* New York: David McKay.

LONG, D. (1999). "School Finance Litigation." National Center for Education Statistics. Education Finance Statistics Center. (http://nces.ed.gov/edfin/litigation/litigation.asp)

MACKEY, S. (1998). "The School Money Puzzle." *Government Finance Review.* (2), 39–42.

MORRIS, G. (1989). "The Blackboard Jungle Revisited." *National Review.* 41(8), 18–19.

MOSTELLER, F., LIGHT, R. J., AND SACHS, J. (1996). "Sustained Inquiry in Education: Lessons From Skill Grouping and Class Size." *Harvard Educational Review.* 66(4), 797–842.

NATIONAL CENTER FOR EDUCATION STATISTICS. (2001a). "Selected Graphics in Education Finance." U.S. Department of Education. Educational Finance Statistics Center. (http://nces.ed.gov/edfin/graphs)

———. (2001b). "Statistics in Brief." U.S. Department of Education. Office of Educational Research and Improvement. NCES 2001.

———. (2002). "Important Aspects of *No Child Left Behind* Relevant to NAEP." (http://nces.ed.gov/nationsreportcard/nclb.asp)

NEW JERSEY DEPARTMENT OF EDUCATION. (2002). *School Report Cards.* Education Information Resources. (www.njevalsoft.com)

NEW YORK STATE DEPARTMENT OF EDUCATION. (1996). *Learning Standards for Languages Other Than English.* Albany: Author.

———. (2001). *New York: The State of Learning (Chapter 655 Report).* Albany: Author.

The New York Times. (2001). "Another Stalled Budget." Editorial, June 2, p. A12.

ODDEN, A., AND PICUS, L. (1992). *School Finance: A Policy Perspective.* New York: McGraw-Hill.

ORFIELD, G. (1994). "Asking the Right Question." *Educational Policy.* (8), 404–413.

ORGANISATION FOR ECONOMIC COOPERATION AND DEVELOPMENT. (2001). *Education at a Glance: OECD Indicators 2001 Edition.* Washington, DC: Author.

———. (2002). *Education at a Glance: OECD Indicators 2002 Edition.* Washington, DC: Author.

O'SULLIVAN, A., SEXTON, A., AND SHEFFRIN, S. (1995). *Property Taxes and Tax Revolts: The Legacy of Proposition 13.* Cambridge: Cambridge University Press.

PARIS, D. (1995). *Ideology and Educational Reform: Themes and Theories in Public Education.* Boulder: Westview Press.

PEREZ-PENA, R. (2001). "Opponents of New Regents Exams Take Protest to Capitol." *The New York Times.* May 8, p. B5.

REID, B., AND ANCHORS, S. (2002). "Urban Schools Rating Lower Than in Suburbs." *The Arizona Republic.* Oct. 19. (Online edition: www.arizonarepublic.com/northphoenix/articles/1019Failing1019Z3.html)

RESCHOVSKY, A. (1994). "Fiscal Equalization and School Finance." *National Tax Journal.* 47(1), 185–197.

Serrano v. Priest. (1971). 5 Cal 3d 584.

SLAVIN, R. (1997). "Can Education Reduce Social Inequity?" *Educational Leadership.* 55(4), 6–10.

SMITH, S. (2001, February). "School Finance Litigation Update." Denver: National Conference of State Legislatures/National Center on Educational Finance.

THEOBOLD, N., AND PICUS, L. (1991). "Living With Equal Amounts of Less: Experience of States With Primarily State-Funded School Systems." *Journal of Education Finance.* 17, 1–6.

TYACK, D. (1974). *The One Best System: A History of American Urban Education.* Cambridge: Harvard University Press.

VENTURA, A. (2002). "School Construction Costs Soar More Than 70 Percent Since 1999." *Inside the Budget.* New York Independent Budget Office. Feb. 4, 1–3.

United States v. Carolene Products. (1938). 304 U.S. 144.

URBAN, W., AND WAGONER, J. (2000). *American Education: A History.* 2nd Ed. New York: McGraw-Hill.

VIADERO, D. (1998). "In Education Spending, U.S. Near the Top, Report Finds." *Education Week.* Jan. 14, 11.

WALSH, E. (2001). "Federal Appeals Panel Finds University's Race-Based 'Point' System Unconstitutional." *Washington Post.* Aug. 28, p. A5.

WEST, D. (2001). "Scarsdale Told to Ensure Students Take State Tests." *The New York Times.* Nov. 4, Sec. 14WC, p. 8.

WILGOREN, J. (2001). "U.S. Court Bars Race as Factor in School Entry." *The New York Times,* March 28, p. A1.

CHAPTER 4

The Academic Achievement Gap: Old Remedies or New

POSITION 1: FOR MAINTAINING EXISTING PROGRAMS

By passing this bill, we bridge the gap between helplessness and hope for more than 5 million educationally deprived children. We put into the hands of our youth more than 30 million new books, and into many of our schools their first libraries. We reduce the terrible time lag in bringing new teaching techniques into the nation's classrooms. We strengthen State and local agencies which bear the burden and the challenge of better education. And we rekindle the revolution—the revolution of the spirit against the tyranny of ignorance.

—JOHNSON, 1965

The Academic Achievement Gap

If you were an African American or Latino teenager in the early 1960s, you probably were prevented from attending an integrated high school (Weinberg, 1977). The laws of your state might have specifically mandated separate schools for black and white students. In other areas school districts enforced regulations prohibiting students from enrolling in schools outside their neighborhoods—and those neighborhoods were segregated by race. There was only a fifty-fifty chance you would graduate from high school. Your chances of finishing college were about four in one hundred (Orfield and Eaton, 1996).

Tests designed to measure academic achievement also documented the gap between students of color and their white counterparts. The National Assessment of Educational Progress (NAEP) testing program was established in 1969 "to monitor the academic achievement of nine-, thirteen-, and seventeen-year-olds currently enrolled in school" (Jencks and Phillips, 1998, p. 152). NAEP annually tests 70,000 to 100,000 students in reading, math, science and writing. It is influential and credible enough to be called "The Nation's Report Card." In the early 1970s the NAEP demonstrated dramatic differences between white students and those of color. In all subjects, across all grade levels, white students outperformed African American and Latino students by 12 to 20 percent (Campbell, Hombo, and Mazzeo, 2000).

In the first half of the twentieth century, the common wisdom was that some students simply were incapable of mastering the standard curriculum. If most were students of color, that was to be expected; they simply were genetically or culturally inferior. Southerners justified segregated schools on that basis (Tyack, 1974). In the North, school districts created vocational and industrial educational programs. Many students of color were automatically assigned to them—and not to schools with college preparatory courses (Tyack, 1974; Angus and Mirel, 1999). Education reflected the reality that America was a racially segregated society. In housing, employment, and social relations, people of color and whites lived separate, and definitely not equal, lives. For the most part, those racial arrangements were not challenged in American public schools (Tyack, 1974; Anyon, 1997; Taylor, 1998; Angus and Mirel, 1999). Faint rumblings, however, could be heard heralding a revolution in American life (Tushnet, 1987).

After World War II, racial attitudes in America began at long last to change. Soldiers of African American and Latino descent had risked their lives for the United States and were unwilling to continue to accept second-class citizenship. Civil rights organizations such as the NAACP began to challenge segregation and inequality in the courts. Inevitably attention turned toward schools (Kluger, 1975; Tushnet, 1987; Taylor, 1998). Members of these groups "rejected earlier diagnoses of the problem of poor [school] performers, especially those that located the trouble in the defects of individuals (whether of character or chromosomes)" (Deschenes, Cuban, and Tyack, 2001, p. 533). Instead they believed discrimination prevented students of color from having access to the kind of schools, instructions, and resources white students had. And they had every intention of changing that situation.

Thanks to pressure from members of marginalized communities and their white allies, changes began that were nothing short of revolutionary. Over the last thirty-five years, we developed laws and programs designed to make equal educational opportunity a reality. The courts declared that laws mandating segregation in schools are illegal. Congress has enacted legislation creating Head Start and Title I, which allocates funds to schools with high concentrations of low-performing students. The executive branch of government established affirmative action programs to remedy historic discrimination against people of color. Some of these programs faced tremendous opposition. It took many legal, political, and social struggles to put them into place. It was a fight well worth having; the combined consequences of these policies and programs have been revolutionary.

Today eight out of ten black adolescents receive their high school diplomas (Haycock, 2001). By the 1980s, the high school graduation rate for African Americans was higher than those of all groups in most European countries (Orfield and Eaton, 1996, p. 86). The percentage of African American and Latino students who took the SATs for college entrance has doubled since the 1960s

(Rothstein, 1993). Almost three-quarters of African American high school graduates go on to college. The gap on the NAEP has decreased by approximately 5 percent (Campbell, Hombo, and Mazzeo, 2000).

Policies creating equal educational opportunity are even more important now than when they began. The gains we have made as a society in eliminating some of the harshest forms of racial and ethnic discrimination have resulted in increased economic possibilities for Latinos and African Americans. We have seen dramatic increase in their earning power and that has, in turn, allowed more families to create stable, middle-class lives. This situation marks a dramatic change from the 1960s when employed African American men, for example, earned only a little more than half of what white men earned. The most noticeable change, however, has been among men whose academic achievement is greatest. In the sixties, black men with higher academic achievement earned two-thirds as much as whites. Now, they earn about ninety-six percent of the white average (Jencks and Phillips, 1998, pp. 5–6). Clearly, it is even more imperative we ensure children of color receive an education that will allow them to take advantage of the improved social climate providing them with so many new possibilities.

Too many African American and Latino students still live in neighborhoods of concentrated poverty where drug violence is rampant. They see few adults in their communities with full-time jobs making living wages. Dependency on government programs such as Food Stamps and medicaid is the norm (Wilson, 1996; Orfield, 1993). They do not have the advantages their white counterparts take for granted. Their parents are undereducated (National Center for Children in Poverty, 2002a) and cannot provide support at home to complement teachers' sometimes heroic efforts. They own fewer books and their public libraries are poorly financed and operate on limited schedules. They attend fewer cultural events—such as concerts, plays or poetry readings—and visit museums, art galleries, zoos, and conservatories even less frequently (Bradley et al., 2001). When they then are forced to "measure up" to more privileged children on standardized tests, it is no wonder they cannot do so (National Center for Children in Poverty, 2002b).

If we want to eliminate poverty and the "underclass" in American society, we need to ensure that every child has equal educational opportunity. The academic achievement gap is the most important civil rights issue of the new century. Integration, affirmative action, Title I, and Head Start are legacies from those who knew school achievement was key to creating a more just society. Maintaining, extending, and even expanding these programs and policies is the best way to close the gap that prevents people of color from taking their rightful place in the United States.

Integration

In 1954 the Supreme Court ruled in the landmark case, *Brown v. Board of Education of Topeka, Kansas,* that laws assigning students to school based on their race were unconstitutional. Segregated schools could never be equal, the Court declared in their unanimous ruling. The laws violated the Fourteenth Amendment's guarantee that the rights of all Americans deserved equal protection. Being separated from white students engendered feelings of inferiority in students of color and jeopardized their futures.

The struggle to carry out the Court's ruling was difficult—at times even violent. Two centuries of belief in white superiority did not disappear overnight and could not be "court-ordered" away. In the South, governors turned students away from schools they attempted to integrate. State troopers protected crowds of angry whites while leaving black schoolchildren vulnerable to expressions of hatred. School districts closed down rather than integrate. Many whites attended newly created private schools exempt from desegregation orders. Children of color were completely shut out. It took almost two decades for every state in the South to begin to comply with court orders to desegregate. In the North, the problem was different, but equally difficult. There, most metropolitan areas were segregated by economics. Schools reflected housing patterns of communities and de facto segregation developed. Courts began to order school districts to assign students to schools outside their neighborhoods to desegregate them and transport them to their new schools. Many urban whites already felt "left behind" in the movement to the suburbs their more comfortable neighbors began in the 1930s and 1940s. Taking away their neighborhood schools was the last straw. In the 1970s, the "busing" issue heated up and sometimes violent protests took place in large cities outside the South. The federal courts' uncompromising commitment in the early desegregation period meant, however, there was no turning back. All across the country school districts attempted to comply with desegregation orders. Creative opportunities for all students resulted including magnet schools whose innovative programs were designed to attract white students to attend integrated schools (Lewis, 1965; Sarratt, 1966; Cecelski, 1994; Taylor, 1998; Orfield, 2001).

Even though it was a tremendous struggle, desegregation was worth the effort. Integration is correlated with dramatic changes in the academic achievement gap. "The gap in standardized test scores between white and black children has nearly halved" (Armor, 1992). Students of color who attended desegregated schools, especially if they began to do so in the early grades, had educational achievement levels one grade higher than they would have attained in a segregated school (Mahard and Crain, 1984). African American and Latino students who attend desegregated schools are less likely to become teenage parents or delinquents. They also are more likely to graduate from high school, enroll in and be successful in college (Liebman, 1990; Orfield and Eaton, 1996; Orfield, 2001).

Despite its success, integration has become increasingly difficult to maintain. Relying only on the limited power of the courts to sustain this policy has resulted in situations with disastrous consequences. The Supreme Court has narrowly defined the role of the judicial branch in creating desegregated schools. The courts can intervene only in cases where segregation results from previous governmental policies. If, for example, a school district constructed schools in racially isolated neighborhoods, then it can be held responsible for the resulting segregation. In such a case, the courts can order integration (*Keyes v. School District No. 1, Denver, Colorado,* 1973). If, however, the segregation is the result of individuals' choices—such as living in a more expensive suburb rather than the city—school districts cannot be forced to remedy the resulting segregation (*Milliken v. Bradley,* 1974). In addition to these understandings of when the courts can order integration, the increasing absence of whites in urban public schools also has caused a decrease in integration efforts. Once a school district has demonstrated it has done everything to desegregate schools and programs, it can be declared "unitary" and released from desegregation orders. School districts then can return to neighborhood school policies, even if they result in resegregation. Districts all across the country—Buffalo, Boston, Louisville and Charlotte, North Carolina, to name a few—are deciding to end efforts to racially balance their schools (Teicher, 1999; Simon, 2001).

The combination of court rulings, school district decisions, and white flight mean we have lost the battle to desegregate schools (Orfield and Eaton, 1996; Applebome, 1997) and that failure is reflected in the academic achievement gap. Differences in test scores between students of color and their white counterparts decreased in the integration era. However, once students who entered through the system during the late sixties and early seventies (the brief period when court-ordered integration had been put in place and cities' populations were still relatively diverse) completed their education, the gap between test scores of students of color and those of white students began to increase again (Campbell, Hombo, and Mazzeo, 2000). (See Figures 4.1 and 4.2.)

It appears that there is a correlation between efforts to desegregate schools and a decrease in the academic achievement gap. Ending racial isolation in schools is desirable for this reason. New strategies, however, appear needed. The

FIGURE 4.1 Long-Term Trend Assessments—Reading.
Differences Between Average Test Scores of Whites, Blacks, and Hispanics (ages 17, 13, 9)

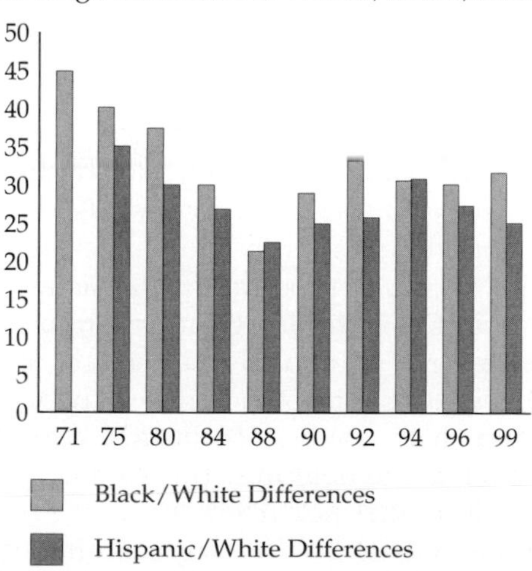

Source: *National Center for Educational Statistics, National Assessment of Educational Progress. 1999 Long-Term Trend Assessment Data.* (N. B. Data not available for Hispanic students until 1975.)

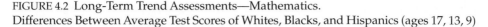

FIGURE 4.2 Long-Term Trend Assessments—Mathematics.
Differences Between Average Test Scores of Whites, Blacks, and Hispanics (ages 17, 13, 9)

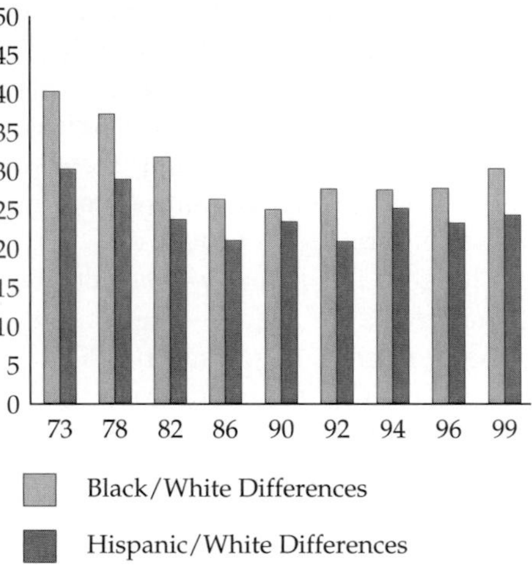

Source: *National Center for Educational Statistics, National Assessment of Educational Progress. 1999 Long-Term Trend Assessment Data.*

Supreme Court has made it clear that court-ordered desegregation was a time-limited remedy and that the clock has run out. Federal courts are releasing school districts from desegregation plans even though "stark racial inequalities remain" and the decisions seem "premature, unwarranted and unjust" (Joondeph, 1998, p. 3). We need to turn to the political process and take up once again the strenuous task of creating a coalition of groups to support new mandates for integration.

Head Start

In 1965, Congress funded an innovative program for preschoolers based on the belief that children born to poor families faced disadvantages that translated into school difficulties. Head Start goes far beyond traditional preschool programs. It attempts to address a multitude of factors affecting poor children and their families. It offers opportunities for 3- and 4-year-old children to become "school-ready" through a variety of programs (U.S. Department of Health and Human Services, 2002). The bill authorizing the program states, "It is the purpose of this subchapter to promote school readiness by enhancing the social and cognitive development of low-income children through the provision, to low-income children and their families, of health, educational, nutritional, social, and other services that are determined, based on family needs assessments, to be necessary" (Head Start Act, 1998).

Classroom-based programs enrich the early learning environment of children from impoverished backgrounds, providing places where children have access to books, toys and equipment for the creative play—such as "dress-up" and "house." Those resources often are difficult for poor parents to provide.

Head Start programs also provide parent education programs to teach ways of interacting with their children to improve their chance at school success. In addition, Head Start programs assist parents in making connections with social service agencies that can help them deal with survival issues such as food, housing, and medical care. "It is Head Start's focus on families and fighting poverty in a comprehensive manner which has led to the program's success in getting children ready for school, improving their literacy and numeracy skills, and giving their parents the skills in becoming their child's first and best teacher" (National Head Start Association, 2002).

Head Start is a remarkably effective program. It may well be the most researched social service program in our history and the conclusions are impressive. Assessments show that Head Start children go to school more ready to learn, like school, try to do their best, and get along well with their teachers and peers (Darlington, 1991; Currie and Duncan, 1994; Marcon, 2000; U.S. Department of Health and Human Services, 2002). Their test scores in reading and math are at or above the national average by the time they reach third grade (Currie and Duncan, 1996; Marcon, 1996; Jacobson, 2002). They are more likely to be enrolled in health-care programs and participate in early screening for health and development problems. They are healthier in general and have fewer health-related absences from school. Even siblings of children who attend Head Start programs appear to benefit, even if they themselves do not participate in the program (Garces, Thomas, and Currie, 2000).

Head Start is a program that works. Clearly, we need to maintain our commitment to such an effective means of closing the academic achievement gap. Head Start also is relatively uncontroversial; it has such bipartisan support that Congress routinely dramatically increases the program's budget proposals. Unfortunately, it also is dramatically underfunded. Head Start operates with the lowest income guidelines the federal government mandates for any assistance programs. The approximately 900,000 children enrolled in Head Start represent only 60 percent of those eligible. About 600,000 children whose families are so poor they are entitled to the program cannot get the assistance they so desperately need. Children whose family income would qualify them for free and reduced lunches in public schools are not eligible for Head Start. Children whose mothers receive WIC (Women, Infants, and Children) assistance aren't either (National Head Start Association, 2002). Politicians who want to take credit for Head Start's success and pat themselves on the back for voting to fund it need to stop kidding themselves and the American people. They need to change the income requirements so more children can be eligible to benefit from Head Start and then need to fully fund the program so that all eligible children can take part. Anything less is simply political smoke and mirrors, not good public policy.

Title I

In 1965, as a follow-up to the Civil Rights Act of the previous year, Congress passed the Elementary and Secondary Education Act. The bill was based on the understanding that inequalities in educational opportunities were responsible for the academic achievement gap between poor and privileged children and between whites and students of color. The federal government, through this legislation, began to provide financial assistance to school districts with large numbers of low-income families. In addition, it provided money for library improvement, instructional materials, educational innovations, and research. It has been revised and reauthorized every five years since. Over time it has come to include funding for bilingual education, drug education, school lunch and breakfast programs. The federal government has also, through this law, increased resources for the education of Native Americans (Sadker and Sadker, 2002). The aspect of this legislation that most directly affects students in schools where families have low incomes is usually referred to as Title I.

For over a generation, Title I has been the largest source of federal funding for poor children in elementary and secondary schools. It serves over 10 million children in over 50,000 schools—95 percent of all school districts in the country receive some Title I funds (Slavin, 1999). Title I funding is in excess of $11 billion. Title I funding is targeted to address the needs of poor children and it does just that. Money from Title I goes to high-poverty schools; more than two-thirds is used for instructional purposes (Chait et al., 2001).

In the 1980s when Title I was experiencing high levels of growth in its funding, it was enabling schools to address the needs of their students. The increase in Title I money occurred at the same time as the increase in the average test scores of children of color. The differences between white and both African American and Latino students narrowed steadily until 1988 (Campbell, Hombo, and Mazzeo, 2000). Title I was an important factor in reducing the academic achievement gap in the 1970s and 1980s (Slavin, 1999).

When progress made in closing the achievement gap stalled in the early 1990s, Title I was revised to reflect increasing knowledge of what kinds of programs actually benefit children. We have moved, for example, away from "pull-out" programs in which disadvantaged students were taken from their classrooms and given extra help to whole school reform programs. Research had shown that the remedial instruction children received was not enough to close the achievement gap between students in high- and low-poverty schools. Studies have found that expectations were lower overall in high-poverty schools and that students who attended them achieved less than students in low-poverty schools, no matter what their own family income level might be (Chait et al., 2001). Now, efforts funded by Title I go toward setting high standards for all children in poor schools and for providing instruction that enable them to meet those goals.

Title I has been critical in reforming high-poverty schools and promoting achievement of their students. "Whenever an inner-city or poor rural school is found to be achieving outstanding results with its students by implementing innovative strategies, these innovations are almost invariably paid for primarily by Title I funds" (Slavin, 1999, p. 6). We must ensure funding for these valuable programs keeps up with schools' needs. Those suggesting money does not make a difference in a child's education need only study improvements made with Title I funds to see how foolish that statement really is.

Affirmative Action

Closing the academic achievement gap also requires we remain committed to remedying past discriminatory practices through affirmative action policies. They are the most controversial of all the political legacies of the civil rights era—perhaps because they have been so effective at disturbing structures of racial and ethnic privilege. They have not always been implemented perfectly and certainly have not ended prejudice and discrimination. "However, there would be no struggle to roll back the gains achieved if affirmative action policies were ineffective" (Kivel, 1996, p. 1).

For forty years Americans have attempted to deal with the effects of discrimination—for almost two centuries people of color were denied employment and educational opportunities because of race or ethnicity while white males received preferential treatment. Before affirmative action, for example, it once was legal to pay white workers more than people of color for doing the same job and to have separate sections in the "want-ads" for each group. Employer's could refuse to hire people because of the color of their skin or the place they or their parents were born. Even private schools, colleges, and universities could refuse to admit students based on race or ethnicity. Schools could set "quotas" limiting their number of nonwhite students. Colleges and universities insisted students abide by segregated housing policies or would transfer a roommate simply because of race or ethnicity (Stephanopoulos and Edley, 1995). White Americans didn't wake up one morning and decide such practices were unfair and had to be eliminated. It took a long, slow process in which people of color and their allies demanded everyone be given the equal protection the Fourteenth Amendment guaranteed.

Even when it became illegal to continue such practices, their consequences lingered and adversely affected people of color. "The disadvantages to people of color and the benefits to white people are passed on to each succeeding generation unless remedial action is taken" (Kivel, 1996, p. 2). Discrimination people's ancestors faced continues to affect them generations later. Because one family faced little prejudice, its members may have, through contacts with their friends, obtained well paying jobs, purchased a home in a neighborhood with good schools, learned about cultural events and institutions, and gone to college. A family that faced more discrimination would have few of those advantages. Their friends would have been as shut out from information about jobs, culture, and education as they were. The cycle would perpetuate itself for many years.

Affirmative action is meant to break this cycle. First, it outlawed discrimination in hiring and admission policies, starting a larger process of creating equal opportunity. If, for example, through heroic sacrifices or extraordinarily good luck, a person of color was qualified for a job or a school, neither an employer nor an admissions officer could turn them down simply because of race or ethnicity (Stephanopoulos and Edley, 1995). If two equally qualified people seek the same benefit, affirmative action requires the job or college placement be offered first to the person of color. The law also allows employers or schools to choose a person of color whose qualifications are roughly comparable, but not exactly equal, to a white person. By providing such opportunities for members of groups who experienced previous discrimination, we would start to end the cycle described before. Now people of color would have access to jobs or education and could begin to accumulate both material and cultural "wealth" to pass on to their descendants, and have a chance to experience the "rising tide that lifts all boats" in America.

Clearly, affirmative action policies are beginning to close the academic achievement gap. Since discriminatory admission policies are illegal, qualified African American and Latino students now can seek admission to any college or university and entertain reasonable expectations of success. Young people condemned by society to attend inferior public schools but who demonstrate commitment and academic potential can be admitted to many schools, even if their test scores are lower than those of their white counterparts. As a result, more students of color are attending and completing college than ever before. Students of color who attend selective schools benefit in many ways: Their achievement is high in every measure of success—attainment of professional degrees, employment, earnings, civic participation, and overall satisfaction (Bowen and Bok, 1998).

Opponents of affirmative action protest that it's not fair. The question is, not fair to whom? These people have few, if any, complaints about policies that are equally "unfair." In this country we have long had preferential treatment for groups we deemed deserving. Colleges have preferential recruiting and admission policies for veterans, children of alumni, and athletes as well as for students whose families are wealthy enough to afford the tuition with no financial help from the school. They do not have to have exactly the same test scores as other applicants to be admitted. Are these policies fundamentally "unfair"? Or do they represent honest attempts by colleges and universities to create winning teams, balanced budgets, and reward school loyalty and patriotism? What makes these reasons morally more acceptable than efforts to eliminate and compensate for institutional effects of racism and ethnic prejudice?

A compelling case can be made that affirmative action in educational settings has benefits for all students, not just those of color. There is a growing body of evidence that students educated in universities, colleges, and graduate programs where there is a diverse population actually experience academic gains. They learn to think in more complex ways. "Students who experienced the most racial and ethnic diversity in classroom settings and in informal interactions with peers showed the greatest engagement in active thinking processes, growth in intellectual engagement and motivation, and growth in intellectual and academic skills" (Sugrue et al., 1999, p. 4). Students who go to college and university in diverse settings are better prepared to participate fully in a pluralistic, democratic society (Sugrue et al., 1999, p. 7). In one important study of graduates from institutions committed to admission policies supporting creation of a diverse study body, over three-quarters of white students affirmed the idea that such policies should be maintained or strengthened (Bowen and Bok, 1998).

Those who attack affirmative action need to reflect carefully before using slogans such as "reverse discrimination." Quite often what they describe is not discrimination but a loss of privilege. Saying you favor equal opportunity but opposing every effort society makes to ensure that equality is hypocritical. Affirmative action has been a symbol of our collective acknowledgment that discrimination did take place in the past and it is a token of our commitment to make sure it ends with us. One generation is hardly enough time to remedy such a long period of deprivation. We need to give this policy more time to work. People of color have a right to expect effective remedies for past policies that have violated their rights and slowed their assimilation into the fullness of American society.

We must continue to work to eliminate the last effects of discrimination in schools, colleges and universities. As we engage in that long struggle for a better future, however, we must keep faith with our present and maintain our commitment to providing short-term remedies through affirmative action policies.

Conclusion

Social change takes place slowly, and closing the academic achievement gap between students of color and their white counterparts constitutes a dramatic change in American society. Although some believe the strong, effective government programs established in this country have outlived their usefulness, nothing could be further from the truth. We are only now beginning to see how these programs have affected the first generation to benefit from them. If they have not created complete equality of achievement in one generation, does that mean we should abandon them and their potential gains? If we remember how long it took other ethnic communities to participate fully in U.S. economic and social life, we know it was longer than thirty years for most. Many people of color did not come to this country voluntarily—instead they were brought here as slaves or migrant workers—as cheap labor. They faced legalized discrimination for over two hundred years and the effects of racism were cumulative. The disparity between them and other citizens widened over time and few efforts were made to bridge them. Surely in a country as wealthy and fortunate as this, we can afford to spend more than three decades making up for two centuries of abuse. Those who argue otherwise may knowingly or not perpetuate inequality and gain advantages for their children while condemning others to lives of poverty and despair. The consequences of abandoning these efforts will fall not only on children of color but on all of us. Hopelessness is a breeding ground for social alienation. Without a stake in society, people have no reason to obey its laws or support it against its enemies. Our own security as a nation demands we maintain our commitment to providing programs that, through education, lift young people out of despair and convince them they are valued. We cannot abandon that effort now.

POSITION 2: FOR INNOVATIVE SOLUTIONS

We must use the moment upon us now to finally deliver on the promise that those who came before us left only halfway done. . . . Our job, in other words, is to find a way to set aside all the old bargains, the old politeness, and do what it takes to make needed change before it's too late for the children and for public education.

—HAYCOCK, 2001, P. 1

Reconsidering the Academic Achievement Gap

The differences in academic achievement between young white Americans and their African American and Latino counterparts are a nagging, persistent reminder of just how ineffective large, bureaucratic governmental programs actually are. On the National Assessment of Educational Progress—"The Nation's Report Card," students of color made progress in closing the gap between them and their white counterparts during the 1970s and 1980s. Then, for almost a decade, progress stalled, and more recently has lost ground. At all ages and in all subjects, the gap now is larger than it was in 1988—in some cases by as much as 50 percent (Campbell, Hombo, and Mazzeo, 2000). The average SAT scores of African Americans is 195 points lower than the average of white test-takers; for Latinos, the difference is 100 points less. Although the gap has narrowed in the last thirty years, African American and Latino students still have lower rates of college entrance and completion and lower grades than do white students (Steele, 1992; Campbell, Hombo, and Mazzeo, 2000; Haycock, 2001).

These statistics paint a gloomy picture. Some gains made through older strategies have been lost and others are too small to be meaningful. It may very well be that the remedies applied in the 1970s and 1980s suited the causes of the achievement gap as we then understood them; our national culture has changed, however, and, in doing so, has altered the reasons for the academic achievement gap. Unless we accurately understand the causes of the problem, we can do little about finding appropriate ways to correct it. In addition, we need to be aware that the political climate has changed in this country since the 1980s. Whether we agree with the current viewpoint or not, there is great pessimism about government's ability to solve problems and more irritation with the ways it interferes with individual freedom. These attitudes are dramatically different from those of the 1960s and 1970s when a liberal optimism pervaded the country, promising that with enough regulation and tax dollars we could fix anything that was wrong with America.

Blaming the Victims

Clearly, there is no one easy answer to the question of why African American and Latino children continue to have lower scores on standardized tests and generally experience less academic success than white students. The reasons are complex and fluid and probably interact with one another in ways we have yet to understand. We can, however, think of them in two categories: sociocultural and school related.

For most of the last thirty years, we emphasized sociocultural causes, believing segregation, discrimination, and effects of poverty were mostly to blame for the low levels of achievement among students of color. Our thinking about these causes resulted in national soul-searching and in making necessary corrections to laws and policies—for example, putting an end to racially separate and unequal schools.

We also focused on what we perceived to be "lacks" in the children and families we hoped to serve. We believed parents' low level of educational achievement, lack of financial resources, and child-rearing practices all contributed to their children's low levels of academic achievement. We thought by creating antipoverty programs such as Head Start, Food Stamps, Job Training, and medicaid, and finding ways of connecting poor people to them, we'd improve children's chances of succeeding in schools.

We thought children of color were themselves partly to blame for their educational difficulties. Linguistic differences between them and the school communities created problems, but the young people were unwilling to give up their unique ways of speaking. They used drugs and became parents themselves in their teens, and appeared to prefer the culture of the streets to the promise of entrance into mainstream America. So we introduced drug and sex education into school curricula, introduced bilingual education, and attempted to teach the values of hard work and perseverance.

The solutions we created in response to our understandings, however, were only partially effective and, in some cases, actually have worsened the problems they were intended to correct. For example, thirty years ago, we believed the academic achievement gap was caused by segregation and discriminatory practices. Segregation isolated children of color and convinced them that they were inferior to whites (*Brown v. Board of Education,* 1954). If we could only get them into integrated schools, then their success rates would soar. So the government mandated desegregation programs all across the county. Most of the policies involved busing children around cities, increasing their time away from home and their studies, removing many urban children from their neighborhoods. In many cases, such policies destroyed the work of generations of city-dwellers who had painstakingly built up connections between their schools and communities (Cecelski, 1994; Taylor, 1998). Parent involvement became more difficult and involved long treks to schools in unfamiliar areas of the city. Eventually, those who could—admittedly, most often whites—voted with their feet and left the cities and "integrated" public schools. As a result, in most cities the majority of the population overwhelmingly consists of people of color. Suburbs are equally segregated; it's just that whites are the majority there (Orfield, 2001).

Consequently, schools are becoming increasingly racially isolated (Applebome, 1997; Orfield, 2001). "More than 70% of the nation's black students now attend predominantly minority schools . . . more than one-third of

Latino students attend intensely segregated schools. . . . Whites on average attend schools where less than 20% of the students are from all of the other racial and ethnic groups combined. On average, blacks and Latinos attend schools with 53% to 55% students of their own group" (Orfield, 2001, p. 2). There are many reasons for these changes in school populations in the 1980s and 1990s. Some are relatively benign, such as people seeking the suburbs' more relaxed lifestyle. Some are more troubling. Forced integration did not change people's minds and hearts; racial prejudice still exists and some whites have expressed their preferences by moving away from neighborhoods with diverse populations. Court-ordered desegregation of schools did not prevent the continued residential isolation between white people and those of color. The Supreme Court's most recent rulings have made it clear that the era of government-mandated integration has come to a close (Weiler, 1998; Orfield, 2001).

That actually may be a good thing. There was a kind of racial superiority implicit in the frantic efforts to get children of color into "good" schools. What supporters really meant, but rarely said, was that children of color needed to go to "white" schools. Supporters of integration did not insist that white students attend schools whose populations previously consisted predominately of students of color. In fact, students of color were moved to "white" schools, even when the facilities were not as good (Cecelski, 1994; Taylor, 1998). Many African American principals and teachers lost their jobs during integration instead of exchanging places with their white colleagues in integrated schools (Hooker, 1970; Arnez, 1976; Haney, 1978). School policies and practices didn't allow students of color to bring their customs and traditions to integrated schools (Wilkerson, 1991; Cecelski, 1994). No wonder many people of color are tired of fighting for integration and want to return control of their children's schools to their own communities (Farkas and Johnson, 1998).

The same sense of white superiority permeates attitudes toward African American and Latino parents. Society judges parenting skills using "white" parenting styles as the norm (Hill, 1999). As a result, African American, Latino, and Asian parents often feel that educators don't respect them or the many efforts they make on behalf of their children. Perhaps that is one reason it is difficult for such parents to become fully involved in their children's schools (Lightfoot, 1978; De La Cruz, 1999).

Affirmative action programs also contain a hidden message of racial superiority. Surely, they communicate the message that some people are simply less able. Without special treatment, they cannot compete with those who are more competent. The existence of such programs makes the achievement of all people of color suspect. On college campuses or in school districts, many assume people of color are there because they have received the "favor" of preferential admissions or hiring because of their race or ethnicity (Cohen, 1999). Those who might benefit from such programs are rejecting them for these very reasons (Connerly, 2000).

Criticisms of young people of color also are often based on a sense that white culture is superior. The way they dress and talk, the music they like, the foods they eat, their choice of recreational activities, and even the ways they relate to one another are seen as problems to be solved before they can learn what "really counts" (Davidson, 1996; Deschenes, Cuban, and Tyack, 2001). Efforts to convince them that if they want to become academically successful, they have to "act white" seem persuasive. These young people find themselves in the impossible position of choosing between their communities and school achievement. Not surprisingly, many cannot reconcile the two and succumb to peer and community pressure (Fordham and Ogbu, 1986; Fordham, 1997; Ferguson, 1998).

For some time, most efforts to "solve" the socioeconomic causes of the academic achievement gap have approached the problem from a belief in the superiority of white culture. These efforts have blamed the victims of discriminatory practices in every conceivable way and robbed them of belief in their individual strengths and those of their communities. At the same time, government funding has decreased for housing, health, and nutrition programs that would address the effects of poverty—the most significant sociocultural cause of the academic achievement gap. In 2000, nearly 12 million American children lived in poverty—almost the same number as in 1967—about 16 percent of all children in the United States in both cases. Black and Latino children make up almost 7.2 million of that number—a whopping 60 percent of all children living in poverty (Children's Defense Fund, 2002). It doesn't appear that Americans have the political will or economic ability to reduce the number of poor children. The consequences of that failure, however, are directly related to the academic achievement gap. "We take students who have less to begin with and give them less in school, too" (Education Trust, 1996). Closing the gap between children of color and their white counterparts depends first and foremost on the quality of schools they attend, the curriculum they study and the teachers who instruct them (Charles A. Dana Center, 1999; Education Trust, 2001).

School-Related Causes of the Academic Achievement Gap

Schools and the educational system contribute in many ways to the academic achievement gap. Educators can and must remedy these problems to close this gap. Significantly, children of color encounter teachers who have lower expectations for them than they do for white students. Teachers, like all of us, are part of this society in which race, ethnicity, and class stimulate certain stereotypes, and teachers appear to regard their students through the lens of those prejudices. Children have a difficult time breaking through their teachers' preconceived notions of their ability or interest (Baron, Tom, and Cooper, 1985; Lightfoot, 1978). Research indicates that teachers perceive white children as more capable, expect more from them, and are more supportive of their efforts to be academically successful. They search less aggressively for ways to help students of color because, on some level, they already have drawn the conclusion that they have less potential. Consequently, the instruction children of color receive is not tailored to their potential for success and does little to reduce the academic achievement gap (Ferguson, 1998). In turn, students of color internalize their teachers' low expectations and do not see themselves as capable of learning. Their low self-expectation interacts with the teachers' underestimation of their abilities to create low academic performance (Arroyo, Rhoad, and Drew, 1999; Presidential Advisory Commission on Educational Excellence for Hispanic Americans, 2000). This problem particularly is destructive in schools where the majority are low-income children of color. In schools with racially mixed populations, teachers' high expectations for their white students appears to result in better instruction overall and higher achievement for children of color in particular (Viadero, 2000). Children of color are less likely than their white counterparts to attend schools with highly qualified, experienced teachers. They are more likely, in high school, for example, to have teachers without a college major—or even a minor—in the subject they are teaching (Kober, 2001). They are twice as likely to have inexperienced teachers, and experience far greater turnover among the faculty of their schools than do their white counterparts. They are far more likely to have teachers with low scores on college entrance and teacher certification examinations (Education Trust, 2001; Kober, 2001). All of these factors—teacher quality, academic preparation, experience, stability, and test scores—affect student performance.

Children of color, because they most often attend schools with more limited resources than do white children, find themselves in classes with larger populations. In such settings even the most qualified teachers with the highest expectations are stretched too thin. They simply cannot provide the individual attention children need and deserve if we are sincerely trying to improve their academic achievement (Achilles, Finn, and Gerber, 2000).

Schools that do not set high standards and encourage or insist that they enroll in challenging courses also handicap students of color. Too many students of color are still engaged in vocational programs intended to prepare them for industrial jobs that no longer exist (Education Trust, 2000). Students of color are less likely to attend schools offering advanced math and science or advanced placement courses (Kober, 2001). Even when the courses are available, students of color are not ready to take advantage of them. They too often have been tracked into "general" or "basic" courses where the curriculum was simplified, teachers covered less material, gave less homework, and rewarded low-level performance with high grades. Students whose preparation is inadequate cannot be successful in higher-level courses. The tragedy is that students who do not take algebra, geometry, trigonometry, chemistry, physics, and other challenging courses have lower scores on standardized tests than those who do. In addition, the difficulty of the course in middle and high school is the best predictor of college success (Kober, 2001). By opting out or being forced out of the more challenging curriculum, students of color are limiting their futures.

Teachers and administrators often complain they are hampered in their efforts to change these school conditions because parents are not actively involved. However, schools serving communities of color often fail to take the most elementary steps to increase parent involvement. For example, when Latino parents come to school to discuss their children's academic programs or progress, they often encounter a staff that speaks only English. There are rarely interpreters for parents whose primary language is not English. How unwelcoming a place school must seem (Lara and Pande, 2001).

School districts where there is high mobility among students—that is, children often move around during their school years and sometimes *within* a year—often have policies that contribute to the academic achievement gap. They do not standardize curriculum, textbooks, or instruction. Students who move from one school to another may find themselves repeating material they already have learned or being challenged to do work for which they have not been prepared. Children who experience such problems often lose heart and stop trying (D'Amico, 2001).

Policies and practices in schools that ignore or disparage children's cultural lives also contribute to low academic achievement and maintain the gap between students of color and their white counterparts. Students who believe their teachers do not value their background or community values feel "disrespected." They find it difficult to respect the requests or suggestions of such adults—even when they are well intentioned and, if taken, actually might lead to improvement in students' life possibilities. Instead they resist, rebel, drop out, or get by. They learn to devalue education because they feel devalued within their schools (Steele, 1992; Locke-Davidson, 1996; Fordham, 1997).

Although this scenario is depressing, it is far from hopeless. By identifying school factors contributing to the academic achievement gap, possible solutions emerge. These remedies will not involve massive dislocation of people against their will, as did forced integration. They will not require explanations that disparage students or their families. "Whiteness" need not be held out as the norm for academic achievement. Instead, policymakers can take the very best from past remedies and use them to create and sponsor new and innovative solutions.

Closing the Academic Achievement Gap: New Solutions

Understanding more clearly the ways in which schools contribute to the academic achievement gap makes it possible to envision how they can contribute to closing it.

In 2002, Congress reauthorized federal assistance to elementary and secondary schools. This bill is the descendant of the original law passed in 1965 during the heyday of the War on Poverty. Teachers and administrators accomplished a great deal with the money they received, especially through Title I. They made significant strides in lessening racial and ethnic differences in academic achievement. In the late 1960s and early 1970s, children of color were not receiving instruction to help them master even the most basic skills. Title I funding paid for paraprofessionals (teachers' aides) who were able to take children out of classrooms for periods of time and, through old-fashioned drill and practice, work with them on very basic skills in reading and math. Progress made by these practices, however, slowed and then reversed; those kind of solutions do not appear to enable students to push forward. The remaining ethnic and racial academic achievement gap is more stubborn because it is different. The differences that now matter are not in the areas of basic, but rather more advanced, skills. Students need to do more than decode words—that is not all we mean by literacy; they need to analyze what they are capable of reading and use higher-order thinking to solve complex mathematics problems. "Pull-out" programs emphasizing memorization will never accomplish those goals. Solving this problem requires far more dramatic changes in the way schools do business (Education Trust, 2001).

The appropriate next steps appear to be setting clear goals for all children and establishing high, but achievable, standards that specify what they are to learn and when they are to learn it. Each state needs to work with local school districts to identify goals for children in their state and then make a commitment that every child in the state will reach them. No longer can there be different expectations for children depending on race, ethnicity, or economic status. That attitude only perpetuates differences in their achievement (Northwest Regional Educational Laboratory, 1997; Education Trust, 2001; Kober, 2001).

Teachers, administrators, and school districts must be accountable for their students' progress, best done through student performance on in-depth, appropriate, and ongoing assessments. Standardized testing is an important part of such accountability. The federal government now requires that all states administer such tests annually to students in grades three through eight. In addition a group of fourth- and eighth-graders in each state must participate in the National Assessment of Educational Progress every other year (*Education Week,* 2002). States must disaggregate the scores of their students. That is, they must report them by race, ethnicity, and income to measure the gaps between and among them. States and local school districts finally are being held accountable for closing the achievement gap. Failure to do so will jeopardize a state's federal funding. This innovative reform is based on the experience and advice of educators, parents, and family advocates in a variety of states. This is reform of education from the "bottom-up" and is long overdue.

Ample evidence suggests implementation of high-standards policies backed up with accountability through assessment will be successful. In school districts in Maryland, Colorado, Arizona, Texas, and Kentucky the academic achievement of poor children and children of color has increased through such efforts (Schmoker and Marzano, 1999; Murnane and Levy, 2001; Annie E. Casey Foundation, 2002). Experiences with standards-based educational reform have shown it can be especially effective with children of color when certain criteria are met. If every student's test scores count, for example, in determining how well educators have been accountable, then the academic achievement of children with limited language proficiency or disabilities will matter in new ways. It will be imperative for districts to attend to their needs. Since children of color are disproportionately represented in these groups, it follows that the academic achievement gap will be affected by efforts to improve their performance. In addition, if high-stakes testing actually measures skills and knowledge that lead to higher levels of educational attainment and increased economic success, then instruction in those skills and knowledge will be increased in schools—especially if the "high stakes" place educators at risk for student failure. Such improvement in instructional techniques will benefit children of color directly (Murnane and Levy, 2001).

Establishment of high standards and specific accountability for those standards therefore will go hand-in-hand with the creation of challenging curriculum for all students. Vocational training programs preparing students for nonexistent jobs will disappear. Every young person, whatever their racial or ethnic background, will take an academic program rigorous enough to allow them to enter college if they so desire (Slavin, 1999; Education Trust, 2001; Kober, 2001). That preparation will begin in elementary school—the goal of any "ability grouping" at that level of education must be to sharpen all students' skills so they are prepared to take challenging high school courses that will make college a possibility.

To be successful in these rigorous classes, students will need highly qualified teachers and proven instructional programs. Accountability and standards in teacher education programs will produce teachers knowledgeable in their academic content area and who are able to work with students of color. Standards-based education also will require low-income districts to recruit, hire, and retain good teachers (Darling-Hammond and Finn, 2000). Policymakers will therefore utilize every effective strategy—salary incentives, lower teaching loads, bans on the hiring of uncertified teachers—to correct the current situation where the best teachers wind up with the least-needy children (Education Trust, 2001). These standards and assessments, and the very public method of reporting them required by the No Child Left Behind legislation, will result in professional development assistance and monetary rewards for teachers who can produce the desired results.

Beyond standards-based education, improvement also is needed in the relationships between schools and the families and communities of children of color. Educators must be able to communicate effectively with them (De La Cruz, 1999) and let them know schools recognize and intend to build on the strengths of their children's heritages. The conflicts between adults that can take place in schools must be minimized by focusing attention on mutual concerns for young people. Schools need to become sites where the differences among the many subcultures of our society are negotiated in peaceful and productive ways (Kober, 2001; Charles A. Dana Center, 1999).

Finally, educators need to deal more effectively with the ambivalence many students of color feel about school. Claude Steele has suggested creation of what he calls "wise" schools—places where students of color feel their full humanity is visible and cherished by their teachers. Such schools would recognize and nurture the ambitions of children of color and help them deal with the inevitable difficulties they encounter on the road to achieving them. "Wise" schools would be as integrated as is possible but even when the student body remains predominantly made up of people of color, the presence on the faculty of whites who would ally themselves with the struggle of the young people would diminish effects of racial prejudice and vulnerability. Finally, in such a school, all aspects of students' lives and cultures would "be presented in the mainstream curriculum . . . not assigned to special days, weeks or even months of the year, or to special-topic courses or programs" (Steele, 1992, p. 15). In such schools, social conditions would be analyzed and remedies would be debated. No one would pretend that all racial and ethnic discrimination is over; no one would ignore the harsh realities of poverty. These schools, however, also would be places where stories of struggle would be told (O'Connor, 1997) and where social justice would be held out as an ideal for society and for schools themselves (Cochran-Smith, 1997). There is ample reason to believe such schools are possible. These ideas represent the best characteristics of African American schools in the segregated South in which so many students of color succeeded in getting an education despite incredible odds (Siddle-Walker, 1996). Research also indicates these qualities can be found in some Catholic schools in the North and that in those schools the academic achievement gap is minimized (Bryk, Lee, and Holland, 1993; Youniss and Covey, 2000). We need to insist the values present in these schools are brought into public schools.

Conclusion

We have entered a new era in American public education. The remedies of the past no longer are suitable. While large government programs and attempts at social engineering reaped some benefits, their usefulness is over. We need fresh ways to look at the academic achievement gap and focus attention where it belongs—on schools and what happens in classrooms. We cannot waste any more time—or any more lives—on inadequate remedies. We must take up the cause of civil rights for all Americans. We cannot champion that cause by spending large sums of money without holding anyone accountable for results, by forcing families to send their children to schools they do not choose, or by making unjust allowances for past discrimination. Instead, we must insist on a new kind of justice—good schooling for all children, regardless of their race or ethnicity. We can settle for nothing less.

For Discussion

1. We might assume Latino children would face many academic challenges due to limited English language proficiency. However, the gap between their test scores and those of white students usually is less than the difference between black students' scores and those of whites. (See Figures 4.1 and 4.2.) How would you account for these findings? What factors might account for the differences?
2. The No Child Left Behind Act of 2002 requires states to report on student performance on standardized tests and to disaggregate that data by "race, gender, and other criteria to demonstrate not only how well students are achieving overall but also progress in closing the achievement gap between disadvantaged students and other groups of students" (U.S. Department of Education, 2002). Will the requirement to provide such data pressure school districts to improve instruction for children of color? Discuss why or why not.
3. Talk to an admissions counselor in your college or university about the institution's policy regarding affirmative action and admissions. Critique the policy from the point of view of its effectiveness in closing the academic achievement gap.

4. Using the NAEP database (http://nces.ed.gov/nationsreportcard/naepdata/search.asp), research the achievement gap in your state. Speculate on factors that may influ ence conditions in your state. Using databases and other sources of information, research and evaluate your state's efforts to close the gap.

References

ACHILLES, C. M., FINN, J. D., AND GERBER, S. (2000) "Small Classes Do Reduce the Test-Score Achievement Gap." Paper presented at the Annual Meeting of the Council of Great City Schools, Los Angeles.

ANGUS, D., AND MIREL, J. (1999). *The Failed Promise of the American High School 1890–1995.* New York: Teachers College Press.

ANNIE E. CASEY FOUNDATION. (2002). "Success in School: Education Ideas That Count." (www.aecf.org/publications/success/stand.htm)

ANYON, J. (1997). *Ghetto Schooling.* New York: Teachers College Press.

APPLEBOME, P. (1997). "Schools See Re-emergence of 'Separate But Equal.'" *New York Times.* April 8, p. A10.

ARMOR, D. (1992). "Why Is Black Educational Achievement Rising?" *Public Interest* 108, 65–68.

ARNEZ, N. (1976). "Desegregation of Public Schools: A Discriminatory Process." *Journal of Afro-American Issues* 4(1), 274–281.

ARROYO, A., RHOAD, R., AND DREW, P. (1999). "Meeting Diverse Student Needs in Urban Schools: Research-Based Recommendations for School Personnel." *Preventing School Failure* 43(4), 145–153.

BARON, R., TOM, D., AND COOPER, H. (1985). "Social Class, Race and Teacher Expectations." In J. Dusek, ed., *Teacher Expectancies.* Hillside, NJ: Erlbaum.

BOWEN, W., AND BOK, D. (1998). *The Shape of the River. Long-Term Consequences of Considering Race in College and University Admissions.* Princeton: Princeton University Press.

BRADLEY, R., ET AL. (2001). "The Home Environments of Children in the United States, Part I: Variations by Age, Ethnicity, and Poverty States." *Child Development* 72, 1844–1867.

Brown v. Board of Education of Topeka, Kansas. (1954). 347 U.S. 483.

BRYK, A., LEE, V., AND HOLLAND, P. (1993). *Catholic Schools and the Common Good.* Cambridge: Harvard University Press.

CAMPBELL, J, HOMBO, C., AND MAZZEO, J. (2000). NAEP 1999 Trends in Academic Progress: Three Decades of Student Performance. National Assessment of Educational Progress. (http://nces.ed.gov/nationsreportcard/pubs/main1999/2000469.asp)

CECELSKI, D. (1994). *Along Freedom Road.* Chapel Hill: University of North Carolina Press.

CHAIT, R., ET AL. (2001). "High Standards for All Students: A Report from the National Assessment of Title I on Progress and Challenges Since the 1964 Reauthorization." Washington, DC: U.S. Department of Education. ERIC Document, ED 457280.

CHARLES A. DANA CENTER. (1999). "Hope for Urban Education: A Study of Nine High-Performing, High-Poverty Urban Elementary Schools." Washington, DC: U.S. Department of Education. (www/ed.gov/pbs/urbanhope)

CHILDREN'S DEFENSE FUND. (2002). "Poverty Status of Persons Younger than 18: 1959–2000." (www.childrensdefense.org/fairstart-povstat1.htm)

COCHRAN-SMITH, M. (1997). Knowledge, Skills and Experiences for Teaching Culturally Diverse Learners: A Perspective for Practicing Teachers. In J. Irvine, ed., *Critical knowledge for diverse teachers and learners.* Washington, DC: American Association of Colleges for Teacher Education.

COHEN, C. (1999). "Race Preference in College Admissions." Heritage Lectures. (www.heritage.org/library/lecture/h1611.html)

CONNERLY, W. (2000). "A Vision for America, Beyond Race." *Intellectual Ammunition: Point of View.* Nov.–Dec. (www.heartland.org/ia/novdec00/connerly.htm)

CURRIE, J., AND DUNCAN, T. (1994). "Does Head Start Make a Difference?" *Labor and Population Program.* ERIC Document ED 382352.

———. (1996). "Does Head Start Help Hispanic Children?" *Labor and Population Program.* ERIC Document ED 404008.

D'AMICO, J. (2001). "A Closer Look at the Minority Achievement Gap." EDRS Spectrum, Educational Research Service. (www.ers.org/spectrum/spg01a.htm)

DARLING-HAMMOND, L., AND FINN, C. (2000). "Two Paths to Quality Teaching: Implications for Policymakers." Education Commission of the States. (http://ecs.org/clearinghouse/12/22/1222.htm/)

DARLINGTON, R. (1991). "The Long-Term Effects of Model Preschool Programs." In L. Okagaki, and R. J. Sternberg, eds., *Directors of Development: Influences on the Development of Children's Thinking.* Hillsdale, NY: Erlbaum.

DAVIDSON, A. (1996). *Making and Molding Identity in Schools: Student Narratives on Race, Gender, and Academic Achievement.* Albany: SUNY Press.

DE LA CRUZ, Y. (1999). "Reversing the Trend: Latino Families in Real Partnerships with Schools." *Teaching Children Mathematics* 5(5), 296–300.

DESCHENES, S., CUBAN, L., AND TYACK, D. (2001). "Mismatch: Historical Perspectives on Schools and Students Who Don't Fit Them." *Teachers College Record* 103(4), 525–547.

EDUCATION TRUST. (1996). *Education Watch: The 1996 Education Trust State and National Data Book.* (www.edtrust.org)

———. (2001). "New Frontiers for a New Century." *Thinking K–16* 5(2), 1–22.

EDUCATION WEEK. (2002). "An ESEA Primer." Jan. 9 (21), 28–29.

FARKAS, S., AND JOHNSON, J. (1998). *Time to Move On : African-Americans and White Parents Set an Agenda for Public Schools.* New York: Public Agenda.

FERGUSON, R. (1998). Teachers' Perceptions and Expectations and the Black-White Test Score Gap. In C. Jencks, and M. Phillips, eds., *The Black-White Test Score Gap.* Washington, DC: Brookings Institution.

FORDHAM, S. (1997). "Those Loud Black Girls." In M. Seller and L. Weis, eds., *Beyond Black and White.* Albany: SUNY Press.

FORDHAM, S., AND OGBU, J. (1986). Black Students' School Success: Coping with the Burden of "Acting White." *Urban Review* 18(1), 176–204.

GARCES, E., THOMAS, D., AND CURRIE, J. (2000). "Longer Term Effects of Head Start." National Bureau of Economic Research, Working Paper (No. 8054).

HAYCOCK, K. (2001). "Closing the Achievement Gap." *Education Leadership,* 58(60). (www.ascd.org/readingroom/edlead/0103/haycock.html)

HANEY, J. (1978). "The Effects of the *Brown* Decision on Black Educators." *Journal of Negro Education* 47(1), 88–95.

HEAD START ACT. (1998). Sec. 636. [42 U.S.C. 9831]. (www2.acf.dhhs.gov/programs/hsb/regs/hsactogc.htm)

HILL, R. (1999). *The Strengths of African American Families: Twenty-five Years Later.* Lanham, MD: University Press of America.

HOOKER, R. (1970). *Displacement of Black Teachers in the Eleven Southern States.* Special Report. Washington, DC: U.S. Office of Education.

JACOBSON, L. (2002). "Study: Early Head Start Children Outpace Peers." *Education Week* June 12. (www.edweek.org)

JENCKS, C., AND PHILLIPS, M., EDS. (1998). *The Black-White Test Score Gap.* Washington, DC: Brookings Institution.

JOHNSON, L. B. (1996). *Public Papers on the Presidents of the United States: Lyndon B. Johnson, 1965.* Vol. I, entry 181, pp. 412–414. Washington, DC: U.S. Government Printing Office.

JOONDEPH, B. (1998). "Skepticism and School Desegregation." *Washington University Law Quarterly* 76(1). (www.wulaw.wustl.ed/WULQ/76-1/761-12.html)

Keyes v. School District No. 1, Denver, Colorado. (1973). 413 U.S. 189.

KIVEL, P. (1996). Affirmative action works! *In Motion Magazine.* (http://inmotionmagazine.com/pkivel.html)

KLUGER, R. (1975). *Simple Justice: This History of Brown v. Board of Education and Black America's Struggle for Equality.* New York: Knopf.

KOBER, N. (2001). "It Takes More Than Testing: Closing the Achievement Gap." A Report of the Center on Educational Policy. Washington, DC: Center on Educational Policy.

LARA, J., AND PANDE, G. (2001). "Latino Students and Secondary Education." *Gaining Ground Newsletter* May–June, 1–4. ERIC Document ED 456349.

LEWIS, A. (1965). *Portrait of a Decade.* New York: Bantam Books.

LIEBMAN, J. (1990). "Desegregating Politics: All-Out School Desegregation Explained." *Columbia Law Review* 90, Column L, Rev. 1463.

LIGHTFOOT, S. L. (1978). *Worlds Apart.* New York: Basic Books.

LOCKE-DAVIDSON, A. (1996). *Making and Molding Identity in Schools.* Albany: State University of New York Press.

MAHARD, R., AND CRAIN, R. (1984). "Research on Minority Achievement in Desegregated Schools." In C. Rossell, and W. Hawley, eds., *The Consequences of School Desegregation,* Philadelphia: Temple University Press.

MARCON, R. (1996). "Head Start Graduates: Making the Transition from the Early to Later Childhood Grades." Paper presented at the Biennial Conference on Human Development, Birmingham. ERIC Document ED 397962.

———. (2000). "Transitions in Early Childhood, Middle Childhood and Early Adolescence: Head Start vs. Public School Pre-Kindergarten Graduates." Paper presented at the National Head Start Conference, Washington, DC. ERIC Document ED 441601.

Milliken v. Bradley. (1974). 419 U.S. 815.

MURNANE, R., AND LEVY, F. (2001). "Will Standards-Based Reforms Improve the Education of Students of Color?" *National Tax Journal* 54, 401.

NATIONAL CENTER FOR CHILDREN IN POVERTY. (2002a). "Early Childhood Poverty: A Statistical Profile." (http://cpmcnet.columbia.edu/dept/nccp/ecp302.html)

———. (2002b). *Ready to Enter: What Research Tells Policymakers About Strategies to Promote Social and Emotional School Readiness Among Three- and Four-Year-Old Children.* New York: Author.

NATIONAL HEAD START ASSOCIATION. (2002). "Chairman of the Board's Address to the 29th Annual Training Conference." (www.nhsa.org)

NORTHWEST REGIONAL EDUCATIONAL LABORATORY. (1997). "Closing the Achievement Gap Requires Multiple Solutions." (www.nrel.org/cnorse/infoline/may97/article5.html)

O'CONNOR, C. (1997). "Dispositions Toward (Collective) Struggle and Educational Resilience in the Inner City." *American Educational Research Journal* 34(4), 593–629.

ORFIELD, G. (2001). "Schools More Separate: Consequences of a Decade of Resegregation." The Civil Rights Project, Harvard University. (www.law.harvard.edu/civilrights)

———. (1993). *The Growth of Segregation in American Schools: Changing Patterns of Separation and Poverty Since 1968.* Cambridge: Report of the Harvard Project on School Desegregation to the National School Boards Association.

ORFIELD, G., AND EATON, S. (1996). *Dismantling Desegregation.* New York: New Press.

PRESIDENTIAL ADVISORY COMMISSION ON EDUCATIONAL EXCELLENCE FOR HISPANIC AMERICANS. (2000). *Creating the Will: Hispanic Achieving Educational Excellence.* Washington: DC: U.S. Department of Education.

ROTHSTEIN, R. (1993). "The Myth of Public School Failure." *American Prospect* 4(13). (www.prospect.org/print/v4/13/rothstein-r.html) March 21.

SADKER, M., AND SADKER, D. (2002). *Teachers, Schools and Society.* New York: McGraw-Hill.

SARRATT, R. (1966). *The Ordeal of Desegregation.* New York: Harper & Row.

SCHMOKER, M., AND MARZANO, R. (1999). "Realizing the Promise of Standards-Based Education." *Educational Leadership* 56. (www.acsd.org/readingroom/edlead/9903/extschmoker.html)

SIDDLE-WALKER, V. (1996). *Their Highest Potential.* Chapel Hill: University of North Carolina Press.

SIMON, P. (2001). "Schools to End Forced Busing." *Buffalo News.* April 22, p. A1.

SLAVIN, R. (1999). "How Title I Can Become the Engine of Reform in America's Schools." Washington, DC: Office of Educational Research and Improvement. ERIC Document ED 456546.

STEELE, C. (1992). "Race and the Schooling of Black Americans." *Atlantic Monthly.* April. (Digital Edition: www.theatlantic.com/politics/reace/steele.htm)

SUGRUE, T., ET AL. (1999). *The Compelling Need for Diversity in Higher Education.* Ann Arbor: University of Michigan Press. ERIC Document ED 435367. (www.umich.edu/~ure/admissions/legal/expert/index.html)

STEPHANOPOULOS, G., AND EDLEY, C. (1995). "Affirmative Action Review: Report to the President." (http://clinton2.nara.gov/WH/EOP/OP/html/aa/aa-index.html)

TAYLOR, S. (1998) *Desegregation in Boston and Buffalo.* Albany: SUNY Press.

TEICHER, S. (1999). "Closing a Chapter on School Desegregation." *The Christian Science Monitor.* (www.csmonitor.com/durable/19997/07/16/fp1s3-csm.shtml)

TUSHNET, M. (1987). *Segregated Education, 1925–1950.* Chapel Hill: University of North Carolina Press.

TYACK, D. (1974). *The One Best System: A History of American Urban Education.* Cambridge: Harvard University Press.

U.S. DEPARTMENT OF EDUCATION. (2002). "No Child Left Behind Act." (Online website: www.ed.gov)

U.S. DEPARTMENT OF HEALTH AND HUMAN SERVICES. (2002). "About Head Start." (www2.acf.dhhs.gov/programs/hsb/about/index.htm)

VIADERO, D. (2000). "Lags in Minority Achievement Defy Traditional Explanations." *Education Week,* March 22.

WEILER, J. (1998). "Recent Changes in School Desegregation." ERIC Digest Number 133. ERIC Document ED 419029.

WEINBERG, M. (1977). *A Chance to Learn.* Cambridge: Cambridge University Press.

WILKERSON, I. (1991). Separate Proms Reveal an Unspanned Racial Divide, *The New York Times.* May 5, pp. 1, 36.

WILSON, W. (1996). *When Work Disappears: The World of the New Urban Poor.* New York: Knopf.

YOUNISS, J., AND COVEY, J., EDS. (2000). *Catholic Schools at the Crossroads.* New York: Teachers College Press.

CHAPTER 5

Gender Equity: Eliminating Discrimination or Making Legitimate Accommodations

POSITION 1: ELIMINATING DISCRIMINATION

Regardless of the sources of gender gaps—whether "nature" or "nurture"—schools have a mission to educate all students to levels of competency and to broaden individual opportunities rather than reinforce group stereotypes about student skills and options.

—AMERICAN ASSOCIATION OF UNIVERSITY WOMEN (AAUW), 1998

Efforts to end gender discrimination in schools have been part of the ongoing struggles for civil rights in the United States. In the last decade young people have begun to reap the benefits of the latest chapter in that quest—however, the attempt to ensure equal educational access, opportunity, and achievement to both men and women faces new challenges. Recent proposals to create single-sex classes and schools and to revise Title IX threaten the progress made. Perhaps these new suggestions are sincere efforts to meet young people's needs; ultimately, however, they violate our country's commitment to "liberty and justice for all."

Gender Roles and Education

Debates about educational gender equity always have been inextricably connected to society's understanding of gender roles—that is, education Americans viewed as gender appropriate was connected to the social roles men and women were assigned. Of course, race and social class prejudices also have affected equity between males and females in schools. In some ways, however, notions of what men and women are expected to be and do have transcended those other categories. Definitions of gender roles have shaped equity in educational access, opportunity, and achievement. An end to discrimination in schools depended on decreased discrimination in society.

In colonial America gender roles were rooted in biblical understanding. Women were seen as subservient to men. "Let a woman learn in silence with all submission. For I do not allow a woman to teach, or go to exercise authority over men; but she is to keep quiet . . . Yet women will be saved by childbearing, if they continue in faith and love and holiness with modesty" (Timothy 2:9–15). In keeping with these admonitions, early Christian colonists refused to provide boys and girls with equal access to schools (Tyack and Hansot, 1992; Spring, 1997; Urban and Wagoner, 2000). Colonial Christianity, however, also required each believer be able to read and interpret the Scriptures for themselves and provide their children with the same ability. Therefore, both men and women had to be literate. As a result women gained limited access to education through education at home or in "dame" schools. In keeping with colonial gender roles, they were expected to learn only enough to perform their religious and domestic duties (Tozer, Violas, and Senese, 2002).

After the American Revolution the social tasks assigned to each gender remained essentially the same, although they now were rooted in a political, not religious, ideology. Men had public responsibilities in the new country. They needed to be moral neighbors, informed voters, and responsible businessmen. Schooling was designed to help boys develop manly virtues such as obedience to authority, respect for the rights of others, an appreciation of "fair play" and patriotism (Tozer, Violas, and Senese, 2002).

Women's responsibilities in the republic remained primarily in the private sphere. They were expected to provide "lessons" at home that would prepare their sons and daughters to be responsible citizens (Douglas, 1977; Evans, 1989; Tyack and Hansot, 1992; Zinn, 1995). Any schooling was expected to prepare them for those domestic duties. Believing both men and women's contributions were vital to the country's well-being, Americans in general supported gender equity in access (Kaestle, 1983; Evans, 1989; Tyack and Hansot, 1992; Zinn, 1995). Coeducational elementary schools became the country's norm (Tyack and Hansot, 1992; Sklar, 1993).

Having decided on equity regarding access to free education, Americans had to determine whether men and women should have the opportunity to study the same curriculum, even if they were going to use those lessons in different ways (Tyack and Hansot, 1992). This question primarily involved secondary education. By the early nineteenth century, upper- and middle-class boys increasingly went beyond elementary school. Pioneers such as Catharine Beecher, Emma Willard, and Mary Lyon worked to ensure the same opportunity for girls, arguing the country's needs required women to extend their duties as "Republican mothers" beyond the confines of their own homes. Educated young women would serve the country by taking their "natural" aptitude for teaching into schools. In response to these arguments, state and local governments began providing public funding for secondary education for women. These schools both reflected and contributed to changes in sex role understandings. Working outside the home as teachers no longer was considered a violation of women's assigned gender role (Kaminer, 1998, p. 2). By the early twentieth century, private single-sex academies were replaced by public high schools that admitted boys and girls on a relatively equal footing (Rury, 1991; Tyack and Hansot, 1992; Spring, 1997; Urban and Wagoner, 2000). Changes in gender role understanding had resulted in greater equity in educational opportunity.

However, as long as equity in educational opportunity remained rooted in the belief that men and women had distinct gender characteristics, suiting them for different work, then it could not be fully achieved. Despite the increased availability of secondary schools, the long struggle to grant women access to colleges and universities (Horowitz, 1984; Solomon, 1986), only few women had the opportunity to pursue education preparing them for professions. For the most part, women were seen as "unfit" for some careers. The right to work in the law, business, medicine and ministry belonged almost exclusively to men (Horowitz, 1984; Solomon, 1986; Tozer, Violas, and Senese, 2002).

At the high school level, after some early equality of opportunity, gender role understandings began to reassert themselves. Progressive Era theories resulted in differences between males' and females' school experiences, although they did reflect some increased options for women's work in the public sphere. Girls were tracked into teacher preparatory programs, nursing courses, "commercial" programs that readied them to be secretaries, receptionists, or clerks, or home economics courses that taught them how to be good wives and mothers (Rury, 1991). Boys took college preparatory courses in larger numbers than girls and participated in vocational programs preparing them for "manly" jobs in industry and the trades (Rury, 1991; Tyack and Hansot, 1992; Ravitch, 2000). The introduction of "girls' electives" such as cooking, sewing, typing, and stenography increased segregation by gender in high school, resulting in a drop of women's participation in more "academic" courses (Rury, 1991). For more than thirty years, gender differences in educational opportunity remained part of American secondary and higher education. This discrimination had serious consequences. For example, although a higher percentage of women completed four years of high school between 1933 and 1965, fewer women than men completed four years of college during that same period (U.S. Census Bureau, 2000).

In the last half of the twentieth century, the relationship between society's view of gender roles and the kind of education appropriate for males and females was renegotiated once again. This time dramatic progress was made in ending educational gender discrimination.

Changes in the nation's understanding of appropriate gender roles underwent a radical shift during World War II. Women took on industrial jobs previously considered too "masculine" for them to perform (Evans, 1989). Universities and professional schools opened their doors to women when prospective male students were in the military. Despite efforts to restore the previous gender order during peacetime (Evans, 1989), once the genie was out of the bottle, there was no going back. Gender issues were rethought by men and women scholars and such activists as Carol Gilligan, Germaine Greer, Gloria Steinem, Betty Friedan, Michael Kimmel, Robert Connell, Martin Mac an Ghaill, and Robert Bly.

The 1960s saw a renewed commitment to the position that biological differences should not affect the kind or quality of education men and women received. Many argued the differences between men and women actually were more social than biological (Miller, 1976; Chodorow, 1978; Gilligan, 1982; Segal,

1990; Connell, 1995). Scholars investigated the policies, practices, curriculum, and student-teacher interactions in schools for explanations for differences in school achievement between boys and girls and reported many gender inequities (U.S. Department of Health, Education and Welfare, 1978; Mac an Ghaill, 1994; Sadker and Sadker, 1982, 1994).

Feminists who did the earliest of this research took particular note of the ways in which discrimination affected females. Women and their accomplishments were missing from textbooks. Girls were still tracked into courses of study associated with traditionally female occupations such as nursing, teaching, secretarial work, or homemaking. Instructional materials virtually ignored women's contributions and experiences. Boys received more teacher attention than did girls. Their learning was supported in more positive ways. In addition, discrimination existed in admission practices, financial aid, regulations, counseling, athletics, and access to programs and courses (Frazier and Sadker, 1973; Howe, 1984; AAUW, 1995; Biklen and Pollard, 1993; Sadker and Sadker, 1994).

Gender discrimination in education was linked to the larger civil rights movement. Americans had come to realize that discrimination on the basis of race violated the most fundamental principles on which the country had been founded. The civil rights movement had awakened the country to the social and economic costs of denying any citizen their individual freedoms. Passage of the Civil Rights Acts in the late sixties legislated an end to policies and practices blocking racial equality. Advocates of gender equity argued that discrimination on the basis of sex was as much a violation of the Fourteenth Amendment as that based on race.

As a result, in 1972, Congress passed Title IX of the Educational Amendment Act. Although most closely identified with efforts to make athletic programs more equal, the bill actually bans discrimination on the basis of sex in *any* program or activity receiving federal financial assistance—meaning neither gender can be denied equal access to any aspect of educational opportunity. Course-taking opportunities, participation in extracurricular activities, eligibility for awards, and college and university admission policies no longer could be determined by a student's gender. In 1974, the Women's Educational Equity Act (WEEA) was passed. This law requires the federal government to provide incentives and guidance to schools to promote educational equity. The WEEA Equity Resource Center has been important to this effort in developing gender-equitable materials for schools and teachers. In addition, WEEA has provided funding for programs to overcome discriminatory policies and practices that prevent women and girls from having equal access or opportunity in education (Valentin, 1997). WEEA and Title IX were the culmination of efforts to ensure gender equity with regard to educational opportunity.

For the first time in American history, the struggle for gender equity in education was fueled not by arguments that women's unique gender role required educational access or opportunity but instead was based on the idea that men and women shared equally in the "unalienable rights" named by the Declaration of Independence and guaranteed by the Fourteenth Amendment. Dramatic progress has resulted in equalizing achievement, the third type of educational equity. There has been movement to greater gender equality in standardized test scores, course-taking, participation in sports and extracurricular activities, and educational attainment. These results indicate reasons for continued commitment to eliminating gender discrimination in schools.

Academic Improvement

The movement for equal rights for men and women has resulted in fewer barriers to women's participation in the marketplace. The same movement also has lowered barriers to females' full participation in schools.

The reduction in gender discrimination in schools due to Title IX meant girls could adjust their course-taking patterns to be better prepared for their new options. They appear to have done so. For example, based on reviews of high school graduates' transcripts, the Department of Education reports more girls are taking physics, a three-credit sequence in science, and advanced mathematics (including calculus). In 1982, only 10.2 percent of girls took physics; in 1998, 26.24 percent did. Twenty years ago only 8 percent of girls took the three-credit science sequence. In the most recent figures available, almost a quarter of them did so. In 1982, only 11.7 percent of girls took advanced math; in 1998 that number rose to 33 percent (U.S. Department of Education, 2001). These gains have brought them much closer to equality with their male counterparts. (See Figure 5.1.)

Ending gender discrimination in schools has had positive effects on both male and female achievement. Standardized test scores demonstrate this effect of ending gender discrimination. For example, the average score of males on the verbal section of the SAT exam in 1967 was five points lower than that of the

FIGURE 5.1 Percentage of Males and Females Taking Selected High School Courses

	Percent Males	Percent Females
1982 Physics	19.1	10.15
1998 Physics	31.79	26.24
1982 Biology/Chemistry/ Physics Sequence	13.61	8.03
1998 Biology/Chemistry/ Physics Sequence	27.57	23.94
1982 Advanced Math	14.80	11.65
1998 Advanced Math	31.3	32.9
1982 Calculus	5.19	4.2
1998 Calculus	11.2	10.6

Source: *U.S. Department of Education 2001.*

average female. However, males' verbal scores rose steadily and in the 1970s and 1980s their average scores were as many as ten points higher than that of girls. By the mid-1990s that gap also decreased, however; between 2000 and 2002, the male average was only five points higher than the female scores (The College Board, 2002). Girls' scores on the math sections of the SATs have been increasing. In 2002, that average reached 500 at last. While a sizeable gap remains between average male and female scores in math, it has lessened since 1967 (The College Board, 2002).

Even more heartening than these test scores, however, are data about changes in the gap between men's and women's educational attainments. In the last thirty years, women have made remarkable progress at achieving degrees in areas once dominated by men. In 1970, women earned 43.1 percent of all bachelor's degrees. In 2000, that figure rose to 57.2 percent (U.S. Department of Education, 2000, 2002).

Gender no longer is the prime characteristic determining a person's college major and subsequent career opportunities. Women have entered professions once overwhelmingly male. (See Figure 5.2.) Men, too, have taken advantage of the changes in gender expectations. For example, in 1966, less than 1 percent of all registered nurses were male. By 2000, men constituted almost 6 percent of all those employed as nurses (U.S. Department of Health and Human Services, 2000).

Gender inequities also have decreased in graduate degree programs, notably those preparing for law and medicine. (See Figure 5.3.)

These remarkable accomplishments result from efforts to end discriminatory practices in elementary and secondary schools. No longer is it legal to prevent students from taking courses because of their gender. In addition, educators differentiate instruction within classrooms so they can meet each student's complex educational needs and have begun developing a repertoire of instructional strategies more effectively to reach each child. The pressure from

FIGURE 5.2 Percentage of Bachelor's Degrees Conferred on Women in Selected Fields of Study

	1970	2000
Engineering	0.7	20.4
Agriculture/Natural Resources	4.1	42.9
Business	9.0	49.7
Computer Science	12.9	28.1
Mathematics	37.4	47.1
Physical Science	13.6	40.3

Source: *U.S. Department of Education, 2000 (Trends in Educational Equity) and 2001 (Completions Survey).*

FIGURE 5.3 Percentage of Graduate Degrees Awarded to Women in Selected Fields

	1970	2000
Law (L.L.B., J.D.)	5.4	44.7
Medicine (M.D.)	8.4	42.6
Computer Science (Ph.D.)	1.9	16.9
Engineering (Ph.D.)	0.7	15.5
Physical Sciences (Ph.D.)	5.4	25.4
Business (M.B.A.)	1.6	39.8

Sources: *U.S. Department of Education 2000 (Trends in Educational Equity); U.S. Department of Education 2002, Integrated Postsecondary Education Data Systems (Completion Surveys).*

feminists for equal educational opportunity for girls has improved the chances of success for all children (Wandle and Carpenter, 2001).

Extracurricular Equity

Extracurricular activities offer students opportunity to interact with their peers, explore and develop their talents and abilities, and participate in community service activities that prepare them for citizenship responsibilities. For those reasons, gender equity with regard to extracurricular activities is an important goal. Although some progress has been made, males and females continue to take part in different types of activities. More girls than boys are involved in community service, music, performing arts, academic clubs, school publications, and student governments (U.S. Department of Education, 2000).

The provisions of Title IX legislation have been applied most noticeably to athletics. Although gender differences still remain, more equitable distribution of resources has dramatically increased girls' participation in scholastic sports programs in the last thirty years. In 1972, fewer than 32,000 women participated in college or university sports programs; in 2001, over 150,000 women did. In the days before Title IX, athletic scholarships for women were nonexistent. In 2001, women received more than 40 percent of the available scholarship money for sports. Before Title IX fewer than 300,000 girls played high school sports. In 2001, that number reached 2.78 million (National Women's Law Center, 2002).

The benefits of gender equity in sports have been significant. The increasing number of athletic scholarships for women has made it possible for more of them to attend college than ever before. Participation in sports also leads to healthier lifestyles and less risk-taking behavior among adolescents. Student athletes are less likely to smoke or use drugs (National Women's Law Center, 2002); female adolescent athletes are less likely to engage in premarital sex or become pregnant during high school (Sabo, 1998). Girls who play sports have "higher levels of self-esteem, a lower incidence of depression and a more positive body image" (National Women's Law Center, 2002). In addition, there are long-term health benefits from women's participation in athletics. Women who take part in rigorous exercise such as provided by sports are less likely to develop heart diseases, osteoporosis, and breast cancer over the course of their lives (National Women's Law Center, 2002). Increased gender equity in sport participation provide benefits that, like academic achievement, are long-lasting.

Gender role expectations affect young people's experiences and achievements in schools and they do so across race, class, and ethnicity (Coley, 2001). Schools adopting a zero-tolerance policy for gender discrimination will enable all students' unique personalities and talents to flourish.

What Remains to Be Done

While there is indeed good news, a look at contemporary American society will show there is still work to be done in achieving gender equity outside of school. Women's earning power still lags behind that of men. The Department of Labor reports women are paid less than men in every occupational category for which there is enough information to calculate such figures. On average, a full-time working woman currently is paid only 73¢ for every dollar earned by a man (National Organization for Women, 2002). They also are less likely than men to be employed in industries offering health-care or retirement benefits. They often are dependent on their husband's health-care plans and lose coverage if divorced or widowed. As they age, women are more likely than men to be poor. Almost 75 percent of senior citizens living below the poverty level are female. Most older women depend on Social Security benefits as their sole source of income. Men are twice as likely to receive a pension as women are (Administration on the Aging, 2002).

Surely, no one can expect that changes in the way schools educate girls and boys can address or correct all these issues. The educational system, however, can help young people become aware of them. In doing so, schools will challenge the remaining patterns of gender-based social inequality.

In addition, school communities can renew their commitments to ending discrimination in their extracurricular programs. For example, although we recently have been made aware of Title IX successes regarding women's athletics (Gavora, 2001), issues remain to be faced. Girls' and boys' teams do not always have the same access to practice time, facilities, and faculty support. In addition, schools, colleges, and universities have played the "blame" game with Title IX. They continue to fund expensive male sports such as basketball, football, and ice hockey, stretching their athletic budgets to the breaking point. Then, prevented by Title IX from spending more on men's sports than on women's, they cut smaller men's teams and blame the law for needing to do so (Gavora, 2001). Consequently, there is sometimes great resentment against women's athletic programs and girls who play sports. The public's attention should be redirected to the vast amounts of money being used to support a relatively small number of male athletes in "first-tier" sports (Weistart, 1998). These programs—not women's field hockey—are draining athletic budgets and preventing men from competing in less prestigious sports such as gymnastics, swimming, and volleyball.

In a school setting where community members endeavor to end gender discrimination, the social activities sponsored by a school can reflect that commitment. Subtle messages about gender stereotyping can be corrected by refusing to "crown" homecoming kings or queens or allow only heterosexual couples to attend formal dances.

Schools committed to ending gender discrimination also can work to eliminate sexual harassment. Eighty percent of students—boys and girls—report they have been victims of sexual harassment in their schools (AAUW, 2001). Although most schools have policies prohibiting and punishing sexual harassment, clearly this is an area in which gender equity advocates must continue to monitor how teachers and administrators enforce the rules they have created.

New Challenges to Ending Discrimination

In 2002 the Department of Education announced its intention "to provide more flexibility for educators to establish single-sex classes and schools at the elementary and secondary level" (*Federal Register*, 2002). For Americans who have participated in the efforts to ensure full gender equality in public schools, this proposal presents a new challenge.

In the last ten years, publicly funded single-sex educational opportunities for young people have increased (Stowe, 1991; Perry, 1996; Streitmatter, 1997, 1998, 1999). Arguments supporting single-sex educational projects generally have been based on public school's failure to meet students' needs. For example, feminist concerns that sexism in schools creates unequal opportunity for girls are the driving force in the creation of single-sex classes for young women. Advocates for classes exclusively for African American boys often cite their need for strong male role models in light of their participation in female-headed households.

However, "(t)here is no evidence that single-sex education in general works or is better than coeducation" (AAUW, 1998, pp. 2–3). Factors other than gender explain whatever academic advantages of single-sex schools or classes have been documented: Single-sex schools tend to be smaller, have more constrained curricula, more personal social relations among school community members, and teaching that allows more student activity (Lee, 1998). Such schools have teachers "who have a willingness to take personal responsibility for all students' learning and a belief that all students can learn what they are taught" (Lee, 1998, p. 48). In addition, students in single-sex schools have made a choice to attend a school where academics, not socializing, are the most dominant aspect of school life. In doing so they buy into the values of such a school and, therefore, their own academic achievement increases (Riordan, 1998, p. 55).

Americans should not let those who propose a return to single-sex settings deter them from their efforts to end gender discrimination in schools. Even if well intentioned, what they are suggesting is dangerous. Their plans risk reinforcing sexual stereotypes and traditional gender roles and have the potential to create the kind of separate and unequal educational settings ruled unconstitutional in *Brown v. Board of Education* (1954).

Many of those who advocate single-sex schools or classes may do so to advance another agenda. They often insist that providing such options increases "parental choice" with regard to children's education (National Association for the Advancement of Single-Sex Public Education, 2002). Those who use the language of choice often support privatization of education—they are often in favor of charter schools, vouchers, and other proposals that provide public funds for nonpublic schools. Currently, most single-sex schools are private schools. If proponents of gender-segregated settings can convince the public of their value, it might become easier to convince voters to allow students to choose to attend one outside the public school system. After all, they will argue, wouldn't it be easier just to give students the tuition money to attend an already existing school than go to all the trouble and expense of creating one? Once that door has been opened, it will be difficult to close and could be pushed open even farther by those who want to dismantle the American public school system completely.

Conclusion

The struggle to achieve gender equity in American public education has been long and difficult. Some progress was achieved by relying on arguments based on beliefs that differences between men and women meant they had different educational needs. The fundamental conservatism of that position, however, limited its usefulness in securing access to schools. Creating equal opportunity resulting in more equal achievement for boys and girls requires the belief that society had no right to create gender roles limiting individuals' freedom. That point of view has been adopted only in the last few decades, but was centuries in the making and is quintessentially American. Eliminating discrimination is faithful to the commitment to guarantee individual liberty. The process of doing so results in more just schools and, ultimately, a more just country.

POSITION 2: FOR MAKING LEGITIMATE DISTINCTIONS

> *We argue, then, that what is good in equal-opportunity programs has to be placed in a new context and in various ways given new aims. In broad terms, it is a question of directly addressing the issues that equal opportunity strategies take for granted.*
>
> —KESSLER ET AL., 1985

There is no question that the efforts of many Americans to end educational gender discrimination have resulted in important gains. All phases of public education—from kindergarten to graduate school—are open to members of both genders. By insisting schools adhere to rigid, often quota-based, policies, however, those who refuse to see the need to make legitimate distinctions have created situations that actually work against the students they claim to be assisting. Pressure from feminists and others who advocate eliminating all differences between boys' and girls' educations have made it almost impossible to create educational situations that actually attend to their needs. In doing so they have relied on the notion that inequity has been based on unjust gender roles imposed on people from someone or something outside of themselves.

In actuality, males and females make choices about and within educational settings that contribute to inequality. In order to allow young people more freedom for making those choices, educators need to be able to make legitimate distinctions between boys' and girls' education. Single-sex schools and classes and modifications to Title IX's application are examples of approaches that allow for the differences in male and female student choices to be examined and supported. These strategies will, in the long term, result in more equity for men and women than rigid dictates of nondiscrimination can provide.

Gendered Experiences in Schools

Despite a generation-long effort to eliminate discrimination from schools, gender still affects students' educational experiences. Even in preschool, differences emerge. Teachers encourage boys to be assertive and independent but discourage girls when they try to take risks. Instead, they reward girls for being "timid, cooperative and quiet" (Tozer, Violas, and Senese, 2002, p. 392). Preschool boys "handle more tools, throw more balls, construct more Lego bridges, build more block towers, and tinker more with simple mechanical objects than do girls" (Kahle, in AAUW, 1995, p. 27). Since teachers often think boys' abilities in these activities are "natural," they do not teach these skills as part of the regular curriculum. As a result, girls do not receive instruction in the skills that do not come "naturally" to them (AAUW, 1995, p. 28). Since these activities have been credited with developing spatial abilities that eventually make it easier to learn mathematics and science concepts, not being part of girls' instruction has serious consequences. Males consistently score higher than females on later tests in math and science—tests that serve as "gatekeepers" for higher education, scholarships, and careers (U.S. Department of Education, 2000).

Girls, however, also bring and develop skills in preschool that boys do not. They are more competent at impulse control, have greater small-muscle development, and are more fluent with language use. Apparently schools are no more successful in helping boys develop these traditionally "female" linguistic skills than they are at helping girls learn skills seen as male. Boys' test scores in the NAEP exams—"The Nation's Report Card"—in reading and writing lag behind those of their female counterparts (Coley, 2001).

Girls have lower tests scores on the SAT and ACT college entrance exams. The math sections of these tests show the most discrepancies between the genders. The SAT and ACT are "gatekeepers"—colleges and universities use them to decide who's in and who's out. Even more troublesome is the fact that these tests are used to determine scholarships and other awards. "High-stakes tests, with disproportionate power to affect students' lives, are the tests that most dramatically reflect gender differences in performance" (AAUW, 1998, p. 35). When women's scores lag behind men's, so do their rewards. They are excluded "from consideration by entire classes of other scholarships, many for study in fields in which men already have a participation of advantage" (Brake, 1999, p. 10).

In elementary school, another gender pattern emerges. Teachers spend more time working with boys, give them more attention and affection, and talk to boys more often than to girls. When boys attempt to complete projects or answer difficult questions, teachers respond by prompting them to think them through on their own. When girls are in similar situations, teachers more often provide the answers or demonstrate how to do the project. Ultimately, this appears to result in the belief among girls that they are less capable than their male peers. In addition, when boys comment on a question by calling out, teachers pay attention to the content of their response. When girls do the same thing, teachers more often respond by scolding them for not following classroom rules (Sadker and Sadker, 1994).

Boys' experiences in grammar school, however, are not completely positive. They are more likely than girls to have their teachers contact parents about behavioral problems, to repeat a grade, and to be labeled as learning disabled (U.S. Department of Education, 2000). Boys are unprepared for class and forget books and other school supplies more often than girls. They do less homework as well (Sommers, 2000).

Students also have gendered experiences in schools through their textbooks. Although the texts rarely discuss gender specifically, they provide representations of masculinity and femininity that do not deeply challenge traditional understandings of gender. There may be pictures and stories about women and men in nontraditional roles but these are presented within a "safety zone"—that is, students may read stories or see illustrations of female doctors or male nurses but are less likely to read about or see female construction workers or male dancers. In addition, curricular materials often do not affirm differences between members of the same gender or integrate the experiences, needs, and interests of both sexes in their material (AAUW, 1995).

By the time they get to middle school, girls are struggling with messages about their academic competency, while being pressured to conform to social expectations that define "feminine" behavior. In their elementary school years, girls know what they feel and want and feel perfectly free to express themselves. But as they move to middle school—at eleven or twelve—they become afraid to say what they think. They are internalizing the social expectation that "good" girls take care of other people before they attend to their own needs. As a result they become tentative about speaking up for themselves—even in situations that present very real dangers. Teachers, even women, reinforce these norms (Brown and Gilligan, 1993).

By the time they are in high school, many girls have adapted themselves so fully to notions of "femininity" that they no longer know what they think or feel. Some of them become quite good at "doing school"—that is, presenting their work neatly, turning it in on time, and regurgitating information on tests. They do not, however, excel in independent or critical thinking and rarely take risks in choosing courses or assignments (Brown and Gilligan, 1993; AAUW, 1995).

During these same periods, boys are "taught" what it means to be a male. They are pressured to take part in sports, whether they like them or not, and are judged by peers based on their ability to compete. Boys are pressured to engage in drug and alcohol use and other risky behaviors. Expressions of emotion are deemed unmanly (Kindlon et al., 1999; Pollack, 1999). They are taught they are supposed to be in power and encouraged to act as if they are through posturing and violence. They are ridiculed for showing interest in "feminine" things such as reading and the arts (Kimmel, 2000).

For young adolescents—male or female—maintaining a gender-appropriate appearance becomes one of their most important "curricula." Young women learn how to buy and apply makeup and choose clothing that "flatters" their bodies. Their "teachers" often are those companies with products—cosmetics, clothes, shoes, and accessories—to sell (Gilbert and Taylor, 1991; Smith, 1991). In addition, advertisements these companies use as their "textbooks" feature models whose appearance is unattainable to most girls. The thinness that photographs so well has become the ideal for too many young women. In an effort to achieve that goal, they starve themselves, often resulting in unhealthy dieting and sometimes in life-threatening conditions such as anorexia or bulimia (Whitehead, 1998; National Organization for Women, 2002). In addition, the success of their "study" depends on the response of others—another aspect of the project that girls do not control. Many feel they are "failing" the course and have no hope of "passing." Their responses are self-destructive.

> Close to 40 percent of college women are frequent binge drinkers, a behavior related to date rapes and venereal disease. Young women suffer higher levels of depression, suicidal thoughts and attempts than young men from early adolescence on. Between 1980 and 1992, the rate of completed suicides more than tripled among white girls and doubled among black girls. For white women between 15 and 24, suicide is the third leading cause of death." (Whitehead, 1998, p. 1)

Males also suffer when they do not match the gender stereotypes laid down for them in the media. Boys who are "too" short, thin, or uncoordinated are targets of other boys' ridicule and the victim of girls' rejection. Like girls they sometimes go to dangerous lengths to fit the view of masculinity they see all around them. Nearly a half million teenagers, mostly boys, use steroids. Many admit they do so to create an image of masculinity they think is acceptable. These drugs have negative impacts on young bodies. They stunt the growth of healthy bones, can cause liver tumors, and sometimes result in irreversible reproductive system damage (Egan, 2002). Like girls, they seek to learn the craft of being gender appropriate. They try to wear the "right" clothes, carry the "right" accessories, and use the "right" products. When they fail to succeed, their sexual orientation often is questioned (AAUW, 1993) with serious consequences. Although fewer boys than girls attempt suicide, boys more often succeed (Sommers, 2000); one of the leading causes of suicide among young men is concern about their sexual orientation (Sell and Becker, 2001).

Behaviors associated with gender also are enforced by and enacted in acts of sexual harassment in schools. Four out of five students report that they have been the victim of such behavior. One-quarter say it happens to them "often" (AAUW, 1993). Students perceived as being outside the socially accepted heterosexual norm especially are victimized (GLSEN, 2001; Human Rights Watch, 2001).

Sexual harassment takes many forms in secondary schools: sexual comments, jokes, gestures, and looks. Students are touched, grabbed or pinched in sexual ways. They are subjected to mooning, flashing, and genital exposure. Students become targets of sexual rumors or written graffiti, have their clothes pulled at or off, are spied on in locker rooms, are shown or given unwanted sexual pictures or notes, and are blocked or cornered in sexual ways. They are forced to kiss someone when they did not want to, and in some cases do something even more sexual than kissing. It seems that no school space is entirely safe. Students report harassment takes place in classrooms, hallways, gyms, cafeterias, locker rooms, parking lots, playgrounds, and buses (AAUW, 1993).

"The consequences can be devastating, as young women struggle to survive in a learning environment they often experience as toxic. When so much of a female student's day is spent fending off diminishing comments, sexual innuendoes and physical pestering, how can she be expected to thrive at school?" (Larkin, 1997, p. 14). Despite more than a decade's worth of efforts to remedy these problems, they remain (Williams, Wasserman, and Goodman, 1997). Boys also suffer from schools' failures to eliminate sexual harassment. In addition to being victimized, they are forced into roles that neither they nor society will really welcome over the long term. When allowed or pressured to take on the role of harasser, boys learn to detach themselves from their victims. "The disrespect or indifference evident in those who sexually harass others suggests a lack of empathy or emotional literacy on their part" (Flood, 2000, p. 4). Boys trained to develop those qualities can grow into men who abuse and hurt others. Masculinity, in this culture, is associated with physical prowess demonstrated by men's ability to dominate women (Fine and Weis, 1999).

There seems to have been some improvement in the stereotypical gender course-taking patterns of students in college preparatory programs (U.S. Department of Education, 2001). Vocational education programs, however, clearly reflect and reproduce traditional gender expectations. Females are overwhelmingly directed or allowed to enter "training programs for historically female—and traditionally low wage—jobs" (Brake, 1999, p. 10). Boys go into courses designed to get them ready for high-paying work as carpenters, electricians, or plumbers. Girls study cosmetology, child care, and practical nursing (U.S. Department of Education, 2001).

Another way gender stereotypes play out in schools is in their treatment of young women who are pregnant or parenting. We no longer may place a "scarlet letter" on these girls, but our behavior toward them still is often punitive. Schools do little to accommodate their special needs. Few schedules are adjusted to allow for the extra time mothers might need to transport their babies to child care. Even fewer provide such centers on site. These young women are more likely to drop out of school than other female students (U.S. Department of

Education, 2000). Research indicates girls with traditional sex role orientations get pregnant more often than those who are more liberated (AAUW, 1995).

In many ways, schools are sites where gender differences are created and maintained. Efforts to create gender equity by eliminating gender discrimination in schools have met with limited success because they do not go far enough in interrupting the forces at work in creating gender.

En-gendering children

For centuries humans have speculated that biological differences between boys and girls are the cause of gender-specific behaviors. Girls play with dolls, it is supposed, because they know they most likely are going to become mothers. Boys practice skills that will stand them in good stead when they seek employment to provide for their family. We can change society in many ways, but so far we have not been able to alter this gender arrangement fundamentally (Goldberg, 1973). There is certainly no denying that biological differences between males and females really exist. Women conceive, gestate, give birth, and suckle new members of the human race. Men do not.

It seems their role in the reproductive process is only one aspect of the physical differences between males and females. Males' and females' brains also differ. Scientists have known for more than a hundred years that men's brains are larger than women's. Recent investigation indicates that men's brain structures allow them to perform better than women when attempting visual or spatial tasks. Women's brain structures help them do better than men on verbal or language-oriented tasks. It also appears that women have greater integration between the hemispheres of their brains resulting in their ability to take a more integrated approach to acquiring and using knowledge. Women's brains also seem to allow them to attend to more than one activity at the same time (Charles A. Dana Center, 2000). It may be too early in the research process to understand completely how the physical differences between men and women are related to thinking and learning. Clearly, however, such differences do exist.

It also is becoming clear that gender is something separate from a person's biological realities—their sex. Many scholars (Chodorow, 1978; Smith, 1989; Mac an Ghaill, 1994; Connell, 1996) have demonstrated that becoming "masculine" or "feminine" is an interaction between individuals and the societies in which they live. Those who rely on gender role prescriptions as the cause of injustice have only half the story. In every culture some patterns of behavior are defined as appropriate for each "sex," and these understandings of masculinity and femininity are created and maintained through such social institutions as families, businesses, churches, and schools. In the United States, people are bombarded with messages about gender through the mass media as well. Print ads, television shows, movies, and sports describe in vivid detail what "real" men and women should wear, look like, want, and do (Smith, 1989; Connell, 1996). The missing piece in the gender role explanation, however, is the response of individuals to these social "inputs." People try to look, act, and feel in ways that match these gender descriptions. That is, individuals become masculine or feminine by working hard at it (Smith, 1989). The preceding discussion of adolescents' efforts to match themselves to social messages about gender appropriateness illustrated this process.

Individuals and society use many aspects of school life to create and maintain gender. School authority structures (male administrators, female teachers), division of labor (teacher or student course assignments based on gender; the kind of work we ask students to do in school), discipline policies (gender-specific responses to infractions), and symbols (gender-based formal or informal dress codes, extracurricular participation, and ways of speaking) all teach school community members how to be "masculine" or "feminine" and impose penalties on anyone who violates that code (Connell, 1996). Members of school communities create their "genders" in response to cues they get from the environment—both in and out of schools.

In turn, individual responses to gender norms reshape the definition of masculinity and femininity. Consequently, the definition of manly or womanly behavior and traits changes (Connell, 1996). For example, women who followed Amelia Bloomer's advice and threw away their corsets and other confining undergarments changed the socially accepted understanding of femininity—even if their choice to do so was based on comfort rather than political conviction. This reworking of gender norms, however, is difficult and requires a kind of support that previous efforts to end gender discrimination simply do not provide. Such attempts to achieve gender equity fail because they do not fully take into account the process by which gender is created.

The Limits of Title IX

During the 1970s, feminists and other civil rights advocates tried to amend the Constitution. They argued that the passage of an Equal Rights Amendment would have prohibited all discrimination on the basis of gender. In doing so, they tried to equate racism and sexism. However, during the decade-long national debate on the ERA, it became clear to most Americans that it sometimes was necessary to make legitimate distinctions between the genders in order to serve the best interests of women and their children.

> Most people recognized that legally equating sex with race would inhibit states from making any distinctions, no matter how reasonable, based on sex, and would discourage states from enacting laws helpful to women. For unlike skin color—a superficial characteristic utterly irrelevant to merit or performance—sex, when it does matter, matters a great deal. (Blair, 1997, p. 1)

A determined campaign by those who saw the dangers to women inherent in the ERA argued that the amendment would prevent the courts from allowing legitimate distinctions to be made in public policies such as child custody, alimony, and workforce accommodations. Their campaign awakened Americans to the problems ratification of the ERA would create. After 1977, no state legislature could be persuaded to ratify the amendment. By 1982, even the most ardent feminists declared the effort to pass the ERA to be at an end (Blair, 1997).

The 1970s, however, did see the passage of legislation designed to end gender discrimination. In 1972, Congress passed Title IX prohibiting discrimination on the basis of sex in any educational institution. The legislation has become the justification for efforts to prove more equitable distribution of educational resources and opportunities. When it has been applied on a rational basis, the consequences have had significant positive impacts on the struggle to create a more just educational system. However, as opponents of the ERA had suggested, legislation that attempts to rule out all legitimate distinctions between treatment of the sexes contains within it inherent difficulties. Title IX had the potential to create situations that are, in fact, unjust.

The limitations and resulting failures of the attempt to create gender equity by relying solely on ending discrimination are particularly obvious in the application of Title IX regulations to athletics. The legislation originally was intended to end discrimination in school sports programs. Over time, however, it has created a "quota system," most often applied at colleges and universities that actually limits opportunity for some students. Through the efforts of feminists and others who support rigid policies of what they call nondiscrimination, the law has been interpreted as requiring strict "proportionality" between the percentage of women in a school's student body and the percentage of women participating in varsity sports. That is, if 55 percent of the students at a given institution are female, then 55 percent of the athletes also must be female. Schools are considered in violation of the law and face loss of government aid if they fail to comply (Gavora, 2002). Despite girls' increased participation in sports, fewer young women than men make the commitment to take part in intercollegiate athletics. Since they ignore the element of individual choice in the creation of gender identities and the influence of those choices on gender equity in educational settings, proponents of rigid nondiscrimination policies blame schools for the differences in student involvement in sports. When colleges cannot entice or coerce enough women to participate in sports, they are forced to achieve proportionality by cutting men's teams. As a result, the NCAA reported that "more than 200 men's teams and 20,000 male athletes disappeared from the ranks of America's colleges" in the 1990s (Gavora, 2001).

The absurdity of the claim that this policy helps achieve justice is obvious. Instead, male athletes are being deprived of their right to choose to participate in sports and to have that participation supported by their schools. The law never was meant to discriminate against men through an insistence on a policy that does not take into account individual freedom. It was meant to ensure equal opportunity for males and females, not to create quotas that are themselves discriminatory.

Single-Sex Schools

Creation of legitimate distinctions between the tasks males and females face in challenging gender norms holds out more possibilities for achieving the goals of the gender equity movement. That is, it is more likely that educational communities where the different needs of males and females are taken into account will provide young people with the ability to create futures allowing them to act as free individuals instead of stereotypes. Single-sex schools and classes appear to be examples of such places.

Although we have not had many opportunities to collect data on academic settings in single-sex public schools, significant research has taken place in single-sex private schools (Riordan, 1990). Researchers over the last thirty years have demonstrated that girls attending private, especially Catholic, single-sex schools have higher levels of academic achievement in reading, math, science, and writing than do those who attend coeducational private or public schools. Some data imply that attendance at a girls' school could increase science achievement by a year's growth (Riordan, 1985; Lee and Bryk, 1986). Girls who attended single-sex schools had higher SAT scores as well than their counterparts at coed schools (Riordan, 1985).

In addition to producing higher levels of academic achievement, single-sex schools also showed a positive effect on students' attitudes toward academics. Young people in such schools were more likely to associate with students committed to their studies. They did more homework and took more math and science courses than students in coeducational schools (Lee and Bryk, 1986). Apparently those students who choose to attend such schools opt to find a setting in which their academic aspirations will be taken seriously regardless of their gender appropriateness (Riordan, 1998).

What appears to happen in single-sex schools is that students are presented with alternatives to traditional ways of being male or female. For example, although most adolescent girls say they feel good about themselves, what gives them high self-esteem depends on what kind of school they attend. The best predictor of self-worth for girls attending coed schools is their satisfaction with their physical appearance; for those in single-sex schools, it is their academic achievement (Cairns, 1990; Granleese and Joseph, 1993). The fact that such an identity is achievable and acceptable in a single-sex school means girls are freer to build their sense of self on their achievements, surely a more reliable source of self-worth than appearance. The ability to create an acceptable self-image—including positive feelings about one's gender identity—results in behaviors with long-lasting positive effects. In single-sex schools, in addition to acquiring knowledge that will result in increased choices about future education and careers, it also is considered within the range of acceptable femininity for a girl to learn how to work hard, discover what kinds of efforts are successful for her, and develop time-management and problem-solving skills. Most importantly in such a setting, young women can come to believe that they have tremendous control over the course of their lives and still be considered feminine.

These attitudes and skills result in behaviors that in other settings would not appear gender appropriate. Karen Stabiner noted that girls she met in a single-sex school "were self-confident, comfortable with themselves in a way I was not used to seeing. They said what they meant, absolved of the social concerns that often make girls tone themselves down. They felt no need to defer or compromise their opinions" (National Association for the Advancement of Single-Sex Public Education, 2002). Robin Robertson claimed she could identify the girls in her classes who had attended all-girls' high schools. "They were the young women whose hands shot up in the air, who were not afraid to defend their positions, and who assumed that I would be interested in their perspective" (National Association for the Advancement of Single-Sex Public Education, 2002).

Teachers and administrators also expand the definition of acceptable gender behavior for girls in most single-sex schools. Students see women teaching subjects such as chemistry, physics, and advanced mathematics that traditionally have not been considered "feminine." Their principals and other administrators are women and as they act with authority they provide girls with examples of powerful women (Lee and Bryk, 1986). In addition, the environment provides girls with adult women with whom they can talk about sexuality, birth control, family, and peer pressure (McCarthy, 1999).

Although there is less research on the experience of boys in all-male settings, some evidence notes it is possible in such spaces to interrupt gender patterns reinforcing social inequity that precedes inequality in schools (Riordan, 1990). In addition there may be a greater range in the definition of masculinity in schools for boys than in coeducational ones. That is, many single-sex schools offer young men the opportunity to take part in activities traditionally defined as "feminine." Boys studying in an all-male setting are more likely to be encouraged to take part in the arts and do community service (Brennan, 2002). Supporters of single-sex schools for boys use anecdotal evidence to argue their case, citing testimonies from boys who describe the freedom to develop talents in single-sex schools that they would have been afraid to explore in coeducational settings (National Association for the Advancement of Single-Sex Public Education, 2002).

In many ways, single-sex educational settings are able to present young people with alternate ideas about gender. That is, in these schools rigid stereotypes about masculinity and femininity can be challenged and changed. When those are altered, students no longer have to conform their behavior or attitudes to them. They appear to be freer to explore other, more liberating, ways of being themselves. There is irony in the insistence that rigid policies of nondiscrimination in coed schools are the only ways to achieve gender equity. Their refusal to consider making legitimate distinctions between the needs of male and female students means that such alternatives have not been explored in public school settings. Therefore, research cannot be conducted that would give the American public any real data on which to base decisions about the allocation of public funds for education.

It is also ironic that advocates of educational equity appear unaware of race and class issues involved in their refusal to allow legitimate distinctions in boys' and girls' education through creation of publicly funded single-sex schools. Despite difficulties in creating publicly funded single-sex situations that meet the requirements of the law, doing so is a matter of justice. There are hundreds of private girls' schools in the United States (National Coalition of Girls Schools, 2002), but only eleven public single-sex schools or public schools in which there are single-sex classes (National Association for the Advancement of Single-Sex

Public Education, 2002). Tuition in the more elite private schools costs over $10,000 per year. Schools with affiliations to religious organizations are more affordable but are unacceptable to families whose faith traditions differ from that of the schools. Only affluent families can afford to make this choice for their daughters.

This fact is particularly troublesome in light of what we know about who benefits most from single-sex schools and classes. Research indicates girls of color from families with limited incomes who attend single-sex schools show the most dramatic difference in academic achievement compared with their counterparts in coeducational settings (Lee and Bryk, 1986; Riordan, 1985).

Liberals who claim to be sensitive to issues of multiculturalism in education also need to take a look at their coed-only stance. There are many new immigrants whose cultures or religions have long-standing bans against educating boys and girls in the same schools or classrooms. Because of the scarcity of such options in public schools, they choose to send their children to private schools, which, due to a lack of funds, sometimes are unable to provide adequate education for their students. In addition, these schools have the effect—intended or not—of isolating young people from others who will share the future of this country with them. The process of Americanization—of incorporating immigrants into our society—has long been one of the missions of public schools. Policies preventing educators from offering these immigrant children educational settings their cultures require create a great, and unnecessary, risk they may never come to see themselves as full participants in their adopted country. It also may guarantee they never have the opportunity fully to understand the U.S. form of government, laws, and the processes by which wrongs are addressed. Such limitations also may deprive some young people—eager to learn what they need to become self-sufficient—contributing members of society, of the schooling that will enable them to do so. That simply is a bad gamble. The stakes are too high.

Conclusion

The effort to create educational gender equity is laudable and rightly has been pursued throughout U.S. history. Eliminating truly discriminatory policies and practices has been a necessary part of that process. It has not, however, proven to be a sufficient one. Eliminating the possibility of making legitimate distinctions between educational needs of males and females has prevented the struggle for educational equality from being as successful as justice demands it be.

Educational gender inequity remains a fact of life in American schools. It will continue to do so until educators are allowed to create settings addressing the total process by which gender differences in schools are produced. By ignoring the tendency of coeducational settings to reproduce society's dominant gender prescriptions, and refusing to permit educators to create settings that resist those stereotypes, we perpetuate pressures that result in students' choices to conform to them. What is needed is a commitment to make public education better able to meet the needs of all the students it serves. Young people deserve nothing less than having an equal right to education that recognizes the complexity of the problem of gender.

For Discussion

1. Although the positions in this chapter allude to the effects race, class, and ethnicity might have on an individual's creation of his or her gender identity, they do not discuss those effects in any detail. Consider how the other facets of a person's identity or situation in life might affect the choices they make about how much or how little to conform to various forms of masculinity or femininity. That is, does a person's race, class, or gender affect how free people feel they are to deviate from gender stereotypes? Depending on your answers, what kinds of changes to the proposals in this chapter do you think are necessary to create gender equity in schools that takes race, class, and ethnicity into consideration?
2. Access information about gender differences in test scores from the Educational Testing Services website, www.ets.org/research. (For example, the report by Richard Coley cited in the References is available there.) In light of the discussions in this chapter, how do you explain such differences? How do you explain the fact that there appear to be little variance among gender differences from one racial/ethnic group to another? What does that suggest to you about ways to remedy gender inequity?
3. Research your college or university's athletic program. Do they seem to be in compliance with Title IX regulations? Have any male teams been cut to achieve "proportionality"? Interview male and female athletes and coaches to get their views on gender issues in the program and to determine for yourself if any discrimination exists.
4. Advantages of single-sex schools are discussed in Position 2. Can you think of any disadvantages of attending such schools? Are they academic or social in nature? Interview friends or classmates who attended single-sex high schools. How do their experiences confirm the arguments made in the chapter? How do their experiences confirm your speculated disadvantages?

References

ADMINISTRATION ON THE AGING. (2002). "Meeting the Needs of Older Women: A Diverse and Growing Population." (www.aoa.gov/factsheets/ow.html)

AMERICAN ASSOCIATION OF UNIVERSITY WOMEN (AAUW). (1993). *Hostile Hallways: The AAUW Survey of Sexual Harassment in America's Schools.* Washington, DC: Author.

———. (1995) *How Schools Shortchange Girls.* New York: Marlowe.

———. (1998). *Gender Gap.* Washington, DC: Author.

———. (2001). *Hostile Hallways: Bullying, Teasing and Sexual Harassment in School.* Washington, DC: Author.

BIKLEN, S., AND POLLARD, D., EDS. (1993). *Gender and Education.* Yearbook of the National Society for the Study of Education. Chicago: NSSE.

BLAIR, A. (1997). "How We Got the ERA." Independent Women's Forum. (www.iwf.org/pubs/twq/sp97a.shtml)

BRAKE, D. (1999). "Women's Equity Digest." Equity Research Center. (www.edc.org/WomensEquity/pubs/digests/digest-singlesex.html)

BRENNAN, P. (2002). "Pupils at Single-Sex Schools Excel Research Shows." NewsMax.com. (www.newsmax.com/archives/articles/2002/5/2/155112.shtml)

BROWN, L., AND GILLIGAN, C. (1993). *Meeting at the Crossroads.* Cambridge: Harvard University Press.

Brown v. Board of Education of Topeka, Kansas. (1954). 347 U.S. 483.

CAIRNS, E. (1990). "The Relationship Between Adolescent Perceived Self-Competence and Attendance at Single-Sex Secondary School." *British Journal of Educational Psychology* 60, 210.

CHARLES A. DANA CENTER. (2000). "Gender and the Brain." *The Dana Brain Daybook* 4, 1–4.

CHODOROW, N. (1978). *The Reproduction of Mothering.* Berkley: University of California Press.

COLEY, R. (2001). *Differences in the Gender Gap: Comparisons Across Racial/Ethnic Groups in Education and Work.* Princeton: Educational Testing Service.

THE COLLEGE BOARD. (2002). "Average SAT Scores of Entering College Classes, 1967–2002." (Online: www.collegeboard.com)

CONNELL, R. (1995). *Masculinities.* Berkeley: University of California Press.

———. (1996). "Teaching the Boys: New Research on Masculinity, and Gender Strategies for Schools." *Teachers College Record* 98, 206–235.

DOUGLAS, A. (1977). *The Feminization of American Culture.* New York: Avon Books.

EGAN, T. (2002). "Body-Conscious Boys Adopt Athletes' Taste for Steroids." *The New York Times.* Nov. 22, p. A1.

EVANS, S. (1989). *Born for Liberty: A History of Women in America.* New York: Free Press.

FEDERAL REGISTER. (2002) "Nondiscrimination on the Basis of Sex in Education Programs or Activities Receiving Federal Financial Assistance: Notice of Intent to Regulate." May 8, 31098.

FINE, M., AND WEIS, L. (1999). *The Unknown City.* Boston: Beacon.

FLOOD, C. (2000). "Safe Boys, Safe Schools." *WEEA Digest.* Nov. 1, 3–6.

FRAZIER, N., AND SADKER, M. (1973). *Sexism in School and Society.* New York: Harper & Row.

GAVORA, J. (2001). "Title IX's Flip Side." *Independent Women's Forum.* (www.iwf.org/pubs/exfemina/April 2001c.shtml)

———. (2002). "The Inequity of Gender Equity." *The Chronicle of Higher Education.* May 3, p. B11.

GILBERT, P., AND TAYLOR, S. (1991). *Fashioning the Feminine.* Sydney: Allen & Unwin.

GILLIGAN, C. (1982). *In A Different Voice: Psychological Theory and Women's Development.* Cambridge: Harvard University Press.

GLSEN. (2001). *National School Climate Survey.* New York: Author.

GOLDBERG, S. (1973). *The Inevitability of Patriarchy.* New York: William Morrow.

GRANLEESE, J., AND JOSEPH, S. (1993). "Self-perception Profile of Adolescent Girls at a Single-sex and a Mixed-sex School." *The Journal of Genetic Psychology* 60:210.

HOROWITZ, H. (1984). *Alma Mater.* New York: Knopf.

HOWE, F. (1984). *Myths of Coeducation: Selected Essays.* Bloomington: Indiana University Press.

HUMAN RIGHTS WATCH. (2001). *Hatred in the Hallways.* New York: Author.

KAESTLE, C. (1983). *Pillars of the Republic: Common Schools and American Society 1780–1860.* New York: Hill & Wang.

KAMINER, W. (1998). "The Trouble with Single-Sex Schools." *Atlantic Monthly.* Digital Edition. (www.theatlantic.com/issues/98apr/singlesex.htm)

KESSLER, S., ET AL. (1985). "Gender Relations in Secondary Schooling." *Sociology of Education* 58(8), 34–48.

KIMMEL, M. (2000). "What About the Boys?" *WEEA Digest,* Nov. 1, 1–2, 7–8.

KINDLON, D., ET AL. (1999). *Raising Cain: Protecting the Emotional Life of Boys.* New York: Ballantine.

LARKIN, J. (1997). *Sexual Harassment: High School Girls Speak Out.* Toronto: Second Story Press.

LEE, V. (1998). "Single Sex Secondary Schooling: A Solution to the Problem of Gender Inequity?" In *Separated by Sex.* Washington, DC: AAUW.

LEE, V., AND BRYK, A. (1986). "Effects of Single-sex Secondary Schools on Student Achievement and Attitudes." *Journal of Educational Psychology* 78(5).

MAC AN GHAILL, M. (1994). *The Making of Men: Masculinities, Sexualities and Schooling.* Buckingham: Open University Press.

MCCARTHY, M. R. (1999). "Feminist Pedagogy in Teachers in Catholic Women's High School." *Journal of Women and Religion* (17), 55–68.

MILLER, J. (1976). *Toward A New Psychology of Women.* Boston: Beacon Press.

NATIONAL ASSOCIATION FOR THE ADVANCEMENT OF SINGLE-SEX PUBLIC EDUCATION. (2002). "Notable Quotes." (Home Page: www.singlesexschools.org)

NATIONAL COALITION OF GIRLS SCHOOLS. (2002). (Home Page: www.ncgs.org)

NATIONAL ORGANIZATION FOR WOMEN. (2002). "Redesigning Liberation: Fact Sheet for the Women's Health Project." (www.nowfoundation.org/health/whp/fact5.html)

NATIONAL WOMEN'S LAW CENTER. (2002). "Title IX and Women's Athletic Opportunity: A Nation's Promise Yet to Be Fulfilled." Washington, DC: Author. (Available Online: www.nwlc.org)

PERRY, W. (1996). "Gender Based Education: Why it Works at the Middle School Level." National Association for the Advancement of Single-Sex Public Education. *Bulletin* 80(577).

POLLACK, W. (1999). *Real Boys.* New York: Dimensions.

RAVITCH, D. (2000). *Left Back.* New York: Simon & Schuster.

RIORDAN, C. (1985). "Public and Catholic Schooling: The Effects of Gender Context Policy." *American Journal of Education* 93(4), 518–540.

———. (1990). *Girls and Boys in School: Together or Separate.* New York: Teacher College Press.

———. (1998). "The Future of Single Sex Schools." In American Association of University Women's Educational Foundation, *Separated by Sex.* Washington, DC: AAUW.

RURY, J. (1991). *Education and Women's Work.* Albany: SUNY Press.

SABO, D. (1998). *The Women's Sports Foundation Report: Sport and Teen Pregnancy.* (www.womenssportsfoundation.org/cgi-bin/iowa/issues/body/article.html?record=883)

SADKER, M., AND SADKER, D. (1982). *Sex Equity Handbook for Schools.* New York: Longman.

———. (1994). *Failing at Fairness: How Schools Cheat Girls.* New York: Touchstone.

SEGAL, L. (1990). *Slow Motion: Changing Masculinities, Changing Men.* London: Virago.

SELL, R., AND BECKER, J. (2001). "Sex Orientation Data Collection and Progress toward Healthy People 2010." *American Journal of Public Health,* 91, 76–82.

SKLAR, K. (1993). "The Schooling of Girls and Changing Community Values in Massachusetts Towns 1750–1820." *History of Education Quarterly* 33(4), 511–542.

SMITH, D. (1989) "Femininity as Discourse." In L. Roman, L. Christian-Smith, and E. Ellsworth, eds., *Becoming Feminine: The Politics of Popular Culture.* London: Falmer Press.

———. (1991). *Texts, Facts and Femininity: Exploring the Relations Ruling.* New York: Routledge.

SOLOMON, B. (1986). *In the Company of Educated Women.* New Haven: Yale University Press.

SOMMERS, C. (2000). "The War Against Boys." *Atlantic Monthly.* Digital Edition. (www.theatlantic.com/issues/2000/05/sommers.htm)

SPRING, J. (1997). *The American School 1642–1996.* New York: McGraw Hill.

STOWE, L. (1991). "Should Physics Classes Be Single-sex?" *Physics Teacher* 29(6), 380–381.

STREITMATTER, J. (1997). "An Exploratory Study of Risk-Taking and Attitudes in a Girls Only Middle School Math Class." *Elementary School Journal* 98(1), 15–26.

———. (1998) "Single-sex Classes: Female Physics Students Make their Case." *School Science and Mathematics* 98(7), 369–375.

———. (1999). *For Girls Only.* Albany: SUNY Press.

TOZER, S., VIOLAS, P., AND SENESE, G. (2002). *School and Society: Historical and Contemporary Perspectives.* 4th Ed. Boston: McGraw Hill.

TYACK, D., AND HANSOT, E. (1992). *Learning Together: A History of Coeducation in American Public Schools.* New York: Russell Sage Foundation.

U.S. CENSUS BUREAU. (2000). "Percent of People 25 Years Old and Over Who Have Completed High School Years 1940 to 2000." (www.census.gov/population/socdemo/education/tableA-2txt)

U.S. DEPARTMENT OF EDUCATION. (2000). "Trends in Educational Equity of Girls and Women." Washington, DC: Author.

———. (2001), "1998 High School Transcript Study." Washington, DC: National Center for Educational Statistics. (nces.ed.gov/pubsearch/pubinfo.asp?oybud=2001498)

———. (2002). "Integrated Postsecondary Education Data Systems, Completion Surveys." (http://nces.ed.gov)

U.S. DEPARTMENT OF HEALTH, EDUCATION AND WELFARE. (1978). *Taking Sexism Out of Education: The National Project on Women in Education.* Washington, DC: Author.

U.S. DEPARTMENT OF HEALTH AND HUMAN SERVICES. (2000). "The Registered Nurse Population." *National Sample Survey of Registered Nurses.* Washington, DC: Author.

URBAN, W., AND WAGONER, J. (2000). *American Education: A History.* New York: McGraw-Hill.

VALENTIN, I. (1997). "Title IX: A Brief History." *WEEA Digest.* Aug., 1–8.

WANDLE, C., AND CARPENTER, M. (2001). "Gender Equity Education: Implications for Risk Prevention for All Kids." Poster Session presented at the Annual Conference of the National Association of School Psychologists, Washington, DC. Eric Document ED453490.

WEISTART, J. (1998). "Title IX and Intercollegiate Sports: Equal Opportunity?" *Brookings Review* 16, 30–43.

WHITEHEAD, B. (1998). "The Generation of Gen X." American Enterprise.

WILLIAMS, L., WASSERMAN, J., AND GOODMAN, L. (1997) "Hands Off: Girls Pass a Gauntlet of Gropes in Schools." *Daily News.* June 15, p. 4.

ZINN, H. (1995). *A People's History of the United States.* New York: Harper.

CHAPTER 6

Standards-Based Reform: Real Change or Political Smoke Screen

POSITION 1: STANDARDS-BASED REFORM PROMISES QUALITY EDUCATION FOR ALL STUDENTS

In 1980, The Gannett newspaper chain sent investigative reporters into twenty-two schools in nine states, where they discovered that academic credit was offered for courses such as cheerleading, student government, and mass media. . . . [T]he only statewide requirement for graduation was two years of physical education. . . . The largest proportion [of California's high school students], 45 percent, was in the general track, where a typical student took courses such as typing, cultural awareness, homemaking, beginning restaurant management, food for singles, exploring childhood, and clothing.

—RAVITCH, 2000, PP. 408–409

Americans have faith in their public schools but they have never been entirely satisfied with them. Education always has been the focus of reform. Earlier generations of school reformers were concerned with access, and for good reason. One hundred years ago, only 10 percent of Americans attended secondary schools, and barely 2 percent received degrees (Gardner, 2002). Fewer still could think realistically about college. Before the twentieth century, race, gender, and economic circumstances combined to make it unlikely many students would continue their education beyond elementary school. Previous reforms focused on making schools affordable and accessible to all students, and those efforts were largely successful. Today's reformers have turned their attention to school quality, kindergarten through high school, and this too is for good reason. Americans now ask schools to do more than enroll large numbers of students and pass them along from one grade to another. For citizens to thrive personally and for the nation to prosper as a whole, schools must ensure students have an adequate command of the sciences, social sciences, and humanities. Our economic and political well-being depends on what is learned in schools. As Diane Ravitch puts it, schools must teach students "what knowledge is of most value, how to use that knowledge, how to organize what they know, how to understand the relationship between past and present, how to tell the difference between accurate information and propaganda, and how to turn information into understanding" (Ravitch, 2000, p. 17). Schools across the country must establish high academic standards, and must be accountable for teaching specified levels of content to all the children they enroll.

Standards-Based Reform and America's Underachieving Schools

> Standards can support better learning if they are used to direct teaching toward worthy goals, to promote teaching that is responsive to the ways students learn, to examine students in ways that can be used to inform instruction, to keep students and parents apprised of progress, to trigger specific support for students who need them, and to evaluate school priorities. (Falk, 2002, p. 612)

The 1983 publication of *A Nation at Risk* was the catalyst for today's standards-based reform movement. A short 63-page book, written in direct, simple language without academic jargon, or confusing statistics and tables, it called public attention to serious deficiencies in schools. "Our nation is at risk," the report begins,

> Our once unchallenged preeminence in commerce, industry, science, and technological innovation is being overtaken by competitors throughout the world. . . . What was unimaginable a generation ago has begun to occur—others are matching and surpassing our educational attainments.
>
> If an unfriendly foreign power had attempted to impose on America the mediocre educational performance that exists today, we might have viewed it as an act of war. (National Commission on Excellence in Education, 1983, p. 5)

A sobersided panel of educators, which included college presidents and public school administrators, brought together by the secretary of education, used alarming language to describe the state of K–12 education. Americans were shaken from their quiescence and self-satisfaction. The panel found a host of problems in schools. Among other things, achievement scores on standardized tests were down and international comparisons were embarrassing. Thirteen percent of all 17-year-olds were functionally illiterate, and many of their literate peers could not "draw an inference from written material, write a persuasive essay, or solve a math problem that required more than one or two steps." The report's directness attracted attention of parents, educators, and elected officials. Recommendations for public education were straightforward: (1) improve education for all students, and (2) develop more rigorous and measurable standards. American education had to chart a higher, more rigorous, course and measure student progress more systematically.

National changes in education always are painfully slow. Schooling in the United States is left largely to the states. Most of the funding, and until recently, all the expectations for student performance are under the general control of the 50 states and administered by 15,000 school districts. Local control of schooling is part of the American tradition of education. In the 1980s, however,

President George H. Bush was willing to set aside tradition to assert the role of the federal government in encouraging higher national standards for public education. He recognized that states by themselves were not able to bring about necessary national changes.

President Bush believed the nation needed to establish world-class national standards in core subject areas, and to make sure that students were meeting these standards, his administration called for voluntary testing in grades 4, 8, and 12. In 1989, at a conference in Charlottesville, Virginia, President Bush and the nation's governors agreed to six national goals for education. "America 2000," as the goals became known, stipulated that by the year 2000,

1. All children will start school ready to learn.
2. The high school graduation rate will increase to 90 percent.
3. All students in grades 4, 8, and 12 will demonstrate competency in English, math, science, civics and foreign language, economics, arts, history, and geography.
4. U.S. students will be first in math and science achievement.
5. Every adult will be literate.
6. Every school in the U.S. will be free of drugs and violence, and the unauthorized presence of firearms and alcohol. (Jennings, 1998, p. 14)

In 1994, Congress added additional goals to improve the quality of teacher education and increase parental involvement in schools. These proposals would take education reform in a new direction. In the past, government initiatives, at the state and national levels, had focused principally on *minimum* standards, for example, the *lowest* acceptable level of reading or mathematics necessary before schools promoted a student or issued a diploma. America 2000 encouraged high standards and high national expectations for all students. The federal government would not intrude on the states' control of education, but it could urge them to raise the academic bar. The standards proposed by President Bush were not designed to serve as a national curriculum. Instead, they were to be academic models state and local school districts could adopt to raise expectations for teachers and students. Improved state standards promised national reform. Variations would continue to be found across state lines, but students, parents, and teachers in every state would know what was expected of them. Schools of education were asked to equip prospective and in-service teachers with the skills needed to help students meet the new standards. Test makers were asked to develop examinations keyed to the standards. By design, all students were to benefit from the standards movement.

Although the timetable proved to be overly optimistic, President Bush's call for high national standards and assessment of student performance set the stage for substantive reform in the quality of education. In 1992, Bill Clinton was elected president. Mr. Clinton, as governor, had been active in the 1989 education conference. A year later, President Clinton proposed "Goals 2000," a legislative package that, if it had been enacted, would have set into law the six national goals for education agreed to by George Bush and the nation's governors. Under President Bush, the Department of Education provided grants to national organizations of scholars and teachers to develop voluntary national standards in important school subjects. President Clinton's administration provided funds for states to develop standards of their own at about the same time national standards were being released. The issue grew murky with both states and national organizations developing academic standards simultaneously. President Clinton tried to help by agreeing to support state standards as long as states volunteered to go along with national testing. However, the ensuing confusion between state and national standards and difficulty of assessing fifty state systems through one national test hindered the progress of school reform until 2002.

"No Child Left Behind Act," 2002

The No Child Left Behind (2002a) legislation, supported by large majorities of Democrats and Republicans in both houses of Congress, and signed by President George W. Bush, is designed to create a stronger, more accountable education system. It does not call for national standards or national tests, as Presidents Bush and Clinton had advocated. The legislation shifts the action back to the states. Under the new law, states are required to develop their own standards for what students should know at every grade level in math and English/language arts and science. When the specific standards are in place—stipulating the level at which a child should be reading by the end of third grade, for example—the states are to assess every student's progress with exams aligned with state standards. Assessments will be phased in, and by the 2005–2006 school year, states are to conduct annual tests for all children in grades three through eight. States are required to develop a "single statewide accountability system" to ensure schools and school districts—not individual students—are making "adequate yearly progress" in math, reading/language arts, and by 2005–2006, in science. Progress is to be demonstrated for all students, with "separate measurable annual objectives" for (1) economically disadvantaged students, (2) students from major racial and ethnic groups, (3) students with disabilities, and (4) students with limited English proficiency. By 2014, twelve years from the enactment of the legislation, "all students were to meet the proficient level on state tests." The legislation requires each school, school district, and state to make "adequate yearly progress[1]" toward meeting state standards. Parents with children in failing schools are given the right to have them transferred to better-performing schools. Students who have been victims of violent crimes and those who attend persistently unsafe schools also will be allowed to transfer schools (No Child Left Behind, 2002a).

Three presidents, two Republicans and one Democrat, established the priorities for the school reform agenda in the early twenty-first century. They agree that to improve the nation's schools, the United States should develop a system of high state standards and rigorous state testing. Setting high standards for all students nationwide is the appropriate point of departure for building better schools. The

[1]As defined on the "No Child Left Behind" (2002b) website, Adequate Yearly Progress (AYP) is "an individual state's measure of yearly progress toward achieving state academic standards. AYP is the minimum level of improvement the states, school districts, and schools must achieve each year." (p. 2)

standards movement will help *all* students. This is a significant policy shift in itself. Currently U.S. schools sort students into various categories by academic ability, and treat different groups of students differently. The most able students are provided college-preparatory curricula of reasonably high quality. For all other students—in many cases, the vast majority of students—the curriculum is watered down, ineffective, and unlikely to equip them with the skills and knowledge needed for economic success and the common store of knowledge necessary for informed civic participation. The standards movement is designed to bring all students up to higher levels of academic performance, no matter where they begin (Tucker and Codding, 1998). An education built around academic standards will serve students from poor as well as wealthy homes, and it will be especially valuable to students who, in the course of their education, move from school to school or district to district. It should be self-evident that students are likely to learn more when there is common agreement about what they are supposed to learn and high expectations for their achievement. In fact, the logic of standards-based school reform is so obvious and compelling that one may wonder why it is referred to as a *reform movement* (Bennett et al., 1999, p. 586).

Impact on Poor and Minority Children

Support for the standards movement rests on the assumption that the subject matter students learn in school is important: content counts. The store of knowledge possessed by individuals operates to determine success or failure in school and, to a large measure, success or failure in life (Hirsch, 1996). That is to say, individuals who know more, those who have a greater store of knowledge, are more successful in school, and tend to be more successful in getting into college, securing employment, and earning higher-than-average salaries. Subject matter knowledge is the very essence of education. It is important to be able to read, but it is more important what is read. Students who study and understand Dickens, Shakespeare, and Virginia Woolf are more likely to succeed than students who read less important, less challenging works. It is not enough for schools to pass students along from grade to grade simply because they attend regularly and display adequate reading, math, and computer skills. States must establish content standards appropriate for success, and students must demonstrate command of subject matter and academic skills at the level described in the standards. Schools should not focus only on "critical thinking," "library skills," "keyboarding," or other warm and fuzzy objectives. It is the content of education that matters.

When schools focus on process goals—for example, thinking skills, self-esteem exercises, discovery techniques, cooperative learning strategies—all students suffer because they learn less subject matter content (Hirsch, 1996; Bennett, Finn, and Cribb, 1999). Any approach to learning that emphasizes a process approach limits the futures of children by denying them access to intellectual capital—that is, the store of knowledge needed to do well in school and life. All children are harmed by a content-light approach, but children of the poor will be affected the most. Children from middle-class homes can count on their parents to compensate for schools' inattention to subject matter. They are likely to benefit from the company of literate adults, family trips, and private tutors to help them with foreign language acquisition, music and art, and mathematics. The negative effects of watered-down content, low standards, and low expectations fall hardest on the poor and students from less well-educated families. For these students, standards reform can produce dramatic improvements.

Consider one example, from Mount Vernon, New York, a working-class, minority suburb of New York City. Following the national model, New York State developed standards and assessment tests for all children, and initially the tests proved to be an embarrassment to the state's cities. Only 36 percent of Mount Vernon's fourth graders, for example, passed the English/Language Arts (ELA) test. Instead of rolling over and playing dead or attacking the tests, however, Ronald Ross, a newly appointed school superintendent, decided to tackle the real problem head-on. Ross examined the test and decided that it asked reasonable things of students and encouraged the teaching of worthwhile content. For example, fourth graders were expected to read stories and poems, chart the chronology of each, understand their imagery, and write an essay using the content from both the story and the poem. Ross decided that the ELA test was of educational value, and teaching to the test would help students learn more skills and content than they had in the past. Teaching to the test would lead students and teachers along a higher curricular path. Children took books home every night and read for at least 30 minutes; they wrote every day; teachers drilled them, and prepared them to meet state standards. The following year, the fourth graders at the lowest-achieving school improved their passing rate from 13 to 82 percent (Taub, 2002, p. 49).

In the world of education, a phrase such as "teaching to the test" sounds like heresy, and stressing content over process may seem like a renunciation of the progressive pedagogical creed. For decades, teachers have been told to "teach the individual child" and build content around the "interests of each child"—mantralike aphorisms offered by people who are well meaning but misinformed. Unfortunately, the "child-centered" approach led to the "dumbing down" of the school curriculum, and test results indicate students were not learning enough of value. The standards-reform movement asks states and school districts to develop high standards and reasonable tests that hold schools accountable for teaching worthwhile material. It may not be as much fun for students as a child-centered approach to learning, and may not sound lofty and inspiring, but will be more beneficial for children in the long run. As one writer notes, "In the world of education, a great deal of power attaches to practices that are aesthetically appealing; but justice is very often better served by the merely effective" (Taub, 2002, p. 50).

Standards, Indicators, and Test Items: An Example from Mathematics

The standards movement is well under way. The effort to develop academically appropriate standards has been ongoing for more than a decade. Some disciplines are ahead of others, and some states are further along the path to standards-based teaching and assessment, but changes are occurring everywhere. The field of school mathematics offers a good example of progress made in one K–12 discipline. Since 1989, the National Council of Teachers of Mathematics (NCTM) has released a series of documents that has produced high-quality, thoughtful reform. The NCTM recommends that math instruction move away from memorization of isolated facts and focus attention on mathematical problem solving and teaching mathematical concepts. Based on NCTM recommendations states developed their own math standards and curriculum frameworks. State standards usually are written by experts in the field—mathematicians, math educators and math teachers—and cover the range of content knowledge students need to know. The website of one state explains its math standards are designed, "To enable all of [the state's] children to acquire the mathematical skills, understandings, and attitudes they will need to be successful in their careers and daily lives."[2] This very general math objective then is fleshed out, organized by topics, and applied appropriately to various grade levels in the form of "standards "and "grade-level indicators." Consider the standard for "statistics and probability," a subset of the state's more general math objective. It reads,

> All students will develop an understanding of the statistics and probability and will use them to represent and analyze relationships among variable quantities and to solve problems.

Most states have developed between five and fifteen global standards in mathematics, and to make them understandable to students and their parents, and workable for teachers and administrators, each state has developed substandards, referred to as "grade-level indicators" that offer specificity and practical classroom guidance. Consider one "grade-level indicator" that has established expectations for what fourth-graders should know and be able to do in the area of "statistics and probability." It requires students

> Read, interpret, construct, analyze, generate questions about, and draw inferences from displays of data.

This grade-level indicator is quite specific and allows teachers to apply the state's standards to children in their classes. Teachers know what they are expected to teach, what their students should know, and how their students will be assessed. The open-ended test item given here, designed to assess students' command of "statistics and probability" in the fourth grade, is similar to one that appeared on the state exam. It reads,

> Mr. Jones gave each of the students in his class a one-ounce box of raisins. When the students opened the boxes and counted the raisins, they found different amounts. Here are the numbers of raisins they found in 16 boxes: 13, 12, 15, 14, 12, 10, 13, 15, 12, 11, 13, 10, 14, 13, 14, 12. Construct a bar graph to present the students' finding on the grid in your answer booklet. Be sure to label your graph correctly. If you opened another box of raisins, how many would you expect to have? Explain why.

[2]Our examples, typical of the field, are taken from the New Jersey standards in mathematics (New Jersey Department of Education [2002]).

At the eighth-grade level, one of the grade-level indicators for the "statistics and probability" standard reads,

> Select and use appropriate representations for sets of data and appropriate measures of central tendency.

To assess the extent to which eighth-grade students were able to perform at the expected level, the state exam included this short-answer item:

> On five tests of 100 points, José has an average of exactly 90. What is the lowest score he could have made on any one of the five tests?

A multiple-choice item for the same indicator on the state test reads,

> In Mrs. Smith's 7th grade class, students' heights are as follows: 59", 60", 62", 62", 63", 65", 66", 67", 72". For these nine students, the mean is 64", and the median is 63", and the mode is 62". Which of the following describes how the mean, median, and mode are affected if a new student enters whose height is 64"?
>
> a. The mean, median, and mode all remain the same.
> b. The mean and mode remain the same, but the median changes.
> c. The mean and median remain the same, but the mode changes.
> d. Only the mean remains the same.

While math may not become fun for every student, at the very least on a statewide basis, more math will be taught at a higher level to all students. Teachers will know what they are expected to teach; parents will know what their children are expected to learn; and the state math test will measure what is being taught in math classes. All students will receive higher-quality instruction thanks to standards-based reforms. The NCTM believes that mathematics is a subject matter for every student, not just the few who may have the unusual talents needed by future engineers or scientists. All students deserve high-quality mathematics education. The NCTM argues that, "All interested parties must work together to create mathematics classrooms where students of varied background and abilities work with expert teachers, learning important mathematical ideas with understanding, in environments that are equitable, challenging, supportive, and technologically equipped for the twenty-first century" (NCTM, 2002).

The Logic of Standards

Advocates of standards-based reform in education offer several arguments to support their position, and they encourage you to think about the issue with these points in mind:

- Content matters in education. For personal economic success and for the civic well-being of the nation, students should possess a reasonable command of a common store of agreed-upon content in math and literature, and the social, natural and biological sciences.
- States must establish high, appropriate, and reasonable content standards for all students, and hold schools accountable for teaching that body of knowledge.

- Schools will be better places for children when curriculum planners stipulate in the clearest language possible what students should know and be able to do.
- Students are advantaged when schools test what is taught. The goal of assessment is to ensure that students have learned what is contained in the curriculum.
- Teacher-led instruction and other forms of explicit instruction are among the many effective methods for leading students to a consideration of subject matter. Book learning, memorization, and drill are part of successful instruction (Evers, 2001).
- High standards and curriculum-based testing will improve the quality of education for all students. The evidence suggests that common curriculum standards and curriculum-based tests increase academic achievement and decrease the achievement gap between rich and poor students (Hirsch, 2001, p. 201).
- Standards-based reform is more than making sure students do better on tougher tests. The standards-reform movement is less about imposing rigor than it is a program for ensuring academic and personal success for all students.

POSITION 2: STANDARDS-BASED REFORM IS A POLITICAL SMOKE SCREEN

Over the past year, I have been asking members of groups to which I speak to select from four items the one they believe to have the most *promise for improving our schools . . .*

- *standards and tests mandated by all states;*
- *a qualified, competent teacher in every classroom;*
- *nonpromotion and grade retention for all students who fail to reach grade-level standards on the tests; and*
- *schools of choice for all parents.*

From an audience of about a thousand people at the 2001 National School Boards Association conference, one person chose the first. All *the rest chose the second, which usually is the unanimous choice, whatever the group.*

—GOODLAD, 2002, P. 20

Advocates of the standards movement argue that their reform was born in response to a crisis. *A Nation at Risk* (National Commission on Excellence in Education, 1983), the much-cited instigator of standards reform, describes a national crisis brought about by anemic academic standards. The report argues teachers are not teaching well, and students are not learning very much of value in schools. International comparisons of student achievement reflect so poorly on U.S. students that the result is considered a national tragedy for all Americans. The authors of the report argue that Americans face a crisis, economically and politically. They claim schools have let the nation down, and the nation is now in peril. If this were all true, an academic call-to-arms would be in order. The data and arguments of the report, however, defy common sense and do not stand up to even modest academic scrutiny. It's been 20 years since the publication of *A Nation at Risk*. In that time, the United States has experienced unprecedented prosperity and economic growth. American achievements in science, technology, and medicine are the envy of the world. When Nobel Prize winners are announced, you can bet half your SAT score that Americans will figure prominently among the winners. Everything is not perfect in education, but it is not crumbling and certainly not in crisis. The jeremiads are not to be believed.

A Nation at Risk helped promote the myth of a failing public school system, and it is used for political purposes with little if anything to do with academic quality. Berliner and Biddle (1995) argue that the authors of the report distorted the picture of American schools. Standardized test scores are not in decline. In fact, test results from the National Assessment of Educational Progress are inching upward every year. While there are still too many poor and failing schools, there is no evidence of systemic collapse, and overheated rhetoric and questionable comparisons do not match the facts. The charges, the authors say, are "errant nonsense."

> If we go by the evidence, despite greatly expanded student enrollment, the average American high school and college student is now doing as well, or perhaps slightly better than, that student did in previous years. Indeed, not only is student achievement remaining steady or rising slowly across the land, but so also is student intelligence. And when comparative-study evidence is examined carefully, that evidence also confirms impressive strengths of American education. (p. 64)

Errant nonsense or not, *A Nation at Risk* focused attention on school reform for the first time in a generation. The report, widely publicized by journalists, made Americans suspicious of their schools. While some politicians and school reformers saw this as an honest opportunity to create sounder academic standards, others seized on the bad news to attack schools and advance their own agendas. Those on the far right in religion and politics used the "manufactured crisis" as an opportunity to take control of schools and ban ideas they found ideologically distasteful. Only with national and statewide curricula could ultraconservatives be assured that disquieting local voices—advocates of gay rights, abortion rights, and birth control, for example—could be kept out of schools. Other more centrist conservatives wanted schools to return to the "good old days," before they had been captured by "social experimentalists," advocates of whole language, new math, and sex education in schools (Berliner and Biddle, 1995). The report also serves the political agenda of home schoolers, voucher supporters, and other advocates of alternatives to public schools (Bracey, 2000; Gardner, 2002). The publication of *A Nation At Risk* not only fueled the myth of failing schools, it also paved the way for a conservative reform agenda and business solutions to educational problems.

Risks of Business Rationality in Education

> Transformed into classroom managers overseeing student-workers, teachers became further disengaged from the nature of teaching, as they were galvanized to follow prescribed "teaching recipes" in the form of pre-formulated lesson plans. With the rise of pre-packaged instructional materials, intellectual engagement with the curriculum now becomes, for many teachers, a luxury, as they were transformed into the managers of learning. (Weil, 2001, p. 62)

McNeil (2000) and Horn and Kincheloe (2001) provide instructive histories of the Texas standards movement, a statewide effort influenced by Ross Perot, the businessman and onetime presidential candidate. Perot, appointed head of a state commission on education reform, argues that if something is proved to be effective in business management, it must be good for education. Many in Texas were persuaded by this argument, as well as by Mr. Perot's history of business success and his personal style. Perot distrusts middle management. It is a lesson he learned from business. Mr. Perot likes to control things from the top, and he had found mid-level managers an obstacle to change and champions of the status quo. Middle managers in business like things the way they are, he argues, and he believes this also is true in education. Perot places the blame for Texas's education problems at the doorsteps of school administrators, education's middle managers, and he is convinced they are opponents of reform and incompetent. He endears himself to teachers by exempting them from blame and deriding their bosses. He argues that school administrators do not have the ability to lead or the sense to get out of the way. "Half of them," Perot said, poking fun at their backgrounds in coaching, "still have whistles around their necks." (Thomas Toch quoted in McNeil, 2000, p. 179).

The consequences of Perot's reforms have been profound and largely negative. Ross Perot and the school reform committee he chaired advocate top-down management and a centralized system designed to bypass Texas school administrators and hasten school reforms. Schools have to be changed quickly and all at once. Otherwise, he says, middle managers, "the good ol' boys at the local level would incrementalize them to death" (McNeil, 2000, p. 186). Following Mr. Perot's advice, the Texas legislature tried to reform schools as if they were a large, foundering business. Linda McNeil argues that school reform failed in Texas because what works for a business does not necessarily work in education. Texas legislators, she writes, tried to simplify and standardize everything about classroom processes: planning, teaching, and assessment. They attempted to "teacher-proof" the curriculum with a checklist for teacher behaviors and tests of student minimum skills. This might be an effective way to reform a production-line industry, but is the wrong approach for education, and is particularly damaging to the brightest and most thoughtful teachers.

> By doing so, they made schools exceedingly comfortable for mediocre teachers who like to teach routine lessons according to a standard sequence and format, who like working as de-skilled laborers not having to think about their work. They made being a Texas public school teacher extremely uncomfortable for those who know their subjects well, who teach in ways that engage

> their students, who match their teaching to reflect their own continued learning. (McNeil, 2000, p. 187)

A business focus on schools distorts an understanding of teachers' work and the critical role teachers play in education. It fails to take into account teachers' ability to encourage or discourage students, to bring out their potential or thwart it, to open students to new worlds of understanding or to close them off. Business solutions are overly simple, with an emphasis on uniformity of outcomes and achievement measured along a single plane. Success in business is determined by profits and growth. According to a business model, school success could be measured by test scores and increases in the number of test-takers who improve. The emphasis on scores and statewide achievement measures is too narrow a measure for schools. It is, McNeil (2000) writes, as if the multiple dimensions of a well-rounded well-educated child had been reduced to a "stick figure." The narrowness of statewide testing fails to capture important dimensions of learning. While testing may indicate whether children can indent paragraphs or reduce fractions, it does not begin to capture a student's social awareness, civic responsibility, creativity and imagination, and emotional development. Learning reduced to the measurable leaves out more than it can report. As John Goodlad notes, "The American people have looked to their schools not only for the teaching of reading, writing, and figuring, but also for the civilizing of their offspring. They have said over and over that they want it all from their schools: the development of personal, social, vocational, and academic attributes" (Goodlad, 2002, p. 20).

Education's embrace of business models is not surprising. First of all, American business, measured by profits and losses, is both an unqualified success and easy to understand. *A Nation at Risk* (National Commission on Excellence in Education,1983) tied education and business together and frightened readers with threats to their economic comfort. Schooling must attend to the "new basics" or the American system was at risk. According to the report,

> The risk is not only that the Japanese make automobiles more efficiently than Americans and have government subsidies for development and export. It is not just that the South Koreans recently built the world's most efficient steel mill, or that American machine tools, once the pride of the world, are being displaced by German products. It is also that these developments signify a redistribution of trained capability throughout the globe. Knowledge, learning, information, and skilled intelligence are the new raw materials of international commerce. . . . (pp. 6–7)

Think about the best teachers you had in school. It is quite likely they all had high standards for your work, but did they simply take someone else's standards off the shelf and apply them? Did they use prepackaged lessons or did they craft standards based on what they knew about you and your classmates and what they imagined you would like to read, explore, and think about? Were your best teachers the efficient managers of someone else's plan for your education or were they the personal planners and evaluators for you and others in your class? How would you describe your best teachers?

Jonathan Kozol says the best teachers he knows are poets at heart who love the unpredictable aspects of teaching and uniqueness of every child in their classes. That's why, he argues, they are drawn to teaching children and not to business school. Teaching to standards that are not their own will make teachers technicians, and the classroom will lose its best teachers. Kozol writes,

> If we force them to be a little more than the obedient floor managers for industry, they won't remain in public schools. The price will be too high. The poetry will have turned to prose: the worst kind too, the prose of experts who know every single thing there is to know except their own destructiveness. (Kozol, 2000, p. xii, in Cohen and Rogers, 2000)

Costs of High-Stakes Testing

> "Three in a Row? No. No. No." (Three answers of "b" in a row on a multiple choice test? No. No. No.)
>
> One of several cheers taught to students at their daily pep rallies on test taking strategies for the TAAS test [Texas Assessment of Academic Skills]. (McNeil, 2000, p. 229)

In the 1980s, the nation was deluged with reports critical of public education.[3] The standards movement promised a quick fix, and like all quick fixes, it is overly simplistic and accompanied by problems. State accountability systems tied to common standards placed students and school personnel in thralldom to testing companies. Multiple-choice tests have become the assessment tool of choice for most states, and they involve high stakes. Students who do poorly on state tests may not be promoted or graduated. The building principal's salary and his or her job continuation may depend on the school's scores (FairTest, 2002a). Art and music, typically not part of standards assessments, tend to disappear from many schools, and upper-level science electives, such as marine biology or biochemistry, also may fall victim to the standards movement because they are not tested (McNeil, 2000). In many school districts, a good part of the school year is now given over to test preparation. When teachers take weeks and months from the regular curriculum to teach students test-preparation skills, it cannot be known for certain if subsequent gains in test scores result from real advances in learning and improvements in the quality of education or if higher scores reflect the impact of drill and repetition, and an improvement mainly in test-taking skills (McKeon, Marcella, and McLaren, 2001). High-stakes multiple-choice tests have few fans in the education community. Practitioners and researchers in education believe that to capture the full range of a student's skill and knowledge, it is necessary to use

[3]For examples written during the same period that were equally critical of public education, see: Adler, M. J. (1982). *The Paideia Proposal;* Boyer, E. L. (1983). *High School: A Report on Secondary Education in America;* Goodlad, J. L. (1984). *A Place Called School: Prospects for the Future;* Twentieth Century Fund. (1983). *Making the Grade: Report of the Twentieth Century Fund Task Force in Federal Elementary and Secondary Education;* and Sizer, T. R. (1984). *Horace's Compromise: The Dilemma of the American High School.*

an array of techniques, designed by classroom teachers, and administered over time. In addition to standardized tests, assessments should use authentic measures, portfolios reviews, and essay exams that measure academic subtleties and the complexities of thinking (Janesick, 2001a). The education research community has opposed single "high-stakes" measures. Consider Table 6.1, the position the American Educational Research Association, the nation's largest organization dedicated to the scientific study of education.

In some states, the major problem with the standards movement is the poor alignment among its three elements: the standards themselves, resources available to the school for helping students reach the standards, and instruments used to

Table 6.1 High Stakes Testing in Pre K–12 Education Position Statement of the American Educational Research Association (excerpted). Adopted July 2000.

1. Protection Against High-Stakes Decisions Based on a Single Test
   Decisions that affect individual students' life chances or educational opportunities should not be made on the basis of test scores alone. . . . [W]hen there is credible evidence that a test score may not adequately reflect a student's true proficiency, alternative acceptable means should be provided by which to demonstrate attainment of the tested standards.
2. Adequate Resources and Opportunity to Learn
   [I]t must be shown that the tested content has been incorporated into the curriculum, materials, and instruction students are provided before high-stakes consequences are imposed for failing examinations.
3. Validation for Each Separate Intended Use
   Test valid for one use may be invalid for another.
4. Full Disclosure of Likely Negative Consequences of High-Stakes Testing Programs
   Where credible scientific evidence suggests that a given type of testing program is likely to have negative effects, test developers and users should make a serious effort to explain these possible effects to policy makers.
5. Alignment Between the Test and the Curriculum
   Both the content of the test and the cognitive process engaged in taking the test should adequately represent the curriculum. High-stakes tests should not be limited to that portion of the relevant curriculum that is easiest to measure.
6. Careful Adherence to Explicit Rules Determining Which Students Are to be Tested
   When schools, districts, or other administrative units are compared to one another or when changes in scores are tracked over time, there must be explicit policies specifying which students are to be tested. . . .
7. Sufficient Reliability for Each Intended Use
   Reliability refers to the accuracy or precision of test scores. It must be shown that scores reported for individuals or for schools are sufficiently accurate to support each intended interpretation.
8. Ongoing Evaluation of Intended and Unintended Effects of High-Stakes Testing

Source: www.aera.net/about/policy/stakes.htm

assess learning. Often, the rush to develop assessment instruments outpaced the development of new curricula and teaching approaches necessary to implement new high-standards learning (McKeon, Marcella, and McLaren, 2001, p. 5). It has proved to be a far easier process to write multiple-choice tests than to revamp curriculum and instruction. Teachers and administrators, buried in the work of developing new, more rigorous programs, looked up from their curriculum work only to find that evaluation instruments were already in place. As has happened all too frequently in education, the tests were completed and ready to go before the curricula and matching teaching strategies had been designed. The tests were driving the reform, and in many cases the new curricula did not match the new tests. The tests were measuring content and skills that had not been introduced to students. The result has been confusion known as "misalignment": accountability systems not matched to the curriculum or classroom instruction. One set of skills and knowledge is being taught and another set of skills and knowledge is being tested.

Equity

> The back-to-basics movement is historically rooted primarily in the mistaken notion that sameness produces equity. Nothing could be further from the truth. One would have to look far and wide to find evidence that standardization brings up the bottom-scoring students. (Janesick, 2001a, p. 163)

Students come to school with various backgrounds and differing sets of academic advantages and disadvantages. More than 10 percent of children come from homes where English is not the primary language. One in five children lives in poverty. These children typically test poorly and have trouble with math, science, and language arts (McKeon, Marcella, and McLaren, 2001). The nation may well be in crisis, Deborah Meir argues, but it's not the crisis described by the authors of *A Nation at Risk*. The real crisis, she says, is one of equity and justice for our most vulnerable citizens: the children of the poor. The United States spends "less on child welfare—baby care, medical care, family leave—than almost every foreign counterpart," and in the United States, the gap between rich and poor is greater than in other advanced industrial countries, while "our high rate of and investment in incarceration places us in a class by ourselves." (Meir, 2000, pp. 12–13)

The real crisis facing the United States is social, not academic. Children who come to school hungry and poor are not likely to be helped by more rigorous standards. Children with children of their own and children from abusive homes are unlikely to see their lives improve through statewide accountability plans. The real crisis is more appropriately measured not by test scores but by dropout rates, unemployment statistics, and the juvenile incarceration rate. By itself, the standards-based reform movement will not affect deeper social problems. The standards movement can be thought of as a new kind of discrimination. Under the guise of fairness, offering all students the same curriculum, same forms of instruction, and same objective assessments, students from less wealthy homes with less well-educated parents are denied the education they need. With its emphasis on drill and repetitive practice for the exams, the standards movement has increased classroom tedium and time spent on numbing routine. High-stakes testing has added stress and the threat of failure. The negative impact of standards reform has fallen hardest on poor and minority students. In Texas, the graduation rate for minority students has decreased since the beginning of the standards movement (McNeil, 2000). Increasing numbers of poor-performing students have been pushed out of school made less pleasant by the changes brought by standards reform.

This is not a new phenomenon. Variables of class and race have always had high correlations with the dropout rate. SAT scores, for example, of both white and black students are influenced by social class. Low parental income predicts low SAT scores, and the higher the family income, the higher the scores for both races. The black-white test gap narrows at the highest income levels. It helps to have wealthy parents if you want to score well on standardized tests (Lemann, 1999). The relationship between achievement and social factors should not be a surprise in a society where race and class weigh so heavily in so much of life. Supporters of the standards movement pretend that academic achievement is more important than anything else in securing a job. However, educational attainment is less likely to predict who will get into college or land a good job than race and class (Caputo-Pearl, 2001; Ross, 2001). The standards movement is a smoke screen. Under competitive economic systems, not everyone is expected to prosper equally. Supporters of standards pretend to sort winners and losers by academic achievement, as if academic achievement were not proxies for race and class, the real variables that determine who will succeed and who will fail in life.

Standards Alone Cannot Solve the Problems of Schooling

> All too often, standards have "raised the bar" for students, educators, and schools without the accompanying resources and support needed to make standards-based education work. (McKeon, Marcella, and McLaren, 2001, p. 2)

Everyone wants to improve schools and raise the levels of learning. No one is opposed to standards, but higher standards alone are not likely to offer help for the range of school-based problems. We have argued a number of points: (1) the so-called crisis in education that gave rise to the standards movement is largely manufactured; (2) the key to better schools is not likely to be realized through imposition of more rigorous standards; (3) standards-based reform makes inappropriate use of a model borrowed from business; (4) the standards approach to school reform discourages the best teachers; (5) the standards movement has been confusing to everyone involved because of the misalignment of standards, teaching practices, and the means of assessment; (6) high-stakes testing puts unnecessary stress on students; (7) standards ignore issues of equity, and (8) standards-based reformers rarely mention the real problems of schools: poverty, social injustice, and national inattention to issues of equity. In addition, the standards movement has many unresolved issues and questions that should make you cautious. Look carefully at these issues before you jump on the standards bandwagon.

Unresolved Issues

- *Where is teacher and administrator involvement?* Teachers and administrators should be involved in developing local standards for their students. The people at the school level know best what is needed in the community and what will work in classes. To exclude them is to deny their knowledge and skills. To mandate curriculum and the means of assessment at the state level is to intrude on local authority and the academic freedom of teachers and principals.
- *Can coerced reform produce positive changes?* Top-down school reform is arrogant and unwarranted. The failure to bring teachers and administrators into the reform effort decreases the likelihood that standards reform will be effective. Excluding parents and other community members is undemocratic, insulting, and irresponsible (Kohn, 1999).
- *One standard fits none.* Outside of a very few core standards, there is no compelling reason that all students of a state should be held to the same standards. Such uniformity penalizes the highest achieving students as well as those who have the most difficulty in school.
- *Retention in grade may be as bad as social promotion.* No matter how good the tests may be and how poorly a student may perform on them, retention in grade should be used sparingly. The dangers of grade retention may be as great as the risks of social promotion: "Grade retention has repeatedly proven to be counterproductive: students who are retained do not improve academically, are emotionally damaged by retention, suffer a loss of interest in school and self-esteem, and are more likely to drop out of school" (FairTest, 2002b, p. 2).
- *Beware of the promise of "school choice."* This might well prove to be a phoney promise. According to the legislation signed in 2002, "Parents with a child enrolled in a failing school will be able to transfer their child to a better performing public school or public charter school. Charter Schools are independent public schools designed and operated by educators, parents, community leaders, educational entrepreneurs, and others. They are sponsored by designated local or state educational organizations, who monitor their quality and effectiveness but allow them to operate outside of the traditional system of public schools" (No Child Left Behind, 2002a, p. 2). However, the promise of school choice may well prove to be impossible unless there are enough seats in better-performing schools available for all of those who want to transfer.

Reform movements with so many problems and so many unresolved issues should be greeted with suspicion. Who will be served by standards-based reform? Who will be disadvantaged? Is this real reform or the smoke and mirrors of sham reform? Standards-based reform is taking schools in the wrong direction and ignoring the real problems. It seems likely to discourage teachers and administrators while doing little to improve education for most students. We are puzzled how this can be termed "reform."

For Discussion

1. Education writer Alfie Kohn begins one of his books with this description:

   > Abigail is given plenty of worksheets to complete in class as well as a substantial amount of homework. She studies to get good grades, and her school is proud of its high standardized test scores. Outstanding students are publicly recognized by the use of honor rolls, awards assemblies, and bumper stickers. Abigail's teacher, a charismatic lecturer, is clearly in control of the class: students raise their hands and wait patiently to be recognized. The teacher prepares detailed lesson plans well ahead of time, uses the latest textbooks, and gives regular quizzes to make sure the kids stay on track (Kohn, 1999, p. 1).

   Kohn, who argues that tougher standards can be destructive of good education, asks, What's wrong with this picture? And he answers, "Just about everything." What do you think he finds objectionable here? How do you think Kohn would describe Abigail's class if she were enjoying what he believes is a "good education"?
2. Representatives of school districts with a long record of academic success, strong teachers, and solid curricula argue they should be exempted from statewide testing aimed at assessing minimal standards. Representatives of low-achieving and minority districts argue statewide testing is increasing the dropout rate because it frustrates students who score poorly. They too want to be exempted from statewide tests. Should state officials accede to the demands of one side or the other? Both?
3. The United States has a history of local instead of national control of education. Great Britain had moved toward national control, and France has long had a national system of education. Would U.S. education be improved if we moved in the direction of national control with national standards and national examinations?

References

BENNETT, W. J., FINN, C. E., AND CRIBB, J. T. E. (1999). *The Educated Child: A Parent's Guide from Preschool through Eighth Grade*. New York: Free Press.

BERLINER, D. C., AND BIDDLE, B. J. (1995). *The Manufactured Crisis: Myths, Fraud, and the Attack on America's Public Schools*. Reading, MA: Addison-Wesley.

BRACEY, G. W. (2000). *Bail Me Out! Handling Difficult Data and Tough Questions About Public Schools*. Thousand Oaks, CA: Corwin.

CAPUTO-PERL, A. (2001). "Challenging High-Stakes Testing: Building an Antiracist, Progressive, Social Movement in Public Education." In J. L. Kincheloe and D. Weil, eds., *Standards and Schooling in the United States, An Encyclopedia*. Santa Barbara, CA: ABC-CLIO.

COHEN, J., AND ROGERS, J., EDS. (2000). *Will Standards Save Public Education?* Boston: Beacon.

EVERS, W. M. (2001). "Standards and Accountability." In T. M. Moe, ed., *A Primer on America's Schools*. Stanford: Hoover Institution.

FAIRTEST. (2002a). Initial FairTest Analysis of ESEA as passed by Congress, Dec. 2001. (www.fairtest.org/nattest/ESEA.html)

———. (2002b). The Dangerous Consequences of High-Stakes Standardized Testing. (www.fairtest.org/facts/DangerousConsequences.html)

FALK, B. (2002). "Standards-Based Reform: Problems and Possibilities." *Phi Delta Kappan* 83, 612–620.

GARDNER, H. (2002). "Too Many Choices?" *New York Review of Books.* April 11, pp. 51–54.

GOODLAD, J. (2002). "Kudzu, Rabbits and School Reform." *Phi Delta Kappan* 84, 16–23.

HIRSCH, E. D. (1996). *The Schools We Need and Why We Don't Have Them.* New York: Doubleday.

———. (2001). "Curriculum and Competence." In T. M. Moe, ed., *A Primer on America's Schools.* Stanford: Hoover Institution.

HORN, R. A., AND KINCHELOE, J. L., EDS. (2001). *American Standards: Quality Education in a Complex World.* New York: Peter Lang.

JANESICK, V. J. (2001a). *The Assessment Debate: A Reference Handbook.* Santa Barbara, CA: ABC-CLIO.

———. (2001b). "The Standards Movement: Issues, Problems, and Possibilities." In J. L. Kincheloe and D. Weil, eds., *Standards and Schooling in the United States, An Encyclopedia.* Santa Barbara, CA: ABC-CLIO.

JENNINGS, J. F. (1998). *Why National Standards and Tests? Politics and the Quest for Better Schools.* Thousand Oaks, CA: Sage.

KOHN, A. (1999). *The Schools Our Children Deserve: Moving Beyond Traditional Classrooms and "Tougher Standards."* Boston: Houghton Mifflin.

LEMANN, N. (1999). *The Big Test: The Secret History of the American Meritocracy.* New York: Farrar, Straus and Giroux.

MCNEIL, L. M. (2000). *Contradictions of Reform: The Educational Costs of Standardized Testing.* New York: Routledge.

MEIER, D. (2000). "Educating a Democracy." In J. Cohen and J. Rogers, eds., *Will Standards Save Public Education?* Boston: Beacon.

NATIONAL COMMISSION ON EXCELLENCE IN EDUCATION. (1983). *A Nation at Risk: The Imperative for Educational Reform.* Washington, DC: U.S. Department of Education.

NATIONAL COUNCIL OF TEACHERS OF MATHEMATICS. (2002). "A Vision for School Mathematics." (http://standards.nctm.org/document)

NEW JERSEY, DEPARTMENT OF EDUCATION. (2002). "Standards & Assessment." (www.state.nj.us/njed/stass)

NO CHILD LEFT BEHIND. (2002a). (www.NoChildLeftBehind.gov/next/overview/index.html)

———.(2002b). (www.NoChildLeftBehind.gov/start/glossary/index.html)

RAVITCH, D., ED. (1995). *Debating the Future of American Education: Do We Need National Standards and Assessments?* Washington, DC: Brookings Institution.

———. (2000). *Left Back: A Century of Failed School Reforms.* New York: Simon & Schuster.

ROSS, E. W. (2001). "The Spectacle of Standards and Summits." In J. L. Kincheloe and D. Weil, eds., *Standards and Schooling in the United States, An Encyclopedia.* Santa Barbara, CA: ABC-CLIO.

STOTSKY, S. (2000). *What's At Stake in the K–12 Standards War: A Primer for Educational Policy Makers.* New York: Peter Lang.

TAUB, J. (2002). "The Test Mess." *New York Times Magazine.* April 4, Sec. 6, pp. 46–51, 60, 78.

TUCKER, M. S., AND CODDING, J. B. (1998). *Standards for Our Schools: How to Set Them, Measure Them, and Reach Them.* San Francisco: Jossey-Bass.

WEIL, D. (2001). "Couching the Standards Debate in Historical Terms: Developing a Dialectical Understanding of the Standards Debate Through Historical Awareness." In R. A. Horn and J. L. Kincheloe, eds., *American Standard.* New York: Peter Lang.

CHAPTER 7

Religion-Church/State: Unification or Separation

POSITION 1: FOR RELIGIOUS FREEDOM IN SCHOOLS

Congress shall make no law respecting an establishment of religion or prohibiting the free exercise thereof . . .

—U.S. CONSTITUTION, FIRST AMENDMENT

Take out a dollar bill. Turn it over to the back. What do you see when you look beneath the heading "The United States of America"? Printed on the dollar, as on every other denomination of American paper currency, is the motto "In God We Trust." Given the current state of affairs in this country, one day soon we'll have to add the phrase "Except in Public Schools." Court decisions, pressure from special interest groups, and the growing preference by government for a "civil religion" of secular humanism have whittled away at religious freedom in schools to an alarming degree. For the most part, the God on whom we as Americans supposedly rely cannot be discussed or addressed in public schools. Students, teachers, and administrators who attempt to do so face disciplinary action and lawsuits. Claiming to protect the rights of a minority, the courts, especially the federal courts, have trampled on the rights of the majority. This situation must be remedied, and full freedom of religious expression must be restored to all citizens in America's public schools. The First Amendment guarantees protection for the basic human right of religious liberty, and we must insist that its promise be fulfilled.

The First Amendment

The First Amendment to the Constitution was carefully crafted by the Founding Fathers to protect what they considered "inalienable rights" of American citizens. For example, they wanted to protect their countrymen's right to practice the religion of their choice without fear. Aware of British history, they knew one of the greatest impediments to religious freedom was state support of one denomination. To these early Americans, breaking away from England meant, among other things, putting an end to religious conflicts. Therefore, they believed prohibiting governmental support for any individual faith was the best policy for their new republic (Wood, 1969; MacLeod, 2000; Tozer, Violas, and Senese, 2002).

To achieve these dual aims, the founders included two clauses in the First Amendment's statement about religious freedom. The first, called the "establishment" clause, claims that religions and the state should be kept separate so that no religion is seen as having more right than any other. The second clause, the "free exercise" clause, emphasizes that government could not prevent Americans from expressing their religious beliefs in ways that seemed right to them. Reading these two clauses carefully is important in understanding why current attempts to banish religion from public schools violates the founders' intention.

The "establishment" clause says, "Congress shall make no law respecting *an* establishment of religion." Many people, when referring to the clause, quote it incorrectly as saying, "Congress shall make no law respecting *the* establishment of religion." The difference is crucial. The first, and accurate, reading clearly shows the intent was to prevent any one religious "establishment" from receiving governmental support or protection not available to all others. In fact, one of James Madison's original drafts of the religious section of the amendment said, "The civil rights of none shall be abridged on account of religious belief or worship, nor shall any national religion be established" (Robb, 1985, p. 7). Those opposing creation of a strong centralized government believed Madison's original formulation implied the presence of a body strong enough to create a national religion. As part of the many compromises required to create the Constitution, Madison removed the offending wording. His purposes, however, were clear. The "establishment" of any religion through governmental support was to be prohibited because it would negatively affect individuals' freedom of religious expression. The fact that many states already had done exactly that added a sense of urgency to the task of the Constitutional Convention. Madison and others wanted to prevent a repeat of the religious wars in England that resulted from royal support of different Christian denominations (Wood, 1969; MacLeod, 2000).

Clearly, the Founding Fathers had no intention of barring all mention of God from American public life—almost all professed belief in God although many did not identify themselves as members of any religious denomination. They routinely began assemblies with prayers for guidance and inspiration. They asked God's blessing on themselves and their countrymen in their foundational documents. Their language in such settings went beyond the traditional words used in different denominations. They spoke of a God who had created all and maintained the world, a God who was bigger than the claims of any individual group of believers (Farrand, 1986).

For most of our history the Supreme Court did not interfere in state laws regarding religious practices in schools (Batte, 2002). Any act on the part of government supporting one religious denomination at the expense of others was considered unconstitutional. Any act of the government limiting an individual's right to free expression of his or her religious beliefs was equally illegitimate. Recently, however, the balance between the needs expressed in the two clauses has been disturbed, and the rights of many Americans to practice their religions freely has been denied to them within public schools. These wrongs must be corrected and the balance restored. Young people must be able to exercise the freedom of religion guaranteed to them by the Constitution.

The Supreme Court and Religion in Public Schools

In discussing the relationship between public life and religion, the Supreme Court has been clear about a number of things. First, it established the principle that government, including such governmental agencies as public schools, has the obligation to accommodate religion wherever possible (Stronks and Stronks, 1999). Recognizing the good that religious institutions bring to the society as a whole, they have been granted tax exemptions. Despite that accommodation, governmental agencies have continued to provide them with public services such as police and fire department protection.

A second principle established by the courts regarding separation of church and state is that religious speech is as deserving of protection as other kinds of speech. Unfortunately, this principle has not been followed. Students have been prevented from leading prayers at high school graduation ceremonies, even when members of the senior class want to include such devotions. Student athletes are forbidden from praying at sporting events, even in their own locker rooms. School board meetings cannot be opened with prayer or a moment of silent meditation. Other forms of religious speech also are prohibited. Teachers cannot discuss their own religious experiences with children, even if they believe their religion commands them to do so. They cannot use such expressions as "God Bless You" in communications with students or parents. Children cannot read Bible stories to classmates as part of oral communication lessons, nor can they express religious beliefs during a class presentation. In addition, they should not expect to see drawings they've made of religious figures or symbols hanging on the walls of their classrooms or schools. Bibles may not be distributed in public schools during regular operating hours. Teachers and students may not celebrate the religious aspects of such holidays as Thanksgiving, Christmas, or Easter (ACLU Legal Bulletin, 1996; Worona, 1999).

So what has happened to the "free exercise" clause of the First Amendment? Why are so many people in schools prevented from expressing their faith as their conscience dictates?

The two clauses are in tension with one another, and is made worse because contemporary court decisions have emphasized the "establishment" clause to the detriment of the "free exercise" clause. In 1947 in *Everson v. Board of Education*, the Supreme Court ruled using state funds to reimburse parents for the cost of transporting children to religious schools did not violate the "establishment" clause. However, in writing the majority opinion, Judge Hugo Black interpreted that section of the First Amendment in a way that ignored its text. Black wrote that the "establishment" clause created "a complete separation between the state and religion" (*Everson v. Board of Education,* 1947). This interpretation was based on a letter Jefferson wrote ten years after ratification of the First Amendment in which he made his famous "wall of separation" statement (MacLeod, 2000). It reads in part: ". . . I contemplate with sovereign reverence that act of the whole American people which declared that their legislature should 'make no law respecting an establishment of religion, or prohibiting the free exercise thereof,' thus building a wall of separation between Church and State" (Koch and Peden, 1944, p. 307).

Black and others who use this interpretation to limit individual freedom of religious expression would do well to read the rest of Jefferson's quote. He writes, "Adhering to this expression of the supreme will of the nation in behalf of the *rights of conscience,* I shall see with sincere satisfaction the progress of those sentiments which tend to restore to man all his natural rights, convinced he has no natural right in opposition to his social duties" (Koch and Peden, 1944, p. 307). Clearly, Jefferson's words about the strict separation between church and state were not meant to limit individual rights but rather to argue against the possibility that any one religious sect would become a "national religion" through government efforts. When understood in this light, Jefferson's "wall" should be seen as the protector of freedom of religious expression (Marty and Moore, 2000). Instead it has been used to remove religion from public schools in ways that neither he nor the other founders of this nation intended. Other court cases have followed, relying on the interpretation offered by Justice Black in *Everson.* One by one they have created a legal legacy that violates the intentions of our founders.

In *McCollum v. Board of Education* (1948), the court ruled sectarian religious leaders were constitutionally forbidden from conducting voluntary, optional religious instruction in school buildings. Some years later the court held in *Engel v. Vitale* (1962) and *Abington Township School District v. Schempp* (1963) that neither classroom prayer nor Bible readings were constitutional even when students had the option of being excused from participation. Building on the misinterpretation of the "establishment" clause as presented by Justice Black in *Engel,* the Court took the serious step of defining governmental acts to accommodate religious freedom that could be deemed constitutional. In doing so, however, the Court created such narrow parameters that, since *Lemon v. Kurtzman* (1971), almost no religious practices in school have been declared constitutional. The "Lemon test," as the policy has come to be known, consists of three standards that must be met if the action of a school district can be established as protecting religious freedom rather than endorsing religious practices. To be constitutional a policy or activity supported by a school must (1) have a secular purpose, (2) not have the effect of advancing or inhibiting religion, and (3) avoid excessive entanglement between government and religion (ACLU Legal Bulletin, 1996; MacLeod, 2000). Applying the "Lemon test" in other cases has resulted in even more limitations on religious practices in schools.

For example, in *Stone v. Graham* (1980) the Court declared that a state law requiring public schools to post the Ten Commandments was unconstitutional.

Wallace v. Jaffree (1985) struck down a state law requiring a moment of meditation or silent prayer. In *Lee v. Weisman* (1992) the Court ruled that, even when offered by a private individual with no formal connection to the school or government, prayer at public school graduation is unconstitutional. Apparently, asking students to bow their heads, remain silent, and show respect during such a prayer violates the rights of students who do not believe in God. They are, according to the Court, compelled to participate and in so insisting on their participation, the school is "conveying a message that religion or a particular religious belief is favored or preferred" over unbelief (*County of Allegheny v. American Civil Liberties Union, Greater Pittsburgh Chapter*, 1989).

Finally, in *Santa Fe Independent School District v. Jane Doe* (2000) the Court ruled student-led prayer at football games was unconstitutional. Even though participation in such games is purely voluntary, the fact that the school district sponsors and pays for the games makes them governmental actions. So prayer at the games also are government-supported activities that must pass the "Lemon test." The Court says they do not because there is no secular purpose for the prayers, which have the effect of advancing religion because they will be "perceived by adherents . . . as an endorsement, and by nonadherents as a disapproval, of their individual religious choices" (*School District of the City of Grand Rapids v. Ball*, 1985). In 2002 a federal court ruled that the phrase "under God" in the Pledge of Allegiance also fails the "Lemon test" (*Nedow v. U.S.Congress*, 2002).

These Supreme Court cases, based as they are on a interpretation of a text that does not even appear in the Constitution, have created a disastrous situation for America's schools. In an attempt to preserve the rights of a minority of nonbelieving students, we have trampled on the rights of the majority of students, their families, and the taxpayers who provide funds for public schools. Recent polls indicate that most Americans oppose these decisions (*Newsweek*, 2000) and support prayer in school (Tayman, 2000). They believe because of these decisions ". . . public schools have grown increasingly hostile to the rights of students to express religious opinions" (MacLeod, 2000, p. 1).

Wouldn't it be more just if Congress addressed the constitutional issues raised by the Supreme Court's decision? They could craft legislation that allowed decision making about religious practices in public schools to be placed back in the hands of local officials. Community school board members would be able to set guidelines for activities respecting the rights of the minority but at the same time not infringing on the rights of the majority. They would be bound to observe constitutional provisions regarding the "manner" of free speech expression. That is, they could restrict any form of speech, including religious speech, that might put students in physical danger or disrupt the order of the school (MacLeod, 2000). Returning such authority to those officials closest to the communities involved would protect the rights of all citizens, not just a vocal minority. In doing so, we would regain a truly neutral position with regard to religious expression.

History of American Education

Seeing religion banished from all but the most innocuous aspects of U.S. public school life is truly ironic. The very first schools in the English colonies that would become the United States were instituted for religious reasons. The leaders of the Pilgrims, living in the Massachusetts Bay Colony, passed a law establishing schools that would teach children to read their Bibles. Their literacy would protect them from "that old deluder Satan."

In the early days of the Republic, American schools were, for the most part, privately funded and religious practices considered an essential part of the curriculum. Early public schools taught religion from a perspective shared with others influenced by the Enlightenment. For them a shared belief in God was necessary to create the moral discipline living in a democratic society required. The McGuffey *Readers*, the most popular textbooks for most of the nineteenth century, built on a presumption that Americans shared a belief in God to teach children what behavior was expected of them. Concern for the needs and rights of others, honesty, and perseverance despite difficulties were presented as the responsibility of all God's children in America. "It was almost universally accepted that American democracy drew its strength from the general conviction that there was a divine power, the author of the rights of man defined in America's first political document" (McCluskey, 1967, p. 237). Children were taught that each citizen derived his or her rights from their Almighty Father and that no human being had the right to take away those rights. In that era most Americans believed the majority could, on the basis of their religious beliefs, determine basic community norms including the place of religion in the public school curriculum and activities (McCarthy, 1983, p. 7). Since most Americans were Protestant Christians, their beliefs and practices were incorporated into public schools. Teachers led children in daily prayer. The Bible, usually the King James version, was read in schools. Religious holidays were celebrated (Goodman and Lesnick, 2001). State laws not only permitted such practices, they mandated them (McCarthy, 1983). So what happened?

The loss of balance between protecting both clauses of the First Amendment's state on religion began in the first half of the nineteenth century. Immigrant children from Ireland, Germany, and, later, from Italy and Eastern Europe swelled American public school enrollment, especially between 1840 and 1924. Most of these children were not members of mainstream Protestant groups, but instead were Catholics. Loyal to the teachings of their faith, and to the Pope, Catholic religious leaders objected to what they saw as the Protestant character of religion being taught in public schools. Because it offended their religious tradition, they did not understand that the religious dimensions of public school life actually were designed to help their children become part of American life (Kaestle, 1983; Goodman, 2001). Their leaders protested strenuously and began a campaign to create schools that socialized children to their own religious beliefs (Cross, 1965; Sanders, 1977; Tozer, Violas, and Senese, 2002). To many Protestant Americans, these early immigrants seemed to reject becoming part of the very country to which they had turned as a refuge from political and economic oppression (Kaestle, 1983).

Fortunately, the objections of Catholics and Jewish people who saw the value of public education were soon quieted. Schools made some accommodations because of their objections. Some districts eliminated Bible readings altogether to end the Catholics' objections to using the Protestant version of the Scriptures (Wright, 1999, p. 18). By the end of the nineteenth century, some would argue that sectarian education had been ended in public schools (Nord, 1995), although such practices as prayer in school continued.

Most citizens believed a kind of neutrality among religious denominations could be maintained in public schools while still preserving the freedom of all students and teachers to exercise their religious freedom (Goodman and Lesnick, 2001). Prayers were offered in "theistic" rather than "Christian" language, and holidays from both traditions were celebrated. Catholics and Jews who could not make this accommodation sent their children to schools in which their own beliefs could be practiced more freely (Cross, 1965; Sanders, 1977; Zeldin, 1986). In the last half of the twentieth century, however, public schools were faced with new challenges as children from nonbiblical faith traditions began to appear in public schools. It still seemed possible to reach a solution that would preserve the rights of all students and teachers to express their religious beliefs freely. Among those who believe in God or seek divine assistance, common language and practices seem achievable.

The situation, however, was complicated by the growth of an altogether different belief system. The United States, like many other Western countries, experienced the growth of philosophies that were antireligious. Those who accepted these beliefs were concerned about what they perceived to be the vulnerability of children in schools. They worried that schools, by openly supporting free expression of religious beliefs—indeed by mandating them in some cases—were creating situations in which young people were being taught that religious beliefs were normative. They argued such tacit approval of religious faith would pressure young people to profess such beliefs themselves without being given the opportunity to evaluate them.

As we have seen, most Americans—over 90 percent—believe in God. Only a very small number of Americans totally reject the existence of a divine being—however, they constitute a very vocal and powerful minority. They brought many of the lawsuits that have had such negative effects on the free exercise of religion by students and teachers (*McCollum v. Board of Education*, 1947; *Zorach v. Clauson*, 1952; *Engel v. Vitale*, 1962; *Abington Township School District v. Schempp*, 1963; and *Murray v. Curlett*, 1963). Over time the commitment to protect the rights of the minority has taken precedence over the desire to secure the rights of the majority. In attempts to establish "neutrality" toward religions in American public schools, the government has taken a position resulting in an almost total ban on religious speech and practice in schools. The courts have better protected the rights of nonreligious people than those of citizens who want to express their beliefs in God. The consequences have been destructive of one of our most cherished human rights, and we need to correct the error as soon as possible.

To do so, however, will require we understand these "nonbelievers" actually have a very specific faith and that in protecting their rights, the government has deprived believers of theirs.

Secular Humanism as the State Religion

Many who do not believe in God and have argued their right to do so is violated by religious expression in public schools have adopted a philosophy called "secular humanism." Secular humanism is a world view committed to critical investigation, rather than dogma, as the source of solutions for human problems and answers to important human questions (Council for Secular Humanism, 2002). In 1933, in the first Humanist Manifesto, they declared humanism is an alternative to theism—that is, belief in God. In 1973 the second Manifesto announced that faith is God is unproven and out of date. It should be replaced, especially on a national level, by humanism and its ethical process. They argue that not only should intelligent people reject traditional religion but also should replace it with the new beliefs and traditions of secular humanism. Finally, a document issued in 1980 made sure that all understood secular humanism relies not on the guidance of a divine and loving being, but rather on human intelligence and the scientific method (McCarthy, 1983, p. 89). Their own words have shown us that humanism is truly a religion. It has basic beliefs; its followers use the word *faith* to describe it. As a philosophy it gives science the same position as believers give to revelation—it is viewed as a guide to human progress. Secularism is a religion that worships human abilities and achievements the way other faiths worship the abilities and achievements of God (Kussrow and Vannest, 1999).

For the last seventy years secular humanists have been organizing and pushing their radical viewpoint into the very heart of American life. Although secular humanism adherents deny they practice a religion, it functions as one and has been given preferential treatment by the government. In doing so, the government has violated both the "establishment" and "free exercise" aspects of the religious clauses of the First Amendment. Those who care about liberty must help other Americans become aware of the ways in which their freedoms are shrinking while those of some are expanded.

Secular humanism has developed within the larger historical process of secularization—the development of ways of understanding the world that are less dependent on religion and more reliant on the findings of science and philosophy. These developments have resulted in many scientific discoveries and in increased personal freedom for many people. The process is "almost certainly irreversible" (Cox, 1967, p. 20). In fact, this revolution in worldviews was the very basis for the creation of the United States. Secularization, however, does not, of necessity, eliminate the rationality of belief in God. Believers successfully have struggled to incorporate revelations that science, technology, commerce, industry, and politics have produced with belief in God. Secular humanism was only one possible belief system that could evolve from the process of secularization. That is what makes the Supreme Court's protection of the rights of its adherents at the expense of those of religious believers so difficult to reconcile with the First Amendment "establishment" clause.

Most who believe in God have come to accept that sectarian religious education no longer is possible in American public schools. Those who have adopted secular humanism as their belief system have insisted on it and the courts have supported them. They argued their beliefs actually are neutral regarding religion. In actuality, they are hostile to it (Nord, 1995), contending any expression of belief in God is unconstitutional in public settings because, by being exposed to such activities, their children are coerced into accepting the beliefs from which they spring. In most cases the Supreme Court has accepted their arguments. The result is that the most privileged belief system in public schools is secular humanism. The rulings against common prayer, moments of silence, and celebrations of religious holidays in schools establish secular humanists' beliefs as dominant in schools. Of course such a policy clearly is unconstitutional. Several Supreme Court justices have explained what neutrality with regard to religion in public schools really means. Writing in *Everson* Hugo Black states, "State power is no more to be used so as to handicap religions than it is to favor them" (1947). In *Abington v. Schempp,* Tom Clark wrote, "The state may not establish a 'religion of secularism' in the sense of affirmatively opposing or showing hostility to religion, thus 'preferring those who believe in no religion over those who do believe'" (*Abington Township School District v. Schempp,* 1963). It would seem these warnings were ignored. The public school environment has increasingly become hostile to believers, limiting their freedom of expression while allowing secular humanists license to incorporate their beliefs into the curricula.

Curricular Consequences

The perspectives of religious believers have almost been eliminated from public school curricula. In general, textbooks "seldom explain religion's role in shaping human thought and action or as a motivating force" (Sewall, 1998, pp. 81–82). In fact, antagonism to religious approaches exists in most subjects. For example, the origin of human life is a topic in which the legitimate religious perspective is at best ignored and at worst, ridiculed. The "scientific" theory of evolution—in reality a tenet of the secular humanist belief system—is presented as fact while the "scientific" theory of creationism—a tenet of biblically based Jewish and Christian belief systems—is presented as myth.

Health classes are another area of the curriculum in which the beliefs of secular humanists have been privileged. Students, regardless of their religious beliefs, are compelled to hear presentations in which their traditions' attitudes toward abortion, premarital sex, homosexuality, masturbation, and other topics are dismissed as unscientific and irrational. Students are invited to create their own code of ethics instead of being educated in the rich Western tradition of philosophical and religious thinking about moral topics (Concerned Women for America, 2000). Secular humanists have convinced the courts and the courts have convinced school boards that including religious perspectives on such topics constitute breaches in the separation between church and state (Nord, 1995). They ignore the fact, however, that their own beliefs are being supported by the government, a practice that clearly is unconstitutional and should be stopped.

Conclusion

The First Amendment religious clauses clearly establish two duties for government regarding freedom of religion. Government must not favor one religion over others and must not prevent citizens from expressing their religious beliefs. In attempting to reach a balance between these clauses, especially in light of the growing pluralism of religious belief among Americans, the courts have created a situation in which schools cannot carry out their obligation to protect students' freedom of religious expression. Secular humanists have claimed that religious neutrality means students must be prevented from hearing religious speech that is "offensive" to them. The feelings of children who are nonbelievers have taken precedence over the rights of children who believe in and want to express their faith in God. All citizens have an obligation to see that freedom of religious expression is returned to schools as soon as possible. If we fail to do so, the continued existence of public schools is in jeopardy.

Many parents who feel as if their children's religious freedom has been limited are opting out of public school (Detwiler, 1999; Fraser, 1999). They increasingly are supporting voucher plans that will divert money from public to private schools where they believe their children's rights will be better guaranteed. If public schools are a place where Americans learn about their rights, learn to practice them and to protect the rights of others, then it is imperative to prevent their replacement by private schools where only people of like minds gather. Ensuring full freedom of religious expression in public school will achieve that end.

POSITION 2: AGAINST VIOLATING THE SEPARATION BETWEEN CHURCH AND STATE

Even today there are many in this country who would like to restore the old morning exercises—Bible reading, Lord's prayer and flag salute. We should be firm in resisting this demand.

—NODDINGS, 1993, P. 140

To hear members of the religious right complain, you'd think that all religious expression had been totally banned in American public schools. Actually teachers and students enjoy a great deal of freedom to engage in religious speech and practices. In 1999 the Department of Education reissued guidelines on Religious Expression in Public Schools. In doing so, the Department recognized two obligations imposed on schools by the First Amendment. "Schools may not discriminate against private religious expression by students, but must instead give students the same right to engage in religious activity and discussion as they have to engage in other comparable activity. . . . At the same time, schools may not endorse religious activity or doctrine, nor may they coerce participation in religious activity" (Riley, 1998, p. 2).

The freedoms specifically enumerated in the guidelines include: reading Scriptures, saying grace before meals, praying before tests, and discussing religious views in informal settings such as cafeterias and hallways. In addition, students may speak to and try to persuade other students about religious topics, participate in prayerful gatherings before and after school, and express their religious beliefs in homework, artwork, and other written and oral assignments. They also may distribute religious literature to others in the school. They can display religious messages on their clothing and wear religious attire—such as veils or yarmulkes (U.S. Department of Education, 1998, pp. 5–7). A school can limit these expressions of free speech only to the same degree it limits other comparable words or activities. So, for example, if a school has a dress code that is religiously neutral and generally applicable, students need not be exempted from conforming to it based on their religious beliefs or practices. Similarly students have the right to distribute religious literature, hold prayer gatherings on school grounds, and discuss their religious beliefs to the same extent that they could engage in similar activities on comparable topics—such as politics or social issues.

Sounds good, doesn't it? It appears that students who want to engage in religious activities or speak about their faith have lots of freedom to do so. It sounds fair and reasonable—an all-American compromise that respects every student's right to religious liberty. So what's the problem?

Apparently this kind of freedom is not enough for some religious believers. They want schools to be permitted to sponsor religious activities and coerce students to attend those events. For example, they believe school officials should be able to organize or mandate prayer at graduation ceremonies or, alternatively, to organize religious "baccalaureate" ceremonies for graduates, their friends and families. They believe it should be acceptable for teachers or principals to encourage students to participate in prayer gatherings before or after school, want teachers to be able to speak openly about their own religious beliefs in classroom settings, and advocate celebrating religious aspects of holidays in school. "For many religious Americans, the failure of public institutions to acknowledge any blessings that flow from God—and God alone—means that, as individuals and society, we fail . . . . these religious Americans think the nation's education system is complicit in sacrilege and moral decline" (Sewall, 1999, p. 13).

Many of these people fail to understand that complex legal questions arise "when students' rights to attend public school in an environment free from state sponsorship of religion are pitted against claims that accommodation to religious beliefs are required to protect free exercise rights" (McCarthy, 1983, p. 14). They seem incapable of comprehending that religious liberty in America means we are all free to express our beliefs but may not impose them on others. They do not seem to understand public schools are governmental agencies and, as such, are bound by the First Amendment not to take any action that would favor one religion over another—or belief over nonbelief. Intentionally or not, they seem opposed to schools' maintaining the constitutionally required separation of church and state. They want to be able to engage in sectarian behavior at taxpayer expense and not only practice their religion but preach it to others in publicly funded schools.

While those desires might be admirable from a religious point of view, they violate some very basic principles of American life—such as religious liberty and separation of church and state. There is a way, however, to compromise between those values and still bring religion back into the schools. It requires a willingness to apply good educational values such as open-mindedness and critical thinking to religious belief—rewards for doing so will be great.

Teaching About *Religion in Public School Curriculum*

In describing schools that a democratic society requires, John Dewey argued we "must have a type of education which gives individuals a personal interest in social relationships and control and the habits of mind which secure social change without introducing disorder" (Dewey, 1916, p. 115). What are those habits of mind? They include an acceptance that the open flow of ideas is necessary for citizens to be informed sufficiently to participate in democratic collective decision making. Citizens in democracies also need to understand that democracy does not consist of a preexisting ideal to be pursued but is a set of values guiding our common life. In addition, those living in this form of government must be able to use critical reflection and analysis to evaluate ideas, problems, and policies (Apple and Beane, 1995). By teaching *about* religion in public schools in ways that do not promote one set of beliefs over another or belief over nonbelief, we can develop these "habits of mind" in young Americans. By doing so we will strengthen our democracy.

In our justifiable efforts to remedy violations of the First Amendment such as school-sponsored prayer or Bible reading, we have been frightened away from helping young people understand religion's significance in many aspects of life. We have become overly cautious about presenting the variety of perspectives, rooted in belief or nonbelief, from which people look at issues in all areas of the curriculum. "While educational theorists have been ignoring religion as though the Enlightenment project had succeeded, more and more people have actually returned to religion" (Noddings, 1993, p. xiv). Schools have neglected their duty to educate thoughtful, tolerant citizens by failing to provide them with information about religious and nonreligious viewpoints on controversial topics. Educators have not offered students opportunities to hear arguments for and against their own and others' beliefs. We Americans seem to have a great deal of difficulty understanding one another and creating political compromises about social issues that involve religious beliefs. Perhaps it is because we have not learned about various viewpoints nor discussed them in school.

There is general agreement that nothing in the First Amendment prohibits educators from teaching about religion. They rarely do so, however. Many teachers and administrators believe "Religion is bad stuff from the word go some say and the more we can leave it out of the classroom and curriculum, the better off we will be. . . . Introducing religion on curricular terms, others say, only opens the way for proselytizing and witnessing groups to get a foot in the door and to introduce elements of competition to the school scene" (Marty and Moore, 2000, p. 46). Few teachers feel prepared to deal competently with discussions of religious perspectives on topics in their own discipline. Even fewer feel able to address larger conceptual differences between religious and secular perspectives. It's no wonder. Most have little or no experience with the study of religion in educational settings. "Most people in American public schools and universities can get degrees and diplomas without ever confronting a live religious idea" (Nord, 1995, p. 1). Teacher education programs do little to provide teachers with knowledge, skills, and dispositions needed to create learning activities about these topics. Many are afraid they will be challenged, either by the school board or in court, if they attempt to teach about religion in public schools.

Despite these justified fears, there are many good reasons why educators need to begin to develop good instruction about a variety of worldviews. We live in a world in which the inability of people, especially those in positions of political power, to understand others' perspectives on the world has resulted in frustration. All too often that frustration has erupted into violence, often against civilians. Young people deserve an opportunity to develop knowledge and skills to better enable their generation of leaders to deal with such misunderstanding before it results in acts of war. "Because religion plays significant roles in history and society, study about religion is essential to understanding both the nation and the world" (Nord, 1999a, p. 1). Knowledge of the many ways people's actions are affected by religious beliefs or the lack of them "gives students an accurate picture of the world, helps students account for wider, deeper readings of human motivation and action" (Marty and Moore, 2000, p. 64).

In that context, helping students understand the powerful influence religion has exerted on governments and individuals helps them contextualize events and artifacts that are unintelligible without such information. The Holocaust is inexplicable without reference to interpretations of biblical accounts of Jesus' death. The American "work ethic" cannot be understood without some grasp of the aspects of Protestant theology from which it flows. The continuing conflict over a relatively small area of land in the Middle East cannot be comprehended without knowledge of its value to members of three religious traditions. If students do not understand the basic symbols, practices, and scriptures of various religions, references to them in literature, art, and music are lost on them. Their ability to comprehend a writer's or artist's intention is severely limited.

The religious worldview often is critical of "commonsense" approaches to economic issues. When we exclude thoughts of those who approach topics from a religious viewpoint, we deprive students of the possibility of realizing that economists have suggested alternative solutions to problems of the production and distribution of goods and services from those proposed by neoclassical economic theory. By ignoring those alternative solutions, we deprive students opportunity to "create a common language to challenge utilitarian, self-interested, fragmented, individualistic ideologies or values (Nord, 1999a, p. 137).

In approaching the science curriculum, we often deprive students opportunity to "wonder"—that is, to adopt a religious stance toward the material. Our acceptance of the dogma that "when science and religion conflict, only science provides reliable knowledge" (Nord, 1999b, p. 29) shortchanges students. Indeed, they often find out how unsatisfactory "scientific" answers can be when they are faced, in their own lives, with issues of bioethics such as reproduction, life support, and treatment of genetic disorders.

In every instance where teachers address religious worldviews inherent in or critical of curricular material, they must, of course, remain neutral but real neutrality does not mean silence. "To advocate a particular sectarian view is clearly unconstitutional. But to ignore—as we do now—that people have taken such views and that these views, in many cases, have been enormously influential is morally reprehensible" (Noddings, 1993, p. 133). It is bad education.

We simply cannot claim to be providing students with a complete education when we fail to discuss religious aspects inherent in our curriculum Furthermore, we cannot suggest we are fully educating them to be well prepared to function as citizens in as pluralistic society as the United States if we fail to prepare them to deal intelligently with diversity of ideas as well as ethnicities. Public schools must teach a variety of worldviews to provide students the ability to deal with conflicts that arise in our society as a result of our different perspectives. We claim to believe new members of our society must come to understand that in a democracy we practice virtues such as "tolerance, . . . the right of an individual to hold minority views and to be protected in them and the belief that in an open forum truth will win out" (Cox, 1967, p. 100). We cannot assume young people automatically will develop skill at putting those attitudes into practice. In their classrooms students need to experience what it is like when such values are lived out in discussion. Believers and nonbelievers need to learn to listen respectfully to one another, practice asking clarifying questions, finding and articulating areas of agreement, and describing their disagreements in a civil way. They need the help of competent, confident adults. Schools should be one of the social institutions in which they find opportunities to learn such skills under mentors committed to democratic principles. By attending to young people's needs in a neutral, respectful way, educators will be demonstrating that First Amendment freedoms are not merely empty promises. They will create "greenhouses" in their schools and classrooms where the rights and responsibilities described in the religious clauses can grow into sturdy plants.

Practical Implications

If schools are to meet the difficult responsibilities given to them by the First Amendment regarding religious freedom, then several conditions must be met. Teacher education programs must prepare students for this aspect of their professional duties, requiring courses in philosophy and religious studies as well as methods of instruction. They would need to become informed about limits on freedom of religious expression and the meaning of "neutrality" as those principles apply in schools. Several preparation programs have begun the task of educating teachers—new and experienced—to take up teaching about religion in schools in ways that safeguard First Amendment freedoms (Freedom Forum et al., 1999).

We need teachers willing to teach *about* religion. They should seek out textbooks that treat perspectives of believers and nonbelievers fairly, and provide opportunities for students to think critically about various perspectives. Teachers should find primary sources and scholarly secondary sources to supplement text material. Guest speakers with an appropriate background and an understanding of First Amendment guidelines for teaching about religion in schools should be welcome visitors in their classrooms. Teachers should use multiple perspectives in their approach to art, music, literature, or drama, incorporating both religious and secular viewpoints.

The only way teachers can incorporate these practices into their classrooms is if their schools and districts provide clear guidelines and support. The policies must incorporate a commitment to federal guidelines (Riley, 1998) and require that a teacher's approach to religion is academic, not devotional. Administrators must ensure the curriculum strives for student awareness of religion or nonbelief, not acceptance of either point of view. In addition, the policy must guarantee a neutrality such that neither viewpoint is denigrated or supported. To protect teachers and safeguard students' rights, policies may require administrator approval of speakers or activities that introduce multiple perspectives, especially if the topic potentially is controversial. Finally, districts should establish policies that maintain communication between teachers, parents, students, and administrators.

One final implication of arguing that a policy of teaching about religion in schools is appropriate involves those who believe the First Amendment is being violated by omission of the topic. Religious believers especially need to be willing to adhere to guidelines developed by the Department of Education in conformity with the decisions of the Supreme Court. That is, believers must not expect that the introduction of conversation in schools *about* religion is license to violate the rights of nonbelievers or those who come from traditions other than their own. Religious believers also must understand the introduction of religion into classrooms as an academic subject means it will be subject to critical student evaluation as are other perspectives. Students inevitably will hear opinions and beliefs differing from their own; they will be involved in discussions in which positive and negative effects of religion on individual and collective behavior is evaluated; they will be challenged to deal with the contradictions between the teachings of a religious group and behaviors of its members. If those conversations take place within the "neutrality" implied in the First Amendment and spelled out in Court decisions and Department of Education guidelines, then believers must accept the discomfort that might arise as a result. There is no reason to conclude such discussion will automatically endanger the beliefs of students. "Education . . . does not necessarily destroy belief; it may indeed deepen it"(Noddings, 1993, p. 143).

Many religious believers, however, have seemed hostile to exploring religious perspectives with the same critical lens used to evaluate more secular viewpoints. They have waged repeated and unfortunately rather successful campaigns for "abstinence only" sex education programs. Because their religious beliefs prohibit sexual intercourse outside of marriage, groups like Focus on the Family, Concerned Women for America, and the American Family Association oppose education about birth control or sexually transmitted infections (STIs). Members of these and other groups are unwilling to allow young people to compare their perspectives on sexuality with those less influenced by religious beliefs. The same insistence on imposing their views on others can be found in their approach to issues regarding the civil rights of homosexuals (American Family Association of Georgia, 2002; Concerned Women for America, 2000). These actions are "by definition, a suppression of alternative points of view and involves supplanting a method scientifically proven to be effective in decreasing the spread of STIs with another unproven method. Yet this approach is constructed as preserving an atmosphere of intellectual freedom" (Advocates for Youth, 2002). Fear of negative reaction on the part of such vocal opponents often is one of the major reasons why religious points of view rarely are discussed in American schools. Teachers know that if they present these opinions in a noncritical way, they are violating the First Amendment. They also know, however, that if they conduct neutral discussions of such topics, they run the risk of losing their jobs in a tumultuous controversy. So they remain silent and students lose the opportunity to think through their positions on issues of vital importance.

Religious believers who want their views presented as "the truth" are not interested in good education. They are merely interested in preaching. Nowhere is this more apparent than in the creationism debate.

The Creationism Debate

Although the Supreme Court ruled in 1987 (*Edwards v. Aguillard)* that it is unconstitutional for a state or school district to require "equal time" for evolution and "creation science," many Americans still have not fully accepted the ruling. They are convinced that, unless the "theory" of evolution is challenged, then the state is violating their right to religious liberty and perpetuating intellectual fraud. What is going on?

Some people object to evolution because it contradicts the creation account found in Genesis, the first chapter in the Bible. They believe that the world was created 6,000 years ago by a divine being acting purposefully. "They have been told or have somehow acquired the belief . . . that evolution proves there is no purpose to life, that life has no meaning, that they must give up their sense of the divine" (Scott, 2001, p. 2). The Institute for Creation Research, one of the most influential creationist organizations, believes evolution "leads to the notion that each person owns himself, and is the master of his own destiny." That notion, they declare, violates the Bible. They want to see all teaching of evolution banned from public schools because it will be too tempting for young people and those who accept it "must ultimately be consigned to the everlasting fire prepared for the devil and his angels" (Institute for Creation Research,

1999). Another group that lobbies against the inclusion of evolution in K–12 curriculum is the Answers in Genesis group. They argue that belief in evolution is incompatible with belief in Christ and "those who do not believe in Christ are subject to everlasting conscious punishment" (Answers in Genesis, 1998).

Feeling their core beliefs are at stake, those who take the Bible literally think they have no choice but to insist their children be protected from these evil influences in school. Evolution, they argue, is responsible for abortion, the breakdown of the family, homosexuality, lawlessness and pornography (Answers in Genesis, 1998). Consequently, they have lobbied to have textbooks removed from schools if authors do not give "equal time" to creationism, convinced legislators and departments of education to remove evolution from state science standards that strongly influence the curriculum taught in public schools, and have had all mention of evolution removed from statewide tests, thus giving school districts the green light to ignore the topic in their classes without fear that students will suffer. They argue that creationism is a "science" with a different theory of the origin of the world and its living organisms. They portray themselves as victims of discrimination because they are not allowed to air their theory in public schools. They argue for fairness, tolerance for diversity, individual choice, and opposition to censorship (People for the American Way, 1999). And those are very powerful arguments in a society committed to them as part of its core values. The problem is that creationists themselves are not tolerant. In addition, their claims are based on a misunderstanding, deliberate or not, of the differences in criteria used by religion and science to arrive at an understanding of truth.

None of this would matter very much if evolution weren't such an important part of the science curriculum. However, it is one of the most important contributions science has ever made to our understanding of the connections between all living things, and is fundamental to genetics, biochemistry, physiology, and ecology. "It helps to explain the emergence of new infectious diseases, the development of antibiotic resistance in bacteria, the agricultural relationships among wild and domestic plants and animals, the composition of Earth's atmosphere, the molecular machinery of the cell, the similarities between human beings and other primates, and countless other features of the biological and physical world" (National Academy of Sciences, 1999, p. 1). An earth science or biology course that does not include evolution shortchanges students. "They will leave the course having been misled that science largely consists of the tedious memorization of lists of facts, rather than a tool we can use to help us understand the world of nature . . . it turns students away from studying science, and perhaps worse yet, defeats our efforts to produce a scientifically literate society" (Scott, 2001, p. 3). Therefore, the demand that evolution be removed from the science curriculum is an impossible one to meet if we want to give young people a rigorous scientific education.

Even including creationism on equal terms with evolution would distort students' understanding of science. The theory of evolution has been built up through facts such as "the presence and/or absence of particular fossils in particular strata of the geological column. From these confirmed observations we develop an explanation, an inference, that what explains all of these facts is that species have had histories, and that descent with modification has taken place" (Scott, 2001, p. 6). Scientists no longer debate whether evolution has taken place because the data from experimentation and observation is too strong.

When we teach young people evolution, we should help them understand what we mean by a scientific theory. "A theory, in science, is a logical construct of facts and hypotheses that attempts to explain a natural phenomenon" (Scott, 2001, p. 6). We need to clarify that we are not presenting evolution as *a* fact, but rather as an explanation for the facts we have collected through the scientific tools of observation and experimentation (National Academy of Sciences, 1999; Scott, 2001). We also should ensure students understand that it is through such methods that we create scientific knowledge: "explanations that can be inferred from confirmable data" (National Academy of Sciences, 1999, p. 1).

Religion offers people another way of knowing—one that is different from science. Its claims cannot be tested in the same way as those of science. They don't need to be in order to be believable as *religious* truths. A person can accept on faith any explanation they choose for the origin of the world or the relationships between its living things. People can draw on statements based on revelation or religious authority. They can take great comfort from such faith and can be profoundly inspired by its explanations. They can study different expressions of those beliefs, comparing and contrasting them—sifting among them for the one that is most convincing. But what they can't do is call them "science." No set of beliefs that is not open to change if new data, interpretations, or explanations are presented can call itself a science (National Academy of Sciences, 1999). Even the federal courts have said creationists cannot call their ideas a science "if they start with a conclusion and refuse to change it regardless of the evidence developed during the course of the investigation" (*McLean v. Arkansas Board of Education,* 1982). Allowing young people to think differently is to do them a disservice.

Multiple ways of explaining the origin of the world, however, can be explored in schools. Courses in comparative literature, mythology, the history of world cultures are all appropriate places to discuss the various ways people have come to understand how the world began and if, and in what ways, the beings on it are connected to one another. Such disciplines have their own criteria for weighing the merits of these different ideas—and those criteria would be a better fit for the kind of knowledge belief in the biblical version of creation constructs. So there is room in schools for creationism, just not in science classes. Those believers who continue to insist their religion is "scientific" are shortsighted and, ultimately, defeat their stated purpose of including the study of religion in public school curricula.

Conclusion

Nel Noddings argues eloquently that public schools "should play a major role in educating for intelligent belief or unbelief" (Noddings, 1993, p. xiv). "Religious and metaphysical questions may arise anywhere and teachers should assume that students are continually asking such questions implicitly and plan their lessons to include such material" (Noddings, 1993, p. 132). This goal is one that we should all be able to embrace as American if we truly are committed to religious liberty.

However, the Constitution also requires us to be vigilant against allowing government to favor belief over unbelief. We have seen that there was good reason for the caution of the Founding Fathers. Without the restraint provided by the Constitution, systems of belief suggesting they have answers to any question can threaten fundamental aspects of democracy. For example, if a group of people believe they have "the truth," it could be difficult for them to tolerate dissent from those beliefs. Since they are primarily accountable to God and since, to them at least, God has revealed the criteria for "right" and "wrong" actions, they might find themselves facing conflicts between their obligations as citizens and those they have as believers. Ultimately the authority of God will always be superior to the authority of the state. These religions, sure of their correctness, may not see questioning and critical thinking as desirable intellectual habits. These are, however, precisely the qualities a democracy needs in its citizens (Nash, 1999). The reaction of many religious believers to the presentation of a secular view of the world in schools reveals their inability to understand or accept the compromises required in order to protect the rights of all Americans.

We must continue to struggle to achieve the delicate balance our Constitution requires regarding religion and public schools. We must allow individual students freedom to express their religious beliefs through word and action so long as they do not infringe on other students' right to abstain from such behavior. At the same time, we must prevent government, through schools, to support an establishment of religion. We must give both religious and secular views of the world a voice in schools. "Because our culture is so deeply divided, public education should not take sides in our culture wars but should maintain neutrality treating the contending alternatives fairly. Indeed *only by taking each other seriously* can we resolve our national dilemma about religion and education" (Nord, 1995, p. 8).

For Discussion

1. The National Academy of Sciences (NAS) has argued that creationism does not meet the criteria for a scientific theory. Investigate the NAS definition further and determine whether creation scientists could gather facts that would support their theory regarding the origin of life on earth and what type of evidence they would need. Can you find other definitions of scientific knowledge that might be expansive enough to include creation science?
2. The courts have ruled that teachers may not communicate their own religious beliefs to students. What do you think is the basis for those rulings? Research other legal limitations that have been placed on teachers' individual freedoms. Do they reflect society's attempt to balance the rights of individuals and needs of a democratic society? Do you agree with the way that balance has been achieved? What would you do differently?
3. Read or watch a film or video version of *Inherit the Wind,* the dramatization of the Scopes trial. Research the actual event as well. What role did the historical and geographical setting play in the case? Would the case have been brought in a different

location—even during the same period? Speculate on whether geographic differences might exist today regarding the question of religious freedom in public schools. What implications might these differences have for those entering the teaching profession? On what grounds would you base your guesses? How could you verify your thesis?

4. The U.S. Department of Education has issued guidelines for religious expression in public schools. Using those guidelines, take the role of a school superintendent and prepare a set of rules for your school district. Assume that they will need to be approved by your school board and create an explanation for each of the regulations you propose.

References

Abington Township School District v. Schempp. (1963). 374 U.S. 203.

ACLU LEGAL BULLETIN. (1996). "The Establishment Clause and Public Schools." (www.aclu.org.issues/religion/pr3.html)

ADVOCATES FOR YOUTH. (2002). "Abstinence-Only-Until Marriage Education: Abandoning Responsibility to GLBTG Youth." *Transitions* 14(6), 1–3. (www.advocatesforyouth.org/publications/transitions/transitions14046.htm)

AMERICAN FAMILY ASSOCIATION OF GEORGIA. (2002). (www.afafa.or/Homosexuality.htm)

ANSWERS IN GENESIS. (1998). "Creation Evangelism." (http://answersingenesis.org)

APPLE, M., AND BEANE, J. (1995). *Democratic Schools.* Alexandria, VA: ACSD.

BATTE, S. (2002). "School Prayer Decision." The Constitutional Principle of Church and State Website. (http://members.tripod.com/~candst/pray2a.htm)

Brown v. Board of Education of Topeka, Kansas. (1954). 347 U.S. 483.

CARPENTER, D. (2002). "Safe Schools, Free Speech and the Truth." *Focus on Education.* (www.focusoneducation.com/policy/articles/a0001188.html)

CONCERNED WOMEN FOR AMERICA. (2000). "Sex Educators Not Telling Whole Truth." (http://cwfa.org/library/education/2000-09-26_pr_sex-ed.shtml)

County of Allegheny v. American Civil Liberties Union, Greater Pittsburgh Chapter. (1989). 492 U.S. 573.

COUNCIL FOR SECULAR HUMANISM. (2002). "What is Secular Humanism?" (www.secularhumanism.org/intro/what.html)

COX, H. (1967). "The Relation Between Religion and Education." In T. Sizer, ed., *Religion and Public Education.* Boston: Houghton Mifflin.

CROSS, R. (1965). "Origins of Catholic Schools in the United States." *The American Benedictine Review, XVI.* June, 1965.

DETWILER, F. (1999). *Standing on the Premises of God: The Christian Right's Fight to Redefine America's Public Schools.* New York: New York University Press.

DEWEY, J. (1916). *Democracy and Education.* New York: Macmillan.

Edwards v. Aguillard. (1987). 482 U.S. 578.

Engel v. Vitale. (1962). 370 U.S. 421.

Everson v. Board of Education. (1947). 330 U.S. 855.

FARRAND, M. (1986). *The Records of the Federal Convention of 1878.* New Haven: Yale University Press.

FRASER, J. (1999). *Religion and Public Education in a Multi-Cultural America.* New York: St. Martin's Press.

FREEDOM FORUM, ET AL. (1999). *Public Schools and Religious Communities: A First Amendment Guide.* (www.freedomforum.org/newsstand/brochures)

GOODMAN, J., AND LESNICK, H. (2001). *The Moral Stake in Education.* New York: Longman.

INSTITUTE FOR CREATION RESEARCH. (1999). "A Word from the President." (www. irc.org)

KAESTLE, C. (1983). *Pillars of the Republic.* New York: Hill and Wang.

KOCH, A., AND PEDEN, W. (1944). *The Life and Selected Writings of Thomas Jefferson.* New York: Random House.

KUSSROW, P., AND VANNEST, L. (1999). "Can Public Schools Be Religiously Neutral?" Leadership University, Telling the Truth Project. (www.leaderu.com/humanities/neutral.html)

Lee v. Weisman. (1992). 505 U.S. 577.

Lemon v. Kurtzman. (1971). 403 U.S. 602.

MACLEOD, L. (2000)."School Prayer and Religious Liberty: A Constitutional Perspective." Washington, DC: Concerned Women for America. (www.cwfa.org/library/freedom/2000-09-pp_school-prayers.html)

MARTY, M., AND MOORE, J. (2000). *Education, Religion and the Common Good: Advancing a Distinctly American Conversation About Religion's Role in Our Shared Life.* San Francisco: Jossey-Bass.

MCCARTHY, M. (1983). *A Delicate Balance: Church, State and the Schools.* Bloomington, IN: Phi Delta Kappan Educational Foundation.

MCCLUSKEY, N. (1967). "The New Secularity and the Requirements of Pluralism." In T. Sizer, ed., *Religion and Public Education.* Boston: Houghton Mifflin.

McCollum v. Board of Education. (1948). 333 U.S. 203.

McLean v. Arkansas Board of Education. (1982). 529 F. Supp. 1255.

Murray v. Curlett. (1963). 371 U.S. 944.

NASH, R. (1999). *Faith, Hype and Clarity: Teaching About Religion in American Schools and Colleges.* New York: Teachers College Press.

NATIONAL ACADEMY OF SCIENCES. (1999). *Science and Creationism: A View from the National Academy of Sciences.* Washington, DC: National Academy Press.

Nedow v. U.S. Congress. (2002). 293 F. 3d. 597.

Newsweek. (2000). Poll Conducted by Princeton Survey Research Associates. April, pp. 13–14. (www.pollingreport.com/religion.htm)

NODDINGS, N. (1993). *Educating for Intelligent Belief or Unbelief.* New York: Teachers College Press.

NORD, W. (1995). *Religion and American Education: Rethinking a National Dilemma.* Chapel Hill: University of North Carolina Press.

———. (1999a). "The Relevance of Religion to the Curriculum." *School Administrator Web Edition,* Jan., pp. 1–6. (www.aasa.org/publications/sa/1999_01/Nord.htm)

———. (1999b). "Science, Religion and Education." *Phi Delta Kappan* 81(1), 28–33.

PEOPLE FOR THE AMERICAN WAY. (1999). "Sabotaging Science: Creationist Strategy in the '90s." (www.PFAW.org)

RILEY, R. (1998). "Introduction." *Guidelines on Religious Expression in Public Schools.* Washington, DC: Department of Education. (www.ed.gov/Speeches/08-1995/religion.html)

ROBB, S. (1985). *In Defense of School Prayer.* Santa Ana, CA: Parca Publishing.

SANDERS, J. (1977). *Education of an Urban Minority.* New York: Oxford University Press.

Santa Fe Indpendent School District v. Jane Doe. (2000). 530 U.S. 290.

School District of the City of Grand Rapids v. Ball. (1985). 437 U.S. 373.

SCOTT, E. (2001). "Dealing with Anti-Evolutionism." National Center for Science Education. (www.ncseweb.org/resources)

SEWALL, G. (1998). "Religion and the Textbooks." In J. Sears. and J. Carper, eds., *Curriculum, Religion and Public Education: Conversations for an Enlarging Public Square.* New York: Teachers College Press, 73–84.

SEWALL, G. (1998). "Religion and the Textbooks." In J. Sears. and J. Carper, eds., *Curriculum, Religion and Public Education: Conversations for an Enlarging Public Square.* New York: Teachers College Press, 73–84.

———. (1999) "Religion Comes to School." *Phi Delta Kappan,* 81(1), 10–16.

Stone v. Graham. (1980). 449 U.S. 39.

STRONKS, J., AND STRONKS, G. (1999). *Christian Teachers in Public Schools: A Guide for Teachers, Administrators, and Parents.* Grand Rapids: Baker Books.

TAYMAN, L. (2000). "Poll Finds Americans Favor Religion in Schools." *School Administrator.* Web Edition. July 14, pp. 13–14.

TOZER, S., VIOLAS, P., AND SENESE, G. (2002). *School and Society.* New York: McGraw-Hill.

U.S. DEPARTMENT OF EDUCATION. (1998). *Guidelines on Religious Expression in Public Schools.* Washington, DC: Author. (www.ed.gov/Speeches/08-1995/religion.html)

Wallace v. Jaffree. (1985). 472 U.S. 38.

WOOD, G. (1969). *The Creation of the American Republic 1776–1787.* New York: W. W. Norton.

WORONA, J. (1999). "Religion and the Schools—Emerging Issues." *Inquiry and Analysis: The Bimonthly Publication of the NSBA Council of School Attorneys.* Nov., pp. 1–15. Eric Document ED 438609.

WRIGHT, E. (1999). "Religion in American Education: A Historical View." *Phi Delta Kappan* 81(1), 17–20.

ZELDIN, M. (1986). "A Century Later and Worlds Apart: American Reform Jews and the Public School-Private School Dilemma, 1870–1970." Paper presented at the Annual Meeting of the American Educational Research Association, San Francisco.

Zorach v. Clauson. (1952). 343 U.S. 306.

CHAPTER 8

Privatization of Schools: Boon or Bane

POSITION 1: PUBLIC SCHOOLS SHOULD BE PRIVATIZED

In recent years, privatization has been one of the most controversial issues in public management and the delivery of public services at all levels of government. . . . In the years ahead, as in the last decade, state leaders and managers are likely to face tough decisions on whether to privatize certain state services or programs at a greater rate in efforts to improve productivity and cost-efficiency in state government.

—Chi, 2000, p. 13

Privatization means changing public services once operated by governmental agencies to private ownership or operation. This means cutting the high cost to taxpayers, government bloat, and the typical inefficiencies of governmental activities and monopolies. Public education is one of the most tax costly, bloated, and inefficient enterprises of government. It is also monopolistic. For these and other reasons, public education has not fulfilled its social purpose of providing high-quality education. With no competition and a tradition of inefficiency, public schools have become the major burden on, and frustration for, the local taxpayer. Thus, public schools are a prime candidate for privatization.

Privatization of a variety of government services has developed rapidly across the world over the past two decades, with more than 100 nations shifting from public to private ownership or private operation of such major enterprises as telecommunications, railroads, and national airlines. The value of global privatization is about $200 billion, a remarkable number more than double the privatization value in 1995 (Schipke, 2001). It is a movement based on good sense and good economics.

In contemporary society, there are three types of privatization. The first is to transfer or sell state-owned enterprises to private individuals, corporations, or organizations. The second is to contract out for services formerly done by government to a private company (Emmons, 2000). Third, deregulation of much of the public enterprise has offered opportunities for private industry to enter and compete in previously government-controlled monopolies, with less government involvement and control. Outright sale, contracting for services, and deregulation all represent structural reengineering of the public sector in response to market-oriented economics.

School privatization has mainly occurred in the second category of privatization—contracting with private enterprise to provide better education for less money. Public school districts don't see themselves as candidates for a public sale to private companies in the way that nations have divested themselves of governmentally owned telecommunication and transportation systems. Also, a strong private school movement in the United States already exists. Instead, most public schools recognize the values of private operation of some or all of their work, and schools in many states are considering or undertaking the contracting-out approach to privatization. Many other states and districts are developing charter or other parental-choice schools, which represent the deregulation approach in education.

Reasons for the Privatization of American Public Schools

1. Improving Schools for Our Children

The most important reason to involve private enterprise in schools is to benefit our children. Our primary resources, our children, deserve the best schools we can provide. The faceless bureaucracy created for government-operated schools not only overwhelms local budgets, but also does not respond to complaints. Private enterprise could not survive with that approach; its success is linked to ever-increasing efficiency and customer satisfaction. Privatization also increases accountability, making school staffs responsible for meeting performance standards for the benefit of children. Accountability, a keystone of private enterprise, offers a way to clearly identify problems and reward good performance in schools. Instead of weak, vague educational jargon that hides poor school practices, private enterprise sets specific goals and measures how well schools meet them. Schools that work will be rewarded; those that don't will be changed or closed.

The Edison Project, an innovative approach to school privatization, contracts with public schools to operate them with no increase in costs, but with better results. In addition, Edison offers opportunity for stockholders to participate while providing a public good. The Edison purposes are clear and direct: "to offer the best education in the world," "to welcome all students," and "to operate at an affordable price" ("An Invitation to Public School Partnership: Executive Summary," the Edison Project, www.edisonschools.com, undated). This puts the focus on student achievement. The Edison Project includes strict performance conditions in its contracts, which can be terminated on short notice if results are not satisfactory. Chubb (1998) documented the improving quality of schooling in Edison-operated schools of Boston; academic scores of students are improving under Edison leadership. Other major private contractors put performance conditions in their contracts. What public school operation gives the public the same guarantee?

2. Providing Democratic Choice—Breaking the Public School Monopoly

A second reason for privatizing schools is to break the monopoly public education has had in the United States. Privatizing schools offers democratic choices to parents concerned about their children's education but required by location or funds to send them to state-specified schools. School choice is certainly in the best interest of children and their parents, but it also forces schools to compete to attract students and needed financial support.

Law professor John Coons (1988) describes the U.S. education system as a "state-run monopoly" rather than a system of public schools. He argues that state-run schools strip families of authority to choose their children's schools by limiting them to local public school boundaries. The comparatively few private and parochial schools in the nation currently are prohibited from receiving taxpayer money. As a result, they serve a different and more selective clientele than their public counterparts; they don't compete for taxpayer dollars. Without competition, public schools have developed into self-protective havens where performance is not a high priority.

The public schools have had a monopoly for far too long, and have suffered from lack of competition. They have institutional hardening of the arteries, bloated and inefficient operations, and slow bureaucratic response to public concerns. These schools have little reason to provide better public service, increase their efficiency, require higher standards, or eliminate layers of bureaucracy. Privatization offers a way to bring customer satisfaction and state-of-the-art efficiency to such schools without the self-serving bureaucracy. Of course, public schools do not welcome privatization, and their unions continue to fight it (Shanker, 1994a, 1994b).

3. Increasing Productivity in Education

Privatizing will increase productivity in public schools, a place where productivity has not changed for a century. In most public school districts, schools are operated in much the same manner as they were when our grandparents were students. Private industry could not operate in this manner without suffering financial collapse. Expensive, labor-intensive public schools with inflated administrations sap local and state finances. Improvements in technology and communications have revolutionized U.S. business and provided manifold increases in productivity, but there has been virtually no change in public schools. Computers and other forms of high technology speed up all forms of industry, but schools, even with many computers, continue to take the same costly approach. Anderson (1998) notes that most school administrators come through the ranks of education and lack the business background and discipline needed to develop and implement sound strategic planning, efficient resource allocations, monitoring and accountability control, and effective management in schools. That may explain their lack of interest in improving productivity.

In high-cost, high-maintenance buildings, students attend classes about six hours a day for about one-half of the calendar year. Teachers still teach about twenty-five students per hour in separate classrooms using multiple copies of costly printed textbooks, similar to the way in which teachers taught at the beginning of the twentieth century. Those teachers, no matter how good or bad, are paid according to a standard scale, earning from about $25,000 to $75,000 per year for only nine months' employment. The one-size-fits-all teacher pay scale depends on seniority, not on how well each teacher teaches or how well students learn. This compromises good teachers and forces many away from teaching as a career. Competitive schools that reward performance will change that.

4. Meeting Global Competition

Schools will doubtless exert great influence on the future of the United States and its role in the global marketplace. International competition requires the United States to remain on the cutting edge of innovation or suffer future decline. If public schools are not up to the task, we need to find other ways to continue to improve the nation's status. Assuring America's place as a world leader and correcting long-term performance problems in public education underscores the point that privatization of schools is an idea whose time has come. The resounding collapse of the Soviet Union illustrated defects in economic structures that depend on government operation. Now we are in a race to see which nation will provide leadership in private development.

Privatization of public services promises significant benefits in worldwide competition and offers lower taxes, customer-focused service, and greater efficiency.

As democracy and capitalism increase across the globe, privatization will continue to be a strong movement in public life during the twenty-first century. Government-run operations show weaknesses that private enterprise can overcome. Worldwide, leaders recognize private enterprise as the key vehicle for improving citizens' lives while making government more efficient with available funds and resources. Nations from many geographic areas and differing economic traditions are moving toward private operation of a variety of public services. Schools are among the social institutions increasingly undergoing privatization in many nations. England and New Zealand provide excellent examples of this process; the public in each of these nations recognizes the value of private enterprise in more effectively and efficiently operating schools. The United States is actually lagging behind other nations in this global movement.

A Variety of Approaches to School Privatization: Charter Schools to Food Operations

In public-private partnerships, the school board hires private managers to run the public schools under a multi-year contract that specifies performance standards and allows the board to fire the managers with ninety days' notice. Complete privatization offers some distinct advantages, such as allowing districts to hold private managers accountable for student learning, but it is also possible to identify limited segments of current school operations that private contractors could handle to the benefit of students and taxpayers.

Some public schools now contract for selected services that are too costly or too cumbersome to handle under public control. Many school districts contract with computer corporations for payroll and accounting services. Others have found that contracting with popular fast-food companies, such as McDonalds and Pizza Hut, to provide school lunch service is more cost-effective, more acceptable to students, and sometimes more nutritious than the standard school cafeteria food. Private contracts for specific services, from the provision of food to managing all school operations, have proved their value to students, school officials, and taxpayers. Piecemeal privatization of school services has been working well for years in many schools. Now private operation of individual schools, and even entire city school districts, is developing. Charter school programs, in which the state grants specific charters to groups to organize or take over schools, now are legal in many states.

The Massachusetts charter school law allows profit-making companies to apply for charters. Edison, developed by business entrepreneur Chris Whittle, recently won three charters to operate public schools in Massachusetts as part of its original plan to establish up to 200 public, but for-profit, schools nationwide. Whittle's Channel One, the privately sponsored television channel for schools, has been operating successfully in a number of school districts—another example of the privatization of schools. The Edison Project has over 130 schools under its management, educating 75,000 students (Steinberg, 2002), with low costs and good results.

Privatization of individual schools includes the contracts given to Educational Alternatives Inc. (EAI), a private firm headquartered in Minneapolis, to operate individual schools in Baltimore and in southern Florida. But no city had completely privatized its schools until Hartford, Connecticut, took that step in 1994. Educational management organizations, similar to HMOs for medical care, are emerging to improve schools. Sylvan Learning Systems, Nobel Learning Communities, and Knowledge Universe are current examples of private management of education. The twenty-first century should see expansion of school privatization from 13 percent in 2000 to 25 percent by 2020.

Under complete privatization, rigorous contracts with the local board of education guarantee performance. Included in complete privatization would be all activities from managing the school(s), hiring, and evaluating staff, developing the curriculum, evaluating student learning, communicating with parents and the community, and providing custodial and ancillary maintenance.

Clearly, any of these individual items also are excellent candidates for partial privatization of school operations.

Revitalizing the Public Sector: Improving Schools

Privatization is a valid idea for any public sector enterprise that has become stagnant. Public agencies provide needed services where private enterprise can't. This should not mean that public agencies, once established, must always continue. The standard for all public enterprises is whether the quality of service they provide is the best we can get for the price we pay. If public agencies don't measure up against their counterparts in the private sector, we should replace them. That is the essence of privatization. Public agencies often outlive their purposes and become a drain on public funds. As Denis Doyle (1994), a senior fellow at the Hudson Institute, argues:

> While it is the business of the public to provide public service, the question before us should be, Does government need to own and operate the means of production to see that the service is provided wisely and well? To which our answer must be, "Only rarely and in special circumstances." (p. 130)

Doyle submits that police departments and the issuance of currency must remain in public hands, but that construction of public roads, buildings, and bridges can be performed (and already is) mainly by private contractors, as are trash collection and maintenance in many cities. Further, contracting out for services is just good business for many public agencies. In particular, Doyle singles out public schools as places where entrepreneurship clearly is needed to provide innovation and confront unproductive and conformist traditions. He points out that "the uniformity of the school system, once thought to be a virtue, is clearly a liability in the modern era" (p. 129).

Schools consume more taxes than any other agency in local communities, and also account for the largest part of most state budgets. That favored financial position should have made U.S. schools the best in the world, but we all know this is not the case. Evidence shows public schools spend increasing amounts of taxpayer money while becoming more and more mediocre. Privatizing schools is one strong alternative to the spend-and-decline model we have seen in education during the latter half of the twentieth century.

Historically, we could argue, public schools made a contribution to development of our nation by providing access to education for many and offering basic literacy and Americanization to immigrant children. There is good reason to continue to provide mass education in this modern and globally competitive age, but no reason that government must own and operate schools. The government school is an anachronism, held over because of romantic ideas about tradition. This holdover is one we will look back on one day and wonder why it lasted so long and cost so much to maintain. Government schools have come to represent high costs, low efficiency, and bureaucratic layering. It is time to shake up the bureaucrats and consider innovative ways to improve our schools at less cost. Privatization offers just that to schooling.

Obstacles to Privatization of Schools

Obviously, lack of knowledge and public apathy are serious obstacles to any innovation. These obstacles can be corrected through a public information and education program. When people understand that, for less cost, they can have better service and more accountability, they quickly become supporters of the shift to private operation. Other, more difficult, obstacles remain.

Public employee labor unions lobby extensively against privatization of public services, obvious self-interest. Public school teacher unions have been particularly active in opposing school privatization. Teacher unions are among the largest, best-financed, and most active organizations in state legislatures. Many state legislators fear the power of teacher unions. The teacher unions' self-serving approach has not been to the unions' credit. Teacher unions actually have filed suit against school vouchers in Milwaukee, against school management contracts in Baltimore, Hartford, Connecticut, and Wilkinsburg, Pennsylvania, and against school janitorial contracts in California (Eggers and O'Leary, 1996). Members of the teachers union very actively, but unsuccessfully, opposed the shift to privatization of schools in Philadelphia (Steinberg, 2002).

Government bureaucracies also can present obstacles to private enterprise, since bureaucracies may lose some of their power over key decisions. Under charter school laws in many states, charter schools are not subject to some of the bureaucratic regulations that have kept the public school establishment so entrenched. They may establish evaluations holding teachers accountable without worrying about tenure requirements, develop a curriculum without contending with state mandates, and organize classes and provide instruction without meeting some of the trivial specifications that have petrified public education. The public education bureaucracy has built a massive fortress of regulations, with personnel required to draft, monitor, and alter each segment. It is the IRS of the school business. Deregulation is a fearful event to some agency bureaucrats whose influence and positions are in jeopardy.

Privatization Is in America's Interest

President Reagan established the President's Commission on Privatization to recommend the transfer of selected public services to the private sector. The commission's report, *Privatization: Toward More Effective Government* (1988), expressed a concern about government-operated services:

> The American people have often complained of the intrusiveness of federal programs, of inadequate performance, and of excessive expenditure . . . government should consider turning to the creative talents and ingenuity in the private sector to provide, whenever possible and appropriate, better answers to present and future challenges. (p. xi)

The report identified the essential ways to privatize as (1) selling off government assets, (2) contracting work out to private companies, and (3) providing vouchers to purchase private services. Using testimony from some of the United States' most eminent scholars, the commission noted its primary interest in "the American consumer who is in need . . . of education; of loans for school, home, farm, or business; of transportation; of health care; of other social services" (p. xi).

With regard to education, the commission found that:

> The recent record of educational achievement has fallen far short of the basic goals that Americans set for their schools. . . . Despite substantial public spending on education—at all levels of government—the nation's schools were not

> producing commensurate results—educational report cards have turned the 1980s into a decade of dissatisfaction with schools. (Privatization, 1988, p. 85)

The commission's report showed that taxpayer spending on public schools doubled during the prior two decades, but educational results have been far less impressive than expected from that level of public financial support. Expenditures per student in private education are about two-thirds the per-student costs of public education. Although the nation spends heavily on public schools, average SAT test scores declined in the 1980s. These scores have only haltingly started to increase, and a massive infusion of tax dollars over the past decades has not had any effect on them. The National Assessment of Educational Progress (NAEP) and other tests of basic skills also show that U.S. students perform poorly. In the international arena, comparative studies of test scores show that U.S. students rank at the bottom among industrialized democracies (Finn, 1995; Mandel et al., 1995). Pumping more taxpayer money into those schools is not likely to alter their long-term deficiencies. Emily Feistritzer (1987) reported that no apparent correlation exists between education spending and student achievement. At no additional cost, privatization can improve schools, increase teacher motivation, and enhance student learning.

The decline of quality in U.S. education while school costs were rapidly increasing was of great concern to the commission. Public schooling is one area we can improve through expertise in management, cost control, and performance. Schools are a public service that the private sector can help.

Privatization and the Public School Crisis: What Can Privatization Provide for Schools?

The most significant commission recommendations for reforming education involve providing school choice, giving parents vouchers for use at private schools, and allowing private schools to participate in other federal programs. While these are important ideas that we should pursue, they may be insufficient to stem the decline in public education. Although the commission accurately assessed problems in public schools and determined significant change was needed, it did not go far enough in its recommendations for privatization. There are many reasons to seriously question the continuation of public education as it is presently organized and operated (Geiger, 1995).

Public schools are a lockstep system, out of touch with contemporary business management. Current school management follows an archaic and costly pattern, under regulations the education establishment set up early in the twentieth century. Many small schools have separate administrations and budgets for providing essentially the same services. New Jersey, for example, has more than 600 separate school districts. In some states, even tiny schools are mandated to employ a school principal, and often a superintendent and other staff. In large districts, multiple, well-paid school administrative officers never teach a student and seldom visit the district's schools. Organizational structures of schools are more similar to those of inefficient early factories than to structures of modern corporations.

Public schools use an old-fashioned system that relies on politics to get more tax money, elaborate and expensive lobbying in state legislatures to improve teacher salaries and keep teacher unions in power, and coziness with state education agencies to maintain the status quo. Increasing state regulation serves only to further bloat school administrations. And all this is practiced without any accountability. The failings of public schools are revealed in the low test scores of U.S. students as compared with those of other nations, in the discourteous behavior of students, and in low public esteem.

Schools are mired in bureaucracy and self-protective traditional thinking. They are not efficient institutions. Instead of attempting to keep costs down while improving quality, a standard that business sets, schools simply obtain increased tax funds without improving productivity.

There are numerous places to increase productivity and improve school performance in this antiquated system of education. The school day and school year are expensive links to our agricultural past. Most industrialized nations keep students in school for longer days and for more days of the year. Traditional small-group instruction, with one well-paid teacher for each class of twenty-five students, does not take advantage of striking advances in communication technology or flexible management. Interactive computers linked with major libraries and scholars would make better use of limited resources. The lack of merit-based salary recognition for teachers limits teachers' motivation. The inertia of low productivity is built into the current public schools; private enterprise offers a fresh approach.

The Privatization Movement: A Global Context

Schools are not the only public agency that could be improved by privatization. A worldwide privatization movement is already in progress, rapidly improving services in many other areas, such as transportation and communication. Schools are an important part of this movement, and the effort to privatize them should be viewed in the larger context.

The global political economy has changed since the end of the cold war, as the world increasingly recognizes the values inherent in free market enterprise. Privatization is consistent with the realization that communism and socialism are defective political systems. Communism robs people of their individuality, and socialism robs them of their personal motivation. The former communist and socialist nations of the old Soviet bloc realize privatization of wasteful and bureaucratic state-owned industries is the only way to improve their economies and the lives of their people.

As the Soviet Union collapsed in the late 1980s and early 1990s, Russian and other former communist governments tried to embrace capitalistic economics by replacing public ownership with privately held and operated businesses. This experiment has been slow and difficult because of the many years of communist rule and the serious economic decline state socialism caused. Economic analyses (Vickers and Yarrow, 1991; van Brabant, 1992; Earle,

Frydman, and Rapaczynski, 1993) describe the difficulties such nations as Hungary, Poland, Czechoslovakia, and Russia encountered in their massive efforts to restructure a failed system, but economists generally recognize the need to privatize to compete in the global market. Earle, Frydman, and Rapaczynski, for example, note:

> After decades of experience with malfunctioning command economies and unsuccessful attempts to improve their performance through moderate "market socialist" reforms, the countries of Eastern Europe and the former Soviet Union are struggling to radically transform their economic systems. (p. 1)

If the Russian people can persist in their short-term sacrifices, they will be far better off than they were under communism. In 1990, formerly communist East Germany had almost 14,000 state-owned businesses, and just four years later, the number was fewer than 150 (Protzman, 1994). Private enterprise and marketplace competition are replacing inefficient government-controlled business enterprises.

Other nations are engaging in massive privatization of publicly owned industries. Great Britain, suffering under Labour Party governments and socialistic economics for several decades, more recently privatized many publicly owned and operated industries. The British economy has improved significantly as a result. Privatization is an idea taking hold for industries in many nations. Water and waste treatment, for example, are 100 percent privatized in England, while the United States has privatized only about 15 percent (Farazmand, 2001).

The competition that is a hallmark of private enterprise requires efficient operation and consumer satisfaction—two elements lacking in government monopolies. Under privatization, it is possible to maintain and improve public services while cutting taxes. In addition, private enterprise is built on the human desire to succeed and get credit for succeeding. This system motivates people to achieve more and rewards those who show improved work. No wonder privatization is sweeping the world, creating increased global competition.

We should not be content with old structures and the myths that support them if those structures are no longer efficient. Just as an old car must be replaced when it costs more to repair it than it is worth, we need to review some social agencies to see if they are as efficient as possible alternatives.

Schools are basic to the national interest and to international competition. America's leadership depends on top-quality, well-educated people—successful students from achievement-driven schools. The talents and vision of such people are limited by cookie-cutter schools that offer less than the most current and efficient approaches to education. The private sector of the U.S. economy, which demands innovation and efficiency to survive, offers an avenue for reshaping U.S. schools to meet the demands of global competition in the twenty-first century. For many good reasons, privatization of schools is the wave of the twenty-first century.

POSITION 2: PUBLIC SCHOOLS SHOULD BE PUBLIC

Privatisation [sic] increases unemployment, reduces the standard of living and working conditions of public sector workers, and brings them continuous fear for their livelihood. Also, it further increases the enormous differences between the rich, who can afford private education, private health care, etc., and the poor who cannot.

—BICKERSTAFFE, IN HASTINGS AND LEVIE, 1983, P. 7

Is privatization of public services good public policy or just good corporate propaganda? Do corporations do things better than public employees, or are they just better at PR? Are Enron and WorldCom good examples of how privatization might work for education? Do you prefer Arthur Andersen and Company? Should we work out a system for privatizing public schools that would handsomely reward the school CEO and a chosen few insiders, penalize the workers and general stockholders, and allow a failing corporation to walk away from the schools with little responsibility for their failure?

The idea that private operation of public services is superior is a socially destructive myth. Schrag (1999) points out that "the pattern in our society is toward withdrawal from community into private, gated enclaves with private security, private recreational facilities, private everything, even as the public facilities deteriorate" (p. B-11). Social destruction results from the self-serving myth—promoted in the corporate world and corporate-oriented mass media—that private enterprise offers superior services. Krugman (2002) argues that the vast experience in privatization by governments at all levels is that the record does not support claims of improving efficiency. Typically, private contractors submit low bids to get a contract, then move prices up—or have cost-overruns—when government workers have been eliminated and they and their unions are no threat to the corporation. Privatization also may have a hidden agenda of providing a new political spoils system, where civil service rules are avoided and patronage comes back in favor to reward party loyalists (Krugman, 2002).

Private management of public schools seeks shelter under other myths about efficiency, competition, and management. There is no solid evidence of superior performance, higher quality, lower costs, or better management in schools by the private sector. Evidence seems to demonstrate the opposite. Edison Schools, the largest of private corporations running schools, can produce no substantial evidence of improvements in academic performance by students (Miron and Applegate, 2000; Bracey, 2002; Henriques and Steinberg, 2002a,b; Holloway, 2002). Since private companies are supposed to be good in the area of management, look at how well Edison Schools manages itself: This corporation faces financial crises all the time, issuing new stock to finance continuing operations and borrowing immense amounts of money. All the while Edison gets substantial funds from public school district money for, ironically, contracting to manage public schools in a cost-effective way. In 2001, Edison reportedly had to pledge \$61 million as collateral to obtain a loan of only \$20 million—a demonstration of the company's financial problems. No public school would be permitted to do such shaky financing. In addition, Edison sometimes gets subsidies from private charities for running its schools—raising questions about the corporate claim that they can run schools at less cost per pupil than public school (Henriques and Steinberg, 2002a). Bracey (2002) details a long series of Edison difficulties, both financial and educational. He even suggests questionable political arrangements Edison used to obtain contracts in such places as Philadelphia, prompting investigations, and several serious problems in Edison's efforts to provide private schooling in such places as New York, Georgia, Massachusetts, Connecticut, Texas, and Kansas.

In regard to evidence about charter schools, the uncritical reporting by mass media on charter schools describes charters as innovations to improve education, but hides their lack of academic performance. Not all charter schools are private, but many are and there is a false presumption behind all of them that they are somehow better than public education. For many critics of public education, charter schools (especially private ones) are good examples of how privatization would work in education. A vast, 2.5-year study by researchers at UCLA found little support for claims that charter schools improve learning; charter schools neither fulfill their promises nor improve student achievement (Magee and Leopold, 1998). Some charter schools, relieved from many state regulations, have serious problems in finances, student achievement, and operations ("Gateway Academy Raided as State Begins Fraud Investigation," 2002). A Brookings Institute Brown Center Report on American Education (2002), which examined academic achievement in charter schools in ten states from 1999 to 2001, concludes: "in a nutshell, charter schools performed about one-quarter standard deviation below comparable regular public schools on these three years of state tests" (Brown Center Report, 2002, p. 1). Charter schools do not live up to their advertising. Privatizing schools is not improvement or progress, just another avenue for private wealth to gain more control of our society.

Social Purposes and Private Goals

In a capitalistic democracy, some activities fit private enterprise and some deserve public operation and oversight. A striking and sobering book, *Savage Inequalities* (Kozol, 1991), documents how underfinanced public schools in poor areas make a mockery of democratic ideals. Jonathan Kozol, in an interview reported in *Rethinking Schools* (1998), finds no evidence that "a competitive free market, unrestricted, without a strong counterpoise within the public sector will ever dispense decent medical care, sanitation, transportation, or education to the people" (p. 1). We will discover whether privatization can work in providing Homeland Security, perhaps to our regret.

Privatizing public schools is another example of mythology, a siren song of lower costs and better scores. Significantly, the issue shifts attention from the fundamental social purposes of public education in a democracy. While this shift may serve the purpose of those advocating privatization, basic social purposes must be the centerpoint of any substantial debate over privatization. A major test of the public/private balance lies in the fundamental social purposes of an activity. Thus, we can measure public and private operation of schools against the broad social purposes of schooling. Any debate over privatizing public schools should focus on whether public or private control is more likely to move us toward fulfilling those large social purposes.

The clamor to privatize, and a vicious long-term campaign to demonize public schools, has stifled the more significant debate on social purposes (Troy, 1999). Lacking is the necessary long-range social perspective in the pressure to privatize schools (Hunter and Brown, 1995). Shortsighted goals of achieving higher test scores and saving money are simply insufficient reasons for privatizing, even if private schools would assure these results. Of course, they can't; and short-term test score improvement has been shown to be the result of manipulation, not superior schooling. The privatization myth magnifies social and economic problems plaguing public schools for over a century, while it hides significant historical defects of private enterprise.

Despite a century-long tradition of excellent public service in difficult social and financial conditions, public schools have been subjected to a relentlessly negative campaign during the past two decades. Ironically, the privatization myth has protected private enterprise from similar attacks for its many failures and its significant threat to democracy. The history of private enterprise—with its questionable ethics, cavalier treatment of employees and the public, financial manipulation of the political process, and declarations of bankruptcy when in trouble—goes unmentioned in mass media reporting and public discourse on privatization. Much support for privatization of public schools revolves around shallow advertising that capitalizes on negative images of public schools, unsupported claims of potential cost savings, and a paternalistic aura that corporations know best. The evidence does not support the claims. A Brookings Institute study of privatization in public schools, especially big city schools, found that most arguments for school privatization are based on wishful thinking (Ascher, Fruchter, and Berne, 1996). Other studies have shown for-profit schools do not have innovative practices, curriculum, or management programs—except that they are in it for profit (Kaplan, 1996; Zollers and Ramanathan, 1998).

The rush to privatization demands a serious look at rationales, practices, and potentials. In certain situations and under strict and open public regulation and school district supervision, it is reasonable to provide some aspects of public services, such as food service in school lunchrooms, through private contracts. But wholesale privatizing of schools, where a private corporation controls the management, curriculum, and instructional decisions of a whole school or school district, is an extremely hazardous approach to dealing with public services. In areas as important to society's future as education, privatizing may destroy the soul of democratic life (Saltman, 2000; Sudetic, 2001).

To address the lacks in long-range perspective and in maintaining a balanced view, we present two major points: (1) public schools serve significant public purposes, and (2) privatization is being championed under a number of myths that hide its unpleasant characteristics. Our conclusion: that public schools must not be sacrificed to private profiteering.

Privatizing and the Democratic Purpose of Public Education

To be self-governing, a democracy requires a well-informed, active, and free populace. The primary ideals of democracy in the United States include justice, equality, and freedom. Within those high social ideals, the overriding purpose of public education is to prepare students for active and knowledgeable participation in society. In schools, that preparation involves development of language facility, social knowledge, ethical conduct, and sound critical thinking—all in the context of the accumulated wisdom of the arts and sciences. Standardized test scores, of course, reveal relatively little about this significant curriculum or about the social purposes public schools serve. Further, these instructional topics, and related extracurricular life of the school, are baseless without the root purpose of improving civilization by focusing on ensuring and expanding justice, equality, and freedom. To lose sight of that grand democratic ideal by working to trim costs and raise test scores is to undercut the fabric of American society.

This relationship between a democratic society and the need for publicly operated schools has been widely recognized throughout history. Aristotle (1988), the first Western political philosopher, clearly recognized the need to provide schooling for all citizens to preserve a democracy. Among the most compelling statements for public education in a democratic society is John Dewey's *Democracy and Education* (1916). In recent years, leading political theorists and education scholars have reiterated the significance of public education to democracy (Gutmann, 1999; Saltman, 2000).

The goals of improving justice, equality, and freedom are central to the idea of a public school, but not to private enterprise. Clearly, we have a long way to go in public education to meet these high standards; minorities and women have not had equal opportunities or freedom in schools. But we are improving significantly in this area, and we continue to pursue those goals in public education. Privatizing, with its attendant emphasis on cutting costs and improving test scores, is less likely to expand opportunities for the weakest or most disadvantaged. When you take seriously the need to educate the whole society, and not merely the elite, you improve society—but you probably won't increase average test scores or cut the school budget.

In addition to making strong efforts to improve justice and equality, schools allow the freedom of inquiry needed to fulfill the claim of democracy. Education for knowledgeable self-governance liberates us from ignorance, including that perpetuated by propaganda and censorship. Public education for all citizens requires student and teacher freedom of inquiry and critical thinking about social problems. But free, critical study of social problems may not be a goal in corporation-operated schools. Open examination of controversial topics, necessary in democratic society, may conflict with corporate agendas in an ethos in which business knows best. How many corporations encourage criticism, especially public criticism, of their purposes and practices? Saltman (2000) notes an example of "Coke Day" in a high school in Georgia: the school entered a Coca-Cola-sponsored competition by having a day of Coke rallies, speeches by Coke executives, economics and chemistry classes using the Coca-Cola company as a fine example, and an aerial photo of students dressed in red and white and forming the word *Coke.* A few students rebelled, and wore Pepsi shirts at the photo shoot, and the school principal suspended them. This is a minor story, but illustrates the strong influence of corporations on public school life, portending more commercialization when schools are privatized. Saltman rightly condemns the utter commercialization of public education as a major threat to democracy.

Not only has the common schools tradition in the United States been a keystone of democratic society by offering individuals the opportunity to develop skills and knowledge needed to self-govern, but schools also have provided a community-centered service responsible to the community in a variety of ways. Privatization threatens that tradition. Dayton and Glickman (1994) point clearly to one aspect of the threat:

> A fundamental problem with the privatization movement is that it views public education as merely another individual entitlement and ignores the vital public interests served by common public schools. Public education is democratically controlled by the elected representatives of the People. Ultimately it is the People who decide how public education funds are expended. Privatization systems use public funds, but limit public control. Allowing private control of public funds circumvents the democratic control and interests of the People. (p. 82)

A significant question regarding privatization of public schools is whether private management is likely to view justice, equality, and freedom as schools' most important purposes. Public education may have some difficult problems, but its purposes are clear and positive. Can the private sector be trusted to foster these democratic ideals?

Recent Examples of School Privatization: Reasons for Resistance

The two most prominent efforts to privatize public schools in the United States have already been fraying at the edges and engaging in questionable practices that should arouse the public's skepticism about the whole process (Saks, 1995; Toch, 1995; CUPE Report, 1998; Schrag, 1999; Breslau and Joseph, 2001; Shrag, 2001; Bracey, 2002; Henriquez and Steinberg, 2002a,b).

The Edison Project

The Edison Project, the most widely advertised effort to take over and profit from operation of public schools, was established by Christopher Whittle in 1991. Whittle, a strong advocate of free market economics, was known for comments that were "unbelievably hostile to the public school world" (*New York*, 1994, p. 53).

Using Whittle's funds for startup, with the expectation that investors would seize the new money-making opportunity, the Edison Project began by proposing to build new schools. That idea changed quickly to an effort to contract for the complete operation of existing public schools. Whittle had predicted that the Edison Project would be operating 200 private schools by 1996, and would be educating 2 million children by the year 2010. He also pledged to personally finance the education of 100 "Whittle Scholars" for a year at the University of Tennessee (*New Yorker,* 1994). The widely publicized project now appears unable to meet any of its initial projections. Edison reportedly was operating twelve for-profit schools at the end of the twentieth century, with a record of high teacher turnover because of organizational disarray, lack of materials and support, and other related problems (CUPE Report, 1998; Breslau and Joseph, 2001; Shrag, 2001; Bracey, 2002).

In 1992, Whittle persuaded Benno Schmidt, then president of Yale University, to become the Edison Project's chief executive officer, reportedly "in exchange for equity in the new company and a salary that insiders estimate at around 1 million dollars" (*New York,* 1994, p. 53). *The New York Times* (Applebome, 1994) reported Schmidt's salary at $800,000, but whichever figure is accurate, Schmidt's move from Yale president to for-profit education certainly profited him. The Edison CEO salary is over twenty times the average public school teacher's salary and nearly seven times the salary of the highest-paid public school administrators. How can privatization, with such huge executive salaries, bring cost savings to taxpayers without cutting instructional support?

Million-dollar salaries for private school executives, while proposing to lower the costs of school operation, suggests mirrors-and-smoke accounting or major cuts in the most direct services to students. Privatization means even lower pay and higher workloads for teachers and counselors, increased savings on textbooks and materials, cutting or elimination of other services, to help finance higher salaries for executives. This corporate model—excessively paid executives over exploited workers—benefits an elite few, but does not benefit society in general.

Can private business show how to better finance schools with public funds, make a profit, and preserve educational quality? The financial management of Whittle's corporation may provide a perspective. By 1994, Whittle Communications had reached a state of financial collapse. *The New Yorker* magazine (1994) featured a long story detailing this collapse under the title "Grand Illusion," and subtitled with the line, "But the biggest surprise may be that it took so long for anyone to know that things had gone so wrong" (p. 63). The story described Whittle's reputation on Madison Avenue as a "legendary salesman" and one whose "most striking quality may be his charm" (p. 63). This charm has not made the Edison stock worthwhile; it has declined precipitously amid concerns about its profitability and an SEC investigation (Steinberg and Henriques, 2002).

Whittle had earlier established Channel One, a private television channel that "gave" TV equipment to schools on the condition that students be required to watch the channel and its commercials daily. Needing capital to try to save his other ventures, Whittle sold Channel One to K–III Communications. K–III owns *Seventeen* magazine and the *Weekly Reader,* a school newspaper, and is itself under the control of the same corporate body that controls RJR Nabisco. That relationship raised some concerns about corporate interests and influence when the *Weekly Reader* carried a story on "smokers' rights" (*Wall Street Journal,* 1994). But the larger concern is about the broad effort to commercialize public education.

The Edison Project's financial difficulties illustrate some defects inherent in the privatization scheme. Venture capital, with its high risks and potentially high rewards for a few, is not the best model for organizing public schools in a democracy. Public schooling's long-term goals of providing knowledge and encouraging ethical conduct based on justice, equality, and freedom are socially constructive. Are those goals best served by people known as legendary salespeople hostile to public schools? A public education system based on charm and advertising is inconsistent with the democratic purposes of education. The potential damage to youth and to society is too great.

Another Privatization Experiment at Public Cost

The second most visible effort to privatize public schools involves Educational Alternatives, Inc., or EAI, founded in 1986. EAI obtained the first contract for the private operation of an entire public school district—the Hartford, Connecticut, schools. The controversial decision was described as the result of a city "torn between a desperate plight and a radical plan" (*Time,* 1994, p. 48). Hartford's schools suffered from problems similar to those of many urban districts: neglect, intensified social problems, and high costs of maintaining old schools and senior staffs. Per-student expenditures were higher, at about $9,000, than those of the average district in the state, but student test scores were low and dropout rate high. The board of education chose EAI to undertake a five-year contract to pay the bills, shape the curriculum, train the teachers, and then keep whatever money was left in the public school budget, about $200 million per year, as profit.

One question the *Time* article posed was, "What will be the driving motive: improving schools or improving EAI's bottom line?" (p. 49). In a commentary raising questions about the Hartford deal with EAI, Judith Glazer (1994) suggested that "American education is for sale" to "profit-making companies whose bottom line is not education but the strength of their financial performance for their stockholders" (p. 44). Glazer makes a strong point that if Hartford's school problems had become so dire, the public should have held the state governor, state legislature, city council, and local school board accountable for neglecting their duty to provide quality public schools.

EAI's record in school privatization is sketchy. In 1992, the corporation obtained a $135 million contract to take over a few schools in Baltimore. EAI agreed to improve instruction and make school operations more efficient, with any unspent funds going to the company as profit. Judson (1994) reports that the school district uses its public budget to pay EAI the city's average amount per student, or about $6,000. In fact, most non-EAI schools actually receive less than the average total student expenditure because the costs of the central district offices are figured into the averages, but are not counted against EAI's budget. Thus, EAI actually gets about $1 million more per school per year than other schools in the district.

EAI improved physical facilities at the schools, but spent "more than the average amount of money" and "had not begun to deliver on its promise, that private enterprise can do a better job for less in running big-city public schools" (Judson, 1994, p. A13). Albert Shanker (1994b) reported that EAI changed some arrangements after the agreement, putting special education students in regular classrooms and then replacing special education teachers with "interns," recent college graduates paid $7 per hour with no benefits.

EAI initially reported increased scores in EAI schools in Baltimore, but an examination of the scores by the *Minneapolis Star-Tribune* found EAI had inflated the data (Leslie, 1994). EAI later acknowledged its error; data show standardized test scores in EAI schools actually have gone down (Judson, 1994). After this was publicized, the eight schools used to make comparative evaluations with EAI schools were changed by dropping the three non-EAI schools at which students did very well (Shanker, 1994a). This change should make EAI school test scores look better, but not because of improved education. Surprisingly, for all the fanfare about business's hard-nosed accountability for performance in private enterprise, the Baltimore contract does not set any performance standards for EAI to meet (Judson, 1994), and the comparative evaluation program has been compromised.

By 1996, EAI had lost both contracts, Hartford and Baltimore. An AFT report on the Baltimore school project showed EAI had a profit of $2.6 million, teacher morale had declined, and there was no improvement in student test scores. The salary of the CEO of EAI was reported in 1996 to be $325,000, with an additional $193,000 in stock options (CUPE Report, 1998).

Privatization and Private Enterprise: Beyond Schooling

The stories of the Edison Project and EAI are cautionary tales for those considering privatization of public education. Another example comes from Canada, where Alberta is rethinking its charter schools. The largest one in Calgary closed, leaving large unpaid bills and frustrated parents—apparently, no one monitored the money (Sheppard, 1998).

In areas where private enterprise is supposed to afford the best leadership (efficiency, financial acuity, accountability, and performance), these private ventures do not measure up. Instead, evidence of financial manipulation, wastage and inefficiency, and insufficient public accountability crops up. Further, private enterprise has offered no demonstration that instruction actually was improved and at a lower cost when private groups take over. The social purposes of public education, of course, are not addressed in these examples. Where is the concern for justice, equality, and freedom?

Private entrepreneurship is one of the values American society holds dear. We prize the brave individuals who risk their financial security to bring new ideas and products to the public marketplace. Thomas Edison and Alexander Graham Bell are considered heroes who endured sacrifices and hard work to emerge as successful inventors and businessmen. Private entrepreneurs encourage innovation, experimentation, and development. But private entrepreneurship also is marked by unethical and illegal practices, including fraud and scams, graft and corruption, "Let the buyer beware" as a common corporate philosophy, and irresponsible pollution of the environment. The robber baron mentality permeates much of private enterprise, where payoffs and hidden conspiracies for fixing prices or controlling the market are simply ways of doing business. The primary value is personal greed. In these ways, private enterprise has shown little regard for social responsibility. Incompetent private operation and lack of adequate governmental regulation have cost taxpayers billions in government bailouts and subsidies of Chrysler, Lockheed, and the savings and loan associations. Yet private enterprise maintains an aura of respectability that implies it is better than public operations.

Challenging the Privatization Myth

Striking examples of improvements and declines in the quality of human life can be attributed to both private and public enterprise; neither has an automatic superiority in economic, ethical, or social terms. In addition to lack of clear supportive evidence about the extraordinary claims of privatization advocates, questions arise about the ideology of privatization and its consequences for society.

Inherent in privatization mythology is the presumption that if something makes a profit, it must be good for us. How can a democracy sustain the idea that greed offers more to society than social responsibility? Privatization encourages privateering over the public good. Standard Oil's manipulation of the public trust was so massive it resulted in antitrust laws supposed to protect us from further fleecing by private enterprise (Tarbell, 1904). Unfortunately, we have suffered a long history of corporate corruption, fraud, and manipulation of the public even with some protections resulting from antitrust legislation (Adams, 1990; Calavita, 1997; Mitchell, 2001; Sherman, 2001; Palast, 2002).

In 2002, Enron and WorldCom showed us that the corporate world remains ready and eager to gain excessive, some say obscene, profits on public necessities without accepting public responsibility. Enron is only one of the most recent and largest of corporations to use slack regulation and a misguided "market" theology to cover private greed at the public trough. A pattern of Enron political action, including gifts, contributions, and extraordinary lobbying, gave Enron executives access to top politicians. These Enron executives became leaders of the effort to deregulate the energy industry, a necessary public commodity. Their substantial contributions to both political parties assured Enron of a more than equal opportunity to have their side heard in the halls of government. The resulting deregulation, a form of privatization, permitted manipulation of the system of electricity and gas provided to the public, creating manufactured crises, shortages, and windfall profits to companies like Enron. Enron had not been entirely without public blame before the debacle of 2002; three years earlier, Human Rights Watch published a dark story of Enron's involvement in human rights violations (Human Rights Watch, 1999). While other examples of corporate greed are not as large or public as Enron's became, there are many others. WorldCom's hidden losses were, apparently, the largest of any corporation in history and were taken largely by shareholders and employees—not the key executives. We need to exercise great caution in accepting the myth that corporations will look out for the public good.

Exposing the Myths of Privatization

Clever packaging in a period when people distrust government and are concerned about rising taxes has made privatization popular. There are, however, several presumptions that privatization is based on, and they are simply false or at least seriously questionable. The popular media have not challenged these presumptions. They are myths of private enterprise, and deserve to be fully examined before the public purse is opened even wider to private operations.

Myths about privatization include the ideas that privatization is:

- efficient, so it can save tax money while providing quality services.
- market-driven, so it is responsive to the consumer.
- performance-based, rewarding the productive and cutting out the incompetent.
- a success as a worldwide movement.

Myth: Efficiency

Efficiency is the main claim of private enterprise. It is almost an article of faith, but the claim collapses under scrutiny.

Efficiency is a means, not a goal; the mere act of being efficient is inadequate as a rationale for social policy. There has to be a purpose for striving to make human activities efficient. In a democratic society that respects the environment and aspires to equity for its members, efficiency can be a worthwhile pursuit, but effectiveness is more important. Efficient use of resources, human and other, should aim to preserve and improve the environment. That is a worthy goal, and efficiency is an appropriate means to reach it; but environmental improvement by efficiency is not in the interests of many industries. Efficient operation of social services should have the purpose of improving the lot of society as a whole, not just of one class of people. That statement of purpose suggests the kind of social benefits efficiency should supply. We must ask, would efficiency improve civilization by increasing justice, equality, freedom, and life for the common citizen?

Against this measure, the superficial type of efficiency used in the private sector is found wanting. The profit motive defines efficiency as a cost-saving way to increase corporate income. Saving time by requiring dangerous shortcuts may appear to be efficient, but may simply be foolhardy. Efficient slaughter of wild animals, once a pastime of the wealthy and a business enterprise, sped endangerment of many species. Wild animal wall trophies and exotic meat dishes are not worth the price of those forms of efficiency.

Efficient manufacturing has created toxic waste, workplace accidents, worker health problems, overproduction, and waste. Actual social costs of this type of efficiency are seldom calculated. Environmental and human costs of industrial efficiency are hidden in the search for profit. In addition, the public often subsidizes the private sector through corporation-friendly policies on taxes and use of natural resources.

A related concern is whether captains of industry are themselves efficient and productive. Do they seem to practice what they preach for the public sector? Are their homes, cars, boats, and planes evidence of efficiency? Do they lead lives that model efficiency and social improvement? Although it is possible to find examples of wealthy, powerful people who make significant contributions to the improvement of society and who strive for efficient and productive lives, that is not the standard. Large homes, expensive cars, servants, yachts, exclusive clubs, private planes, and legal and financial assistance to take advantage of tax loopholes typify those who gain the most from private enterprise. These are not accoutrements normally found among public school educators, whose lives are devoted to public service. Conspicuous consumption is a characteristic of private enterprise, not of public employment.

Myth: Market-Driven and Consumer-Responsive

Another myth is that the private sector must be superior because it competes in the open marketplace and pleases its customers. However, clearly there is no free and open market in the current economy. The marketplace itself is a myth. Price-fixing, monopolistic trusts, special interest legislation, weak regulatory agencies, and other corporation-protective practices skew the market to benefit the biggest corporations and most politically adept businesspeople. Lobbying, graft, buyouts, control of regulating authorities, and an "old boys' network" combine to deny newcomers equal marketplace opportunity. Most corporate strategies aim to gain control of the market to keep others out, not to encourage free competition. When that doesn't work well, corporations appeal to the government for special treatment or subsidies, or undergo bankruptcy, which hurts small investors but leaves executives wealthy. The free market does not exist.

Public bailouts of failed corporations, such as Chrysler and the savings and loan associations, have enormous public costs, but somehow they are not classified as failures since they were successful at getting taxpayers to cover the cost (U.S. Congress, 1980; Adams, 1990; Long, 1993). These publicly funded bailouts of failed corporations could be called publicization, but they were not made public enterprises—they remained profit-making entities with taxpayers taking the loss. The term used for using public funds to shore up failing or weak private corporations is *corporate welfare.* This is not a term that the business community likes, no matter how accurate. Destruction of the myth that business leaders have superior wisdom, skill, or ethics would help to allay the rush to privatize schools; in many respects, public schools show superior wisdom, skill, and ethics in providing good mass education at a remarkably low cost over a long time with relatively few ethical lapses.

Consumer responsiveness is another figment of the imagination. Marketing to increase consumerism is a high priority in the private sector, but the primary purpose is to increase profits, not to please customers. Enticing consumers to buy things they do not need is one of the purposes. Consumer protection and satisfaction is a public, not a private, concern, fostered by decades of consumer manipulation by private businesses. Every consumer has experienced traumatic confrontations with corporations; they make errors, furnish poor-quality goods or services, are unwilling to correct or replace items, use bait-and-switch tactics, provide weak warranties, list conditions of sale in unreadable fine print on contracts, and inflate credit charges.

Myths: The Performance-Based Corporation, Rewarding Merit, and Cutting Incompetence

Another myth about private enterprise is that it is rigorous about performance, expecting increased productivity and eliminating incompetence. But performance, in business terms, is merely selling more products at less cost with more profit. This goal has nothing to do with quality. Business news is filled with stories of chief executive officers (CEOs) whose corporations underperform, but who still receive large salary increases and bonuses. Incompetence occurs regularly and at high levels, office politics is more important than quality of work, and you can't challenge higher-level decisions even when these decisions obviously are wrong.

If U.S. businesses are so committed to performance, why was there a decline in its quality of manufacture and share of the world marketplace? Why are corporation stockholder meetings a façade while good ideas from ordinary stockholders essentially are excluded? Why is the business of consumer advocate offices increasing? Why are the most meritorious employees often forgotten, while the well-connected earn quick promotions? These and other points suggest that performance is not always the corporation's focus, and is not a major principle in big business.

Myth: The Successful Worldwide Movement

The vaunted privatization of public services in many nations has been unraveling. Britain's problems with the privatization of public services illustrate public loss for private gain. After World War II, Britain moved to public ownership of many enterprises to provide better accessibility to education, health care, and social services. Fifteen years of the Thatcher and Major governments produced privatization, and public services found themselves under assault.

Ellingsen (1994a) examined this privatization program and found: "Britain's passion for privatization has produced no payoff for the public . . . the public is starting to realize not only that the sell-offs have made millionaires of those who run former state enterprises, but have cost consumers something like $9 billion" (p. 21). The minister responsible for most of the privatization, Lord Parkinson, admitted after retiring that auctioning public businesses had not gone as planned; private shareholders did well, but the customers did not. British Telecom, auctioned in 1984, had embarrassingly high profits, while customers paid about $1 billion more than necessary. Water authorities, after privatization, saw their profits soar, while "customers are paying an extra $640 million for service that, as yet, has not fundamentally improved" (p. 21).

As a result of privatization, London Electricity executives saw their salaries rise from averages well below those in the private sector—to over $4 million annually for each of the twelve top officers. One executive retired on a $3 million pension, about $200,000 per month for each month he was in the privatized corporation. Public utilities were sold at excessively low prices that allowed quick profits, and executive income was linked to those profits in a charade claim of performance—all essentially at taxpayer expense (Ellingsen, 1994a). The greed of privatization has transformed the benevolent post–World War II British welfare state into a nation plagued by increased separation between the social classes, illegal child labor, hidden sweatshops, and crime and drugs (Ellingsen, 1994b).

Australia's experience with privatization also is problematic. Although studies concluded that a Sydney harbor tunnel was not economically viable, a private firm was proposed to build and operate one. After two years of private operation, taxpayers learned they will pick up a previously unreported tab of $4 billion to cover extra expenses during the thirty-year life of the private contract. Following that disclosure, alarms were sounded about other privatization efforts because of secrecy, hidden costs, and lack of scrutiny of private contracts for public services, such as building and operating hospitals, prisons, airports, railroads, and water services ("Auditor Criticises Secrecy on Public Works Contracts," 1994; "Public Funds, Public Works," 1994; "Why Parlt [Parliament] Must Scrutinize Projects with Private Sector," 1994). The public services employees' organization warned that a proposed bill to privatize state utilities (gas, electricity, and water) could lead to destruction of the public sector without adequate protection for consumers or public funds or provision of quality service ("Competition May Kill Utilities: ACTU," 1994).

Citizens of other nations also have suffered under privatization. In Eastern Europe and the former Soviet Union, privatization created high unemployment, extraordinary inflation, pyramid schemes that enriched a few and caused financial disaster for many, and social unrest (van Brabant, 1992; Earle, Frydman, and Rapaczynski, 1993).

These myths of privatization should become part of the public debate before we take irretrievable actions to dismantle public schools. Privatizing public schools is another example of mythology, a siren song of lower costs and better scores.

Ideology or Sound Thinking?

After studying the economics of public service privatization for over six years, Sclar (1994) dismissed the claim that privatizing would save money while improving services. He found this promise to be ideological hype, a starkly conservative agenda unsupported by research or practice. Sclar suggests that real competition in the global marketplace will require an improved public infrastructure, not its decimation by privatization. Undercutting public services, increasing in actual total costs, and raking in windfalls for the well-connected do not offer a quality of life that encourages global leadership. Sclar concludes: "Finally, it is the public sector that is the dispenser of social justice. It is difficult to envision America sustaining itself as a progressive democracy with that role impaired" (p. 336).

In a system of democratic capitalism, where the relationship between public and private sectors is delicate, there are many tensions. Private enterprise has some virtues and advocates, but it creates severe economic disparity among people and carries a history of exploitation. Similarly, public enterprise offers virtues and has supporters, but creates tax burdens and opens itself to bureaucratic bungling. Each sector serves different needs of individuals and society at large. Increasing the proportion controlled by the private sector comes at a cost to the public. For a democracy, the cost of privatizing public education is too high.

For Discussion

1. Dialogue Ideas: Even if we find that it costs more to educate children under private operations, this clearly would show the public the need to better finance schools. Either way, it benefits education.

   Are there logical flaws in this argument? What are the implications of the position?
2. Table 8.1 shows categories and examples of government services that are candidates for privatization.
   a. What are the advantages and disadvantages of privatization in regard to each of the examples?
   b. What criteria should be used to determine the advantages and disadvantages?
   c. How do these criteria fit a discussion of privatizing schools?
   d. Who should be empowered to make the decisions about privatization?

Table 8.1 Government Services and Privatization.

Category of Service	Example Activities for Privatization
Defense	military support, training
Health	public hospitals, FDA operations
Transportation	airports, Amtrack, FA, urban mass transit
Recreation	parks service, public land development
Justice	crime control, prisons
Communication	public radio, monitoring airwaves
Taxes	collection enforcement, IRS audits

3. Shanker (1994b) noted that a public-private venture called "performance contracting" was started during the Nixon administration to save public schools. The idea was for private firms to contract to improve student test scores in specific subjects. The result, says Shanker, was scandalous: repetitive test taking, or drill teaching of answers to test questions, because the companies were good at marketing, but knew little about education. If we are to privatize public schools, what conditions should be established or regulated?
4. The Government Accounting Office (1996) found five studies conducted between 1991 and 1996 that compared public and private prisons in California, Texas, Washington, Tennessee, and New Mexico on the criteria of operational costs and quality of service

provided. The GAO drew no conclusions from these studies because they found little or no differences in operational costs or in quality of service provided. How does this report support public or private operation of prisons?

5. The Milwaukee parental-choice program, a voucherlike plan that uses state funds for sending a small group of children from poor families to private schools, has been evaluated in three independent studies. Evidence shows parents in the privatization program are more satisfied with school than those not in the program, but evidence also shows no difference between public and private schools in actual student achievement. What could account for these findings? What implications can we draw from the evidence? What does this say about privatization?

References

ADAMS, J. R. (1990). *The Big Fix: Inside the S & L Scandal.* New York: Wiley.

ANDERSON, C. (1998). "Schools Need Privatization Lesson." *North County* (CA) *Times.* Nov. 28, pp. A–14.

APPLEBOME, P. (1994). "A Venture on the Brink: Do Education and Profits Mix?" *The New York Times.* Oct. 30, p. 28.

ARISTOTLE. (1988). *The Politics.* S. Everson, ed. Cambridge, England: Cambridge University Press.

ASCHER, C., FRUCHTER, N., AND BERNE, R. (1996). *Hard Lessons: Public Schools and Privatization.* Washington, DC: Brookings Institute Press.

"Auditor Criticises Secrecy on Public Works Contracts." (1994). *Sydney Morning Herald.* Oct. 18, p. 1.

BRACEY, G. (2002). "The 12th Bracey Report on the Condition of Public Education." *Phi Delta Kappan* 84(2) 135–150.

BRESLAU, K., AND JOSEPH, N. (2001). Edison's Report Card: Problems in San Francisco and Elsewhere." *Newsweek* 138(1) July 2, pp. 48, 49.

BROWN CENTER ANNUAL REPORT ON EDUCATION IN THE UNITED STATES—CHARTER SCHOOLS (2002). (Brookings Institute Website: www.brook.edu/gs/brown/bc)

CALAVITA, K., ET AL., EDS. (1997). *Big Money Crime.* Berkeley: University of California Press.

CHI, K. S. (2000). "Restructuring, Quality Management, and Privatization in State Government." In P. J. Andrisani et al., eds., *Making Government Work: Lessons from America's Governors and Mayors.* Lanham, MD: Rowman and Littlefield.

CHUBB, J. (1998). "Edison Scores and Scores Again in Boston." *Phi Delta Kappan* 80(3), 205–213.

"Competition May Kill Utilities: ACTU." (1994). *Sydney Morning Herald.* Oct. 29, p. 39.

COONS, J. (1988). "Testimony, Hearings on Educational Choice. December 22." Cited in Privatization: Toward More Effective Government. Washington, DC: U.S. Government Printing Office.

CUPE REPORT. (1998). Canadian Union of Public Employees. (www.cupe.ca)

DAYTON, J., AND GLICKMAN, C. D. (1994). "American Constitutional Democracy: Implications for Public School Curriculum Development." *Peabody Journal of Education* 69, 62–80.

DEWEY, J. (1916). *Democracy and Education.* New York: Macmillan.

DOBEK, M. M. (1993). *The Political Logic of Privatization.* Westport, CT: Praeger.

DOYLE, D. (1994). "The Role of Private Sector Management in Public Education." *Phi Delta Kappan* 76, 128–132.

EARLE, J., FRYDMAN, R., AND RAPACZYNSKI, A. (1993). *Privatization in the Transition to a Market Economy.* New York: St. Martin's Press.

EGGERS, W., AND O'LEARY, J. (1996). "Union Confederates." *American Spectator.* March.
ELLINGSEN, P. (1994a). "Making Profit in Private." *Sydney Morning Herald.* Nov. 26, p. 21.
———. (1994b). "Rule Britannia—A Nation of Despair." *Sydney Morning Herald.* Oct. 29, p. 28.
EMMONS, W. (2000). *The Evolving Bargain.* Boston: Harvard Business School Press.
FARAZMAND, A., ED. (2001). *Privatization or Public Enterprise Reform?* Westport, CT: Greenwood Press.
FEISTRITZER, E. (1987). "Public vs. Private: Biggest Difference Is Not the Students." *The Wall Street Journal.* Dec. 1, p. 36.
FINN, C. (1995). "The School," *Commentary* 99, 6–10.
"Gateway Academy Raided as State Begins Fraud Investigation." (2002). *The San Diego Union-Tribune.* Jan. 25, p. A8.
GEIGER, P. E. (1995). "Representation and Privatization." *American School and University* 67, 28–30.
GIBBS, N. (1994). "Schools for Profit." *Time.* Oct. 17, pp. 48–49.
GLAZER, J. (1994). "The New Politics of Education: Schools for Sale." *Education Week* 14, 44–ff.
GOVERNMENT ACCOUNTING OFFICE. (1996). "Private and Public Prisons: Studies Comparing Operational Costs and/or Quality of Service." Report GCD-96-158. Report to the Subcommittee on Crime, Committee on the Judiciary, House of Representatives. Washington, DC: August.
GUTMANN, A. (1999). *Democratic Education.* 2nd Ed. Princeton: Princeton University Press.
HASTINGS, S., AND LEVIE, H., EDS., (1983). *Privatisation?* Nottingham, England: Spokesman.
HENRIQUES, D. B., AND STEINBERG, J. (2002a). "Woes for Company Running Schools." *New York Times on the Web.* May 14, pp. 1–4.
———. (2002b). "Operator of Public Schools in Settlement with SEC" *New York Times on the Web.* May 15, pp. 1–4.
HOLLOWAY, J. H. (2002). "Research Link: For-Profit Schools." *Educational Leadership* 59(7), 84, 85.
HUMAN RIGHTS WATCH. (1999). The Enron Corporation: Corporate Complicity in Human Rights Violations. New York: Human Rights Watch.
HUNTER, R. C., AND BROWN, F. EDS. (1995). "Privatization in Public Education." *Education and Urban Society* 27, 107–228.
JEFFERSON, T. (1939). *Democracy.* New York: Greenwood Press.
JUDSON, G. (1994). "Hartford Hires Group to Run School System." *The New York Times.* Oct. 4, pp. B1, B6.
KAPLAN, G. (1996). "Profits r Us." *Phi Delta Kappan* 78(3), K1–12.
KOZOL, J. (1991). *Savage Inequalities: Children in America's Schools.* New York: Crown.
KRUGMAN, P. (2002) "Victors and Spoils." *New York Times Online.* Nov. 19, p. 1. (www.nytimes.com)
LESLIE, C. (1994). "Taking Public Schools Private." *Newsweek.* June 20, p. 7.
LONG, R. E., ED. (1993). *Banking Scandals: The S & Ls and BCCI.* New York: H. W. Wilson.
MAGEE, M., AND LEOPOLD, L. S. (1998). "Study Finds Charter Schools Succeed No More than Others." *San Diego Union-Tribune.* Dec. 4, pp. A–1, 15.
MANDEL, M., ET AL. (1995). "Will Schools Ever Get Better?" *Business Week.* April 17, pp. 64–68.
MIRON, G., AND APPLEGATE, B. (2000). *An Evaluation of Student Achievement in Edison Schools Opened in 1995 and 1996.* Kalamzaoo, MI: The Evaluation Center, Western Michigan University.
MITCHELL, L. E. (2001). *Corporate Irresponsibility: America's Newest Export.* New Haven, CT: Yale University Press.

New York. (1994). "Has Benno Schmidt Learned His Lesson?" Oct. 31, pp. 49–59.

New Yorker. (1994). "Grand Illusion." Oct. 31, pp. 64–81.

PALAST, G. (2002). *The Best Democracy Money Can Buy.* London: Pluto Press.

Privatization: Toward More Effective Government. (1988). Report of the President's Commission on Privatization. Washington, DC: U.S. Government Printing Office.

PROTZMAN, F. (1994). "East Nearly Privatized, Germans Argue the Cost." *The New York Times.* Aug. 12, pp. D1, D2.

"Public Funds, Public Works." (1994). *Sydney Morning Herald.* Oct. 18, p. 18.

Rethinking Schools. (1998). "The Market Is Not the Answer: An Interview with Jonathan Kozol." (www. rethinkingschools.org)

SAKS, J. B. (1995). "Scrutinizing Edison." *American School Boards Journal* 183, 20–24.

SALTMAN, J. (2000). *Collateral Damage: Corporatizing Public Schools—a Threat to Democracy.* Lanham, MD: Rowman and Littlefield.

SCHIPKE, A. (2001). *Why Do Governments Divest?* Berlin: Springer.

SCHMIDT, P. (1994). "Hartford Hires E.A.I. to Run Entire District." *Education Week* 14, 1, 14.

SCHRAG, P. (1999). "Private Affluence and Public Squalor." *San Diego Union-Tribune* 8(8), Jan. 8, B11.

———. (2001). "Edison's Red Ink Schoolhouse." *The Nation* 272(25), June 25, pp. 20–24.

SCLAR, E. (1994). "Public-Service Privatization: Ideology or Economics?" *Dissent,* Summer, pp. 329–336.

SHAFER, G. (1999). "The Myth of Competition and the Case Against School Choice." *The Humanist* 59(2), 15+.

SHANKER, A. (1994a). "Barnum Was Right." *The New York Times.* Oct. 23, p. E7.

———. (1994b). "A History Lesson." *The New York Times.* March 6, p. E7.

SHERMAN, M. (2001). *White Collar Crime.* Washington DC: Federal Judiciary Center.

SHEPPARD, R. (1998). "A School Failure." *MacLeans* 111, 52–53.

STEINBERG, J. (2002). "Private Groups Get 42 Schools in Philadelphia." *New York Times on the Web.* April 18, pp. 1–3.

STEINBERG, J., AND HENRIQUES, D. (2002). "Edison Schools Gets Reprieve." *New York Times Online.* June 5, p. 1. (www.nytimes.com)

SUDETIC, C. (2001). "Reading, Writing, and Revenue." *Mother Jones* 26(3), May/June, pp. 84–95.

TARBELL, I. M. (1904). *The History of the Standard Oil Company.* New York: McClure, Phillips and Company.

Time. (1994). "Schools for Profit." Oct. 17, pp. 48–49.

TOCH, T. (1995). "Taking Public Schools Private: A Setback." *U.S. News & World Report* 117, 74.

TROY, F. (1999). "The Myth of a Failed Public School System." *Church and State.* Jan., pp. 17–20.

U.S. CONGRESS. SENATE. (1980). *Chrysler Corporation Loan Guarantee Act.* Washington, DC: U.S. Government Publications Office.

VAN BRABANT, J. V. (1992). *Privatizing Eastern Europe.* International Studies in Economics and Econometrics, No. 24. Boston: Kluwer Academic Press.

VICKERS, J., AND YARROW, G. (1991). "Economic Perspectives on Privatization." *Journal of Economic Perspectives* 2, 111–132.

Wall Street Journal. (1994). "A KKR Vehicle Finds Profit and Education a Rich But Uneasy Mix." Oct. 12, pp. A11, A12.

"Why Parlt [Parliament] Must Scrutinize Projects with Private Sector." (1994). *Sydney Morning Herald.* Oct. 18, p. 19.

ZOLLERS, N., AND RAMANATHAN. A. (1998). "For-Profit Charter Schools and Students with Disabilities." *Phi Delta Kappan* 80(4), 297–315.

PART TWO

What Should Be Taught?

Knowledge and Literacy

About Part Two: School curriculum battles are the outward sign of competing social forces. Knowledge, intelligence, literacy, and learning are complementary concepts—but they often have differing definitions and interpretations. These concepts are the currency of education, whether that education is provided in schools or out. Schools, as formal agencies of education, are necessarily involved with definitions of these four terms and with disputes over those definitions. Topics covered in Chapters 9 through 14 of Part Two concern the idea of knowledge, and its relation to intelligence, literacy, and learning. This section includes the topics of basic education, reading and language, multicultural education, values, and technology. Each issue involves both theoretical and practical concerns, since the curriculum identifies the most important school knowledge as it describes what is to be taught in schools.

This introductory essay explores social and psychological contexts for the idea of knowledge and its corollaries, political and philosophic contexts for school curriculum decisions, and ideological and practical contexts of curriculum control.

INTRODUCTION

Teaching is, of course, more than telling or testing. And learning is more than listening and recalling. Poor-quality teaching and learning could be described as only telling and listening, but good education requires more thought about what should be taught and why, and consideration of what is to be learned and how. Since we usually think we are obviously well educated, we could assume that what should be taught is what we were taught—and learned as we did; the answer to why is because we are so well educated. That self-congratulatory response does answer a question about the central purpose for schools—what should be taught?—but it is not a satisfactory answer in contemporary society.

If the best education is simply what we were taught and recall, then teaching could be only telling and testing of what we already think we know. There would be no sense trying to make changes in schools, curriculum, or teaching. Education would be static. There also would be no reason for a book on educational issues—there would be no issues. But we all know there are enormous, important issues about schooling; what should be taught is one of the most enormous and important. What we were taught, or the different information taught to our parents and grandparents, represented an idea at those times of important school knowledge to prepare literate and intelligent students. But knowledge changes—and so do our conceptions of intelligence, literacy, and learning. Schools, from day care to graduate school, exist to determine, examine, convey, question, and modify knowledge. That responsibility is the root of issues surrounding what should be taught.

Communicating knowledge, most people agree, is the core purpose of schools. And that interactive communication depends on our definitions of knowledge, intelligence, literacy, and learning. It isn't surprising to find that a book about schooling spends considerable space on knowledge, but what makes knowledge an issue? Issues arise because of major theoretical, practical, and ideological disagreements over how knowledge is to be defined, whose ideas of knowledge should prevail in schools, how to package knowledge, and how to organize and teach knowledge. In addition to disputes about the nature, value, and expression of knowledge are disagreements about how to define and measure human intelligence and literacy, and how to identify and stimulate the best kinds of learning. This complex of disputes is often at the center of various school wars, since the control of knowledge is the control of society.

Significant arguments arise over such issues as

- What knowledge should we teach, in what sequence, and who gets to decide?
- Which knowledge should be required study, which should be elective, and which should be censored?
- Who should get access to which kinds of knowledge?
- How do we know if and when that or other knowledge is learned?

These are not only theoretical concerns linked directly to decisions about school curriculum, they are also practical concerns basic to teaching and learning, success and failure.

Schools should provide teaching in the most valuable knowledge, but that begs the questions of who decides what is worth knowing and on what grounds. The struggle to control what is accepted as valued knowledge is inevitably a struggle for power. As philosophers, politicians, salesmen, and activists have realized for centuries, control of people's minds is control of their expectations, behavior, and allegiance. Deciding which students get access to which knowledge has a powerful impact on social policy and politics, with results that can lead in opposite directions:

more social egalitarianism or more elitism, more social-class separation or more social integration. Such decisions can enable or restrict individual achievements and enhance or detract from democracy. Thus, these decisions have enormous implications for individuals and society.

Should schools aim to produce broadly educated people, specialists in academic subjects, social critics, book learners, industrial workers, college material, athletes, consumers, patriots, or something else? Should schools emphasize the classics, computer technology, basic skills, moral behavior, employable job skills, test taking, citizenship, the arts, science, language, recreational activities, or some combination of these or other topics? Who should be selected for admission to programs in law, medicine, teacher education, auto mechanics, flower arranging, or accounting? Who should decide?

NONSCHOOL KNOWLEDGE AND UNINTENDED SCHOOL LEARNINGS

School, of course, is not the only place where knowledge is gained, intelligence developed, literacy honed, and learning productive. Glynda Hull and Katherine Schultz (2002) summarized the large volume of research on learning in and out of school commenting:

> During the last two decades researchers from a range of disciplines have documented the considerable intellectual accomplishments of children, adolescents, and adults in out-of-school settings, accomplishments that often contrast with their poor school-based performances and suggest a different view of their potential as capable learners and doers in the world . . . school has come to be such a particular, specialized institution with its own particular brand of learning. . . . " (pp. 575, 577)

All of us experience nonschool settings where we gain significant knowledge; families, friends, peers, work groups, and media are but a few excellent examples. We learn from our earliest days to the last, and formal schooling accounts for less than 10 percent of that learning period for most people. School time certainly is significant for acquisition of recognized knowledge, but is not the only source. In addition to out-of-school knowledge, some wisdom we have gained came to us in school, but is not what the school intended for us to learn—this is the hidden curriculum of schooling. Some students learn dishonesty and cheating as a result of experiences in school life, but the school did not intend that result.

Learning in nonschool settings and through the hidden curriculum in schools challenges many of our limited conceptions about school as the prime location for knowledge, intelligence, literacy, and learning. Schooling is but one dimension of this process of development, but school is the organized agency given responsibility for defining, transmitting, and changing knowledge deemed important in a society. Our focus, in this section, will be on disputes over what should be taught in schools, but we must not mistake that for the whole of knowledge or intelligence.

Knowledge, of course, depends on intelligence since it is only through intelligence that we gain, interpret, and use knowledge. Yet, there are as many disputes about intelligence as there are about knowledge. As Ken Richardson (2000), notes:

> There has probably been a concept of intelligence, and a word for it, since people first started to compare themselves with other animals and with one another. We know this at least since thinkers first began to theorize about the nature of the mind. . . . the existing ground does not offer a firm foundation for anyone seeking to answer the question: "What is intelligence?" Indeed, it is a complex confusion. (pp. 1, 20)

As psychologist Howard Gardner (1993, 1999) eloquently argues, we really have multiple intelligences, not just a single form. He also suggests that intelligences are actually potentials for people to develop processes to solve problems or create things; they are not completed events, nor are they clearly observable or testable, and they are relatively independent of each other. Some kinds of intelligence (such as logical-mathematical and linguistic) are especially useful in satisfying school academic requirements, and others (such as intra- and interpersonal, musical, and bodily-kinesthetic) are more useful in other settings in and out of school. If Gardner is correct, this level of complexity makes "intelligence" testing, and other efforts to standardize and measure schooling more difficult, if not impossible. As Gardner puts it, "intelligence is too important to be left to the intelligence testers" (1999, p. 3).

Similarly, we have multiple literacies and multiple learning processes (Hull and Schultz, 2002). Literacy can be defined in many ways: as basic reading/writing skills, as computer skills, as economic ability, as cultural capabilities, as historical cognizance, or as artistic or critical literacy (Gee, 1996, 2000). Critical literacy provides a way to use basic school knowledge to identify and correct significant power disparities between haves and have-nots (Freire, 1970; Freire and Macedo, 1987). Multiple learning processes are obvious to anyone who observes children acquire walking, speaking, reading, creative, and interpretive abilities. This sophisticated concept of multiple intelligences, literacies, and learning processes not only makes definitions of knowledge, intelligence, literacy, and learning very problematic, it also raises important questions about school curriculum, national and state standardized testing, and teaching.

THE SCHOOL CURRICULUM: KNOWLEDGE AND POLITICS

The school curriculum of each society reflects the definitions of formal knowledge and literacy prevalent in that society and in that time—and they reflect political decisions. These definitions often conflict—arts versus sciences, practical versus theoretical, socialization versus individual independence. In an age of witchery, a literate, intelligent person is one who shares the language and values of the sorcerer's form of knowledge. In an age of technology, a literate and intelligent person may be defined as one who shares the language and values of technological knowledge. Thus, the term *literate* may be thought of as a verbal badge given to those who possess knowledge considered socially valuable. Schools provide literacy credentials in the form of diplomas, degrees, and various types of professional certificates. When magic and witchcraft were socially credible, sorcerers enjoyed great power and status. Their pronouncements often became laws and policies. Only a select few had the opportunity to learn their secret rites. When knowledge of witchcraft came to be viewed as evil, sorcerers were burned. In modern societies where scientific knowledge is prized, "sorcerers" are considered interesting eccentrics. The postmodern society suggests new definitions and a new school curriculum for meeting the needs of the twenty-first century (Stanley, 1992; Greene, 1994).

Typically, traditional school subjects coexist in the curriculum until new topics or arguments arise challenging that emphasis. In our seventeenth-century secondary schools, classes were taught in Latin, and Greek was required along with moral philosophy. In the last decades of the twentieth century, when test scores revealed deficiencies in the basic skills of reading, writing, and arithmetic, most elementary schools decreased the curriculum time spent on science, social studies, and the arts and shifted it to reading and arithmetic. When computers became more socially valuable, schools made space to fit computer study into a crowded school curriculum. Other additions such as driver's education, physical education, drug education, and character education illustrate curriculum changes based on redefinitions of knowledge and the politics of schools. The specific mix of courses and emphasis within the curriculum depend on prevailing visions of the "good" individual and the "good" society. In every age, people hold disparate views on what kinds of individuals and society are most desirable. Some want individuals to be free, independent, and critical; others advocate behavior modification to control deviation and ensure social conformity. Some demand prescribed moral values and beliefs; others demand release from moralisms and prescriptions. Some desire respect for authority; others prefer challenges to authority. Driving each of these competing views are concepts of the "good" individual and the "good" society.

PRACTICAL, THEORETICAL, AND MORAL SCHOOLING

The literature of all societies is filled with disputes over how school should develop the good individual and the good society. Aristotle considered the state the fulfillment of our social drives and saw education as a state activity designed to provide social unity. He said that "education is therefore the means of making it [the society] a community and giving it unity" (Aristotle, 1962, p. 51). In *The Politics*, Aristotle discussed the controversy over whether schools should teach practical knowledge, moral character, or esoteric ideas:

> The absence of any clear view about the proper subjects of instruction: the conflicting claims of utility, moral discipline, and the advancement of knowledge . . . At present, opinion is divided about the subjects of education. All do not take the same view about what should be learned by the young, either with a view to plain goodness or with a view to the best life possible; nor is opinion clear whether education should be directed mainly to the understanding, or mainly to moral character. (pp. 333–334)

Contemporary curriculum debate continues to focus on the relative emphasis schools should give to practical, theoretical, and moral schooling. What type of knowledge will best fulfill the needs of individuals and society to (1) develop the skills for doing practical work; (2) pursue advanced, theoretical knowledge in such areas as mathematics, literature, logic, and the arts; and (3) provide a set of moral guidelines and ethical values for judging right from wrong?

No one has resolved the disputes over the kinds of knowledge schools should convey. Contemporary comprehensive public schools offer some useful applied educational programs, such as reading, music, wood shop, home economics, computer operation, physical education, and vocational training. They also offer the study of theoretical concepts in English, math, social studies, the arts, and science. And schools provide various forms of moral education; students study materials conveying ideas of the good person and the good society, and learn from school rules and teachers to be respectful, patriotic, loyal, and honest. The exact mix of these forms of education varies as different reforms become popular and as local communities make changes.

School reform literature of the 1980s and reactions of the 1990s were marked by arguments over whether to emphasize practical, theoretical, or moral knowledge in schools. One high-profile national commission proposed the following high school graduation requirements: four years of English, three years of mathematics, three years of science, and a semester of computer science (National Commission on Excellence in Education, 1983). They ignored vocational education, a prominent feature of school reforms of the 1930s and 1940s, and physical education, an emphasis in major school reforms between 1910 and 1920. The arts received only passing reference in the report. The emphasis on computer science was support of a practical course, not unlike the business education proposals of the 1920s and 1930s. This was framed as a way to restore America's competitive edge in international business and national defense. These are practical and political purposes, and suggest that the required core of courses should tend toward knowledge useful in business. Economic utility, as Goodlad (1999) notes, continues to be the "drumbeat" of school reform.

Another view describes four essential functions of a high school—to help students:

1. Develop critical thinking and effective communication skills.
2. Learn about themselves, the human heritage, and the interdependent world.
3. Prepare for work and further education.
4. Fulfill social and civic obligations. (Boyer, 1983)

These functions incorporate practical, moral, and higher or theoretical knowledge. Boyer's curriculum proposal includes required courses in writing, speech, literature, the arts, foreign language, U.S. and world history, civics, science, technology, and health, as well as a seminar on work and a senior-level independent applied project.

Curricular reforms of the 1980s were seen by many as essentially mechanistic and "top-down." The presumption was that the president, governors, legislators, and national commissions could tell the schools what and how to teach in order to correct educational ills. Their prescriptions—for increased course requirements, longer school days and school years, more homework, more testing, and force-feeding knowledge to students in factory-like schools—did not prove their curative abilities. Edward B. Fiske (1991), former education editor for *The New York Times*, argues:

> The time for tinkering with the current system of public education is over. After a decade of trying to make the system work better by such means as more testing, higher salaries, and tighter curriculums, we must now face up to the fact that anything short of fundamental structural change is futile. We are trying to use a nineteenth-century institution to prepare young people for life in the twenty-first century. (p. 14)

Fiske argues against highly centralized school authority, standardization, and bureaucracy. He presents a case for students who can think for themselves; decentralized and shared school decision making, with teachers taking responsibility for making the most important school decisions; for cooperative learning; and for moving beyond multiple-choice standardized testing to measure student knowledge.

Individual schools do not make a separate determination of the relative values of parts of the curriculum; a number of factors influence what most schools teach and contribute to a relatively standard curriculum in U.S. schools. States mandate certain courses state legislatures believe are necessary for all students, such as English and American history. Many states also encourage or require other courses, such as drug and alcohol education, providing special funding or applying political pressure to add these courses to the curriculum. Accrediting agencies in each region examine schools periodically, and review the curriculum to see if it conforms to their standards. Publishers, aiming at a national market, produce teaching materials that fit a national curriculum. Schools deviating from that pattern will have trouble finding textbooks. And school district curriculum coordinators and department heads attend national con ferences and read journals that stress standard curricular structures. Thus, a broad outline exists for a general national curriculum based on common practices, even though specific curricula in each state differ.

In these beginning years of the twenty-first century, external forces still largely determine the formal curriculum in American schools. We now have national and state standards, increasing external accountability for student learning, and more complex ideas of socially expected literacy. Since Colonial times, the curriculum has evolved from a narrow interest in teaching religious ideals to multiple, and often conflicting, interests in providing broad knowledge, skills, and values relevant to nearly every aspect of social life. In U.S. schools, the medieval curriculum of "seven liberal arts"—rhetoric, grammar, logic, arithmetic, astronomy, geometry, and music—has given way to a list of subjects too long to enumerate. And the formal curriculum is certainly not all that students are expected to learn in school.

THE HIDDEN CURRICULUM

In addition to the formal school curriculum there is also a hidden curriculum consisting of unexpressed and usually unexamined ideas, values, and behaviors conveyed more informally to students. These are subtle, often unintended, things students (and teachers) learn as they go about their lives in school. They represent underlying ideologies, root ideas about human values and social relations.

A few brief examples illustrate the hidden curriculum at its simplest level. Teachers tell students to be independent and express their own ideas, but they often chastise or punish the student who actually exhibits independence and expresses ideas the teacher doesn't like. In history courses, students hear that justice and equality are basic American rights, yet they see that compliant and well-dressed students earn favored treatment. In school, students are told that plagiarism is an academic sin; then the news shows prominent and award-winning historians (probably quoted in the high school history textbook) who plagiarized from others. Students are told to not smoke, by teachers who do. The hidden curriculum is a vast, relatively uncharted domain often much more effective than the formal curriculum in shaping student learning and knowledge.

At a deeper level, discrepancies between what a teacher says and what that teacher does may raise a more significant concern about competing ideologies. Often, the hidden curriculum conflicts with the stated purposes of the visible curriculum. The stated curriculum may value diversity; the hidden curriculum expects conformity. The stated curriculum advocates critical thinking; the hidden curriculum supports docility. The visible curriculum emphasizes equal opportunity; the hidden curriculum separates students according to social-class background, gender, race, or other factors.

Critical literature examines the hidden curriculum and its ideological bases (see, for example, Young, 1970; Cherryholmes, 1978, 1988; Anyon, 1979, 1980; Giroux and Purpel, 1983; Popkewitz, 1987; Giroux, 1988; Apple, 1990; Stanley, 1992). From this critical view, the "great debates" about schooling extensively covered in the media and mainstream educational literature are actually narrowly constructed differences between liberals and conservatives. At bottom, public debates do not raise ideological concerns about the control of knowledge and its social consequences; they tinker with the stated curriculum but leave the powerful hidden curriculum intact. That is the reason superficial school reforms do very little to change schooling, and neither mainstream liberals nor conservatives really want much change.

At the surface level, where much school reform debate occurs, a discussion about whether to spend more school time on computers, math, and English and less on the arts and social studies is a comparatively trivial matter; it hides more fundamental disputes about whose interests are served and whose are maligned. Shallow arguments about whether the curriculum should stress the basics, provide vocational courses, allow electives, or emphasize American values should lead to deeper, more critical examinations of who controls the school curriculum and consequences of that control. In mainstream discourse, those basic issues (surrounding class, gender, race, and age controls) are hidden.

A central issue in the struggle for control of knowledge is whether traditional knowledge provides enduring wisdom or promotes social oppression. In opposition to the traditional use of literacy as a tool of the dominant class to separate and control the masses is the idea of literacy as a tool for liberation, Paulo Freire's revolutionary concept (Freire and Berthoff, 1987). Freire, born in one of the most impoverished areas of Brazil, came to know the plight of the poor. He vowed to dedicate his life to the struggle against misery and suffering, and his work led him to define the "culture of silence" he saw among the disadvantaged.

Freire realized the power of knowledge and recognized that the dominant class used education to keep the culture of silence among the victims—the poor and illiterate. He developed a program to teach adults to read in order to liberate them from their imposed silence. As a professor of education in Brazil, he experimented with this program to erase illiteracy, and his ideas became widely used in private literacy campaigns there. Freire was considered a threat to the government and was jailed after a military coup in 1964. Forced to leave his native country, he went to Chile to work with UNESCO, came to the United States, and then joined the World Council of Churches in Geneva as head of its educational division. Freire's program involves the development of critical consciousness, using communication to expose oppression. Teacher and student are "co-intentional," sharing equally in dialogues on social reality and developing a critical understanding that can liberate them from the culture of silence.

Henry Giroux, citing Freire, argues that we need a redefinition of literacy to focus on its critical dimensions. Mass culture via television and other electronic media is under the control of dominant economic interests, and offers only immediate images and unthoughtful information. This creates a "technocratic" illiteracy that is a threat to self-perception, critical thought, and democracy. Giroux (1988) states:

> Instead of formulating literacy in terms of the mastery of techniques, we must broaden its meaning to include the ability to read critically, both inside and outside one's experiences, and with conceptual power. This means that literacy would enable people to decode critically their personal and social worlds and thereby further their ability to challenge the myths and beliefs that structure their perceptions and experiences. (p. 84)

CURRICULUM CONTROL

Control of knowledge, and the school curriculum, is a product of both prevailing social goals and prevailing social structures. During most of the United States' formative years, religion was the basis. Although differences existed among the colonies, most people expected all young children to be taught religious precepts at home or at dame or writing schools. The purpose was to thwart the efforts of "that ould deluder, Satan," who sought to keep human beings from knowledge of the scriptures. After learning to read and write, however, most girls were not permitted further education. They returned home to learn the art of homemaking, while boys from more affluent homes continued their schooling at Latin grammar schools. African Americans and Native Americans were virtually excluded from schools.

Historically, the struggle for the control of knowledge has paralleled social-class differences (Anyon, 1980; Spring, 1998). The assumption was that workers needed practical knowledge, the privileged class needed higher knowledge, and both needed moral knowledge, but with great disparity in the kinds of moral knowledge they required. Craft apprenticeships to acquire practical knowledge were for the masses. Formal schooling to learn critical thinking and study philosophy, science, and the arts was for the aristocratic class. In terms of moral instruction, the masses were to gain the moral character to obey, respect authority, work hard and be frugal, and suffer with little complaint. Members of the privileged class were supposed to gain the moral character to rule wisely, justly, and with civility.

One of the central purposes of schooling is to prepare future leaders of society. When the powerful class controls education and decides what is to be taught, the essential curricular question is: What should members of the ruling class know? In more democratic societies, involved in mass education, the curricular questions revolve around what all members of the society need to know to participate fully and actively.

Even in democratic societies, however, curricular needs of those identified as potential leaders receive special attention. We can see this in the higher academic tracks and honors programs characterizing many modern high schools. The correlation between social expectations, social-class structure, and what schools teach deserves ongoing examination. Marrou (1956/1982), for example, notes that in ancient Arabia the "upper class is composed of an aristocracy of warriors, and education is therefore of a military kind . . . training character and building up physical vigour rather than developing the intelligence." He found similar conditions in ancient Asian, Indian, and Western educational systems (pp. xiv, xv).

R. H. Tawney (1964), criticized the elite "public boarding-school" tradition of the wealthy in England, and advocated improvements in the developing system of free schools for the working classes. He saw how the very nature of the elite system was a part of the hidden curriculum, teaching the sons of the wealthy "not in words or of set purpose, but by the mere facts of their environment, that they are members . . . of a privileged group, whose function it will be, on however humble a scale, to direct and command, and to which leadership, influence, and the other prizes of life properly belong" (1964, p. 83).

Social class is not the only major factor lying behind curricular decisions. Race, gender, national origin, and religion are other conditions that influence decisions about which people receive what knowledge in a society. The concept of privilege, and the education that privilege brings, has been linked to racism and sexism in American and other national histories. Educational discrimination against racial minorities, women, Jews, Catholics, Native Americans, Eskimos, and others is a sorry tradition in a democratic society.

About half a century ago, psychologist Kenneth Clark, whose studies were a significant factor in the Supreme Court decision that found segregated schools unconstitutional (*Brown v. Board of Education*, 1954), put the case clearly:

> The public schools in America's urban ghettos also reflect the oppressive damage of racial exclusion. . . . Segregation and inferior education reinforce each other. . . . Children themselves are not fooled by the various euphemisms educators use to disguise educational snobbery. From the earliest grades a child knows when he has been assigned to a level that is considered less than adequate. . . . "The clash of cultures in the classroom" is essentially a class war, a socioeconomic and racial warfare being waged on the battleground of our schools, with middle-class and middle-class-aspiring teachers provided with a powerful arsenal of half-truths, prejudices, and rationalizations, arrayed against the hopelessly outclassed working-class youngsters. (Clark, 1965, pp. 111–117)

Similar condemnations of educational discrimination based on religion, nationality, and gender are common in the critical literature (Hofstadter, 1944; Clark, 1965; Katz, 1971; Feldman, 1974; Spring, 1976; Apple, 1979, 1990; Sadker and Sadker, 1982; Walker and Barton, 1983; Grimshaw, 1986; Giroux, 1991; Weiler, 1991; Lather, 1991; Spring, 1998). As Rosemary Deem (1983) comments: "Women have had to struggle hard against dominant patriarchal power relations, which try to confine women to the private sphere of the home and family, away from the public sphere of production and political power" (p. 107).

Weiler (1991) essentially agrees in a critique of the Western system of knowledge, arguing that feminist pedagogy is rooted in a critical, oppositional, and activist vision of social change. Schooling that provides different types of knowledge and skills to students who differ only in race, gender, class, religion, or nationality contributes to continued inequality of treatment and stereotypes.

SOCIAL EXPECTATIONS

Should schools concentrate on subject knowledge of historic and socially approved value, or on material encouraging critical thinking and student interest? If individual students are expected to develop independent and critical judgment so they can participate actively in improving the democratic society, we should expect schooling that leads to that goal, and can expect educated individuals to have an impact on society. If society values a structure in which only a few people have power and most people are expected to be docile and conform to social norms, we should expect schooling that leads to that end, and the resulting society.

Those two hypothetical statements seem to suggest the choice is simple; it is not. There are complex and changing relationships between the kinds of individuals we desire, the society we want to develop, and schooling we provide. These relationships often send conflicting signals to schools, and the conflicts become enshrined in the school curriculum. Society wants students to become self-sufficient individuals—but not too self-sufficient too early, so students have little latitude in deciding what to study until they reach college. We desire a society that is democratic and inspires voluntary loyalty, but we do not trust open inquiry, so we require courses stressing nationalistic patriotism.

Prior to the American Revolution, religion was waning as the primary social glue. National political interests emerged. After the Revolution, and into the nineteenth century, nationalism replaced religion as an educational force. Literacy became important not for religious salvation, but for patriotism, preservation of liberty, and participation in democracy. The political-nationalistic tradition remains strong in U.S. schools, with a call for renewed emphasis each time social values seem threatened. The War on Terrorism is a prime contemporary example; there is a redoubled effort to require allegiance pledges and patriotic exercises in schools.

There are many other examples of political uses of schools. During the period of overt racism in the United States, and as a reaction to the abolition of slavery, some regions used literacy tests to restrict voting rights. Since slaves had been prohibited, by law in some states, from receiving an education, these tests were intended to keep former slaves and the poor from voting. Their proponents also used them to limit participation of immigrants. David Tyack (1967) quotes an imperial wizard of the Ku Klux Klan as saying, "Ominous statistics proclaim the persistent development of a parasitic mass within our domain. . . . We have taken unto ourselves a Trojan horse crowded with ignorance, illiteracy, and envy" (p. 233).

The "Red Scare" of the 1920s, McCarthyism in the 1950s, and anticommunist political rhetoric in the 1980s were also periods when people perceived social threats; the effect was to strengthen a nationalist viewpoint in history, government, literature, and economics curricula. International competition in technology and trade threatens Americans today and translates into an increased curricular emphasis on mathematics, science, technological subjects such as computers, and foreign languages.

SUMMARY

The formal curriculum is one of the most visible parts of a school, indicating the relative value schools put on various forms of knowledge, and definitions of intelligence and literacy. There is far more to knowledge and literacy than what schools organize and teach, but schools provide legitimacy to the knowledge they select and teach, and credentials to those students who are successful in school. This means debates over school knowledge often are political, with ideological undercurrents.

Some people enjoy mathematics. For others, reading history or literature is a great joy. Some like to dissect white rats in biology class, saw wood in shop, or exercise in gym. Others are completely baffled or utterly bored by textbooks and teachers. Different strokes, as they say, for different folks. But aren't there some things that everyone should know, whether they enjoy it or not? Is there a set of skills that all should master? Should we require that anyone who graduates from high school be literate? Who should decide the criteria for literacy? What does it take to be educated in this beginning decade of the twentieth-first century?

The chapters of Part Two examine some of the current curriculum disputes that have emerged as part of reform movements in education. These disputes illustrate the question of what knowledge is most valuable in our society, a question that, in turn, relates to our differing visions of what constitutes the good individual and the good society.

References

ANYON, J. (1979). "Ideology and U.S. History Textbooks." *Harvard Educational Review* 7, 49–60.

———. (1980). "Social Class and the Hidden Curriculum of Work." *Journal of Education* 162, 67–92.

APPLE, M. (1979, 1990). Ideology and Curriculum. 2nd Ed. New York: Routledge.

———. (1982). *Education and Power.* London: Routledge & Kegan Paul.

ARISTOTLE. (1962). *The Politics of Aristotle.* E. Barker, translator. Oxford: Oxford University Press.

BERNSTEIN, B. (1977). *Class, Codes, and Control.* Vol. 3. London: Routledge & Kegan Paul.

BOURDIEU, P., AND PASSERON, J. (1977). *Reproduction in Education, Society, and Culture.* London: Sage.

BOWLES, S., AND GINTIS, H. (1976). *Schooling in Capitalist America.* New York: Basic Books.

BOYER, E. L. (1983). *High School.* New York: Harper & Row.

Brown v. Board of Education of Topeka, Shawnee County, Kansas, et al. (1954). 74 Sup. Ct. 686.

CARNOY, M. (1975). *Schooling in a Corporate Society: The Political Economy of Education in the Democratic State.* 2nd Ed. New York: McKay.

CARNOY, M., AND LEVIN, H. (1985). *Schooling and Work in America.* Stanford, CA: Stanford University Press.

CHENG, L. (1998). "Beyond Multiculturalism." In V. Pang, and L. Cheng, *Struggling to Be Heard.* Albany: State University of New York Press.

CHERRYHOLMES, C. (1978). "Curriculum Design as a Political Act." *Curriculum Inquiry* 10, 115–141.

———. (1988). *Power and Criticism: Poststructural Investigations in Education.* New York: Teachers College Press.

CLARK, K. (1965). *Dark Ghetto.* New York: Harper & Row.

DEEM, R. (1983). "Gender, Patriarchy and Class in the Popular Education of Women." In S. Walker and L. Barton., eds., *Gender, Class and Education.* London: Falmer Press.

EDELSKY, C., ALTWERGER, B., AND FLORES, B. (1991). *Whole Language, What's the Difference?* Portsmouth, NH: Heinemann.

FELDMAN, S. (1974). *The Rights of Women.* Rochelle Park, NJ: Hayden.

FISKE, E. B. (1991). *Smart School, Smart Kids.* New York: Simon & Schuster.

FREIRE, P. (1970). *Pedagogy of the Oppressed.* M. B. Ramos, translator. New York: Herder and Herder.

FREIRE, P., AND BERTHOFF, D. (1987). *Literacy: Reading and the World.* South Hadley, MA: Bergin & Garvey.

FREIRE, P., AND MACEDO, D. (1987). *Literacy.* South Hadley, MA: Bergin & Garvey.

GARDNER, H. (1993). *Frames of Mind.* New York: Basic Books.

———. (1999). *Intelligence Reframed: Multiple Intelligences for the 21st Century.* New York: Basic Books.

GEE, J. P. (1996). *Social Linguistics and Literacies.* 2nd Ed. London: Falmer Press.

———. (2000). "The New Literacy Studies" In D. Barton, et al., eds., *Situated Literacies.* London: Routledge.

GIROUX, H. (1981). *Ideology, Culture, and the Process of Schooling.* Philadelphia: Temple University Press.

———. (1988). *The Teacher as Intellectual.* South Hadley, MA: Bergin & Garvey.

———, ed. (1991). *Postmodernism, Feminism and Cultural Politics.* Albany: SUNY Press.

GIROUX, H., AND PURPEL, D. (1983). *The Hidden Curriculum and Moral Education.* Berkeley: McCutchan.

GOODLAD, J. (1999). "Flow, Eros, and Ethos in Educational Renewal." *Phi Delta Kappan* 80(8), 571–578.

GREENE, M. (1994). "Postmodernism and the Crisis of Representation." *English Education* 26, 206–219.

GRIMSHAW, J. (1986). *Philosophy and Feminist Thinking.* Minneapolis: University of Minnesota Press.

HANSON, F. A. (1993). *Testing, Testing: Social Consequences of the Examined Life.* Berkeley: University of California Press.

HOFSTADTER, R. (1944). *Social Darwinism in American Thought.* Philadelphia: University of Pennsylvania Press.

HALL, G., AND SCHULTZ, K., EDS. (2002) *School's Out.* New York: Teachers College Press.

KATZ, M. B. (1971). *Class, Bureaucracy, and Schools.* New York: Praeger.

LANGER, J., ED. (1987). *Language, Literacy and Culture: Issues of Society and Schooling.* Norwood, NJ: Ablex.

LATHER, P. (1991). *Getting Smart: Feminist Research and Pedagogy Within the Postmodern.* New York: Routledge.

MARROU, H. (1956/1982). *A History of Education in Antiquity.* G. Lamb, translator. Madison: University of Wisconsin Press.

NATIONAL COMMISSION ON EXCELLENCE IN EDUCATION. (1983). *A Nation at Risk.* Washington, DC: U.S. Department of Education.

NELSON, J., CARLSON, K., AND LINTON, T. (1972). *Radical Ideas and the Schools.* New York: Holt, Rinehart and Winston.

OAKES, J. (1985). *Keeping Track: How the Schools Structure Inequality.* New Haven, CT: Yale University Press.

POPKEWITZ, T. (1977). "The Latent Values of the Discipline-Centered Curriculum." *Theory and Research in Social Education* 13, 189–206.

———. (1987). *The Formation of School Subjects.* New York: Falmer Press.

RICHARDSON, K. (2000). *The Making of Intelligence.* New York: Columbia University Press.

SADKER, P., AND SADKER, D. M. (1982). *Sex Equity Handbook for Schools.* New York: Longman.

SPRING, J. (1976). *The Sorting Machine.* New York: McKay.

———. (1998). *American Education.* 8th Ed. New York: McGraw-Hill.

STANLEY, W. (1992). *Education for Utopia: Social Reconstructionism and Critical Pedagogy in the Postmodern Era.* Albany: SUNY Press.

TAWNEY, R. H. (1964). *The Radical Tradition.* London: Allen & Unwin.

TYACK, D. (1967). *Turning Points in American Educational History.* Waltham, MA: Blaisdell.

WALKER, S., AND BARTON, L. (1983). *Gender Class and Education.* London: Falmer Press.

WEILER, K. (1991). "Freire and a Feminist Pedagogy of Difference." *Harvard Educational Review* 61, 449–474.

YOUNG, M. F. D., ED. (1970). *Knowledge and Control.* London: Collier-Macmillan.

CHAPTER 9

Basic Education: Traditional or Critical

POSITION 1: TEACH THE BASIC DISCIPLINES

> *. . . the idea of liberal arts education for all slowly fell out of fashion after the first two decades of the twentieth century, as the pervasive influence of "progressive" education began to take hold. Since then, the story of American public schools has largely been the story of content-light education. . . .*
>
> —EVERS, 2001, P. 209

The primary purpose of schooling in a democratic society is to provide competence in basic knowledge to every child. Schools may be able to do more, and may harbor a misplaced desire to do far more social welfare or personality adjustment for students. But the focus must remain on developing academic competence. This competence is, at its root, democratic. As Hirsch (2001a) has eloquently argued, the common knowledge "characteristically shared by those at the top of the socioeconomic ladder in the United States" (p. 24) should be readily available to all citizens because people who lack it suffer serious handicaps. This "core knowledge" is needed for productive communication and in establishing fundamental equality as citizens. That is the content of basic education and should be the primary focus of schooling. This, Hirsch points out, is not a matter of being politically liberal or conservative, it is just good sense based on solid research in cognitive psychology.

Stress the Basics and Necessary Skills

No solid argument contradicts the wisdom of teaching traditional skills of reading, writing, and arithmetic. Disputes may arise as to how we should teach these skills, for how long, and how to measure their mastery, but even hard-core "child-centered" advocates agree children need to be able to communicate in language and numbers. This agreement would seem sufficient to guarantee a strong emphasis on these skills in schools. Unfortunately, that is not the case. The basics are not adequately taught in school. So it is no wonder large numbers of students are not acquiring this necessary knowledge and skills to use it, and will suffer as they try to make their way in society. Society suffers as well, since these otherwise productive workers will lack the capability to contribute satisfactorily in the workplace (Szabo, 1992) and will be at a continuing disadvantage in society. In addition to this illiterate group of students, another group does manage to pick up some fundamental skills, but not enough to be competitive. This combined body of functionally illiterate and semiliterate young people are destined to take marginal positions in society and to be the main recipients of social welfare programs.

Paige (2002), serving as United States Secretary of Education, puts the problem this way:

> There is no doubt that our system is in urgent need of repair . . . our system is still failing too many children. According to the most recent National Assessment of Educational Progress (NAEP), only 32% of fourth graders can read proficiently, and the proportion in urban areas is even lower. . . . Our high school seniors scored lower on the 2000 NAEP math assessment than their predecessors in 1996. (pp. 710, 711)

One reason schools fail in this basic curriculum is that they spend insufficient time ensuring children master these skills. Second, these skills are taught in isolation from the disciplines of knowledge students will confront as they move through school. Instead of reading literature or history, children learn to read from texts especially designed to avoid ideas and to present only insipid stories using "a limited vocabulary." A third reason for failure, tied to the second, is that schools do not expect enough of many students, and children become bored and shut out education. Students in earlier periods of history could read complicated material that stretched their minds. Today's texts, "dumbed down" to meet a minimal standard, are demeaning to students and stultify their development. In addition to these reasons for failure, there are too many distractions from academic work at school. These include extensive athletic and social activities, an emphasis on personal and social "adjustment," and using the school curriculum as a dumping-ground for ill-conceived attempts to solve social problems.

Ensure the Fundamentals

Not only do we need to reemphasize the fundamental skills in elementary schools, but we also need to insist on rigorous evaluation of those skills before we allow students to continue in school. The purpose for requiring that students obtain skills in the early years is to permit full use of those skills in further study of important knowledge. Thus, we do a disservice to students who have not mastered the skills, as well as to those who have, if we merely pass these students on to higher grades. Social promotion, based on a loose and disorganized curriculum, produces inadequate education and a disdain for schooling.

Knowledge acquired over a long period, and with great effort, is collected in the major disciplines schools traditionally have taught. All new generations must learn this intellectual and cultural heritage to preserve and extend the culture. Development of disciplines has helped to establish categories of knowledge and study methods that make access to the cultural heritage easier and more systematic. Learning is difficult work, and it should be, but study of the basic disciplines provides a logical avenue to reach understanding. As students master the basics, they find learning easier and more enjoyable. They are no longer failures; if you can't read and calculate at grade level, you won't like school.

The basic disciplines represent differing ways humans have organized wisdom, and together they offer the means to intellectual power. Among these disciplines are:

- math, because we live in a world where quantity and numerical relationships are important.
- language, because accumulated knowledge is communicated in various languages.
- sciences, because they provide an understanding of our environment and its workings.
- history, because an understanding of current life requires us to study the past.

Of course, one can study other disciplines as well in the process of becoming an educated person, but the basic four deserve particular attention in schools and in evaluating how well schools are doing. These are the liberal arts disciplines, meant to liberate people from ignorance. Although the liberal arts have changed over time, they still represent the storehouse of knowledge an educated person should have. Modern society needs citizens grounded in math, language, science, and history to take on the responsibilities and challenges of democratic governance.

A thorough understanding of mathematical and scientific principles is necessary for life in a rapidly changing technological world. Understanding the humanities, represented by literature and history, is necessary if we are to comprehend the human condition and communicate effectively. This combination is the essence of education. To proceed with schooling that fails to educate our children in these areas is to short-circuit the educative process and condemn our children to ignorance.

Continuation of a Major Problem

In a well-reasoned book published a half-century ago, historian Arthur Bestor (1953) called attention to this educational issue:

> The disciplined mind is what education at every level should strive to produce. . . . The idea that the school must undertake to meet every need that some other agency is failing to meet, regardless of the suitability of the classroom to the task, is a preposterous delusion that in the end can wreck the educational system without in any way contributing to the salvation of society. . . . The school promises too much on the one hand, and too little on the other, when it begins to think so loosely about its functions. (pp. 59, 75–76)

Bestor further proposed identification of the fundamentals needed in schools: "Educational reform must begin with the courageous assertion that all the various subjects and disciplines in the curriculum are *not* [original author's emphasis] of equal value. Some disciplines are fundamental. . . ." Those fundamental studies in science, math, language, and history should return to primacy in schools. Bestor directed his attack toward the progressive educationists who claimed they should "teach children" and not "teach history." He correctly pointed out the inanity of this claim. Clearly, the idea of teaching children is vapid; children must be taught something. Bestor argued strongly for intellectual content. He supported public education, but not education about nothing. Nor did he support education about everything, but with no intellectual focus or structure.

Thirty years later, Gilbert Sewall (1983), education editor of *Newsweek,* visited about thirty schools in eight states and reviewed many contemporary writings about schools. In summarizing his findings, Sewall wrote of the contemporary American schools:

> For youngsters of all backgrounds and capabilities, academic outcomes are low and, at least until very recently, have been shrinking. Why? To begin with, few pupils at the secondary level are required to take courses in the basic subjects—language, math, history, science—in order to qualify for a high school diploma. . . . Even more disturbing, curricular revisions have steadily diluted course content. New syllabuses in basic subjects have appeared, purged of tedious or difficult units. Vacuous electives have proliferated, allowing some students to sidestep challenging courses altogether. . . . Endless courses in family life, personal adjustment, consumer skills, and business have crowded out more rigorous subjects, notably in science and foreign language. (Sewall, 1983, pp. 6, 7)

Sewall concludes his book with strong support for teaching fundamental disciplines and basic subjects, with high expectations and clear standards for student performance. He argues that schools have taken on "new and distracting duties to care for every unfortunate and antisocial child, increasingly acting as flunkies and surrogates for self-absorbed, overburdened, or negligent parents" (p. 177). Schools should return to their primary purpose, allow other social institutions to conduct their proper social welfare functions, and recognize that the best route to a satisfying vocation is solid preparation in fundamental knowledge.

Now, some twenty years after Sewall and fifty after Bestor, we shouldn't have to read Herbert Walberg (2001) making the same point:

> Students should be able to read, write, calculate and reason skillfully; they should possess deep and wide knowledge of standard subject matter. . . . For a country that leads the world in the competitiveness and productivity of many old and new industries, it is shocking that American schools are so inefficient. Among the consequences is that schools fail to pull their weight in improving the quality of American life. Their graduates are less literate, less skillful, less informed as citizens, voters, and workers than they should be. (pp. 43, 56, 57)

And Hirsch (2001b) points out a continuing reason: "The curricular chaos of the American elementary school is a feature of our public education that few people have been even aware of, and the growth of that awareness has been one of the origins of the standards movement." Evers (2001) finds that much of the blame for these disturbing lacks in basic education in public schools lies with the "child-centered" notions of progressive educators: "Child-centered progressives do not believe there is a culturally established body of knowledge that students need to learn; therefore they oppose the idea of standards and accountability" (p. 219). In contrast, Evers points out that "Traditionalists believe in systematic and sequential teacher-led instruction . . . that there is a culturally established body of knowledge that students should learn; they believe that successful instruction involves lectures and book learning; and they believe that memorization, drills, and practice are effective learning tools" (Evers, 2001, pp. 220, 221).

Schools continue to fail at the one thing society charges them to do—provide students with a basic education. Declining test scores and painfully obvious evidence of basically illiterate citizens demonstrate serious deficiencies in U.S. schooling. As a recent report of the Center for Educational Reform notes, "Intellectually and morally, America's educational system is failing far too many people" (1998). Despite the enormous amount of money we pour into our schools, our students do not compare favorably with students in Japan, Germany, or most modern industrialized nations. We spend more than most nations do on our schools, ranking fourth among the Organisation for Economic Cooperation and Development (OECD) nations (Hoff, 1998), but we have less to show for it. Academically, the United States ranks with developing countries.

We are a third-rate nation producing generations of graduates who can't read, write, compute, or respond intelligently to questions about history, geography, economics, or literature (Paige, 2002). Our 17-year-olds are incompetent in the humanities (Ravitch and Finn, 1987); in science and math, they are even worse, and they also perform poorly when tested on general information about society and contemporary affairs (*Fortune,* 1990; *National Review,* 1990; *USA Today,* 1990; Samuelson, 1991; Perry, 1993; Peltzman, 1994; Finn, 1995; Center for Educational Reform, 1998; McNamara, 1998; Walberg, 2001).

Baker and Smith (1997) performed a comprehensive analysis of multiple studies of math and science achievements, comparing U.S. schools with schools in other nations over a recent three-year period. They note that "U.S. performance ranks in the middle of each study and never among the best-performing countries" (p. 16). The Third International Mathematics and Science Scores (TIMSS) rated the performance of U.S. students as "among the worst in the world" (McNamara, 1998). These depressing data on academic achievement show the enormous lack in our educational system. Even in an area that the United States used to excel in, high school graduation rates, we are now declining behind other nations ("U.S. Drops in Education Rankings," 1998). Although high school graduation rates in the United States hide the weak program of studies that many U.S. students take, we still have fallen behind other nations whose students take much stronger academic programs (Hoff, 1998; Walberg, 2001).

The basic purpose of schools is to teach fundamental knowledge and skills to the young, including the body of important information and values that stems from our cultural heritage. Fundamental skills, such as mature reading, writing, and computation, are necessary to survive and be productive in contemporary society. Our cultural heritage has evolved over time and also has served society well. It incorporates history, literature, and elements of national character that make the United States what it is. Yet, even in these basic tasks of schools, we see failure.

A History of School Failure in the Basics

Despite two decades of increased funding and attention, the "rising tide of mediocrity" in American schools has not been stemmed. In 1983, a national panel provided a devastating analysis of educational performance (National Commission on Excellence in Education, 1983) that identified thirty-seven different study findings, including these:

- Average academic achievement test scores are lower than in 1957, when *Sputnik* was launched.
- SAT test scores were in continual decline from 1963 to 1980.
- Remedial math courses in college increased by almost 75 percent.
- In international comparisons on nineteen academic achievement tests, U.S. students never scored first or second, and they scored last seven times.
- Textbooks have been written at lower reading levels ("dumbing down") to accommodate declining reading abilities.
- About half the new teachers of math, science, and English are not qualified to teach these subjects.

Since publication of the National Commission report, school funding and teacher salaries have increased, national goals have been set, and some states have set new requirements to improve schools with high-stakes testing of academic subjects. Still, there has been a bureaucratic and ideological reluctance of "progressive" school people and protective teachers' unions to actually return the basics to their rightful place in the curriculum (*Time,* 1989; Perry, 1993; Shaw, 1993; Ravitch, 2000; Evers, 2001).

Fifteen long years after the 1983 report on the dismal state of public education, a conference sponsored by the Heritage Foundation, the Center for Educational Reform, Empower America, and the Thomas G. Fordham Foundation produced *A Nation Still at Risk: An Educational Manifesto* (Center for Educational Reform, 1998), following up the startling report of the National Commission. They found no improvement. This 1998 Manifesto reported that many educators and commentators responded to the persistence of mediocre performance in schools by engaging in "denial, self-delusion, and blame-shifting" (1998, p.1). Such notable intellectuals as William Bennett, Chester Finn, E. D. Hirsch, and Diane Ravitch, part of this distinguished and concerned group, offered practical suggestions to deal with the continuing educational problem:

1. Set and maintain high standards, national competitive assessments, and strict accountability.
2. Provide plural avenues to schooling, competing with public schools and offering choice to parents (for example, charter schools, school choice, vouchers).

3. Require rigorous subject field tests for teachers.
4. Reinstitute order and discipline in schools.
5. Institute merit pay for teachers and administrators.
6. End the monopoly of colleges of education over teacher education.
7. Limit the excesses of such school efforts as bilingual education and multicultural education.
8. Teach the essential academic skills and knowledge.

Shaw (1993) points out that despite the failure of schools, Americans have become educated through the media and interactions with their families and peers. Industrial growth has continued even though we have seen a steady decline in reading scores since 1930. Consider what might have happened if schools were doing their job. There is a superficial idea that schools have improved, but it is similar to the sham of grade inflation that engulfed schools; magically, grade-point averages increased while real student achievement declined. The much-heralded and temporary fads hide underlying erosion of school quality. Schools move like sludge, and the 1990s showed no better overall student performance in academic subjects.

The Dumping-Ground School

Clearly, schools have taken on far too many tasks, failed in the most significant ones, and been forced into the position of replacing parents, church, and society. Schools just do not have enough time or resources to deal with every possible topic. We need to decide which areas are important, and focus our schools' energies on doing them well, meaning we must decide what to jettison and what to improve.

Instead of teaching necessary academic skills and knowledge, today's schools serve as places to learn a set of ideological ideas and engage in utopian, liberal pet projects, including such preposterous and intellectually squishy topics as:

Saving the environment and establishing world peace

Self-respect and adjusting to society

Getting a job

Sex education

Driving a car

Ironically, schools' attempts to fulfill these more frivolous tasks also have been unsuccessful. Further, the frivolous deflect from the basic purpose of education. Some may desire to have schools assume all responsibilities for children, but don't recognize the threat this represents to our free society. Government-operated or -supervised schools have a severely limited capacity to know what's best. Financing those behemoth operations strains the tax budget without improving solid learning. Samuelson (1998), noting that the United States spends over half a trillion dollars each year on its schools, found waste and test failure are typical outcomes.

Unfortunately, the school curriculum has become a dumping ground for every special interest group's pet idea for solving a human problem. If we have a problem with crime, we think we can solve it by teaching about crime in schools. When teenage sex and pregnancy show up on the front pages of newspapers, a new course is proposed for schools. A war occurs somewhere in the world, and we find calls for "peace education" in schools. The AIDS epidemic leads to special courses and instructions on using condoms; meanwhile, the epidemic of actual school failure is ignored. Some students fail tests, and the schools respond not by giving the student additional work on the subject area, but by taking up curricular time with courses on study habits and how to take tests.

If one could find evidence that these frill courses actually eliminated crime, teenage pregnancy, war, academic failure, and AIDS, there might be some grounds for including them in the curriculum. But the simpleminded idea that schools should use their valuable time to address each social problem, or that they actually could deal effectively with social problems, has put the real curriculum in danger. While students starve for quality academic work, schools crowd their time with frills and foolishness. Some of these topics are important social issues, but the school is ill-equipped to address them.

There are several reasons we need to get the schools out of the social welfare business and back into teaching students the basics. First, schools have limited time and have other, more significant, purposes. Second, these topics are heavily laden with values, and our children should not be subjected to a teacher's interpretation of "proper" values. And third, it is folly to believe students with difficulty reading and calculating, or lacking basic knowledge and experience, can adequately deal with such topics as crime and nuclear war.

Courses with no important social value but which pander to fads and fun include Being Me, Making Conversation, Informed Shopping, Hairstyling, or All About Cars. Spending valuable curricular time on driver's education, school safety, baton twirling, school newspaper production, marching band, sports, home maintenance, and the like drains valuable time and energy from the study of literature, history, math, and science.

Schools Fail Even in the Nonessentials

Even if we agreed schools were appropriate places in which to study society's problems or help students with low self-esteem, have those problems been solved by tackling them in schools? If anything, we have even more social problems. Schools have not been successful in teaching fundamentals, nor have they been successful in the misguided effort to correct all of society's ills or to produce happy and confident students.

In examining the list of excessive tasks taken on by schools, we find only one that they have performed moderately well—though at great cost. Driver's education may help young drivers slightly in driving more safely and gaining lower insurance premiums, but that has been accomplished by sacrificing valuable school time, using expensive teachers in very inefficient settings with a small number of students, eliminating a skill area parents could teach to their children, and saddling school budgets with unnecessary costs for automobiles, insurance, equipment, and teaching time. This is not a diatribe against teaching students how to drive, but is an example of limited and costly success in a mistaken area of the school curriculum. School is not the best place to use time and money to teach students how to drive.

Is school the best, or even a good, place for children to learn parenting, self-respect, drug avoidance, safe sex, and morality? Parenting, self-respect, and morality have declined in American society, even as schools have sought to teach these subjects. Clearly, drug usage has not abated after years of school efforts to teach its dangers, and students' unsafe sex practices seem to be epidemic. Beyond this, the backbone of American society, the family, has eroded because schools, not families, have taken responsibility for these educational areas.

Family life has declined in the twentieth century as schools have begun to take over many family responsibilities. Home often consists of providing a place to sleep and eat, watch television, and wave goodbye as parents go to work or the child goes to school. The historic and appropriate tasks of families include providing security and nurturing. The nurturing purpose is essentially educative, as families provide guidance and values for the young. Families that take nurturing seriously risk the teaching of a different set of values in school. Obviously, this is a particular problem for religious families.

Adjustment and Conformity

Among extraneous school responsibilities are teaching students to adjust to society, get along with others, obtain a job, and appreciate the arts. This list smacks of Big Brother. Who is to decide what adjustment, behaviors, and arts we should honor? Do we want monolithic schooling that requires each student to adjust to whatever the school determines is good for society? Life adjustment education, brought in by the "progressives" just after World War II, assumed educators knew what society needed and could determine how students would adjust. This was a form of social engineering that failed. This movement opposed academic study and substituted such trivial activities as learning to dance, playing party games, selecting good movies, and relieving tensions. Thankfully, this period of silly curricula passed, but remnants still remain in schools, and "omission of subject matter continued" (Evers, 2001, p. 207).

A school curriculum built on current fads and latest social issues has no lasting value and cannot hope to prepare young people for productive lives. Similarly, a curriculum designed simply to make students feel better about themselves does not develop maturity; rather, it likely exaggerates personal problems and dependency on others. Meanwhile, these kinds of curricula rob students of time and energy better devoted to real education. Students should be learning important subjects and skills consistent with education's basic purposes. We need to identify essential skills needed for learning and time-tested knowledge all educated citizens should acquire. This is the basic rationale for compulsory schooling; otherwise, why require all children to attend school?

Summary

The distressing list of curricular failures in areas of fundamental knowledge indicates our nation is still at risk. We must move to correct education's accumulated problems by refocusing on the basics. Basic school studies take time and concentration. One cannot master fundamental skills and principles of our cultural heritage on a part-time basis, while devoting considerable time to learning how to "get along with others," or "improve self-respect," or even "learning how to learn." The focus on current fads and personal problems trivializes our heritage, consumes precious school time, and compromises our children's and our society's future. Furthermore, schools clearly have not solved social problems and, as a result of spending time trying to, are not very successful in teaching the basics.

The most valuable education for individual students and for society is to build basic skills and emphasize the liberal arts disciplines.

POSITION 2: TEACH FOR CRITICAL THINKING

> *Behind much of what we do in school lie some ideas that could be expressed roughly as follows: (1) Of the vast body of human knowledge, there are certain bits and pieces that can be called essential, . . . (2) the extent to which a person can be considered educated . . . depends on the amount of this essential knowledge that he carries about with him; (3) it is the duty of the schools, therefore, to get as much of this essential knowledge as possible into the minds of children. . . . These ideas are absurd and harmful nonsense . . . children quickly forget all but a small part of what they learn in school. It is of no use or interest to them; they do not want, or expect, or even intend to remember it. The only difference between bad and good students in this respect is that the bad students forget right away, while the good students are careful to wait until after the exam.*
>
> —HOLT, 1982, PP. 288–289

A democratic nation cannot long survive simply on math and reading skills, or on a body of memorized and easily tested standard information. The world requires thinking people to critically examine issues and policies, which means actively engaging students in inquiry. Of course, fully engaging in inquiry without developing good reading, writing, and calculation skills is impossible. So it is absurd to argue basic skills and knowledge are not important areas of learning in schools that promote critical thinking. But it also is absurd to argue that we should define basic education as the severely limited study of traditional fields of knowledge, taught and tested only in a certain old-fashioned way (Sirotnik, 2002). A better definition of *basic education* is that set of knowledge, skills, values, and attitudes required for students to live active, productive lives in a changing society. That definition assumes a reality, a context, a usefulness, a dynamic of knowledge, and a need for critical skills. What could be more basic in American society?

Unfortunately, "basic education" has become a code term to describe a sterile, conformist school environment that feeds externally defined skills and lists of information to children. It depends heavily on indoctrination and regurgitation; there is, presumably, one right way to learn and one set of right "facts" to obtain. *Critical thinking,* however, is defined as "reasonably reflective thinking that is focused on deciding what to believe or do" (Ennis, 1991, p. 6). It depends on engagement of the thinker in the process and requires valid use of fundamental knowledge and skills. We, therefore, advocate critical thinking as the most important goal of education, in opposition to the narrowly defined basic education. And critical thinking demands examination of problems.

You can't just tell someone to think critically in the same way that teachers in traditional schools try to explain history or science. Critical thinking requires active involvement in the reflective act and goes well beyond mechanical recitation of information imparted by a teacher or textbook—student interest must be stimulated to activate participation. Students, then, have a serious stake in critical thinking, and schools cannot ignore student interests and motivations. Critical thinking cannot operate in top-down schooling, which has no regard for learners or for real learning situations.

The narrow and intellectually invalid perspective that basic education is a set of predetermined subjects historically taught in a prescribed sequence to previous generations ignores the most thoughtful work on learning and intelligence (Gardner, 1999). The call for "basic education" seriously compromises a good education by using a fantasy "golden age" concept that old-time schools were better. This effort to return U.S. schools to memorization, recitation, and skill drill is misguided and educationally restrictive. There are good reasons for selective use of memorization, recitation, and skill practice in developing some student abilities, but that approach to teaching should not be the dominant form. Obviously, schools must include strong academic work in educating youngsters, but the focus on a very small group of separate traditional disciplines is only one way to organize and learn knowledge. And it has many limitations. Had basic education in its narrow form been continued from seventeenth-century Latin Grammar schools, we now would have classes taught in Latin, and students would get a very different view of world history, geography, politics, science, and life.

Political turmoil surrounding school reform over the past twenty years has obscured schooling's most important purpose. In the clamor to improve test scores that require students to recall bits of information, we have ignored developing students' abilities to engage in critical inquiry. Backward-looking, rigid disciplinarians should not be allowed to put intellectual blinders on the critical work of schools to push their school and social agenda. Traditionalists would like us to move back to drill and memorization in a few selected school subjects to raise test scores. They want to restrict new generations to old ideas, filtered through their narrow vision of education, limit controversy and thinking, control teachers, and make schools dull and deadly places where test scores rule. But controversy, as Nel Noddings (1999) properly comments, is necessary to democratic education.

Sheffler (1985) made the point twenty years ago:

> The democratic ideal precludes the conception of education as an *instrument* [italics in original]; it is antithetical to the idea of rulers shaping or molding the mind of the pupil. The function of education in a democracy is rather to liberate the mind, strengthen its critical powers, inform it with knowledge and the capacity for independent inquiry, engage its human sympathies and illuminate its moral and practical choices. (p. 124)

This is a complicated, difficult, but necessary responsibility for schools to undertake. The return to basics with memorization of predigested information in a standardized curriculum with excessive amounts of testing of often trivial material takes precious time and energy from this more important role for contemporary schools (Hatch, 2002). The highly traditional curriculum also destroys student interest and motivation, resulting in boredom, disruption, resentful acquiescence, and even dropping out (Sirotnik, 2002). This is a combination we cannot afford. Eisner (2002) puts it well:

> If all that students get out of what they learn in history or math or science are ideas they rapidly forget and cannot employ outside of the context of a classroom, then education is a casualty. The point of learning anything in school is not primarily to enable one to do well in schools—although most parents and students believe this to be the case—it is to enable one to do well in life. (p. 581).

The learner-centered critical-thinking curriculum is strongly intellectual. It engages students' intellects and challenges their ideas. The essential concern in education should not be what we teach, but what students learn. For too long, we have posed the wrong question in considering the school curriculum. Certainly we need to consider what is, or should be, taught, but that is a secondary issue. The primary focus should be on what is, or should be, learned. We can't properly address what we want to teach in schools without first determining the nature of learning and of the learners. Curriculum artificiality is borne on the presumption that we can ignore children's needs, interests, and long-term development in favor of a set of pronouncements on what subjects they must learn.

The premise for education must be the child's development, not the adult's wish to mold the child's knowledge, values, and behavior. When we focus on subjects that "must" be taught, we are inclined to forget about students and thinking. We are more likely to produce lists of concepts imposed on us that we now wish to impose on students. We introduce the teacher as an authority, rather than a wise guide. And we structure schools to systematically destroy children's creative interests by forcing them all to learn the same material.

Natural and Unnatural Learning

A substantial battle has raged in the long history of educational thought between those who think people learn naturally from within and those who believe external force must be brought to bear to assure learning. This battle is illustrated currently by the difference of opinion between those who want students to be free to pursue their natural inclinations to learn and those who want to impose a set of conditions and ideas on the minds and actions of students. This battle also is illustrated by a quote from Nat Hentoff (1977):

> One afternoon as we were walking down the street, Paul Goodman turned to me and said, "Do you realize that if the ability to walk depended on kids being taught walking as a subject in school, a large number of citizens would be ambulatory only if they crawled." (p. 53)

Support of student freedom for learning does not mean letting students do whatever they please. Among the false criticisms of progressive education and of John Dewey's work is the claim that the child determines everything. That is either a misreading or a calculated attempt to discredit the position. Dewey insisted that the most mature person in the classroom, the teacher, must ultimately take responsibility for what is taught, but that the teacher's decision must be predicated on the child's needs and interests. The child, or learner, determines what is learned. Thus, the child-centered, or learner-centered, curriculum is designed with the child's development first in mind. The teacher must, in this curriculum, remain sensitive to the learner. License to do whatever one pleases, whether teacher or learner, is inconsistent with this view. Freedom encourages innovation and stimulates critical thinking.

The learner-centered curriculum stands in opposition to the subject- or discipline-centered curriculum, which begins by considering how the discipline is organized according to a select group of scholars. The traditional discipline-centered curriculum represents imposition of information, categories, and ideas without concern for the learner. Thus, it is an unnatural, external structuring of what is learned. The learner-centered curriculum rests on the conviction that students want to learn. What destroys that natural curiosity is the authoritarian nature of traditional approaches to schooling.

Student and Teacher Experiences

The primary way people learn, as opposed to being taught, is through experience. Learning is an active, not a static, process. When we are involved in some physical activity, such as organizing a group project, building a model village, playing a game, or measuring a room, we are learning. We make errors, seek advice, modify actions, and gain understanding in a real situation. Most teachers will admit, for example, that they learned the most about a subject when they had to teach it, not when they were sitting in a college class. We learn more about cars by trying to fix them than by hearing how to fix them.

Not all experiential learning involves physical activity or actual situations. Such vicarious experiences as reading a book or listening to a speaker can provide pertinent learning. And, of course, it is impossible, and would not even be desirable, for students to physically experience all learning situations. Active engagement, mental or physical, is what produces learning.

Curiosity, interest, or the need to resolve a problem makes reading or listening a learning situation in which active engagement can take place. Simply being told something is important, or something must be learned for a test, does not necessarily stimulate active engagement. Perfunctory reading of a book or listening to a teacher may appear to be learning, but students with an active mind may be off on a different tangent. Teachers teach and assign readings; students appear to listen and read, but what do they learn? Students learn to cope with dry, uninteresting material in a school filled with boring routines. That is not the experience good teachers desire, and many are themselves tired of dullness and boredom. Certainly, it is not the experience students desire. But too many traditional schools operate this way.

Clearly, not all experiences are equally beneficial as learning situations; some are actually detrimental. We may like the taste of excessively fatty and salty foods, but that can lead to poor nutritional habits. Smoking cigarettes may lead to health problems. It may take only one experience of jumping out of a window to stop learning entirely. It is not simply experience that matters, but the quality and developmental nature of that experience. The teacher's role, then, becomes one of seeking and providing experiences for students that stimulate their interest and enrich their learning. Success, of course, depends on the teacher's wisdom, knowledge, and sensitivity to the students.

Knowledge and Problems

To focus on what areas of knowledge are important for students to use in dealing with human problems we must start with those problems and determine what knowledge exists that can help us understand and address them. That is certainly different from the old-fashioned approach, which starts with categories or subjects and presumes students need to learn them regardless of their value to the learner. Real human problems cannot be treated simply as literature or history or chemistry problems. Under the traditional curriculum, teachers resort to contrived "problems" in each of the subjects in an attempt to motivate student interest. Standard math story problems are notoriously unreal; U.S. history usually presents problems students see as already resolved and unrelated to current life. Why not start with a problem students can easily identify, and then find knowledge—regardless of its subject field—that we can utilize in solving that problem? This method recognizes knowledge as interrelated and useful, not as compartmentalized and ornamental.

The adult, traditional manner of organizing knowledge into apparently discrete categories, such as English and American literature, physics, biology, algebra, European and U.S. history, chemistry, and drama, may work well for those who devote their careers to advanced study in one of these areas. These distinct categories may not be as useful for students in elementary and secondary schools, where the need is greater to see that knowledge is seamless and valuable in examining life's problems. Some pervasive human problems revolve around such values as justice, equality, freedom, democracy, and human rights. And a myriad of individual problems are related to these broader human challenges. To solve them will require knowledge from such fields as math, science, history, economics, psychology, literature, the arts, and politics—and skills in reading, writing, calculating, organizing, categorizing, and critical thinking. As students mature, they develop interests in different problems, different types of knowledge, and different levels of skills. An active problems approach to learning, based on student interests and freedom to choose, leads to development of critical thinking

Anti-intellectualism and the Back to Basics Movement

In the tightly organized and past-oriented traditional curriculum, the meticulously structured content largely has no meaning in students' lives, and memorizing material for a test is scarcely intellectual. A properly developed learner-centered curriculum, however, requires students' intellectual involvement in examining topics they can comprehend and utilize. The traditional back to basics curriculum is filled with what Alfred North Whitehead so eloquently derided in his 1929 classic, *The Aims of Education:* "'inert ideas'—that is to say, ideas that are merely received into the mind without being utilised, or tested, or thrown into fresh combinations" (Whitehead, 1929, p. 13). Whitehead goes on to note that education is "overladen with inert ideas." And he states that "education with inert ideas is not only useless: it is, above all things, harmful. . . ." This is anti-intellectual.

School reform efforts of the past two decades have been dominated by a focus on learning sterile trivia—inert ideas—to pass tests designed by and for an earlier generation of students. We are so driven by silly concepts of competition in test scores that we limit time left for creativity, innovation, intellectual stimulation, and reflection on matters of importance to the child and to our society. Critical thinking has been abandoned by the one social institution that should most defend it. In an educational absurdity, students must seek opportunities to develop critical thinking by looking outside the school (Caywood, 1994).

The traditional school is filled with inert ideas, bits and pieces of information that fit no pattern and have no vitality for most students. Every class period of inert ideas is followed by another period of different, apparently unrelated, inert ideas. Each teacher acts as though his or her ideas are very important, and will soon appear on a test, and students go through the expected motions. Schools are like giant jigsaw puzzles, except the box cover with the picture of the completed puzzle is missing.

Subjects taught in the traditional manner are not intellectual; they do not stimulate thinking and consideration of diverse ideas. Intellectual vitality arises from life, not from unrelated segments of knowledge we throw at students. That does not mean we would ignore or destroy information gained from scholarly study of a subject; it means we need to help students understand the connections that make knowledge valuable and learn how to utilize that knowledge in solving problems.

That schools are not preparing students in basic subjects is a myth. On a wide variety of measures, including but going beyond test scores, U.S. students stack up very well. For political and ideological purposes, conservatives manufactured a fictitious crisis in American education in the 1980s (Berliner and

Biddle, 1995). Misinterpretations of test quality, student scores, and differing contexts in different nations and times have misled the public. Researcher Gerald Bracey's annual reports on the condition of public education and his many articles clearly show no massive failure in schools (Bracey, 1998, 1999, 2002). Lemann (1998) notes in an article about American schools in *Atlantic Monthly*, "The rhetoric of failure is simply wrong. . . . Public education is by far the largest and most important function performed by government in this country. In no way is it in systemic crisis" (pp. 92–93). Ideologues and much of the media have maligned public schools. The mistreatment helps people get elected, sells newspapers, and furthers the right-wing agenda to gut public education and control social values. At its center, the back to basics movement is an ideological effort to limit critics and critical thought.

The artificiality of traditional basic education in schools is obvious. These schools are disconnected from society, from children's lives, from families, and from reality. Children are drilled to memorize terms that hold no meaning for them. Tidiness and punctuality substitute for thought. Platitudes abound about a life that is not recognizable in the children's experience. Students are required to learn categories of information that do not relate to their lives, and are tested on trivial details. The public then falsely presumes students' scores represent what they know about the world, and we pretend this is preparation for life. School takes children who are living a real life and gives them artificiality, claiming this is education.

The Impact on Students

Students thus begin to dread school, hating the regimen of rules, boredom, inert ideas, and stuffiness. We all start with immense curiosity about the world, and most of us are eager to start school. That curiosity is quickly stifled and eagerness dulled as we progress through schools that deny us the chance to engage in critical thinking. Isn't that incredibly ironic? The institution intended to stimulate learning about the world is, instead, the institution presenting the most obstacles to that learning.

Academically successful students in such schools usually are not the most curious or creative, but ones best able to follow the teacher's directions and remember what the books say when it's time for a test. Schools reward conformity and obedience, not diversity and independence. Schooling becomes training, not education. The student is a bystander in schooling. Sizer's (1984) study of high school students showed they were compliant, docile, and lacked initiative. He attributed this to the heavy emphasis on getting right answers and to too little emphasis on being inquisitive. Goodlad (1983), after examining data from observations in over a thousand classrooms, documented the high degree of passivity among students and lack of time or concern afforded student interests and opinions.

Students need, and deserve, to participate actively in the learning process, and require materials that stretch their imaginations, preexisting conceptions, and intellectual capacities (Duckworth, 1987; Bamberger, 1991; Begley, 1993;

Tice, 1994). These are basic elements in developing critical thinking. School reform at the beginning of the twenty-first century has glossed over these elements in favor of old-fashioned basic skill drills and test scores.

False Critiques

The false presumption behind the idea that schools should be reformed to teach basic reading, writing, and arithmetic skills is that schools are not now teaching these skills. In fact, schools have devoted significant time and energy to teach these fundamental areas for generations. Communication and mathematics are necessary parts of an education, but are too limited to be schooling's only goal. These skills are important because of their value to individual children in making sense of their experience and in the critical thinking necessary for social improvement. They are not important simply because previous generations had to learn them. Information is essential, but why must everyone know the same things?

Certainly individual school districts, schools, and classrooms may be unsatisfactory and need correction and improvement, but there is no large-scale decline across our schools. If a problem exists in education now, it is that traditionalist school reforms, stimulated by the fictional crisis, have stifled teacher creativity and chilled efforts to improve schools in their most important functions.

A backward-looking curriculum and lack of mental stimulation combine to rob contemporary students of their right to a liberating education. School has become an onerous period of separation from reality. What students learn does not prepare them for understanding or reflecting on life. As Howard Gardner (1991a) expresses it: "Specifically, school knowledge seems strictly bound to school settings" (p. 119). Gardner's studies show that school knowledge may show up in students' scores on school-related tests, but that school knowledge has limited relation to improved knowledge of the real world (Gardner, 1991b). The movement to mandate national standards of basic education is restrictive, counterproductive, and, ultimately, a national folly (Ohanian, 1999)

Backward Steps

Students were the most hidden part of the school reform movement of the 1980s and 1990s; in fact, students were essentially invisible. The most ignored curriculum concern was critical thinking. Virtually every report, government statement, and proposed legislation focused on basic skills, the school organization, or school officials. The concern was to make some organizational or operational change in the institution's structure. No interest was shown in the students or their lives in school, and developing critical judgment as a primary school goal was lost in pages of test score data. More tests, higher standards set by adults outside school, longer school days and years, more homework, more stress on teachers and administrators, and less enjoyment in learning were the major educational achievements of the past two decades.

In a particularly clear-eyed review of the 1980s reform movement, English teacher Susan Ohanian (1985) summarized this point:

> We must be ever wary of wasting some youngster's life just because of a dubious notion that a rigorous, regimented curriculum will help restore to the U.S. a better balance of trade. . . . At best, the recommendations of the commissions and task forces on school reform are hallucinatory; at worst, they are soul-destroying. Let us teachers not succumb to the temptation of asking what we can do for General Motors; let us continue to ask only what we can do for the children. (p. 321)

Over half a century ago, John Dewey's remarkably cogent book, *Experience and Education,* differentiated between traditional and progressive education. Dewey divided the two on the basis of a long-term schism that "is marked by opposition between the idea that education is development from within and that it is formation from without . . ." (Dewey, 1938, p. 17). He notes traditional education consists of information and skills that "have been worked out in the past," its standards and rules of conduct are prescribed by adults, and schools operate as though they were separate from children's lives and the rest of society. Schools impose subject matter and rules of conduct on children, and pupils' attitude must "be one of docility, receptivity, and obedience" (p. 18). The school molds or forms the child.

Progressive education, Dewey says, arose out of discontent with this traditional approach:

> To imposition from above is opposed expression and cultivation of individuality; to external discipline is opposed free activity; to learning from texts and teachers, learning through experience; to acquisition of isolated skills and techniques by drill, is opposed acquisition of them as a means of attaining ends which make direct vital appeal; to preparation for a more or less remote future is opposed making the most of opportunities of present life; to static aims and materials is opposed acquaintance with a changing world. (p. 20)

Unfortunately, schools have never taken progressive education—developing learners from within—seriously. Cosmetic changes have made schools appear more humane, but they have not shed their basic, misplaced authoritarian efforts to impose selected information and morals on children. Traditional education seeks to pour information into students, discouraging critical thinking and creativity. Schools continue to teach as though education were not part of life itself, but preparation for some later event. They ignore individual children in favor of standardization of curriculum and test scores.

A Summary of the Multiple Defects in the Traditional Structure of Schooling

The discipline-centered school has several defects. It imposes an externally determined body of information on children, ignores natural learning interests and stifles curiosity and creativity, and requires schools to be authoritarian. If one starts with the premise that children are curious, imaginative, and eager to learn, what happens to make schools impose so many restrictions on students?

The main reason is that schools traditionally have been expected to homogenize individual children into an adult view of what society should be.

The structure of traditional schooling is consistent with the old-fashioned view that schools should be cheerless places where the young are trained to become adults by learning what adults think they should know and behaving in ways adults think they should behave. Schools are expected to impart to the younger generation skills and information based on past ideas; they are expected to train students to behave according to a set of rules and standards; and they are to do it all as efficiently as possible to save time and tax money.

From this viewpoint, schools are organized to distill the adult world for children, impose a set of ideas and morals on them, and require them to undergo processing as though they were in a food-packing or auto-assembly plant. As a result, schools classify students by grade and test scores to make teaching more efficient, set up severe time schedules, and rely on teacher or textbook presentation of standard information, required courses, and excessive testing to ensure all students are trained the same way.

Traditional schools are static institutions stressing conformity and adult concepts with limited meaning in students' lives. Yet students are dynamic, growing, and concerned about their own individuality. Remarkably, the resilience of youth permits them to survive in such a stifling environment. Good teachers recognize the paradox between traditional schooling and needs of youth, and they try to find ways to match static material with a changing society. They also ameliorate the demand for conformity by trying to recognize individual differences among their students, and attempt to enlarge students' horizons by building on their experiences. But the efforts of good teachers are undermined by schooling's traditional structure, standardized tests, and pressure from vocal advocates of the past.

In traditional schools, the main purpose is for students to get the "right answers," not to encourage them to engage in critical thinking. Thinking students might challenge the way the school operates, uninteresting material, stress on conformity, and why certain answers are "right." Schools are not usually prepared to respond to such challenges, and often resort to fear, ridicule, repression, and isolation to squelch them. Students learn quickly that it does not pay to raise serious questions, and withdraw into the safer haven of going along with the system.

Schools present artificial barriers to learning, and stimulate fear and repression. The typical student responds to school in one of these ways:

- Drop out or fail
- Slip through without meaningful engagement
- Please the teacher and succeed
- Resist school rules and suffer penalties
- Wait for something more interesting

None of these responses represents the best form of intellectual development. Do we think our schools are excellent when large numbers of students drop out, fail, or set aside their curiosity?

The material taught—which is different from the material learned—is a series of disconnected and lifeless bits of information with little meaning for students. Students learn that English is separate from history, which is separate from economics, science, math, the arts, and physical education. And students learn that school is separate from life, and certainly from social and individual problems. How can students understand and try to resolve a personal or a social problem using traditional school subjects? Are shyness, feelings of failure, apprehension, death in the family, and acne the kinds of problems traditional subjects can address? Do students see problems of poverty, alcoholism, war, and human rights as resolvable by using bits and pieces learned in math or science or history or English as taught in schools? Is it reasonable or desirable for students to suffer through school and look forward to life outside of school? That inverts what school should be, and what knowledge should provide.

The Essential Point

Traditional schooling continues to emphasize rote memory, achieving high scores on tests over relatively trivial material, and amassing information taught for its own sake. This type of schooling fails to connect to students and their lives, and suppresses critical thinking because that type of thinking disrupts the teacher's authoritarian role. Schooling should, instead, open ideas that stimulate students to examine their own experiences and engage in critical examination of social problems. This goal requires a new focus on students and on critical thinking.

Students come with a variety of personalities, backgrounds, and interests. We need a curriculum that recognizes this individuality as an opportunity and sees students as a dynamic resource. The static, traditional curriculum pushes them into molds and stamps them with a list of subjects studied. The learner-centered critical-thinking curriculum develops students' inner curiosity and energy and their ability to utilize knowledge in addressing human problems.

For Discussion

1. Dialogue Ideas: How do you define basic education? From what sources have you come to this definition? What are the arguments against your definition? Which typical school subjects fit your definition and which are left out?
2. Construct and defend hypothetical school curricula that you believe would ensure these:
   - **a.** Graduates would be able to operate successfully in society.
   - **b.** Individual students' rights and interests would be given credible expression.
   - **c.** Critical thinking would be a high priority for all students.
   - **d.** Basic education would be at the core of the curriculum.
3. You have had experiences as a student in several different levels of schooling. Which of these potential school topics would you identify as a frill? Which are, to you, fundamentals? On what basis do you make the distinction?

   Athletics

   Group play

Penmanship
Landscaping
American history
Writing letters
Games and rules
Reviewing movies, newspapers, and television
Literary classics
Balancing a checkbook
Advanced science and math
Japanese, Russian, Chinese, and Spanish languages
Astrology
Myths and legends
Latin and Greek
Social living
Economic theory
Parts of speech
Clothing design

What would you add that is clearly a frill? What could you add that is obviously a fundamental?

4. If the roles of adults and children were reversed to allow children to determine what adults should know for a basic education, what would the curriculum be like?

References

BAKER, D. P., AND SMITH, T. (1997). Trend 1: The condition of Academic Achievement in the Nation. *Teachers College Record* 99(1), 14–17.
BAMBERGER, J. (1991). *The Mind Behind the Musical Ear.* Cambridge, MA: Harvard University Press.
BEGLEY, S. (1993). "Doin' What Doesn't Come Naturally." *Newsweek* 122, 84.
BERLINER, D., AND BIDDLE, B. J. (1995). *The Manufactured Crisis: Myths, Fraud, and Attack on America's Public Schools.* Reading, MA: Addison-Wesley.
BESTOR, A. (1953). *Educational Wastelands.* Urbana: University of Illinois Press.
BRACEY, G. (1998). "The Eighth Bracey Report." *Phi Delta Kappan.* October.
———. (1999). "The Demise of the Asian Math Gene." *Phi Delta Kappan* 80(8), 619–620.
———. (2002). *The War Against America's Public Schools.* Boston: Allyn and Bacon/Longmans.
CAYWOOD, C. (1994). "Critical Thinking: A Critical Need." *School Library Journal* 40, 46.
CENTER FOR EDUCATIONAL REFORM. (1998). *A Nation Still at Risk: An Education Manifesto.* Washington, DC: Author.
DEWEY, J. (1938). *Experience and Education.* New York: Macmillan.
DUCKWORTH, E. (1987). *The Having of Wonderful Ideas and Other Essays.* New York: Teachers College Press.
EISNER, E. (2002). "The Kind of Schools We Need." *Phi Delta Kappan* 83(8), 576–583.
ENNIS, R. (1991). "Critical Thinking: A Streamlined Conception." *Teaching Philosophy* 14, 5–24.

EVERS, W. M. (2001). "Standards and Accountability." In T. Moe, ed., *A Primer on America's Schools.* Stanford: Hoover Institution Press.

FINN, C. (1995). "The School." *Commentary* 99, 6–10.

Fortune. (1990). Special Issue: "Saving Our Schools." Spring, p. 121.

GARDNER, H. (1991a). "The Tensions Between Education and Development." *Journal of Moral Education* 20, 113–125.

———. (1991b). *The Unschooled Mind.* New York: Basic Books.

———. (1999) *Intelligence Reframed: Multiple Intelligences for the 21st Century.* New York: Basic Books.

GOODLAD, J. (1983). *A Place Called School.* New York: McGraw-Hill.

HATCH, J. A. (2002). "Accountability Shovedown." *Phi Delta Kappan* 83(6), 457–462.

HENTOFF, N. (1977). *Does Anybody Give a Damn?* New York: Knopf.

HIRSCH, E. D. (1996) *The Schools We Need: And Why We Don't Have Them.* New York: Doubleday.

———. (2001a). "Seeking Breadth and Depth in the Curriculum." *Educational Leadership* 59(2), 22–25.

HOFF, D. J. (1998). "U.S. Graduation Rates Starting to Fall Behind." *Education Week on the Web,* Nov. 25.

HOLT, J. (1982). *How Children Fail.* Rev. Ed. Reading, MA: Perseus Books.

LEMANN, N. (1998). "Ready, Read!" *Atlantic Monthly* 282(5), 92–104.

MCNAMARA, J. B. (1998). "The Morality of Mediocrity." *Vital Speeches of the Day* 64(16), 497–501.

NATIONAL ASSESSMENT OF EDUCATIONAL PROGRESS. (1994). *NAEP 1992 Trends in Academic Progress.* National Center for Educational Statistics. Washington, DC: U.S. Department of Education.

NATIONAL COMMISSION ON EXCELLENCE IN EDUCATION. (1983). *A Nation at Risk.* Washington, DC: U.S. Department of Education.

National Review. (1990). "Knowing So Much About So Little (Poor Performance of American Schools)." 42, 14–15.

"A Nation Still at Risk: An Educational Manifesto." (1998). *Policy Review* 90, 23–29.

NODDINGS, N. (1999). "Renewing Democracy in Schools." *Phi Delta Kappan* 80(8), 579–583.

OHANIAN, S. (1985). "Huffing and Puffing and Blowing the Schools Excellent." *Phi Delta Kappan* 66, 316–321.

———. (1999). *One Size Fits Few: The Folly of Educational Standards.* Westport, CT: Heineman.

PAIGE, R. (2002). "An Overview of America's Education Agenda." *Phi Delta Kappan* 83(9), 708–713.

PELTZMAN, S. (1994). *USA Today.* 122, 22–25.

PERRY, N. J. (1993). "School Reform: Big Pain, Little Gain." *Fortune* 128, 130–135.

"Political Factors in Public School Decline." (1994). *The American Enterprise* 4, 44–49.

RAVITCH, D. (2000) *Left Back: A Century of Failed School Reforms.* New York: Simon & Schuster.

RAVITCH, D., AND FINN, C. (1987). *What Do Our 17-Year-Olds Know?* New York: Harper & Row.

SAMUELSON, R. J. (1991). "The School Reform Fraud." *Newsweek* 117, 44.

———. (1998) "The Wastage in Education." *Newsweek* 132, 49.

SEWALL, G. T. (1983). *Necessary Lessons: Decline and Renewal in American Schools.* New York: Free Press.

SHAW, P. (1993). "The Competitiveness Illusion: Does Our Country Need to Be Literate in Order to Be Competitive? If Not, Why Read?" *National Review* 45, 41–45.

SHEFFLER, I. (1985). *Of Human Potential.* Boston: Routledge and Kegan Paul.

SIROTNIK, K. A. (2002). "Promoting Responsible Accountability in Schools and Education." *Phi Delta Kappan* 83(9), 662–673.

SIZER, T. (1984). *Horace's Compromise: The Dilemma of the American High School.* Boston: Houghton Mifflin.

SZABO, J. C. (1992). "Boosting Workers' Basic Skills." *Nation's Business* 80, 38–41.

TICE, T. N. (1994). "Critical Plus Open." *Education Digest* 59, 42–44.

Time. (1989). "Mixed Review: Some Progress, More Needed." 133, 68.

"U.S. Drops in Education Rankings." (1998). *San Diego Union Tribune* 7(328), 1, 17.

USA Today. (1990). "Skills Lacking for Tomorrow's Jobs." 119, 11+.

WALBERG, H. (2001). "Achievement in American Schools." In T. Moe, ed., *A Primer on America's Schools.* Stanford: Hoover Institution Press.

WHITEHEAD, A. N. (1929). *The Aims of Education.* New York: Macmillan.

CHAPTER 10

Reading: Phonics or Whole Language

POSITION 1: THE PHONICS ARGUMENT

> *When Alexis Muskie talks about her daughter's experience learning to read, she begins to cry. Muskie, whose father-in-law was the late Senator and Secretary of State Edmund Muskie, lives in Peterborough, New Hampshire. Before her daughter, Olivia, entered first grade, it became apparent that she would need some extra help, and so she received phonics tutoring in addition to her classroom instruction. But the school district had adopted the "whole language" approach to teaching reading. "There was a conflict between the special-ed teacher and the whole language teacher," Muskie says. "The whole language teacher was saying I can't send her to that program." The tutoring ended, but Olivia's reading didn't improve, and in second grade she became scared and frustrated. "She was literally pulling her hair out," Muskie remembers, her voice cracking. A year later, Muskie found a reading clinic that used a phonics method. "It took them six days," Muskie says, "and Olivia could read."*
>
> —COLLINS, 1997, P. 1

We all learn to use oral language through a natural process. We imitate the sounds we hear in our environment, connect those sounds to things and people, and eventually utter them in patterns others can understand. We learn informal oral communication skills without any direct instruction. You are unlikely to hear people arguing about "the best way to teach young children to speak" or discussing the "speaking crisis in our schools," and you may never run across a book entitled *Why Johnny Can't Speak!* Learning to read, on the other hand, is not an automatically acquired, natural process. The relationship between sounds and letters is an arrangement by convention; there is nothing natural about the letters assigned to sounds of the English language. Left to themselves, children will not automatically learn to associate sounds with letters, a fundamental prerequisite for successful reading. The weight of research evidence indicates that children will not learn to read without direct instruction

(Grossen, 1998). Children need to be taught explicitly how to break the code of letters we use to represent the sounds of our language.

Reading instruction is a matter of serious concern. Nothing better predicts the future academic success of children than their ability to read. Unfortunately, as many as one in five children have reading difficulties, and those children are likely to be headed for a life of academic struggle and a world of diminished promise. Children behind in reading at an early age, in kindergarten and first grade fall further behind every year they are in school. A review of research conducted by the National Institute of Child Health and Human Development found that nearly three-fourths of children diagnosed as "reading disabled" in third grade remained disabled in ninth grade (Grossen, 1998, p. 6). What makes this all the more unfortunate is that we know how to teach young children to read. Recent research evidence is overwhelming. To become good readers, children need to be taught the "alphabetic principle"; that is, schools need to teach students that words are made up of letters, and letters correspond to speech in consistent and specific ways. In experimental treatments comparing direct instruction in letter-sound correspondence (phonics) and less direct methods (whole language), the children receiving direct instruction "improved in word reading at a faster rate and had higher word-recognition skills" than the other children (Foorman et al., 1998, p. 37).

Why do children need to know the sounds of letters? The answer is disarmingly straightforward: Words and syllables are composed of short sound units called phonemes. Research indicates that deficits in phonemic awareness—the ability to understand how to break words into component sounds—is at the heart of most reading problems (Grossen, 1998, p. 6). For children to become successful readers, teachers need to begin reading instruction with direct, explicit lessons in the relationships between sounds and letters. As one researcher points out, children who are not taught to link sounds and letters are in academic trouble: "You have to understand what happened to kids who don't learn sound awareness. . . . They just don't make it. They don't make it in school and they don't make it in life. It is extremely important and it is not something you can 'pick up'" (Gursky, 1998, p. 12).

Reading is a technical field, but don't be thrown by terms such as *letter-sound relationships, phonemic awareness,* and *phonics.* These terms are nothing more than the ways reading scholars describe how oral language relates to written language. Consider this example of several phonemic awareness tasks for young children. On the left side are the technical terms for the phonics subskills. On the right side are the classroom questions a teacher would ask to help students develop those skills.

1. Phoneme deletion:	What word would be left if the /k/ sound were taken away from *cat?*
2. Word-to-word matching:	Do *pen* and *pipe* begin with the same sound?
3. Blending:	What word would we have if we put these sounds together: /s/, /a/, /t/?
4. Sound isolation:	What is the first sound in *rose?*

5. Phoneme segmentation: What sounds do you hear in the word *hot?*
6. Phoneme counting: How many sounds do you hear in the word *cake?*
7. Deleting phonemes: What sound do you hear in *meat* that is missing in *eat?*
8. Odd word out: What word starts with a different sound: *bag, nine, beach, bike?*
9. Sound-to-word matching: Is there a /k/ in *bike?* (Grossen, 1998, p. 10)

The Romance of Whole Language

Are you familiar with *Emile,* by Jean-Jacques Rousseau? *Emile,* an educational romance, describes the raising of a young boy based on the principles of nature. One section reads,

> Everything is good as it leaves the hands of the Author of things; everything degenerates in the hands of man. He forces one soil to nourish the products of another, one tree to bear the fruit of another. He mixes and confuses the climates, the elements, the seasons. He mutilates his dog, his horse, his slave. [Man] turns everything upside down; he disfigures everything; he loves deformity, monsters. He wants nothing as nature made it, not even man; for him, man must be trained like a school horse; man must be fashioned in keeping with his fancy like a tree in his garden. (Rousseau, 1979, p. 37)

You may well wonder what this has to do with reading. Rousseau (1712–1778) might seem an unlikely source in a discussion of today's "reading wars," but his insistence on the "natural" goodness of man and children's "natural" inclination to take the right educational path provide some background to the current dilemma. Rousseau's pedagogic focus on the wishes of the child and his insistence that children learn best when allowed to do exactly what they want provides the ideologic basis for present-day progressive education and whole-language reading instruction. Emile, Rousseau's hypothetical pupil, was led by a tutor to discover scientific and moral truths by following his inherent creativity and curiosity. Emile learned by observing nature, by cultivating a garden and discovering nature's rules about competition and survival, and by experiencing the world around him. He also learned useful trades and the principles of good character formation. The basic purpose of education, according to Rousseau, is to facilitate the happiness of humankind. True learning is the road to happiness, and it could only be discovered individually. False learning is prescribed, standardized, and taught by drill and repetition.

Whole-language thinking is a direct descendant of Rousseau's philosophy, by way of modern-day progressive educators. Whole-language methods do not require a private tutor for every child, but teachers are asked to draw on the natural curiosity of each individual child in the classroom. Whole-language advocates reject drill and phonics worksheets as corrupting and unnatural, in the same way that Rousseau rejected the conformity of schooling and rules of civilized society. The whole-language approach to reading is based on the false analogy equating learning to speak with learning to read. While children naturally learn oral language, it is an illusion to regard beginning reading as anything but a difficult, artificial process (Hirsch, 2002). Whole language may be attractive at first glance, and it would be a very compelling classroom methodology if it were effective in teaching children to read, but it is not. In fact, the appeal of whole language does not extend beyond its rhetoric, and in practice it nearly visited disaster on the children from one state that adopted it.

Whole-Language Problems in California

> Why are California's schoolchildren reading so poorly? The whole-language method. (Grossen, 1995, p. 43)

California's experience offers an interesting case study of the failure of whole-language instruction as a practical method for teaching reading. During the 1980s, William Honig, the Superintendent of Public Instruction in California, was responsible for the education of the state's 5 million school children. Honig was not an expert on reading, but he was taken by what he heard about whole language. He was impressed by whole-language arguments that children would benefit from spending more time reading "real books" and less time performing repetitive classroom drills. The skill-and-drill approach to reading made an easy target. The image of classrooms filled with joyful children reading "real literature" was appealing, and the siren call of a literature-based whole-language approach to reading was hard to resist. Honig was taken with whole-language optimism about schooling and the argument that whole-language instruction would bring young children the joy of reading real literature. To Honig and others, whole language seemed both innocent and promising.

By 1987, California bought into whole language hook, line, and sinker. A committee Honig appointed recommended the state abandon phonics and adopt the recently designed English-Language Arts Framework, a curriculum approach based largely on the principles of whole language (Lemann, 1997). Teachers were told to discard their old phonics methods and texts and embrace the new literature-based classroom methods. Schools cast aside phonics and research on reading as the state adopted untested whole-language approaches.

As phonics educators had warned, the approach did not go well. The failures of whole-language methods were not immediately apparent to outsiders, and it was not until the state published nationally normed test results that Californians learned about the problem and were shocked into action. The reading portion of the National Assessment of Education Progress exam (a test discussed in Chapter 14) placed California children in a tie for last place in the nation. Whole-language reading instruction was not working; children's reading skills were declining. As one member of the California State Board of Education later put it, "Unfortunately for California children, the unsubstantiated claims and enthusiastic visions of whole language ideologues proved to be disastrous when applied to real children" (Palmaffy, 1997, p. 3). California's experience provides a clear message: When reading teachers ignore phonics instruction, reading scores plummet.

William Honig would turn away from whole language and acknowledge that phonics teaching was a prerequisite for developing successful readers. Before they can become proficient readers, children need to learn phonics.

In 1995, California enacted legislation that required the State Board of Education to exercise greater control over reading instruction and include "systematic, explicit phonics" (Grossen, 1995, p. 43). California later strengthened the language of this legislation to ensure reading instruction in grades K–6 conformed to the rules of phonics, and teachers provided direct instruction in letter-sound correspondence, letter by letter, word by word. During a typical phonics lesson under the new regulations, teachers ask children to produce the sounds of letters that appear both singly and combined in words. Phonics was back. Fad was out. Trust in reading research was restored. To become readers, children need to master a variety of important skills, and teachers need to direct their activities and press them to achieve higher levels of accomplishment. According to the National Institute for Literacy, children need to

- use language in conversation
- listen and respond to stories read aloud
- recognize and name the letters of the alphabet
- listen to the sounds of spoken language
- connect the sounds to letters to figure out the "code" of reading
- read often so that recognizing words becomes easy and automatic
- learn and use new words
- understand what is read (National Institute for Literacy, 2002, p. 1)

These skills demand practice. In addition, children need to be challenged with increasingly difficult reading material. This is part of the hard work of reading, but it is essential for progress, and it is here that whole language lets children down. Whole-language teachers pride themselves in being "student centered." Children in the earliest grades are allowed to choose comfortable rather than demanding materials. The classroom emphasis is on self-esteem and learner choice. These are certainly laudable and worthy goals, but only if they do not come at the expense of achievement. In comparisons of student achievement in whole-language schools where children were free to choose their reading material and more traditional schools in which teachers direct children's reading and push them to increasingly difficult materials, the traditional students outperform whole-language students (Stahl, 1999). Pleasant school reading environments and healthy attitudes are not sufficient preparation for a competitive world in which success is directly related to one's skills.

Research on Reading

For over thirty years, at a cost of more than $200 million, the National Institute of Child Health and Human Development (NICHD) has conducted research supporting the essential link between learning to read effectively and systematic phonics instruction. The NICHD program was formed in 1965 to study children experiencing reading difficulties. In 1985, its mission was expanded to examine ways to improve the quality of reading research. NICHD division head Reid Lyon, described as a "nightmare figure for the whole language movement" because of his insistence on scientific evidence, led as many as one hundred researchers in several fields, including medicine, psychology, and education (Lemann, 1997, p. 132). Working in fourteen different centers, Lyon and his colleagues designed longitudinal studies to uncover the factors that were causing 20 to 40 percent of the population to exhibit persistent reading problems.

The findings are interesting: Children's reading difficulties appear to occur independent of IQ or other academic abilities such as listening comprehension or mathematics. Children's difficulties in reading relate to an inability to decode the sound-letter relationship; disabled readers typically have trouble "sounding out" single words. For example, when asked to say *cat* without the /t/ sound, good readers have no problem, while disabled readers have difficulty. This difficulty indicates their trouble with "phonological awareness," a skill closely associated with phonics and typically overlooked in whole language (Grossen, 1998, p. 5). Based on these studies, Lyon has become an opponent of whole-language methods and an enthusiastic supporter of the teaching of phonics (Lemann, 1997). Lyon's findings are by no means new or unique. For many years, researchers have documented the success of phonics instruction over any competing approach. In 1985, the U.S. Department of Education released a report, "Becoming a Nation of Readers," which concluded that "the issue is no longer . . . whether children should be taught phonics . . . [but] how it should be done" (Palmaffy, 1997, p. 3). In another study of 285 first- and second-graders, the greatest reading gains were found among children receiving direct instruction on the correspondence between letters of the alphabet and the sounds they make. These children learned to recognize words at a faster rate and with a higher degree of accuracy than children receiving instruction of other sorts, including whole-language techniques (Foorman et al., 1998; Jones and Littel, 2000).

The weight of research evidence increasingly points to the effectiveness of phonics instruction. Reid Lyon and the Secretary of Education impaneled a group of researchers to review the reading research in several areas. Known as the National Reading Panel (NRP), the researchers, with congressional funding, conducted a meta-analysis, a critical review of independent scientific research, in several areas, including systematic phonics instruction. Congress wanted to know if there was enough credible research evidence to offer teachers and parents sound recommendations about beginning reading instruction. The NRP answered affirmatively: In research studies published over a ten-year period, involving students from a variety of backgrounds and family income levels, "systematic phonics instruction helped children learn to read better than all forms of control group instruction, including whole language." The NRP report recommended that phonics "should be implemented as part of literacy programs to teach beginning reading as well as to prevent and remediate reading difficulties" (Ehri et al., 2001, p. 393). On the basis of these studies and others, the National Institute for Literacy, an independent national organization, now tells parents that in the early grades, they should expect to see teachers systematically teaching phonics and helping students learn letter-sound relationships, and they should help their children by pointing out letter-sound relationships "on labels, boxes, newspapers, and signs" (National Institute for Literacy, 2002, p. 2).

Phonics Instruction

> Good people do believe in alchemy at various points in our history. (California's State Superintendent of Public Instruction, quoted in Lemann, 1997, p. 133)

You may well ask, If the weight of research evidence in support of phonics is so overwhelming, why are the voices in opposition so insistent? The answer may be quite simple: For a long time, reading teachers have known children must learn written letters correspond to the sounds in spoken words, but in the past, phonics-based teaching methods have been anything but stimulating. Consider this example:

> It is October 1921, and forty first-graders are seated at rows of desks. The teacher stands at the front of the class and points with a long wooden pointer to a wall chart that contains columns of letters and letter combinations. As she points to a column of short vowel and consonant b combinations, the class responds with the sound of each combination: /ab/, /eb/, /ib/, /ob/, /ub/. She goes to the next column and the class responds, /bab/, /beb/, /bib/, /bob/, /bub/. Then the teacher asks, "What's the rule?" The children respond in unison, "In a one-syllable word, in which there is a single vowel followed by a consonant . . ." So it went day after day, "with letter-sound relationships and pronunciation rules done to death." (Diederich, 1973, quoted in Beck and Juel, 1995, p. 24)

Phonics theory was tarnished by the dreariness of early phonics instruction. Phonics became a synonym for "skill and drill" and "heartless drudgery." None of us wants to teach or be taught with these methods. We know today that children do not learn to read by memorizing abstract rules about the sounds of letters. Children need lots of practice with interesting materials to help them learn the patterns of written language. Today's phonics instruction and the basal programs using phonics convey the principles of phonics through better teaching approaches. Instead of memorizing strings of abstract rules, children are introduced to meaningful reading, and they practice with real books and real words that teach sound-letter relationships.

We note here some of the characteristics of a phonics-based basal approach to teaching beginning reading, highlight some of its assumptions, and describe the array of materials available to teachers. If you have not already explored these materials on your own, your courses on reading methods will provide greater detail. You may be surprised and pleased by the explicit link between the research evidence about how children learn to read and the reading materials now available to teach young learners. No matter who the publisher is, today's phonics materials are unlike the basals you may have used as a student, and phonics instruction is designed to match the variety of learner needs (Dahl et al., 2001). You also may be surprised to find most new phonics-based basals incorporate the best teaching ideas formerly associated with whole language.

The publisher of "Open Court"[1] states that the series uses a "blended variety of approaches to reading instruction and that . . . whole language and phonics need not be mutually exclusive." The new balanced approach to basals offers a rich resource for teachers in kindergarten through sixth-grade classrooms who want to give their students a sound introduction to phonics and an exposure to authentic classic and contemporary literature. These examples of the newer basals, taken from "Open Court," are typical of the materials you will find for children in first grade:

- *Real literature in a phonics base:* Children are reminded that literacy is a powerful tool gained through learning the written code. Children's literature experience begins with Big Books (oversize story books) and extends to both contemporary and classic fiction and nonfiction. Literature selections include such familiar works as "Hey, Diddle, Diddle" and "The House That Jack Built," as well as poetry by William Blake (1757–1827) and selections from some of today's award-winning children's authors.

  The literature cuts across subject lines and affords children an integrated curriculum. The Big Book *Animals* introduces students to biology, and *Captain Bill Pinckney's Journey* introduces social studies concepts through the tale of a solo sail around the world. In addition, children learn natural reader-response to literature by watching the teacher and their classmates respond as they read authentic texts.
- *Research-based phonics instruction:* As one of the basal authors notes, "In order for children to learn to read, they have got to break the code. And by teaching them about how the sound structure of their language works, you're only making it much easier for them to break the code" (Hirshberg, 1995, p. 17F). This basal series offers direct instruction in phonics through a variety of research-validated techniques. For example, sound/spelling cards introduce students to the sounds and spellings of English phonemes. Students are taught to be active learners and to construct meaning from multiple sources. They are encouraged to use "inventive spelling" and to explore the relationships between sounds and words and the application of phonics knowledge to writing.
- *Teacher support:* Even the most able and best-prepared new teacher needs help in weaving together the complex activities of a beginning reading program. Phonemic awareness cards, phonics cards, sound/spelling cards, learning framework cards, activity sheets, Big Books, individual sound/spelling cards, letters cards, alphabet flash cards, take-home phonics books, and the like can form a dizzying array of materials. Teacher's guides offer practical advice about how to structure and pace a lesson, how to individualize instruction, and how to integrate the various aspects of the basal program. In addition, a series of fifteen letters to parents (written in English and Spanish) solidify the home/school connection by informing parents what's going on in the classroom and how they can help their child learn to read.

[1]The "Open Court" basal series is published by the Open Court Publishing Company, Chicago and Peru, Illinois, a division of SRA McGraw-Hill.

Phonics instruction is based on sound, research-based teaching strategies, and the new basal series is nothing short of a bonanza for the new teacher. The new basals are an effective component of phonics instruction that incorporate the best of whole-language approaches (invented spelling, constructed knowledge, authentic literature, reader response) while eliminating the dull routine formerly associated with phonics. Using phonics to teach reading is not new; however, today's basals help to make it an exciting approach to beginning reading. Check this approach out thoroughly.

POSITION 2: THE WHOLE-LANGUAGE ARGUMENT

When Carol Avery talks about her goddaughter's experience learning to read, she . . . begins to cry. Avery, from Millersville, Pennsylvania, recently served as president of the National Council of Teachers of English. Like most members of that organization, she is a committed, sincere believer in whole language. "Mary knew how to read when she got to the first grade," Avery says. "I asked her what she read in school, and she said, 'We don't read stories; we do papers.'" By "papers" Mary meant phonics worksheets. "She had a terrible time that year," Avery continues, now holding back tears. "She cried every night. She had to stand in the corner with her nose against the wall for having too many mistakes on her worksheets. That's the sort of experience I fear too many children will have with what's happening with phonics now."

—COLLINS, 1997, PP. 1–2

Whole language is a perspective on reading and education that assumes, among other things, that learning to read and write is not very different from learning to talk. The roots of whole-language reading instruction can be traced to the work done in the 1970s by Frank Smith of the University of Victoria in British Columbia and Ken and Yetta Goodman of the University of Arizona. For most people, whole language did not become widely known in the United States until the late 1980s. The whole-language approach to reading is harder to define than the phonics approach. It is not a program or a commercial package of materials for the classroom. It is easier to think of whole language as a perspective on the ways children learn and teaching methods that spring from that perspective (Watson, 1989).

Whole-language theorists and researchers argue that children learn to read by interacting with the world of print in natural exchanges. One instructional key to whole language is to encourage students to do real reading and real writing and not waste effort on repetitive exercises and isolated drills commonly found in basal programs. Whole-language teachers use genuine texts—children's literature, song lyrics, poetry, and story books—not artificially written material designed only for instructional purposes. The real difference between phonics and whole language, however, is not necessarily in the material, but in the ways teachers use the materials. Whole-language teachers and phonics teachers may read the same poem with their students. The whole-language teacher is likely to have selected the poem so children can learn from it and enjoy its message. Phonics teachers are likely to use it to isolate its rhyming patterns, letter sounds, or some other feature (Edelsky, Altwerger, and Flores, 1991, p. 8). In whole-language classrooms, teachers expect children to do real reading, real writing, and real learning. Students and teachers pursue whole texts at the very beginning of reading instruction. Whole-language teachers do not try to break texts into fragments. They do not use "readiness activities" to prepare children for reading someplace down the road. They begin with texts and other materials designed to interest readers, not skills that can discourage students from learning to read. Whole-language teachers do not rely on basals.

"Let's not beat around the bush," writes Ken Goodman, "basal readers, workbooks, skills sequences, and practice materials that fragment the process are unacceptable to whole language teachers" (Goodman, 1986, p. 29). Reading is not a mechanical process acquired in isolated steps. Bright, creative teachers find themselves dulled by drills, scripted lessons, and worksheets typically found in basal readers. As one reading educator writes, "I 'test drove' Open Court[2] [a commercially prepared basal program] and found myself nodding off as I was teaching. The program was boring!" (Garan, 2002, p. 30).

Definition of Reading: Constructed Meanings

> Reading is not a matter of "getting the meaning" from text, as if that meaning were *in* the text waiting to be decoded by the reader. Rather, reading is a matter of readers using the cues print provides and the knowledge they bring with them . . . to construct a unique interpretation. (Edelsky, Altwerger, and Flores, 1991, pp. 19–20)

The real difference between the whole-language approach and the phonics approach to reading lies in separate and competing perspectives and differing definitions of what it means to read. If someone were to ask you, "Can you read English?" How would you interpret the question, and how would you answer? Would you think that the questioner was referring to your ability to *pronounce* English words? In that case, you might respond that you could read not only English but you could also claim to "read" a host of languages including Spanish, French, Portuguese, Romansch, and Latin. Most of us can sound out words in those languages although we may not know what they mean, and we ordinarily do not confuse the languages we can read with those we can merely *pronounce.*

Do you believe reading means decoding the words to find out what the author meant when she wrote them? Do you believe that meaning is embedded in the word and to "read English" is to engage in a code-breaking process of unlocking the author's intent? Many people accept this definition, and if you are among them, you may be comfortable with the phonics arguments about reading. The conception of reading as decoding or unlocking the meaning embedded in text and a phonics approach to reading instruction go hand in glove.

[2]The "Open Court" basal series is published by the Open Court Publishing Company, Chicago and Peru, Illinois, a division of SRA McGraw-Hill.

On the other hand, if you believe that reading is a process in which a person brings meaning to the text, you are likely to be more comfortable in the whole-language camp (Braunger and Lewis, 1997, p. 7). The view of reading as a way to construct meaning is one of the unifying threads among whole-language advocates. For whole-language teachers, reading occurs when written language comes alive in the minds of readers (Myer, 2002, p. 26). The text has a certain inherent meaning for whole-language teachers—it is a product of the author's interpretation or imagination—but understanding text depends mainly on what the individual reader brings to it. Not every child can be expected to respond and interpret written material in the same way. Teachers encourage students to develop "individual understanding" of text instead of working only to unlock the "author's intent" in their reading. Whole-language teachers do not expect or reward conformity; they are comfortable in classrooms reflecting multiple student interpretations and understandings of printed material. These ideas may be threatening to those who prize consensus, conformity, and authority.

Whole language is based on research principles derived from several fields, including linguistics and cognitive psychology. Whole-language teachers are a diverse, creative group, and not all whole-language classrooms look the same, nor should you expect them to. If you spend time with a whole-language teacher, you are likely to see a wide range of classroom activities designed to encourage reading and writing, but not every teacher uses the same set of classroom strategies. You are likely to find, however, that whole-language teachers do share a number of perspectives and principles about literacy. For example:

- Learning to read is a natural, social process, much like learning to speak. Children approach reading and speaking as ways of communicating meaning. Children will learn to read when teachers and other literate adults capture their interests and find ways to engage them in written language (Edelsky, Altwerger, and Flores, 1991; Freeman and Freeman, 1998).
- Reading is not a decoding of text. It is a construction of meaning from text that requires readers to be active and build their own understandings (Braunger and Lewis, 1997, p. 29).
- Researchers find that when readers focus on phonetic accuracy, they lose the meaning in the text. Readers who ask themselves questions about plot and characters may lose phonetic accuracy, but their comprehension increases (Strauss, 2001).
- Phonics teaches children unreal relationships between the sounds of oral language and the letters of written language. It is silly to teach that "when two vowels go walking, the first does the talking." (That is, when two vowels come together, the first vowel is long and the second is silent.) This "rule" holds in limited cases, and the reader must know the exceptions to make sense of the rule (Goodman, 1986, p. 37).
- "Sounding out" words, a phonics technique, is useful to readers only as far as letters correspond to sounds. English contains too many exceptions for this to be the only strategy for teaching reading. (Try sounding out *pneumonia* and *salmon.*) Letters and the sounds of language are not linked together directly

by lawlike rules. Teaching students to link speech sounds to letters is useful but English has thousands of exceptions that confuse readers trying to learn *the* sounds of letters. Consider, for example, the sound of the final /s/ in books and beds, and the different letters used to form the same sounds in common words: *meet/meat/mete* and *peak/peek/pique* (Strauss, 2001, p. 28).

- Whole language focuses on children, and whole-language teachers plan with children what they will read and write. Students are allowed to choose the books they read and often read silently, since these are characteristics of most reading in "real life" (Goodman, 1998).
- Some classroom practices support reading instruction; others do not. The International Reading Association lists practices that hinder reading development: "Emphasizing only phonics, drilling on isolated letters or sounds . . . focusing on skills rather than interpretation and comprehension, constant use of workbooks and worksheets, fixed ability grouping, blind adherence to the basal program . . ." (Braunger and Lewis, 1997, p. 65).
- Basal readers, workbooks, and skill sheets are not needed to teach reading. Children are better served when classrooms are filled with books children want to read—real literature, such as poetry, fiction, and nonfiction, some books specially designed for schools, such as beginning dictionaries, and some real-world texts, such as phone books (Goodman, 1986, p. 33).
- The effectiveness of whole-language methods is supported by over sixty years of research. If reading is defined as pronouncing words found in print, phonics is the more effective teaching method; if reading is making sense of print, whole language is more effective (Daniels, Zemelman, and Bizar, 1999; Moustafa, 2002).

What Are Whole-Language Methods?

> One must certainly wonder . . . how the first readers ever learned to read, having no one to teach them the alphabetic principle (Strauss, 2001, p. 28).

Whole language is not a single method, a series of methods, a package, or even a program. As noted earlier, it may be more helpful to think of whole language as a perspective on language and learning. Although whole language has no core methods, some classroom approaches fit better than others with a whole-language teaching. In your reading classes, you will learn about methods commonly associated with whole language, such as self-selected reading, literature studies, theme cycles, interactive journal writing, Big Books, predictable texts, and creating literature-rich environments (Edelsky, Altwerger, and Flores, 1991, p. 42). We do not go into great detail on those methods here. Our goal is to provide an overview and an introduction that will assist in your own exploration of whole-language teaching.

As Ken Goodman notes, the organization of the whole-language classroom may not be obvious to the casual observer (1986, p. 31). Beliefs rather than specific methods distinguish different kinds of reading teachers. A whole-language teacher and a skills teacher may both use phonic activities and decoding strategies. The difference between the teachers will be the role they assign to these activities and whether such activities are the focus of instruction. A whole-language teacher, for example, would not teach phonics in isolation apart from the text or as a prerequisite skill for reading and writing. Whole-language teachers are more likely to use phonics "opportunistically," that is, when questions arise during reading that can be answered with a phonics explanation.

Other visible differences may also appear subtle at first glance. A skills-oriented phonics teacher may try to correct every error a child makes in oral reading. Phonics teachers expect readers to strive for accuracy as they decode the printed text and convert it into oral language. Because whole-language teachers are more interested in having the reader derive meaning from the text, they are less concerned about whether the child reads every word correctly. Whole-language teachers consider teacher-corrected errors in reading (referred to as "miscues") a distraction from the central task of making sense of the text. Goodman emphasizes student self-correction. "When they [the students] realize something has gone wrong, they will take the opportunity to locate the problem and fix it. There's no good reason to call their attention to miscues that don't disrupt the process of making sense" (1996, p. 115).

What Really Happened to the Reading Ability of California's Children?

In the mid 1990s, critics of whole language tried to blame whole-language teaching for California's problems in reading achievement. California had introduced a new English–Language Arts Framework that shifted the focus of literacy instruction from a skills-based to a literature-based approach to reading, writing, and language arts. Scores on the National Assessment of Educational Progress (NAEP) indicated the reading levels of California's fourth-graders were very low. In 1992, California's students ranked fifth from the bottom nationally. After the next NAEP exam, an analysis of reading scores found California students tied for last place among students from the fifty states, and ahead only of students from Guam (Lemann, 1997). California's own statewide test, the California Learning Assessment System, also indicated student problems in reading (McQuillan, 1998).

Something had to be done. William Honig, the Superintendent of Public Instruction who had endorsed the literature-based reading, an approach associated with whole language, was no longer in office. Both economic conditions and California electoral politics had changed. Less money was available for public schools. A new superintendent was in office, and a conservative had replaced a liberal governor. NAEP reading scores were low, and state officials blamed the literature-based approach to teaching reading. Critics quickly condemned whole-language instruction as a mistake that caused the decline in reading scores. Whole language provided a scapegoat, and phonics promised a quick remedy. Unfortunately neither problem nor the solution was academically responsible or warranted.

If you have taken a course in logic, you probably have learned about errors of reasoning, sometimes referred to as "logical fallacies." Among these errors is one referred to as the *post hoc, ergo propter hoc* fallacy ("after this, therefore because of this"). You are guilty of committing this error in logic if your reasoning holds that because event A precedes event B, then A must be the cause of B. For example, if A, a rooster crowing in the morning, is followed by B, a sunrise, it would be false to conclude that A caused B. When California politicians and school leaders blamed declining scores on whole-language instruction, they were committing this logical fallacy. When the legislature of California enacted legislation mandating phonics instruction in 1995, they were sacrificing sound logic to political expediency.

California's experience reveals little about the effectiveness of whole language. First, it is not clear that California's reading test scores actually declined. California's children were not doing well, to be sure, but to attribute a decline in test scores to a curriculum change, test data must be collected over time—both before and after the implementation of the new curriculum. No such test data existed for California children taking the NAEP exam. The NAEP data do not provide evidence of a decline, only scores that were low and that continued to be low. On the California state test, reading scores were stable despite the introduction of the whole-language curriculum in 1987. Students were performing at about the same level in 1985, before the adoption of the framework, as they were in 1990, after the introduction of the new curriculum (McQuillan, 1998, p. 13). The scores were not good, but they were not declining.

In the rush to indict whole language, critics ignored two interesting findings from the NAEP assessment: (1) In 1992, as part of the assessment, fourth-grade teachers were asked to indicate their methodological approach to teaching reading and to identify the term that best described their approach: whole language, literature-based, or phonics. The average scores for children of teachers using each approach were then compared; children in classrooms with a heavy emphasis on phonics did the worst (McQuillan, 1998, p. 14). (2) A major feature of whole language is silent reading of student-selected books. NAEP results indicate students who read silently in school and students who choose their own books to read had higher test scores on average than students who did not participate in these features of instruction (Goodman, 1998, p. 6).

Despite the heated rhetoric and political maneuvering, no real evidence indicates that California's reading scores have declined over the past ten years or that whole-language teaching methods are to blame for any reading problems. However, phonics advocates castigated whole language while ignoring many factors that affect student performance. For example, California, once a leader in public education, had experienced dramatic changes in its classrooms. In the 1970s, under spending-limit initiatives proposed by then-Governor Ronald Reagan, the state spent less money on public education. In 1965, California was fifth in the nation in per capita spending on public education; by the time of the 1992 NAEP exam, its rank had slipped to thirty-seventh (Lemann, 1997, p. 134).

The new Language Arts Framework was introduced as California was experiencing further budget cuts. As a result of an economic downturn in the

1980s and early 1990s, California's schools were not as well funded as they had been, and many teachers found themselves teaching between thirty-two and thirty-six students in cramped classrooms where it was not uncommon to hear three or four different languages. During this period, California's schools realized a dramatic increase in the number of children living in poverty and children from homes where English was not the first language (Boyd and Mitchell, 2002). To make matters worse, Californians had fewer library books per child than called for by national standards, and California ranked dead last in the number of librarians per pupil (Freppon and Dahl, 1998).

It is hard enough to switch to a literature-based reading approach in large classes, without adequate books or library facilities, but to make matters worse, California's teachers were asked to change the emphasis of their reading instruction without being given adequate support to help them make the transition. Fewer than 2 percent of the teachers were introduced to whole-language principles and techniques during in-service workshops (Murphy, 1998, p. 165). As one teacher educator admitted:

> Many beginning teachers were not well-prepared to teach reading. In California, the teaching credential is earned in fifth-year programs after earning a bachelor's degree. This results in one (or possibly two) literacy courses in that fifth year. . . . It's simply not possible to teach everything beginning teachers need to know about reading in a single course. (Freppon and Dahl, 1998, p. 246)

Did the reading scores of California's schoolchildren really decline? If they did, what was the cause? Unfortunately, no one can answer the first question with certainty because no longitudinal data exist. Clearly, California's children were not doing well on standardized tests, but no one can say for sure whether spending cuts, class size, lack of support for teachers, or the implementation of a literature-based reading instruction and a deemphasis on phonics was to blame.

The Politics of Reading

> "God Believes in the Beauty of Phonics" . . . The primary push for intensive, systematic phonics comes originally—especially—from the religious right . . . and more generally from the far right, which currently wields considerable influence and power in our national and state governments. (Weaver and Brinkley, 1998, pp. 128–129)

Whole-language teaching came to public attention through media accounts of the NAEP assessment data and the California's Reading–Language Arts Framework. Newspapers and magazines reported a new "school crisis." Children were at risk; whole-language teachers were villains; parents were understandably alarmed. Whole-language teachers and teacher educators were taken unawares. Certainly they knew that not everything was right with reading in the schools. They agreed students should read more, with greater understanding, and derive more pleasure from reading. Whole-language teachers were stunned, however, that the media had declared a "reading crisis." Teachers who kept up with research knew that U.S. children were reading as well as their parents had a generation ago (see Berliner and Biddle, 1995). A review of the NAEP testing from 1971 to 1996 showed some fluctuations in performance, but it failed to indicate a national decline in reading scores (McQuillan, 1998).

Whole-language teachers were further surprised to learn from media accounts that they were at "war" with phonics advocates. Although whole-language teachers begin reading instruction with real literature, not by teaching the sounds the letters make, they are not opposed to phonics teaching and certainly not to phonics teachers. Most whole-language educators found themselves comfortable with a National Council of Teachers of English resolution calling for all students to learn a range of reading strategies, including phonics, but that phonics be considered only one part of the socially constructed intellectual process we call reading (Taylor, 1998). Does that sound like the rhetoric of a war?

Whole-language educators have come to realize that the reading crisis was largely a media invention, and if whole language was at war, it was not necessarily at war with other reading camps. Whole-language teachers might instead be in a battle with commercial publishers on one front and the far right on another. Given their support for children's choice in literature and individualized reading assignments, whole-language teachers are likely to favor increases in library budgets and filling libraries floor-to-ceiling with trade books. They may not support schools spending money on commercially prepared (and expensive) basals. Reading represents a large, lucrative market. Publishers invest heavily in instructional reading materials for schools, and they expect significant financial returns. Four corporations currently dominate textbook publishing: McGraw-Hill, ScottForesman, Houghton-Mifflin, and Harcourt (Allington, 2002). If schools adopted whole language more widely, children would be reading more, but they would be using commercially prepared basals less.

Other whole-language adversaries represent the extremes of the political and religious right. Whole-language instruction emphasizes a child's individual interpretation of literature. Readers are encouraged to bring their own meanings to texts and develop their own constructions of what is important in the books they read. This approach may raise the ire of those who believe texts have definite, embedded meanings that learners are to unlock. For some, the interpretative nature of whole language is a threat to the authority, control, and tradition of text materials. For others, whole language represents an attack on the notion of "absolute truth" and "literal interpretation of text" (Weaver and Brinkley, 1998, pp. 129, 132). Whole-language instruction embraces the freedom for teachers and students to select and interpret reading materials, thereby posing a threat to traditional hierarchies (Wolfe and Poynor, 2001). As one whole-language educator notes:

> One reason that fundamentalist Christian parents value reading so highly and favor an emphasis on phonics and spelling is that they believe these skills will lead to a more careful reading of the Bible. Studying biblical texts closely, attending to precision in language, and carefully weighing the meaning of each word are especially valued, since fundamentalists depend on their accurately reading and interpreting Bible messages as a way to keep them focused on God's will for their lives. (Brinkley, 1998, p. 59)

Phonics is associated with order and structure and a less interpretative, more direct "transmission model" of education, a notion that what is taught is learned just as the textbook authors and curriculum planners intended (Weaver and Brinkley, 1998). Phonics also is comforting to parents because it reminds them of their own experiences in school: weekly spelling tests, red-ink corrections, and worksheets (Allington, 2002). Some whole-language critics believe that phonics will afford them greater control over what children learn and think because it limits the range of children's interpretations. Many on the far right see phonics as a way to control the messages of the school curriculum (Taylor, 1998, p. 319). Several states and many school districts now require teachers to use prepackaged phonics kits exclusively in teaching reading and to follow the teachers' manual verbatim. Teachers' skills and knowledge have become less valued and respected. Teachers are not allowed to decide which students in their classes would profit from intense phonics and which would not. "Boxed programs" for teaching reading or any other subject demand teacher and student compliance and they ensure greater centralized control over what is taught in schools (Meyer, 2002). Mandated methods insult teachers' intelligence and discourage their creativity. As one teacher argued,

> If I don't know anything . . . , how can they trust me with thirty-two first graders? Why am I teaching if they do not have enough trust in me to allow me to adjust what I'm doing based on what I see? . . . These days, it can be hard to be a smart teacher. I almost feel as if I should be stupid. Then I'd be glad to follow their scripts, whether or not they work. But I'm not stupid. And I can't be responsible for doing a good job and yet be prevented from responding to what I see my kids need. (Calkins, 2001, p. 530)

The so-called "reading wars" are a reminder to educators that they cannot separate the processes of teaching and learning from politics and economics. The contest over teaching reading and writing to young children is much more than a set of academic differences between phonics teachers and whole-language teachers. The battle over reading is really about controlling the school curriculum, and ultimately about regulating the flow of information and determining what counts as knowledge. Whole-language teachers need to do a better job of explaining the value of real reading and literature-based instruction to parents and the media. Literacy teachers are among society's least combative people, but others have drawn them into battle. Whole-language teachers did not initiate the conflict, but they will continue to fight back and defend their approaches to teaching reading and writing because these approaches are best for children.

For Discussion

1. As you have read, phonics advocates argue that successful readers need to understand the sound-letter relationships in words. Guessing a word from context does not always equal word recognition. In the following text, taken from Jack London, the blanks indicate parts a child was unable to decode (Grossen, 1998, p. 14). Is it possible to predict the missing words from context, as whole-language teachers advocate?

He had never seen dogs fight as the w_____ish c_____f_____t, his first_____ex t_____t him an unf_____able l_____n. It is true, it was a vi_____ ex_____, else he would not have lived to pr_____it by it. Curly was v_____. They were camped near the log store, where she, in her friend _____ way, made ad_____ to a husky dog the size of a full-_____ wolf, th_____ not so large as _____he. _____ere was no w_____ing, only a leap in like a flash, a met_____clip of teeth, a leap out equal_____swift, and Curly's face was ripped open from eye to jaw.

2. In 1998, the California State Department of Education prohibited schools from spending funds for any teacher development program that uses reading methodologies

FIGURE 10.1 Comparing Basal and Whole-Language Approaches

Traditional Basal Approach	**Whole-Language Approach**
Reading Materials	
Traditional basals	Trade books only
Word-Recognition Instruction (Most Notably Phonics)	
Typically sequenced, isolated skills work	No sequence of skills and no isolated skills work
Ability Grouping	
Often three relatively fixed ability groups	Not used
Assessment	
Standardized tests and objective tests that come with the basal	Performance-based subjective assessment
Student-Centered Orientation	
Primarily teacher-centered	Strongly student-centered
Active, Constructive Teaching and Learning	
Most teachers endorse these principles	
Integrating Reading and Writing, and Other Language Arts the Curriculum as a Whole, and the World Outside of School	
Most teachers endorse these principles	

Source: *Excerpted from Graves, Juel, and Graves, 2001, p. 71.*

emphasizing contextual clues in place of decoding, or encourages inventive spelling in writing instruction. Whole-language teachers argue state and federal government should not be involved in defining what is and what is not good reading instruction (Taylor, 1998). Whole-language advocates further contend decisions about the most appropriate reading programs are academic decisions that should be left to classroom teachers and reading educators. Do you agree? Should classroom teachers have the right to choose the methods of reading instruction? What about parents? Should they have the right to select the methods of instruction for their children? Who should select the books children read in elementary schools?

3. William Honig, the former Superintendent of Instruction for California, among others involved in the debate about reading instruction, now advocates a "balanced approach" to reading instruction. Honig recommends one hour a day of direct instruction on teaching letter-sound correspondence (phonics) and an additional hour a day for shared reading, reading children's literature, and writing instruction (a literature-based strategy characteristic of whole-language teachers. (Freppon and Dahl, 1998, p. 242). A survey of elementary teachers indicates that the majority prefer such a "balanced approach" to reading instruction (Baumann et al., 1998). Consider Figure 10.1, which compares a traditional basal approach with a whole-language approach. Do you think a balanced approach is possible? Do you think this approach would resolve the "reading wars"? Interview teachers in public schools and colleges of education to learn their opinions.

References

ADAMS, M. J., AND BRUCK, M. (1995). "Resolving the 'Great Debate.'" *American Educator* (Summer), pp. 7–20.

ALLINGTON, R. L. (2002). Does State and Federal Reading Policymaking Matter? In T. Loveless, ed., *The Great Curriculum Debate.* Washington, DC: Brookings Institution.

BAUMANN, J. F., ET AL. (1998). "Where Are the Teachers' Voices in the Phonics/Whole Language Debate? Results from a Survey of U.S. Elementary Teachers." *The Reading Teacher* 51, 636–651.

BECK, I. L., AND JUEL, C. (1995). "The Role of Decoding in Learning to Read." *American Educator* 8, 21–25, 39–42.

BERLINER, D., AND BIDDLE, B. (1995). *The Manufactured Crisis: Myths, Fraud, and the Attack on America's Public Schools.* Reading, MA: Addison-Wesley.

BOYD, W. L., AND MITCHELL, D. E. (2002). "The Politics of the Reading Wars." In T. Loveless, ed., *The Great Curriculum Debate: How Should We Teach Reading and Math?* Washington, DC: Brookings Institution.

BRAUNGER, J., AND LEWIS, J. P. (1997). *Building a Knowledge Base in Reading.* Newark, DE: International Reading Association.

BRINKLEY, E. H. (1998). "What's Religion Got to Do with Attacks on Whole Language?" In K. Goodman, ed., *In Defense of Good Teaching: What Teachers Need to Know About the "Reading Wars."* York, ME: Stenhouse.

CALKINS, L. M. (2001). *The Art of Teaching Reading.* New York: Longman.

COLLINS, J. (1997). "How Johnny Should Read: A War Is On Between Supporters of Phonics and Those Who Believe in the Whole-Language Method of Learning to Read. Caught in the Middle—The Nation's Schoolchildren." *Time.* Oct. 7, pp. 1–7. (http://web.lexis-nexis.com)

DAHL, K. L., ET AL. (2001). *Rethinking Phonics: Making the Best Teaching Decisions.* Portsmouth, NH: Heinemann.

DANIELS, H., ZEMELMAN, S., AND BIZAR, M. (1999). "Whole Language Works: Sixty Years of Research." *Educational Leadership* 57, pp. 32–37.

EDELSKY, C., ALTWERGER, B., AND FLORES, B. (1991). *Whole Language, What's the Difference.* Portsmouth, NH: Heinemann.

EHRI, L. C., ET AL. (2001). "Systematic Phonics Instruction Helps Students Learn to Read: Evidence from the National Reading Panel's Meta-Analysis." *Review of Educational Research* 71, 393–447.

FOORMAN, B. R., ET AL. (1998). "The Role of Instruction in Learning to Read: Preventing Reading Failure in At-Risk Children." *Journal of Educational Psychology* 90, 37–55.

FREEMAN, D., AND FREEMAN, Y. S. (1998). "California Reading: The Pendulum Swings." In K. Goodman, ed., *In Defense of Good Teaching: What Teachers Need to Know About the "Reading Wars."* York, ME: Stenhouse.

FREPPON, P. A., AND DAHL, K. L. (1998). "Balanced Instruction: Insights and Considerations." *Reading Research Quarterly* 33, 240–251.

GARAN, E. M. (2002). *Resisting Reading Mandates: How to Triumph with the Truth.* Portsmouth, NH: Heinemann.

GOODMAN, K. (1986). *What's Whole In Whole Language.* Portsmouth, NH: Heinemann.

———. (1996). On Reading, *A Common-Sense Look at the Nature of Language and the Science of Reading.* Portsmouth, NH: Heinemann.

———. ED. (1998). *In Defense of Good Teaching: What Teachers Need to Know About the "Reading Wars."* York, ME: Stenhouse.

GRAVES, M. F., JUEL, C., AND GRAVES, B. B. (2001). *Teaching Reading in the 21st Century.* (2nd Ed.) Boston: Allyn & Bacon.

GROSSEN, B. (1995). "Preventing Reading Failure." *Effective School Practices* (Fall), 43–44.

———. (1998). "30 Years of Research: What We Know About How Children Learn to Read." *The Center for the Study of the Future of Teaching & Learning,* Nov. 11. (www.cftl.org/30years/30years.html)

GURSKY, D. (1998, March). "What Works for Reading." *American Teacher* pp. 12–13.

HIRSCH, E. D. (2002). "The Roots of the Education Wars." In T. Loveless, ed., *The Great Curriculum Debate: How Should We Teach Reading and Math?* Washington, DC: Brookings Institution.

HIRSHBERG, J. (1995). *Framework for Effective Teaching: Grade 1—Thinking and Learning About Print, Teacher's Guide, Part A.* Chicago: Open Court.

JONES, W. H., AND LITTEL, S. W. (2000). "A Meta-Analysis of Studies Examining the Effect of Whole Language on the Literacy of Low-SES Students," *Elementary School Journal* 101, 21–33.

LEMANN, N. (1997). "The Reading Wars." *The Atlantic Monthly.* Nov., pp. 128–134.

MCQUILLAN, J. (1998). *The Literacy Crisis: False Claims, Real Solutions.* Portsmouth, NH: Heinemann.

MEYER, R. J. (2002). *Phonics Exposed: Understanding and Resisting Systematic Direct Intense Phonics Instruction.* Mahwah, NJ: Lawrence Erlbaum.

MOUSTAFA, M. (2002). Contemporary Reading Instruction. In T. Loveless, ed., *The Great Curriculum Debate.* Washington, DC: Brookings Institution.

MURPHY, S. (1998). "The Sky is Falling: Whole Language Meets Henny Penny." In K. Goodman, ed., *In Defense of Good Teaching: What Teachers Need to Know About the "Reading Wars."* York, ME: Stenhouse.

NATIONAL INSTITUTE FOR LITERACY. (2002). "Helping Your Child Learn to Read, A Parent Guide, Preschool Through Grade 3." (www.nifl.gov/nifl/research/reading_first2.html)

PALMAFFY, T. (1997). "See Dick Flunk." *The Journal of American Citizenship Policy Review,* Nov.–Dec., pp. 1–12. (http://web.lexis-nexis.com)

ROUSSEAU, J-J. (1979). *Emile, or On Education.* A. Bloom, translator. New York: Basic Books.

STAHL, S. A. (1999). "Why Innovations Come and Go (and Mostly Go): The Case of Whole Language." *Educational Researcher* 28, 13–22.

STRAUSS, S. L. (2001). "An Open Letter to Reid Lyon." *Educational Researcher* 30, 26–33.

TAYLOR, D. (1998). *Beginning to Read and the Spin Doctors of Science: The Political Campaign to Change America's Mind About How Children Learn to Read.* Urbana, IL: National Council of Teachers of English.

WATSON, D. (1989). "Defining and Describing Whole Language." *The Elementary School Journal* 90, 208–221.

WEAVER, C., AND BRINKLEY, E. H. (1998). "Phonics, Whole Language, and the Religious and Political Right." In K. Goodman, ed., *In Defense of Good Teaching: What Teachers Need to Know About the "Reading Wars."* York, ME: Stenhouse.

WOLFE, P., AND POYNOR, L. (2001). "Politics and the Pendulum: An Alternative Understanding of the Case of Whole Language as Educational Innovation." *Educational Researcher* 30, 15–20.

CHAPTER 11

Multicultural Education: Democratic or Divisive

POSITION 1: MULTICULTURALISM: CENTRAL TO A DEMOCRATIC EDUCATION

Multiculturalism is . . . the only way to reduce the misunderstanding across subcultures, the only way to build bridges of loyalty across the ethnicities that have so often divided us. Multiculturalism of this sort—pluralism, to use an older word—is a way of making sure we care enough about people across ethnic divides to keep those ethnic divides from destroying us.

—APPIAH, 2000, P. 291

The U.S. population has grown more in the past ten years than in any previous decade in its history. The overall gain was about 13 percent, a 3.4 percent increase for the white population and a 35 percent increase for the non-Hispanic white population. The recent surge of immigration has placed on the schools' doorstep the largest number of immigrant children it has ever been asked to educate. Schools are working with children from all over the world.

Consider Figures 11.1 and 11.2. The foreign-born population of the United States is projected to swell from 28.4 million in 2000 to 56.5 million in 2050; every year the nation is becoming more racially and ethnically diverse (Edmonston, 2000).[1] The census data paint a vivid picture of an increasingly multicultural nation. Not only will there be more Americans in the future, they will differ from one another more than ever before in history. The United States already is multicultural, and it will become even more so. Multicultural approaches to education are not an option; the only question concerns the form it will take.

Multicultural education can take many forms. Some scholars in the field, for example, believe multicultural education should focus mainly on the concept of culture and problems resulting from the clash of cultures. They believe students

[1]The author of this report argues that although race is no longer regarded as a meaningful biological concept, self-reported racial identity has significant social and economic correlates.

FIGURE 11.1. Foreign-Born Population of the United States and the Percentage of Foreign-Born Population of the Total Population, 1850–2050

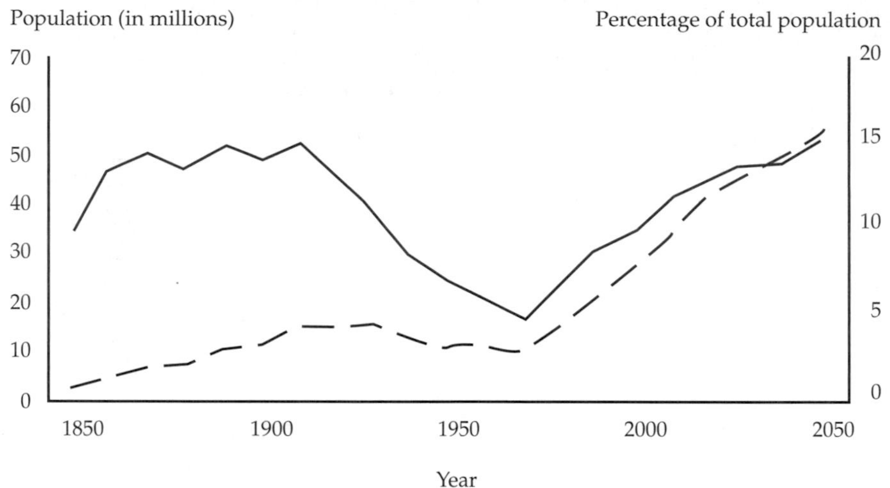

Note: *The bars represent the total population with the scale shown on the left; the line represents the percent of the total population with the scale shown on the right.*
Source: *Historical reconstruction of the U.S. population described in Jeffrey S. Passel and Barry Edmonston, "Immigration and Race: Recent Trends in Immigration to the United States," in Barry Edmonston and Jeffrey S. Passel, eds.,* Immigration and Ethnicity: The Integration of America's Newest Arrivals, *chapter 2 (Washington, DC: Urban Institute Press, 1994); and population projection of the U.S. population described in Barry Edmonston and Jeffrey S. Passel, "The Future Immigrant Population of the United States," in Barry Edmonston and Jeffrey S. Passel, eds.,* Immigration and Ethnicity: The Integration of America's Newest Arrivals, *chapter 11 (Washington, DC: Urban Institute Press, 1994). In Anderson (2000) p. 78.*

should examine the conflicting demands of home versus school culture, as well as the conflict between cultures of the powerful and the powerless, and unequal treatment afforded certain groups because of race, gender, and sexual preference (Spring, 2000). For other scholars, multiculturalism is less about the study of culture than a vehicle for change. It is the method for critiquing and reforming society that includes political and moral correctives to assist working class and nonwhite students attain social and economic advancement (Sleeter, 1996; Giroux, 1997; Willett, 1998; Steinberg and Kincheloe, 2001). Taking a more inclusive approach to studying multiculturalism, Glazer (1997) argues that "we are all multiculturalists," because whether you may favor or oppose it, multiculturalism is here, necessary, and unavoidable. All groups—ethnic, religious, racial—belong in any study of American culture because of their unique contributions and perspectives. Glazer argues that some groups have been denied appropriate recognition. "Multiculturalism," Glazer writes, "is the price America is paying for its inability or unwillingness to incorporate into its society African Americans, in the same way and to the same degree it has incorporated so many groups" (p. 147).

FIGURE 11.2. Racial Composition of the U.S. Population, 1850–2050

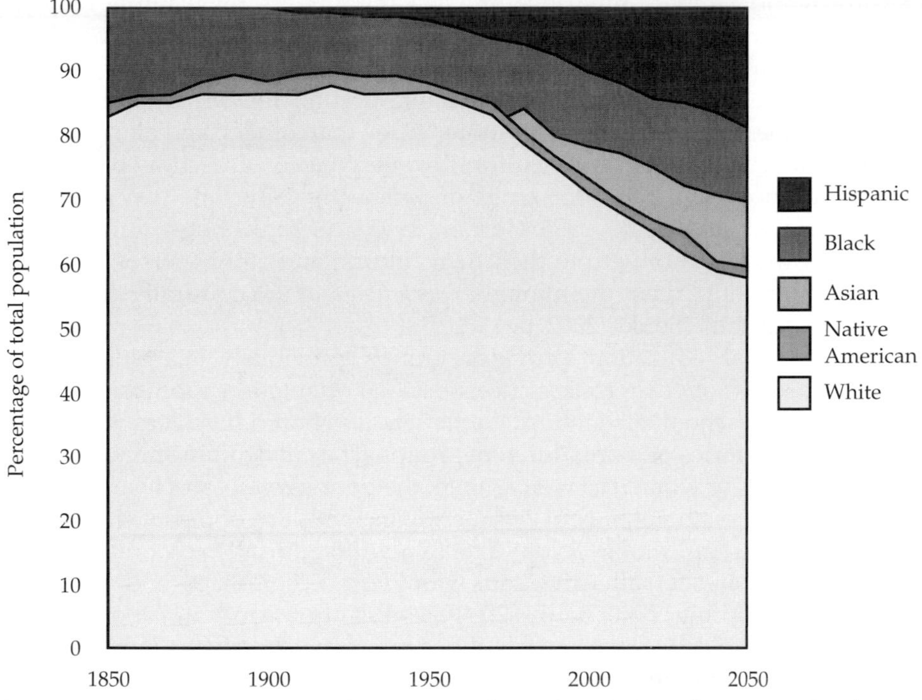

Source: *Historical reconstruction of the U.S. population described in Jeffrey S. Passel and Barry Edmonston, "Immigration and Race: Trends in Immigration to the United States," in Barry Edmonston and Jeffrey S. Passel, eds.,* Immigration and Ethnicity: The Integration of America's Newest Arrivals, *chapter 2 (Washington, DC: Urban Institute Press, 1994); and population projection of the U.S. population described in Barry Edmonston and Jeffrey S. Passel, "The Future Immigrant Population of the United States," in Barry Edmonston and Jeffrey S. Passel, eds.,* Immigration and Ethnicity: The Integration of America's Newest Arrivals, *chapter 11 (Washington, DC: Urban Institute Press, 1994). In Anderson (2000) p. 79.*

Although there are many approaches to multicultural instruction in schools, this section draws upon Professor James Banks's definition, who writes that multiculturalism

> is a reform movement designed to restructure educational institutions so that all students, including white, male and middle-class students, will acquire the knowledge, skills, and attitudes needed to function effectively in a culturally and ethnically diverse nation and world. . . . Multicultural education . . . is not an ethnic- or gender-specific movement, but a movement designed to empower all students to become knowledgeable, caring, and active citizens. . . . (Banks, 2002, p. 5)

The Best That Is Thought and Known?

Multiculturalists agree that people see the world from slightly different perspectives. Everyone brings understandings to events based on their personal and academic experiences and on other interpretive lenses through which they view the world. Women, minorities, and new immigrants, for example, may see the world from a different vantage point than men, majority-group members, and long-established American families. Everyone develops separate frames of reference and different perspectives for interpreting the social and political world. No one frame of reference is more "true" than others, and all deserve to be heard and understood. Multiculturalism may be considered as part of the struggle to incorporate a wider range of perspectives into the way we make meanings in school (Takaki, 1993; Gordon, 1995). As Banks notes, "Individuals who know the world only from their own cultural and ethnic perspectives are denied important parts of the human experience and are culturally and ethnically encapsulated" (Banks, 2002, p. 1).

Multicultural education provides groups previously marginalized or excluded because of gender, class, race, or sexual orientation appropriate representation in the school curriculum. Public schools should be places where students hear the stories of many different groups. The curriculum should present the perspectives of women as well as men, the poor as well as rich, and should celebrate the heroism not only of conquering generals but of those who are victorious in the struggles of everyday life. In a multiculturally reconfigured curriculum, the voices of all Americans would find legitimacy and academic consideration (Spring, 2000; Banks, 2002). Multiculturalism is not about pitting one group against others or claiming that any one perspective is more valid or more valued. Multicultural education is about fairness and justice. In the past, schools have done a disservice to students by assuming a single view of truth and ignoring students' need to create their knowledge of the world by considering multiple truths and multiple perspectives. A multicultural society will inevitably have competing views of truth and multiple sources of knowledge.

Different Voices

If you were to believe the critics of multiculturalism, you might conclude that multiculturalists are bent on destroying not only the schools but the whole of Western civilization. Samuel P. Huntington castigates multiculturalism as an immediate and dangerous challenge to America's sense of itself. Multiculturalists, he writes, have "denied the existence of a common American culture and promoted racial, ethnic, and other subnational identities and groupings" (1996, p. 305).

Huntington is not alone. Other traditionalists see multiculturalism as a threat to national identity, one that will divide the nation. E. D. Hirsch (1987, 1996), for example, tried to convince his readers that the nation would disintegrate unless schools required all students to study a common curriculum. Allan Bloom (1987) warned that multiculturalism poses the threat of cultural relativism, a disease, he says, that regards all values as equally valid, and that would likely cause the decline of the West. Another critic of multiculturalism, Diane Ravitch, argues that multiculturalism would lead to the death of education and fragmentation of American society. Professor Ravitch touts the elementary school curriculum of what she believes was a better time, the first decade of the twentieth century, when children were exposed to a common culture and high expectations:

> Most children read (or listened to) the Greek and Roman myths and folklore from the "oriental nations." . . . The third grade in the public schools of Philadelphia studied "heroes of legend and history," including "Joseph; Moses; David; Ulysses; Alexander; Roland; Alfred the Great; Richard the Lion Hearted; Robert Bruce; William Tell; Joan of Arc; Peter the Great; Florence Nightingale." (Ravitch, 1987, p. 8)

This represents a rich literature, to be sure, but, like the canon championed by Huntington, Hirsch, and Bloom, it is skewed toward a white, Western, male orientation. No people of other races were represented in classroom readings during the "good old days," and for women to find their way into the curriculum, they either had to be burned at the stake or to pioneer as nurses! Multiculturalists find little that was good in the so-called "good old days" of schooling. Very few students experienced schools that had high standards and excellent teachers. The good old days were good for only a privileged handful—the high-achieving children of English-speaking families of means. For most others it was a time of alienation caused by a denial of their ethnic heritages. Henry Louis Gates, Jr. refers to the nostalgic celebration of the good old days as the antebellum aesthetic position, "when men were men, and men were white . . . when women and persons of color were voiceless, faceless servants and laborers, pouring tea and filling brandy snifters in the boardrooms in the old boys' clubs" (Gates, 1992, p. 17).

Multicultural Perspectives

What do the multiculturalists want? Are they a threat to schools and the social cohesion of the country? Are they trying to impose political correctness on all Americans? Take a look at some of the multiculturalist arguments for curriculum change in the schools and decide for yourself.

As noted earlier, multiculturalists are a diverse group that includes feminists, Afrocentrists, social critics, and many people who defy labels but who simply want to transmit the variety of American culture more faithfully to their children. The charge that multiculturalists want to purge the school curriculum of Western culture is simply false. Multiculturalism, as the term is used here, does not require schools rid the curriculum of stories of white males and substitute the experiences of women, gays, African Americans, and other exploited and disadvantaged persons (Sobol, 1993). Multiculturalism is not a euphemism for white–male bashing or a movement against the West. Multiculturalists ask only for a fair share of curricular attention, an honest representation of the poor as well as the powerful, and reasonable treatment of minority as well as majority culture perspectives. Whatever the outcome of the current struggle over cultural representation in the curriculum, the world American students know already is multicultural (Gates, 1992, p. xvi). The curriculum must change to reflect this society, or it becomes irrelevant to students' lives.

You might think of the multiculturalist reaction against the traditional curriculum as a "victims' revolution," a repudiation of the top-down approach to literature, art, music, and history. It demands change by those discounted and otherwise harmed by traditional approaches to schooling. Multiculturalists ask schools to tell the cultural tale in a way that weaves experiences of the disadvantaged and marginalized into the tapestry of the U.S. rise to prominence. Multiculturalism is a call for fairness and a better representation of the contributions of all Americans. Multiculturalists do not disparage the school's role in developing a cohesive, national identity. At the same time, however, they recognize schools must ensure *all* students preserve, as well, their individual ethnic, cultural, and economic identities (Banks, 1994, 2001; Pang and Cheng, 1998).

Schools are obligated to teach multiple perspectives in the name of academic fairness and historical accuracy. Few events of significance can be understood considering only one perspective, and viewing any event from diverse, competing viewpoints leads to a fuller, more complete representation of truth. For example, school textbooks typically emphasize the role nineteenth-century white abolitionists played and discuss how whites struggled to achieve integration in the twentieth century. This is, of course, appropriate; many whites have played and continue to play vital and significant roles in the struggle for social justice. But these same textbooks typically minimize the stories of African American resistance to slavery, as well as their efforts to achieve integration and equality (Asante, 1987, 1991). These omissions alienate young African American students and present an inaccurate picture to their white peers. The story of slavery must be told from many sides, including the perspective of African Americans as agents in their own history and not simply as people who were colonized, enslaved, and freed by others (Asante, 1995). A multiculturally educated person would be able to see the slave trade from the view of the white slave trader as well as from the perspective of the enslaved people. The point is not to replace one group's story with another, but to tell the whole story more fully. To include women, the poor, and minorities is not to eliminate the lessons of culture or history; it is simply a way to make them richer and more complete.

Monoculturalism and Minority Alienation

> Read our faces. We don't see ourselves on the faculty. We don't read about ourselves in the books you're requiring us to read, and we don't hear our voices in the lectures. (*Harvard Educational Review*, 1997, pp. 170–171)

Curriculum change may come from the top down or from the bottom up, but it never comes easily. The goal of multiculturalists is to bend education around the lives of students so all students can experience a real chance at school success. Anyone familiar with schools knows the most effective way to teach is to make the curriculum relevant to students. Curricula have more meaning when students find characters like themselves in the books they read, and instruction has a better chance of engaging students when the subject matter speaks to their experiences. Exclusion of particular groups of students and their history from the literature alienates students and diminishes academic achievement. Children who find themselves and their culture underrepresented in the school curriculum cannot help but feel lost and resentful. Without a multicultural emphasis, minority children feel like outsiders. As Asante (1991) writes:

> The little African American child who sits in a classroom and is taught to accept as heroes and heroines individuals who defamed African people is being actively decentered, dislocated, and made into a nonperson, one whose aim in life might be to one day shed that "badge of inferiority": his or her Blackness. (p. 171)

Everyone benefits from multicultural education: Children of immigrants from northern and Western Europe need to hear tales that resonate with their experiences. They also need to learn about the experiences of others and how they view their lives. Children of new immigrants from Asia and Latin America need to learn about the lands they left, their new home, and varied new neighbors. They must examine their cultural baggage so they can better understand how it fits into the cultures that shape America. All children should be able to learn in school that a pluralistic society welcomes cultural differences, and that they do not have to distance themselves from their families and cultural traditions and homogenize to be considered "good Americans." Schools in a democratic society have no choice but to be multicultural.

A Responsible Multicultural Curriculum

Multicultural education reform has spread to many states (Banks and McGee-Banks, 1995) and nations (Cornwell and Stoddard, 2001). The experience of New York State is an interesting example because of the state's ethnic complexity and its combination of urban, suburban, and rural school districts. In the late 1980s, the New York State Commissioner of Education invited scholars and curriculum writers to review the appropriateness of the state's K–12 social studies curriculum and recommend any needed changes.[2]

The report, *A Curriculum of Inclusion, 1989,* recognized New York's curriculum was not fairly representing minorities. Although the state had opened its doors to millions of new immigrants, their ways of life, foods, religions, and histories were not found in the curriculum. Instead, the new immigrants were socialized along an "Anglo-American model" (New York State Social Studies Syllabus Review and Development Committee, 1991). New York was asking new immigrants to exchange their families' habits and rituals for a homogenized

[2]Task Force members were asked to examine the curriculum and address questions about its fairness and balance. Did this curriculum speak to the varied needs of female as well as male students, African Americans and Asian Americans as well as European Americans, the disadvantaged as well as the advantaged? On the basis of the reviewers' recommendations, New York developed a new curriculum promising a fresh focus on the treatment of all students in the state. To compare New York's approach with a more rural state, see the "Nebraska Multicultural Education Bill" (Banks, 2002, pp. 128–130).

American culture. The unstated curricular message asked new immigrants to abandon their forebears' cultures and learn to prize the literature, history, traditions, and holidays of the Anglo-American Founding Fathers.

This is a familiar model of cultural assimilation. Proponents of state-funded education in the nineteenth century encouraged schools to teach immigrants social behaviors and patriotic rituals designed to encourage "Americanization." Such assimilation worked reasonably well for white Europeans who came to this country in the nineteenth century, but it did not work for other immigrants. Now, in the face of new immigration patterns, it seems to be an untenable ideal. A significant demographic difference distinguishes today's immigrants from those of the past. In the nineteenth century, most of the nation's voluntary immigrants came from Europe, and socialization toward an Anglo-American model of behavior may not have been terribly discontinuous with their heritage. Now, the majority of immigrants are from Asia and South America. People newly arrived from Korea and Colombia are less likely to find resonance in the Anglo-American cultural ideal than those who came to the United States from Ireland, Germany, and Italy.

New York State curriculum planners and teachers debated the design and implementation of a multicultural approach for the better part of twenty years. The new curriculum acknowledges the importance of socialization and nation building for an increasingly diverse population, but also fosters respect for cultural diversity. The New York State curriculum recognizes that to teach the nation's history appropriately requires teaching from multiple perspectives. Classroom attention must be focused on a wide range of people, their culture, and perspectives that make up the nation. The curriculum recommends that the social studies, K–12,

> should go beyond the addition of long lists of ethnic groups, heroes, and contributions to the infusion of various perspectives, frame of reference, and content from various groups . . . Effective multicultural approaches look beyond ethnic particularism, examine differences in light of universal human characteristics, focus on multiple perspectives, and attend to the mutual influences among groups within and across national boundaries. (New York State Education Department, 2002, p. 5)

The multiculturalist argument is not that Eurocentric views are wrong or evil or that children of Asian or African descent should not learn about the European cultural legacy. Multiculturalism asks schools to subscribe to one simple educational truth: Tolerance cannot come without respect, and respect cannot come without knowledge of others and their point of view (Gates, 1992, p. xv). Multiculturalism begins by recognizing the cultural diversity of the United States, and asks that the school curriculum explore that diversity. To be well educated in a multicultural sense means to learn about the histories, literature, and contributions of the varied people who have fashioned the complex tapestry of American life. All students should sample broadly from all of the cultures and all of the ideas that have contributed to the making of the United States.

POSITION 2: MULTICULTURALISM IS DIVISIVE AND DESTRUCTIVE

When multiculturalism was first promoted as an educational philosophy, its stress seemed to be on the positive contributions of minority groups in this country and on a balanced portrayal of a variety of cultures around the world. But over the years, multiculturalism acquired an additional meaning. Instead of emphasizing the positive contributions of America's minority groups and a balanced range of social groups from around the world, the version of multiculturalism now promoted . . . posits an animus against what are perceived as Western values, particularly the value placed on acquiring knowledge, or analytical thinking, and on academic achievement itself.

—STOTSKY, 1999, P. XI

Schools and the Cultural Heritage

For the past 150 years, public schools have had three broad objectives: to educate individual citizens for democratic participation; encourage individual achievement through academic competition; and promote, encourage, and teach the values and traditions of the American cultural heritage. The United States has been enriched by every ethnic and racial group to land on these shores, and the immigrants, in turn, have been well served by the nation and the nation's schools. The public schools have their share of detractors, to be sure, but the multiculturalists' attack on the schools' curriculum seems misguided. Any fair assessment would find it difficult to fault the success schools have had in passing the common culture of the United States to new generations of Americans—immigrants and native-born citizens alike. No mean accomplishment, the transmission of the cultural heritage requires an appreciation for the complex aspects of U.S. history, literature, and political traditions (Ravitch, 1990; Schlesinger, 1992; Ravitch and Viteritti, 2001). American culture is, after all, a hybrid—a mix of European, Asian, and African cultures—and the school's job is to transmit this cultural legacy faithfully in all its complexity. The school's role in cultural transmission has been one of brilliant success for well over a century.

Nineteenth-century proponents of public education recognized the United States was a dynamic nation, with succeeding waves of immigrants changing and invigorating American culture. The new arrivals came from every corner of the world, and brought energy, talent, and cultural variation never before gathered in one nation. When they arrived in the United States, they spoke different languages, were of many races, and practiced many religions. What they shared was an eagerness to succeed economically and politically, and to learn how to become "American," to fit into a unique, unprecedented cultural amalgam.

Nineteenth-century common schools influenced by Western ideas of philosophic rationalism and humanism, were an expression of optimism about human progress and democratic potential. Advocates of mass public education saw schools as a vehicle of social progress, and shared a common belief in education, "an education, moreover, which was neither a privilege of a fortunate few nor a crumb tossed to the poor and lowly, but one which was to be a right of every child in the land" (Meyer, 1957, p. 143). The common schools succeeded beyond anyone's expectations. Children of the poor as well as the rich received a public education; children of immigrants read the same texts and learned the same lore as the children of native-born Americans. The mix of immigrants now coming to the United States is far richer and more diverse than the founders of the common schools could ever have envisioned. The need for schools to transmit the common culture has never been greater; the preservation of democratic tradition has never been more difficult.

The United States always has been a haven for those seeking political freedom and political expression. In the nineteenth century, millions of immigrants came to this country, in large measure, to enjoy the fruits and accept the burdens of participating in a democratic society. This still is true today, but unlike the immigrants of former times, today's new arrivals typically have had little or no direct experience with democratic traditions. For example, in the 1840s, after the collapse of the Frankfurt diet, immigrants from Germany flocked to America seeking the democratic political expression they had been denied in their homeland. Today's immigrants may want democracy, but when they come from autocratic regimes in Asia and South America, they have had no experience with the responsibilities of democratic living. They are less prepared for assuming a role in a democratic society than any previous generation of immigrants. Clearly, it is up to schools to induct the children of the new immigrants into the complexities of a democratic society.

Although schools should expose children to the common culture, they need not pretend to a cultural homogeneity or deny individual students' ethnic experiences. Schools are obligated to represent the range of cultural voices—male and female, African American, Asian American, and European American—but these voices must be trained not for solo performances but to be part of a chorus. Schools must encourage individual identification with one central cultural tradition, or the United States might fall prey to the same ethnic tensions undermining the sovereignty of Afghanistan and the nations of Eastern Europe and Africa. Students should learn about the common Western ideals that shaped the United States and bind us together as a nation: democracy, capitalism, and monotheism.

Particularism

> What happens when people of different ethnic origins, speaking different languages and professing different religions, settle in the same geographical locality and live under the same political sovereignty? Unless a common purpose binds them together, tribal hostilities will drive them apart. Ethnic and racial conflict, it seems evident, will now replace the conflict of ideologies as the explosive issues of our times. (Schlesinger, 1992, p. 10)

The United States stands to benefit—economically, politically, and socially—from the infusion of talent brought by new immigrants, as it has in the past. Assimilated new immigrants pose no threat to U.S. growth or nationhood. Instead, the United States faces a threat from those who deny that schools should teach a common American tradition or that a common culture even exists! Diane Ravitch calls these people particularists; they argue that teaching a common culture is a disservice to ethnic and racial minorities. "Particularism," writes Ravitch, "is a bad idea whose time has come" (Ravitch, 1990, p. 346).

Particularists demand public schools give up trying to teach the commonalities of cultural heritage in favor of teaching a curriculum centering on the specific ethnic mix represented in a given school or community. Students in predominantly white schools would have one focus, children in predominantly African American schools another, and so on. It is not at all clear where the particularists would stop in the Balkanization of the curriculum. Would a school with a predominantly Asian population have an Asian-focused curriculum, or would they further divide the curriculum into separate strands of Korean, Chinese, Vietnamese, Filipino, and Cambodian culture (Fox-Genovese, 1991)?

The extreme arguments of the particularists do not lend support to the unifying and democratic ends that the founders of the common schools envisioned. Asante, for example, advocates an Afrocentrist curriculum that would teach young African American children about their African cultural roots at the expense of teaching them about Western traditions. He denounces those African Americans who prefer Bach and Beethoven to Ellington and Coltrane. African Americans, he believes, should center on their cultural experience; any other preference is an aberration. Asante argues majority as well as minority students are disadvantaged by the "monoculturally diseased curriculum." He writes that few Americans of any color "have heard the names of Cheikh Anta Diop, Anna Julia Cooper, C. L. R. James, or J. A. Rogers," historians who contributed to an understanding of the African world (Asante, 1991, p. 175). He is probably right, but for better or worse, the most enduring mainstream white historians—for example, Spengler, Gibbon, Macaulay, Carlyle, and Trevelyan—are not likely to enjoy greater recognition.

The cultural focus of the curriculum is a serious matter, and although petty and irrational arguments exist on all sides, the real issue is the role schools must play in transmitting the common cultural heritage. Schools must teach children that regardless of race, gender, or ethnicity, one can achieve great feats. This is the record of the past and promise of the future. The public school curriculum should allow all children to believe they are part of a society that welcomes their participation and encourages their achievements. As Ravitch (1990) writes, "In their curriculum, their hiring practices, and their general philosophy, the public schools must not discriminate against or give preference to any racial or ethnic group. . . . They should not be expected to teach children to view the world through an ethnocentric perspective that rejects or ignores the common culture" (p. 352).

Schools cannot fulfill their central mission to transmit the common culture if they cater to particularist demands for teaching the perspective of every minority group. Ravitch argues that in the past, generation upon generation of minorities—Jews, Catholics, Greeks, Poles, and Japanese—have used private lessons, after school or on weekends, to instill ethnic pride and ethnic continuity in their children. These may be valuable goals, but they have never been the public schools' province, nor should they be. Public schools must develop a common culture, "a definition of citizenship and culture that is both expansive and *inclusive*," one that speaks to our commonalities and not our differences (Ravitch, 1990, p. 352). The public school curriculum must not succumb to particularists' demands to prize our differences rather than celebrate our common good.

Anticanonical Assaults

Among the greatest absurdities the particularists have produced is their attack on the canon, denouncing it as racist, sexist, Eurocentric, logocentric, and politically incorrect. Before we put these distortions to rest, a few words about the nature of the canon: The term *canon* (from the Greek word *kanon*, meaning a measuring rod), which originally referred to the books of the Hebrew and Christian Bibles, meant Holy Scripture as officially recognized by the ecclesiastic authority. Today, it has taken on secular and political meanings. The canon represents, first of all, the major monuments to Western civilization, great ideas embodied in books forming the foundation of our democratic traditions. The "great books" of the Western tradition (for example, the writings of Plato, Aristotle, Machiavelli, and Marx, to name but a few) have shaped our political thinking, whether we trace our origins to Europe, Africa, or Asia; Homer, Sophocles, George Eliot, and Virginia Woolf inform our sense of literature whether we are male or female. Every major university offers courses in the Western canon, and as the late Alan Bloom notes, generations of students have enjoyed these works. He writes, "wherever the Great Books make up a central part of the curriculum, the students are excited and satisfied, feel they are doing something that is independent and fulfilling, getting something from the university they cannot get elsewhere. . . . Their gratitude at learning of Achilles or the categorical imperative is boundless" (Bloom, 1987, p. 344).

The particularists' attack on the canon is new and somewhat surprising. The value of the canon has long been taken for granted as the cornerstone of quality education. As the philosopher John Searle writes, educated circles accepted, almost to the point of cliche, that there is a certain Western intellectual tradition that goes from, say, Socrates to Wittgenstein in philosophy, and from Homer to James Joyce in literature, and it is essential to the liberal education of young men and women in the United States that they receive some exposure to at least some of the great works in this intellectual tradition; they should, in Matthew Arnold's overquoted words, know the best that is thought and known in the world. (Searle, 1990, p. 34)

In the past, support for the canon was an article of faith, not belabored or examined at length. People considered these works and the ideas they contained to be of enduring worth, part of a timeless literary judgment—as Samuel Johnson spoke of it—and quite apart from the hurly-burly of politics. Canonical authors were acknowledged representatives of the evolution in the thought of ideas shaping Western civilization. No longer. Particularists and multiculturalists attack the canon at every turn. Searle writes that the cant of the anticanonicals runs something like this:

> Western civilization is in large part a history of oppression. Internally, Western civilization oppressed women, various slave and serf populations, and ethnic and cultural minorities, generally. In foreign affairs, the history of Western civilization is one of imperialism and colonialism. The so-called canon of Western civilization consists of the official publications of the system of oppression, and it is no accident that the authors in the "canon" are almost exclusively Western white males. . . . [The canon] has to be abolished in favor of something that is "multicultural" and "nonhierarchical." (Searle, 1990, p. 35)

The particularists and multiculturalists are trying to do to the public school curriculum what they tried unsuccessfully to accomplish at universities: to politicize and bias the curriculum. In the name of justice and equity, they encouraged universities to broaden the curriculum and include non-Western as well as Western authors. This might not be so offensive if school *could teach everything*, but curriculum is a zero sum game; that is, if a school adds something, it also must take something else out.

The case of Stanford University is instructive. In the late 1980s, Stanford proposed adding authors from developing countries and both women's and minority perspectives into the curriculum of the Western Culture course. These changes would come at considerable cost. Plato's *Republic* and Machiavelli's *Prince* would be replaced by works such as *I, Rigoberta Menchu,* the story of the political coming-of-age of a Guatemalan peasant woman, and Franz Fanon's *Wretched of the Earth,* a book that encouraged violent and revolutionary acts among citizens of third world countries (D'Souza, 1991). Although campus radicals demonstrated in support of the proposal, chanting, "Hey, hey, ho, ho, Western Culture's got to go," cooler heads won the day. The required course in Western Culture retained its reading list but added some optional assignments that provided a non-Western focus.

Stanford's approach to curriculum reform underestimated the value of Western literature, the ability of great books to capture the imaginations of majority as well as minority students, and the ability minority students have to appreciate Western classics. Sachs and Thiel, Stanford students during the time of the "great curriculum wars," argue that Stanford multiculturalists rejected the universalism of Western culture and the power of ideas. They write:

> There exist truths that transcend the accidents of one's birth, and these objective truths are in principle available to everyone—whether young or old, rich or poor, male or female, white or black; individual (and humanity as a whole) are not trapped within a closed cultural space that predetermines what they may know. (1995, p. 3)

Misguided Curriculum Change in the Name of Multicultural Reform

Stanford successfully resisted the multiculturalists' social engineering, as have most universities; public schools have been less successful. New York State barely survived an attempt to radicalize its schools. The curriculum was headed in a strident multicultural direction when reason prevailed and the radicals lost. New York State had plunged headlong into the maelstrom of multiculturalism in reaction to a report critical of the state's social studies curriculum. The New York proposal was filled with problems. Consider a few: One of the guiding principles of the report is that "[t]he subject matter content should be *treated as socially constructed* and therefore tentative—as is all knowledge." The document had gone on to assert: "Knowledge is the product of human beings located in specific times and places; consequently, much of our subject matter must be understood as tentative" (New York State Social Studies Syllabus Review and Development Committee, 1991, p. 29). Supporters of this view believe we should teach students all knowledge is socially constructed—made up, fabricated—and that there is no overarching and agreed-upon sense of truth or right moral action.

This is distressing. What are we passing on to succeeding generations if not the fruits of our culture's pursuit of truth? According to social constructionists, all concepts of "truth and falsehood, "right and wrong," and "good and bad" are products of the human mind, as varied as human experience, and equally valid. As Glazer (2001) notes, "As the absolute ground of truth and morality weaken, one will find students (and teachers) who will question the automatic disapproval of practices once considered abhorrent (human sacrifice among the Aztecs?) because they have been taught that every culture has its own standard, and that there are no absolute grounds for judgment (p. 174). The New York State curriculum proposal (*One Nation, Many Peoples: A Declaration of Cultural Independence,* New York State Social Studies Syllabus Review and Development Committee, 1991) would have taken the state in inappropriate directions. Its most extreme positions were beaten down by critics, and the current (2002) curriculum contains less of the inflammatory language and ratiocinations of previous drafts. Many educators joined together and successfully denounced the earlier plan for its intellectual dishonesty and potential for divisiveness.

Albert Shanker, the late president of the American Federation of Teachers, argued that "multiculturalism" is an appealing idea but is likely to degenerate into stereotyping about minority views when applied in the classroom:

> For a teacher presenting a historical event to elementary school children, using multiple perspectives probably means that the teacher turns to each child and asks the point of view about the event. To the African American child this would mean, "What is the African American point of view?" To a Jewish child, "What is the Jewish point of view?" And to the Irish child, "What is the Irish point of view?" (Shanker, 1991, p. E7)

Shanker pointed out that multiculturalism is, in practice, a racist approach: It assumes that every single African American child shares the same perspective, as do all members of any religious and/or ethnic group. The rhetoric of cultural relevance and a curriculum centered around the child's sociocultural experience is, on the surface, attractive. Such an approach, however, treats culture as a heritable or biological characteristic. This is a cruel distortion. Culture is learned, much as language is learned. Ravitch reminds us that adoption of multiculturalist assumptions limits our ideas of human freedom and potential and "implies a dubious, dangerous form of cultural predestination" (Ravitch, 1990, p. 346).

Political Correctness

Before it was amended in 2002, the New York State curriculum proposal had enshrined the shrillest voices of the political correctness choir, forcing adherence to the political attitudes and social mores of the liberal left. Political correctness is not entirely bad; it has made us more sensitive about the language we use. We can credit it with making people realize how inappropriate it is to refer to mature women as "girls" and black men as "boys." However, there seems to be no stopping the tidal wave of "correctspeak" and politically correct behavior. You no doubt have heard some wag report it is no longer acceptable to call people "short"; instead they are "vertically challenged humans." The deceased may be labeled "permanently horizontal"! We could take this lightly if it were not such a serious matter. Political correctness, which has become the multiculturalists' enforcement arm, has narrowed the range of acceptable public discourse—things we can speak about openly—and has enlarged the American lexicon of neologisms. It also protects people from a range of tyrannies never before imagined. For example, Smith College in Northampton, Massachusetts, calls students' attention to several types of "oppression," including "ableism," "heteroism," and "lookism." Consider these definitions:

> Ableism: Oppression of the differently abled by the temporarily able.
>
> Heteroism: Oppression of those of sexual orientation other than heterosexual, such as gays, lesbians, and bisexuals; this can take place by not acknowledging their existence.
>
> Lookism: The belief that appearance is an indicator of a person's value; the construction of a standard of beauty/attractiveness; and oppression through stereotypes and generalization of both those who do not fit that standard and those who do. (Schlesinger, 1998, pp. 120–121)

One shudders to think what would happen if ableism and lookism ever were to be ruled violations of the Constitution. Would medical schools be forced to accept applicants no matter what their ability? Would Miss America contests be decided by lottery?

Consider another example of an adventure into the misguided world of political correctness. A New Jersey high school decided not to announce the names of graduates in alphabetical order at senior commencement because to do so would group together the school's large number of Asian-Indian students. It seems that during past commencement ceremonies, members of the audience would snicker at the large number of graduates with the last name

Patel. "As each got up, some people would yell 'Patel number one,' 'Patel number two,' and so on," reported one school administrator. The school superintendent said, "We were teaching students about sensitivity to race and ethnic background. [We] were grouping the students by last names. It was a type of segregation. It didn't make sense" (Jaffe, 1994, p. 14).

The whole business does not make sense. Why did the school need a special new policy? What happens in schools where the most common surnames are Smith, Jones, and Johnson? Do administrators there consider calling names randomly at commencement? Or does political correctness force a new, self-conscious, and unnatural attention to these matters?

* * *

The historian Arthur Schlesinger, Jr. argues that the defining experience for Americans has not been ethnicity or sanctification of old cultures, "but the creation of a new national culture and a *new* national identity." It is foolish, he argues, to look backward in empty celebration of what we once were. Instead, schools need to look forward and blend the disparate experiences of immigrants into one American culture (New York State Social Studies Syllabus Review and Development Committee, 1991, p. 89). Schools should continue to serve the nation by passing on to children elements of the common culture that defines the United States and binds its people together. This is not to say schools should be asked to portray the culture as unchangeable or force students to accept it without question. The culture of a nation changes as a reflection of its citizens; U.S. culture will continue to change. School curricula will of necessity expand and sample more broadly from the various influences that have shaped our culture. However, to turn the schools away from Western ideals of democracy, justice, freedom, equality, and opportunity is to renounce the greatest legacy one generation ever bequeathed to the next. No matter who sits in American classrooms—African Americans, Asian Americans, Latin Americans, or European Americans—and no matter what their religion or creed, those students and their nation have been shaped by democratic and intellectual traditions of the Western world, and they had better learn those traditions or risk losing them.

For Discussion

1. According to John Searle (1990), these are characteristics of a well-educated person:
   - **a.** The person should know enough of his or her cultural traditions to know how they evolved.
   - **b.** The person should know enough of the natural sciences that he or she is not a stranger in that world.
   - **c.** The person should know enough of how society works to understand the trade cycle, interest, unemployment, and other elements of the political and economic world.
   - **d.** The person should know at least one language well enough to read the best literature that culture offers in the original language.
   - **e.** The person needs to know enough philosophy to be able to use the tools of logical analysis.
   - **f.** The person must be able to write and speak clearly and with candor and rigor.

Do you agree or disagree with Searle's characteristics of a well-educated person? Who should determine what it means to be "well educated"—the individual? the school? the parents? the state? the federal government?

2. According to one survey, by 2000, more than half of colleges and universities required students to study diversity issues (Conciatore, 2000). What arguments support a "multicultural education" course as a college/university graduation requirement? What courses at your institution would you recommend to satisfy that requirement? Would you include courses on feminism? What about modern language courses or courses in ancient Greek? Would you allow a Mexican American student to satisfy the requirement by taking a course in Hispanic studies? Should courses in gay and lesbian studies be counted as a multicultural course for straight people?
3. Steinberg and Kincheloe identify five positions in the public discourse about multicultural education (2001, pp. 3–5). From these following excerpts, do you find yourself more comfortable with one or more of these positions than others? Does your teacher-education program adhere more closely to one or more of them?
   - **a.** *Conservative multiculturalism of monoculturalism position:*
     believes in the superiority of Western patriarchal culture
     promotes the Western canon as a universal civilizing influence
     targets multiculturalism as the enemy of Western progress
   - **b.** *Liberal multiculturalism position:*
     emphasizes the natural equality and common humanity of individuals from diverse race, class, and gender groups
     argues that inequality results from lack of opportunity
     maintains that problems individuals from divergent backgrounds face are individual difficulties, not socially structured adversities
   - **c.** *Pluralist multiculturalism position:*
     exoticizes difference and positions it as necessary knowledge for those who compete in globalized economy
     contends the curriculum should consist of studies of various divergent groups
     avoids the concept of oppression
   - **d.** *Leftist-essential multiculturalism position:*
     maintains that race, class, and gender categories consist of a set of unchanging priorities (essences)
     assumes that only authentically oppressed people can speak about particular issues concerning a specific group
   - **e.** *Critical multiculturalism position:*
     grounds a critical pedagogy that promotes an understanding of how schools/education works by the exposé of student sorting processes and power's complicity with the curriculum
     makes no pretense of neutrality, as it honors the notion of egalitarianism and elimination of human suffering
     analyzes the way power shapes consciousness
4. When multicultural educators use the term *white supremacy,* they are not referring to groups like the Klan or the Aryan Nation. Duarte and Smith (2000) define "white supremacy" (also known as "whiteness") as an approach to understanding racism "that shifts the focus from individual prejudice to structural domination . . . [W]hite people are systematically privileged and advantaged within society's institutions because of their skin color and its relationship to historical patterns of oppression and exploitation" (p. 357). Whiteness is typically an unexamined, taken for granted set of assumptions that may be less obvious to white people than to people of color. "When

George W. Bush, Dick Cheney, and William Bennett refer to family values, they are speaking of a white entity, a white norm missing in nonwhite homes (Steinberg and Kincheloe, 2001, p. 18).

Whiteness is often expressed naively by white people. bell hooks (2000) uses the example of an English professor who "wants very much to have 'a' black person in 'their' department as long as that person thinks and acts like them, shares their values and beliefs, and is in no way different" (p. 111).

What role should whiteness studies play in multicultural education? Do you believe that "whiteness" should be studied as an ethnicity or as a racial group with its own socially constructed values, customs, and cultural norms? Or do you think that "whiteness" studies do not merit classroom attention in public schools?

References

ANDERSON, M. J., EDITOR-IN-CHIEF. (2000). *Encyclopedia of the U.S. Census.* Washington, DC: CQ Press.

APPIAH, K. A. (2000). "Culture, Subculture, Multiculturalism: Educational Options." In E. M. Durate and S. Smith, eds., *Foundational Perspectives in Education.* New York: Longman.

ASANTE, M. K. (1987). *The Afrocentric Idea.* Philadelphia: Temple University Press.

———. (1991). "The Afrocentric Idea in Education." *Journal of Negro Education* 60(2), 170–180.

———. (1995). *African American History: A Journey of Liberation.* Maywood, NJ: The Peoples Publishing Group.

BANKS, J. A. (1994). "Transforming the Mainstream Curriculum." *Educational Leadership* 51(8), 4–8.

———. (2001). *Cultural Diversity and Education: Foundations, Curriculum, and Teaching.* Boston: Allyn & Bacon.

———. (2002). *An Introduction to Multicultural Education.* 3rd Ed. Boston: Allyn & Bacon.

BANKS, J. A., AND MCGEE-BANKS, C. A., EDS. (1995). *Handbook of Research on Multicultural Education.* New York: Macmillan.

BLOOM, A. (1987). *The Closing of the American Mind.* New York: Simon & Schuster.

CONCIATORE, J. (2000). "Study Shows More than Half of American Colleges Now Have Diversity Requirements." *Black Issues in Higher Education,* Nov., v. 17. (http://web3.infotrac.galegroup.com)

CORNWELL, G. H., AND STODDARD, E. W., EDS. *Global Multiculturalism: Comparative Perspectives on Ethnicity, Race, and Nation.* Lanham, MD: Rowan & Littlefield.

D'SOUZA, D. (1991). "Illiberal Education." *The Atlantic Monthly.* March, 51–79.

DURATE, E. M., AND SMITH S., EDS. (2000). *Foundational Perspectives in Education.* New York: Longman.

EDMONSTON, B. (2000). "Composition of the Population." In M. J. Anderson, ed., *Encyclopedia of the U.S. Census.* Washington, DC: Urban Institute Press.

FOX-GENOVESE, E. (1991). "The Self-Interest of Multiculturalism." *Tikkun* 6(4), 47–49.

GATES, H. L., JR. (1992). *Loose Canons: Notes on the Cultural Wars.* New York: Oxford University Press.

GIROUX, H. A. (1997). "Rewriting the Discourse of Racial Identity: Towards a Pedagogy and Politics of Whiteness." *Harvard Educational Review* 67(2), 169–187.

GLAZER, N. (1997). *We Are All Multiculturalists Now.* Cambridge: Harvard University Press.

———. (2001). "Problems in Acknowledging Diversity." In D. Ravitch and J. P. Viteritti, eds., *Making Good Citizens: Education and Civil Society.* New Haven: Yale University Press.

GORDON, B. M. (1995). "Knowledge Construction, Competing Critical Theories, and Education." In J. A. Banks and C. A. McGee-Banks, eds., *Handbook of Research on Multicultural Education.* New York: Macmillan.

HARVARD EDUCATIONAL REVIEW. (1997). "Ethnicity and Education Forum: What Difference Does Difference Make?" *Harvard Educational Review* 67(2), 169–187.

HIRSCH, E. D., JR. (1987). *Cultural Literacy: What Every American Needs to Know.* Boston: Houghton Mifflin.

———. (1996). *The Schools We Need, and Why We Don't Have Them.* New York: Doubleday.

HOOKS, B. (2000). "Overcoming White Supremacy: A Comment." In E. M. Durate and S. Smith, eds., *Foundational Perspectives in Education.* New York: Longman.

HUNTINGTON, S. P. (1996). *The Clash of Civilizations: Remaking of the World Order.* New York: Touchstone.

JAFFE, J. (1994). "Flunking Bigotry." *The Newark Star Ledger.* June 22, p. 14.

MEYER, A. E. (1957). *An Educational History of the American People.* New York: McGraw-Hill.

NEW YORK STATE EDUCATION DEPARTMENT. (2002). *Social Studies: Resource Guide with Core Curriculum.* Albany: The State Education Department.

NEW YORK STATE SOCIAL STUDIES SYLLABUS REVIEW AND DEVELOPMENT COMMITTEE. (1991). *One Nation, Many Peoples: A Declaration of Cultural Independence.* Albany: The State Education Department, State University of New York.

PANG, V. O., AND CHENG, L. L. (1998). *Struggling to be Heard: The Unmet Needs of Asian Pacific American Children.* Albany: State University of New York.

RAVITCH, D. (1987). "Tot Sociology, Grade School History." *Current* (Dec.), 4–10.

———. (1990). "Multiculturalism, E Pluribus Plures." *American Scholar* (Summer), 337–354.

RAVITCH, D., AND VITERITTI, J. P. (2001). *Making Good Citizens: Education and Civil Society.* New Haven: Yale University Press.

SACHS, D. O., AND THIEL, P. A. (1995). *The Diversity Myth, "Multiculturalism" and the Politics of Intolerance at Stanford.* Oakland, CA: The Independent Institute.

SCHLESINGER, A. M. (1992/1998). *The Disuniting of America.* New York: W. W. Norton.

SEARLE, J. (1990). "The Storm Over the University." *The New York Review of Books.* Dec. 6, pp. 34–41.

SHANKER, A. (1991). "Multiple Perspectives." *The New York Times.* Oct. 27, 1991, p. E7.

SLEETER, C. E. (1996). *Multicultural Education as Social Activism.* Albany: State University of New York Press.

SOBOL, T. (1993). "Revising the New York State Social Studies Curriculum." *Teachers College Record* (Winter), pp. 258–272.

SPRING, J. (2000). *The Intersection of Cultures: Multicultural Education in the United States and the Global Economy.* 2nd. Ed. New York: McGraw-Hill.

STEINBERG, S. R., AND KINCHELOE, J. L. (2001). "Setting the Context for Critical Multi/Interculturalism: The Power Blocs of Class Elitism, White Supremacy, and Patriarchy." In S. R. Steinberg, ed., *Multi/Intercultural Conversations.* New York: Peter Lang.

STOTSKY, S. (1999). *Losing Our Language: How Multicultural Classroom Instruction is Undermining Our Children's Ability to Read, Write, and Reason.* New York: Free Press.

TAKAKI, R. (1993). *A Different Mirror: A History of Multicultural America.* Boston: Little, Brown.

WILLETT, C., ED. (1998). *Theorizing Multiculturalism, A Guide to the Current Debate.* Malden, MA: Blackwell.

CHAPTER 12

Values/Character Education: Traditional or Liberational

POSITION 1: TEACH TRADITIONAL VALUES

While reading, math, and science can give our children strength of mind, character education is necessary to give them strength of heart. It is time for schools to return to teaching children that character, honesty, and integrity are important. Good character is not something you are born with; it is something you must learn from those who have it.

—PAIGE, 2002, P. 712

In the twenty-first century, American public schools commonly operate without an ethical compass. Relativism keeps such schools and their students adrift in a sea of personal and social temptations. Relativism in schools reflects the ideas that (1) all values are relative, with none superior; (2) there is no enduring set of ethical standards; and (3) personal character is a matter of individual choice and particular situations. It incorporates situational ethics and egotistical rationalization to justify any values or actions.

Sommers (1998), in a perceptive analysis of the moral and educational chaos facing young people, summarizes this position: "The last few decades of the twentieth century have seen a steady erosion of knowledge and a steady increase in moral relativism" (p. 33). She demonstrates the link betwen a host of other school problems and the fact that Johnny can't read, write, or count; continuing: "it is also true that Johnny is having difficulty distinguishing right from wrong. . . . Along with illiteracy and innumeracy, we must add deep moral confusion to the list of educational problems" (p. 31). This is a very serious problem that will continue to haunt American society until it is adequately addressed. As Hansen (2001) notes, "Studies suggest that teaching is inherently a moral endeavor" (p. 826). Morality cannot be escaped by pretending schools are outside its sphere.

That schools are an important bearer of values to the young is clear. We are not born with a set of values, they are all—good and bad—learned. Although we learn values in many places, from many people, and through many media, schools form a particularly significant institution for imparting values. This has been recognized for a long time; as Simon Blackburn (2001) points out, Aristotle "emphasized that it takes education and practice in order to become virtuous" (p. 113). More recently, Former Secretary of Education William Bennett (1992) highlights the tradition of common schools as the basis of common values, with leaders of the common school movement coming mainly from business, the clergy, and civic positions—people who "saw the schools as upholders of standards of individual morality and small incubators of civic and personal virtue; the founders of the public schools had faith that public education could teach good moral and civic character from a common ground of American values" (p. 58). Education Secretary Rod Paige (2002) supports this point as he argues for a return to solid character education.

Yet, as Bennett documents, schools have lost this central purpose in a contemporary welter of value-neutral, value-relative, and anything-goes approaches to values education. The former position of schools was to be stalwart conveyors of good values and sound character, with exemplary moral and ethical modelling by school teachers and administrators. That has been replaced by an institutional blind eye to values and educator disinterest in, or fear of, maintaining high standards of morality and ethics for themselves and their students. Far too many public schools lack a central core of fundamental morals and give students no ethical basis for guidance through life. Instead, secular domination of education mistakenly keeps religious values at bay, while self-absorption becomes a primary focus for students. Is it any wonder that society is crumbling, violence is increasing, families are in disarray, and civility has disappeared?

Education emphasizing selfishness, personal freedom, and permissiveness is a major contributor to the significant decline in social and family values (Sowell, 1992). Increased crime and abuse is a natural outcome of schooling that preaches self-indulgence. Charles Colson (1994) argues that secularization of American society is responsible for the increase in violent crime. Where can one gain a deep respect for other people, property, and social traditions if schools assume the relativist stance that these things do not matter?

Liberalism and Moral Decline

The liberal view of education—that traditional values don't matter and students should decide basic value questions for themselves without guidance from educators, religious leaders, or parents—has an eroding effect on the cornerstones of American society. Liberalism itself is a culprit; in education it does significant damage to American morality (Falwell, 1980; Bennett, 1993; Bork, 1996; Himmelfarb, 1999). It does not take a rocket scientist to recognize that common values undergirding civility, manners, and courtesies once dominant in the United States have given way to self-indulgent values of greed, destruction, consumption, and distrust of authority. This erosion has been the companion of permissive attitudes fostered in schools since progressive education concepts enveloped schools in the 1930s (Bennett, 1994).

No wonder family values have declined in the face of a long-term educational philosophy based on individualism and libertine lifestyles (Rafferty, 1968; Anderson, 1994; Roberts, 1994). Evidence of moral disaster surrounds us: extraordinarily high divorce rates, child and spouse abuse, lack of ethics in business and government, drug and alcohol addiction, out-of-control teenage pregnancy rates, excessive reliance on child care outside the home, acceptance of immorality on television and in the arts, cheating scandals and explosive violence in schools (Colson, 1994). We even have a recent U.S. president who admitted to moral corruption in his private life and deception in his public life, even as important public figures claimed that his behavior did not matter. This is a snapshot of life when we do not provide a strong education in traditional values.

Schools have lost their moral focus and, thus, their ability to educate youth in the most important of areas—morality. Without a moral focus, other learnings are shallow. Bryce Christensen (1991), director of the Rockford Institute Center on the Family in America, argues persuasively that schools have become ideological centers for crusades against family and traditional values. He buttresses his points with numerous quotations, including an apt insight from sociologist Kingsley Davis: "One of the main functions of [the school system] . . . appears to be to alienate offspring from their parents" (p. 6).

Christensen raises important questions about teachers who presume to supersede parents in implanting moral values in children. Further, he cites the work of Paul Vitz and Michael Levin, who document an aggressive feminist bias in school texts and teachings—a feminist bias in opposition to traditional American family values. Traditional parenthood and family life are virtually censored from school materials, while available teaching materials convey romantic images of adventurous single women. Similarly, reports Christensen, traditionalist parents have good reason to worry about amoral messages in literature, music, and arts that denounce religion and espouse adultery or other antifamily values.

Radical feminism is not the only culprit in the theft of morality from schools; it is just one of several modern amoral attitudes. Similar attacks on American family values have appeared under the banners of "diversity," "multiculturalism," and "sexual orientation." These banners share the root idea of moral relativism, the idea that all views are equally valid in the classroom—from killing by euthanasia or abortion to gay and lesbian advocacy. As it destroys traditional values, moral relativism substitutes amorality or immorality as a guide to life. Even in this, there is rank logical inconsistency in the advocacy of value neutrality by many liberals. While claiming that no values are more important than any others, liberal advocates still propose a set of special interests they claim deserve special treatment in classrooms and textbooks: minorities, women, disabled, gay and lesbian. This special treatment constitutes a set of values they consider more valuable. Further, they accept mercy killings, abortions, and homosexuality as examples of perfectly acceptable topics of study and conduct, while praying in school is not. This is hypocrisy.

Noted moral education scholar Tom Lickona (1991, 1993) outlined the kinds of problems that demonstrate a decline in values among youth. He includes violence, vandalism, bad language, sexual promiscuity, peer cruelty, stealing, and cheating. He linked this decline to a series of factors, including:

Darwinism and the relativistic view that springs from it,

A philosophy of pseudo-scientific logical positivism that separates "facts" from "values,"

Personalism, emphasizing individual rights over social responsibilities and moral authority,

Pluralism, suggesting multiple values and raising a question of which ones we should teach, and

Secularization, which falsely separates church and state and offers no religious guidance.

American schools were not always cavalier about values. Syndicated columnist William Murchison (1994) points out that the earliest schools were designed to impart strong positive feelings about patriotism and American democracy, and many people still look to public schools to fight to "reverse the moral trends of the day" (p. 145). But Murchison also notes that institutions and social conditions have changed and moral authority no longer is acknowledged in schools, nor is it practiced by teachers and parents. This predicament represents a major erosion of respect for traditional values, parental authority, and teachers' purpose in character education. This, he argues, is related to the continuing decline of all types of standards, academic and ethical, in schools and in life—a reflection of cultural and moral relativity.

Traditional Values Can Be Restored to Schools

There is a tight relationship between good families and good schools in a society based on common values. The increasing disillusionment many Americans feel concerning the drift of the nation and decline of schools causes them to want to stem the downward trend. The good news is that efforts to bring schools and society back to their moral base can yield positive results. Although we can differentiate among definitions of values, ethics, morals, and character, school programs bearing labels such as "values education," "ethics education," "moral education," and "character education" often use the same principles, purposes, and general practices. Often they are so similar as to be interchangeable, and we will treat them as such unless the terms are used as covers for value-free or value-neutral programs. At the core of the best of the good programs is an effort to restore traditional values to schools and students; and these good programs work. Lickona's (1993) work as director of the Center for the 4th and 5th Rs (respect and responsibility), shows much promise in restoring "good" character to its historic place at the center of schooling. Leming and Silva (2001) reported excellent results from a five-year study on teaching a special Heartwood Foundation ethics curriculum to fifth-graders; compared with other students, the program produced more caring and respectful actions and fewer disciplinary referrals, and the teachers' approach to ethics teaching changed in a positive way.

Over a decade ago, a coalition of groups supporting family values and school morality were successful in elections in San Diego County, California, putting strong citizens in about two-thirds of the open seats on school boards and city councils. Pat Robertson's Christian Coalition described San Diego as a model of what we can do in local communities to reestablish morality in schools and society. Local agendas now include maintaining traditional values in the school curriculum, fighting to bring religion back as basic to schooling, and stemming the tide of such antifamily education as providing birth control classes (Rabkin, 1995). A continuing series of U.S. elections replacing liberal politicians with more conservative ones reflect the general discontent with the direction taken during the Progressive Period.

Among the agenda items in the new movement for family values is the restoration of religion to U.S. schools. The Freedom Alliance works to restore America's first principles: traditional morality, close and strong families, free enterprise, solid schools, and vigorous national defense (see www.freedomalliance.com). There is a strong link among personal character, family values, and national patriotism. Other indicators of success include the increasing number and quality of educational materials available for teachers and parents. The Character Education Institute provides teaching materials aimed at instilling universal values in students: honor, honesty, truthfulness, kindness, generosity, helpfulness, courage, convictions, justice, respect, freedom, and equality (Character Education Institute, 1998). The Bureau of Essential Ethics Education in California maintains a Character Education Center on the Internet. The Education Index listed the Center as one of the best education-related sites on the Internet, and *USA Today* featured it as a "Hot Site." The Bureau advocates core ethical values, and has created a system to help children understand these values by relating them to parts of the body:

1. Positive mental attitude (mind)
2. Respect (eyes and ears)
3. Integrity (mouth)
4. Compassion (heart)
5. Cooperation (hands)
6. Perseverance (stomach or guts)
7. Initiative (feet)

The Bureau's research studies followed children over a twenty-year period, the most comprehensive ethics education study ever done in the United States. The studies found extraordinarily high levels of success in students' ability to identify and write knowledgeably about these ethical values after participating in the Bureau's educational programs. Other Internet sites offer assistance (see www.goodcharacter.com; www.character.org; www.aimcenter.com; www.ethicusa.com). Leming (2002), working for the Character Education Partnership, developed and maintains a database at www.character.org, which includes descriptions and analyses of various instruments that can be used to assess character education.

A variety of private foundation and government grants have emerged to assist in the movement for improved character education. Model centers and special programs for character education are under way in a number of states, including North Carolina, California, Iowa, New Mexico, Utah, Connecticut, Maryland, Washington, Missouri, Kentucky, New Jersey, and South Carolina. The centers sponsor such activities as programs devoted to creating safe and orderly school environments, encouraging students to take responsibility for their conduct and for others, preventing violence, and reinforcing efforts to curb drug abuse and weapons in school. Character education is developing quickly into one of the most important new projects in the schools.

What Should Be Taught: Traditional Values as the Focus

Clearly, schools need to rediscover their proper role and function in a moral society. The United States was founded on Judeo-Christian ideals. We have survived, and thrived, because of these ideals. They form the basis of our concepts of justice and democracy. Schools were established to transmit those values to the young to preserve values and society. A belief in God and support for traditional values gave early American schools a clarity of purpose and a solid direction. Children did not receive mixed messages about morality and behavior, and did not get the impression they could make up and change their values on a whim.

Renewing character education should include a prominent focus on traditional values at all levels. In elementary school, reading material should emphasize ideals (Anderson, 1994). Stories of great heroes, personal integrity, resoluteness, loyalty, and productivity should dominate. The main emphasis should be on the positive aspects of U.S. history and literature, showing how individuals working together toward a suitable goal can succeed. Teachers should stress and expect ethical behavior, respect, and consideration (Lickona, 1991). Classes should study various religions with the purpose of understanding their common values and how those values apply to life. Providing time in school for children to reflect on personal religious beliefs would be appropriate.

Signs and symbols in school should reinforce American values. Pictures, displays, and assemblies on morality offer students a chance to see how important those values are to society and school. Inviting speakers into classes, showing films, and taking students to see significant monuments to American values are techniques that can help. Teachers can emphasize good values by providing direct instruction on moral precepts and rewarding students for good citizenship.

At the secondary level, emphasis on traditional values should continue with more sophisticated materials and concepts. There is no need for a special course on sex education if family values are covered in other courses and at home. A student honor roll, citing acts of outstanding school citizenship, might be as prominently displayed as athletic trophies. Libraries are good places for displays of books featuring the kinds of thoughts and behaviors we seek to encourage.

Literature classes should teach U.S. and foreign literature portraying rewards of moral behavior and negative consequences of immorality. American history classes should express ideals for which we stand and our extraordinary historical achievements. Science courses should feature stories of hard work and perseverance in making scientific discoveries, as well as stories of how basic values and religious views have guided many scientists in their work.

The arts are a rich place to show values through study of paintings, compositions, sculptures, and other art forms that express the positive aspects of human life under a set of everlasting ideals. Religious music and art can be a part of the curriculum, as can nonreligious art idealizing such values as the golden rule and personal virtue. Vocational subjects afford numerous ways to present good attitudes toward work, family, responsibility, loyalty, decency, and respect. Sports are an especially important place in which to reaffirm these same values; numerous professional and college teams pray together before matches, and many players are leading figures in setting high standards of moral conduct.

Teachers for American Values

We need teachers who demonstrate a strong personal commitment to traditional values and whose behaviors and lives exhibit that commitment. These teachers are the key to improved values education. Changes in curriculum or teaching materials will have no impact if teachers who work directly with the young do not meet strong moral standards. Obviously, determining a teacher's moral beliefs goes beyond examining his or her college transcripts, since the subjects a person studies bear little relation to his or her moral conduct.

To preserve and protect American values in schools, states have a right to require high moral standards from those who obtain state licenses to teach in public schools. Colleges preparing teachers should examine potential students' records and deny entry to those with criminal or morally objectionable backgrounds (for example, a history of cheating, dishonesty, or sexual misconduct). Applicants for teaching credentials should be expected to submit references that speak to their moral character. Since we ask this of lawyers who take state bar exams, why shouldn't we expect it of people going into teaching? Schools should require applicants to prepare essays discussing their values. Clearly, student teaching and the first few years of full-time teaching provide opportunity to screen young teachers to ensure they uphold moral standards. If these criteria are clearly and publicly stated, they have fair warning. Teachers found wanting should find employment in some other occupation. They should not be retained in positions where they can influence young people's ideals.

With a strengthened corps of teachers, we can rebuild American values. These teachers will demand better curricula, better teaching materials, and better student behavior. This renewed commitment to ethical behavior will have an infectious quality that will influence parents, government, and the media. The schools have a rich opportunity.

Schools Are Rooted in Moral Values

Schools in America were founded to provide a moral foundation, and they were effective. Colonial schools had as their core a firm commitment to morality, ethics, and traditional values. The first school laws, passed in Massachusetts in 1642 and 1647, mandated that communities provide schooling for young people and that those schools preserve religious and social values. The *New England Primer,* the colonial schoolbook used to teach the alphabet and reading, incorporated moral virtues in its teaching of basic skills. All schoolbooks followed this pattern for many generations. Early Americans clearly recognized the link between a good society and solid religious, family, and school values. Religion continues to be a firm foundation for teaching traditional values, and should not be kept out of public school classrooms (Schiltz, 1998).

From the *New England Primer* through McGuffy's *Readers,* the content studied in school was consistent with America's traditional values. We can learn much from the moral stories these old works present. Children learned it was wrong to misbehave at home, in the community, and at school. They learned the consequences of affronting the common morality by reading about what happened to those who did. They gained respect for proper authority in families, churches, society, and school. We need to reject permissiveness and valuelessness of current schools and return to emphasizing moral precepts and proper behavior. The crisis in education has the same origin as the crisis in society: a decline in basic values. Correction in schools is the main avenue to correction in society.

Religion affords a good moral base for young people, but isn't the only source of traditional values. Ethical personal behavior also derives from deep-rooted family and social values. The good society depends on citizens who have developed keen concern for others, awareness of personal responsibility, and habits of moderation (McFarlane, 1994). Etzioni (1998) argues that values education has broad and deep support among the American public, and he proposes "we just teach the values that most Americans agree upon" (p. 448). Sommers (1998) presents a clear case for classical moral education for students, the "core of noncontroversial ethical issues that were settled long ago. . . . We need to bring back the great books and the great ideas" (pp. 33, 34).

Basic ethical traditions undergirding strong, positive character traits are necessary in a civil society, but many in our modern, selfish, and individualistic world have forsaken them. Not all families or social groups exhibit values conducive to the good society because they themselves are in deep moral decay. That is why schooling to preserve and protect traditional values is so essential. Schools, unfortunately, have fallen prey to the same selfish and corrupting ideas that have destroyed some families and some segments of society.

Secular Humanism and the Loss of Values

Schools no longer lead in reaffirmation of traditional family and religious values, but instead have become leaders in spreading secular humanism and its selfish pursuits. Secular humanism, with its relativistic and narcissistic values, has corrupted much of public life. It has permeated public schools; it has fostered permissiveness and kept students from developing a personal core of values. This is certainly one reason why family life has fallen apart and why religious involvement has declined. Most young people of the post–World War II generation were indoctrinated with secular humanism in school, even though they may not have recognized its pernicious influence. Thus, it is easy to understand how family and religious life would suffer as that generation became parents. Now at least two generations have gone through the program, and American society is reaping the social discontent that secular humanism can produce.

Secular humanism holds that the state is more important than religion, and humans can create and change their values without reference to a greater being. This means any current fad can become the ethical code for society. If enough people want to do something, they simply do it, no matter how much it may damage society or moral law. If what they want to do is illegal, they flout the law and put pressure on public officials to ignore higher values. In some instances, they alter the law to erode basic values further. Legalized gambling and easy abortions are examples of this practice.

Secular humanism, and the relativistic values it promotes, caters to the basest of human desires. Because it provides no guidelines for behavior or thought, it represents permissiveness at its most extreme. Secular humanism is now the dominant view in the public schools.

Jerry Falwell (1980) described the destruction of American education:

> Until about thirty years ago, the public schools in America were providing . . . support for our boys and girls. Christian education and the precepts of the Bible still permeated the curriculum of the public schools. . . . Our public schools are now permeated with humanism. . . . children are taught that there are no absolute rights or wrongs and that the traditional home is only one alternative. (pp. 205, 210)

Senator Strom Thurmond, a strong Constitutionalist, wrote a ringing criticism of Supreme Court decisions that "assault the Constitution." Among the decisions he criticizes as leaving the country open to communism, collectivism, and immorality are the Court's actions to prohibit prayer and Bible reading in public schools. He asserts:

> They [parents] ought to have a right to insist that their children are educated in the traditions and values of their own culture. Above all, they have a right to see that their children are not indoctrinated in a secular, Godless point of view which contradicts the values that are taught at home. (Thurmond, 1968, p. 28)

How Schools Destroy Values: Values Clarification and Moral Obfuscation

In many schools, children are taught that values they learn at home or church are a matter of choice. Through teachings such as "values clarification," children are led to believe that right and wrong are purely matters of individual opinion. There is no moral guideline for conduct or thought. In values clarification, teachers may ask children to publicly identify situations when their father or mother was wrong and to present their own view of what the parent should have done. Teachers ask children personal questions about their family lives and private thoughts. There are no criteria children can use to weigh right and wrong. Instead, teachers encourage children to determine their own set of values. Bennett (1992), describes values clarification:

> Schools were not to take part in their time-honored task of transmitting sound moral values; rather, they were to allow the child to "clarify" his own values (which adults, including parents, had no right to criticize). The "values clarification" movement didn't clarify values, it clarified wants and desires. This form of moral relativism said, in effect, that no set of values was right or wrong. (p. 56)

In class discussions on values, children who present their personal opinions with conviction can influence other children, and the teacher is not to intercede for fear of impeding the "clarification" of values. An entire class can agree that tying cans to a cat's tail, euthanizing people who are old or ill, or remaining seated during the salute to the flag may be acceptable behavior. Children also learn to report on their parents and to ridicule those who support traditional values concerning discretion and privacy. Obviously, without clear and consistent standards of acceptable behavior and belief, our society is doomed to ethical destruction. Can one argue seriously that a life of dishonesty and cheating is morally equal to a life of honesty and integrity? How can schools adopt a position of neutrality regarding values and character development? Yet that absurd view is behind values clarification and other relativistic approaches to dealing with values in schools.

It is ridiculous to assert that young children can exert self-restraint and make critical judgments without proper training. Government requires school attendance but neglects and undercuts the moral basis required for a proper education in values.

Confusing Values in the Current Curriculum

School curriculum and textbooks currently present a wide array of relativistic values that only confuse children. Secular humanism, relativism, and liberalism are not defined as school subjects, and schools offer no courses with those titles. Instead, these insidious ideas filter into nearly all courses and often go unrecognized, even by teachers. Because no specific curriculum stresses traditional morals and values, teachers and courses easily present differing views, leading students to believe there are no eternal or universal values, only personal ones. If courses and teachers do not attest to a common core of morality, students are left morally rudderless. This spawns confusion or self-indulgence at best, and scorn for morality at worst.

Teaching materials children learn from often are either vapid, without any connection to moral thought and behavior, or confusing, displaying multiple values of supposedly equal weight. Current school reading materials include trash directing attention to the values of the worst elements of society, and adult stories well beyond children's moral development. In civics and history, the focus is on political power, not virtue. Children are taught how to manipulate others and how interest groups get their way. History texts are bland and noncommittal concerning basic values and treat religion with disdain. Sex education instruction tends toward the belief that students will engage in promiscuity and sexual freedom, not exercise abstinence and responsibility (Whitehead, 1994). Science ignores religious views and substitutes the "value-free" ideas; any scientific experiment is okay. Instead of protecting and encouraging innocence, schools savage and debase it.

Results of this permissive and selfish education are apparent. We are subject to increasing abuse in contemporary life. We have seen a startling increase in child abuse, so prevalent we now have twenty-four-hour telephone hotlines to report it. Spousal abuse is another item featured almost daily in newspapers. Animal abuse is so common it no longer makes news. And sex and drug abuse have become epidemic.

Other abuses currently abound. We abuse our ideals, respect, heroes, national honor, and religious base. Political and business leaders abuse the public trust through cheating and corruption. Young people no longer understand why we fought wars to protect our liberties. Some children refuse to recite the Pledge of Allegiance or to sing the "Star-Spangled Banner." Graffiti covers many of our national monuments and our statues of heroes. Children no longer honor their parents or respect their elders.

Summary

The obvious decline in values among the young results from a number of factors. Foremost is that schools have forsaken the responsibility to teach solid values, instead, substituting highly relativistic opinions that undermine parental and religious authority. Children are taught all values are equal, so whatever they value is fine. We can't hold children responsible for this rejection of common morality because their natural tendency is to be selfish. Parents must teach children to share and to respect traditional social values. Historically, we relied on schools to reinforce and extend the basic ethical code families, churches, and other religious institutions teach. In those unfortunate circumstances when parents are unable, or refuse, to teach children right from wrong, schools usually have supplied this important function. Those who now run the schools have forgotten their history, and people who forget will repeat mistakes of the past.

With current high divorce rates and parental lack of attention to their children's moral development, schools should be expected to play an even more significant role in conveying American values to children. In times of family and social stress, schools should exert expanded influence to ensure continuation of our heritage. Active membership in religion is beginning to increase as people recognize the insidious moral vacuum created during the most recent period of permissiveness. But many of our young parents grew up during the 1960s and 1970s, when there was a sharp decline in religious participation and a significant increase in immorality. Without the value base provided by strong religious and national traditions, the United States will be in trouble. Schools must assume an increased responsibility for training students in traditional values. There are some positive and promising new developments in character education, and these deserve strong support.

We must restore basic American values to schools and to our young people, and it is possible. But a potential opportunity is not enough. It is crucial that we move quickly to reinvigorate our school leaders with the resolve to do it. We are facing a crisis of values in society, and the crisis is reflected in our schools. Our society is extremely vulnerable. Schools must reassume their original responsibility for moral teachings.

POSITION 2: LIBERATION THROUGH ACTIVE VALUE INQUIRY

> *. . . the morally good man must try to think out for himself the question of what he ought to do. This "thinking out" is a difficult task. It requires, first, information. . . . I must assess it and bring it together with whatever moral views I hold. . . . this may involve a calculation of which course of action produces greater happiness or less suffering; or it may mean an attempt to place myself in the positions of those affected by my decision; or it may lead me to attempt to "weigh up" conflicting duties and interests.*
>
> —SINGER, 2000, PP. 4, 5

School is not a neutral activity. The very idea of schooling expresses a set of values. Social and individual decisions to provide and to participate in education are based on a set of values. The daily activity of education is value-laden. Everything schools do and decide not to do reflects a set of values. No school is value-free; neither are teachers or students. We educate and are educated for some purpose we consider good. We teach what we think is a valuable set of ideas. How else could we construct education? It would be absurd to have schools without goals, teaching without purpose, curriculum without objectives.

Schools, then, are heavily involved in a series of value-based decisions related to the kind of person and society we want to produce. Schools provide values education through a variety of forms, whether intended and thoughtful or not. When education about values is thoughtful, it incorporates society's primary ideals expressed and examined by students in a rational, respectful approach. That requires it to be an intelligent approach respecting student learning and maturity, consistent with basic moral and democratic principles. Rather than preach morality and goodness, it expects students to develop reasoned recognition of core civilizing values and correlated ethical behavior.

Students come to school with a collection of values and opinions on good and bad; these have been acquired from family, TV, friends, and other experiences. Students do not come to school as empty moral vessels, waiting for proper values to be poured in. Even primary-grade children have a pretty clear sense of right and wrong; in fact, they are almost too clear in their determination of what is fair and what is not and who should get punished and for what infractions. There are few gray areas. Try playing a game with young children and see how rules are interpreted. Maturity brings a more sophisticated sense of justice, morality, ethics, and values—much of which is honed among families, friends, media, and such institutions as formal religion and schools.

Good character is a work in progress, exhibited in actions in situations where morals, values, and ethics are tested. Values education should critically examine traditional and contemporary moral ideas, and test and refine a set of personal beliefs about ethical conduct. Attempted indoctrination by slogans, moralisms, and dogmatic piety does not meet that high standard and can result in nonthinking knee-jerk reactions. Examples of unethical and immoral actions by some clergy and corporate executives over the past decade show that moral righteousness can be spoken by everyone, but moral action requires a higher level of principles and fortitude. There are no guarantees, but more likely good results from value inquiry than from programs of moralisms and authoritarian pronouncements. Sociologist J. S. Victor (2002) points out that "It is much more useful to offer our children a path to follow than a battery of abstract values . . . a way of thinking rather than a code of rules to follow" (p. 31).

Liberation = Education

Education's primary purpose is liberation. Liberation from ignorance is the foundation beneath freedoms from slavery, dictatorship, and domination. Freedom to know underlies the freedom to participate fully in a democracy, enjoy and extend justice and equality, live a healthy and satisfying life, and provide the same opportunities to others. These are all solid values students can examine and relate to their own lives. But that inquiry requires freedom. Freedom to think and freedom to act are based on freedom to know. Any society intending to be free and democratic must recognize an elemental equation: liberation = education. Schools that restrict and contort the minds of the young oppose that principle, and democratic civilization is the victim. Since students learn a lot about values by observing the operation of values in the world about them, unreasonably authoritarian schools convey antidemocratic values inconsistent with many basic moral principles, in addition to being disrespectful of student intelligence.

Clearly, this is not an essay in favor of abandoning the civilizing characteristics of human society, including decency, respect, responsibility, courage, and magnanimity. Indeed, it is the opposite—a plea in favor of values inquiry that offers to empower students to develop and enhance civilization without hypocrisy. We cannot impose traditional values on schoolchildren without allowing criticism of those values. Students, in traditional values indoctrination courses, learn conformity to authority, not thinking. Value inquiry into basic values of civilization will yield stronger, more realistic convictions among students than mere sloganeering and student conformity. Often, as a result of student passivity and obedience, such moral problems as social injustice and inequality are ignored. Instead of questioning and acting to improve society, students are expected to sponge up moralisms and be quiet. Philosopher Maxine Greene (1990) argued moral choice and ethical action should be products of careful and critical thought. That occurs when the community provides freedom and encouragement for individual students and teachers to engage in such thinking.

There are, of course, reasonable limits and conditions to this concept of freedom, as there are to all freedoms. Very young children require guidance and direction in basic good habits. And the small number of people whose development has been arrested at an equivalent level of infancy or young childhood may require some caring authoritarian control for their own safety and well-being over much of their lives. We should expect the vast majority of children and school students, however, to mature in terms of intellect and values, progressing beyond fixed habits and adopting a reasoned understanding and independent judgment of suitable values and ethical conduct.

That maturing requires the opportunity to question, challenge, and critically examine moral pronouncements within the context of a considered view of right and wrong. Does that mean we support a school approach to values as anything goes? Absolutely not. It means students need to fully comprehend social mores and values and recognize and take responsibility for the consequences of their actions. It also means they must understand and reason through moral principles undergirding adequate ethical conduct and values. Such principles as humanity and human rights, justice, equality, freedom, and civilization deserve considerable and rational deliberation in terms of how they can be used as standards against which to weigh ethical conduct and values in given situations. Confronted with a choice between rational deliberation and emotional outburst, few thinking students will pick emotion. They want to reason, even as emotion plays some role in their decisions. Given a choice between freedom and slavery, most will pick freedom—and for good reasons. Value inquiry involves the original thinking through of fundamental moral principles, testing those principles in the cauldron of value conflicts in society and daily life, providing opportunity to rationally criticize, and developing a more consistent set of values and operational ethics. This is not license to do whatever one wants, and it is clearly not blind obedience to authority.

As social scientist Alan Wolfe (2001) found in interviews across the United States, a concept of moral freedom is evolving. Moral freedom draws from ideas similar to those political, economic, and religious freedom ideas flowing from the revolutionary ideas in the founding of this society—a recognition that freedom and democracy are necessary cohabitants. Wolfe notes that previous ideas of character formation required unthinking obedience to institutional authoritarianism, based on the idea that individuals were basically evil and needed correction:

> ". . . character formation involved the alchemist task of making something good (virtue) out of something bad (human nature) . . . the process of character formation, premised on individual weakness, always sits uncomfortably in a liberal democratic society. . . . Highly structured systems of moral authority require

> that we repress our instincts and needs for the sake of authority. But if we believe ourselves to be inherently good people—or at the least neither good nor bad—why can't we trust ourselves more and learn to trust institutions, which are capable of abusing the power they have, less?" (Wolfe, 2001, pp. 179, 180)

We have certainly seen enough authoritarian institutions who have abused their power in the past decades. From churches to government to corporations, there are plenty of examples of abuse. Some who preach morality, ethics, and responsibility have been found to be wanting in exactly those areas. But this new moral freedom from such authoritarianism does not lead to personal anarchy or irresponsibility, with no central values. Many key traditional moral precepts remain, but, as Wolf points out for those he interviewed: "In an age of moral freedom, moral authority has to justify its claims to special insight" (p. 226). Legitimacy and credibility are necessary conditions for sound moral authority. Wolf found respondents had strong feelings supporting such traditional values as loyalty, self-discipline, honesty, and forgiveness. They had consulted authorities and institutions, but did not simply obey them, in arriving at these values. They were struggling with how to apply them to everyday life in a variety of situations, but felt free to do that and question them at the same time. This is a form of value inquiry based on the concept of liberation, consistent with the research of Coles (1997) and Piaget (1997) on how moral reasoning develops. As Eisgruber (2002) comments,

> One of the defining characteristics of liberal democracy is that persons must give reasoned justification for the power they seek to exercise; they behave undemocratically insofar as they rely only on personal status or authority . . . the liberal democratic state teaches most powerfully by example, not by sermonizing. (pp. 72, 83)

Principles of liberation and education operate whether students are learning basic skills and knowledge, or values, ethical conduct, morality, and character development. While it may be possible to develop basic skills and rote information in dogmatic and dictatorial schools, that denies the concept of independent thinking necessary to a democracy. It is, therefore, undemocratic to teach academic subjects in that system. Similarly, it is possible to indoctrinate students with values and ethical standards, but that approach is inconsistent with democracy and independent thinking. In addition to being undemocratic, teaching values and ethics in authoritarian settings that brook no challenge also is counterproductive. The purpose of values education is to get students to understand, examine, derive, and thoughtfully adopt a set of socially positive values that can be translated into ethical behavior. Authoritarianism is in opposition to that purpose; it requires only obedience, blindly.

The Humanist magazine, in 1998, reprinted a 1947 article by Thayer (1947/1998) persuasively arguing that effective character education (1) grows out of active relationships; and (2) is positive, not negative. Thayer's premise grew from educational philosopher W. H. Kilpatrick's observation that children learn what they live and live what they learn. This expresses the idea that children's values and ethics are influenced by their real environments, not by the dogma of hypocritical pronouncements, moralisms, or memorized do-nots. This is a sound, commonsense position for values education in the twenty-first century also.

School Decisions About Values Education

The issue is not whether schools should be engaged in values education, since all are by their very nature. Rather, the issues are what kinds of values should be central to schoolwork, and how should they best be taught and learned. Teachers, textbooks, and schools in general all teach some set of values to young people. Schools can be organized and operate in ways that develop conformity, obedience to external authorities, and passive, docile behavior. Schools also can work to develop thoughtful critics of society's problems, students who are willing to challenge social norms and pursue continued improvement of humankind into the future (Kidder, 1994; Haydon, 1995). There are many variations on these purposes of either socializing students to conform to social values or liberating them to engage in social improvement.

Unfortunately for those who believe schools have more significant social purposes, much contemporary school activity is devoted to producing docile, passive students who will be unlikely to challenge the status quo or raise questions even in the face of unreasoned authoritarianism. Current materials for teaching values and character in schools often are intended to protect the status quo, make students vessels for conformist behavior, and offer a noncritical perspective on religious views. Kohn (1998), for example, provides ample evidence that "conventional character education rests upon behaviorism, conservatism, and religious dogma" (p. 455). Even more unfortunately for students and society, schools often are successful in this purpose. School life focuses far too much on conformity, placing extreme pressure on all students to think, behave, and view life in the same way. This not only is hypocritical, since many adult citizens and educators do not adhere to the moralistic standards prescribed, but it destroys our young people's creativity and energy. It also leads to passivity in civic life—a serious malady in a democracy.

John Stuart Mill (1859/1956) defines the commonplace conformist education of his time:

> A general State education is a mere contrivance for moulding people to be exactly like one another; and as the mould in which it casts them is that which pleases the predominant power in the government—whether this be a monarch, a priesthood, an aristocracy, or the majority of the existing generation—in proportion as it is efficient and successful, it establishes a despotism over the mind, leading by natural tendency to one over the body. (p. 129)

Mill's comments still are appropriate today. Sadly, many schools aim to produce obedient citizens to assure social control, not critical thinking to enhance the society.

In traditional schools, students are force-fed moralisms and value precepts inconsistent with what they see in society. Poorly paid teachers preach honesty while wealthy financiers, bankers, and politicians loot the public. Well-heeled or well-connected people who commit so-called white-collar crimes seldom are punished, although a few may be sent to luxurious detainment centers for brief stays. However, people from lower-social-class backgrounds who commit nonviolent crimes often receive long and debilitating sentences in standard prisons, where they learn more criminal behavior. Even recent U.S. presidents who engage in questionable ethical behavior—sexual or corporate—are given credibility, as though the behavior is acceptable. These obvious disparities in our concept of justice, and in our other values, is evident to students. Similar examples of disparity in equality, justice, honesty, and citizenship abound in our national life. Students are well aware of these inequities. A moralistic slogan or required reading in school does not hide the defect.

Liberation Education and Critical Pedagogy: Values Inquiry

Liberation education offers opportunity to examine social problems and conflicting values. It is linked well with ideas of critical pedagogy, a program to assist teachers to engage students in this examination (Shor, 1987; Burbules and Berk, 1999; see www.perfectfit.org; www.csd.uma.org). Liberation education is not a prescribed set of teacher techniques, a specific lesson plan, or a textbook series for schools to adopt. There is no mechanistic or teacher-proof approach that will produce liberation. Critical pedagogy is anything but mechanical and teacher-proof; it is dynamic and teacher-oriented. Devious and robotlike educational theories, such as behavioral objectives and mastery learning, are not part of liberation education or critical pedagogy. Liberation is the emancipation of students and teachers from the blinders of class-dominated ignorance, conformity, and thought control (Shor, 1987; Clark, 1990; Ahlquist, 1991). Its dynamic quality views students and teachers as active participants in opposing oppression and improving democracy (Giroux, 1991). Applied to values, it proposes students inquire into basic moral concepts, apply them to disparities in society's values, examine alternative views, and arrive at a valid and usable set of ethical guidelines. It is grounded in reason, based on well-examined beliefs. A very popular ethics course at Harvard appropriately includes work on liberation education (www.ethics.harvard.edu).

Liberation education is complex, because the social forces it addresses are complex. The central purpose is to liberate the individual and society and to broadly distribute liberating power (Freire, 1970; Glass, 2001). It requires a set of values, including justice and equality, to serve as ideals in opposition to oppression and authoritarianism, and a critical understanding of the many cultural cross-currents in contemporary society and mechanisms of manipulation that hide ideological purposes. Liberation education and critical pedagogy uncover myths and injustices evident in the dominant culture. They also embrace the expectation that the powerless can, through education, develop power. This requires us to recognize that forms of knowledge and schooling are not neutral, but are utilized by the dominant culture to secure its power.

Schools must become sites where we examine conflicts of humankind in increasing depth to understand ideological and cultural bases on which societies operate. The purpose is not merely to recognize those conflicts or ideologies, but to engage in actions that constrain oppression and expand personal power. This profound, revolutionary educational concept goes to the heart of what education should be. Schools themselves need to undergo this liberation, and we should take actions to make them more truly democratic. Other social institutions also merit examination and action. Obviously, liberation education, a redundant term, is controversial in contemporary society. Liberated people threaten the traditional docility and passivity schools now impose.

What Should Be Taught

Liberation education for values inquiry requires us to blend curriculum content with critical pedagogy. We cannot separate what students study from how they study it. The basis of this approach to schooling is to engage students in critical study of the society and its institutions with the dual purpose of liberating themselves from blinders that simply reproduce old values that continue such ethical blights as greed, corruption, and inhumanity; and liberating society from oppressive manipulation of people by government, corporate, and institutional propaganda.

Critical study involves both method and content. It expects an open examination and critique of diverse ideas and sees the human condition as problematic. That places all human activity within the scope of potential curriculum content and makes all activity subject to critical scrutiny through a dynamic form of dialectic reasoning.

Obviously, students cannot examine all things at all times. Thus, selection of topics for study depends on several factors, including what students previously have studied, and the depth of those investigations; which contemporary social issues are significant; students' interests and maturity level; and the teacher's knowledge. There is no neatly structured sequence of information all students must pass through and then forget. Knowledge is active and dynamic; it is complex and intertwined. Students should come to understand that, and to examine the nature of knowledge itself. That can lead to liberation. And liberation develops strong character.

Among topics of early and continuing study should be ideologies. Students need to learn how to strip away layers of propaganda and rationalization to examine root causes. Ideology, in its most literal sense, is the study of ideas. Those ideas may be phrased in a language intended for mystification, or designed to persuade people. Racism and sexism are not considered acceptable public views in the United States, and yet they often lie behind high-sounding pronouncements and policies. Test scores from culturally biased tests are rationalized to segregate students for favored treatment in neutral-sounding nonracist and nonsexist terms, but basic causes and consequences are still racist or sexist. Imperialism is not considered proper in current international relations, but powerful nations do attempt to control others through physical or political-economic means while labeling their actions defensive or even "freedom fighting." Ideological study can help students situate events in historic, economic, and political settings deeper and richer than surface explanations.

Mainstream Mystification

Too little in popular educational literature speaks to liberation, opposition to oppressive forces, and improvement of democracy. Most mainstream educational writing raises no questions about the context schools sit within; the writers seem to accept the conservative purposes of schools and merely urge us to "fine-tune" them a bit. Standard educational writing does not examine our schooling system to the depth of its roots, ideologies, and complexities. Instead, teachers and teachers-in-training read articles on implementing teaching techniques and making slight modifications in curriculum. There is nothing critical in these pieces, and no liberation of the mind from strictures of a narrow culture. The dominant concern is to make schools more efficient, mechanical, factory-like, and conformist.

Mainstream educational literature rests on a mainstream of thought in American society. This thought is bound by a narrow band between standard conservative and liberal ideas. Those who go outside this band are labeled radical or "un-American" and viewed with suspicion. Outside ideas and criticisms have no public credibility. Neither conservatives nor liberals are pleased to see schools critically examine American democracy.

Conservatives and liberals do seem to agree that U.S. schools should support democracy. Numerous platitudes about schools preparing citizens for democracy, or about schools as a minidemocracy, fill mainstream literature. This literature can be classified as mystification because it uses high-sounding phrases to cover its ideology, a continuation of status quo and power of the already dominant class. It is not active democracy, with its liberation values, that this literature commends. The real purpose of this line of thought is to keep the masses content as uncritical workers who believe themselves to be free but actually are bound and powerless. The function of mainstream writing, in other words, is to mystify readers with a rhetoric of freedom while maintaining domination of the powerful.

Current educational terms, such as *excellence, standards, humanistic,* and *progressive,* fill mainstream periodicals. Although the terms may be useful in discussing education, they often serve as camouflage. Conservatives use the terms excellence and standards to mask the interests of the dominant classes in justifying their advantages and the interests of business in production of skilled but docile workers. Liberals use the terms humanistic and progressive to hide a soft, comfortable individualism that ignores society's basic problems and conflicts. Together, the terms combine the business ideology dominating schools and society and narcissism preventing groups from recognizing defects in that ideology. That is *mystification*—an effort to mystify the public and hide the real school agenda.

That agenda is to maintain what Joel Spring (1976) calls a "sorting machine," sorting different social classes into various categories of citizenship. Raymond Callahan (1962) documents this agenda as a business orientation in schools, designed to prepare the masses to do efficient work and the elite to manage. Jean

Anyon (1980) exposes the actual curriculum of docility and obedience taught to the lower classes. Henry Giroux (1988) describes the hidden curriculum imposing dominant class values, attitudes, and norms on all students. And Aronowitz and Giroux (1991) identify the need for a strong schooling in criticism to buttress students against crippling effects of traditional values society imposes.

The mass media amplify conservative and liberal arguments about schooling, but, in fact, little separates them. Schools can and do, by making slight modifications every few years, accommodate each side for a while. The pendulum swings in a narrow arc from the center, but schools remain pretty much the same, with only cosmetic changes. When conservatives are in power, people express more concern about competition, grading, passing tests, and knowing specific bits of information. Liberals try to make students feel happy, allow more freedom in the curriculum, and offer more student activities.

With regard to democracy and schooling, differences between conservative and liberal views lie in how narrowly democracy is defined and at what age students are to begin practicing democracy. Conservative rhetoric calls for a narrower definition and inculcation of good habits and values among students at an early age. Liberals call for a somewhat broader definition and for establishment of schools as places where students pretend to practice a form of democracy.

Neither conservative nor liberal mainstream views raise questions about democracy's basic nature or the means we use to achieve it. Neither view is critical of existing class domination over knowledge and schools. Neither sees democracy as problematic, deserving continuing critical examination to improve it. Both views assume there is a basic consensus on what democracy is, and that schools are an agency for achieving it. As a result, conservative and liberal views about schooling in a democracy differ very little. The two groups express only shallow differences over what subjects schools should emphasize and how much freedom students should have. Those may sound like important differences, but debates over such matters as how tough grading practices should be or whether students need extra time for reading drill do not address serious, significant issues of democratic life. Ideologically, conservatives and liberals share basic beliefs. Their form of values education is devoted to the status quo to avoid confronting more serious social problems of injustice and inequality.

Reactionary Indoctrination and Cultural Reproduction

Only the far-right reactionary fringe appears to desire schools and a society that are basically undemocratic in purpose and operation. At least the far-right wing is honest and direct, if wrong in their approach. These reactionary groups, including religious fundamentalists, are clear that a hierarchical social order must be imposed on children in schools. There is nothing democratic in that premise. Right-wingers are open advocates of indoctrination and censorship. If you know the truth, why would you present other ideas? Dissent, of course, should be stifled because it confuses children of all ages, and deviation cannot be tolerated. This view has potentially disastrous consequences for any democracy and its schools.

Interestingly, both conservatives and liberals expect indoctrination, but are loath to tell anyone because it sounds undemocratic. Instead, since they control schools and society, they can impose their dominant views by more subtle means. Through state laws, this coalition controls school curriculum, textbook selection, school operation, and teacher licensing. State agencies—for example, a state department of education—monitor schools and prescribe limits. The news media, which also are dominated by mainstream conservative and liberal forces, persuade the public that democracy is working relatively well. Basic ideological disputes on social values are not confronted because no real disputes arise between standard conservative and liberal views.

So schools are expected to indoctrinate students into mainstream culture, and the mainstream has the power to require conformity. "Cultural reproduction" means each generation passes on to the next the dominant cultural ideology that was imposed on it. In the United States, this cultural reproduction takes two forms: (1) a set of positive beliefs that the United States is a chosen country, with justice and equality for all and the best of economic systems; and (2) a set of negative beliefs that any views raising troubling questions about American values are automatically anti-American. This twofold reproduction ensures teachers and students will not engage in serious critical thinking, but will merely accept dominant ideologies. Thus, the very nature of democracy, and means for improving it, are perceived as naturally existing and beyond the school's scope of inquiry.

In school, students read mainstream literature, hear mainstream views from teachers and peers, see mainstream films, listen to mainstream speakers, and engage in mainstream extracurricular activities. The school library carries only mainstream periodicals and books. Finding an examination of highly divergent ideas is virtually impossible. When students are not in school, they read the mainstream press, watch mainstream TV, and live in families of people who were educated in the same manner. Teachers prepare in colleges where they study mainstream views of their subjects and the profession of teaching. No wonder schools are prime locations for cultural reproduction; they contain no other sources of ideas. To have mainstream ideas broadly represented in schools is certainly not improper, but to suppress critical examination of those ideas, and limit students to such a narrow band of ideas, is not liberating.

Students often are surprised to stumble on a radical journal or book legitimately challenging basic assumptions about capitalism and U.S. politics and their impact on justice and equality. Those students rightfully are concerned about an education that did not permit them to consider opposing values and ideologies. Unfortunately, the vast majority of students never come across radical materials, or they automatically and unthoughtfully reject any divergent views because schools have effectively sealed their minds.

Mainstream Control of Knowledge

Not only do schools sort and label students and limit the range of views that undergo examination, but they also provide class-biased knowledge to differing groups of students. Michael F. D. Young (1971), a British sociologist, has argued that "those in positions of power will attempt to define what is taken as knowledge, [and] how accessible to different groups knowledge is. . . ."

Essentially, those in power in schools guard knowledge they consider high status and use it to retain power and differentiate themselves from the masses. Although some auto mechanics, for example, must use complex skills and knowledge, it is not considered high-status knowledge. Law and medicine, which also utilize complex skills and knowledge, are considered high status. Access to these professions is restricted. As Michael Apple (1990) notes, a relationship exists between economic structure and high-status knowledge. A capitalist, industrial, technological society values knowledge that most contributes to its continuing development. Math, science, and computer study have demonstrably more financial support than do the arts and humanities. A master's degree in business administration, especially if from a "prestigious" institution, is more valuable than a degree in humanities. Technical subjects, such as math and the sciences, are more easily broken into discrete bits of information, and are more easily testable than are the arts and humanities. This leads to easy stratification of students, often along social class lines. The idea of school achievement is to compete well in the "hard" technical subjects where differentiation is easiest to measure. Upper-class students, however, are not in the competition, since they are protected and usually do not attend public schools. The upper middle class provides advantages for its children; the working-class child struggles to overcome disadvantage.

Separation of subjects in the discipline-centered curriculum serves to legitimize the high status of hard subjects and academic preparatory sequence. Few critically examine the organization of knowledge or understand it as class-based or problematic. Instead, schools present information in segments and spurts, testing on detail and ranking students on how well they accept the school's definitions. We pretend that knowledge is neutral, that numerous subject categories and titles are merely logical structures to assist understanding. This separates school learning from social problems, reinforces the existing authority's domination over what is important to know, and maintains students as dependent and uncritical thinkers.

The Dynamic Dialectic

Liberation education requires teachers and students to engage in a dynamic form of dialectic reasoning to uncover ideological roots of significant values. A dynamic dialectic opens topics to examination. It does not impose a set of absolutes with a known truth, but operates more like a spiral, digging deep into rationales. It examines the topic in its total social context, not in segments as in the discipline-centered curriculum. And it requires a vision of liberation allowing students to dig beneath the topic's surface to uncover its basic relationships to society's structure and to dominant interests. The purpose of the dialectic is to encourage students to transcend their traditional nonactive, sterile roles and accept active roles as knowledgeable participants in the improvement of civilization. In theory, the dialectic is never-ending, since civilization is in continual need of improvement. In practice in the schools, the dialectic is limited by time, energy, interest, and topics under study.

Liberation education expects schools will explore highly divergent ideas. But this in itself is insufficient. These divergent ideas must be examined in a setting where they can be fully developed and are perceived as legitimate, rather than strange or quaint. Adequate time and resources must be available, and censorship and authoritarianism kept at bay.

To ensure a truly liberated society, one cannot expect less of schools than education for liberation. Critical pedagogy offers a major opportunity to move in that direction. An emancipatory climate in schools will regenerate students and teachers to fully use their intellects and creativity. Those are fitting and proper goals for schools, unachievable under restricted mainstream forms of schooling our society now practices. This is values inquiry for liberation.

For Discussion

1. You have been asked to recommend ten members to a local advisory council on Values and Character Education. The council's charge is to identify how schools should approach teaching values and character development.
   a. What process would you go through to find the best people?
   b. What kinds of people would you select, and how many of each? Why?
   c. What educational background should be required?
   d. What occupations should be represented, and in what proportions?
   e. What groups or agencies should be represented, and in what proportions?
   f. What age, gender, or ethnic categories should be represented, and in what proportions?
   g. What other characteristics would you look for?
   h. What kinds of people would you want to exclude? Why?
2. Paulo Freire, a major advocate of liberation education, claims that traditional teaching is fundamentally "narrative," leaving the subject matter "lifeless and petrified." Freire writes:

   > The teacher talks about reality as if it were motionless, static, compartmentalized, and predictable. Or else he expounds on a topic completely alien to the existential experience of the students. His task is to "fill" the students with the contents of his narration—contents which are detached from reality. . . . The more completely he fills the receptacles, the better a teacher he is. The more meekly the receptacles permit themselves to be filled, the better students they are. (1970, pp. 57, 58)

   Does this description fit your experience in schools? What evidence can you provide? Criticize Freire's view of this "banking" form of education. Has he properly characterized what happens in schools? Should it happen? What are the social costs of changing to liberation education? What are the costs of not changing? What would be an example of an antithetical position to Freire's?
3. Many agree we should teach values in school, but disagree about which values and who makes that choice. Some propose everlasting universal values; others propose utilitarian short-term values; some propose general and vague social values; and still others propose values based on individual or immediate circumstances. What is a

reasonable way to determine what kind of values education we should teach in U.S. schools? What possible social consequences can you foresee for the various forms of values education? Who should decide on which values should be taught?

4. Values and character are two very important dimensions of education. If indoctrination is one view of how values should be imparted—a thesis—and relativistic open inquiry is another—an antithesis—what are some possible school approaches that could represent a synthesis view? How do your justify your proposal?

References

AHLQUIST, R. (1991). "Critical Pedagogy for Social Studies Teachers." *Social Studies Review* 29, 53–57.

ANDERSON, D. (1994). "The Great Tradition." *National Review* 46, 56–58.

ANYON, J. (1980). "Social Class and the Hidden Curriculum of Work." *Journal of Education* 162, 67–92.

APPLE, M. (1990). *Ideology and Curriculum.* 2nd Ed. London: Routledge & Kegan Paul.

ARONOWITZ, S., AND GIROUX, H. A. (1991). *Postmodern Education: Culture, Politics, and Social Criticism.* Minneapolis: University of Minnesota Press.

BENNETT, W. J. (1992). *The De-Valuing of America.* New York: Summit Books.

———. (1993). *The Book of Virtues.* New York: Simon & Schuster.

———. (1994). "America at Risk." *USA Today* 123, 14–16.

BLACKBURN, S. (2001). *Being Good.* Oxford: Oxford University Press.

BORK, R. (1996). *Slouching Toward Gomorrah: Modern Liberalism and American Decline.* New York: Regan Books.

BURBULES, N., AND BERK, R. (1999). "Critical Thinking and Critical Pedagogy." In T. Popkewitz and L. Fendler, eds., *Critical Theories in Education.* New York: Routledge.

CALLAHAN, R. (1962). *Education and the Cult of Efficiency.* Chicago: University of Chicago Press.

CHARACTER EDUCATION INSTITUTE. (1998). (Available online at http://www.charactereducation.com)

CHRISTENSEN, B. (1991). "Pro: The Schools Should Presume that Parents have the Primary Authority to Determine the Cultural Traditions to Be Transmitted to Pupils." Debates in Education. *Curriculum Review* 31, 6–10.

CLARK, M. A. (1990). "Some Cautionary Observations on Liberation Education." *Language Arts* 67, 388–398.

COLES, R. (1997). *The Moral Intelligence of Children.* New York: Random House.

COLSON, C. (1994). "Begging for Tyranny." *Christianity Today* 38, 80–81.

DALAI LAMA. (1999). *Ethics for the New Millenium.* New York: Riverhead Books/Penguin Putnam.

DIAMOND, S. (1999). *Not by Politics Alone: The Enduring Influence of the Christian Right.* New York: Guilford Press.

EISGRUBER, C. L. (2002). "How do Liberal Democracies Teach Values?" In S. Macedos and Y. Tamir, eds., *Moral and Political Education.* New York: New York University Press.

ETZIONI, A. (1998). "How Not to Discuss Character Education." *Phi Delta Kappan* 79, 446–448.

FALWELL, J. (1980). *Listen, America!* Garden City, NJ: Doubleday.

FREIRE, P. (1970). *Pedagogy of the Oppressed.* New York: Herder and Herder.

GIROUX, H. (1988). *Teachers as Intellectuals.* Granby, MA: Bergin & Garvey.

———. (1990). "Curriculum Theory, Textual Authority, and the Role of Teachers as Public Intellectuals." *Journal of Curriculum and Supervision* 4, 361–383.

———. (1991). "Curriculum Planning, Public Schooling, and Democratic Struggle." *NASSP Bulletin* 75, 12–25.

GLASS, R. D. (2001). "On Paulo Freire's Philosophy of Praxis and the Foundations of Liberation Education." *Harvard Education Review* 20(2), 15–25.

GREENE, M. (1990). "The Passion of the Possible." *Journal of Moral Education* 19, 67–76.

———. (1991). "Con: The Schools Should Presume that Parents Have the Primary Authority to Determine the Cultural Traditions to Be Transmitted to Pupils." Debates in Education. *Curriculum Review* 31, 6–10.

HANSEN, D. T. (2001) "Teaching as a Moral Activity." In V. Richardson, ed., *Handbook of Research on Teaching*. 4th Ed. Washington, DC: American Educational Research Association.

HAYDON, G. (1995). "Thick or Thin: The Cognitive Content of Moral Education." *Journal of Moral Education* 24, 53–64.

HIMMELFARB, G. (1999). *One Nation, Two Cultures.* New York: Knopf.

KIDDER, R. (1994). "Universal Human Values." *The Futurist* 28, 8–14.

KOHN, A. (1998). "Adventures in Ethics Behavioral Control." *Phi Delta Kappan* 79, 455–460.

LATHER, P. (1991). *Getting Smart: Feminist Research and Pedagogy Within the Postmodern.* New York: Routledge.

LEMING, J. (2002). Assessment Database. Character Education Partnership. (www.character.org)

LEMING, J., AND SILVA, D. (2001). "A Five Year Follow-up Evaluation of the Effects of the Heartwood Ethics Curriculum on the Development of Children's Character." Character Education Partnership. (www.character.org)

LICKONA, T. (1991). *Educating for Character.* New York: Bantam.

———. (1993). "The Return of Character Education." *Educational Leadership* 51(3), 6–11.

MCFARLANE, A. (1994). "Radical Educational Values." *America* 171, 10–13.

MILL, J. S. (1859/1956). *On Liberty,* C. V. Shields, ed. Indianapolis: Bobbs-Merrill.

MURCHISON, W. (1994). *Reclaiming Morality in America.* Nashville, Thomas Nelson.

PAIGE, R. (2002). "An Overview of America's Education Agenda." *Phi Delta Kappan* 83(9), 711–714.

PIAGET, J. (1997). *The Moral Judgment of the Child.* Free Press Paperbacks.

RABKIN, J. (1995). "Let Us Pray." *The American Spectator* 28, 46–47.

RAFFERTY, M. (1968). *Max Rafferty on Education.* New York: Devon-Adair.

READ, L. (1968). *Accent on the Right.* Irvington-on-Hudson, NY: Foundation for Economic Education.

ROBERTS, S. V. (1994). "America's New Crusade." *U.S. News & World Report* 117, 26–29.

SCHILTZ, P. (1998). "Don't Leave Religion Out of the Classroom." *U.S. Catholic* 63, 22–23.

SHOR, I. (1987). *Pedagogy for Liberation.* South Hadley, MA: Bergin & Garvey.

SINGER, P. (2000). *Writings on an Ethical Life.* New York: Ecco Press/HarperCollins.

———. (1989). "Developing Student Autonomy in the Classroom." *Equity and Excellence* 24, 35–37.

SOMMERS, C. H. (1998). "Are We Living in a Moral Stone Age?" *Current* 403, 31–34.

SOWELL, T. (1992). "A Dirty War." *Forbes* 150, 63.

SPRING, J. (1976). *The Sorting Machine: National Educational Policy Since 1945.* New York: McKay.

THAYER, V. T. (1947/1998). "The School as a Character-Building Agency." *The Humanist* 58, 42–43.

THURMOND, S. (1968). *The Faith We Have Not Kept.* San Diego: Viewpoint Books.

TOWNS, E. T. (1974). *Have the Public Schools "Had It"?* New York: Nelson.

TYACK, D., AND HANSOT, E. (1982). *Managers of Virtue: Public School Leadership in America, 1820–1980.* New York: Basic Books.

VICTOR, J. S. (2002). "Teaching Our Children About Evil." *The Humanist* 62(4), 30–32.

WEILER, K. (1991). "Freire and a Feminist Pedagogy of Difference." *Harvard Educational Review* 61, 449–474.

WHITEHEAD, B. D. (1994). "The Failure of Sex Education." *The Atlantic Monthly* 274, 55–80.

WOLFE, A. (2001). *Moral Freedom: The Search for Virtue in a World of Choice.* New York: W. W. Norton.

YOUNG, M. F. D. (1971). *Knowledge and Control.* London: Collier-Macmillan.

CHAPTER 13

Technological Literacy: Necessary or Excessive

POSITION 1: FOR FULLY INTEGRATED TECHNOLOGICAL LITERACY: TECHNOLOGY HOLDS THE PROMISE

Schools that functionally reflect the culture of the past, rather than the demands of the future, will not prepare students to thrive in the digital age.

—CEO FORUM POLICY PAPER, 2001, P. 1

There are many possible ways to consider technology and schooling including using technology in classroom instruction, student research or distance learning, improved school design and operation, virtual education and beyond. Technology has the potential to completely reconstruct what we normally think of as schooling, learning, and teaching. From simply using a video, calculator, or computer to help a lesson or do homework to the multiple applications of complex research on brain activity, technology has myriad uses in improving teaching and learning. Inherent in these illustrations is technology's obvious importance to education; it is even more important to society. A major curricular consideration arises from this point: Technology has become so important that we must fully integrate it into the central purposes of schooling. It is knowledge, and is also a major means to knowledge.

No longer can we treat technology as just a collection of devices occasionally used to illustrate a lesson—it is not merely peripheral to fundamental knowledge students must have to survive and thrive in our society. Technological literacy itself is fundamental and should be deeply incorporated in all the main courses of study in schools. There is a historic parallel in the Writing Across the Curriculum project, a very popular movement, which advocates that writing is so important to individuals and society that it should not be limited to English courses, but should be emphasized in all areas studied by students. Technological literacy deserves no less than full integration into schools, a basic part of courses, programs, and activities.

Technological literacy is a prescription for education's future, linked directly to society's future. Our lives are based on technology; we use it extensively; we thank it; we love it; and we have come to expect more with better results and higher quality. Further, the economics and politics of international competition demand that the United States remain in the forefront of technological innovation and development. We cannot let our current status as world leaders in technology slip because we failed to see how important technological literacy is for education and society. This is a fundamental responsibility of schools, one that has far-reaching implications. Through technological innovation, we can put the best schooling in the hands of all children, rural, suburban, or urban. Rich or poor, children can have access to fine teachers, excellent culture, significant science, and interesting learning. Technological literacy deserves to be one of the core subjects of the school.

Defining Technological Literacy

What is technological literacy? It includes a set of *knowledge, skills,* and *attitudes* related to appreciating, understanding, using, and improving technology.

The *knowledge* part involves a working understanding of current technical and operational language, a comprehensive understanding of common technological equipment and related software, a grasp of fundamental scientific and mathematical principles on which technology rests, and an understanding of the history of technology and its impacts on society.

Necessary *skills* are the techniques useful in efficient and effective operation of various technical devices, and those useful in dealing with the results of that work. This would include the ability of all students to comfortably operate widely available technology, from computers and telecommunication to image reproduction and robotics. It also includes skills used in evaluating, reporting on, and correcting or repairing technological material.

The *attitudes* portion includes an awareness of the need for continued technological innovation, an openness to change and a desire to improve technology, and an optimistic sense that recognizes the value of technology to social and individual lives. (Hunter, 1992)

This functional set of knowledge, skills, and attitudes represents technological literacy, necessary to all citizens in contemporary society. Technology should be included in the basic education required of all students throughout their school careers. For schools, that is a dynamic responsibility because technology is constantly changing—and so must education.

Good Reasons for Fully Integrating Technological Literacy into Schools

Social Value

The United States requires a populace well informed about new technologies, their use, and social value. Education is society's front line in technological advancement. Technological literacy is the beginning point and schools are the obvious place to start. No other institution in society has taken such broad responsibilities for the development of various literacies—the ability to read, write, speak, understand, and apply information—among the young. Schools have a long, proud tradition of providing a common curriculum in necessary and important learnings: language use, civic responsibility, computation skill, scientific and economic understanding, and appreciation of the arts. Each involves literacy, with schools offering the means to student comprehension and use. Because of technology's obvious and increasing significance to human life and societal well-being, schools must undertake basic education in technology.

Technological education also offers more chance for improving democracy. It provides the means for equalizing educational opportunity, something American schools have tried to do with moderate success for over a century. It can be the great equalizer society has been seeking, far better than busing. With proper facilities in schools, public places, and homes, technological schooling can replace schooling that has become segregated by race or class. The machines do not differentiate among users, except for those more proficient than others, and proficiency develops with experience and good guidance. Without specific intervention by humans, machines do not shut off a student quest for information because that student is a member of a minority group or is from a family in poverty.

Improved Learning and Teaching

An extensive body of research shows student achievement, improved teaching, and more efficient and effective use of schools result from integration of technology into schools. Johnson and Barker (2002), examining studies of about 100 educational technology projects funded by government sources, present a wide range of studies reporting positive results from using technology: improved student outcomes in cognitive knowledge and information access, and improved teaching. Their work offers a sourcebook on measures of the impact of technology on teaching and learning. Mann (1999) reports on a statewide West Virginia longitudinal study showing "technology-enhanced" students achieved significantly higher scores on standardized basic knowledge tests in several grades than those without the enhancement. Ringstaff and Kelley (2002) analyzed findings from a large variety of research studies on the use of technology on learning and teaching, finding substantial improvements in most subjects. Chaika (1999), summarizes many research studies showing beneficial learning and teaching resulting from the use of technology in schools to support her contention that technology "does" make a difference in schooling.

The Apple Classrooms of Tomorrow (ACOT) study, concluded in 1998 after 13 years, was one of the longest continuing educational research projects of its kind. One particularly important conclusion of this study was that "introduction of technology into classrooms can significantly increase the potential for learning—especially in collaboration, information access, and expression and representation of student's thoughts and ideas" (Apple Classrooms of Tomorrow Study, 2000; Sandholtz, Ringstaff, and Dwyer, 1997). Rinstaff and Yocam (1996), in ACOT Report number 22, studied teachers who used technology and found improvements in classroom organization, increasing level of teacher use of technology, and positive differences in personal philosophy toward teaching—more excitement, feelings of capability and accomplishment.

Economics, Business, and Global Competition

Among those supporting a strong role for schools in technological literacy are major educational associations and businesses. The CEO Forum, consisting of members from such diverse and influential organizations as the National Education Association and the National School Boards Association, and such corporations as IBM, Dell, AOL, Hewlett-Packard, and Apple, was founded in 1996 to provide leadership to ensure that America's schools "effectively prepare all students to be contributing citizens and productive workers in the 21st century" (CEO Forum, Policy Paper, 2001). A Forum document shows the reasons and presents recommendations:

> **Reasons**
>
> The emergence of new information technologies, the evolution of the global digital economy, and the global competition for technically skilled workers creates a national urgency to improve our educational system. . . . This is an issue of preeminent national importance. . . . Unless we continue to ensure that our educational system improves student achievement for all students, the future of our nation and our children is threatened.
>
> **Recommendations**
>
> 1. Broaden our definition of student achievement to include 21st century skills. The Department of Education should establish accountability models for the inclusion of 21st century skills as an additional discipline.
> 2. Expand federal support for education technology investments. The federal government should double the national investment in education technology.
> 3. Increase investment in research and development and dissemination. The federal government should increase its investment in dedicated education technology research and development to at least $100 million. (CEO Forum Policy Paper, 2001)

Opening Horizons

Looking at one example of the impact of technology on education, the Pew Research Center (2002) issued a study of student use of the Internet showing that by September 2001:

94% of students used the Internet for school research;

71% used it as a major source for their most recent school project;

58% used a website set up by their school or class;

34% downloaded study aids; and

17% have created a web page related to a school project.

This aspect of technology provides significant resources for schooling, resources students recognize. The U.S. Department of Education also recognizes this potential, assisting in the wiring of all schools and achieving a remarkable result: In 1994 about 35 percent of public schools had Internet access, by fall 2001 99 percent of public schools had access. And the ratio of students to computer has decreased, from 12.1/1 in 1998 to 5.4/1 in 2001.

The Office of Educational Research and Improvement (OERI) of the U.S. Department of Education offers a vision for educational technology that includes three purposes:

1. Integrate current and future information and communication technologies into *everyday* (emphasis in original) teaching and learning;
2. Create programs that capture opportunities offered by appropriate emerging technologies; and
3. Reform the *context* (emphasis in original) in which technology is being integrated into schools.

This, the OERI argues, should enable schools to:

Customize and improve teaching;

Individualize and improve learning;

Achieve equity; and

Effect systemic change. (Johnson and Barker, 2002)

Full integration of technology and technological literacy into the heart of schools benefits society and students. In addition to Internet connections, schools with state-of-the-art equipment and teaching materials, a suitable technology curriculum, and teachers well-prepared in the use and value of various technologies are a necessity. Schools play a particularly important role in diagnosis, delivery, and development of technological literacy. Qualified teachers diagnose the students' technical knowledge and skill in reference to national standards, deliver appropriate learning to improve student mastery, and develop innovative and interesting teaching materials and techniques for continuing improvement. Further, schools must provide a supportive, sustaining environment for technology, assisting teachers and other staff to acquire and improve their own knowledge, skills, and attitudes to further that education for students.

Setting Standards for Technological Literacy

National educational standards have a major impact on schools, providing focus for curriculum and instruction and offering accountability to society. Any subject not included in approved national standards is destined to be marginalized in schools. English, history, math, and science have approved standards. Technology has demonstrated its importance to society and schools; we need national standards for technological education to offer accountability for technological literacy and avoid marginalization.

The National Educational Technology Standards (NETS) project of the International Society for Technological Education (ISTE) provides the basis for standards documents in over 80 percent of the states. These standards pursue the idea that technology enables students to become capable users, information seekers, problems solvers, communicators, analyzers, evaluators, and decision makers—thus, informed, responsible and productive citizens (National Educational Technology Standards, 2002).

ISTE standards for students are grouped by type, and include these:

1. Basic Operations and Concepts, e.g., *standards*
   Demonstrates knowledge (sound understanding) of the nature and operation of technical systems
   Is proficient in the use of technology
2. Social, Ethical, and Human Issues, e.g., *standards*
   Understands social, cultural and ethical issues related to technology
   Practices responsible use of technology, information, systems, and software
   Develops a positive attitude toward technology and uses that in support of collaborative efforts, personal pursuits, lifelong learning, and increased productivity
3. Technological Communication Tools, e.g., *standards*
   Uses telecommunication effectively and efficiently
   Uses a variety of media
4. Technological Productivity Tools, e.g., *standard*
   Uses technological tools to enhance learning and promote creativity

The full set of proposed standards, and any updates, are available at www.cnets.iste.org (Oct. 2002; updated Dec. 2002).

The ISTE Standards project includes specific student performance indicators by grade level, to guide teachers and school staff in shaping a technological curriculum to meet the standards and make accountability clearer. Examples include:

> By grade 2: Students will use input devices (mouse, keyboards, etc.) to successfully operate technical equipment like VCRs and computers.
> By grade 5: Students will discuss basic issues related to the responsible use of technology and information
> By grade 8: Students will apply strategies for identifying and solving common hardware and software problems; and will exhibit ethical behavior when using technology and information.
> By grade 12: Students will identify the capabilities and limitations of current and developing technological resources and evaluate the potential of these in meeting personal, lifelong, and workplace needs.
> Students will be able to make informed decisions among technological systems and services.
> Students will collaborate with others to contribute to a substantial knowledge base by using technology. (National Educational Technology Standards, 2002)

The ISTE performance indicators just exemplified provide schools with a logical, consistent sequential system for developing technological knowledge, skills, and attitudes—technological literacy. High national standards for technological education will give a substantial boost to technological literacy for students and society. Until the political process for federal approval is completed, these are some clear criteria and performance objectives for student achievement in technological literacy.

An Expanding Role for Technological Education

Seymour Papert (2002), noted MIT mathematician and pioneer in artificial intelligence, expects even more of our schools in this work. He argues that most discussion of technology's role in schools has been related to two valuable but short-term purposes:

1. Improving existing practice in schools (e.g., how to teach content subjects); and
2. Introducing very simple forms of literacy for using computers or technology, set up as "vocational knowledge" to help workers.

Papert considers these two purposes insufficient, lacking the necessary vision of what technology can bring to schools. In contrast, he thinks technology can:

1. Change the whole system of schooling to improve learning and teaching (e.g., show that knowledge is interdisciplinary with no need for separate, compartmentalized subjects; that the learning process has continuity without a need to segregate students by age).
2. "Mobilize powerful ideas" (e.g., use virtual reality to try things out, offer immediate feedback from multiple sources).
3. Encourage "children to become a driving force for educational change instead of passive recipients" (e.g., students teach along with teachers, children's curiosity stimulates innovative uses for technology).

From this view, technological literacy goes beyond basic operations and information to expand and engage students and teachers in redesigning the very nature of schooling and learning. That is a tall order, but Papert is an enthusiastic, reasonable, and infectious advocate. His position illustrates the potential of a well-developed technological literacy program in schools.

Obstacles to Technological Literacy: Cost and Staffing

There are, however, several obstacles to adequate technological literacy, including financing, adequate staffing, suitable curriculum, technological fear, and the traditional slow speed of educational change.

Financing the cost of massive technological literacy is an important issue, but must be weighed against the social costs of not preparing students for twenty-first century technical life. If such literacy is not provided, we expand the digital divide between the well-to-do and the poor. A ten-year national investment in wiring schools has helped to close that divide (Edutopia, 2002), and Internet access in public schools has increased each year, moving from less than one-third of all schools in the mid 1990s to virtually all schools now ("2020

Visions," 2002). Another effort is the development of Community Tech Centers (www.CTCNet), under an NSF grant, to establish a national network of over 600 affiliates and more than 4,000 locations (Edutopia, 2002). One project involving the National Urban League, Boys and Girls Clubs, YMCA and YWCA groups, and others, with help from the Bill and Melinda Gates Foundation, will technologically link over 7,000 libraries (Edutopia, 2002). Schools have help in this literacy work, but adequate financing must be found for continued support in schools.

Another obstacle to technological literacy is that some teachers fear, or are reluctant about, technology, and are not prepared to properly educate students. A teacher who is fearful of technology avoids it as much as possible. Some teachers disparage new computer or telecommunications devices as useful only for "entertainment" or "self-indulgence." Teacher-imposed classroom rules often prohibit students from bringing in technological equipment; school rules may limit use of such equipment in the building. McKenzie (1999) points out that "Except for a hardy group of pioneers who have shown what is possible, the bulk of our teachers lack the support, the resources, or the motivation to bring these intruders (new technologies) into the classroom core" (p. 1). Several of McKenzie's (1999, 2000, 2001) books are designed to assist schools and teachers in overcoming this obstacle with practical ideas and classroom suggestions.

Research into how teachers use laptop computers provided by the district show teachers mediate the value and use of school computers through their own concepts of what counts as legitimate learning and their views of technology (Windschitl and Sahl, 2002). A sizable number of teachers see laptop computers merely as a "presentation" tool and "marginalize every aspect of the laptop" in their classrooms (p. 197). Others may find laptops somewhat useful, but only as a supplement within their standard approach to teaching. And some would use them effectively, but they would have to rethink what they considered good pedagogy and change their teaching styles in substantial ways. Without broad support, the likelihood of that happening across a school district is not very high.

Some schools unintentionally create obstacles to student use. In many current schools, students find it difficult to get access to various media devices and experimentation is not permitted. The school computer room is separate from the real classwork areas, limited to select students or use or times, and is heavily controlled and monitored. It also has far too few computers, often older models, with creaky programs and little maintenance. Only certain students get special training on computers, and none is permitted to alter the programs, settings, or school standard operating arrangements for computers, even to repair them. This is hardly a setting that encourages technological literacy or advancement.

Most schools now have computers, but seldom enough for each student to have easy access at convenient times, during class lessons, or for long periods. Computers often are used for "special" work, "events," or personal use for homework and e-mail in the library. That hardly ties them into the ongoing educational activity in classrooms. Sometimes computers and other equipment are kept under lock and strict supervision to "protect" them from student misuse.

Teachers and administrators often perceive technical equipment as expensive and separate from standard schoolwork. They don't trust the students, and they may be uncomfortable around the equipment themselves. Sometimes they suspect students are using computers and other equipment inappropriately, as in "surfing" the Internet and finding something interesting. There may even be a moralist orientation with concerns about student access to sexual, drug, or other "banned" material. This fear adds fuel to efforts to limit and control student use, and student technological literacy.

Many students learn advanced technology through home computers and communications equipment; they have some skill in manipulating new technology; and their attitude is one of positive curiosity and eagerness about the latest advances. But some of these students attend schools where the chalkboard is king, where teachers teach and keep records in the most labor-intensive way, and where teachers fear or scorn technology. We are, then, in the ludicrous position where schools may be far behind students' level of technological knowledge and skill.

Without easy access to up-to-date learning equipment, technologically prepared and inspired teachers, and the necessary positive attitude about technology, these schools limit their students. Students get education shock, equivalent to culture shock, when they leave these schools for work and discover the level of technological skill needed in the workplace: The rest of us suffer from an unprepared workforce.

Obstacles: Slow Pace of School Change and Fast Pace of Technological Change

Technological change seems to be happening faster and faster, but not school change. The time gap between discoveries in science and their application has been shortening at an increasing rate as a result of computers and other new technology. It took more than one hundred years before scientific discoveries about light in the eighteenth century were transformed into technology for photography. Over sixty-five years passed between nineteenth-century science behind electric motors and technology that provided them for everyday use. The gap between discovery and technology that produced radios was some thirty-five years. In the twentieth century, the gap between discoveries in atomic theory and technology for atomic weapons was only six years, and from science to technology on transistors was only three years (Gleick, 1999). The science-technology gap is narrowing; what of the schooling gap?

Papert (1993) compares a hypothetical doctor and a teacher who come from 1900 into today; the doctor would be amazed at changes in medicine and health care, but the teacher would notice little fundamental change in schools. Technology transformed medical practice, but has only superficially changed schools. Recent developments in computers, lasers, robotics, gene research, telecommunications, and transportation influence everyday lives of virtually all people. Schooling should keep up with these developments. Some current schools, however, operate in patterns reminiscent of the schools from the

Victorian period to World War II (Papert, 2002). The teacher and chalkboard, student desks with paper and pen, group-based classwork, and a bell-ring schedule for work continue. The speed of technological change is awesome; the slowness of school change is debilitating.

Nearly all the technology we now consider state-of-the-art will be completely redesigned in the next decade or so; that is a pattern shown historically. *The Futurist* magazine ("50 Trends Shaping the World," 1991), based on history, predicted that all technology now in use will make up only 1 percent of what will be available by 2050. Internationally, studies show that only a handful of nations, such as Canada, Finland, and Slovenia, have arranged to have all schools connected to the Internet (Pelgrum, 2001). In the nations surveyed, the most significant obstacles to improving information and communication technology in schools were the lack of computers (identified by 70 percent) and teachers' lack of knowledge or skills (66 percent). Table 13.1 shows the highest-ranking obstacles identified by school principals and school experts in technology in twenty-four nations surveyed.

The research, redesign, and expansion of technology during your lifetime will be done largely by people who are now in school and those who follow them. The future of our society and individual students is bound up in what schools provide. But schools are old-fashioned, balky, and heavily bureaucratic. They stress slow-moving, labor-intensive, and boring approaches to knowledge. Much time is wasted on inefficient school operations and classroom activities. Students can graduate technologically illiterate, unprepared for life and jobs in a society based on high technology. Use of the latest in contemporary technology, and instruction designed to stimulate further technological innovation, would improve school operation, provide significantly better education for students, and benefit society's continued growth.

Table 13.1. Obstacles to Information and Communication Technology Improvement*

Rank	Obstacle
1	Insufficient computers available
2	Teachers lack knowledge or skills
3	Problems integrating into curriculum
4	Getting computer time into schedule
5	Insufficient equipment or software
6	Insufficient teacher time available
7	Lack of supervisory staff and technical assistance
8	Outdated network
9	Insufficient training opportunities
10	Lack of adequate school space

*Identified by school principals and school technology experts in 24 nations

Source: Pelgrum, W. J. (2001). "Obstacles to the Integration of ICT in Education." *Computers and Education* 37(2), p. 173.

Obstacles: Gaps in Achievement

We have a continuing deficiency in U.S. scientific and technological education. Comparative tests of math and science achievement show American students well behind some European countries and Japan. Over the past quarter-century, science has declined in the amount of classroom time spent in elementary schools. Technological education was discounted, turning it into training programs to handle nonacademic students or those who misbehave—training on obsolete equipment with ill-prepared teachers. Math, science, and technology are very significant subjects; the United States should not be behind in these areas.

Buck and colleagues (2000) note the predicament faced in this effort: "For some reason, Americans generally have difficulty understanding science . . . for many people, science courses are dreaded high school and college classes" (pp. 73, 74). Yet we have a fascination with science and such products of science as new technologies. Schooling has not brought students the enjoyment and practical value of scientific understandings, perhaps because school makes such study too formal and uses cumbersome, theoretical language. Technological literacy is a literacy of practice; it involves doing things, operating devices, and trying out innovations. It requires the application of scientific knowledge. Few people fully understand the scientific theories that provide remote controls on our TVs, global positioning that maps routes in our new cars, or wireless digital transmission of correspondence. But most can use and maintain these and a multitude of other contemporary technological devices.

We have to address serious deficiencies in our schools that lead to fear or distaste for science, math, and technology; find ways to increase technological literacy to destroy the digital divide that separates ethnic groups and social classes, forcing many into illiteracy, and provide modern laboratories, equipment, learning materials, and scientifically and technologically competent teachers for all students. We should revamp schools to feature advocacy of technological improvements and offer incentives to those who do it successfully.

Developing Technological Literacy

Education occurs in a variety of locations, under a number of circumstances, at any time, and through uncountable individual interests. Technology not only is a necessary subject to be taught, it offers the means and variety to improve and expand all learning for twenty-first-century schools. Devices offer virtual situations and simulations that approximate real life and provide extraordinary learning experiences not available from books and teachers. Computer programs exist in English literature and grammar, histories of all types, math beyond belief, philosophy, multiple combinations of sciences, any of the arts, foreign language and culture, homemaking and home construction, and any other topic deemed important or interesting. Distance learning programs allow students to stay at home, sit on a beach, wait in a line, sip some milk and eat cookies, or be anywhere and still connected for learning.

Some progressive schools plan to provide a laptop computer for each student from the fourth to seventh grade, a move that will significantly alter how classrooms operate, if we can find able teachers (Windschitl and Sahl, 2002). Students can gain understanding, via technology, of the most theoretical and most applied knowledge. And that knowledge can be rerun as often as students desire until it is mastered or revised.

Not only are available technological options for education more interesting and involving, they are lower in cost and time than many equivalent educational activities. A trip to Italy to use Italian and see art can be simulated by computer at far less than by plane and guide. Designing a building or city is more efficient by computer. Reconstructing historical events is possible and educationally entertaining by computer. Obviously, technology can't fully substitute for real experience, but is far better than the unreality typifing standard schooling, and is safer and more open to multiple tries and modification than real experience. It allows rapid rethinking with "what-if" possibilities, stretching student thinking and creativity.

Available technology in schooling also is intellectually stimulating, interactive, visually stunning, pleasing in sound, and engaging of mind. It is tuned to individual student interests, tastes, and levels of knowledge—it is customized education that can be reorganized and resorted to fit changes in interests or level of understanding. Such education can occur at various times in libraries, on laptops, in centers, at home, by hand-held device, and multiple other means, locations, and times (O'Neil and Perez, 2003). In addition, there is evidence that introduction of technology into classrooms has many other educational benefits, including a significant increase in the potential for learning (Apple Classrooms of Tomorrow Study, 2000).

Good examples of school-related programs aimed at improving technological literacy include FIRST (For Inspiration and Recognition of Science and Technology), a national championship robotics competition among school students. About 650 high schools from the United States and Canada compete, using students to design, build, and operate robotic devices of all types. Over 16,000 people attend the national event (Kirsner, 2002). Another interesting idea for matching school ideas with technology is offered by Warlick (2002) through a website at www.landmark-project.com, which provides students and teachers the opportunity to redesign an old-fashioned school to one they desire to suit contemporary society. Your imagination can visualize well-equipped classrooms where you would enjoy learning. It is likely to be a far cry from the rows of seats, walls of chalkboard, and a lone 21-inch TV on a rolling cart that we know too well. You can also go on to design a complete technologically advanced school, a place of excellent education and a model for enriching the minds of this century. Virtual schooling is not beyond real possibility; some fourteen states have state-sanctioned virtual high schools now, and 40,000 to 50,000 students are in virtual education (Winograd, 2002).

Education and Technological Development in Society

Any large-scale effort to stimulate scientific achievement, improve technology, and make business more efficient has a basic reliance on schooling. To expand new ideas beyond the inventor's desk or laboratory requires some form of education. What might have happened to the lightbulb, automobile, and calculator if there was no way to educate people in their manufacture, proper use, maintenance, and repair? Inventors must rely on a well-educated workforce and consumers to have success in the marketplace. An innovation that cannot be taught or learned has serious limitations in it use. New inventions also depend on education. Representing the White House Office of Science and Technology at the 200th Anniversary of the U.S. Patent and Trademark Office, Richard Russell said that 52 percent of the nation's growth since World War II has come through invention (Leary, 2002). Several of the nation's most influential inventors advocated educational programs to provide students with strong backgrounds in science, math, and technology to encourage invention. Noting that Robert Solow won the 1987 Nobel Prize and the President's Medal in Science in 2000 for "establishing that technology and related innovation are responsible for at least half of US economic growth," Bonvillian (2002), points out that "the spirit of inquiry behind science is not self-sustaining, it is increasingly dependent on societal support" (p. 28). Technological literacy offers the opportunity to extend the benefits of technological improvements throughout the whole society.

Technology has changed our lives, and that will continue. It is impossible to imagine modern life without phones, washers, television, or computers. We expect to travel thousands of miles in a few hours by plane; someday we see travel on space flights. We can find cheaper, more exotic, or more personalized trips on the Internet, have our itineraries sent electronically to inform relatives, arrange payment for the trips with a credit or debit card, electronically pay that bill from a bank account, with frequent flyer mileage and special bonuses credited to other accounts, and have the whole process taken care of in minutes without paperwork or driving from place to place. Robotic devices can largely handle the manufacture of dangerous, difficult, and specialized equipment that make our lives better, more secure, and more satisfying. We communicate by voice, document, photo, and personal interaction instantly with people all over the world. Our trade, communications, transportation, social infrastructure, and daily lives involve extensive use of new technology. Even more significant than obvious lifestyle improvements are the enormous advances in health care through technology over the past decades ("The Telesurgery Revolution," 2002; "Cyberkinetics," 2002). Longer life, better health, easier body repair, and improved quality of life are all the result of technological improvements.

There is no better way to assess the future development of American science and technology than by examining our educational system. The future of American enterprise exists in the schools. We can tinker with current technology for short-term improvements, but long-lasting development depends on new generations of scientists, inventors, business leaders, skilled workers, and knowledgeable consumers. If schools falter, we are committed to continuing decline in society and in world leadership.

Summary

Technological progress requires talented people, with solid educations, and substantial resources in funds, facilities, and encouragement. Schooling is the key to continuing scientific achievements. In the past century, expansion of public schooling and a shift toward science and technology, new attitudes among workers and management about technology in the workplace, government encouragement of research and development, improved patent systems, and incentives for innovation helped make America powerful (Williams, 1982, p. 396). Bromley (2002), points out how we overtook European nations in new knowledge in science and technological innovation after World War II by effective use of technology, giving us a jump-start on the emerging global economy.

The United States has the good fortune to be populated by people with entrepreneurial spirit and scientific curiosity. Our schools were noted for their early interest in scientific and technological education. And we have had a government and economic system that encourages individuals to develop new ideas for consumer goods and services. These ideas have made life easier, better, and more comfortable for American citizens. They also have produced many opportunities for hardworking people to have jobs and attain good incomes. And our democracy is stronger with technology's equalizing power if we can distribute that knowledge widely. We are all better off from this combination of factors. But the United States faces greater competition in technology, development, and manufacturing. This poses a threat to our standard of living and international leadership.

School is a location where the young learn to share and acquire the cultural tradition while preparing to shape the future. Technology is a significant element in defining our culture, identifying and preserving our traditions, and rethinking our future. We must address our current state of technological education and change to a much more aggressive approach to technological literacy for all and advanced work for those who can benefit. More than a simple educational issue, technology is an issue of national and international development. We need and deserve a school curriculum that makes technological literacy a major goal; that is best done by fully integrating it into our schools.

POSITION 2: AGAINST TECHNOLOGICAL EXCESS: FOR CRITICAL TECHNOLOGICAL EDUCATION

> *. . . without a broader vision of the social and civic role that schools perform in a democratic society, our current excessive focus on technology use in schools runs the danger of trivializing our nation's core ideals.*
>
> —CUBAN (2001, P. 197)

Raising Questions

Education about technology can be a useful effort, especially in a society so heavily invested in technology. Schools should be preparing people to live well in the contemporary world and participate in improvements into the future. These are broad educational goals that transcend, but include, technology. Living well and participating in future progress requires an education in the humanities and sciences that offers criteria, knowledge, and processes for making judgments about a good quality of life, including critical assessments of a technological society. That education encourages thoughtful questions about technology and society to help people reason through the value, use, and impact of technological innovation.

However, a school curriculum heavily dependent on and highly focused on technology is unlikely to offer such questioning or critical evaluation. Although there is strong commercial interest in having schools adopt a technology-heavy and noncritical school program, educational needs of students and society are not met in such an environment. We must actively and persistently raise questions about technology and such sponsorship, and question whether devotion to technology is the best use of curricular time for students and public finances for schools. Integration of technology into the whole of the school is, in addition to being a major corporate interest, an effort to hide the serious warts and blemishes of educational technology and diminish challenges teachers and students should be raising about technology in school and society. It also will take away precious time from an already crowded academic agenda and sap financial resources.

Despite the view presented by heavy marketing, technology is not always positive for individuals, society, or schools. Some technology has positive attributes but also carries very negative consequences—sometimes hidden by advocates. We need to raise such questions as whether the human costs and benefits of any technology favor the benefits, why the technology is being advocated, and who really benefits from it?

Technological literacy, that basic familiarity with machines and skills used to operate them, may be sufficient for limited vocational purposes to produce workers capable of taking orders for fast food, keyboarding information, or taking inventories. Or it may be enough for entertainment or recreational use: playing games, seeing videos, listening to music, or sending e-mails. But it is not enough for full education. Uncritical technological literacy can produce true believers, technology consumers, and facile users—a satisfactory result for manufacturers and marketers of technology. But unsatisfactory for a democratic society that expects knowledgeable, thoughtful citizens, and that must demand more of education.

A good life is far more than the ability to read manuals and operate new devices, and technological education is more than just recreational or vocational training to use machines. Education is rich and intellectually rewarding, entailing posing of questions, examination of issues, and search for adequate evidence. These are elements of critical thinking, needed in the study of technology in society and school. Technological issues, both social and educational, are suited to examination in classes because schools exist to help students comprehend and deal with aspects of their environment, and technology has certainly become a major player in all of our environments.

The Need for Critical Technological Education: in Society and in Classrooms

Advocated here is the idea of *critical* technological education, where serious questions are raised about technology and its multiple impacts on individuals, society, and schools. The addition of the word critical to the idea of technological education or literacy changes the concept in basic ways. This phrase connotes an analysis of technology that does not varnish over or ignore important negative implications. It does not simply accept excessive claims made for technical improvements, as though there were only benefits and no social, human, or educational costs. Critical technological education expects students to fully examine claims and evidence provided by advocates and opponents of more technology, measured in terms of supportable criteria derived from civilizing individual and social values.

This essay is not antitechnology; it is against the overselling of technology with little critical examination. It also is against development of a school curriculum or school system where technology is a main ingredient, for similar reasons. The headlong and uncritical plunge into technology over the past decades has had mixed results. We can identify many splendid achievements through new technology, such as some medical breakthroughs, but the negative side of our compulsive lurch into techno-ecstacy often is overlooked. Toxic and waste-littered environments are but one example; antibiotic-resistant bacteria and privacy-jarring surveillance instruments and cell phones are others. Has the wonder of technology stimulated our enchantment with it, or just extraordinarily good salesmanship? Have we been sold a bill of goods, the cost of which comes back to haunt us? A residue of social and educational problems follows the technological explosion.

Schools should be the best places for students to engage these kinds of questions without commercial or ideological interference or influence. The mass media, corporations, and those with strong linkage to technological development cannot be expected to provide both sides of this argument fairly; forces related to the marketplace and ideology limit media and business presentation of negative ideas about technology they like or in which they have huge investments. Current and future social impact of technology is directly related to the kind of instruction and questioning that goes on in technological education.

Good educators want good schools with students engaging important ideas; such teachers also want students to learn, use, and improve their critical thinking. Whether working with students on the study of technology or using technology in the classroom to explore another topic, responsible teachers recognize the importance of critical thinking on significant ideas and issues. Where technological innovation serves those ends in classrooms, teachers will pursue it with relish. But educators realize educational technology is not a panacea, and does not exist in a social vacuum. There are large-scale issues beyond the classroom use of machines, issues involving the use, value, and impact of technology in society. Critical examination of the social context of technological innovation and the instructional use of technology are both topics of importance to educators.

Using a machine that is fast and fancy in providing information is insufficient as an educational goal and it is equally insufficient as a social goal. Technology offers tools that can be used to provide a better educational or social environment, but the same tools can be used for frivolous or malevolent purposes—they are only tools. Criminals and police both use technology. Terrorists and intelligence agents also use technology, as do couch potatoes and research scientists. We should subject technology to critical examination in terms of education and society. The essential question is: Does the new technology improve or diminish the quality of life for most people? If it does, then we need to ask whether or not the technology is worth its various costs. Answering those questions involves dealing with many other questions about technology, history, social values, and making choices. We cannot expect students to use and improve their critical thinking if teachers don't use it themselves on such issues as the role and impact of technology.

Each improvement in technology requires a trade-off. Some are worth it, others are not. Unfortunately, the United States has a long love affair with technology that often blinds us to a full understanding of the trade-offs. Technological marketing has worked very well. Infomercials and other advertising ignore or gloss over negative side effects and consequences to show new technology in its most favorable light. Commercial and corporate financial support for obtaining classroom television, computers, teaching equipment and materials, and other resources places schools in a position that can tax the resolve of good educators. Many schools run the risk of commercialization that dims the critical opportunity for education. Strong corporate encouragement and funding for expansion of technology in schools has added to the massive advertising myth that technology is nearly always beneficial and contains the answers to human problems. We are a society that seems drawn to the newest, most dazzling gimmick promising to save us work, pain, time, and thinking. In education, however, we have an obligation to provide as full a story as we know, offer students divergent views, and encourage challenges. Critical technological education offers an solid alternative.

Underachievement of Technology in Schools: The Hype and the Reality

In schools, technology has overwhelmed but underachieved its forecast educational dream. It has not fulfilled the many promises made, such as improving learning and lowering schooling costs. In 1922, Thomas Edison predicted that "the motion picture is destined to revolutionize our educational system and that in a few years it will supplant largely, if not entirely, the use of textbooks" (Lee, 2000, p.48). Edison was a brilliant inventor, and a wise businessman who financed educational films and understood that his work on motion pictures would be significantly enhanced if they did supplant textbooks. But he was not much on prediction. Movies have changed much of American life and influenced teaching, but they have not replaced books, libraries, or reading.

Other "seers" have predicted at one time or another that radios, phonographs, audiotapes, television, video courses, programmed textbooks, teaching machines, and/or computers would each replace teachers and classrooms (Frank, 1935; Cuban, 1986; Light, 2001). These devices certainly have helped schools and teachers in their work, but have not replaced them. A presumption behind the idea that technology will replace teachers or schools is that technological devices offer more variety and consistent quality, and are more efficient, cheaper, controllable, and generally better than teachers. Had those characteristics actually been demonstrated in use, teacher replacement would have occurred long ago with movies, radio, or TV. Most of these innovations have evolved into forms of entertainment, useful in, but not central to, education. And many of these former wonder devices now sit unused in school storage closets or tossed onto trash dumps. As Julie Landry (2002) noted, "Yet, after hundreds of exhaustive studies, there remains no conclusive proof that technology in the classroom actually helps to teach students. In fact, in some cases it hinders learning" (pp. 37, 38). There is more to good education than mechanical presentation, even when that presentation uses all kinds of eye-and-ear-catching accompaniments.

The current expensive effort to wire all schools for Internet access and provide massive numbers of computers for student use is predicated on the idea that learning will be improved by an increase in technology availability and use. Corporations and government have given much support to this program, arguing it is essential to education and competition with other nations. Increasingly, one measure of whether schools are doing well is their level of investment in technology. And it is a heavy investment, costing much more in maintenance, updating, facilities, software, new equipment, staff and student time, and related expenses than most schools and taxpayers realize. Not only will the national wiring of all schools cost billions, school districts will take on the burden of paying extremely large amounts of money to maintain and improve connections. Further, the Northwest Education Technology Consortium ("Equity Gap in Technology Access," 2002), organized under the National Technology Corps and affiliated with Americorps and VISTA, noted that only 6 percent of all wired schools have trained personnel to put in the available curricular material.

There is another, perhaps more important, toll on the teaching profession and on educational policy when public perception of good schools focuses more on technology than learning. Even some supporters of technology in education agree the focus should not be on technology; as Jamie McKenzie (2001), editor of *From Now On—The Educational Technology Journal,* notes, ". . . it is wrong-minded and shortsighted to make technology, networking, and connectivity the goal" (Introduction). This problem is illustrated by the current craze to get more computers into schools, without providing well-prepared teachers, effective educational program, and critical literacy elements McKenzie and others advocate.

Computers in Classrooms

Significant expansion of computers in schools often is accompanied by a blind and mistaken belief in technology and collateral decline in support for the academic work of schools (Apple, 1991). Computer specialist and skeptical critic Clifford Stoll (1999) recognizes the danger of technology overselling and a school obsession with machines:

> I shrug when businesses blow fortunes on dubiously useful gee-gaws, but I'm furious to watch our schools sold down the river of technology. Throngs of educators, lemming-like, line up to wire their schools. . . . Meanwhile English teachers must deal with the cry for computer literacy while coping with semi-literate students itching to play with computers who can't read a book. . . . A computer can't replace a good teacher. But that's what happens when a fifty minute class gets diluted with a fifteen minute computer break. . . . I believe that a good school needs no computers. And a bad school won't be much improved by even the fastest Internet links." (p. xiii, xiv).

Stoll argues that computers do not even belong in schools for a number of reasons, including:

They distract from the more important thinking goals of education;

They have limited use in learning and excessive use in simple entertainment; and

They require only low-level skills of transitory value to operate them.

In terms of academic learning, there is little evidence that computers add much. Cuban (2001) studied classroom use of computers in the place most likely to be in the forefront of educational technology: the Silicon Valley in Northern California. His research found no strong, consistent evidence students increased academic achievement by using information technologies. Even in classrooms where teachers were serious computer users, students mainly used the machines for word processing to complete assignments, play games, or get information from the Internet or CD-ROMs. Computers did not become the classroom's central feature. The concept of the computer as an interactive online teaching/learning machine that replaces or minimizes teachers and significantly expands students' educational horizons was not demonstrated. This result occurred even in the home region of computers, the one location in the United States where one would expect to find extraordinarily good computer-based education. Despite large expense and heavy promotion of computers, Cuban found that less than 5 percent of teachers actually integrated computers into regular classroom routines and less than 5 percent of students had computer experiences that could be classified heavily technological, and those were usually activities in nonacademic areas or school support service. Cuban concludes the study by commenting, ". . . overall, the quantity of money and time have yet to yield even modest returns or to approach what has been promised in academic achievement, creative classroom integration of technologies, and transformations in teaching and learning" (p. 190).

Computer use in schools also has shown inadequate return on the investment in other nations. Economists Angrist and Lavy (2002) studied computer use in Israeli schools a few years after the national lottery provided about 35,000 computers for many schools—at a cost of $3,000 per computer, not counting wiring and maintenance. A statistical analysis showed that "There is no evidence, however, that increased educational use of computers actually raised pupil test scores" (p. 3). Indeed, there was surprising evidence of a negative effect of computer use regarding math scores at the fourth- and eighth-grade levels, more surprising since the fourth grade was where the computers were reported to have the largest impact on teaching methods. One explanation offered was that computer-assisted instruction (CAI) "may have consumed school resources or displaced educational activities, which, had they been maintained, would have prevented a decline in achievement" (p. 23). The cost of the computers was about $120,000 per school, equivalent to four teacher salaries, and the annual depreciation rate of the computers and software was calculated at 25 percent; thus, Angrist and Lavy summarize, the flow cost of these computers is about one teacher per year. They conclude ". . . the question of future impacts remains open, but this significant and ongoing expenditure on education technology does not appear to be justified by pupil performance results to date" (p. 27). In contrast, the authors note that research has shown that reductions in class size and more teacher training do benefit student learning.

This recent research follows a troubling history of similar findings that computer use adds little to learning. Healy (1998), in a work summarizing much of the research on computers and learning, says:

> It is less amusing to realize that research to be cited throughout this book demonstrates how computer "learning" for young children is far less brain-building than even such simple activities as spontaneous play or playing board games with an adult or older child. "Connecting" alone has yet to demonstrate academic value, and some of the most popular "educational" software may even be damaging to creativity, attention, and motivation. . . . Even for older children and teens, research has yet to confirm substantial benefits from most computer-related products at school or at home. (pp. 20, 21)

Schools often use computers simply for workbook kinds of activity, wherein students try to find answers to posed questions by using signals in the computer program. Some have excellent visuals and interesting narratives, impressive sets of information, can stimulate mental activity, and create good puzzles for students to address. Still, most students realize that the whole of the material is contained in the program, and their work is not to think outside that box. A few program manufacturers try to actively involve students in learning, but these often are very complicated and take much more class time and teacher involvement to perform adequately. Most programs, however, use the workbook format, though in a more seductive form. Students develop an inclination to get the quickest, most efficient right answer that they know is hidden in the program. Speed, not thought, becomes more important. This can translate into a distaste for intellectual work that requires struggle or time, uses resources outside of the classroom, and may have no right answer. They lose the richer context of human issues not mathematically computable. It becomes easy just to let machines take over, giving instant gratification and demanding little in response.

School computer use is usually individual and lacks social involvement (Healy, 1998). So-called interactive educational programs are actually highly programmed and provide a limited set of responses to predictable keyboard or mouse entries, with an air of unreality and superficiality. Imagine learning to play tennis using only the computer and not going outdoors to swing a racquet. It could be fun, but it is not tennis. The same occurs in learning chemistry, biology, physics, and many more subjects by computer without labs or outdoors for real experience. Learning by machine does not provide the quality of educational experience that a classroom or lab of live students offers in the various questions and interchanges and experiments. It is a good supplement to classroom vitality, but is not a substitute.

Cutting Costs with Technology: Distance Education

Distance learning is one example of a claim that technology lowers educational costs. For expensive school buildings, teaching staffs, buses, and other school-like activities, we can substitute computers and video systems offering excellent teachers onscreen with professional-quality visuals and vast libraries of virtual resources on call and in locations in or near each student's home. Instead of paying 200 teachers an average $50,000 per year to sit in a room and have students in groups of 25 wander through a building needing maintenance, custodians, cafeterias, and study halls, thousands of students interactively work on computers costing $1,000 with $250 worth of high-quality programs. That appears to be efficient and effective, but would you want to be educated like that over the course of several years?

Where students live vast distances from schools, as in Australia's outback or sparsely settled parts of the United States, there is a good reason to provide the highest-quality TV and computer courses that can be arranged. Similarly, continuing education for professionals and preliminary classes for students who just want to try out a subject for interest may be good places for electronic schooling. For many specific topics and in certain circumstances, distance learning is the best way to organize educational work. But for mass public education, it often is touted as a way to save money and standardize education. Neither of these is an adequate reason to limit our students by massive distance learning. School, of course, is more than a set of taped lectures, an interesting keyboard or mouse activity, some "interactive" homework, and answering questions on a keypad. This trade-off is not worth it.

Distance learning and other forms of technological replacement of schools will be shown, in the long run, to be neither efficient nor effective. The Western Governors Virtual University, a heavily financed program of four states to establish a college available only through technology was expected to enroll 5,000 students, but only ten had registered at the opening. Temple University started a prototype virtual college, but closed it after determining it would not make a profit (Ohman, 2002). At the precollegiate or collegiate level, well-done distance education takes more resources and money—not less. Where it does cut costs, large volume and cheaper distance learning may mean that only the rich can afford real schools and real teacher contact; the rest get terminals.

Speed, Efficiency, and Schooling

Skewed corporate thinking about efficiency, unfortunately, already dominates schools, making them even more factory-like than before. Callahan (1962) provided ample historical evidence that business influences damage education's central purposes by such things as a myopic focus on time-saving and lower costs. The time-motion measurement of nineteenth-century Taylorism still misleads people about efficiency in business and schools. Saving time is, of course, a relative concept and not the only or best measure of efficiency.

Gleick (1999) makes a good point about wasting time, using phoning as an example:

> When you dial for technical support, you may not get through. The telephone has created, along with many forms of supposed time-saving, one of the most peculiar and misunderstood forms of time wastage. The software industry alone leaves Americans waiting on hold for an estimated three billion minutes a year. Then there are the computer hardware manufacturers, the airlines, the utility companies, the telephone companies themselves, and an incalculable number of government agencies. Like Dante's hell, the state of being On Hold has different levels. . . . So modern telephones come with a button that could hardly have been imagined in the early days of telephony: the button that redials the same number again and again. (pp. 234, 236)

School time has a similarly peculiar notion of time-wasting. Field trips, which students identify as one of the most educational of activities, often are considered time-wasting by adults. Recess, the arts, cultural events, long-term deliberation over a philosophic issue, and reflective quiet sometimes are seen as time-wasters in school. Thinking also can be seen as a time-waster because we don't appear busy.

A better concept of efficiency includes a concern for purpose; why do we want efficiency? Efficiency should not be confused with effectiveness but technology has dulled this difference; we now desire more speed and lose patience easily—often losing effectiveness also. Technology, including the more precise measurement of increasingly smaller bits of time as well as miniaturization of a student's entire school career into one SAT score, encourages us to expect simple and quick fixes. This denigrates all but the accumulation of memorization and simplistic, often useless information—in addition to technical skill developed from practice taking tests. It is anti-intellectualism dressed up in technology and corporate language.

Other Problems in Technology-Based Education

In addition to reasonable skepticism about claims for improved learning, lowered costs, equivalence in high-quality education through technology, and efficiency, several other significant issues are posed by technology's intrusion into schooling. Virtual/technology-based education, whether in distance education or on school campuses, lacks the vitality and educative quality of live class and instructor interaction, cutting the opportunity for interpersonal involvement.

We also can expect curriculum changes from a focus on technology, with a decline in time devoted to critical thinking and a neglect of humanities, arts, health, and exercise. One of the educational drawbacks of new technology is that it often is self-protective, while being seductive. It conveys information to students very quickly, develops skills of machine and program usage, and has excellent visual and auditory features. But it does not encourage questioning or critical examination; certainly not examination of the technology itself. We become true believers because we have no other obvious choice. Seymour Papert (1993), a mathematician who supports computer learning, still has reservations about noncritical true believers, "Across the world children have entered a passionate and enduring love affair with the computer. . . . In many cases their zeal has such force that it brings to mind the word *addiction* to the minds of concerned parents" (p. ix). This is echoed by Clifford Stoll (1999), who cautions: "I worry about a naive credulity in the empty promises of the cult of computing. I'm saddened by a blind faith that technology will deliver a cornucopia of futuristic goodies without exacting payment in kind" (p. xi).

Another significant problem resulting from the overselling of technology in schools is deprofessionalization of teachers, a decline in respect for teachers, teaching skill, and the value of academic/professional judgment. This problem is exacerbated by the too-easy manipulation of students, teachers, and curriculum as a result of corporate pressures and institutional control of electronic educational sources and testing. If operation of a machine is all there is to good education, where does that leave teachers at any level? Academic knowledge, teaching experience, instructional theory and practice will come to mean less, leading to no need for credentialed teachers, no respect for the position, no tenure to protect academic freedom, and no security. What happens to schools and education? Erosion of intellectual freedom for teachers and students is a very serious possibility, denying of the open pursuit of knowledge because technology substitutes sterilized and canned material easily controlled and censorable. A related problem is the question of intellectual property; who has economic and editorial rights to material produced for technology and who can change it? With increasing technological incursions into schools, administrators are more likely to become like corporate vendors and teachers will be less likely to make academic decisions about their courses or their students. Teachers will lose instructional freedom and responsibilities for actual education, but are likely to remain accountable for any test results and school failures.

Further problems occur in the corporatization of schooling, technology providing an easy means to make corporations more influential in education by control over machines, software, faculty, and intellectual property (Werry, 2002). Corporate control of Internet content and teaching is not likely to lead to critical education. Michael Apple (1991) raises an important question about technology in schools: Who benefits? His answer is that those already in power gain more and the rest lose more. More than $5 billion per year is spent for computer technology in classrooms, providing great benefits to tech companies (Landry, 2002). Expensive equipment, programs, and maintenance divert scarce resources from other educational activities. Corporate intrusions into education are abundant, but few have been so successful and so generally supported by government and school officials as the effort to computerize all schools.

Technology and the Schools: The Digital Divide

In addition to major educational problems created by uncritical expansion of technology in schools are social and personal problems involving schooling about technology in society. One widely held assumption is that more computers means more democratic technological development. The digital divide, however, has not diminished. It separates high-income people from low, those living in urban or suburban locations from the rural, the young from the old, and the otherwise privileged from those who are not. It is sometimes hidden by the veneer of corporate advertising that implies their products are necessary for all people for a better life. Bill Gates predicted in 1995 that the Internet would assist rural people to stay in small communities, since they would have equal advantage with city dwellers in terms of their access; his foundation provided substantial support to wire and equip many small-town libraries. But recent evidence suggests new computers may aid the exodus from rural areas as people go online to find jobs in other locations (Egan, 2002).

Schools that can afford it add more technology and frills, and those that can't are separated even further. Another divide in the technological workforce also has an educational component. Most jobs created by technology actually will be low-paid and boring work in such areas as maintenance; fewer jobs will occur in well-paid high-tech positions, and these will require more-advanced education. Should schools be responsible for training workers for low-paid, boring corporate jobs and not provide those students with critical-thinking skills challenging that system? Education should work to provide equity by enhancing equality of opportunity. The digital divide seems to move schools in the opposite direction. It separates races and classes even more—producing a new class of poor, the technologically illiterate, with increased disparity between managers and workers. Critical technology literacy offers equalizing in the exercise of critical thinking about technology.

Some Personal Costs of Technology

Our dependence on technology contains the seeds of narcissism, self-love with individuals becoming unconnected to others' political, economic, social, and personal problems. Social responsibility is ignored in the rush for self-satisfaction. Much new technology used in American society separates people and softens the reality of human suffering. We can control TV photos of the reality of starvation or warfare by using our remotes to switch stations. We use computer games of the most unrealistic violence as pleasure time. We have little personal engagement beyond using the dials and controls. The most popular shows often are ones requiring the least mental effort to watch. Standard news shows feature short two- to three-minute summaries of the most important news along with features intended to attract those wanting entertainment. There is a stultifying homogenization of the important with the trivial, little continuity or depth; usually no opposing views are presented. There is a penchant to feature the violent, criminal, and freakish to attract attention and gain viewership—measured by technological instruments mounted on the TV sets of a few select homes.

Not only does technology threaten society and human decency, it contains threats to individual freedoms and privacy. Secret surveillance and invisible recording of personal information, buying habits, interests, and contacts with others now are easily possible through technology. This capacity connotes more than just annoying targeted telemarketing calls, it abrogates basic rights to personal privacy and from illegal search in addition to exerting an unnecessary caution on your exercise of rights to free speech, assembly, and association. It can also be used to steal your personal identity, alter your records, confound your credit, and cause you substantial misery and trouble. Further, censorship by electronic screening of material restricts your access to ideas. Whether by commercial, criminal, or governmental action, technological intervention has multiple implications for personal life.

Social Costs of Technology

In addition to the costs of technology in personal loss of independence, ingenuity, and intellectual stimulation, there are various social costs. When individualism overcomes social responsibility, we lose the contribution many people could have made to improve society. The separating quality of much new technology has fragmented people's lives and added to isolation and alienation. We have become accustomed to expecting increased speed in everyday life, have lost the patience and focused attention that thoughtful reflection or social interaction require, and have seen dissolution of the family and home setting for maintaining social values and attitudes. Social bonds have deteriorated and there are increases in violent and technology-based crime, technologically produced drug abuse, and noninvolvement in community affairs. Technology saps the core of culture, too great a loss for the limited benefits (Postman, 1992).

Technology permits work at all hours, from home or on plane, or anywhere—but has a resulting decline in free time, leisure, and family involvement. We have a common TV dinner syndrome without family discourse or shared interests, and two-worker families necessary to fund new devices. Increasing productivity by use of technology and robots can lead to social discontent when people are displaced from jobs. A West Coast longshoremen's strike and employer's lockout in 2002 was primarily over the issue of replacing jobs by machines. We can expect more strife if we don't alter the way we look at work and income as technology changes the workplace. There is also an apparent decline in social contact and civility by use of technology. We now have meetings by Internet and conference calls, Internet-purchased home delivery of groceries and all other goods, cell phone interruptions that disrupt social or cultural events, increasing forms of public "rage" as a result of technology glitches, a fixation on speed that diminishes enjoyment and support of arts, culture, and a declining interest in crafts and activities that require time and patience.

Technology has been used to monitor and help clean the environment, but has also created significant threats to the environment and ecosystem, including ozone depletion, various pollutions, and health hazards. Other threats include the possibility of inappropriate cloning and inadequate ethics for technological medical research; insufficient regulation of gene research; racist, sexist, humanly degrading content on the Internet; military development of laser, nuclear, biological weapons making mass destruction simple and distant. There are other social costs to technology. Consider the multiple health problems associated with it and related costs in life quality, time, energy, and money. For the users of computers and other equipment, we now have unusual muscle and eyestrain problems, headache, fatigue, crippling hand and arm pain, and potential of other long-term problems from monitor radiation. Cell phones are being investigated for causing some new health problems. Workers in high-tech manufacturing are subject to safety problems from chemical and radiological materials along with many ailments related to that work. In many industries, workers must have protective gear—but we don't know the longer-term results of that protection. Gleick (1999) points out, "Modern times have brought certain maladies that might be thought of as diseases of technology: radiation poisoning (Marie Curie's truest legacy); carpal tunnel syndrome (descendant of Scrivener's palsy) . . ." (p. 102). Beyond the examples suggested, there are many other personal and social costs to technology; school offers opportunity to consider them.

Critical Technological Education

Critical technological education is the full examination of issues involving the use and value of technology in schools, and the many issues that arise in considering technology in the larger society. The overpromise and underachievement of technology in schools represent a major concern for education, one that goes far beyond financing problems. It includes questions about the nature and quality of learning that results, unfortunate alterations in the culture of schools that deprofessionalize teachers and restrict intellectual freedom, and the corporatization of schools and increases in the digital divide. Critical technological education also provides for full study of multiple personal and social costs of technology.

We need education that provides knowledge and skeptical judgment about all forms of technology. This means critical examination of issues created by technology, and taking seriously the vigilant role of a citizen concerned about human society and our futures. Schools are intertwined in the progress and regress of society. Training people to use, accept, and desire new technology is insufficient; it is not education. Education is not served when we simply pass information on to students uncritically. Developing critical judgment is one of the main goals of education; indeed, it is the most important.

For Discussion

1. Technology, some argue, is neutral—it simply exists. The real question revolves around how the technology is used. From that perspective, draft a short statement that addresses these questions:
   a. How should schools organize their use of technology?
   b. What are the best criteria for judging the most educational use of technology?
   c. Should technological innovators be free to develop any technology?
   d. Should technology advertising be regulated to prohibit misleading or incomplete information?
   e. Should education about technology be changed; how?

   Now, draft a short statement of opposite positions, based on the perspective that technology is not neutral. This view would hold that every technology has some value orientation, from potato peelers to hydrogen bombs. For example, hydrogen bombs have a political purpose; new potato peelers make value assumptions about the market, the users, and how time should be used. Contrast the two statements to see if you can find a workable synthesis.
2. Dialogue Ideas: The essays in this chapter propose distinctly different projections about the possible social and educational consequences of a school curriculum heavily weighted toward technology. Select some examples of technology in schools, either from the essays or from your own experience, and present a discussion of your views of the projections. How likely is either of them to occur? Are the potential consequences mostly positive or negative? On what grounds do you determine positive or negative? Do you have some suggestions for enhancing the positives and diminishing negatives?
3. Is there a digital divide? What evidence can you find that supports your contention? How do you define it? If you find a divide:
   a. What are its characteristics—those identifying elements like social class, race, gender, age?
   b. What are the measures you used to identify it—for example: differences in computer skill level, job expectation, number in training programs or jobs, and so on.
   c. Does the divide seem to be increasing or decreasing?
   d. Do you think it is a natural, cultural, or educational divide?
   e. What would you propose doing about a divide?

   If you do not find a digital divide:
   a. What criteria and what resources did you use to get evidence?
   b. What explanation would you have for public concern about a divide?
   c. What policies would you propose to prevent a divide?
4. What would you think if a local school offered programs to prepare students to

   build and use crystal sets to collect radio waves?
   study by whale oil light, with only one copy of a book available for the class?
   build wood fires to heat the classroom?
   weave and construct their own daily clothing?

   What would you think if a local school offered programs for students to

   stay away from school for all courses and all years, with school-provided technology?
   have an implant to permit instant information transfer to the brain?
   get full school credit for Internet game scores?
   graduate only if they invent one important technological innovation?

Using your sense of the development of technological education over the next thirty to fifty years, present your view of a school of the future. Include physical features and curriculum.

5. How would you define technological literacy? Interview several friends to see how they define it. Compare the definitions according to such criteria about the interviewees as:
   a. age and gender
   b. relative amount of technological expertise
   c. any other obvious differences

   Given the comparison of views, what tentative conclusions can you draw about the definition that schools should use in preparing students in this area?

References

ANGRIST, J., AND LAVY, V. (2002). "New Evidence on Classroom Computers and Pupil Learning." *The Economic Journal* 112, 1–31.

APPLE, M. (1991). "The New Technology." *Computers in the Schools* 8, 59–79.

APPLE CLASSROOMS OF TOMORROW STUDY. (2000). (www.apple.com/education/k12/leadership/ACOT.html2000)

BONVILLIAN, W. B. (2002). "Science at a Crossroads." *Technology in Society* 24(1–2), 27–39.

BROMLEY, A. (2002). Science, Technology, and Politics. *Technology in Society* 24(1–2), 9–26.

BROWN, C., AND CAMPBELL, B. A. (2002). The Impact of Technological Change on Work and Wages. *Industrial Relations* 41(1), 1–33.

BUCK, J. A., ET AL. (2000). "Communicating Science." *Science Communications* 22(1), 73–87.

CALLAHAN, R. (1962). *Education and the Cult of Efficiency.* Chicago: University of Chicago Press.

CHAIKA, G. (1999). "Technology in the School: It *Does* Make a Difference." *Education World.* (www.education-world.com)

CEO FORUM ON EDUCATION AND TECHNOLOGY. (2002). Five Year Project. (www.ceoforum.org)

CEO FORUM POLICY PAPER. (2001). "Education Technology Must be Included in Comprehensive Education Legislation." (www.ceoforum.org) March.

CUBAN, L. (1986). *Teachers and Machines.* New York: Teachers College Press.

———. (2001). *Oversold and Underused: Computers in the Classroom.* Cambridge: Harvard University Press.

"CYBERKINETICS." (2002). *Technological Review* 105(3), 20–21.

"DEFINING THE TECHNOLOGY GAP." (2002). Benton Foundation Website. (www.benton.org) April.

EDUTOPIA. (2002). George Lucas Foundation. (http://glef.org) Oct.

EGAN, T. (2002). "Bill Gates Views What He's Sown in Libraries." *New York Times Online.* Nov. 6.

"EQUITY GAP IN TECHNOLOGY ACCESS." (2002). (Northwest Educational Technology Consortium website: www.netc.org) April.

ERIKSEN, T. H. (2001). *Tyranny of the Moment.* London: Pluto Press.

FERNANDEZ, R. (2001). Skill-Biased Technological Change and Wage Inequality. *American Journal of Sociology* 107(2), 273–320.

"50 TRENDS SHAPING THE WORLD." (1991). *The Futurist* 25(1), 13–18.

GLEICK, J. (1999). *Faster: The Acceleration of Just About Everything.* New York: Pantheon.

HEALY, J. M. (1998). *Failure to Connect: How Computers Affect Our Children's Minds—For Better and Worse.* New York: Simon & Schuster.

HUNTER, J. O. (1992). "Technological Literacy." *Educational Technology* 32, 26–29.

JOHNSON, J., AND BARKER, L. T. (2002). *Assessing the Impact of Technology in Teaching and Learning.* Ann Arbor: Institute for Social Research, University of Michigan. (www.dlrn.org/star/sourcebook.html)

KIRSNER, S. (2002). High Schools Vie to Build a Robotic Champ. *The New York Times.* April 18, G1.

KORSCHING, P. F. (2001). New Technologies for Rural America: Boon or Bane? *Technology in Society* 213(1), 73–77.

LANDRY, J. (2002). "Is Our Children Learning?" *Red Herring* (No. 116), pp. 37–41.

LEARY, W. E. (2002). "The Inquiring Minds Behind 200 Years of Inventions." *New York Times Online.* (www.nytimes.com) Oct. 21.

LEE, L. (2000). *Bad Predictions.* Rochester, MI: Elsewhere Press.

LIGHT, J. (2001). "Rethinking the Digital Divide." *Harvard Educational Review* 71(4), 709–733.

MANN, D., ET AL., (1999). West Virginia Story: Achievement Gains from a Comprehensive Instructional Technology Program. (Milken Family Foundation Website: www.mff.org)

MCCAIN, T. (2000). *Windows on the Future: Education in the Age of Technology.* New York: Corwin Press.

MCKENZIE, J. (1999). *How Teachers Learn Technology Best.* Bellingham, WA: FNO Press.

———. (2000). *Beyond Technology.* Bellingham, WA: FNO Press.

———. (2001). *Planning Good Change with Technology and Literacy.* Bellingham, WA: FNO Press.

NATIONAL EDUCATIONAL TECHNOLOGY STANDARDS. (2002). (www.cnets.iste.org) Oct., Dec.

NOBLE, D. F. (1997). *The Religion of Technology.* New York: Knopf.

OHMAN, R. (2002). "Computers and Technology." *Radical Teacher* (No. 63), p. 206.

O'NEIL, H., AND PEREZ, R., EDS. (2003). *Technology Applications in Education.* Mahwah, NJ: Lawrence Erlbaum.

PAPERT, S. (1993). *The Children's Machine: Rethinking School in the Age of the Computer.* New York: Basic Books.

———. (2002). "Technology in Schools: To Support the System or Render it Obsolete." Milken Exchange. Milken Family Foundation. (www.mff.org/edtech)

PELGRUM, W. J. (2001). "Obstacles to the Integration of ICT in Education." *Computers in Education* 37(2), 163–178.

PEW RESEARCH CENTER. (2002). Study of Student Use of Internet. (www.pewinternet.org)

"POLICY SOLUTIONS FOR BRIDGING THE DIGITAL DIVIDE." (2002). (Children's Partnership Website: www.techpolicybank.org) April.

POSTMAN, N. (1992). *Technopoly: The Surrender of Culture to Technology.* New York: Knopf.

RINGSTAFF, C., AND KELLY, L. (2002). "The Learning Return on Our Educational Technology Investment: A Review of Findings from Research." #IR021079. (www.ERICIT.org)

RINSTAFF, K., AND YOCAM, K. (1996). "Integrating Technology into Classroom Instruction." ACOT Report #22. (www.apple.com./education/html)

SANDHOLTZ, J. H., RINGSTAFF, C., AND DWYER, D. (1997). *Teaching with Technology.* New York: Teachers College Press.

SIEGEL, L., AND MARKOFF, J. (1985). *The High Cost of High Tech: The Dark Side of the Chip.* New York: Harper & Row.

STOLL, C. (1995). *Silicon Snake Oil: Second Thoughts on the Information Highway.* New York: Doubleday.

———. (1999). *High Tech Heretic: Why Computers Don't Belong in the Classroom.* New York: Doubleday.

TENNER, E. (1997). *Why Things Bite Back: Technology and the Revenge of Unintended Consequences.* New York: Vintage Books.

"THE TELESURGERY REVOLUTION." (2002). *The Futurist* 36(1), 6, 7.

"2020 VISIONS." (2002). U.S. Department of Commerce. Washington, DC: Department of Commerce. (www.ed.gov/technology) Sept. 17.

WARLICK, D. (2002). "New Century Schoolhouse." (www.landmark-project.com)

WERRY, C. (2002). "The Rhetoric of Commercial Online Education." *Radical Teacher* (No. 63), Spring.

WILLIAMS, T. I. (1982). *A Short History of Twentieth-Century Technology.* Oxford: Oxford University Press.

WINDSCHITL, M., AND SAHL, K. (2002). "Tracing Teachers' Use of Technology in a Laptop Computer School." *American Educational Research Journal* 39(1), 165–205.

WINOGRAD, K. (2002). "ABCs of the Virtual High School." The Technology Source. (http://ts.mivu.org)

CHAPTER 14

Standardized Testing: Restrict or Expand

POSITION 1: FOR RESTRICTING TESTING

> *A young Ojibwa student . . . was tested by several professionals and classified as having certain learning and behavioral problems. In part, this classification was based upon his staring into space, completing tasks very slowly, and giving "non-reality-based" responses to questions. As it turned out, the boy had a special relationship with his traditional Ojibwa grandfather, who encouraged his dreaming. . . . In Ojibwa thought and language,* ga-na-wa-bun-daw-ming, *which means seeing without feeling (objectivity), carries less value than* mu-zhi-tum-ing, *which means feelings that you do not see (subjectivity).*
>
> —McShane, 1989, cited in Madaus, 1994, p. 80

Vexing Tests

In a witty attack on standardized testing, Banesh Hoffmann (1962) recounted a debate played out on the pages of the London *Times.* A letter to the newspaper's editor asked for help in solving a multiple-choice problem from a battery of school tests the letter-writer's son had taken. At first glance, the question seemed to be straightforward and not surprising to anyone who has taken school tests. It asked, "Which is the odd one out among cricket, football, billiards, and hockey"?

The letter writer believed the answer must be billiards because it is the only one of the four games played indoors. He admitted to being less than sure of his answer, and reported there was no agreement among his acquaintances. One of his neighbors argued the correct choice was cricket, because in all of the other games the object was to put a ball in a net. The writer's son had selected hockey because it was the only one that was a "girls' game." The letter writer asked readers of the *Times* for help. Ensuing letters and arguments succeeded only in muddying the waters, since the logic supporting one choice was no more compelling than the logic supporting any other. For example, billiards could be considered the odd one out because it is the only one of the four games listed that is not ordinarily a team game. It is the only one in which the color of the ball matters. It is the only one in which more than one ball is in play, and it is the only one played on a green cloth rather than a grass field. Unfortunately, equally convincing briefs could be submitted in behalf of the other choices.

Hoffmann fumed about the inherent bias in the question. He assumed the test was designed to measure reasoning ability and not sports knowledge, but he argued that the test-taker might be disadvantaged by too little experience with athletics; for example, not all students with good reasoning skills may know how cricket is played. Test-takers who know too much about sports also might be disadvantaged; they might choose hockey as the odd one out because it is really two different games that share the same name—in England and in several other countries, hockey is a game typically played on grass by players who receive no salary; elsewhere it is a game played on ice, often by professional athletes.

The language of this test item also may trip up students, preventing it from measuring reasoning ability. For example, many working-class students may not be familiar with either cricket or billiards. Items of this sort favor the language and culture of the middle and upper-middle classes, and low scores may reflect measures of social standing more than achievement or ability (Neill and Medina, 1989). Americans also could be disadvantaged by the test item wording, which asks test-takers to select the "odd one out." A similar test item in the United States probably would read, "Which of the following does not belong?"

Test questions of this sort seem silly. There is no readily discernible "right" answer, and test takers have no opportunity to demonstrate the thought processes that led to their decisions. As Hoffmann noted, "What sense is there in giving tests in which the candidate just picks answers, and is not allowed to give the reasons for his choice?" (Hoffmann, 1962, p. 20). Multiple-choice questions are an unnatural problem-solving format incongruous with solving real-life problems. Rarely are life's dilemmas delineated by four answers, one of which is guaranteed to be correct. Good problem solvers in the real world seldom are locked away, deprived of books, computers, and human contact; they seldom are told to respond to a set of timed, multiple-choice questions with no practical meaning.

If multiple-choice questions, such as the one that vexed *Times* readers, were nothing more than a parlor game, a form of Trivial Pursuit played for amusement, few would object to them. Standardized testing, however, has serious consequences, and for public school students, the stakes are particularly high. Standardized test results help determine placement in reading groups, admission to the college-track programs in public high schools, entrance into selective colleges, scholarship awards, admission into medical and law schools, and licensing to practice a profession or trade.

If Testing Is the Answer, What Was the Question?

In the early twentieth century, defining "native intelligence" and attempting to measure it "scientifically" through standardized examinations instigated one of the most controversial legacies of the testing movement (Gould, 1981). Sir Francis Galton in England and Alfred Binet in France attempted to measure mental capacities through standardized tests (Cremin, 1961). Binet developed his test, at the request of the French government, to identify those children who were "mentally subnormal" and not able to function adequately in regular classrooms. Louis Terman translated Binet's tests into English for American students, and he and his colleagues adjusted the tests to comport with their own sense of how intelligence was distributed. For example, Terman believed men are more intelligent than women and rural people are less intelligent than urban dwellers. Therefore, when girls outscored boys, Terman changed the test items on which girls scored unusually well. He made no changes on items where urban children outscored rural children (Garcia and Pearson, 1994). Terman argued that intelligence tests make schools more efficient. He claimed the tests could be used to sort children into differentiated curricula designed to prepare them for their appropriate lot in life:

> Preliminary investigations indicate that an IQ below 70 rarely permits anything better than unskilled labor; the range of 70–80 is preeminently that of semiskilled labor; from 80–100 that of skilled or ordinary clerical labor; from 100–110 or 115 that of semiprofessional pursuits; and that above all of these are grades of intelligence which permit one to enter the professions or other large fields of business. (Terman, 1922, in Wolf et al., 1991)

Psychologists working for the United States government during World War I introduced the first wide-scale use of standardized intelligence tests. The army was interested in classifying all new recruits, giving special attention to two groups: those of exceptional ability and those unfit for military service. Binet and Terman had used individual IQ tests that were not well suited to large-scale testing; under the direction of American psychologists, the army developed the first mass-testing program in history (Gumbert and Spring, 1974, pp. 87–112). The army test came in two forms: The Army Alpha was a written, objective exam; the Army Beta was a pictorial exam designed for illiterate recruits and non-English speakers.

The army used the tests to answer questions about the placement of soldiers: Who would best fit where? Who should be discharged on the grounds of mental incompetence? How could the army best use the varied talents and abilities recruits brought with them? The results helped determine who should be in the infantry and who should go to the army language school.

> It is unclear to what extent the army actually acted on such recommendation. Nevertheless, some disturbing conclusions emerged from the army testing program. The average mental age of white Americans turned out to be 13 (barely above the level of morons). Test results revealed immigrants to be duller still (the average age of Russians being 11.34, Italians 11.01, and Poles 10.74), and Negroes came in last with an average mental age of 10.41. These findings fueled debates about immigration quotas, segregation, eugenics, and miscegenation for years to come. (Hanson, 1993, p. 212)

After the war, colleges and universities bought the surplus exams, and found the language of the army tests required only slight modification for use in schools. The original instructions given to soldiers read:

> Attention! The purpose of this examination is to see how well you can remember, think and carry out what you are told to do in the army. . . . Now in the

> army a man often has to listen to commands and carry them out exactly. I am going to give you these commands to see how well you carry them out....

In schools, these instructions were changed to read:

> Part of being a good student is your ability to follow directions.... When I call "Attention," stop instantly what you are doing and hold your pencil up—so. Don't put your pencil down on the paper until I say "Go." ... Listen carefully to what I say. Do just as you are told to do. As soon as you are through, pencils up. Remember, wait for the word "Go." (Gumbert and Spring, 1974, p. 94)

For many years, schools used IQ tests to track children based on their test performance. Intelligence was viewed as the "raw material" required for schooling, and students judged to have less intelligence received less education. This reliance on IQ tests was designed to make education more objective and more efficient; it produced the unintended result of limiting students' educational access (Darling-Hammond, 1994). Students performing at the lowest levels on IQ tests received an education designed to prepare them to be tractable, unskilled laborers. Only the highest-achieving students would be introduced to the most complex skills. Intellect was viewed as a biological trait much like height or eye color: It was thought to be inherited, measurable, and fixed. IQ tests allowed schools to sort students into appropriate curricula and thus into their later place in society (Callahan, 1962; Wolf et al., 1991). Too frequently, these tests excluded the majority of students from the best opportunities the school offered. More often than not, the best education and the most promising futures were reserved for those who performed well on high-stakes[1] standardized tests, and standardized testing typically has worked to the disadvantage of most minority groups.

In the United States, African Americans score below 75 percent of Americans of European descent on most standardized tests, IQ tests, and achievement tests alike (Jencks and Phillips, 1998, p. 1). There also are significant gaps between standardized test scores of European Americans, Mexican Americans, and Native Americans. Some researchers claim the tests themselves are biased, arguing the tests "reflect the language, culture, or learning style of middle- to upper-class whites. Thus scores on these tests are as much measures of race or ethnicity and income as they are measures of achievement, ability, or skill" (Neill and Medina, 1989, p. 691). Gardner (1983, 1999) argues that children have multiple forms of "intelligence," and schools typically ignore all but two of these. To date, no single explanation successfully accounts for the gap between white and black scores on standardized exams. There are as many explanations as there are disciplinary orientations of the researchers (Lee, 2002). Educators know one thing for certain: No matter how good their grades, students are at a disadvantage in school if they do not score well on standardized tests. And the higher the stakes, the greater the disadvantage. The negative consequences of testing is likely to fall

[1]Tests are referred to as "high stakes" when they have serious consequences for the test-takers, for example, ability grouping, college admission, and scholarships. Chapter 6 contains a discussion of the relative merits of high-stakes testing and accountability.

hardest on the economically disadvantaged. The legacy of poor test performance is enduring, serving as painful memories of humiliation and a sense of inadequacy (Hanson, 1993).

Teachers of poor and minority children report they spend more time teaching to the test and are more likely to rely on data from standardized tests than do teachers of students from moderate- and high-income families (Garcia and Pearson, 1994). Poor and minority children spend more time on workbook exercises and busy-work assignments. They are less likely than middle-class students to have access to classes where they can discuss what they know, read real books, write, or solve problems in mathematics, science, or other school subjects (Darling-Hammond, 1994). Students from poor families and children of minorities have been awarded an education of less substance because of their poor performance on standardized tests. As Madaus (1994) points out, "Clearly, the unintended negative outcomes brought about by the widespread policy use of IQ tests disproportionately disadvantaged minority populations. Despite Binet's original purpose to identify children in need of instructional assistance, the IQ test in this country led to blacks and Hispanics being disproportionately placed in dead-end classes for the 'educable mentally retarded'" (p. 86).

Misleading Test Results

Until the last few years, despite questions about the validity of individual items on standardized tests (Crouse and Trusheim, 1988; Hoffmann, 1962; Nairn and Associates, 1980; Owen, 1985), test-takers never were able to see a list of the "right" answers after they had taken the exams. The Educational Testing Service (ETS)[2] of Princeton, New Jersey, and other test developers published only a few sample questions, claiming full disclosure would compromise the tests. To make the tests reliable,[3] they argued, many items had to be repeated from year to year, and the answers therefore must be held back from public scrutiny. The ETS acknowledged it was possible to construct new equivalent exams every year; however, it would be an expensive process, and test-takers ultimately would bear the costs.

[2]The Educational Testing Service (ETS) of Princeton, New Jersey, is the world's largest testing company. Formed in 1947 to develop and administer college entrance exams for returning World War II veterans, the company now administers over 9 million exams annually and reports earnings of $600 million. The ETS maintains a website at www.ets.org. You also may want to check the website of the National Center for Fair and Open Testing (FairTest) at www.fairtest.org. On its website, FairTest is described as "an advocacy organization working to end abuses, misuses, and flaws of standardized testing and ensure that evaluation of students and workers is fair, open, and educationally sound."

[3]Reliability in testing can be thought of as a synonym for stability, consistency, or dependability. Kerlinger's simile might be useful in understanding this concept. He writes: "A test is like a gun in its purpose. When we measure human attributes and abilities and achievements, we want to measure 'true' amounts of attributes that individuals possess. This is like hitting a target with a gun. With a test we want to hit the attribute. If a gun consistently hits a target—the shots cluster close together at or near the center of the target . . . we say it is reliable. Similarly with psychological and sociological measures. If they hit the target, they are reliable." (Kerlinger, 1979, p. 133)

Recognizing the power standardized exams have on the lives of individual test-takers, and failing to be persuaded by ETS's arguments, New York and California enacted legislation allowing test-takers to see the answers after they had taken the exams. These truth-in-testing laws revealed ambiguity in test items. In some instances, more than one answer was correct. The ETS and other test-makers took the issue to court, and in 1990 a federal district court judge in New York set aside the requirements of the test disclosure law on the grounds that it interfered with copyright laws. The truth-in-testing laws have cast doubt on the ability of tests to measure what they claim to measure, and have opened the issue of validity[4] to public examination.

There is good reason for public suspicion. Some people have intentionally used results of standardized tests to mislead the public. Take the case of the "magic mean," uncovered by a physician in West Virginia. Local newspapers reported students in his state were performing above the national average on standardized tests. This intrigued him, considering that West Virginia had one of the highest rates of illiteracy in the nation. Further checking revealed that no state using the test was reported to be below the mean. The tests compared student achievement with outdated and very low national norms. Therefore, the test results made even the worst test-taker (and the school systems that bought the tests) appear to be above average. As one testing critic notes, "standardized, nationally normed achievement tests give children, parents, school systems, legislatures, and the press inflated and misleading reports on achievement levels" (Cannell, 1987, p. 3).

Indeed, by the late 1990s, it was hard to find any school districts or states scoring below the mean on nationally normed standardized tests. These data have contributed to what has been termed the Lake Wobegon Effect, after the mythical Minnesota town created by Garrison Keillor in which "the women are strong, the men are good looking, and all the children are above average" (Fiske, 1988; Mehrens and Kaminski, 1989; Phillips, 1990). Testing designs of this type are not uncommon, and educators need to exercise caution before making inferences about quality of education based on data from standardized testing (Linn, 1993; Judson, 1996). For the past fifty years, psychometricians and companies that market tests have convinced the public that short-answer tests are objective, scientific measures deserving of public confidence and faith, when in fact these tests suffer from vagueness, ambiguity, imprecision, and bias. In truth, there is nothing scientific or objective about these items; highly subjective human beings write, test, compile, and interpret each item (Owen, 1985).

[4]Validity refers to the ability of a test to measure what the test maker wants to measure. Kerlinger uses the following example: "Suppose a group of teachers of social studies writes a test to measure students' understanding of certain social concepts: justice, equality, and cooperation, for instance. The teachers want to know whether their students understand and can apply the ideas. But they write a test of only factual items about contemporary institutions. The test is then not valid for the purpose they had in mind." (Kerlinger, 1979, p. 138)

Bias

The SAT and the ACT claim to be:

a. measures of academic achievement by students.
b. predictors of whether students will graduate from college.
c. reliable predictors of college performance, race notwithstanding.
d. measures of academic rigor of local school systems.
e. none of the above.
(Chenoweth, 1997, p. 20)

Standardized testing programs discriminate against women and minorities and the poor while often failing to deliver on the promises of scientific measurement and prediction. Consider the test you took as part of your college application process (SAT I, SAT II, and/or ACT). The SAT, the nation's oldest standardized test used in college admissions, is essentially an aptitude test divided into two sections: verbal and math. The SAT II and ACT, subject matter tests, are designed to measure more closely what students have learned in high school. Although high school grades are a far better predictor of college success, test-makers argue that exam scores are very useful in estimating first-year college grades. Consequently, SAT and ACT scores often are part of the data colleges use in making admission and scholarship decisions. According to ETS, students with higher SAT scores should earn higher grades during their first year in college. In fact, the SAT, similar to the ACT exam, measures only how well a student is likely to do during the first year of college, and it does so accurately only about half the time (Chenoweth, 1997).

For women, the SAT *underpredicts* their first-year grades. In one study, the gap between average male and female scores on the test is 61 points. Female test-takers scored 50 points lower on the math section and 11 points lower on the verbal section of the exam. If the SAT accurately predicted grade point average, males would have higher first-year grade point averages than female students. But this is not the case. Despite lower scores on the SAT, women earned higher grades than men (Rosser, 1987). The SAT does not predict what it is supposed to predict: success in college. The scores students get on SAT exams have less meaning than ETS has promised. Rosser concluded that because of sex bias on the SAT exam, women have less chance of receiving financial aid, being accepted to college, and being invited to join programs for the gifted. Because of an invalid exam, women are likely to earn less money and lose out on appointments to positions of leadership. In 1989, a federal district court ruled that New York State's Regents Scholarship, based on a student's performance on the SAT exam, discriminated against women. Women had previously won only 43 percent of the scholarships. After the decision, which required the State of New York to consider high school grades as well as standardized test scores, women won 51 percent of the awards (Arenson, 1996).

The problem of discrimination is made worse by "coaching"—the process of improving individual scores through test-preparation programs, some costing nearly $1,000. Unfortunately, college admissions officers cannot separate applicants who were coached from those who were not. It is not possible to know if an individual's test score was the product of his or her own effort or the work of one or more professional coaching companies. Coaching may raise a student's score by 100 points or more on the SAT (FairTest, 2002a), creating a clear but unfair advantage in admissions for those who can afford to pay.

Tests, Curricula, and Learning

Despite their problems, standardized tests continue to exert great influence on schools. Every teacher knows that testing drives the curriculum: What is tested is taught. No teacher wants his or her students to perform poorly on standardized achievement tests, and no school administrator wants his or her school to rank below others in the state or district. Everyone in education knows that, too often, newspapers report results of statewide testing in much the same way they report basketball standings. "We're Number One" or "County Schools Lowest in State" are not uncommon headlines in many local newspapers. To avoid such invidious comparisons, schools gear instruction to the test. Over time, material not tested tends not to be taught. If only math and language arts are to be tested, other subjects, such as art and music, science and social studies, are likely to be deemphasized or eliminated. Teachers and administrators fall victim to test-makers' promises and the public's misplaced faith in testing. In truth, there is no compelling reason to subject students to large-scale multiple-choice exams.

National testing has become a national obsession. In the 1990s, President George Bush encouraged the education community to develop "New World Standards" in each of five core subject areas. President Clinton, in his 1997 State of the Union address, urged states to adopt higher standards and implement testing programs to ensure the standards were met. The Elementary and Secondary Education Act passed in December 2001, during the presidency of George W. Bush, and referred to as the No Child Left Behind Act, requires each state to establish standards for all students in math and reading or language arts. Science standards are to be added by 2005–06. To measure the extent to which students are making "adequate yearly progress" toward meeting the standards, states are to conduct "academic assessments in grades three to eight and once in high school." The results of this legislation should be a bonanza for test-makers who are likely to fall over themselves in a mad scramble to rush standardized testing plans to market. Many believe few outside of the test-makers will benefit from this legislation. FairTest argues that states will destroy local curricula and individually crafted teaching through their implementation of mandated standardized tests. The result is likely to sort students out into winners and losers rather than help all children get a high-quality education (FairTest, 2002b). Monty Neill of FairTest, among others, argues that all the proposals to bring about school reform through a renewed emphasis on assessment are based on premises that an examination of recent history does not support:

> During the 1980s, U.S. schoolchildren became probably the most overtested students in the world—but the desired educational improvement did not

> occur. FairTest research indicates that our schools now give more than 200 million standardized exams each year. The typical student must take several dozen before graduating. Adding more testing will no more improve education than taking the temperature of a patient more often will reduce his fever. (Neill, 1991, p. 36)

There is an antidote to standardized testing that does not sacrifice accountability. In every community, teachers, parents, and administrators should select appropriate content based on students' interests, experiences, goals, and needs. Teachers should teach that content with all the skill at their command, and evaluate the extent of student learning with a wide variety of instruments. Students should be encouraged to demonstrate their ability to think through written exercises, verbal expression, and informal papers, and should be given ample opportunity to demonstrate the reasons for their choices. Assessment of student learning requires educators develop a broader, richer array of measures (Mabry, 1999; Ardovino, Hollingsworth, and Ybarra, 2000; Janesick, 2001). State and federal legislation should not try to reduce student achievement to a single numerical score. Multiple-choice tests cannot tell the story of academic success. Many students simply do not test well, and all students should be given multiple ways to demonstrate what they have learned. Assessment programs should be designed to improve student learning, not measure one student against another or measure a student's progress against some arbitrary standard.

Assessment programs should focus on the individual student and examples of what they actually have produced. A student's record of school achievement should include a rich portfolio of papers, essays, videos, poems, photographs, drawings, and tape-recorded answers, not a series of test scores. When parents want to know how well their child is doing in school, they should be able to review a portfolio of their child's work with the teacher or at least receive a written narrative from the teacher. Parents should be suspicious of schools that confuse the scores on a norm-referenced examination with a child's progress in the classroom. Parents should not worry about a teacher who does not rely on standardized tests; they should worry more about teachers who believe standardized tests measure the ways in which a child's mind works (Kohn, 2000). Educational decisions should not be based solely on test scores. Testing alone cannot convey to students, parents, college admissions officers, or anyone else adequate information about individual achievement and ability. Standardized testing is a threat to educational improvement, and their use should be restricted.

POSITION 2: FOR EXPANDING TESTING

> *In the American context [standardized, objective] tests are necessary to achieve excellence and fairness. They function as achievement incentives for students and teachers, as ways of monitoring students' progress in order to remedy their deficiencies, and as essential helps in the administrative monitoring of classrooms, schools, and districts. Without effective monitoring, neither good teaching nor*

educational administration is possible. Finally, and above all, objective tests are needed for academic fairness and social equity—the chief reasons that Americans, to their credit, have been pioneers in developing objective tests.

—HIRSCH, 1996, P. 117

According to the results of a survey sponsored by Educational Testing Service (ETS), Americans are not satisfied with public schools, giving them a letter grade no better than "C" (Hart and Teeter, 2001). Academic standards have slipped, and students are passing from grade to grade without mastering the content they need to be successful in life. The public schools, it has been generally concluded, are in need of reform. Many educators recognize that the nation's schools must have high standards for student achievement and scrupulously fair assessments of student performance or the nation will lose its competitive place in the world. Previous generations of education reformers concerned themselves with making education available to children of all classes and races, and to a large extent they were successful. By the 1990s, a higher percentage of students were completing high school than ever before. The issue is no longer *availability;* the current generation of reformers now is forced to consider the *quality* of school experiences. As Mortimer Adler (1982) argues, we cannot satisfy the legal mandates for education simply by guaranteeing all children access to education. In order to satisfy the educational responsibilities of a democratic society, public education must demonstrate that each student is acquiring requisite skills and knowledge. Schools must guarantee the education they offer has a demonstrably positive effect on a student's ability to read, write, and do mathematics, and that moving up the academic ladder from grade to grade is based on merit rather than social promotion. The issue of educational quality raises a broad range of questions:

- How good is the education provided students in kindergarten through grade 12?
- How do the students of today compare with former students?
- Do students know enough to earn a high school diploma?
- How do students in School A or District A or State A compare with others?
- How can prospective employers know that students who graduate from high school possess a minimum level of skills, knowledge, and ability?
- How can taxpayers know that the dollars given over to public education are well spent?
- If changes are made in public education, how can educators determine whether the changes are having a positive effect on learning?

Answers to these questions must be based on high-quality hard data. Schools need quantifiable measures of student performance and documentation of teacher effectiveness if they hope to maintain public support. Policymakers must have objective information in order to make intelligent decisions. Although no single means of data collection is sufficient, data from well-designed standardized tests are crucial to an understanding of school outcomes.

FIGURE 14.1. Public Support for Testing

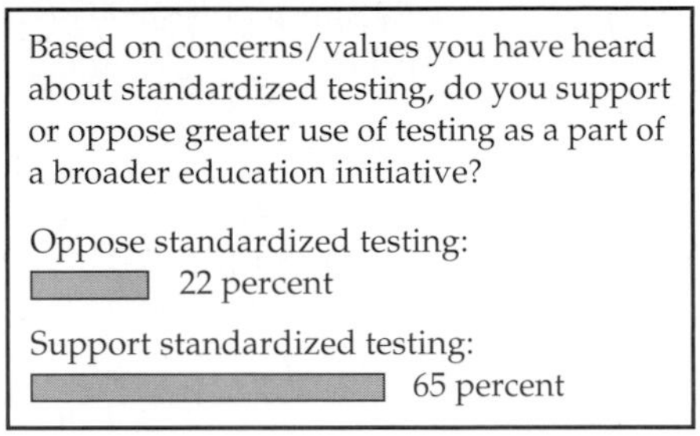

Based on concerns/values you have heard about standardized testing, do you support or oppose greater use of testing as a part of a broader education initiative?

Oppose standardized testing: 22 percent

Support standardized testing: 65 percent

Source: *Hart and Teeter (2001), p. 27.*

Good tests and good testing programs permit schools to gather information about curricula and students not available to them through other means. Without these data, schools cannot make appropriate decisions about curriculum quality or power of specific programs to enhance learning. This is a popular position. Consider the results of a survey reported in Figure 14.1. The public, by a ratio of 3:1, supports expansion of testing in public schools.

Standardized testing is part of the scientific base that supports the art of teaching. Scientific testing permits measurement of the teacher's art, complementing as well as assessing classroom practice. Formal testing programs were introduced into schools in the nineteenth century to counter charges of examiner bias and subjectivity.[5] Today, standardized testing programs also provide the yardstick society uses to chart the progress and shortcomings of education, and their results allow schools to report the status of education to public officials and parents. Test and measurement experts are often at odds with others in education, and have suffered abuse from critics skeptical about the power of testing and fearful of the testing agencies' power to influence public policy. The purpose here is not to answer the critics or submit a brief in support of the Educational Testing Service or the National Assessment of Educational Progress. Instead, we will argue that (1) standardized testing is an essential tool for examining the measurable dimensions of education; and (2) education has entered an era of accountability. School officials must demonstrate that the money taxpayers spend for education is paying dividends in quality.

[5]Nineteenth-century Britain, in the throes of an expanding domestic economy and of becoming an international empire, found it could not satisfy the demand for large numbers of middle-class managers through the traditional patronage appointments. There simply were not enough privileged males—the sons of civil servants, members of Parliament, or others of wealth and connections—to fill the vacancies worldwide. Competitive exams were introduced to open the civil service to a broader range of male applicants.

The United States also used testing to democratize the selection of government workers. Political abuse, through patronage, was rampant in the nineteenth century. Civil Service reform began with the Pendleton Act of 1883, which established competitive exams for prospective government employees.

Testing for the Good of Schools and Students

Standardized testing is an essential element of rational curriculum work. The data testing programs generate help curriculum planners determine whether the measured outcomes of a given set of instructional inputs match the intended goals. In other words, tests can help educators find out if a specific program is working the way it was designed to work. When taxpayers are asked to foot the bill for a new science program in high schools or a new math program in elementary schools, they should be informed of the anticipated effects of these programs and how the results will be measured. The public demands accountability. The public views education reform proposals as incomplete without the means to hold teachers and administrators accountable (Hart and Teeter, 2001). This is a simple matter of cost accounting and fiscal responsibility.

Effective change does not occur by chance. Educational decisions must be made about student progress, rate of achievement of proximate goals, and the best choice among competing paths to the next objective. Educational planners need to choose appropriate measures of student attainment. Impressionistic data are not sufficient; anecdotal evidence is not scientific. It is not enough that a program "seems to be working" or teachers "claim to like" this method or that approach. Schools need to have better answers to direct questions about the curriculum and student learning. At what grade level are students reading? What do diagnostic and prescriptive tests tell us about a child's performance in academic skill areas? How much of the required curricula have students mastered?

Standardized testing should not be viewed as a report card but as part of an assessment system that permits schools to make decisions about curriculum and instruction. Standardized achievement tests are objective measures of performance. Standardized tests are designed to measure the extent to which the nation is meeting its goals and responsibilities to provide educational quality to all children.

Shooting the Messenger

Since 1969, the federal government has financed an assessment program known as the National Assessment of Educational Progress (NAEP).[6] Administered since 1983, by the Educational Testing Service of Princeton, New Jersey, the NAEP gathers data about the knowledge, skills, and attitudes of students across ten subject areas: art, career and occupational development, citizenship, literature, mathematics, music, reading, science, social studies, and writing. Students in four age groups (ages 9, 13, and 17) take the tests. NAEP serves the nation as its "only ongoing monitor of student achievement across time" (Campbell, Hombo, and Mazzeo, 2000, p. ix). NAEP collects valid, scientific data about how well students

[6]The most up-to-date assessment data from NAEP, "The Nation's Report Card," can be found on the Worldwide Web at http://nces.ed.gov.nationsreportcard.

are performing today and how they compare with previous generations of test-takers, and offers educational planners information needed to evaluate schools and improve education.

Unfortunately, much of the test data has been negative; increased spending has not been matched by increases in test scores. NAEP data indicate that math and science scores declined in the 1970s, improved modestly during the 1980s and early 1990s, but have leveled off since. Gains in reading are modest at best, and overall scores in all subject areas tested are still low (Campbell, Hombo, and Mazzeo, 2000). Although these findings grab headlines and cause a great deal of collective hand wringing, they should be viewed as a step toward school reform rather than ends in themselves. The NAEP is designed to help educators reconsider the quality of teaching and learning in public schools.

Has education gotten better or worse? Do students know more or less than students of previous generations? Among the most interesting NAEP assessment techniques are those that collect data about student performance across time. Thus, NAEP allows policymakers and educators to compare the performance of 13-year-olds, for example, of one generation with others across a thirty-year period in school subjects such as reading, mathematics, and science (Campbell, Hombo, and Mazzeo, 2000). To compare the knowledge of today's students with their counterparts of a decade ago, NAEP released the results of a "Civics Assessment" in 1998. The test was first used in 1988, and administered to a similar cohort of students in grades 4, 8, and 12. The test items were designed to tap four content areas central of civics understanding: (1) democratic principles and the purpose of government; (2) knowledge of the structure and function of political institutions; (3) political processes; and (4) rights, responsibilities, and the law. The good news is that students tested in 1998 know as much about these civics areas as students did ten years earlier. NAEP concludes that "Despite evidence of low political engagement [e.g., voting], low levels of interpersonal trust [e.g., attitudes toward elected officials], and relatively low levels of civics knowledge, there is little to suggest that today's youth are less knowledgeable than their predecessors" (Weiss et al., 2001, p. 2).

The bad news is that despite all the increases in education spending on facilities, salaries, hardware and software, student learning has not improved. The nation invested mightily in K–12 education in the decade spanning the first and second tests. Spending on elementary and secondary education increased 44 percent between 1988 and 1998, from about $209 billion to about $377 billion, and in the area of civics education, there was nothing to show for it (http://nces.ed.gov/pubs2001/digest). The 1998 test results indicate little change from 1988, despite significantly increased spending. This is distressing news, especially if you consider the low level of information called for in the test items. (See Figures 14.2 and 14.3.) For example, 50 percent of the twelfth-graders in 1998 could identify the source of a quote from the Declaration of Independence, and only 38 percent could provide a correct response to a multiple-choice question asking test-takers to define bicameralism. Seventy-two percent of the twelfth-graders sampled in 1998 knew that Congress is made up of the House of

FIGURE 14.2. Grade 12 Sample Questions, 1988 and 1998
Content Area: *Democratic Principles and the Purpose of Government*

	Percentage of Students 1988		1998
"We hold these truths to be self-evident, that all men are created equal, that they are endowed by their Creator with certain unalienable Rights, that among these are Life, Liberty, and the Pursuit of Happiness." This quotation is taken from the			
(A, filled) Declaration of Independence	59	>	50
(B) United States Constitution	19		21
(C) Bill of Rights	17	<	21
(D) Articles of Confederation	5	<	8
Bicameralism is best defined as a			
(A) government composed of two principle branches	31		30
(B) multilevel judicial system containing a higher court for appeals	14		12
(C) system of checks and balances between two branches of government	21		21
(D, filled) legislative system composed of two houses or chambers	34		38

> 1988 significantly greater than 1998.
< 1988 significantly less than 1998.
Source: *National Center for Education Statistics, National Assessment of Educational Progress (NAEP), Civics Assessments—1988 and 1998. In Weiss et al. (2001), p. 14.*

Representatives and the Senate, but only a quarter of the respondents could identify the department most concerned with foreign affairs.

Standardized test results cannot be ignored. One of the goals of the NAEP Civics Assessment is to provide baseline data for future assessments of student knowledge of democratic principles, purposes of government, and structure and function of political institutions. Although testing is far from a perfect science, at present there are no measures that can compete with standardized tests for gathering economical, valid, and reliable data about what children have learned in school. Unfortunately, the testing community has been charged with delivering an unpleasant message.

Limits to Authentic Assessment

Most of us are familiar with tests that indirectly measure what we know. For example, a test-maker who wanted to determine students' woodworking ability

FIGURE 14.3. Grade 12 Sample Questions, 1988 and 1998
Content Area: *Political Institutions (Structures and Functions)*

	Percentage of Students		
The U.S. Congress is made up of which of the following?	1988		1998
(A) The House of Representatives and the Supreme Court	8		10
● The House of Representatives and the Senate	77	>	72
(C) The Senate and the Cabinet	5		6
(D) The President and the Cabinet	3	<	5
(E) I don't know	7		7
Which of the following departments is MOST concerned with foreign affairs?			
● Department of State	35	>	25
(B) Department of Commerce	45		50
(C) Department of Agriculture	6		8
(D) Department of the Treasury	5		5
(E) I don't know	9	<	13

> *1988 significantly greater than 1998.*
< *1988 significantly less than 1998.*
Source: *National Center for Education Statistics, National Assessment of Educational Progress (NAEP), Civics Assessments—1988 and 1998. In Weiss et al. (2001), p. 17.*

might devise a test composed of a series of multiple-choice items. Students might be asked which of the following tools would be needed to make a wooden bowl: (a) a ball peen hammer, (b) a lathe chisel, (c) a screwdriver, or (d) a wrench? Other questions might probe the students' knowledge of various types of wood, appropriate procedures for using power tools, types of finishing materials, and safety procedures. These items taken together might indicate a student's knowledge of bowl making, but the student's score would tell the test-maker very little about the student's actual ability to fashion a wooden bowl. A more direct measure of that ability would entail taking students into a fully equipped woodworking shop to watch them set about making a bowl from a block of wood. This authentic measure of performance would allow the test-taker to demonstrate actual ability in a real-life situation, and would allow the test-giver to ask why students followed certain procedures or omitted others (Cizek, 1991).

Since 1988, Vermont has been developing statewide performance programs in mathematics and writing. Careful reviews of the Vermont process highlight some problems with performance evaluation. When evaluators want to determine the quality of student writing, a performance review of actual student writing collected over time has clear advantages over a multiple-choice exam that covers the rules of grammar and the mechanics of writing. Unlike scoring standardized exams, however, the evaluation of writing samples is highly subjective and very expensive. A single reviewer may not offer a reliable assessment of writing, and it is often difficult to find two reviewers who agree about the quality of written work. Independent evaluations of Vermont's performance evaluation effort found that it does not produce consistent assessment of student learning (Supovitz and Brennan, 1997). Portfolio assessments are not necessarily less biased or more fair than standardized testing programs (Popham, 2002).

Assessment of student learning always entails problems. Although policymakers would prefer easy, accurate, and inexpensive assessments, their designs must be complex to account for variations among students, teachers, and curricula (Linn, 1993; Koretz et al., 1994). Performance assessment promises the education community a rich picture, but taken alone, results of performance testing offer a snapshot too grainy to shape policy. As yet, there are no substitutes for objective data, standardized tests, and measures that allow test-takers to know where students stand in comparison to others and that permit policymakers to gauge the progress of educational change.

Assessment programs are changing: In 1994, the verbal section of the SAT began to place greater emphasis on reading and reasoning; the mathematics section now emphasizes data interpretation and real-life mathematics, and students are asked to demonstrate how they arrived at correct answers. Beginning in 2005, the SAT battery will include an assessment of writing, a retooled reading section, and items assessing high-level thinking in math (Hoover, 2002). Psychometric test designers continue to produce better, more reliable, testing instruments. Standardized testing is both necessary and beneficial for schools and the students they serve.

For Discussion

1. When parents and others want to know how a good a school is, they often turn to standardized test scores and other quantitative (numerical) measures, such as per-pupil expenditures, teacher-student ratios, the number of teachers with master's degrees. One writer argues that the evaluation of schools and the business of education is far too complex for such measures to be of value. He suggests ten questions that should be asked to gain a fuller picture of a school. Consider the list:
   - **a.** Can administrators explain the school's mission in plain language?
   - **b.** Do teachers know their subject matter?
   - **c.** Are the tests well-constructed and thoughtful?
   - **d.** What's the school's academic record?
   - **e.** What's on the walls?
   - **f.** Who does the talking in classes?
   - **g.** Is the school safe?
   - **h.** Is the principal on the move (in and around the building)?
   - **i.** How large are classes?
   - **j.** How dedicated are the teachers? (Merrow, 2002)

Would answers to these questions provide useful information in measuring the quality of a school? Would you add questions to this list to provide better information? Are answers to these questions likely to provide information about school quality that is as useful as results of standardized testing programs?

2. Some research indicates parents want tests that produce information about how well their children are performing, how well they can solve problems, and where they need additional help. In one example, parents were asked to compare two sample items from a standardized test:
   a. How much change will you get if you have $6.55 and spend $4.32? (1) $2.23, (2) $2.43, (3) $3.23, (4) $10.87, and
   b. Suppose you couldn't remember what 8 × 7 is. How could you figure it out?

   Parents preferred the second question because they believed it to be more challenging and would likely lead teachers to a better understanding of children's thinking about mathematics (Kohn, 2000, p. 45).

   As a student do you prefer question a or b? Which is more common? Are both formats necessary? Are they both compatible with a standardized-testing format?
3. Students demand fairness in testing and grading, and often argue evaluations of their written work are subjective and that an essay one professor evaluates negatively might be awarded a better grade by another. In a controlled study of "writing ability," 53 different evaluators graded 300 student papers (15,900 evaluations overall). More than one-third of the papers (101) received every possible grade from A through D, and no paper received fewer than five different grades (Hirsch, 1996, pp. 183–184).

   Hirsch argues research findings such as those just described cast doubt on the validity and reliability of performance assessments to measure writing ability. To demonstrate your writing ability, do you prefer to write essays, constructed and evaluated by your teacher, or do you prefer to take commercially prepared, standardized multiple-choice exams scored by a neutral party? Could each form of assessment be reliable and valid? Does your preference for essay or short-answer evaluation extend to other subject areas? Should students have a choice between standardized multiple-choice exams and essay exams to assess their performance in classes?

References

ADLER, M. J. (1982). *The Paideia Proposal: An Educational Manifesto.* New York: Macmillan.

ARDOVINO, J., HOLLINGSWORTH, J., AND YBARRA, S. (2000). *Multiple Measures: Accurate Ways to Assess Student Achievement.* Thousand Oaks, CA: Corwin.

ARENSON, K. W. (1996). "College Board Revises Test to Improve Chances for Girls." *The New York Times.* Oct. 2. (www.nytimes.com)

CALLAHAN, E. (1962). *Education and the Cult of Efficiency.* Chicago: University of Chicago Press.

CAMPBELL, J. R., HOMBO, C. M., AND MAZZEO, J. (2000). *NAEP 1999 Trends in Academic Progress: Three Decades of Student Performance.* Washington, DC: U.S. Department of Education. Office of Education Research and Improvement. National Center for Education Statistics.

CANNELL, J. J. (1987). *Nationally Normed Elementary Achievement Testing in America's Public Schools: How All 50 States Are Above the National Average.* 2nd Ed. Daniels, WV: Friends for Education.

CHENOWETH, K. (1997). "A Measurement of What?" *Black Issues in Higher Education* 14, 18–22, 25.

CIZEK, G. J. (1991). "Innovation or Enervation? Performance Assessment in Perspective." *Phi Delta Kappan* 72, 695–699.

CREMIN, L. (1961). *The Transformation of the School: Progressivism in American Education,* 1876–1957. New York: Knopf.

CROUSE, J., AND TRUSHEIM, D. (1988). *The Case Against the SAT.* Chicago: University of Chicago Press.

DARLING-HAMMOND, L. (1994). "Performance-Based Assessment and Educational Equity." *Harvard Educational Review* 64, 5–30.

FAIRTEST. (2002a). "The SAT: Questions and Answers." (www.fairtest.org/facts/satfact.html)

FAIRTEST. (2002b). "Initial FairTest Analysis of ESEA as Passed by Congress, Dec. 2001." (www.fairtest.org/nattest/ESEA.html)

FISKE, E. B. (1988). "America's Test Mania." *The New York Times.* Education Life, April 10, pp. 16–20.

GARCIA, G. E., AND PEARSON, P. D. (1994). "Assessment and Diversity." In L. Darling-Hammond, ed., *Review of Research in Education.* Washington, DC: American Educational Research Association.

GARDNER, H. (1983). *Frames of Mind: The Theory of Multiple Intelligences.* New York: Basic Books.

———. (1999). *Intelligence Reframed: Multiple Intelligence for the 21st Century.* New York: Basic Books.

GOULD, S. J. (1981). *The Mismeasure of Man.* New York: W. W. Norton.

GUMBERT, E. B., AND SPRING, J. H. (1974). *The Superschool and The Superstate: American Education in the Twentieth Century, 1918–1970.* New York: John Wiley and Sons.

HANSON, F. A. (1993). *Testing Testing: Social Consequences of the Examined Life.* Berkeley: University of California.

HART, P. D., AND TEETER, R. M. (2001). "A Measured Response: Americans Speak on Education Reform." (http://www.ets.org/aboutets/measure.html)

HIRSCH, E. D., JR. (1996). *The Schools We Need and Why We Don't Have Them.* New York: Doubleday.

HOFFMANN, B. (1962). *The Tyranny of Testing.* New York: Crowell-Colliers.

HOOVER, E. (2002). "College Board Approves Major Changes for SAT," June 28. (http://chronicle.com/cg:2-bin)

JANESICK, V. J. (2001). *The Assessment Debate: A Reference Handbook.* Santa Barbara, CA: ABC-CLIO.

JENCKS, C., AND PHILLIPS, M., EDS. (1998). *The Black-White Test Score Gap.* Washington, DC: Brookings Institution.

JUDSON, G. (1996). "What Makes the School Shine? Test Tampering, Officials Say." *The New York Times.* May 1. (www.nytimes.com)

KERLINGER, F. N. (1979). *Behavioral Research.* New York: Holt, Rinehart and Winston.

KOHN, A. (2000). *The Case Against Standardized Testing: Raising the Scores, Ruining the Schools.* Portsmouth, NH: Heinemann.

KORETZ, D., ET AL. (1994). "The Vermont Portfolio Assessment: Findings and Implications." *Educational Measurement: Issues and Practice* 13, 5–16.

LEE, J. (2002). "Racial and Ethnic Achievement Gap Trends: Reversing the Progress Toward Equity? *Education Researcher* 31, 3–12.

LINN, R. L. (1993). "Educational Assessment: Expanded Expectation and Challenges." *Educational Evaluation and Policy Analysis* 15, 1–16.

MABRY, L. (1999). *Portfolio Plus: A Critical Guide to Alternative Assessment.* Thousand Oaks, CA: Corwin.

MADAUS, G. F. (1994). "A Technological and Historical Consideration of Equity Issues Associated with Proposals to Change the Nation's Testing Policy." *Harvard Educational Review* 64, 76–95.

MEHRENS, W. A., AND KAMINSKI, J. (1989). "Methods for Improving Standardized Test Scores: Fruitful, Fruitless, or Fraudulent?" *Educational Measurement: Issues and Practice* 8, 14–22.

MERROW, J. (2002). "Taking the Measure of a School: Standardized Test Scores Don't Tell the Whole Story." *The New York Times.* Jan. 13, 58.

NAIRN, A., AND ASSOCIATES. (1980). *The Reign of ETS: The Corporation that Makes Up Minds.* Washington, DC: Nairn and Associates.

NEILL, D. M. (1991). "Do We Need a National Achievement Exam? No: It Would Damage, Not Improve Education." *Education Week.* April 24, pp. 36, 28.

NEILL, D. M., AND MEDINA, N. J. (1989). "Standardized Testing: Harmful to Educational Health. *Phi Delta Kappan* 70, 688–697.

OWEN, D. (1985). *None of the Above.* Boston: Houghton Mifflin.

PHILLIPS, G. W. (1990). "The Lake Wobegon Effect." *Educational Measurement: Issues and Practice* 9, 3, 14.

POPHAM, W. J. (2002). *Classroom Assessment: What Teachers Need to Know.* 3rd Ed. Boston: Allyn & Bacon.

ROSSER, P. (1987). *Sex Bias in College Admissions Testing: Why Women Lose Out.* 2nd Ed. Cambridge, MA: FairTest.

SUPOVITZ, J. A., AND BRENNAN, R. T. (1997). "Mirror, Mirror on the Wall, Which Is the Fairest Test of All? An Examination of Portfolio Assessment Relative to Standardized Tests." *Harvard Educational Review* 67, 472–502.

TERMAN, L. M. (1922). *Intelligence Tests and School Reorganization.* Yonkers-on-Hudson: World Book.

WEISS, A., ET AL. (2001). "The Next Generation of Citizens: NAEP Civics Assessments—1988 and 1998." Washington, DC: U.S. Department of Education.

WOLF, J. B., ET AL. (1991). "To Use Their Minds Well: Investigating New Forms of Student Assessment." In G. Grant, ed., *Review of Research in Education.* Washington, DC: American Educational Research Association.

PART THREE

How Should Schools Be Organized and Operated?

School Environment

About Part Three: In Chapter 1, we argue that educational issues can be understood only by examining them against a larger social backdrop. Schooling and school policy are part of the political and economic context of society, and while issues in education may at first glance seem to concern mainly matters of teaching and learning, we believe schools always reflect the societies in which they are located and political systems that sustain them.

School leadership, academic freedom, teacher unions, inclusion and mainstreaming, and school violence are issues about the school environment that you will consider here. Similar to issues in other sections of the book, they call your attention to relationships between education and politics, schools and the state. The five chapters in this section focus on ways in which schools are organized and operated. One set of questions about the school environment concerns the nature of teaching and organization of teachers' work. You are asked to consider a variety of questions: Should teachers have decision-making authority that goes beyond their classrooms or would granting teachers this authority represent an unwarranted intrusion on school superintendents' and building principals' management prerogatives? Are students better served by teachers with union representation or do unions distort the working relationship of teachers and schools to the detriment of students? Should schools assume the challenge of including the broadest possible range of the community's children, independent of exceptionality and physical or mental characteristics? Or, as others would have it, are these gestures toward inclusion merely the latest education fad that work ultimately to undo the academic quality of education of all students? Whom should schools serve, and how should schools be organized and managed to serve those populations?

Schools are closely tied to societies that bring them into existence, and the academic ends of schools are always a political reflection of the community. The goals of any educational system are inseparable from society's goals, and organization of the school environment mirrors society's beliefs and values. A society, such as the United States, for example, in which economic rewards are distributed on the basis of contest and merit will insist schools prize competition in their grading system as well as on athletic fields. Schools are expected to teach the virtues of competition and its essential place in finding one's way into the best colleges as well as winning economic success, the right spouse, and the good life.

PUBLIC EDUCATION AND PUBLIC PURPOSE

The link between the ideal state and kinds of schools necessary to support it was described by Plato (427–347 B.C.E). Although Plato often is referred to as the "first philosopher of education," he is less interested in schools than their role in supporting the state. Plato's views of education spring directly from his ideas about the just society. He believes democracy was dangerous and unnecessary, and argues that the great mass of people are not able to move beyond the enjoyment of bodily pleasure to the pleasure of honor, and only a few of the latter group are capable of enjoying the truest pleasure, that of the intellect (Curren, 2000, p. 51). Democracy is dangerous to Plato's way of thinking; it could produce chaos by allowing people freedom to choose their own direction in life as well as their own leaders.

Plato argues public education "is necessary to a just city because it is essential to good order, consensual rule and human virtue, happiness and rationality" (Curren, 2000, p. 53). Compare Plato's sense of justice with ways we framed justice in the Introduction to Part One. There we asked you to consider justice not as a fixed and permanent condition for the good of the state, but as a changeable set of criteria defined differently in other times and places. You may recall we argued that "Burning witches at the stake was considered justice at one time; using the rod to physically punish misbehaving students was an accepted schoolmarm's role in the school justice systems of the past. The ultimate punishment, death, is considered too uncivilized to be justice in some nations; others use it routinely."

Most contemporary definitions of justice involve the equal treatment of individuals and relationship among individuals. That is, justice is related to the principle of each person getting what he or she is due—no more, no less. Most modern writers try to situate justice in an individual context. They ask, what should the state do (or refrain from doing) to determine who should enjoy the benefits and shoulder the burdens of society when other citizens have equally good claims to them (Rawls, 1971; Nozick, 1974)? In America, we often think of justice both as a right of citizens and an obligation of the state. Justice demands certain actions by the state to ensure fairness. By law, American citizens are to be treated equally. Their behavior, right or wrong, is to be judged independent of gender or race or social class. The just society treats everyone fairly. Of course we can all think of exceptions to this principle of justice. It is a safe bet there are more paupers than millionaires on death row, and we can all name individuals who have escaped minor infractions of the law because of who they are or who they know. Our notion of modern justice, however, is rooted in the principle of fair treatment by the state for all individuals, and we are taught to accept no less.

In Part One, we argue schools should serve the interests of justice and equity, and we invited you to consider competing perspectives on seven specific issues. We ask, whose interests should schools serve based on what was just and equitable. In Part Two, we ask you to consider what knowledge is of most value and what should be taught. The organization of this book reflects our belief that any notion of schooling begins with questions about the goals society expects students to achieve. Schools and teachers then define the knowledge and select methods to help students reach those goals. Finally, schools develop an organization and a management system to produce a school environment appropriate for reaching the state's goals. It seems reasonable to expect different conceptions of justice will produce vastly different goals for students. Different societies will prize different forms of school knowledge and classroom instruction, and will embrace different ideas about the organization of the best school environment. Plato's goal, like ours, is justice, but because we might not share his view of justice, we might not share his vision of the ideal school.[1]

Of particular interest in Part Three is the job of teaching. One set of questions running through Chapters 15 through 19 asks you to consider the role teachers should play in schools. What should be the nature of teachers' work? How much decision-making authority should teachers have? How free should teachers be to select content and teaching methods? How should the work of teachers be organized and managed to maximize student learning? Consider Plato's recommendations for teaching subject matter. In Book II of the *Republic,* Plato argues, "we must set up a censorship over the fable-makers, and approve any good fable they make, and disapprove the bad; those which are approved we will persuade the mothers and nurses to tell the children, and

[1]Karl Popper, the late British philosopher (1902–1994), argues Plato's sense of justice is not based on fairness for the individual or right action by the state to protect the individual, but is instead a justification for what is good for the state and the ruling aristocracy. Plato's justice, according to Popper, is designed to protect the state from any change and to hold firm the rigid class structure of Craftsmen, Guardians, and Rulers. Plato's justice is a property of the state necessary to ensure its own best functioning and ultimate survival. Citizens of Plato's state fall into social classes because of their natural talents and abilities, and are all expected to serve the state in different, fixed, and predetermined ways. Some men will naturally be weavers; others will be warriors; and a few will be selected to lead. Craftsmen will never become warriors; leadership will be left to the leaders. Justice is the harmonious and selfless toil of individuals in support of the state (Popper, 1966).

to mould the souls of the children by the fables even more carefully than the bodies by their hands. Most of those they tell now must be thrown away" (Plato, 1984, p. 174). Plato recognizes that stories have great influence on children's behaviors, and many childhood behaviors carry into adulthood. Plato urges censorship of all stories that were either (a) false, or (b) true, if the truth of the story is not in harmony with the needs of the state. The poets and other storytellers, Plato tells us, are dangerous because their writing is so beautiful and engaging. The charm of their words, when false, could lead children to adopt the wrong attitudes, but even when they speak the truth, they could lead children astray (Copleston, 1993).

For Plato, censorship helps to create a positive educational environment. It protects a vulnerable class of young citizens from dangerous effects of an inappropriate body of literature: stories that harm the individual and myths that undermine the state. Children are sheltered from stories in which the gods are portrayed as deceivers or dissemblers, changeable or fickle. In school, the gods always are represented as eternal simplicity and truth. To portray the gods in a bad light would harm the child and ultimately the state. It was nothing less than the duty of schools to prevent damage, as long as the methods of prevention are no more harmful than the evils they were to guard against (Copleston, 1993). Platonic education has specific aims. It is designed to form character and judgments about good and evil in harmony with virtues of both the individual and the state. Education, according to Plato, is designed to "induce an admiration for what is admirable and hatred for what is shameful, and by means of this harmony with reason, as receptivity to reason which will mature into a capacity to grasp why some things are to be admired and others condemned" (Curren, 2000, p. 52).

Plato represents the oldest traditions of education: the view that teachers are nothing more than obedient servants of the state. Plato urges teachers to follow the curriculum slavishly. Warning his readers that any deviation could only be for the worse, he writes: "When the poet says that men care most for 'the newest air that hovers on the singer's lips,' they will be afraid lest he be taken not merely to mean new songs, but to commending a new style of music. Such innovation is not to be commended, nor should the poet be so understood. The introduction of novel fashions in music is a thing to beware of as endangering the whole fabric of society" (Cornford, 1968, p. 115).

Few people today would deny teachers the right to select appropriate teaching methods and be innovative in the classroom. Unlike Plato, most people believe in the potential of progress and value of change. Many believe, however, that control of the curriculum remains the rightful province of the state or community and not the teacher. To empower teachers with authority over the curriculum is to disempower taxpayers, their elected community representatives (boards of education), and school administrators. Consider yourselves, for a moment, not as teachers or prospective teachers, but as taxpayers with children in public schools. Would you be comfortable paying school taxes while having little or no say in the education of your children? Would you be willing to leave decisions about curriculum, textbooks, teaching methodology, and evaluation to teachers who are not directly accountable to you? Or would you prefer to have these policy matters rest in the hands of school administrators and elected school boards who are responsible to you as a citizen and community resident? Clearly, a strong case can be made for community control of schools.

Others will argue with equal conviction that school reform has failed in the past largely because reformers have ignored the role teachers play. For today's schools to become more satisfying and more thought-provoking for children, they must first become better places for teachers. Teachers must be allowed to assume their rightful place as professionals with genuine authority in schools; they should control matters of curriculum, instruction, and policy. Teachers should be able to assume a responsible role in shaping the purposes of schooling (Aronowitz and Giroux, 1985). Would you want to teach in a school district that refused to listen to you about matters of curriculum and instruction?

Arguments about the organization and management of schools lie along a continuum of political thought. The left or liberal end of the continuum includes those who tend to be sympathetic toward the rights of workers and toward teacher empowerment. It also includes those with positive views of unions and union involvement in school policy matters, as well as those who champion academic freedom for public school teachers. The right or conservative end of the continuum includes those more comfortable with the traditional exercise of authority in the schools. They tend to oppose any attempt to weaken community control of schools, such as granting greater power to teachers. Those on the right tend to be less sympathetic toward unions, often viewing them as the protectors of incompetent teachers and as unwise meddlers in local school management. Conservatives typically share a less than charitable view toward extending academic freedom to public school teachers, regarding it as an overused shield for spreading ill-founded and even dangerous ideas in the classroom. Of course, we need to be cautious about painting with too broad a brush. Our goal is not to label school critics, but to make you more aware of competing perspectives in education. As you think about what teaching should be, look to the arguments of both left and right. Where do you find yourself along the spectrum of opinion on each issue?

THE ISSUES OF SCHOOL LEADERSHIP, ACADEMIC FREEDOM, AND TEACHER UNIONS

Teaching has been described as a "careerless profession," a good entry-level job that offers only limited opportunity for promotion or increases in authority and salary (Etzioni, 1969; Lortie, 1975). Upon graduation from college, most people pursue a series of work experiences and job-related career moves that bring them additional responsibilities and greater compensation. A few teachers—mainly those who move from classroom teaching through the principalship to central office administration—follow a similar ascent. However, most teachers typically do not have access to a promotion path that includes a series of increasingly rewarding positions. In the past, the public largely ignored issues about teaching and teachers' work. If the public was satisfied with the quality of schools and the performance of teachers, its satisfaction was expressed inaudibly. When schools appeared to be functioning well, communities rarely considered the problems of a teaching career. As long as student learning appeared to be high and student discipline was relatively unproblematic, few people outside of education concerned themselves with the role teachers should play in schools or the difficulty of attracting and retaining talented faculty.

Beginning in the 1980s, researchers uncovered a variety of problems with public schooling. Educational expenditures had never been higher, but scores on standardized achievement tests were hitting all-time lows. Restive teachers demanded higher salaries, while the popular press delighted in printing stories of increases in school violence, crime, and the numbers of poorly educated students. Studies criticized everything from student learning to teacher preparation (Boyer, 1983; National Commission on Excellence in Education, 1983; Goodlad, 1984; Sizer, 1984; Goodlad, 1990; Archibold, 1998). Schools were said to be in crisis, and the nation was declared at risk because of the poor quality of teaching and learning. Teachers were held up to public scrutiny, and their work was weighed, measured, and assessed. Everywhere, researchers found dull, lifeless teaching; an absence of academic focus; bored, unchallenged students; and teachers mired in routine and paperwork. An inescapable conclusion of the 1980s research was that teachers were not doing, or were not able to do, the job expected of them. The conditions of teaching were revisited as objects of policy reform, and teachers' work has been reopened for debate (Tye and O'Brien, 2002). Is there something wrong with the model of schools that separates teaching from school management? Would schools be better places for students if teachers were granted greater decision-making authority in running schools? Would teaching be a more attractive career choice if teachers were allowed to play empowered roles in school management and school reform? In short, should schools be organized to include classroom teachers as school leaders and managers or are schools and students better off when leadership is left to others?

Plato introduces the topic of censorship in education. Modern democracies pay less attention to school censorship than they do to the other side of the coin: the right to inquire freely in schools. What place should academic freedom play in defining the teacher's role? If you view teachers as the leaders in education, then you are likely to believe they have a "right to teach," based on their special skills and knowledge, and this right should be protected. If, instead, you see teachers as craftsmen or practitioners who merit little authority over the curriculum, then you may be less willing to grant them the same freedoms enjoyed by those who teach in colleges and universities. "Academic freedom," as commonly applied to higher education, is a contemporary term for the classical ideal of the right to teach and learn (Hofstadter and Metzger, 1955). Socrates, Plato's teacher, charged with impiety and the corruption of Athenian youth, defended himself by claiming he and his students had the freedom to pursue truth and all wickedness is due to ignorance. Socrates argued the freedom to teach and learn is essential to uncover knowledge and improve society. His fellow citizens were not persuaded and sentenced Socrates to death. Academic freedom has fared better; though regularly attacked and battered, it has survived. Academic freedom, as applied to American higher education today, typically refers to several related freedoms: (1) the freedom of professors to write, research, and teach in their field of special competence; (2) the freedom of universities to determine policies and practices unfettered by political restraints or other outside pressures; and (3) the freedom of students to learn.

Advocates argue that academic freedom ensures freedom of the mind for both students and scholars and therefore is essential to the pursuit of truth, the primary mission of higher education (Kirk, 1955; MacIver, 1955). The American Civil Liberties Union (ACLU), on the other hand, objects to limiting academic freedom to university settings. The ACLU claims academic freedom should extend to public schools, which they describe as the "authentic academic community" for young people. "If each new generation is to acquire a feeling for civil liberties," the ACLU argues, "it can do so only by having a chance to live in the midst of a community where the principles are continually exemplified" (ACLU, 1968, p. 4). The issue of academic freedom raises a series of difficult questions about the organization of the school environment: What is academic freedom and whom should it protect? Is it a right that can be extended to teachers at all grade levels? Does academic freedom clash with the community's right to determine what to teach its children? Who decides what is an appropriate education for minor children? Can higher education continue to claim academic freedom as a special right reserved for university experts (Hook, 1953)? Or is this an essential right in all learning environments?

What role should unions play in education? How do teacher unions affect the school environment? Unions originated in industry, and were effective in improving workers' salaries. The number of union workers has declined nationally in all fields except public education. The issue we ask you to consider here is not whether teachers should or should not belong to professional work associations, but whether unions are good for education. Conservatives typically argue that unions are undemocratic organizations working against the best interests of pupils, parents, and teachers. Collective bargaining is not for the public good, nor will it contribute to school reform; it should be restricted if schools are to serve the children and the community. Liberals, on the other hand, argue that unions have had a positive effect on education, and collective bargaining and union influence should extend beyond wages and hours to include matters of school policy and reform.

For those on the left, the success of school reform is linked to participation of unions in the reform agenda.

ORGANIZING SCHOOL ENVIRONMENTS FOR STUDENTS WHO ARE "HARD TO TEACH"

Among the great debates about schooling is one that asks what schools should do with students who are hard to teach. One side in the debate argues that schools are designed and organized to teach subject matter, and may weed out or exclude those students who do not show sufficient compliance or the ability to learn. The other side counters that schools are student-centered institutions, and therefore must bend subject matter and programs around all the students. The argument has been going on for over 100 years. It was central in the discussions about schools throughout the twentieth century, and so far has resisted resolution in the early twenty-frst century. In 1902, John Dewey characterized the dispute as argument between two "sects." The subject-matter sect wanted to organize schools by academic topics, subdivided into separate lessons, with each lesson having its own set of facts for students to learn. Children were to proceed step by step in the mastery of individual facts until they had covered the prescribed academic terrain. The other sect, Dewey argued, focused on the individual child as the starting point, middle, and end of education. The academic terrain was irrelevant compared to the needs and interests of individual learners (Loveless, 2001, p. 1). The way in which you see this argument is likely to determine your position in the debate about the obligations schools have to students who are harder to teach and those who are more difficult to manage.

Among other things, we ask that you consider how school should provide the most appropriate education for students who have "special needs." Children with particular mental or physical disabilities, are emotionally disturbed, or have other specific needs fall into this category. Sometimes the term *exceptional* is applied to this group of children in educational literature; usually, this term includes children identified as gifted and talented. The main reason for trying to identify and evaluate children with special or exceptional needs is to provide them with special educational assistance. For physically disabled students, that may mean special equipment such as magnification devices for the visually impaired. For learning disabled children, it may mean specially prepared teaching materials. For gifted and talented children, it may mean special artistic tutoring or advanced academic work. The fundamental question is one of degree: How much should school environments be modified to accommodate learners? When schools try to meet the needs of all students, do they run the risk of serving no student very well? Does a focus on children with special needs dilute the academic quality of public schools?

As you can see, in the twenty-first century, public schools are being asked to do more with a wider range of students than ever before. In the heavy-handed state idealized by Plato, citizens received an education appropriate to their social class and intellectual skills. Teachers in the *Republic* believed justice was served when every citizen and every class of citizens functioned harmoniously, each being educated and performing according to his or her abilities and inclinations for the harmonious good of the state. Athenian education was not to produce citizens who were "to go their own way," as Plato put it. American society and its schools, along with others in the West, have adopted a different understanding of justice and relationships between the individual and the state. Influenced by philosophers who followed Plato (in particular, his student, Aristotle, and later, Immanuel Kant) justice has been identified less frequently as something that exists in the state and more often as something that resides within the individual. Education in democracies requires individuals make their own decisions about vocation and training and type of schooling to be received. Interests of the individual are considered paramount, and the state is thought to be just only when the majority of citizens are served well. Public schools are designed to serve all students. Clearly, problems arise at the margins. How should schools tend to special needs children, the unusually disaffected, the gifted as well as the troubled? We know students are at a terrible disadvantage if they are not graduated from high school, but what should be done with students whose very presence in school works to the academic detriment of others? Chapter 19 will ask you to look at the issue of school violence.

As you are no doubt aware, violence has become one of the most troubling problems facing American educators. Schools, once safe havens from the outside world, now must contend with acts of bullying and violence at every grade level. With school violence on the increase, experts continue to debate its causes and how schools should handle violent students. Many teachers and criminologists argue the time has come to crack down on the most violent offenders and expel them from school. They argue that the school's job is to teach academic subject matter to those who are at least minimally willing to cooperate. Others argue that educators are responsible for helping students with whatever problems they bring to school, even if this means expanding the role of schools into nonacademic areas.

In 2002, pollsters gathering information for the 34th Annual Phi Delta Kappa/ Gallup Poll interviewed respondents individually. They read off several of the problems facing public schools, and asked if that problem in their community was "very serious," "serious," "somewhat serious," or "not serious at all." Seventy-six percent of the respondents rated the "lack of student discipline" as very or somewhat serious, and 63 percent rated the problem of "fighting, violence, gangs" in the same categories (Rose and Gallup, 2002, pp. 51–52).

Clearly, the public sees school violence as a problem. Do you believe schools have an obligation to reduce school violence? Do they already possess a range of effective strategies for doing so? Or is it not the school's job to protect the majority of students from the violent minority?

******

Although this book is divided into three parts, we believe the parts are related to one another in important ways, and also believe you are better able to understand schools and issues surrounding education by considering the interrelationships. Part One focuses on the interests schools should serve; the chapters in Part One ask you to consider the nature of justice and equity and what they mean for people interested in public education. Justice is one of the oldest of the social virtues. Philosophers and students of philosophy have been debating its meaning at least since the time of Plato and Aristotle. If justice is about social fairness, with each getting what he or she is due, how is this related to the practical matters of education? The chapters in Part One ask you to examine competing perspectives about the interests schools should serve, and ask you to decide which positions seem to you to be the more just and offer greater equity.

Part Two asks what knowledge schools should teach. Those on one side of the debate argue that knowledge is neutral and American society in the early twenty-first century has an agreed-upon body of knowledge important for all citizens and should be taught in all schools. Not everyone believes there is or should be one uniform body of knowledge. Picking up a philosophic argument as old as Heraclitus, a pre-Socratic philosopher, and amplified by Friedrich Nietzsche, those on the other side of the argument claim that all truth is perspectival. For them, a single or absolute truth does not exist; what we call knowledge is the perspective or interpretations made by various groups and classes of people reflecting such individual factors as age, race, nationality, religion, and gender. Schools, for those who subscribe to this view, should not pretend to teach knowledge as if it were an agreed-upon, objective, and neutral representation of reality. There are many competing realities, and schools must teach multiple views of what is true. Joel Spring (2002a, 2002b), for one, argues that social knowledge is never neutral. Knowledge always serves one interest or another from the Christian Coalition and conservative think tanks to the National Organization for Women and advocates of Indiocentricity/Afrocentricity. For Spring and others, schools will always be places of conflict among those who subscribe to competing notions of justice, equity, and forms of knowledge flowing from those perspectives.

Part Three asks you to consider the human environment of schools, specifically the rights and roles of teachers and whether or not we can teach all students in public schools. These issues are likely to be related to your positions on the nature of knowledge, the content you believe schools should teach, and ultimately your views of justice and equity. We hope you will find the arguments on both sides convincing and engaging, and encourage your thoughtful deliberations and disagreements. As we wrote in Chapter 1, if you like arguments, you'll love the study of education.

References

AMERICAN CIVIL LIBERTIES UNION (ACLU). (1968). *Academic Freedom in the Secondary Schools.* New York: Author.

ARCHIBOLD, R. C. (1998). "Getting Tough on Teachers." *The New York Times.* Nov. 1, Sec. 4A, pp. 22–25, 30–31.

ARONOWITZ, S., AND GIROUX, H. A. (1985). *Education Under Siege: The Conservative, Liberal, and Radical Debate Over Schooling.* South Hadley, MA: Bergin & Garvey.

BOYER, E. L. (1983). *High School: A Report on Secondary Education in America.* New York: Harper & Row.

COPLESTON, F. (1993). *A History of Philosophy, Vol. I: Greece and Rome.* New York: Doubleday.

CORNFORD, F. M., ED. AND TRANSLATOR. (1968). *The Republic of Plato.* New York: Oxford University Press.

CURREN, R. R. (2000). *Aristotle on the Necessity of Public Education.* Lanham, MD: Rowan and Littlefield.

ETZIONI, A., ED. (1969). *The Semi-Professions and Their Organization: Teachers, Nurses, Social Workers.* New York: Free Press.

GOODLAD, J. I. (1984). *A Place Called School: Prospects for the Future.* New York: McGraw-Hill.

———. (1990). *Teachers for Our Nation's Schools.* San Francisco: Jossey-Bass.

HOFSTADTER, R., AND METZGER, W. P. (1955). *The Development of Academic Freedom in the United States.* New York: Columbia University Press.

HOOK, S. (1953). *Heresy, Yes—Conspiracy, No.* New York: John Day.

KIRK, R. (1955). *Academic Freedom: An Essay in Definition.* Chicago: Henry Regnery.

LORTIE, D. (1975). *Schoolteacher.* Chicago: University of Chicago Press.

LOVELESS, T., ED. (2001). *The Great Curriculum Debate: How Should We Teach Reading and Math?* Washington, DC: Brooking Institution.

MACIVER, R. M. (1955). *Academic Freedom in Our Time.* New York: Columbia University Press.

NATIONAL COMMISSION ON EXCELLENCE IN EDUCATION. (1983). *A Nation at Risk: The Imperative for Educational Reform.* National Education Association. Washington, DC: U.S. Government Printing Office.

NOZICK, R. (1974). *Anarchy, State, State and Utopia.* New York: Basic Books.

PLATO. (1984). *Great Dialogues of Plato.* W. H. D. Rouse, translator. E. H. Warmington and P. G. Rouse, eds. New York: Mentor.

POPPER, K. (1966). *The Open Society and Its Enemies.* Princeton: Princeton University Press.

RAWLS, J. (1971). *A Theory of Justice.* Cambridge: Harvard University Press.

ROSE, L. C., AND GALLUP, A. M. (2002). "The 34th Annual Phi Delta Kappa/Gallup Poll of the Public's Attitudes Toward the Public Schools." *Phi Delta Kappan,* 84, 41–56.

SIZER, T. R. (1984). *Horace's Compromise: The Dilemma of the American High School.* Boston: Houghton Mifflin.

SPRING, J. (2002a). *Political Agenda for Education; From the Religious Right to the Green Party.* 2nd Ed. Mahwah, NJ: Lawrence Erlbaum.

———. (2002b). *Conflict of Interests, The Politics of American Education.* Boston: McGraw-Hill.

TYE, B. B., AND O'BRIEN, L. (2002). "Why Are Experienced Teachers Leaving the Profession?" *Phi Delta Kappan,* 84, 24–32.

CHAPTER 15

Instructional Leadership: Teachers or Administrators

POSITION 1: FOR TEACHERS AS INSTRUCTIONAL LEADERS

When teachers are given the opportunity to exercise their professional talents beyond the classroom, everyone benefits. All too often, outstanding teachers leave the public schools because use of their leadership capabilities and professional skills has been limited only to a single classroom.

—WILLIAMS-BOYD, 2002, P. 29

The authority to act as school leaders was originally placed in the hands of building principals and district superintendents. It was division of labor related to gender. Throughout the history of public education, most teachers have been women—especially in the lower grades—and principals and superintendents have been primarily men. Education was traditionally thought of as "women's work." Women were considered more nurturing and better suited to be moral guides for children. In the early days of public schools, with few other work opportunities open to them, women were ready recruits. Educated only slightly better than the students they would eventually teach, women were hired to work for very low wages and expected to serve in schools without tenure or any promise they could assume positions of leadership. Today, while women make up two-thirds of U.S. teachers, they still are underrepresented in school and district administration (Kowalski, 2003, p. 14).

Although there were male teachers in the early days of public education, teaching was not considered fully respectable work for men, and nineteenth-century authors crafted unflattering portraits of male teachers. Consider, for example, Charles Dickens's teacher in *Hard Times,* Thomas Gradgrind. Gradgrind was a callous and pedantic martinet who prepared his students for a world of the grimmest practicalities: Schooling was designed to do little more than make children ready for dreary and dangerous work in factories. In a chapter entitled "Murdering the Innocents," Dickens offers this description of Gradgrind's teaching:

> "Girl number twenty," said Mr. Gradgrind, squarely pointing with his square forefinger, "I don't know that girl. Who is that girl?"
>
> "Sissy Jupe, sir," explained number twenty, blushing, standing up, and curtsying.
>
> "Sissy is not a name," said Mr. Gradgrind: "Don't call yourself Sissy. Call yourself Cecelia."
>
> "It's father as calls me Sissy, sir," returned the young girl in a trembling voice, and with another curtsy.
>
> "Then he has no business to do it," said Mr. Gradgrind. "Tell him he mustn't. Cecelia Jupe. Let me see. What is your father?"
>
> "He belongs to the horse-riding, if you please, sir . . ."
>
> "Very well, then. He is a veterinary surgeon, a farrier, and horse breaker. Give me your definition of a horse."
>
> (Sissy Jupe thrown into the greatest alarm by this demand.)
>
> "Girl number twenty unable to define a horse!"
>
> said Mr. Gradgrind, for the general behoof of all the little pitchers. "Girl number twenty possessed of no facts, in reference to one of the commonest of animals! Some boy's definition of a horse. Bitzer, yours . . ."
>
> "Quadruped. Graminivorous. Forty teeth, namely twenty-four grinders, four eye-teeth, and twelve incisive. Sheds coat in the spring, in marshy countries, sheds hoofs too. Hoofs hard, but requiring to be shod with iron. Age known by marks in mouth . . ."
>
> "Now, girl twenty," said Mr. Gradgrind, "you know what a horse is."
>
> She curtsied again, and would have blushed deeper, if she could have blushed deeper than she had blushed all this time. (Dickens, 1854, pp. 1–4)

Hard Times was less an attack on teachers than an indictment of the harsh factory system of nineteenth-century England and schools all too willing to prepare students for work in them. There is no denying, however, that Mr. Gradgrind is an offensive character. Indifferent to his students' needs for esteem, insensitive to the imaginative side of childhood, and unaware of even the most obvious aspects of human nature, Dickens's Gradgrind is an unflattering image of public school teachers.

"Unmarriageable Women and Unsaleable Men"

Although education is currently at the top of the nation's policy agenda, teaching has not always been among America's most admired forms for work. During the nineteenth century, it was assumed that those who taught school would do so for only a short time. Women typically chose marriage and homemaking after a few years in the classroom. Ambitious men were expected to move from teaching to loftier, better-paying occupations. Classroom teaching was seldom the chosen lifetime work of the more able. Teaching was considered as employment for workers who were "passing through"on their way to more serious pursuits (Holmes Group, 1986, p. 32).

At best, teaching was seen as a good short-term job, but most people disparaged it as a career choice, and those who chose to stay in the classroom for more than a few years often encountered social derision. In 1932, sociologist Willard Waller observed that teachers were not treated like other workers, and certainly not like professionals. He noted that in small towns, unmarried teachers were expected to live in a teacherage—a special boardinghouse—apart from other single adults who held nonteaching jobs. Waller also noted the popular prejudice against teachers commonly held by wealthier and better-educated members of the community. "Teaching," he wrote, "is quite generally regarded as a failure belt . . . the refuge of unmarriageable women and unsaleable men" (Waller, 1932, p. 61). For many years, teaching was a temporary job for a series of young women and managed by the men in the offices of the principal and the superintendent of schools.

Well before the new millennium, the nature of teaching and the teaching workforce changed dramatically. Today, more women and men look at teaching not just as a job to pursue in their youth, but as a lifelong career. Those who work in public schools today must complete (in most states) five years of higher education. Certification as a beginning teacher now requires at least a bachelor's degree with a strong general education component, specialized academic course work, professional study, and extensive practical experiences in schools. Many teachers have master's degrees, and more than a few have doctorates. Today's teachers are unlike their predecessors. They are well educated and able, and pursue teaching as a career, not as a short-term job. Classroom teachers are experts in the practical matters of teaching and learning, and are the most authoritative source for helping new teachers learn the tricks of the trade. Teachers rightfully expect a greater voice in all matters of education, including school management and school reform.

National Board Certification for Teachers

In a simpler time, it may have been possible for the head of a school to offer appropriate instructional support for most if not all of its teachers. In the 1830s, the term "principal teacher" was first used to indicate the teacher who served as the school overseer (Williams-Boyd, 2002, p. 102). Even to suggest this possibility today is either an indication of arrogance or an admission of ignorance about the complexities of what goes on in classrooms. Effective teachers need to know about the latest developments in instruction, student learning, classroom management, academic assessment, and what constitutes the best and most effective practices in all of these areas. They need to command subject matter and an equal measure of appropriate pedagogy so that all students can learn at the highest levels.

In 1987, a National Board for Professional Teaching Standards was formed to strengthen teaching and improve schools based on what the most accomplished teachers know and are able to do in the classroom. Classroom teachers hold the majority of places on the board. Joined by academics, policymakers, and corporate leaders, the board developed standards in both content and pedagogy needed by classroom teachers. Teaching was recognized as complex and specialized, based on content and pedagogical knowledge and refined by practitioners through actual classroom practice and reflection. The board established standards for teaching content fields from "Art" to "World Literatures other than English," and also developed standards for the pedagogical knowledge needed to teach content to various age groups from Early Childhood, ages 3 to 8, to Adolescent and Young Adult, ages 14 to 18+ (National Board for Professional Teaching Standards, 2002).

Beginning with the Standards, the board created a process by which classroom teachers could earn National Board Certificates in the areas they teach. Available to all teachers with a baccalaureate degree and three years of classroom teaching experience, the rigorous certification process, endorsed by both the National Education Association and the American Federation of Teachers, recognizes the subtleties and complexity of teachers' knowledge (American Federation of Teachers, 2002). By 2003, national certification tests were available or under development in fifteen fields, across as many as four different age levels (National Board for Professional Teaching Standards, 2002). To be certified, teachers must successfully complete as many as six thirty-minute examinations to demonstrate their knowledge of developmentally appropriate content across the range of their teaching area. In addition, teachers seeking certification must submit portfolios that include videotapes of their actual teaching, samples of student work, evidence of their ability to analyze their own teaching, and documentation of their contributions to the profession.

National Board Certification is a time-consuming process, taking at least one year to complete and costing \$2,300 (in 2002), and is valid for only ten years. Certification is not something to be considered lightly, and is likely to be attractive to only the most accomplished classroom teachers. National Board Certification places great faith in teachers. It recognizes that practicing teachers are the best source of content knowledge about the subjects they teach as well as the pedagogical knowledge about how to teach. Certification also demonstrates the commitment of teachers to teaching and student learning (National Board for Professional Teaching Standards, 2002). Nationally Board Certified Teachers have no rivals when it comes to the ability to help other teachers and to lead instruction in schools.

Shared Decision Making Needed to Reform Schools

> Teachers need to be intimately involved in the conceptualization and direction of school reform, which means that teacher isolation, a norm of the profession, must give way to shared decision-making. . . . Teacher knowledge has to be an integral part of the process. (Reed, 2000, xii)

By the 1990s, a growing number of educational theorists and researchers had come to realize that tapping classroom teachers' intellectual understandings and creative energies would lead to improved education (Barth, 1990; Schlechty, 1990; Smylie, 1994). The traditional top-down leadership model of public schools had outlived its usefulness. School faced a wider array of vexing issues than ever before. The problems of education had become far too complex for one or two "leaders" to manage, no matter how skilled and able they might be. In addition, most people recognized that teachers too had changed: Not only were they invested in teaching as a career, they were well educated and possessed curricular expertise and immediate classroom experiences essential to school improvement. School administrators may have been good teachers at one time, but removed from the day-to-day life of instruction, their knowledge of what works and what needs to be done pales in comparison to what teachers know. Above all, experience has shown that for reforms to be successful, the reform agenda must be widely shared by everyone in the school. The best ideas and most worthwhile proposals for change are doomed to failure if viewed as the "principal's plan" rather than a plan shaped and shared by everyone. No single person—no matter how thoughtful and creative that person may be—has a vision that can measure up to the teacher's collective visions of how to help students learn. School leadership is the work of everyone in the schools (Lambert, 2002; Neuman and Simmons, 2000).

Currently, school reform agenda aims at changing schools' governance structure so local teachers and administrators can share authority in making decisions about their students and the ways they are taught. Shared decision making is not an end in itself. It is the way schools can harness talents of teachers and administrators to ensure all students are successful learners. Referred to as "distributed leadership" (Neuman and Simmons, 2000), "teacher leadership" (Guiney, 2001), and more commonly as "shared decision making," advocates of democratic school governance argue schools are unlikely to change for the better without the inclusion of teachers in the change process. Making schools better places for students is the natural work of teachers. Teachers are purposeful, professional creatures for whom school leadership is a reasonable extension of who they are and an essential part of their professional lives (Lambert, 2002).

The shared decision-making (SDM) movement, first proposed in the 1990s, reflects the accumulated evidence about what makes schools effective in teaching children (Marsh et al., 1990; Hatry et al., 1994). Although the level of teacher involvement varies from district to district, teachers in general are beginning to participate more and more in decisions about curriculum, instruction, personnel, and educational policy. Schools increasingly are using teachers' talents, and teachers are more involved in selecting classroom materials, planning in-service workshops, designing evaluations, and assisting new teachers in mastering the art and science of teaching. In some districts, teachers form study groups to examine the research literature and make policy recommendations about approaches to reading, new developments in subject-matter teaching, or schoolwide discipline strategies. Instead of waiting to have change directed from above, teachers in many schools have formed research teams to examine problems in their schools and solutions used by other teachers facing similar problems. In some unionized school districts, collective bargaining agreements have been crafted to ensure teacher participation in school leadership. (See Table 15.1.)

SDM is a promising grass-roots phenomenon that harnesses the energy of both teachers and administrators to reform schools on the local level. No longer can schools be run from offices removed from the classrooms where students learn. Teacher authority is on the rise. Teachers' knowledge about students and about teaching is being transformed into educational policy. SDM involves

Table 15.1. Sample Contract
Cincinnati, Ohio Federation of Teachers
Collective Bargaining Agreement

(Role of the Instructional Leadership Team [ILT])
Instructional Leadership Teams (ILTs) shall be established so that the principal, teachers, and other members may share leadership and make decisions in these areas:

- to develop, review, and evaluate the instructional program
- to monitor and improve school operations and procedures that might impact on instruction
- to plan and monitor training of staff
- to develop and monitor school budget
- to create and maintain a safe and orderly school environment
- to oversee the formation of teams, in team-based schools within given parameters
- to perform all other responsibilities assigned by the contract to the ILT

Source: www.aft.org/research/models/contracts/teacher/cincinnati/150.htm (9/26/02)

more work for teachers; in addition to the demands of the classroom, they now contribute to the management and design of education. An expanded role in school management may not be right for all teachers, but those who choose to take on extra nonteaching tasks and participate in SDM do so because they believe it will improve schools.

Teacher involvement in SDM cannot help but deliver better education. The logic of the SDM reform impulse rests on several interrelated assumptions:

- The demands placed on schools are too complex for any one person to be the leader.
- Teachers have a great store of the practical knowledge about students, curriculum, and instruction necessary to improve schools. No one is more able than teachers to help new teachers, assist struggling colleagues, and make sure that all students learn at high levels. (National Board for Professional Teaching Standards, 2002)
- Schools will become more effective when everyone associated with the school—administrators, teachers, and staff—assume leadership responsibility for student achievement (Neuman and Simmons, 2000).
- Teaching will become a more attractive job when teachers assume greater authority in directing the course of schooling. Increasing numbers of talented undergraduates will choose teaching as a career in direct proportion to the authority we give teachers to manage schools. When teachers are treated as professionals, with greater control over their work, they will use this power to make school better for all learners.

Power

The school reform movement is replete with buzzwords such as "shared decision making," "school-based management," and the "professionalization of

> teaching." Inherent in these concepts, but often overlooked in discussions of their implementation, is the issue of power. Power is a limited commodity in schools, and the established hierarchy places teachers in a low-power position, making it difficult for teacher leaders to be acknowledged as credible forces of change. (Troen and Boles, 1995, p. 371)

Over time, the education community has come to realize that school reform depends on expanding teachers' roles and assigning to them greater responsibilities in schools and the opportunity to direct change. Research evidence suggests that when teachers are given responsibility for school change, there is a greater likelihood these changes will be positive and enduring (Sarason, 1982; Lambert et al., 1997; Reed, 2000). It is reasonable to predict that if schools are restructured so teachers assume greater responsibility for essential school processes—from curriculum to staffing and assessment—students will receive an improved education. Common sense tells us that people work harder and feel better about their work when they have a personal investment in what they do and a sense of identification with the product of their efforts (Foster, 1991; Carr, 1998). Teachers are likely to work toward educational improvement in direct proportion to their involvement in school processes and decision making. The empowerment of teachers through SDM cannot help but pay dividends in improved education for students. SDM is the final repudiation of the nineteenth-century view of teaching. Today's teachers are well educated, well trained, and fully capable of directing their working lives. SDM casts aside forever the view of teachers as social outcasts. SDM recognizes teachers are prepared and able to participate in the management of their careers. As one teacher put it, "Teachers are thinking people and they don't need . . . someone from the top telling them what to do because they know what children need" (Reed, 2000, p. 24).

POSITION 2: FOR PRINCIPALS AS INSTRUCTIONAL LEADERS

> *Informal teacher-leaders insist on high standards in their daily performance, and in knowledge, beliefs, and practice. . . . Yet when these same people are asked who the leaders in the school are, for the most part they will not point to themselves but rather to the administrators—the principal and the vice principal.*
>
> —WILLIAMS-BOYD, 2002, P. 35

Exercising Authority for the Good of Students

"Restructuring schools" and "empowering teachers" are slogans that may fall pleasantly on some ears, but they do not reflect demands placed on schools, authority vested in administrative offices, and research on school reform. School leadership is not a struggle for control between administrators and teachers; it is the exercise of authority necessary to establish appropriate conditions for all children to learn. Public schools are hierarchical by design. They were not structured to be workplace democracies that function to serve teachers. It is not within the role of teachers to shape policy or control schools. Teachers are not entitled to vote on decisions about school procedures, curriculum issues, or the vacation schedule (Owens, 2001). No reasonable school administrator would ignore teachers or deny them a voice in school matters, but to pretend they have legislative power in schools would be to distort school authority and the ends for which schools were established.

"Authority" in this context means the legally designated exercise of responsibility. In public education, the state has given school administrators the authority to run schools and provide effective instruction (Abbott and Caracheo, 1988). Americans generally assume those given authority will use it properly to produce desired ends. If individual school administrators fail to provide quality education, they should be replaced. If, over time, administrative authority is proved to be structurally unsound or unable to promote conditions necessary for student learning, then the state can make changes in the authority structure of schools. However, research findings indicate no need for such changes. The public is generally satisfied with schools. In a national survey, 71 percent of parents gave an A or B letter grade to the school attended by their oldest child (Rose and Gallup, 2002, p. 42). Schools are not without their problems, and the solution for school problems, now and in the future, will most likely be realized through the leadership school principals and superintendents exercise (Weiss, 1993).

Good management principles demand that, in large organizations, one person or one small group of people have the authority to direct corporate outcomes. It is part of the culture of American life to view management as accountable for organization's success or failure. Parents know that this is the pattern in government and industry, and they expect the same rules to apply to education. In schools, authority and responsibility rest with the administration. When parents have questions about school policy, or curriculum, they call the administrators. Parents demand accountability, and expect school administrators to manage teachers and conduct the educational process for the good of the children.

One of the key roles for any administrator is to transform and inspire the efforts of teachers (Smylie and Hart, 1999; Hoy and Hoy, 2003). Good schools could not exist without good teachers, but excellent teachers are not sufficient to provide good education. In the same way a winning baseball team is more than the sum of players' athletic skills, a good school is more than the total of teachers' abilities. Someone has to direct, organize, and criticize the efforts of the baseball team and the school so that the whole will be at least as good as the sum of its parts. Some person or group of people always will have to manage school operations, measure their effectiveness, and chart the course of change. It is hard to manage and play simultaneously; each of these activities requires complete concentration and a separate set of skills. Although managing a baseball team may not be a perfect metaphor for administering a school, both leaders share a similar downside risk: When the team or the school is not doing well, critics often vent their frustrations on the most visible leader, demanding replacement of the manager or principal.

Unfortunately, all is not well with schools, but before making changes in their authority structures, consider demands now placed on school administrators. School administration has become very complex. It was considerably less difficult to manage schools in the past—in 1910, for example, when only 9 percent of the population completed high school, or in 1950, when only 59 percent completed four years of high school. In those days, high schools were far easier to administer. Schools served mainly good and compliant students who were preparing for college (Williams-Boyd, 2002). Today, with three out of four students remaining in school for twelve years, school administrators must oversee programs for students who in previous generations would have dropped out or been forced out of schools. In the past, administrators did not have to contend with drugs, AIDS, guns, or students with children of their own. Society has visited all of its failings on schools, yet now demands all high school graduates meet higher academic standards and acquire marketable skills. More than ever before, schools need trained experts in the field of administrative leadership and educational policy who can bring out the best in teachers and ensure the community is well served.

Unbridled Teacher Power: A Threat to Community Control

> American education is awash in faddish innovations that regularly sweep through the profession like tropical storms: "whole-language reading," "constructivist math," "mixed-ability grouping," "multiculturalism," and so on. The faddishness gives the education system the appearance of ceaseless change. Yet few of these innovations improve academic performance. And nearly all of them are being undertaken within the organizational framework of a rigid, governmentalist monopoly. . . . America's elected officials exert far greater leverage over their welfare, sanitation, and transportation services than over their public schools." (Finn, 1997, pp. 1–2)

In addition to managing teachers' work, protecting the safety of children, and maintaining academic standards, public school administrators must guarantee schools are run in the best interests of the community. As Milton and Rose Friedman have pointed out, taxpayer support for public schooling in the United States was won on the promise that the local community would control education. Distrustful of the socialist philosophies supporting state-controlled education in Europe, Americans would support public schooling only if it were a part of a decentralized education system. The U.S. Constitution was designed to limit the role of the central government in education, and states allowed local communities to control their schools. Schools were designed to be essentially democratic institutions, responsible to parents whose constant vigilance guaranteed schools' service to community interests (Friedman and Friedman, 1979, pp. 154–155).

Over time, the power to run schools has shifted from the local communities to increasingly more centralized authorities. The city, county, state, and federal governments, combined with teacher militancy, have diminished community control over education. Effective administrators must preserve community control over important aspects of education, and must assure parents that schools are still in their service. Parents and other citizens rightfully fear the encroachments of big government and organized labor. They have seen the diminution of their authority and rise of unseen professionals and bureaucrats who control more and more aspects of their lives. Government has become at once more remote and more controlling. One of the last areas citizens typically exercise a measure of real control over is the public school system, and it is the people's right to control their schools; the schools in their neighborhood belong to them. In the American education system, authority was granted to public school administrators—building principals and district superintendents—to keep schools out of politics and protect them from the political arena (Kowalski, 2003, p. 115). School administrators guard the community's interests against both political pressure and the incessant steam of educational fads.

Sacrificing Individual Freedom to Collective Power

In public education, "power" often refers to the ability to either produce or resist instructional outcomes. School boards and state departments of education have the power to deliver new programs of instruction, but teachers have the power to disregard these initiatives by private noncompliance. Schools are not run by the brute force of administrators, and teachers and school administrators know that each teacher has a great deal of autonomy. When teachers close the doors to their classrooms, they have power over instruction unmatched by anyone in the school system, including the superintendent and the board of education. Teachers can control what students learn through the ways they pace instruction, group students, determine levels of difficulty, and set criteria for assessment.

Classroom autonomy is among the key defining characteristics of the teacher's job, and one of the most closely protected. Teachers enjoy the power to teach and to control instruction. Much to the frustration of administrators, attempts to diminish this autonomy—by introducing accountability measures or introducing new curricula, for example—often meet with resistance from teachers. For many teachers, the freedom to teach is among the most attractive aspects of the job. In the past, teachers have purchased this power over their classrooms by relinquishing influence at the school or district level (Corwin and Borman, 1988). The current demands for restructuring schools require that teachers be granted collective power to influence schools. Not only do such ideas run counter to tradition, but they also threaten teacher power in the classroom. If teachers became school leaders, they would have to relinquish the individual control they now enjoy over their own classrooms.

Cries for restructuring schools ignore the contributions administrators make to education. Educational administration is the art and science of applying specialized academic knowledge to solve school problems. School administration requires the experience of a teacher, or at least a deep appreciation of the teacher's art; in addition, it demands a strong knowledge of human behavior, management theory, school law, and organizational leadership. Administrators should understand teaching from a teacher's point of view, but they also must be able to lead teachers and bring findings from administrative theory and research to bear on schools and on the problems of teaching and learning.

Administrators are trained to understand the ways in which school organizations function and how to build on the strengths of individual teachers. Administrators can improve schools by linking the successes of many teachers who work in isolated classrooms (Kowalski, 2003).

The False Promise of Shared Decision Making

> A school administrator is an educational leader who promotes the success of all students by facilitating the development, articulation, implementation, and stewardship of a vision of learning that is shared and supported by the school community. (Standard 1, Interstate School Leaders Licensure Consortium, 1997, quoted in Green, 2001, p. 5)

The public believes that effective administrators can change schools, and research evidence continues to document the successes of effective school leaders in improving the education of children (Manassee, 1985; Weiss, 1993). Researchers also have identified specific administrative behaviors that lead to school improvement. These behaviors include "being visionary, providing individual consideration, engaging in collective problem solving, ensuring goal achievement, and establishing a culture or ethos of improvement" (Blase and Blase, 2001, p. 16). Administrators make a positive difference. The problem with schools is not that principals control them, and it is not likely schools would improve if we handed control over to teachers. In the final analysis, administrators are responsible for schools, and must exert leadership and accept consequences for educational outcomes. Schools need effective leaders who can encourage learning, support and reward good teaching, and ensure schools serve the community.

Although there is strong evidence effective principals are key to student learning, their potential in school reform often is underestimated. Americans tend to view school administration as a "quasi-profession" and principalship as a low-status job (Kowalski, 2003, p. 23). Much of this stems from the stereotype of the old-style school principal. For too long, the image of the public school administrator was that of the rigid disciplinarian, a man who kept students in line with bluff and bluster, the retired coach who jollied the board of education with sports talk and assurances that everything was operating smoothly. Borrowing management models from industry, old-time public school administrators often emphasized control of teachers rather than educational leadership. In the early twentieth century, Frederick W. Taylor, an engineer by training, developed "principles of scientific management." Previous generations of public school administrators took Taylor's recommendations to heart. Among other things, Taylor had recommended that administrators:

- Establish a clear division of responsibility between management and workers, with management doing the goal setting, planning, and supervising, and workers executing the required tasks.
- Establish the discipline whereby management sets the objectives and the workers cooperate in achieving them. (Taylor quoted in Owens, 2001, p. 36)

Previous generations of school leaders divided school employees along the lines suggested by Taylor. Administrators led, and teachers followed. Everyone now recognizes the alienating and dispiriting effects of "scientific management" on teachers. This was certainly not a suitable way to treat professionals. Schools abandoned these conceptions of educational administration long ago. The image of powerless teachers and the bullying, despotic principal exists largely in anecdotes, a fiction recreated by special interest groups who would like to seize control of schools. The stereotype fails to acknowledge the changed nature of educational administration. Modern organizational theory emphasizes an understanding of schools as collaborative systems in which the principal is less a manager than a collegial leader. Today's school administrators view teachers as personal colleagues and the human capital essential to the education of children. Today's principals are trained as instructional leaders who orchestrate the various teachers' talents and create the best climates for student achievement (Smylie and Hart, 1999; Blase and Blase, 2001; Fullan, 2001).

Effective administrative leadership continues to be the most essential ingredient in school reform (Murphy, 1991; Weiss, 1993; Owens, 2001). The conflicting expectations that the state, community, teachers, and students exert on schools demand a specially trained group of managers. Without intelligent leadership from educational administrators, schools would be unlikely to meet any of their academic and social goals. Without trained, carefully selected administrators to lead educational reform, change becomes less likely. School improvement is a very complex process, and it depends largely on the principal's ability to create and manage the conditions necessary for sustained reform (Fullan, 2002). Teachers may determine the success or failure of any education reform or change in school policy, but the burden of leadership falls mainly on administrators. "Above all, the principal must communicate a clear vision of instructional excellence and continuous professional development consistent with the goal of improvement of teaching and learning" (Hoy and Hoy, 2003, p. 2). School administrators play a complex, demanding role in learning and instruction. It is a role that requires special skills and talents. (See Table 15.2.)

Doubtless, you have heard empowering teachers and giving them votes in school decision-making issues will solve many school problems. At first glance, this may seem democratic and appealing. Workplace democracy and shared decision making would expand the supply of good ideas and bring frontline professionals into the conversations about school reform. However, it is impractical. As one principal notes, "Democratic decision making doesn't work! I can't hold a meeting and call a vote every time we need to make a decision; they haven't got time for *that* either" (Owens, 2001, p. 287). Most teachers would agree: They neither want to nor have time to be involved in every aspect of school leadership. Most faculty do not want to be involved in decisions not affecting them, such as the technicalities of tasks remotely related to the classroom or the teacher's welfare (Drake and Roe, 1999, pp. 122–123).

Table 15.2. Council of Chief State School Officers Interstate School Leaders Consortium Standards for School Leaders (excerpts)

A school administrator is an educational leader who promotes the success of all students by:

1. Facilitating the development, articulation, implementation, and stewardship of a vision of learning that is shared and supported by the school community.
2. Advocating, nurturing, and sustaining a school culture and instructional program conducive to student learning and staff professional growth.
3. Ensuring management of the organization, operations, and resources for a safe, efficient, and effective learning environment.
4. Collaborating with families and community members, responding to diverse community interests and needs, and mobilizing community resources.
5. Acting with integrity, responding to, and influencing the larger political, social, economic, legal, and cultural context.

Source: www.ccsso.org/standards.html (2002)

Even in schools that have tried to empower teachers and enlist their aid in decision making, most new ideas still come from administrators. The research shows that shared decision making does not improve teacher morale, nor does it necessarily lead to school reform or improved learning (Weiss, 1993; Smylie, 1994).

Today's school leaders are likely to share responsibilities with teachers, but are not about to give up their role as instructional leaders. School administrators determine the areas in which they have clear authority, where they should consult teachers, and where they should defer to committees of teachers (Hill and Gutherie, 1999). It is still up to administrators to lead schools and school reform. Practicing teachers gladly give their support to administrators who assume the role of instructional leader (Fullan, 2001). Teachers want to be consulted, but they do not want to abandon teaching to run the schools. Teachers want a voice in school matters; they do not want to be administrators.

Good administrators will always recruit the most talented teachers to join in alliances for improvement of schools, but there is insufficient evidence to warrant turning over total control of schools to teachers or running schools as if they were democratic organizations. Advocates of shared decision making seem to forget that teaching is a full-time, energy-draining job. To reserve part of a teacher's day to do administrative work or debate and vote on every issue in the school would mean teachers would have less time to teach and think about the children in their class. This would be cumbersome and impractical, and contrary to the purposes of public education. Schools are run for the benefit of the students, not the teachers. Research thus far does not support the claim that teacher management increases instructional effectiveness (Smylie, 1994). Unless democratic school governance and the greater empowerment of teachers proves to increase student learning, school leadership should remain in the hands of school administrators.

For Discussion

1. According to studies of leadership, the likelihood of school improvement and reform is increased when leaders demonstrate certain personal characteristics and traits. Consider this list of characteristics associated with positive school change. Can these characteristics and traits be taught? Do you think they are more common in teachers or administrators? Should we select school administrators based on whether or not they possess these traits? If not, how should we select and educate those who would like to lead schools?

compassion	accuracy	judgment
persuasion	influence	logic
insight	trust	communication
sensitivity	knowledge	tact
respect	vision	diplomacy
creativity	management	predictability
rapport	dignity	courage
credibility	consistency	decisiveness
organization	fairness	equity
morality	diversity	honesty
support	planning	openness
reasoning	timeliness	adaptability
reliability	accountability	

Source: Green, 2001, p. 22.

2. Eleven states[1] and the District of Columbia require candidates for school principal and school superintendent pass a standardized examination as part of the licensure process. The School Leaders Licensure Assessment was developed by the Educational Testing Service of Princeton, New Jersey, to "evaluate the relevant knowledge, skills, and abilities of each potential principal, superintendent, and school leader" (Educational Testing Service, 2001a). Consider one of the sample exercises from the exam and the scoring rubric used to evaluate candidate's response:

Sample Exercise

Read this vignette and briefly and specifically answer the question that follows:

It is early December and the students in an elementary school are practicing for the annual holiday concert. A parent phones the school to insist that her child not be required to sing any of the Christmas songs. The principal excuses the child from participation in music practice.

Do you agree with the principal's action? Give a rationale, citing factors that are relevant to a principal's decisions in such situations.

[1]Arkansas, California, Indiana, Kentucky, Maryland, Mississippi, Missouri, North Carolina, Pennsylvania, Tennessee, and Virginia.

Scoring Guide

Score 2:

Response specifically cites the civil and/or religious rights of the parent/student, and includes at least one of these:

- meeting with the parent and student to discuss the objective
- suggesting some alternative activity for the student
- examining the content of the concert to determine its appropriateness for all students

Score 1:

Response specifically cites one of these:

- the civil and/or religious rights of the parent/student
- meeting with the parent and student to discuss the objections
- suggesting some alternative activity for the student
- examining the content of the concert to determine its appropriateness for all students

Score: 0

Response is vague, or omits reference to any of the essential factors. (Educational Testing Service, 2001b, p. 10)

What should principals be expected to know and be able to do? Can the knowledge and skills necessary to be a good administrator be measured by standardized exams? If teachers themselves want to be involved in school decision making, should they be required to take and pass exams required of school principals and other administrators?

3. Most school reforms in the United States have been initiated by school administrators, state legislators, university scholars and others who typically bypass classroom teachers. In Japan, public school teachers have been given primary responsibility for improving classroom practices in their schools. Japanese teachers sometimes take the lead and invite school administrators and university personnel to participate in the teacher-directed school improvement process. (McGhan, 2002). As a classroom teacher, would you prefer to focus your energies on teaching and leave school improvement to others, or would you prefer a system that charges teachers with school improvement in addition to their teaching responsibilities?

References

ABBOTT, M. G., AND CARACHEO, F. (1988). "Power, Authority, and Bureaucracy." In N. J. Boyan, ed., *Handbook of Research on Educational Administration.* New York: Longman.

AMERICAN FEDERATION OF TEACHERS. (2002). A Candidate's Guide to the National Board Certification, 2001–2002. (www.aft.org/edissues/downloads/nbpts.pdf)

BARTH, R. (1990). *Improving Schools from Within: Teachers, Parents, and Principals Can Make the Difference.* San Francisco: Jossey-Bass.

BLASE, J., AND BLASE, J. (2001). *Empowering Teachers.* 2nd Ed. Thousand Oaks, CA: Corwin.

CARR, D. A. (1997). "Collegial Leaders: Teachers Who Want More than Just a Job." *The Clearing House* 5, 1–5. (Lexis-Nexis)

CORWIN, R. G., AND BORMAN, K. M. (1988). "School as Workplace: Structural Constraints on Administration." In N. J. Boyan, ed., *Handbook of Research on Educational Administration.* New York: Longman.

DICKENS, C. (1854). *Hard Times.* New York: Harper.

DRAKE, T. L., AND ROE, W. H. (1999). *The Principalship.* 5th Ed. Upper Saddle River, NJ: Prentice Hall.

EDUCATIONAL TESTING SERVICE. (2001a). *Registration Bulletin: School Leaders Licensure Assessment* [and] *School Superintendent Assessment.* Princeton: Author.

———. (2001b). School Leadership Series: *School Leaders Licensure Assessment* [and] *School Superintendent Assessment.* Princeton: Author.

FINN, C. A., JR. (1997). "Learning-Free Zones." *The Journal of American Citizenship Policy Review.* Sept./Oct., pp. 1–7. (Nexis-Lexis)

FOSTER, A. G. (1991). When Teachers Initiate Restructuring. *Educational Leadership* 48, 27–31.

FRIEDMAN, M., AND FRIEDMAN, R. (1979). *Free to Choose.* New York: Harcourt Brace Jovanovich.

FULLAN, M. (2001). *Leading in a Culture of Change.* San Francisco: Jossey-Bass.

———. (2002). "The Change Leader." *Educational Leadership* 59, 16–20.

GREEN, R. L. (2001). *Practicing the Art of Leadership: A Problem-Based Approach to Implementing the ISLLC Standards.* Upper Saddle River, NJ: Prentice Hall.

GUINEY, E. (2001). "Coaching Isn't Just for Athletes: The Role of Teacher Leaders." *Phi Delta Kappan* 82, 740–743.

HATRY, H. P., ET AL. (1994). "Implementing School-Based Management: Insights into Decentralization from Science and Mathematics Departments." *Urban Institute Report* 93–94. Washington, DC: The Urban Institute.

HILL, P. T., AND GUTHERIE, J. W. (1999). "A New Research Paradigm for Understanding (And Improving) Twenty-First Century Schooling." In J. Murphy, and K. S. Louis, eds., *Handbook of Research on Educational Administration.* San Francisco: Jossey-Bass.

HOLMES GROUP. (1986). *Tomorrow's Teachers: A Report on the Holmes Group.* East Lansing, MI: Author.

HOY, A. W. AND HOY, W. K. (2003). *Instructional Leadership: A Learning-Centered Guide.* Boston: Allyn & Bacon.

KOWALSKI, T. J. (2003). *Contemporary School Administration: An Introduction.* 2nd Ed. Boston: Allyn & Bacon.

LAMBERT, L. (2002). "A Framework for Shared Leadership." *Educational Leadership* 59, 37–40.

LAMBERT, L., ET AL. (1997). *Who Will Save Our Schools? Teachers as Constructivist Leaders.* Thousand Oaks, CA: Corwin.

LIEBERMAN, A., AND MILLER, L. (1990). "Restructuring Schools: What Matters and What Works." *Phi Delta Kappan* 71, 759–764.

MANASSEE, A. L. (1985). "Improving Conditions for Principal Effectiveness: Policy Implications of Research." *Elementary School Journal* 85, 439–463.

MARSH, C., ET AL. (1990). *Reconceptualizing School-Based Curriculum Development.* New York: Falmer Press.

MCGHAN, B. (2002). "The Fundamental Education Reform: Teacher-Led Schools." *Phi Delta Kappan* 83, 538–540.

MURPHY, J., AND LOUIS, K. S., EDS. *Handbook of Research on Educational Administration.* 2nd Ed. San Francisco: Jossey-Bass.

MURPHY, J. T. (1991). "Superintendents as Saviors: From the Terminator to Pogo." *Phi Beta Kappan* 72, 507–513.

NATIONAL BOARD FOR PROFESSIONAL TEACHING STANDARDS. (2002). (Home page: www.nbpts.org)

NEWMAN, M., AND SIMMONS, W. (2000). "Leadership for Student Learning." *Phi Delta Kappan* 82, 9–12.

OWENS, R. G. (2001). *Organizational Behavior in Education: Instructional Leadership and School Reform.* 7th Ed. Boston: Allyn & Bacon.

REED, C. J. (2000). *Teaching With Power: Shared Decision-Making and Classroom Practice.* New York: Teachers College Press.

ROSE, L. C., AND GALLUP, A. M. (2002). "The 34th Annual Phi Delta Kappa/Gallup Poll of the Public's Attitudes Toward the Public Schools." *Phi Delta Kappan,* 84, 41–56.

SARASON, S. B. (1982). *The Culture of the School and the Problem of Change.* 2nd Ed. Boston: Allyn & Bacon.

SCHLECHTY, P. S. (1990). *Schools for the 21st Century: Leadership Imperatives for Educational Reform.* San Francisco: Jossey-Bass.

SMYLIE, M. A. (1994). "Redesigning Teachers' Work: Connections to the Classroom." In L. Darling-Hammond, ed., *Review of Research in Education.* Washington, DC: American Educational Research Association.

SMYLIE, M. A., AND HART, A. W. (1999). "School Leadership for Teacher Learning and Change: A Human and Social Capital Perspective." In J. Murphy, and K. S. Louis, eds., *Handbook of Research on Educational Administration.* 2nd Ed. San Francisco: Jossey-Bass.

TROEN, V., AND BOLES, K. C. (1995). "Leadership from the Classroom: Women Teachers as a Key to School Reform." In D. M. Dunlap and P. A. Schmuck, eds., *Women Leading in Education.* Albany: State University of New York Press.

WALLER, W. (1932). *The Sociology of Teaching.* New York: John Wiley and Sons.

WEISS, C. H. (1993). "Shared Decisions About What? A Comparison of Schools With and Without Teacher Participation." *Teachers College Record* 95, 69–92.

WILLIAMS-BOYD, P. (2002). *Educational Leadership: A Reference Book.* Santa Barbara, CA: ABC-CLIO.

CHAPTER 16

Academic Freedom: Teacher Rights or Responsibilities

POSITION 1: FOR TEACHER RESPONSIBILITY

Academic freedom, like every other prescriptive right, has its boundaries and its corresponding duties. When liberty declines into license, then it must be restrained. . . .

—Kirk, 1955, p. 27

Responsibility and Power in Teaching

Teaching is one of the most influential positions in society. In terms of carrying values and ideas from generation to generation, teaching is next to parenting in its power. In some respects, teachers exert more influence on children's views and values than parents do. Parents have great control over what their children see, hear, and do during the earliest years, but after the child starts school, parents relinquish increasing amounts of that influence to teachers. That should be a good thing, with children becoming more mature and independent while studying under responsible, committed teachers. Parents retain strong interests in what their children see, hear, and do long after primary school, and good schools and teachers give them nothing to fear. The influence of teachers goes well beyond the classroom doors, school grounds, and school term; teachers exert influence that can last for years, even lifetimes. This capacity to influence the young carries heavy responsibilities.

Society gives teachers authority to develop sound knowledge and values in children, and school is compulsory for that purpose. The child, being weaned from parental influence, looks to teachers for guidance. This is a particularly important responsibility. Teachers bear duties to parents, society, and the child to provide a suitable education. They also have ethical duties to the profession of teaching. These multiple responsibilities require accountability from teachers and schools.

All rights and freedoms are connected to responsibilities. Otherwise, where no social restraint exists, anarchy reigns. That is not freedom; it is a jungle without rules or ethics. Civilization demands both freedom and responsibility. Within that civilization, teachers' freedoms must be tied to their responsibilities, and their rights and freedoms are conditioned on their acceptance of those responsibilities. Teachers' freedoms are supported and limited by their responsibilities to parents, society, the child, and to the profession.

Parents have general, moral, and legal rights and obligations to and for their children, rights and obligations that teachers and schools must not undermine. Parents are expected to provide for the child's safety and welfare—physical, emotional, spiritual, and moral. Provision of food, clothing, and shelter is a parental obligation given up only when parents are incapable. Parents have moral obligations and rights, including instructing their children in determining right from wrong, good from bad. Parents instruct their children in ethical conduct by providing them with a set of socially acceptable behaviors, including integrity, honesty, courtesy, and respect. Under the law, parents can be held accountable for lack of adequate and appropriate care of their children; they can even be held legally responsible for their children's acts.

Because parents are presumed to have the child's interests at heart, they are given great latititude in providing care and upbringing. Parents are even permitted to exercise appropriate corporal punishment, more than any other person would be permitted to inflict upon a child, under the legal idea that the parent has broad responsibilities and rights. At the root of laws regarding parents' rights and obligations is the idea that they are responsible for their children's upbringing, morality, and behaviors. Teachers, however, act as surrogate parents only in certain situations, with a number of limitations, and should not deviate from the norms of the good parent in the good society.

School as a Positive Parent Surrogate

The good society is made up of good families, and good schools are extensions of those families. Social institutions confirm and sustain the family, even when specific families fail to live up to their responsibilities. Foster homes, family welfare programs, and other social services represent society's attempt to deal with these responsibilities when families fail. These institutions try to do a good job of surrogate parenting, but are working with the results of a difficult situation. Such institutions exist to make up for problems in families and society; the more we have the worse the society is. Schools, however, are a positive social institution. They encourage children's development, extending the family influence to produce good citizens and good members of future families. Children are not put in schools as punishment, or as a way to make up for family irresponsibility. Schools, therefore, must continue the cultural heritage by inculcating positive and supportive social and family values in the young.

The comparative youthfulness of students, influential role of teachers, and authoritative nature of instruction make schools and teachers even more responsible to social and parental values and interests. Especially in public schools, where attendance is mandatory, schools and teachers need a greater sensitivity to the role of positive parental surrogate. Thus, public school teachers are even more accountable than private ones to the community and to parents for what they teach and how.

Teacher Responsibilities to Parents

Schools, then, have a special obligation to be responsive to parents' concerns for their children. This reasoning lies behind the legal concept that teachers act in loco parentis, or in place of the parent. That concept, with deep social and legal roots, protects teachers in handling student discipline and evaluation. It also requires teachers to remain sensitive to parental interests. Parents do not usually consider their obligations as merely technical requirements; they have strong emotional commitments to their children transcending legal and social expectations.

Teachers, standing in place of the parents, take on similar responsibilities for children's development and protection. Teachers have responsibilities for providing a safe, healthy classroom environment, and they assume protective moral, ethical, and legal duties. In addition, they have educational responsibilities: They must teach children necessary knowledge and skills. Discharging these responsibilities demands responsiveness to parental concerns about the kinds of knowledge and values taught.

Teachers cannot have license to do anything to students, physically or mentally. No one today would argue that teachers should be permitted to abuse children physically. Teachers can require students to be attentive to lessons, be orderly, and be civil, but they are prohibited from abusive activities, such as striking students. Malevolent teacher behavior is outside the standards of professional conduct.

Mental abuse of students is equally abhorrent, but is less easy to detect. Scars of mental abuse are not as obvious as those from physical damage. Mental abuse is no less harmful, however, to students, parents, or society. It can consist of vicious verbal personal attacks, indoctrination in antisocial values or behaviors, or manipulation of children's minds against parents or morality. Parents have a right to insist teachers not subject their children to these tactics, but often are unaware of them until after the damage has been done. Good teachers would not contemplate such misuse of their influential role in children's lives; it would be unprofessional.

Parents have a right to monitor what schools are teaching their children, hold the school accountable for it, and limit potential for damage to their children. Beyond necessary limits on teachers, schools also must be subject to limits that conform to social mores. For example, book, video, and film purchases for school libraries should be continuously and vigilantly screened so only proper material is made available to our children. A solid parent review committee can be used to determine which books are suitable, with opportunity for any parent to complain about library materials and have that complaint acted on effectively.

We need not only worry about what teaching materials are used in classrooms, we also must be vigilant about other areas of schools where underage students have access. In school media centers, there is an increasing problem with Internet access. The Internet can be a valuable resource for children. There are many excellent websites for adding educational quality in such areas as science, history, the arts, literature, math, and other subjects. The opportunity to observe geographic locations, ancient art and culture, current news, scientific experiments and achievements, and to engage in available educational work via the Internet is exceptional and otherwise not available. However, there exists a serious problem in Internet usage when websites containing inhumane, anti-American, racist, antiauthority, sexual, antireligious, or other inappropriate material are available in schools. Parents can exert control in their children's computer use at home to screen out undesirable sites; schools have a greater responsibility in screening out any such sites from their computers since schools serve a broad cross section of children.

Teacher Responsibilities to Children

The paramount responsibility of teachers is to their students. Because students are immature and unformed, teachers must carefully exercise their influence and temper freedom with responsibility. Teachers hold great potential power over children's lives, and teacher authority needs to be weighed heavily in teacher decisions as to what to teach and how. Teachers derive power from maturity, physical size, and position. Children are vulnerable.

In forming and testing ideas, attitudes, and behaviors, children look to teachers for direction. Children naturally are curious and positive, but cannot yet fully discern between good and bad, proper and improper. Teachers have a responsibility to continue the moral and ethical education that good parents have begun.

Teacher Responsibilities to Society

Society, as well as parents, has a significant interest in children's education. Schools were established to pass on the cultural heritage; to provide the skills, attitudes, and knowledge needed to produce good citizens; and to prepare children to meet their responsibilities in family, work, and social roles. Schools are social institutions, financed and regulated to fulfill social purposes. Society has values, standards of behavior, and attitudes that schools must convey to children. These standards have evolved over a long period, and they represent our common culture. Society charges schools and teachers to ensure that social standards, and ideals these standards represent, are taught by example and by word.

Schools do not exist as entities separate from society, able to chart their own courses as though they had no social responsibilities. They were not intended to instruct students in antisocial, anti-American, or immoral ideas or behaviors, nor will society allow them to continue to do so. Society trusts teachers to develop the young into positive, productive citizens. Those few teachers who use their position to attempt to destroy social values or create social dissension are violating that trust. Those who sow the seeds of negativism, nihilism, or cynicism also are violating that trust. Society has the right to restrict, condemn, or exclude from teaching those who harm its interests.

Teacher Responsibilities to Their Profession

The teaching profession has an extensive and illustrious history. It is based on the idea of service to children and society. The teachers' code of ethics recognizes teacher responsibilities as singularly important. Teachers want to convey the cultural heritage to their students, along with a strong sense of social responsibility. Teachers can ask no less of themselves.

A basic responsibility of the teaching profession is to prepare young people for life in society. That includes teaching students social values and knowledge, and teachers' personal conduct should exemplify society's ideals. The teaching profession recognizes both children's needs and society's needs. Teachers have an obligation not to go beyond professional bounds, and to reject those who would tarnish the profession's reputation.

Teachers are the key to good education. They are also the key to poor education. When teachers are excellent, a school is excellent. But, as is widely known, many schools are not excellent, and many teachers are weak and ineffective. In fact, much of the great problem in U.S. education is due to teachers who should not be in classrooms. These teachers should be weeded out, but tenure laws and teacher unions protect the weakest and ensure poor educations for many of our children. These protections not only burden students, parents, and citizens, they pose a more serious threat to decency, patriotism, and social values.

Zealotry and Teacher Irresponsibility

Consider the enormous problem created for students, parents, and society when weak teachers are also zealots for causes that undermine American values—teachers eager to sell their beliefs to young people and irresponsible in their accountability to society. Pied Piper teachers are not weak in their beliefs and sales techniques, but often are weak in their intellectual capabilities and acceptance of fundamental responsibility to society and its values. These teachers fail to recognize the proper role of a teacher. Not only does tenure cover up poor teaching, it also protects socially dangerous teachers. They use the hollow claim of academic freedom to camouflage their attempts to distort the minds of the young. Weak teachers who actually believe they have a special freedom to do as they wish in the classroom are a major threat to our culture.

Teachers can be captured by radical ideas, and have a captive audience of immature minds. Oftentimes the academically weak teacher misunderstands the threats of anarchism, atheism, satanism, socialism, communism, and other extreme positions. They often have a simplistic utopian view and want their students to adopt the same, so impose their radical views on vulnerable young people. They may advocate extreme views of politics, economics, religion, family relations, drug use, sexual preferences, and other controversial topics. Students are expected to recognize the teacher's authority and may not be in a position to challenge the teacher's opinions. This denies the concept of education and threatens society. Nevertheless, state laws and unions protect teachers, no matter how radical and socially detrimental their concepts are. This protection, under tenure laws and the false cloak of academic freedom, allows miseducation in schools. Tenure laws make it almost impossible to rid schools of poor teachers or those who are zealots.

The false claim that academic freedom gives teachers the right to do what they wish does not take into account the real history of academic freedom. The historic idea of academic freedom protects scientists and university scholars in pursuing and publishing their research. Even in this restricted setting, there are some limits for researchers; they cannot do any research they might want, certainly none that knowingly harms people. Academic freedom in its original conception has little to do with schoolteachers and their work. Nor does the historic sense of academic freedom reflect social responsibilities attendant on teaching in public elementary and high schools. Because young, impressionable children must attend school by law, we demand greater accountability from public school teachers than we do from teachers in colleges, where students may be old enough to resist brainwashing. Students are a captive audience of relatively unsophisticated children; they are the ones who need protection. The appropriate definition of academic freedom applies solely to the protection of university scholars as they research their specialties. It was never intended to cover schoolteachers and their students.

Academic Freedom as License

A license to teach is not a license to impose one's views on others. Corruption of the young is at the least a moral crime; it is ethically reprehensible. The majority of teachers accept this and discharge their duties with integrity and care. For them, teaching is a calling to instruct the young in society's knowledge and values. This represents the best in the profession and is a great support to the well-being of the community and nation. Unfortunately, some teachers do not subscribe to the values of their profession.

There are teachers who are caught in drug raids, who have cheated on their income tax returns, and who have committed robbery—but these are exceptions. Most teachers are not criminals. When teachers do engage in criminal conduct, they are subject to criminal penalties and possible loss of employment. They do not receive special treatment. However, there is another form of crime, intellectual crime, that teachers may engage in under the guise of academic freedom. Intellectual crimes include ridiculing student or family values, advocating antisocial attitudes, indoctrinating children in secular humanism, and influencing students to think or act in opposition to parent and community norms. These crimes may have an even greater, more devastating, effect on children and society than legal transgressions because they tear at the nation's moral fiber. Perpetrators should not have special protection. There is nothing academic about confusing and confounding children about their families and society; teachers who commit such crimes deserve no consideration under the rubric of academic freedom. Distorting the minds of the young is misteaching and should be penalized.

A child brought up to revere the family, believe in marriage, support the United States, and respect people in authority may find it traumatic when a teacher expresses approval of such activities as participating in homosexual acts, supporting abortion rights, espousing anti-Americanism, engaging in civil disobedience, or sexually using children (Leo, 1993). Teachers should not have the right to damage children in this manner. When it happens, teachers should be dismissed. Stretching the idea of academic freedom to protect such teachers is an affront to the true meaning of academic freedom.

Some schoolteachers and their unions want to open a large umbrella of academic freedom to cover anything a teacher does or says. Their claims to protection are not justified, but make school administrators wary. Administrators do not want the American Civil Liberties Union or other local vigilante groups interfering in school affairs. Thus, radical teachers often get away with their preaching and mind-bending for years because the administration is afraid to reprimand them. Instead, the problem is hidden. Parents who protest are allowed to have their children transferred to other classes, but unsuspecting parents fall prey to these unprofessional classroom Fagins. It takes a courageous, persistent parent to thwart such a teacher. Often, public disclosure of the teacher's actions will arouse the community and force school officials to take action.

Radical teachers also have misused state tenure laws, which typically place excessive impediments to obstruct efforts to dismiss a teacher. As a result, very few school districts find it worthwhile to try to fire even the most incompetent teachers, and radical teachers recognize this. Tenured teacher firings are very rare; the radical teacher merely has to sit tight until tenure, and then anything is permissible. Tenure laws create burdensome requirements that save teachers' jobs even when those teachers have demonstrated a lack of respect for parents, students, and community values. This is a travesty. We need to abolish or change these laws to make it easier to dismiss teachers who behave irresponsibly.

Parading under the guise of academic freedom, special treatment would give teachers license to engage in a variety of forms of educationally disruptive behavior. Certainly, teachers may have views that differ from community norms, but the classroom is not the place in which to express them. Teachers should not have the freedom to preach radical ideas in schools. Schools are not meant to be forums for teachers whose viewpoints differ sharply from those of the community. Instead, schools are intended to express and affirm community values. Malleable students are a captive audience; teachers must not have the right to impose contrary views on the young (McFarlane, 1994).

Academic Freedom and Teacher Freedom

We must bear two important considerations in mind in any discussion of academic and teacher freedom in the schools. First, academic freedom provides limited protection to university-level scholars who are experts in their specialized fields, and it is inappropriate to apply the concept to teachers below the college level. Second, other freedom for teachers below the college level is not unlimited or unrestrained; it is necessarily related to traditional teacher responsibilities.

There is no doubt that, within the limits of responsibility, teachers deserve respect and some freedom to determine how to teach. That is, teacher freedom can be separated from academic freedom, which is intended to protect the rights of experts to present their research results. This separation does not denigrate teachers any more than it denigrates lawyers, doctors, and ministers as respected people with no claim to special freedom in their work. Teacher freedom is protected by community traditions and the constitutional protection of free speech. Teachers do not need additional protections.

The U.S. Constitution's protections of free speech for all citizens are more than sufficient for teachers. Under the Constitution, any of us can say what we wish to say about the government, our employers, or the state of the world, provided it is not slanderous, imminently dangerous, or obscene. Obviously, we cannot say false things about someone without risking a libel suit, and we cannot yell "Fire!" in a crowded theater or "Bomb!" in an airport without risking arrest. Though we have the freedom to say them, we also must accept the consequences for our other statements.

Public expression of controversial views, as in letters to a newspaper editor, is a right of all people in the United States. Teachers, of course, have the same right. But that does not mean that teachers are any different from other citizens or more deserving of job security no matter how inane or anti-American their public statements. Teachers' jobs are not safe regardless, any more than are jobs of those employed by private firms who make controversial public statements. Keeping a particular job regardless of one's actions is not a right the Constitution guarantees. Anyone who wishes to make public statements must recognize the risks involved. Teachers, more than most citizens, should be aware of the responsibilities surrounding public discourse. A teacher's inflammatory comments can lead to public outrage. For public school teachers, the public is the employer.

Schoolteachers should not expect job guarantees when they make negative comments about schools, the community, or the nation. They also should not expect job protection when they teach children by using propaganda or inaccurate or provocative material. Classroom statements by teachers are actually public statements, subject to the same conditions as letters to the editor or public speaking. There is no special privilege granted to teachers merely because they close the classroom door. Good teachers realize their public and social responsibilities to uphold appropriate standards and ideals.

Private schools can expect their teachers to uphold school and parent values because private school administrators and boards have more latitude in dismissing teachers they consider unsatisfactory in teaching or in judgment. State tenure laws do not apply to them. Public school boards and administrators are under some constraints because of those tenure laws and active teacher unions, but they should be more aggressive in weeding out poor teachers and those who engage in controversial acts. Each board of education has a responsibility to provide children with information, skills, a set of social values, and a moral code that strengthen society. Teachers cannot abrogate that responsibility.

Academic Freedom as a Function of Academic Position

Academic freedom protects scholars who recognize the academic responsibilities inherent in it. Scholars who have developed expert knowledge in a subject field may conduct research challenging accepted views—this is how we continue to refine knowledge. Academic freedom allows such scholars to publish or present their research without fear of losing their positions. But even these scholars have academic freedom only in those areas in which they have demonstrated expert knowledge. Academic freedom does not extend to everything they do or say. They have no greater freedom than any other citizen in areas outside their own expertise. An English professor who joins an activist group blocking traffic in an environmental protest has no claim to academic freedom for that activity—the professor is no different from any other citizen. The Constitution protects everyone's speech, but does not and should not protect a faculty job. There is a difference between academic freedom and license, and no academic freedom should exist for those who indoctrinate others. Kirk (1955), Hook (1953), and Buckley (1951), provide philosophic grounds for limiting teacher freedom to expert scholars engaged in publication of their research. They would deny scholars or any other educators the right to proselytize or indoctrinate students under special protection of academic freedom.

In specialized subject areas where a scholar has demonstrated expertise, he or she may need the protection of academic freedom to publish or present research results differing from those of prior research. A few public school teachers may have developed this expert knowledge and be conducting research, but this is not true for the vast majority. As philosopher Russell Kirk has eloquently argued, not all subjects are equally deserving of academic freedom:

> The scholar and teacher deserve their high freedom because they are professors of the true arts and sciences—that is, because their disciplines are the fields of knowledge in which there ought always to be controversy and exploration; and their especial freedom of expression and speculation is their right only while they still argue and investigate. But if this body of learned men is trampled down by a multitude of technicians, adolescent-sitters, . . . and art-of-camp-cookery teachers (whose skills, however convenient to us, do not require a special freedom of mind for their conservation and growth) . . . then the whole order of scholars will sink into disrepute and discouragement. (Kirk, 1955, pp. 79, 80)

Summary

Unfortunately for teachers and scholars, the idea of academic freedom has been abused in current times. Teacher unions and lawyers, attempting to save the jobs of teachers who are incompetent or who espouse antisocial propaganda, have clouded the positive idea of academic freedom. Academic freedom should not become a shield for incompetent, antisocial, or un-American teaching. Rather, academic freedom should offer protection only for expert scholars in the search for truth. Separating the idea of teacher freedom from academic freedom, and requiring concommitant teacher responsibilities and accountability is a much sounder approach to the protection of teachers and integrity of society.

Law professor Stephen Goldstein (1976), in a well-reasoned article on this topic, argues that academic freedom is unsuited to elementary and secondary schools because of the age and immaturity of the students, the teacher's position of authority, the necessarily more highly structured curriculum, and the dominant role of schools in imparting social values. These factors cannot be easily dismissed. Elementary and secondary school teachers are different from university scholars in their training, functions, employment status, and responsibilities. Elementary and secondary schools have broad responsibilities to parents, community, and state that do not permit us to give license to teachers to do what they wish. Schools and teachers serve in capacities that require support for and advocacy of social and family values. Rhetoric about academic freedom does not diminish that significant responsibility.

Good teachers deserve respect and appreciation for their contributions to society, decent salaries, and comfortable working conditions. They deserve the protection the Bill of Rights gives to all U.S. citizens: freedom of speech, association, and assembly. For all of us, including teachers, these freedoms entail responsibilities. Teacher responsibilities to students, parents, school officials, the teaching profession, and to society make classroom teachers one of our most treasured resources. No one would argue that good teachers should be treated like prisoners, without freedom to express their creativity. Creativity that stimulates children to learn is one of the hallmarks of good teaching. Teachers do not, however, merit special treatment in regard to their freedom. Tenure should not protect them from losing their jobs for subverting students, advocating radical ideas, insubordination, or proselytizing. The myth of academic freedom for classroom teachers is damaging to teachers and society.

POSITION 2: FOR INCREASED ACADEMIC FREEDOM

Since freedom of mind and freedom of expression are the root of all freedom, to deny freedom in education is a crime against democracy.

—JOHN DEWEY, 1936

A Necessity, Not a Frill

A society cannot be free when its schools are not. The need to provide strong support to academic freedom for teachers and their students should seem obvious to anyone who supports a free society. Ideas are the primary ingredients of democracy and education and the realm of ideas is protected by academic freedom. This simple, elegant concept is not well enough understood by some of the public, and even by some teachers. Academic freedom requires diligent effort, exercise, and expansion in schools. It is under constant threat.

The continuing development of American democracy requires that academic freedom be further expanded in schools for both students and teachers. Noddings (1999) points out that democratic education requires debate and discourse—only with teacher freedom can this happen. The basic principles are clear—enlightened self-governance is basic to democracy and academic freedom is basic to enlightened self-governance. Freedom to teach and learn is basic to good education.

We are well beyond the period when teachers were prohibited from marrying, dancing, or participating in politics. In contemporary schools, teachers are expected to do more than force-feed students memorized material; we have come to expect education and critical thinking. Yet there remain strong efforts to censor and restrain educators in performance of their profession.

Pat Scales (2001), a school librarian honored by the American Library Association's (ALA) Intellectual Freedom Award, writes:

> The problem is obvious. Censors want to control the minds of the young. They are fearful of the educational system, because students who read learn to think. . . . As educators, we cannot for the sake of the students, allow ourselves to be bullied into diluting the curriculum into superficial facts. We must talk about the principles of intellectual freedom. We must challenge students to think about the intent of our forefathers when they wrote the Bill of Rights. (p. 2)

Unfortunately, some people and groups with strong moralistic or other narrow agendas have increased their efforts to restrict schools and impose censorship on students and teachers. They hope to advance their own political, religious, or economic views and to deny the views of others. They see education as a way to indoctrinate the young to become noncritical believers or as a way to inoculate and insulate students from controversial ideas. They see evil or controversy in anything that differs from their own beliefs.

Zealots on different sides of political, economic, and religious fences have tried to use schools as agents to impose their views and values on the young. They don't want schools to present opposing views or conflicting evidence, and are against real critical thinking. That zealotry has increased the vulnerability of teachers who realize good education requires dealing with controversial issues (Thelin, 1997).

The good teacher, willing to examine controversial topics, runs risks far beyond those who are fearful, docile, and self-censoring. Teachers who fulfill the basic educational responsibility to provide intellectual freedom may encounter threats, ostracism, or ridicule. Ominous overt threats and subtle pressure from administrators, school boards, parents, special interest groups, and even peer teachers can cool a teacher's ardor for freedom of ideas. Teacher self-censorship—where fearful teachers screen ideas from classroom use in order to avoid controversy—is a common but hidden threat to academic freedom. Teachers hear about others being fired or threatened and often try to avoid any topic that could have similar repercussions for them. It is true that a few teachers have been fired for doing what our society should expect all good teachers to do. It is also true that many times these firings are reversed when the teacher is given due process and facts become known. Still, such events produce a chilling effect on other teachers, restricting academic freedom for themselves and their students. It takes courage to remain professional in the pursuit of education, but it is necessary. When the censors win, education and democracy lose.

The Essential Relationship of Academic Freedom to Democracy

One inescapable premise in a democracy is that the people are capable of governing themselves. That premise assumes people can make knowledgeable decisions and select intelligently from among alternative proposals. Education and free exchange of ideas are fundamental to the premise. To think otherwise is to insult the essential condition of democracy.

Academic freedom is the right to "liberty of thought" claimed by teachers and students, including the right to "enjoy the freedom to study, to inquire, to speak . . . to communicate . . . ideas" (*Dictionary of the History of Ideas,* 1973, pp. 9, 10). It is the freedom of teachers to teach, of schools to determine educational policies and practices unfettered by political restraints or censorship, and the freedom of students to engage in study of ideas. It is essential to democracy. The basic idea of academic freedom must be examined from the perspective of a society that prizes freedom and self-governance, even when those ideals are not always evident in the everyday practice of the society. A restrictive or totalitarian society demands a restrictive or totalitarian education system. But a society that professes freedom should demand no less freedom for its schools (Rorty, 1994).

The U.S. Supreme Court demonstrated its commitment to the principle of academic freedom in a 1967 decision, finding that a state law that demanded teachers take a loyalty oath was unconstitutional. The Court noted that academic freedom is a "transcendent value":

> Our nation is deeply committed to safeguarding academic freedom, which is of transcendent value to all of us and not merely to the teachers concerned. That freedom is, therefore, a special concern of the First Amendment, which does not tolerate laws that cast a pall of orthodoxy over the classroom. . . . The classroom is peculiarly the "marketplace of ideas." (*Keyishian v. Board of Regents,* 1967)

Propaganda and public deceit are practiced in all countries, including democracies, but citizens of a democracy are expected to have the right and the ability to question and examine propaganda and expose those deceits. Dictatorial regimes do not need, and do not desire, the masses to have an education enabling them to question information the government presents. Totalitarian states maintain their existence by using raw power and threats, utilizing censorship and restriction, and keeping the public ignorant. Governments in democracies can attempt the same maneuvers, but they run the risk of exposure and replacement. The more totalitarian the government, the more it uses threats, censorship, and denial of freedom in education. The more democratic the society, the less it employs threats, censorship, and restriction of education. This litmus test of a democracy is also a significant measure of the level of academic freedom.

The Evolution and Expansion of Academic Freedom

Academic freedom has evolved and expanded from early American education when a narrow definition limited it to a few scholars in colleges, and even there it was not well practiced. It has since become a fundamental educational concept embracing both the general framework of schooling and work of teachers at all levels. We are closer now to the historic dual German intellectual freedoms—*lehrfreiheit* and *lernfreiheit*—the freedom of teachers to teach and of learners to learn without institutional restriction (Hofstadter and Metzger, 1968). The American concept of academic freedom evolved from this dual and mutually supportive freedom for teachers and students (Daly, Schall, and Skeele, 2001). It still has not evolved sufficiently to assure educators and the public that schools are places of real and critical education, but it is significantly more embedded in the culture of schools and educated society than it was.

Socrates, charged with impiety and corruption of youth, defended himself by claiming that he and his students had the freedom to pursue truth. All wickedness, he argued, was due to ignorance; freedom to teach and learn would uncover knowledge, eliminate ignorance, and improve society. The judges did not agree and Socrates was sentenced to death. Academic freedom, over time, has fared better. Though it is regularly battered, it has survived and expanded.

Unfortunately, differences in state laws and confusing court opinions have produced a mixed view of what specific actions are legally protected under the idea of academic freedom in the United States (O'Neil, 1981; *Newsletter on Intellectual Freedom,* 2000, 2001, 2002, 2003). The broad concept of academic freedom is generally understood, but practical application of that freedom in classrooms and schools often is contested and local and state court decisions often are murky. While some courts have supported school board discretion over curricular and student newspaper matters, in general, courts have exhibited an expanding awareness of the need for academic freedom in schools and have provided protection for teachers. If this good trend continues, and educators remain vigilant, this foretells a proper expansion of the concept to cover the work of competent teachers across the nation.

Courts often have been highly supportive of academic freedom for public school teachers. Justices Frankfurter and Douglas (*Wieman v. Updegraff,* 1952) argued that all teachers from primary grades to the university share a special role in developing good citizens, and all teachers should have the academic freedom necessary to be exemplars of open-mindedness and free inquiry. In *Cary v. Board of Education* (quoted in Rubin and Greenhouse, 1983), the decision included:

> To restrict the opportunity for involvement in an open forum for the free exchange of ideas to higher education would not only foster an unacceptable elitism, it would fail to complete the development of those not going to college, contrary to our constitutional commitment to equal opportunity. Effective citizenship in a participatory democracy must not be dependent upon advancement toward college degrees. Consequently, it would be inappropriate to conclude that academic freedom is required only in colleges and universities. (p. 116)

At the global level, a recent statement adopted by the International Federation of Library Associations and Institutions (IFLAI) holds that: "Human beings have a fundamental right to access to expressions of knowledge, creative thought, and intellectual activity, and to express their views publicly" (IFLAI Statement, 1999). Academic freedom for all teachers is consistent with this position. It needs continual nurturing, expansion, and vigilance in support of global democratization.

Educational Grounds for Academic Freedom

Where, if not in schools, will new generations be able to explore and test divergent ideas, new concepts, and challenges to propaganda? Students should be able to pursue intriguing possibilities under the guidance of free and knowledgeable teachers. Students can test ideas in schools with less serious risks of social condemnation or ostracism. In a setting where critical thinking is prized and nurtured, students and teachers can engage more fully in intellectual development. This is in society's best interests for two fundamental reasons: (1) new ideas from new generations are the basis of social progress, and (2) students who are not permitted to explore divergent ideas in school can be blinded to society's defects and imperfections and will be ill-equipped to participate as citizens in improving democracy.

Although teaching can be conducted easily as simple indoctrination, with teachers presenting material and students memorizing it without thought or criticism, that leads to an incomplete and defective education. Teaching also can be chaotic, with no sense of organization or purpose—this, too, is incomplete and defective education. Neither of these approaches to teaching offers education. Education consists of ideas and challenges, increasingly sophisticated and complex. Indoctrination stunts the educational process, shrinking knowledge and constricting critical thinking. Chaotic schools confuse the educational process, mix important and trivial ideas, and muddle critical thinking. A sound education provides solid grounding in current knowledge and teaches students to challenge ideas as a part of the process of critical thinking.

The defining quality of academic freedom is freedom in the search for knowledge. This freedom extends to all students and teachers engaged in the quest for knowledge. The search for knowledge is not limited to experts, but is the primary purpose of schooling. Learning best occurs as people test new ideas against their own experiences and knowledge—that testing requires academic freedom. This active learning does more than just help clear up student confusion. If offers intellectual involvement and ownership. In addition, it is often students who recognize flaws in existing knowledge or who find new ways to understand. When only experts control knowledge or when censors limit ideas, we risk conformity without challenges or conflicting opinions. We may not like challenges to ideas we find comfortable, but those challenges are the stuff of progress. Limiting the search for knowledge to a cadre of established experts is not in the interest of student learning, human progress, or social development.

Most young people encounter radical ideas in conversations with friends or in films, TV, and other media. In an educational setting, students can more fully consider controversial ideas, and they have the opportunity to criticize each view. The real threat to society is that students will not examine controversial material in schools, and that students will come to distrust education and society as places for free exchange of ideas. Daly and Roach (1990) call for a renewed commitment to academic freedom to pursue these social and educational ends.

The Center of the Profession

Academic freedom is at the heart of the teaching profession (Nelson, 1990). Professions are identified by the complex, purposeful nature of the work, educational requirements for admission, and commonly held ethics and values. Medical professionals, for example, work to protect and improve health, have a specialized education in medical practice, and share a commitment to life. Attorneys work in the realm of law, have specialized training in the practice of law, and are dedicated to the value of justice. Teachers work to educate children, have subject knowledge and specialized education in teaching practice, and share a devotion to enlightenment.

The nature of teachers' work and their shared devotion to enlightenment require a special freedom to explore new ideas in the quest for knowledge. This freedom deserves protection beyond that provided to all citizens under the constitutional guarantee of free speech. Unlike other citizens, teachers have a professional obligation to search for truth and assist students in their search for truth (Zirkel, 1993). The National Science Teachers Association (NSTA) state: "As professionals, teachers must be free to examine controversial issues openly in the classroom" (www.nsta.org). The National Council for Social Studies (1974) notes: "Basic to a democratic society are the freedoms of teachers to teach and of students to learn." Similar statements advocating academic freedom for classroom teachers appear in the major documents of most national teacher associations. The Foundation for Individual Rights in Education (FIRE) maintains a website that archives such academic freedom statements from all over the world (www.thefire.org). Teachers' jobs must not be at risk because they explore controversial material or consider ideas outside the mainstream.

A general misunderstanding of the central role schools play in a free society causes teachers and students to live a peripheral existence in the United States. Teaching has been viewed as less than professional; oftentimes teachers are considered low-level employees, hired to do what managers ask. Excessive restrictions are sometimes imposed on what teachers can teach and methods of instruction they can use. School boards and administrators try to censor teachers and teaching materials. And students are virtually ignored, are treated as nonpersons, or are expected to exhibit blind obedience. There may have been some historic reason to treat teachers as mere functionaries; some came as indentured servants and others had inadequate academic preparation. Now all states require undergraduate degrees and a majority of teachers have graduate degrees. Increasingly rigorous teacher credential regulations and improved professional study and practice offer no grounds for demeaning restrictions on a teacher's work. Academic freedom, the essence of the teaching profession, has been insufficiently developed as a necessary idea in our society and in teacher education. A dual educational effort would increase public awareness of the need for academic freedom and inform and inspire the people who go into teaching.

Academic Freedom and Teacher Competency: The Tenure Process

Provision of academic freedom for teachers is not, however, without limits or conditions. Not all persons certified to teach nor every action they take deserve the protection of academic freedom. The basic condition for academic freedom is teacher competence. Incompetent teachers do not deserve and should not receive that extra protection; they should be dismissed if a fair and evidential evaluation finds them incompetent. A license to teach is not a license to practice incompetence.

Teacher competence is a mix of knowledge, skill, and judgment. It includes knowledge of the material and of the students in class, professional skill in teaching, and considered professional judgment. Competence depends on more than just accumulation of college credits; it includes a practical demonstration that teachers can teach with knowledge, skill, and judgment. As in other professions, competence is measured by peers and supervisors, and continues to be refined as teachers gain experience. In teaching, initial competence is expected as the new teacher completes the teaching credential program. That program of four or more years includes subject field and professional study and practice teaching under supervision. Then, according to the laws of various states, teachers serve full-time for several years under school supervision and are granted tenure only if they are successful. This long test of actual teaching should be sufficient to establish competence. Incompetent teachers should not get tenure.

The main legal protection for academic freedom in schools is state tenure law. Under tenure laws, teachers cannot be fired without due process and legitimate cause. The tenured teacher who is threatened with firing has a right to know specific allegations, a fair hearing, and an evidentially based decision. This protects tenured teachers from improper dismissal as a result of personality conflicts or local politics. Grounds for dismissal, identified in state law, usually include moral turpitude, professional misconduct, and incompetence. The allegation must be clearly demonstrated and documented for the dismissal to be upheld. There should be a high standard for becoming a teacher and for obtaining tenure; there also should be a high standard for dismissing a teacher. Teachers should not be dismissed on the basis of personal or political disagreements with administrators or others.

Nontenured probationary teachers also deserve the general protection of academic freedom because they, too, are expected to engage in enlightening education. However, they do not have the same legal claims as tenured teachers. Tenured teachers serve on "indefinite" contracts that schools need not renew formally each year. Dismissal or nonrenewal of the probationary teacher's one-year contract can occur at the end of any given school term, often without specifying cause for dismissal. Dismissal for dealing with controversial topics in a competent manner should, however, be prohibited by school policy as a condition for all teachers. Many excellent schools districts honor this concept. Tenured faculty, protected from improper interference, need to assure that nontenured teachers are not subjected to dismissal for performing their proper teaching function. It is a professional responsibility.

Obstacles to Academic Freedom

Notwithstanding the compelling reasons that support academic freedom, there are historical, political, and economic pressures that can be overwhelming. Sadly, censorship, political restraint, anti-intellectualism, and illegitimate restrictions on teacher and student freedom have a long and sordid history in the United States. Early schools, under religious domination, imposed moralistic requirements on teachers, firing them for impiety, for not attending religious services, or for not exhibiting sufficient religious zeal. In the nineteenth century, many contracts required teachers to remain single, avoid drinking and smoking, attend church each Sunday, substitute for the minister on occasion, not associate with "bad elements," and avoid controversy. Communities required strict conformity to social norms, and teachers could be dismissed for dating, visiting pool halls, or simply disagreeing with local officials. Teachers whose political views differed from those with power in the community were summarily fired. No recourse was available to stop vigilante school boards or administrators.

In the first half of the twentieth century, political restraint and censorship replaced religious and moralistic restrictions on teachers (Pierce, 1933; Beale, 1936; Gellerman, 1938). College teachers often fared no better, and many suffered great indignities at the hands of college officials (Veblen, 1918/1957; Sinclair, 1922; Hofstadter and Metzger, 1955). Academic freedom was an ideal, not a common practice. John Dewey and a few other widely known scholars founded the American Association of University Professors in 1915 for the primary purpose of organizing to protect the academic freedom of college teachers. Dewey recognized even then that all teachers, not just those in colleges, needed academic freedom.

As the twenty-first century emerges, teachers clearly have gained much in professional preparation and stature, but they are not yet free. Significant threats to academic freedom continue to limit education and place blinders on students. The ALA *Newsletter on Intellectual Freedom* tracks censorship in schools and libraries, reports on news about censorship, and follows court cases related to censorship issues. It is a depressing document to those who believe that an open democracy requires full academic freedom for teachers and students. *Newsletter* reports show censorship attempts have been launched in virtually every state. Some states have numerous censorship attempts each year, and thousands of teachers and students are restricted by actions of vigilante groups, school boards, and school administrators.

Current Examples of Censorship and Restrictions on Intellectual Freedom

Newsletter issues published in the past five years have identified dozens of examples of attempts to censor schools, teachers, and libraries; the listing includes these examples:

- *Harry Potter,* the best-selling series of books by J. K. Rowling, became the book most often challenged for censorship in the United States because of its focus on magic and wizardry.
- Nobel Prize winner Toni Morrison's book, *Beloved,* won the Pulitzer Prize in 1987—but a school board member in Maine challenged its use in schools because of some of its language.
- Parents in Oakley, California, want John Steinbeck's *Of Mice and Men* removed from schools because of racial epithets.
- A self-identified Christian group sent thousands of protests to school board chairs, homes, and churches in Largo, Florida, to urge the forced disbanding of a Gay and Straight Alliance student group at Largo High School.
- In Oklahoma an African American student was asked to not recite Martin Luther King's "I Have a Dream" speech because it may have "racial overtones."
- Words about puberty and homosexuality were cut at the last minute from a New York high school production of *A Chorus Line;* one student danced a part in silence.

Censoring activities occur most frequently on the topics of sex, religion, race, patriotism, and economics. Materials that censors want taken out of the hands of teachers and students include classic writings by renowned authors, standard works that most educated people have read, and popular publications readily available on local newsstands or in public libraries. Oftentimes, local censorship advocates have not read the whole work, but object to selected segments or they parrot organizations who object. Examples of teaching materials banned or challenged in recent years include such standard and popular works as *The Adventures of Huckleberry Finn; A Farewell to Arms; Anne Frank: Diary of a Young Girl; Harry Potter; The Chocolate War; The Color Purple; Catch-22; The Catcher in the Rye; From Here to Eternity; The Great Gatsby; Of Mice and Men; The Sun Also Rises; To Kill a Mockingbird; Native Son; I Know Why the Caged Bird Sings; The Firm; Deliverance; The Martian Chronicles;* and *Slaughterhouse Five.* Other common targets for censors include texts and reference works, such as *Focus on Algebra; Merriam-Webster's Collegiate Dictionary;* and *Human Anatomy and Physiology.* Some popular magazines censors want to ban include *Cosmopolitan; Editor and Publisher; National Enquirer; People;* and *Playboy.* And films such as these continue to bring out the censors: *1900; Glory; Lolita; Schindler's List;* and *The Tin Drum.* (*Newsletter on Intellectual Freedom,* 1996, 1998, 2000, 2002, 2003; Foerstel, 1994, 2002).

Other kinds of censorship and excessive restriction plague schools, teachers, and students. Field trips at a Pennsylvania high school to see *Macbeth* and

Schindler's List were cancelled because of local citizen complaints. A school production of *A Thousand Cranes,* which includes a Japanese girl dying after the U.S. bombing of Hiroshima, was attacked by locals because it might give the idea that "America was unjust." In 1992, the South Carolina legislature considered a bill to ban relaxation techniques and meditation from classrooms because these are used by "New Age" religions. Student newspapers often are censored; and science and art classes have been subjected to censorship and restriction on religious grounds (Sherrow, 1996; *Newsletter on Intellectual Freedom* 2001, 2002, 2003). Figure 16.1 shows institutions receiving the most complaints and challenges to materials being available between 1990 and 2000; schools are the leading institutions for efforts to censor.

Textbook publishers shy away from controversial content to avoid censors, Texas censors forced a major American history textbook by highly respected historians to be stricken from Texas high schools because of two paragraphs (out of 1,000 pages) suggesting prostitution was rampant in the West in the late nineteenth century (Stille, 2002). Teacher self-censorship, noted earlier, continues apace as threats emerge. And many local politicians and self-appointed moralists pressure school boards and administrators to squelch teachers.

The Internet is the most recent focus of censors, with scare tactics used to block access to many legitimate Internet sites. A 1999 report of the Censorware Project shows that Utah blocks access for all public schools and some libraries to such material as: The Declaration of Independence, The U.S. Constitution, the Bible, the Koran, all of Shakespeare's plays, and Sherlock Holmes ("Censored Internet Access in Utah Schools and Libraries," 1999). Websites which protest such censor intrusion into libraries include the Electronic Frontier Foundation (www.eff.org), the Foundation for Individual Rights in Education (www.thefire.org), and Peacefire (www.peacefire.org).

Topics that arouse the censors vary over time and across locations, and span both ends of the political spectrum. Socialism and communism were visible targets in the 1920s and again in the 1960s, surfacing again in the Reagan administration. Sexual topics and profanity are constant targets of school censors. A

FIGURE 16.1. Which Institutions are Targets of Censorship?

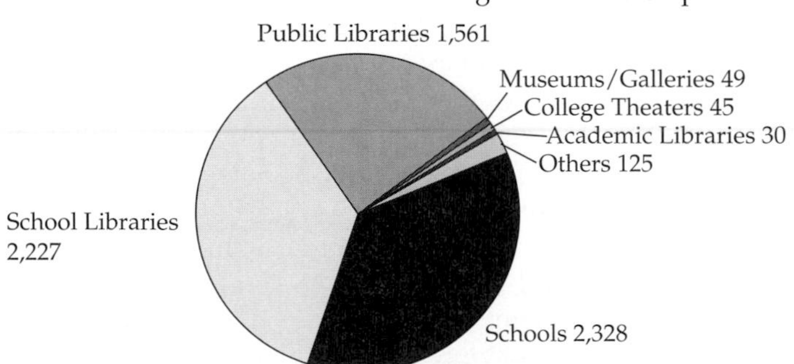

Source: *Office of Intellectual Freedom, American Library Association. In Foerstel, H. N. (2002).* Banned in the USA. *Westport, CT: Greenwood Press. Data from 1990–2000.*

more recent issue is the charge that schools teach secular humanism—teachers and materials are anti-God, immoral, antifamily, and anti-American. Among other current topics stimulating people who want to stifle academic freedom are drugs, evolution, values clarification, economics, environmental issues, social activism, and the use of African American, feminist, or other minority literature (Jenkinson, 1990; Waldron, 1993; Japenga, 1994; Sipe, 1999).

Publicized censorship and restraint activities have a chilling effect on school boards, administrators, and even many teachers (Whitson, 1993). The possibility of complaints on a controversial topic leads to fear. Daly (1991) found that few school districts had policies to protect teacher and student rights to academic freedom. As a result, teacher self-censorship denies students and society the full exploration of ideas. Many teachers avoid significant topics, or they neutralize and sterilize them to the point of student boredom. Table 16.1 indicates that parents are the people most likely to initiate censorship efforts in schools and libraries, at least that was true during the ten years from 1990 to 2000.

A statement by the American Association of University Professors (AAUP, 1986) in support of academic freedom for precollege-level teachers identified a variety of political restraints imposed on such teachers. The American Civil Liberties Union (www.aclu.org) has a long tradition of support for academic freedom for teachers and students, and assists in court proceedings to redress censorship and political restriction. Since 1970, the frequency of reported censorship incidents has tripled. Moreover, estimates suggest that for each incident formally reported, about fifty other censoring activities go unreported (Jenkinson, 1985). The National Coalition Against Censorship (www.ncas.org), affiliated with dozens of professional and scholarly associations, formed because of this increase in censorship.

Studies confirm the fragile state of academic freedom in schools. Censorship of literature continues ("Censorship," 1990; Hymowitz, 1991; Flagg, 1992; Waldron, 1993; Simmons, 1991, 1994); school boards and administrators keep trying

TABLE 16.1. Who Initiates Challenges to School and Library Materials?

Rank	Initiator	Number of Challenges over Ten Years
1	Parents	3,891
2	Patrons	936
3	Administrator	596
4	Board Member	232
5	Teacher	176
6	Pressure Group	175
7	Other Group	162
8	Religious Organization	108
9	Clergy	92
10	Government	53

Source: Office of Intellectual Freedom, American Library Association. In Foerstel, H. N. (2002). *Banned in the USA.* Westport, CT: Greenwood Press. Data from 1990–2000.

to expand their control over instructional material (Daly, 1991; Mesibov, 1991); and courts render inconsistent decisions on the protection of teacher freedoms (Mawdsley and Mawdsley, 1988; Melnick and Lillard, 1989; Sacken, 1989; Turner-Egner, 1989; "Censorship," 1990; Pico, 1990). Is it worth the effort to strive for academic freedom? No other school battle is so worthy.

A Free Society Requires Academic Freedom

Despite the often weak protection of academic freedom and often powerful political pressures brought to bear to stifle it, attaining freedom for teachers and students is worth the strenuous effort it demands. There are compelling democratic, educational, and professional grounds for expanding the protection of academic freedom to competent teachers and all students. And there are important social reasons why the public should support academic freedom in public education. Academic freedom is more than a set of platitudes, state regulations, and court decisions. It should be a fundamental expectation of schools in a free society. Academic freedom is a central truth for the profession of teaching.

For Discussion

1. Dialogue ideas: Should there be any restrictions on what a teacher can discuss in class? What set of principles should govern establishment of those limits? Should students have the same freedoms and limits? Is student age or teacher experience a significant factor in this determination?
2. Louis Menand (1996), distinguished Professor of English at the City University of New York, argues:

   > Academic freedom is not simply a kind of bonus enjoyed by workers within the system, a philosophical luxury universities could function just as effectively, and much more efficiently, without. It is the key legitimating concept of the entire enterprise. Virtually every practice of academic life that we take for granted—from the practice of allowing departments to hire and fire their own members to the practice of not allowing the football coach to influence the quarterback's grade in math class—derives from it. (p. 4)

   a. What evidence is available to determine whether this view of academic freedom at the university level is consistent with principles and practices at the higher education institution you attend?
   b. Discuss why this view of academic freedom is or is not suited to teachers in precollegiate schools.
   c. What other implications for K–12 schooling does this concept of academic freedom convey?
3. Which, if any, of these topics should be banned from schoolbooks or class discussion?

Explicit sexual material	Violence
Sexism	Anti-American views
Racism	Antireligious ideas
Fascism	Socialism
Inhuman treatment of people	Animal, child, or spouse abuse

What are the grounds for justifying censorship of any of these? Who should decide? What are some good examples of thesis and antithesis statements about censorship? How would you construct a dialect on this topic?

4. What role should teachers play in learning about and responding to efforts at censorship? Should censors be censored? How should a teacher be prepared to deal with censors and political restraint?

References

AMERICAN ASSOCIATION OF UNIVERSITY PROFESSORS (AAUP). (1986). *Liberty and Learning in the Schools.* Washington, DC: Author.

ATTACKS ON THE FREEDOM TO LEARN. (1985–1994). Washington, DC: People for the American Way.

BEALE, H. (1936). *Are American Teachers Free?* New York: Scribner's.

BUCKLEY, W. F. (1951). *God and Man at Yale.* Chicago: Regnery.

"Censored Internet Access in Utah Schools and Libraries." (1999). Report, Censorware Project. (Available online at www.censorware.org) March 23.

"Censorship: A Continuing Problem." (1990). *English Journal* 79, 87–89.

DALY, J. K. (1991). "The Influence of Administrators on the Teaching of Social Studies." *Theory and Research in Social Education* 19, 267–283.

DALY, J. K., AND ROACH, P. B. (1990). "Reaffirming a Commitment to Academic Freedom." *Social Education* 54, 342–345.

DALY, J. K., SCHALL, P., AND SKEELE, R. (2001). *Protecting the Right to Teach and Learn.* New York: Teachers College Press.

DEWEY, J. (1936). "The Social Significance of Academic Freedom." *The Social Frontier* 2, 136.

DICTIONARY OF THE HISTORY OF IDEAS. (1973). I. Weiner, ed. New York: Scribners.

FLAGG, G. (1992). "'Snow White' is the Latest Title Under Attack in Schools." *American Libraries* 23, 359–361.

FOERSTEL, H. N. (1994). *Banned in the USA.* Westport, CT: Greenwood Press.

———. (2002). *Banned in the USA.* Westport, CT: Greenwood Press.

GELLERMAN, W. (1938). *The American Legion as Educator.* New York: Teachers College Press.

GOLDSTEIN, S. (1976). "The Asserted Right of Teachers to Determine What They Teach." *University of Pennsylvania Law Review* 124, 1, 293.

HENTOFF, N. (1991). "Saving Kids from Satan's Books." *The Progressive* 55, 14–16.

HOFSTADTER, R., AND METZGER, W. (1955; 1968). *The Development of Academic Freedom in the United States.* New York: Columbia University Press.

HOOK, S. (1953). *Heresy, Yes—Conspiracy, No.* New York: Day.

HYMOWITZ, K. S. (1991). "Babar the Racist." *The New Republic* 205, 12–14.

IFLAI STATEMENT. (1999). "Libraries and Intellectual Freedom." International Federation of Library Associations and Institutions, The Hague, Netherlands. 25 March.

JAPENGA, A. (1994). "A Teacher at War." *Mother Jones* 19, 17.

JENKINSON, E. B. (1985). "Protecting Holden Caulfield and His Friends from the Censors." *English Journal* 74, 26–33.

———. (1990). "Child Abuse in the Hate Factory." In A. Ochoa, ed., *Academic Freedom to Teach and to Learn.* Washington, DC: National Education Association.

Keyishian v. Board of Regents. (1967). 385 U.S. 589.

KIRK, R. (1955). *Academic Freedom.* Chicago: Regnery.

LEO, J. (1993). "Pedophiles in the Schools." *U.S. News & World Report* 115, 37.

MAWDSLEY, R. D., AND MAWDSLEY, A. L. (1988). *Free Expression and Censorship: Public Policy and the Law.* Topeka, KS: National Organization on Legal Problems of Education.

McFarlane, A. (1994). "Radical Educational Values." *America* 171, 10–13.
Melnick, N., and Lillard, S. D. (1989). "Academic Freedom: A Delicate Balance." *Clearing House* 62, 275–277.
Menand, L., ed. (1996). *The Future of Academic Freedom.* Chicago: University of Chicago Press.
Mesibov, L. L. (1991). "Teacher–Board of Education Conflicts Over Instructional Material." *School Law Bulletin* 22, 10–15.
National Council for the Social Studies (NCSS). (1974). "The Freedom to Teach and the Freedom to Learn." Washington, DC: Author.
Nelson, J. (1990). "The Significance of and Rationale for Academic Freedom." In A. Ochoa, ed., *Academic Freedom to Teach and to Learn.* Washington, DC: National Education Association.
Newsletter on Intellectual Freedom. (Bimonthly). Chicago: American Library Association.
Noble, W. (1990). *Bookbanning in America.* Middlebury, VT: Paul Ericksson.
Noddings, N. (1999). "Renewing Democracy in Schools." *Phi Delta Kappan* 80(8), 579–583.
O'Neil, R. M. (1981). *Classrooms in the Crossfire.* Bloomington: Indiana University Press.
Pico, S. (1990). "An Introduction to Censorship." *School Media Quarterly* 18, 84–87.
Pierce, B. (1933). *Citizens' Organizations and the Civic Training of Youth.* New York: Scribners.
Reichman, H. (1993). *Censorship and Selection: Issues and Answers for Schools.* Chicago: American Library Association and American Association of School Administrators.
Rorty, R. (1994). "Does Academic Freedom Have Philosophical Presuppositions?" *Academe* 80, 52–63.
Rubin, D., and Greenhouse, S. (1983). *The Rights of Teachers: the Basic ACLU Guide to a Teacher's Constitutional Rights.* Rev. Ed. New York: Bantam.
Sacken, D. M. (1989). "Rethinking Academic Freedom in the Public Schools." *Teachers College Record* 91, 235–255.
Scales, P. (2001). *Teaching Banned Books.* Chicago: American Library Association.
Sherrow, V. (1996). *Censorship in Schools.* Springfield, NJ: Enslow Publishers.
Simmons, J. (1991). "Censorship in the Schools: No End in Sight." *ALAN Review* 18, 6–8.
———, ed. (1994). *Censorship: A Threat to Reading, Learning, Thinking.* Newark, DE: International Reading Association.
Sinclair, U. (1922). *The Goose-Step.* Pasadena, CA: Sinclair.
———. (1923). *The Goslings.* Pasadena, CA: Sinclair.
Sipe, R. B. (1999). "Don't Confront Censors, Prepare for Them." *Education Digest* 64(6), 42–46.
Stille, A. (2002). "Textbook Publishers Learn to Avoid Messing with Texas." *New York Times Online.* (www.nytimes.com) June 29.
The Rights of Students. 3rd Ed. (1988). Washington, DC: American Civil Liberties Union.
Thelin, J. (1997). "Zealotry and Academic Freedom." *History of Education Quarterly* 37(3), 338–420.
Thomas, C. (1983). *Book Burning.* Manchester, IL: Crossway Books.
Turner-Egner, J. (1989). "Teachers' Discretion in Selecting Instructional Materials and Methods." *West's Education Law Reporter* 53, 365–379.
Veblen, T. (1918/1957). *The Higher Learning in America: Memorandum on the Conduct of Universities by Businessmen.* New York: Sagamore.
Wieman v. Updegraff. (1952). 244 U.S. 183.

WALDRON, C. (1993). "White Teacher's Use of *Ebony* to Teach Tolerance at Texas School Ignites Uproar Among Parents." *Jet* 84, 10–16.
WHITSON, J. A. (1993). "After Hazelwood: The Role of School Officials in Conflicts over the Curriculum." *ALAN Review* 20, 2–6.
ZIRKEL, P. (1993). "Academic Freedom: Professional or Legal Right?" *Educational Leadership* 50, 42–43.

CHAPTER 17

Teacher Unions: Detrimental or Beneficial to Education

POSITION 1: TEACHER UNIONS ARE DETRIMENTAL

Unions are dedicated to protecting the jobs of all their members. The rules they insist upon, as a result, make it virtually impossible for schools to get rid of even the most poorly performing teachers, not to mention those that are merely mediocre.

—MOE, 2001, P. 163

Self-Serving and Unsupported Claims

Teacher union officials say that when public monies are spent to improve working conditions for teachers, children are the ultimate beneficiaries. Their arguments are, no doubt, familiar: Public school students suffer because teachers are underpaid. Hardworking, devoted teachers deserve greater compensation. Unless teachers earn higher salaries, not only will the current crop of teachers become discouraged, but the brightest college graduates will not go into education. Union leaders further argue that teachers need a stronger voice in school affairs. They claim teachers will be more effective if allowed to join administrators in all areas of school management, including curriculum reform and supervision and evaluation of teaching.

The logic in these examples is simple: What is good for teachers is good for children. If the public wants better education for its children, the public should support union efforts to improve education through increased remuneration and greater authority for teachers. Collective bargaining practices, picket lines, work stoppages (strikes), and expansion of union control over schools should be considered beneficial to the community, parents, and students.

Convincing? Not really. Making schools better places for teachers does not necessarily serve the public interest. The public's interest is not measured in teachers' job satisfaction but in the quality of learning provided to students.

Despite the rhetoric of organized labor, teacher unions do not have a positive effect on student achievement nor do increased teacher salaries improve the quality of teaching. More money for teachers does not translate into better schooling. Researchers find negligible differences in achievement between public school students in union and nonunion schools. While research indicates evidence collective bargaining improves teachers' salaries, benefits, and working conditions, it is more difficult to find a consistently positive influence of unions on student learning (Stone, 2000). Unions cannot claim to make a difference where it counts most: students' academic performance. Despite failures of teacher unions to prove their worth in student achievement, the positive wage-effect of unions—that is, their power to improve teachers' pay—clearly ensures unions will remain players in education. Less clear is whether or not unions are good for schools and if they will hinder school reform or merely be irrelevant (Finn, 1985).

Although only about 15 percent of American workers belong to unions, most teachers in America's schools are unionized. Over 80 percent of teachers belong to an affiliate of the National Education Association (NEA) or the American Federation of Teachers (AFT), and with millions of dues-paying members, unions have great resources and great power. Not only can teacher unions exert influence on the day-to-day workings of schools, their political activities have given them unrivaled influence in the local, state, and federal governments. As Terry Moe points out, "The key to the unions' preeminence in American education is that they are able to combine collective bargaining and politics into an integrated strategy for promoting unions objectives" (Moe, 2001, p. 166). He goes on to point out that "On education issues, the teacher unions are the 500-pound gorillas of legislative politics, and especially in legislatures where the Democrats are in control, they are in a better position than any other interest group to get what they want from government" (Moe, 2001, p. 175).

Unions work mainly for the benefit of teachers. Don't be misled when unions call for more rigorous training of teachers or stricter licensing standards. While there is little evidence such changes would result in better education or improved student learning, there is abundant evidence to indicate these policies would make good economic sense for teachers. Stricter standards for teacher certification, whether academic (requiring all teachers to have master's degrees) or arbitrary (requiring all teachers to be over 6′5″ tall) would result in a diminished supply of teachers at a time when demand is increasing. Obviously, unions are hopeful that market forces will result in improved salaries. It is hard for the public to trust unions. Who can say with certainty that union advocacy of smaller class size represents a desire to help children or if it is simply a way to make teachers' work easier and, concurrently, increase the demand for more teachers. Consider another union recommendation: mentorship programs through which experienced classroom teachers help new teachers learn the ropes. When teachers serve as mentors for other teachers, does it benefit students or is this simply driving up the cost of education through featherbedding—the addition of unnecessary workers? Who really benefits from teacher unions, students or teachers? (Ballou and Podgursky, 2000).

From Bread-and-Butter to Policy Issues

Encouraged by their ability to improve teachers' salaries—the union-wage effect is in the neighborhood of 5 to 10 percent—unions have extended their influence beyond bread-and-butter work issues. Past union efforts typically were limited to traditional labor concerns: wages and hours, working conditions, fringe benefits, grievance procedures, organization rights, and such specific work-related issues as extra pay for extra duty (athletic coaching or directing school plays, for example). Over time, teacher unions began to demand a voice in policy issues, including curriculum reform, class size, disciplinary practices, textbook selection procedures, in-service training, teacher transfer policies, and personnel matters—including hiring and awarding tenure (Kerchner, 1986; Kerchner and Koppich, 2000). Today, affiliates of both the NEA and the AFT want teachers to expand their activities and participate in discussions about education reform, political lobbying, and shared decision making. These demands go well beyond the traditional bargaining issue of salaries and working conditions. Some union contracts give teachers the right to make decisions about how schools spend money, how teachers teach, and how students are to learn. In strongly unionized urban districts, union contracts can be hundreds of pages long (Moe, 2001). Under the familiar argument that collective negotiations will create a better education for children, union leaders now claim that increased teacher participation in all the decision-making and managerial aspects of education also will reform schools. The public has greeted the new union arguments with a healthy skepticism. Unions grew up on industrial principles. They have used organizing and negotiating techniques borrowed from industrial unions in mining and manufacturing—collective bargaining and the threat of strikes—to improve their members' working conditions. There is every reason to be suspicious that unions can use the same tactics to improve the quality of schools.

Unfortunately, representatives of the NEA and AFT have been trained to regard local communities with disdain and to treat school boards as the enemy. Turning schools over to unions would distort the authority structure of public education. No matter how it is packaged, capitulating to demands for teacher empowerment destroys community control of education. The unions were not hired by the community, and they may not represent the most effective classroom teachers. Over the years, teacher unions have become stronger, and teachers have increased their political power. While teachers were winning, parents and the community were losing (Friedman and Friedman, 1979; Baird, 1984; Moo, 1999). If unions are allowed to bargain collectively regarding policy and curriculum reform, schools will become less responsive to the community and more an agency of the unions. Responsibility for running schools should be entrusted only to those the voters have chosen. Collective bargaining must not steal the community's right to control the education of its children.

Apologizing for Bad Teachers

Unions have become apologists for poor teaching and an obstacle to school reform. On the one hand, unions heap praise on the magical effect good teachers have on children's lives. On the other hand, they fail to admit weak teachers may be a cause of many of the schools' shortcomings. Everyone familiar with public schools knows the quality of classroom instruction varies tremendously. Nestled among the great teachers, the good teachers, and the marginally adequate teachers are those who fail to convey enthusiasm for learning and, unfortunately, more than a few who have neither the personal qualities nor the skills and knowledge necessary to teach children. While the good teachers whet students' appetites for academic achievement, bad teachers kill interest, leave students with enormous gaps of information, and tarnish the reputation of the profession.

Unions talk about boosting teacher morale and teacher self-esteem, but they regularly oppose merit pay for good teachers. Some districts have proposed pay-for-performance plans that would reward unusually successful teachers—those who produce above-average learning gains in students—with higher raises, whereas those who evidence less success would earn lower-than-normal raises. Typically, teacher unions reject these plans, claiming the plans are "subject to administrator bias" or that the concept of a "good teacher" is too subjective to measure (Lieberman, 1997; Harshbarger, 2000). The public believes schools are designed to treat each child individually and to make judgments about those who should be rewarded and those who should fail. It suspects schools would benefit if teachers were subject to similar judgments. Good teachers should reap the fruits of their individual talent; bad teachers should be fired. As one advocate of performance pay notes:

> And people wonder why public education is going down the tubes. Of course it is. The Union leadership and the dolts who follow the leader seem to think that teaching is the only profession in the world that shouldn't be subject to performance-based pay or goals-based bonus systems. We have teachers who are teaching solely because of the pay, and no matter how good or poor that teacher is, he/she will get the same pay as everyone around him/her. No wonder there's been no true innovation in education in the last 100 years, there's no incentive to do so. When pay is based solely on number of years in the profession, there's no reason to do a good job. It's akin to socialism, and we've seen what that does to economies. (Dwyer, 2001)

The public is generally sympathetic to teachers, but not to teacher unions, and it is not hard to understand why. Trade unionists in education are hard put to account for the numbers of poor teachers in their ranks. Typically, they place the blame either on weak university programs in teacher education or hiring practices of public school administrators. The sad fact remains that too many schools have teachers who are not able to do the work expected of them. Unfortunately, because of unions and tenure laws, even the poorest teachers will probably stay on the job until retirement. Left to their own devices, unions are unlikely to rid the profession of bad teachers. The principal job of the union is not to improve the teaching profession but to protect teachers. Given this goal, unions can hardly refuse to fight dismissals, even when the teacher involved is obviously incompetent. As a result, it is nearly impossible to fire a tenured teacher. A typical school district nationwide might have to spend between $10,000 and $50,000 in legal fees to get rid of its worst teacher (Lieberman, 1985). In New York, it takes well over a year's time and costs the schools almost $195,000 to prosecute a single teacher accused of misconduct (Dillon, 1994). Between 1991 and 1997, only 44 of Illinois' 100,000 tenured public school teachers were dismissed for cause. In Florida only 0.02 percent of the tenured teachers are fired in a typical year (Goldstein, 1998).

Union opposition to culling incompetents from classrooms has forced school districts to decide whether to spend money on new books and programs or on litigation. In many states, union rules have brought administrative actions against ineffective teachers to an absolute halt (VanSciver, 1990). Unions cry for greater involvement in restructuring schools, but their opposition to pay-for-performance plans and refusal to allow dismissal of tenured but incompetent teachers cast great doubt on their potential contribution to reform. The public would be more supportive of unions if unions were as concerned about the quality of teaching as they are about protecting individual teachers.

Resisting Change

Unions and teaching do not fit together gracefully. They may have been useful in earlier times, but they have become anachronisms. Today, unions are more appropriate for heavy industry, such as auto or steel production, where all workers perform similar tasks under much the same circumstances. The net effect of poor work or lazy workers is more destructive in teaching than it would be in factory occupations. One bad steel worker could make his or her coworkers' jobs more difficult, but he or she is unlikely to hurt the industry as a whole. An incompetent teacher who teaches dozens of children a year may have a much more harmful effect on many lives for many years.

Teachers should be treated individually, not collectively. Good teachers should be recognized for their professional competence and financially rewarded according to the quality of their performance. Weak teachers should be helped or weeded out, and labor negotiations should not consume the energies of teachers and administrators. Parents and other members of the community have every reason to be suspicious of unions' potential for championing school reform. To deal unions a hand in school reform would not be unlike hiring wolves to work as shepherds. Unions cannot be trusted to represent anything but teachers' interests. That has been their historic mission, and they have served it well. The claim that they have reinvented themselves to serve the cause of school reform rings hollow. Until unions start talking about ridding the classroom of poor teachers and replacing lifetime tenure with renewable short-term contracts, the public will not be convinced they are serious about reform. Unless unions demonstrate they are on the side of students as well as teachers, they should be held at bay or they will hijack school reform.

POSITION 2: TEACHER UNIONS ARE BENEFICIAL TO EDUCATION

Our challenge is clear: Instead of relegating teachers to the role of production workers—with no say in organizing their schools for excellence—we need to enlist teachers as full partners, indeed as co-managers of their schools. Instead of contracts that reduce flexibility and restrict change, we—and our schools—need contracts that empower and enable. . . . This new collaboration is not about sleeping with the enemy. It is about waking up to our shared stake in reinvigorating the public education enterprise. It is about educating children better, more effectively, more ambitiously.

—CHASE, 1997

Forcing Teachers to Unionize

In the early part of this century, teachers were trained to believe that sacrifice was the essence of their profession. Teachers worked long hours; their classes often numbered fifty or more students; their salaries were low; and schools were at times poorly heated, poorly ventilated, and unsanitary. Women teachers were not allowed to go out unescorted (except to attend church) or frequent places where liquor was served; and in many communities, when women teachers married, they were forced to resign from their jobs. In addition to living truncated social lives, teachers served at the whim of school boards, without any promise of tenure or health or retirement benefits. They were not considered worthy of participating in the book selection process and were excluded from the more substantive deliberations about curriculum.

As school systems developed into large bureaucratic organizations, conditions worsened. School principals became managers. Once referred to as the "principal teacher" or the "main teacher," the head of a school became a manager who shared few of the problems of teachers and none of their perspective. Most of the new school administrators were male; most of the classroom teachers were female. Administrators treated teachers as low-skilled workers who needed to be told what to do. The authority to run schools was vested in men in administrative offices, and teachers were not to challenge their authority. Over time, teachers realized what they were being asked to give up in the name of professionalism was not good for them or their students, and through collective action, schools could be improved for everyone.

Teachers have been organized for well over one hundred years, but their earliest organizations were not really unions. The National Education Association (NEA), for example, was established in 1857, to represent the views of "practical" classroom teachers and administrators. Annual NEA conventions were not union meetings but settings for the exchange of ideas about teaching. Members typically avoided discussing labor issues or how teachers could influence decisions about their work or wages. The NEA was less concerned with the personal welfare of classroom teachers than it was with advancing the profession of education. In its early years, the NEA was a male-dominated organization for teachers that was led by school superintendents, professors of education, and school principals (Wesley, 1957). As one critic of the NEA notes, the role of classroom teachers, especially women teachers, was "limited to listening" (Eaton, 1975, p. 10). Since the 1960s, the NEA has moved more aggressively to represent the views of all classroom teachers, advocating collective negotiations, and encouraging its local affiliates to serve as bargaining agents for teachers.

Teacher unionism dates to the early twentieth century, when Chicago teachers organized to fight for better working conditions. In 1916, the American Federation of Teachers (AFT) was formed as an affiliate of the American Federation of Labor. Initially, the older NEA and the upstart AFT cooperated. The NEA focused on professional and practical sides of teaching; the AFT concentrated on improving economic aspects of teachers' lives (Engel, 1976). Over the years, local affiliates of the NEA and the AFT have become rivals in their efforts to become the teachers' bargaining agents. More than 80 percent of U.S. teachers belong to either the NEA or the AFT, and more than 60 percent work under a formal collective bargaining agreement.

Teachers were never eager to join unions; they were forced to because the culture of administrative managers was at odds with the culture of working teachers (Jessup, 1978; Urban, 1982; Murphy, 1990). Teachers urged their colleagues to use unions and collective bargaining to improve their working conditions and gain a voice in improving education. This letter, typical of the calls for teachers to organize, was written in 1913:

> On the ground that teachers do the every-day work of teaching and understand the conditions necessary for better teaching, we propose the following principles for the new organizations: Teachers should have a voice and a vote in determination of educational policies. The granting of legislative opportunity to the teachers would inevitably contribute to the development of a strong professional spirit, and the intelligent use of their experience in the interest of the public. We advocate the adoption of a plan that will permit all teachers to have a share in the administration of the affairs of their own school. In no more practical way could teachers prepare themselves for training children for citizenship in democracy. . . . ("A Call to Organize," *American Teacher,* December 1913, p. 140, quoted in Eaton, 1975, pp. 13–14)

Today, teacher organizations often bear a greater resemblance to professional associations (for example, the American Bar Association or the American Medical Association) than to labor organizations (the International Ladies Garment Workers Union or the United Automobile Workers). Leaders of the old AFT, however, identified with unionized workers in other industries. They believed problems common to all workers could be solved through cooperation and collective action. They wanted teacher organizations to provide economic benefits for their members, and argued that teacher unions also could assist labor by improving the education offered to working-class children. Despite numerous efforts to organize teachers and revitalize education, including development of a workers' college and special public schools for workers' children,

AFT membership declined in the 1920s and remained flat throughout most of the 1930s. Teachers were reluctant to join unions, and most school administrators were openly hostile to organized labor. In the 1920s, fearing worker radicalism and union activity, many school superintendents demanded teachers, as a condition of employment, sign "yellow dog contracts," agreements they would not join a union.

The National Labor Relations Act (NLRA) of 1935 changed the status of unions by recognizing workers in private industry had the right to bargain collectively. In collective bargaining, employees, as a group, and their employers negotiate in good faith about wages and employment conditions (Lieberman and Moscow, 1966, p. 1). Employees are at a disadvantage when they bargain singly with employers, working alone against the power and resources at management's hand. Collective bargaining laws recognize workers have the right to join together and elect a bargaining agent (a union) to negotiate with management on their behalf. The NLRA required employers and unions to "meet at reasonable times and confer in good faith with respect to wages, hours, and other terms and conditions of employment."

Questions about its constitutionality clouded the NLRA's early history. The Supreme Court eventually decided the issue, judging the act constitutional (*NLRB v. Jones and Laughlin Steel Company*, 1937). This was a major victory for organized labor, and represented a great change in the thinking of the courts. In earlier cases the courts had ruled unions were illegal and workers who joined unions were guilty of entering into an illegal "conspiracy" to improve their wages. By the mid-nineteenth century, courts no longer believed that those who advocated collective bargaining were involved in criminal conspiracies (*Commonwealth v. Hunt*, 1842), but unions and collective negotiations did not earn full legitimacy until the Supreme Court's 1937 decision.

The NLRA affects only workers in the private sector. It does not cover employees of federal, state, or local government, so this law did not guarantee collective bargaining for public school teachers. Public schools are considered extensions of the state. School boards are, in a sense, state employers, and thus they are excluded from federal labor legislation. It has been left up to the states to regulate employment relations in public education. Following Congress's lead, the majority of state legislatures have taken action to recognize the rights of workers to organize and negotiate with employers. By the late 1990s, thirty-four states had laws legally protecting the rights of teachers to bargain collectively; nine states had laws making collective bargaining illegal; and six states were officially silent, neither denying or enabling collective bargaining, instead leaving the decision to local school districts (Lieberman, 1997, p. 48).

The organization of teachers in New York City in 1960 is considered a watershed for public school unions (Lieberman and Moscow, 1966, p. 35). The United Federation of Teachers (UFT), a local affiliate of the AFT, was made up of several New York City teacher organizations. The UFT asked the Board of Education to recognize the teachers' rights to bargain collectively and conduct an election to determine which organization should represent them. The board was unsure how to implement collective bargaining, and it did not move swiftly. The unions accused the board of stalling, and on November 7, 1960, the UFT declared the first strike in the history of New York City education.

It was a brief but effective job action: The next day, teachers were back in the classrooms. The board had agreed to hold elections and not to take reprisals against striking teachers. Union estimates put pickets at about 7,500, and it was claimed that another 15,000 teachers stayed home (Eaton, 1975, p. 165). The strike alerted the nation to the power of unions, and teachers began to recognize the advantages of collective negotiation as well as the power potential of the strike. Collective bargaining changed the relationship between classroom teachers and administrators. It promised teachers more pay, better job security, and an audible voice in education. As one labor historian puts it, "It essentially refined and broadened the concept of professionalism by assuring [teachers] more autonomy and less supervisory control" (Murphy, 1990, p. 209).

The New York City strike reverberated nationally. The results encouraged teachers, and sent the two largest unions, the NEA and the AFT, scrambling for members. The NEA represents about 2.6 million teachers, about twice the number represented by the AFT. These organizations differ on specific issues. An examination of the views of each union can be found in the journal The *NEA Today* and the AFT's *American Teacher.* Regular columns by the AFT president appear in *The New York Times;* columns by the NEA president appear in the *Washington Post.* (You may want to take a look at the AFT website at www.aft.org and the NEA website at www.nea.org).

The decision to join the labor movement no doubt came hard to many teachers. Teachers tended to be politically conservative, first-generation college graduates who identified with management more than with labor (Rosenthal, 1969; Aronowitz, 1973). They belonged (and still belong) to a special category of white-collar employees called "knowledge workers." Paid for what they know and how they use their knowledge to produce value, these workers, as a group, are highly individualistic, and difficult to unionize and organize into collective action (Kerchner, Koppich, and Weeres, 1997, p. 34). Strikes are anathema to most members of teacher unions (Rauth, 1990). The fact that the union movement has succeeded in recruiting teachers speaks well for unions; teachers believe unions are necessary and useful. Most teachers now belong to some sort of union, despite a decline in union membership in other fields and continued middle-class antipathy toward unions.

Protecting Teachers' Rights

Unions have been good for classroom teachers. The research literature indicates unions have had a positive effect on teachers' working conditions. As a result of collective bargaining, teachers' salaries have increased,[1] and teachers have

[1]Teachers' salaries are better, but still not good. In 2001, a teacher at the top of the salary schedule, with a master's degree, in a typical big-city school, earned about $52,000 annually. In the preceding ten years, teachers' had salaries increased at a rate of 3.2 percent annually, barely ahead of inflation, while the yearly average for all workers had annual increases averaging 3.7 percent over the same period (Nelson and Gould, 2001).

gained protection against unreasonable treatment. Unlike the pre-union days, teachers cannot be dismissed simply because they consume alcohol or change their marital status. Unions also have been good for education. They have put the faculty squarely in the front ranks of the battle for better schools and better education for children. Unions have given faculty a collective voice in matters of curriculum and school policy.

Teacher unions have always attracted some bad press. Some of it is traditional antilabor rhetoric, and some is simply misinformed. No doubt you have heard unions are to blame for declining student performance and that unions have hurt education by protecting weak teachers who deserve to be fired. This is not the case. In fact, it is mystifying when unions are blamed for protecting weak teachers. Before teachers are awarded tenure, they must be graduated from state-approved teacher education programs, convince administrators to hire them, and survive an extended probationary period, typically from three to five years. Unions play virtually no part in any of these processes. Weak teachers may make it through this system, but they do so with no help from organized labor. Teacher unions are embarrassed by poor teachers, just as the American Bar Association and the American Medical Association are discomfited by ineffective, corrupt, or lazy members in their ranks. No responsible union wants to protect incompetent workers.

In the mid-1990s, unions in several cities initiated a peer assistance process to identify weak teachers and refer them for help or possible dismissal. Endorsed by the AFT and the NEA, peer assistance programs reaffirm the unions' role in the establishment and enforcement of high standards for teachers' work. Who is in a better position than experienced teachers to assist new or struggling teachers? And who are more able than teachers to judge when a foundering teacher can be rescued or should be dismissed? Today's unions no longer defend members uncritically; their primary responsibility is to improve the teaching quality. As one union leader notes, "unconditional love and acceptance should be expected only from one's mother—not one's union" (Adam Urbanski, quoted in Birk, 1994, p. 10).

On the other hand, without union guarantees of due process, many good teachers likely would be subject to dismissal for political or personal reasons. Therefore, unions protect all teachers' rights to a fair hearing when their jobs are at stake. Teachers should not be fired because of arbitrary or capricious actions by administrators or members of the board of education. Unions recognize an obligation to stand behind teachers to ensure any dismissal is the result of sufficient, demonstrable cause, not administrative whim, retribution, or discrimination. Union support for the employment right of teachers guarantees fairness in the workplace.

You may have heard someone say, "Those who are good teachers have no need for tenure, and those who have need for tenure are not good teachers." This is dangerous rhetoric. Tenure refers to the laws shielding public school teachers from termination-at-will (Larue, 1996). Unions steadfastly support tenure because without it teaching would be too chancy for all but the independently wealthy or the hopelessly foolish. Tenure is among the more misunderstood aspects of teaching. It is not designed to provide teachers with a sinecure, a lifetime job free from the threat of dismissal. Tenured teachers can be fired for incompetence, but tenure guarantees that teachers are free to use appropriate teaching methods and take reasonable academic positions in classrooms without fear of administrative reprisals. Union support for tenure helps to staff the nation's classrooms with practitioners secure in the knowledge that they are free to teach, governed by norms of academic responsibility and unfettered by political constraints. It also assures the public that schools will remain forums dedicated to democratic processes and open inquiry.

Extending Workplace Democracy

Most school boards now accept that teachers have the right to bargain over working conditions, but many remain unconvinced of the legitimacy of labor's voice in policy issues and matters of school reform. Some administrators argue the traditional roles of school employees and employers must be preserved. Superintendents and principals should be executives and managers, and teachers should be the workers; policymaking is the rightful province of the former, and implementation is the task of the latter. Administrators claim that policy should not be subject to the art of compromise, the democratic give-and-take of collective bargaining. Policymaking, they say, is not for teachers.

Even if it were desirable to separate policy issues from teachers' work conditions, it is not possible. Teachers' concerns extend far beyond hours and wages; they are directly affected by a broad range of educational policy decisions. Restricting collective bargaining to bread-and-butter issues of working conditions, wages, and hours is based on a naive view of how schools function. Issues of school policy, from adoption of a new basal series to recruitment of a new building principal, influence every teacher's work. How could teachers' work fail to be affected by changes in materials used in class? Textbooks, curriculum packages, student assessment, teacher evaluation, and school disciplinary policies all affect teachers' daily lives. Policies regulating schools' organization are central to teaching and must be considered as the rightful province of collective negotiations. Children are better served when teachers have a voice in shaping policy and in making decisions about curriculum and personnel (Maeroff, 1988).

Unions have insisted teachers be given a voice in school reform, but in doing so they are not depriving administrators of their authority. They are simply, in the best democratic sense, extending decision making to a broader constituency. Research suggests that workplace democracy has positive payoffs for schools. Collective bargaining about policy issues appears to produce a greater sense of professional efficacy in teachers; they feel better about their jobs, and use their new authority to give more of themselves to the school and their students (Johnson, 1988; Tuthill, 1990).

Unions' Stake in Education Reform

Unions have always recognized their role in school reform, and continue to insist teachers have a collective voice in bringing about better schooling. Teachers' direct daily contact with students provides them with powerful data about which policies and programs work. Teachers know what schools need to do to improve schooling, and their unions want them to use their knowledge to solve school problems. Affiliates of the NEA and AFT have been active in involving teachers in school reform movements (Rauth, 1990; Watts and McClure, 1990; Kerchner and Koppich, 1993). Unions realize that unless teaching becomes a better job for practitioners, it will be increasingly difficult to keep good teachers in the classroom. A sad fact of teaching is that too often the best teachers leave the field after only a few years. Lured by more lucrative careers or seduced into administration, where they can still effect change while earning better pay, many of the most able teachers look for ways out of the classroom soon after landing their first teaching jobs.

The teacher union in Rochester, New York, has pioneered a new approach to keep teachers in the classroom by granting them more authority to run the schools. The union-conceived "career ladder plan" is designed to tap the knowledge of the best teachers. Senior teachers with at least ten years of teaching experience and five years in the district assume leadership functions in school that combine administrative work with classroom instruction. The plan calls for selected teachers to spend half their time working in administrative or supervisory capacities and the other half teaching in classrooms. Their out-of-classroom work includes mentoring new teachers and developing and consulting on curriculum in specialty areas such as math, reading, and science. For their additional responsibility, and their eleven-month contracts, these lead teachers receive a 20 percent pay differential based on their regular salary. The Rochester teacher union has made it clear they want teachers to work in a decision-making capacity in schools. Teachers no longer are willing to be merely advisors. They will assume greater responsibility, but want greater authority and a salary structure that reflects their new role in schools. By the early 1990s, some Rochester teachers were earning salaries that were more than double the national average.

Today's teacher unions are dedicated to school reform and improved education as they are to serving teachers. In fact, they realize the best way to serve teachers is to improve schools. The relationship between schools and unionized teachers is not unlike the new relationship forged between the United Auto Workers (UAW) and the General Motors (GM) Saturn assembly plant. Both GM and the UAW recognized that to compete against foreign and domestic automakers in a fiercely competitive market, both sides needed to develop a new labor-management relationship (Kerchner, Koppich, and Weeres, 1997, p. 113). The old us-versus-them antagonism has given way to a new and cooperative partnership. The goal is to make a better product. For teacher unions, the goal is to build better schools.

FIGURE 17.1. Right to Work States

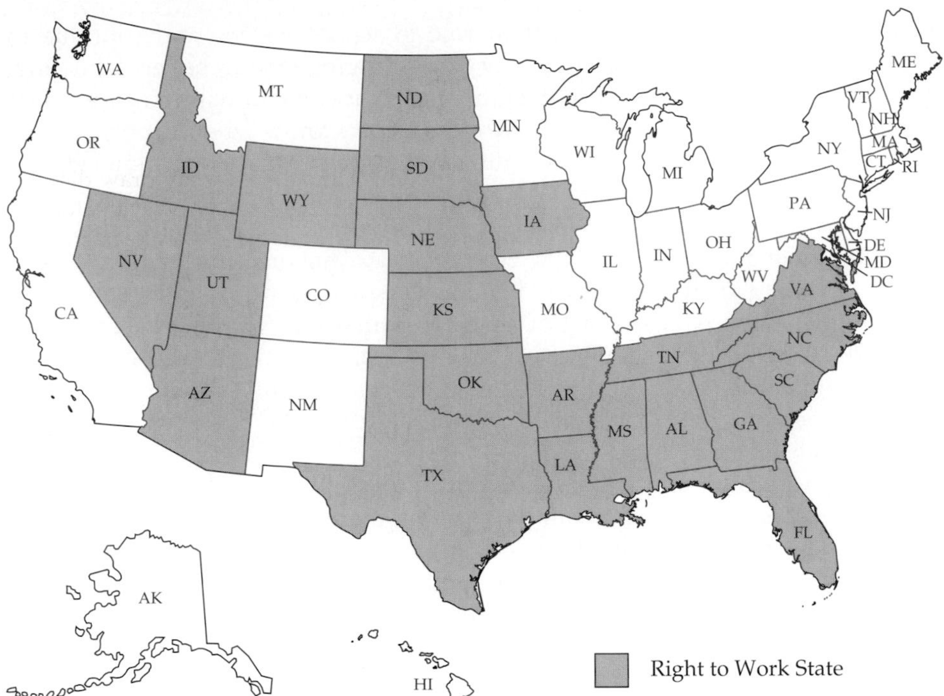

Source: *National Right to Work Organization, (2000). (http://www.nrtw.org/rtws.htm)*

For Discussion

1. Teachers are not required to join unions either to get a job or to keep the one they have. Some states allow teacher unions to require that employees either (a) join the union and pay union dues, or (b) pay an "agency fee" as a condition of employment. (The fee represents the employee's share of what it costs the union to provide collective bargaining and other union benefits.)

   In "right to work" states shown in Figure 17.1, teachers are not required to join a union or pay the union/agency fee. Teachers in these states, however are entitled to benefit from union-negotiated salaries and use union-sponsored grievance procedures. No one has to join a union but everyone receives negotiated benefits. Those with pro-union sympathies refer to these laws as the "right to bargain for less laws" because workers in states with these laws earn less than similar workers elsewhere (Murray, 1998, p. 158). Does your state have "right to work" laws? Do you think "right to work laws" are good or bad for teachers?
2. The laws of many nations give teachers the right to strike. Teacher strikes are legal, for example, in Australia, Canada, France, Germany, Greece, Israel, Italy, Mexico, and Sweden. However, in the United States, only four states consider strikes by public employees legal (Hawaii, Montana, Oregon, and Pennsylvania). In all other states, strikes by public employees, including teachers, are illegal (Shanker, 1992, p. 287).

The strike is undeniably labor's most powerful weapon. What arguments can you offer to support the right of teachers to strike? What arguments would you use to deny teachers the right to strike?

3. Unions typically support a uniform salary structure, a pay scale based on years of service and additional increments for postbaccalaureate college work. As one supporter of this system argues,

> A salary schedule is based on experience and education. It does not draw distinctions on anything else. And it is almost totally objective so that no evaluator or biased administrator can pick-and-choose what criteria he might like in any given year. Salary schedules are clear and predictable and are established on the theory that if you promise to pay people more for every year they stay in teaching, they may be inclined to work for cheaper starting salaries and to make teaching their career. (Harshbarger, 2001)

Do you favor a uniform salary structure for teachers based on experience and education or would you prefer a performance-based salary systems based on criteria that could change year by year?

References

ARONOWITZ, S. (1973). *False Promises: The Shaping of American Working Class Consciousness.* New York: McGraw-Hill.

BAIRD, C. W. (1984). *Opportunity or Privilege: Labor Legislation in America.* Bowling Green, OH: Social Philosophy and Policy Center.

BALLOU D., AND PODGURSKY, M. (2000). "Gaining Control of Professional Licensing and Advancement." In T. Loveless, ed., *Conflicting Missions?* Washington, DC: Brookings Institution.

BIRK, L. (1994). "Intervention: A Few Teachers' Unions Take the Lead in Policing Their Own." *The Harvard Education Letter* 10, Nov./Dec., p. 10.

CHASE, B. (1997). "The New Unionism—A Course for School Quality." (www.nea.org/newunion)

Commonwealth v. Hunt. (1842). 445 Mass (4 met.) 111, 38 Am. Dec 346.

DILLON, S. (1994). "School Board Said to Misuse Consultants." *The New York Times.* Aug. 10, pp. B1–B2.

DWYER, G. (2001). NEA Today Debate Question. (http://nea.org/neatoday) Oct. 15.

EATON, W. E. (1975). *The American Federation of Teachers, 1916–1961: A History of the Movement.* Carbondale: Southern Illinois University Press.

EBERTS, R. W., AND STONE, J. A. (1984). *The Effects of Collective Bargaining on American Education.* Lexington, MA: D. C. Heath.

ENGEL, R. A. (1976). Teacher Negotiation: History and Comment. In E. M. Cresswell and M. J. Murphy, eds., *Education and Collective Bargaining.* Berkeley, CA: McCutchan.

FINN, C. E. (1985). "Teacher Unions and School Quality: Potential Allies or Inevitable Foes?" *Phi Delta Kappan* 66, 331–338.

FRIEDMAN, M., AND FRIEDMAN, R. (1979). *Free to Choose.* New York: Harcourt Brace Jovanovich.

GOLDSTEIN, A. (1998). "Ever Try to Flunk a Bad Teacher?" *Time.* July 20, p. 25.

HARSHBARGER, B. (2000). "NEA Today Debate Question." Feb. 23. (www.nea.org/neatoday)

———. (2001). "NEA Today Debate Question," Sept. 30. (www.nea.org/neatoday)

JESSUP, D. K. (1978). "Teacher Unionization: A Reassessment of Rank and File Education." *Sociology of Education* 51, 44–55.

JOHNSON, S. M. (1988). "Unionism and Collective Bargaining in the Public Schools." In N. J. Boyan, ed., *Handbook of Research on Educational Administration.* New York: Longman.

KERCHNER, C. T. (1986). "Union-Made Teaching: Effects of Labor Relations." In E. Z. Rothkopf, ed., *Review of Research in Education,* Vol. 13. Washington, DC: American Educational Research Association.

KERCHNER, C. T., AND KOPPICH, J. E. (1993). *A Union of Professionals: Labor Relations and Educational Reform.* New York: Teachers College Press.

———. (2000). "Organizing around Quality: The Frontiers of Teacher Unionism." In T. Loveless, ed., *Conflicting Missions?* Washington, DC: Brookings Institution.

KERCHNER, C. T., KOPPICH, J. E., AND WEERES, J. G. (1997). *United Mind Workers: Unions and Teaching in the Knowledge Society.* San Francisco: Jossey-Bass.

LARUE, A. H. (1996). "The Changing Face of Tenure." (www.aft/org/research/reports/tenure/laruep.htm)

LIEBERMAN, M. (1985). "Teacher Unions and Educational Quality: Folklore by Finn." *Phi Delta Kappan* 66, 341–343.

———. (1997). *The Teachers Unions: How the NEA and the AFT Sabotage Reform and Hold Students, Parents, Teachers, and Taxpayers Hostage to Bureaucracy.* New York: Free Press.

LIEBERMAN, M., AND MOSCOW, M. H. (1966). *Collective Negotiations for Teachers: An Approach to School Administration.* Chicago: Rand McNally.

MAEROFF, G. I. (1988). *The Empowerment of Teachers: Overcoming the Crisis of Confidence.* New York: Teachers College Press.

MOE, T. M. (2001). "Teachers Unions." In T. M. Moe, ed., *A Primer on America's Schools.* Stanford: Hoover Institution.

MOO, G. G. (1999). *Power Grab: How the National Education Association is Betraying Our Children.* Washington, DC: Regnery.

MURPHY, M. (1990). *Blackboard Unions: the AFT and the NEA, 1900–1980.* Ithaca, NY: Cornell University Press.

MURRAY, R. E. (1998). *The Lexicon of Labor.* New York: The New Press.

NELSON, F. H., AND GOULD, J. C. (2001). *Teacher Salaried, Expenditures and Federal Revenue in School Districts Serving the Nation's Largest Cities, 1900–91 to 2000–01.* Washington, DC: American Federation of Teachers. (www.aft.orgreports/download/urban_salary.pdf)

NLRB v. Jones and Laughlin Steel Company. (1937). 301 U.S. 1, 57 S.Ct.615.

RAUTH, M. (1990). "Exploring Heresy in Collective Bargaining and School Restructuring." *Phi Delta Kappan* 71, 781–784.

ROSENTHAL, A. (1969). *Pedagogues and Power: Teacher Groups in School Politics.* Syracuse, NY: Syracuse University Press.

SHANKER, A. (1992). "United States of America." In B. S. Cooper, ed., *Labor Relations in Education: An International Perspective.* Westport, CT: Greenwood Press.

STONE, J. A. (2000). "Collective Bargaining and Public Schools." In T. Loveless, ed., *Conflicting Missions?* Washington, DC: Brookings Institution.

TUTHILL, D. (1990). "Expanding the Union Contract: One Teacher's Perspective." *Phi Delta Kappan* 71, 775–780.

URBAN, W. J. (1982). *Why Teachers Organized.* Detroit: Wayne State University Press.

VANSCIVER, J. H. (1990). "Teacher Dismissals." *Phi Delta Kappan* 72, 318–319.

WATTS, G. D., AND MCCLURE, R. (1990). "Expanding the Contract to Revolutionize School Reform." *Phi Delta Kappan* 71, 765–774.

WESLEY, E. B. (1957). *NEA: The First Hundred Years.* New York: Harper and Brothers.

CHAPTER 18

Inclusion and Mainstreaming: Special or Common Education

POSITION 1: FOR FULL INCLUSION

Before the federal government intervened in 1975, perhaps a million disabled children were being denied a public education because of their handicaps. But special education, as a great boon, has ballooned into a massively costly and ineffective program.

—"The Special Education Fiasco." *Wilson Quarterly*, 2002, p. 118

Exceptionality among individuals is a constant in human history. This condition of "abnormality" has historically been the basis for a variety of destructive actions by those in power, from infanticide to institutionalization. Winzer's (1993) comprehensive history of special education is based on a pertinent principle: "A society's treament of those who are weak and dependent is one critical indicator of its social progress. Social attitudes concerning the education and care of exceptional individuals reflect general cultural attitudes concerning the obligations of a society to its individual citizens" (p. 3). This, in the United States and in the civilized world, is a civil rights issue based on the most fundamental documents and foundational moral principles.

Would you like to be excluded, hidden, or separated from other children in school? Would you like to be classified and labeled in a way that limited your participation? Would you want your child to be so treated? That predicament has been the plight of "exceptional" children in U.S. society. They have been evaluated, classified, separated, and hidden in our schools. Equality loses meaning when this happens.

Full inclusion of all children into school life is a fundamental principle in a free, democratic society. Full inclusion means that students classified "special" or "exceptional" because of individual physical or mental characteristics would not be isolated into separate schools, separate classes, or pull-out sessions. They would be full citizens and members of the school community, not only in regular classes but also as legitimate participants in schools' multiple activities. Inclusion is consistent with fundamental principles of our society and with the law (Vargas, 1999; Kluth et al., 2002). The United States should do no less than provide full inclusion (Grossman, 1998).

As a matter of human concern and fairness, we should not separate those who differ from the rest. In making the argument for inclusive schools that recognize the richness in human diversity, Cushner, McClelland, and Safford (2000) offer a philosophic and historic case for the inclusion of exceptional children:

> From its inception, a fundamental characteristic of American schooling has been its intended inclusiveness, across social boundaries, of gender, class, and—belatedly—race. Today, the term inclusion refers to the practice of including another group of students in regular classrooms, those with problems of health and/or physical, developmental, and emotional problems. . . . Like societal inclusion, inclusive education implies fully shared participation of diverse individuals in common experiences. (pp. 161, 163)

Not only is inclusion a matter of fundamental principles and law, it is better educationally—for students and teachers. Sandy Merritt (2001), an elementary grade teacher, writes of her experiences:

> Many general education teachers are frightened by the prospect of including students with disabilities in the general classroom because they have no formal training in dealing with the challenges that these students face. Yes, inclusion can be a frightening endeavor. Nevertheless, for me, a 1st grade teacher of 29 years, inclusion has provided some of the best experiences of my career. (p. 67)

Inclusion Is More than Mere Addition

Full inclusion expects far more of good education than merely adding classified students to general classes or mandating all students to run, climb, read, write, draw, or compute in only one way and at the same speed. Full inclusion assumes schools will provide high-quality, individualized instruction, with well-prepared teachers, suitable and varied teaching materials, and appropriate schedules to support the idea that all students are capable of success. Thoughtful parents and serious educators recognize the principle of full inclusion merely extends the democratic principle of quality education for all to include children with special needs. If we attempt such an education for the majority of students, why not for all?

Kluth and colleagues (2002) note that the 1994 policy guidelines established by the U.S. Department of Education specify schools may not use lack of resources or personnel as an excuse for not providing free and appropriate education—in the least restrictive environments—to students with disabilities (p. 24). But school districts have been very slow to follow the law and the policies. During the twelve year period, 1977 to 1990, there was an actual decline of only 1.2 percent in the number of students with disabilities who were moved from separate to regular classrooms. A National Council on Disability study reported in 2000 that "every state was out of compliance with the requirements of the Individuals with Disabilities Education Act and that U.S. officials were not enforcing compliance" (reported in Kluth et al., 2002). The common excuses of schools simply do not meet the standards set by the law: "we don't provide inclusion"; "this child is too disabled to be in a regular classroom"; "we give them special programs." The law, and supporting court decisions, requires inclusion unless the severity of the disability precludes satisfactory education in regular classes. This high standard does not allow schools to ignore or dismiss the requirement to provide inclusion for the vast majority of students with disabilities (Kluth et al., 2002).

The concept of inclusion involves a set of school practices that Stainback, Stainback, and Jackson (1992) described:

1. All children are to be included in the educational and social lives of their schools and classrooms.
2. The basic goal is to not leave anyone out of school and classroom communities (thus, integration can be abandoned since no one has to go back to the mainstream).
3. The focus is on the support needs of all students and personnel.

Full inclusion does not mean schools should bring in students with special needs only to insist on blind conformity to a single standard for all students; nor does it mean nonconforming students should be ignored or mistreated in "regular" schools. Rather, the concept of inclusion assumes that the individual needs of every student, whether classified "special" or not, seriously must be considered to provide a quality education. This assumption undergirds the idea of full inclusion for students who are "special" or "exceptional."

The Legal Basis for Full Inclusion

Over the past quarter-century, the U.S. Congress clearly has shown its intent that all children with disabilities be provided a free and appropriate education in public schools. A series of modifications in supportive legislation, from 1975 to the present, have improved the educational rights of children with disabilities and their families. Full inclusion is the next logical step. Turnbull and Turnbull (1998) defined this evolving policy as "Zero Reject" and noted an important effect was "to redefine the doctrine of equal educational opportunity as it applies to children with disabilities and to establish different meanings of equality as it applies to people with and without disabilities" (p. 92; emphasis in original). Earlier laws relied on a concept of equality that meant equal access to different resources; children attended separate special education classes and schools. The newer laws assume equal access means full access to regular resources—regular classes and schools, but with special support, to help students "more like than different from people without disabilities" (Turnbull and Turnbull, 1998, p. 93).

The principle of inclusion goes well beyond the mainstreaming that has developed since the 1975 landmark federal legislation, the Education of All Handicapped Children Act (Public Law 94-142). At the time Congress was considering this law, 1 million out of 8 million disabled children under age 21 were completely excluded from the U.S. public school system. They were "outcast children" (Dickman, 1985, p. 181). Mainstreaming grew out of an important clause of the law, offering the concept of the "least restrictive environment"—meaning students with special needs who "demonstrate appropriate behavior and skills" should be in general classrooms rather than segregated programs. The law gave children with special needs the educational, emotional, and social advantages offered to other students. It also gave parents the right to be advocates in fashioning an appropriate education for their differently abled children.

Amendments and modifications to the 1975 law have included changes in the language—for example, replacing handicapped with disabled and renaming the law, calling it the 1990 Individuals with Disabilities Education Act (IDEA). Other important changes in the law have increased the expectations for mainstreaming and led toward full inclusion. The 1990 IDEA law requires schools offer a set of placement options to meet the needs of students with disabilities, and that to the maximum extent appropriate, children with disabilities are to be educated with other children. Further, the law expects schools to provide supplementary aids and services for disabled children when needed; and it requires that any separate schooling or other removal of children with disabilities from the regular environment occur only when the child cannot learn in regular classes even with supplementary aids and services. This sets a high standard for schools to meet in order to exclude disabled students from regular classes.

Laws and court decisions are becoming more expansive in their recognition of individual and social benefits of inclusion. *Mills v. Board of Education of the District of Columbia* (1972) produced a judgment in class-action litigation based on the foundational arguments of equal opportunity and due process. The judge in the Mills case decreed that children with physical or mental disabilities had a right to a suitable and free public education, and lack of funds was not a defense for exclusion. Mainstreaming offered an interim process toward inclusion.

Parents have pursued full inclusion and drawn increasing support from the courts. In a case about a New Jersey boy with severe disabilities, *Oberti v. Board of Education of the Borough of Clementon School District* (1993), a federal judge provided a ringing endorsement of full inclusion. The decision was based on the IDEA law and other laws that guarantee disabled persons access to institutions using federal funds.

Democratic Purposes for Inclusion

At the center of education in a democracy are the concepts of equal opportunity and justice. Democracy, by its very nature, requires all citizens to have the opportunity to be fully educated. Full education cannot be reserved for the favored majority who happen to be nondisabled. Equal opportunity and fairness underscore the idea of inclusion. There are many other important reasons for inclusion of special students in regular school classes and activities, but the fundamental premise of democracy expects no less (Burrello et al., 2001).

Thomas Jefferson, in the Declaration of Independence, wrote: "We hold these truths to be self-evident, that all men are created equal; that they are endowed by their creator with certain inalienable rights, that among these are life, liberty, and the pursuit of happiness." This idea was basic to constitutional objectives of providing for justice, blessings of liberty, and general welfare. Education is the primary means for realizing the great goals of the Declaration of Independence and the Constitution. Isolating special education students not only labels and stigmatizes them, it limits their full interaction with others during their most formative years. This clearly is detrimental to these students, and also is detrimental to the perceptions of nonexceptional students about life in the full society.

In addition to the obvious educational value of allowing all students to participate fully in the schools, inclusion is also a civil rights issue. Discrimination against persons with disabilities has been legally outlawed in the United States. The 1990 Americans with Disabilities Act (ADA) barred such discrimination, just as other laws barred discrimination based on race, gender, or age.

Some institutions meet the access requirements of ADA on purely physical grounds, providing ramps and elevators as well as stairs and modifying doors and bathrooms. This minimal approach would be the equivalent of simply removing "White Only" signs after racial discrimination was ruled illegal and doing nothing more; it still would not deal with underlying, more pervasive instances of institutional discrimination restricting access and opportunity. In a larger context, education is a primary means of access to all of society's opportunities. Separate-but-equal education for African Americans was actually separate but not equal; similarly, separate special education is also separate but not equal.

There are many parallels between how our society has treated minority children and how it has treated disabled children in schools. One of the striking things about school-based classification of children into special education classes, programs, or schools is that students placed in the special category come disproportionately from minority ethnic and social class groups of society (Educational Testing Service, 1980; Heller, Holtzman, and Messick, 1982; Anderson and Anderson, 1983; Brantlinger and Guskin, 1987). Obviously, this combination of class, race, and classification as disabled becomes a recipe for discrimination. Summarizing a substantial amount of research data gathered over twenty years, Wang (1990) notes that "Bias in assessment strategies, placement decisions, and referral rates are frequently cited as reasons that students from selected ethnic and social class status groups traditionally have been overrepresented in special education" (p. 5). This parallel discrimination should be addressed as a civil rights issue on principle and a political issue in practice. Class and ethnicity have been used politically to limit the full participation of groups without wealth and power. Children with special needs have been subject to a similar political agenda restricting access, opportunity, and fulfillment of the democratic ideal (Barton, 1988).

Social Policy Considerations

Beyond the obvious democratic and civil rights concerns raised by separating special needs children from their peers in schools, are other defects in this policy. As a matter of social policy, separation is inconsistent with the larger-scale interests of the United States. Sailor, Gerry, and Wilson (1991) note that U.S. social policy goals include:

- Maximizing economic, social, cultural, and political productivity of all citizens; maximizing the choices for personal freedom and independence (interdependence) of all citizens
- Assuring the integration and participation of all citizens within the social, economic, and political fabric of American communities
- Ensuring fairness and equity (justice) within the operation of the social, economic, and political institutions of the society
- Providing citizen access in governmental decision making to the smallest unit of government consistent with fairness and equity goals. (p. 180)

These broad social policy goals underlie the tenets of inclusion for special needs youth in all society's activities and institutions. Full participation in the society requires full inclusion in the schools. Denying those rights to the disabled denies society the skills, the economic productivity, and the social and political values inherent in full participation of individuals with disabilities.

In the period before 1910, the United States had a pattern of institutionalizing children with disabilities in isolation from society. Families of these children hid them, provided private care, or sent them to institutions where they would live out their lives away from public view or participation. Changing public attitudes regarding our social responsibility for persons with disabilities, as well as a recognition of the general economic value in providing training for disadvantaged people, led to a variety of alterations in social policies and educational practices. This occurred at the same time as public schooling expanded in the early twentieth century. For the disabled, this meant segregation in separate schools and/or separate classes, teachers, and programs. The intent may have been benign, but is inadequate as a social policy. Segregation may be better than complete exclusion, but still offends a basic premise of a civilized society, offers little opportunity for participation in the full society, and reinforces the stigma associated with segregated schools, teachers, and programs. In current times, the stigma of separation has marginalized special education students and robbed society of their energies. Segregation does not match the social policy goals that Sailor, Gerry, and Wilson identified.

Social and Psychological Arguments for Inclusion

In addition to persuasive arguments based on fundamental democratic principles and on fair social policy in favor of full inclusion, social and personal psychology offer other important arguments. Separation of exceptional children from the mainstream of children in schools has been recognized as traumatic for those separated, whether by race, gender, or abilities. In the landmark Supreme Court decision that declared racially segregated schools and the concept of "separate but equal" unconstitutional (*Brown v. Board of Education,* 1954), Chief Justice Earl Warren argued that separation in schools can cause children to "generate a feeling of inferiority as to . . . status in the community that may affect their hearts and minds in a way unlikely ever to be undone" (p. 493). Senator Lowell Weicker stated: "As a society, we have treated people with disabilities as inferiors and made them unwelcome in many activities and opportunities available to other Americans" (quoted in Stainback and Stainback, 1990, p. 7).

Obviously, perceptions of special needs children are strongly influenced by their separation. It goes beyond individual feelings of insecurity to the concept that society values them less and prefers them out of sight. Ethnographic research in a separate class of Trainable Mentally Handicapped students, the Explorer group, illustrates this social ostracism. The Explorer group was established as a separate entity in a regular school for over a year when researchers recorded these observations:

> There was little friendly contact between these young people and the regular student body. From what we had heard about Explorer, it sounded like what we called a "dump and hope" situation: someone had dumped the disabled students and an unmotivated teacher there, and then hoped that things would work out of their own accord. . . . Mr.——, the class's special education teacher . . . said the district had transferred him against his will from another high school where he had taught students who were mildly retarded. He felt unprepared to teach the students with more severe disabilities and doubted they could ever make friends with nondisabled peers. . . .
>
> Classroom materials designed for young children, which stigmatize teenagers with disabilities by causing peers to view them as more incompetent than they really are (Bates et al., 1984), were commonly used. . . . Worst of all, Mr.—— and other staff (such as the school's speech therapist) seemed deliberately to convey their negative evaluations of the students' capabilities to the nondisabled kids. (Murray-Seegert, 1989, pp. 4, 5)

Other research confirms children with special needs do better in both academic work and social adjustment in mainstreamed schools and in regular classes. Semmel, Gottlieb, and Robinson (1979) report results from several studies showed regular class placement was a factor in superior academic achievement among special students, and special needs students did at least as well in academic work in regular classes as they had in special classes. In addition, Carlberg and Kavale (1980) found social adjustment of special needs youth was improved by mainstreaming into the school's life. If social interaction improves for these students, while academic achievement improves or remains at least as high, then inclusion is a positive school practice. Wang, Reynolds, and Walberg (1990) report multiple studies supporting inclusion.

Avoiding Foreseeable Failures in Inclusive Practices

Positive inclusion in schools depends on collaborative efforts by regular and special education teachers, parents, and administrators. Negative results developed in ill-prepared, poorly organized past efforts at mainstreaming; these must be avoided in inclusion. Teachers need to be prepared to work with special needs children in full inclusion schools, but Villa, Thousand, and Chapple (1996) note that few teacher education programs prepare teachers for the new schools. Teacher preparation and in-service programs should move quickly to integrate the most useful knowledge from special education research and practice and should emphasize special methods for dealing with a wide range of students and for individualizing lessons.

Not only are there serious detrimental consequences for the individual exceptional children who are placed in isolated or separated situations, but "average" children are likewise deprived of realistic social interaction and a more compassionate understanding of others' lives. Additionally, the community as a whole suffers from the suspicion, distrust, and misunderstanding created by separation (Risko and Bromley, 2001).

The "Exceptional" and the "Average"

Identification and measurement of exceptionality is a tradition in modern society, though it varies to some extent by nation and time period. Currently, in the United States, *exceptionality* usually refers to observable or measurable differences in physical, mental, emotional, or other abilities. In school terms, exceptional children differ from nonexceptional ones based on school achievement, for example, in reading, writing, listening, sitting attentively, seeing and hearing, and so on. Exceptionality in the United States has included both extremes of mental ability—the severely mentally or learning impaired and the gifted and talented. Both get special treatment and school support. The category of exceptional children also includes those with a variety of measured physical differences from "average" children, including differences in sight, hearing, and use of limbs, but does not include those with extraordinary physical abilities. Similarly, only one end of the potential spectrum of emotional abilities is included in the exceptional category; only those labeled emotionally impaired. There are some problems, then, with consistency in the way we apply the definition of "exceptional."

Causes of exceptionality include genetics, at-birth disabilities, improper medical practice, disease, parental irresponsibility, accidents, and inadequate health care. These exceptionalities are not self-inflicted; they are often chance happenings, as in afflictions caused by accidents, birth defects, or childhood disease. Although exceptionality, in these terms, is relatively rare, it should not create a wall of separation from the rest of society; human variety is extraordinarily complex and incredibly wide ranging. We have improved our measures, but the extent of human variability remains unknown. Further, the classifications themselves reflect cultural norms and prejudices.

The category of "disabled," "exceptional," or "handicapped" depends on the society, time period, and societal norms. *Disability,* according to Dickman (1985), is a deficit that occurs at birth or through disease or some other event, while handicaps are the secondary problems that occur because of discrimination, mistreatment, or help that is denied or delayed. The term *handicapped,* by this definition, represents a social problem of bias and discrimination, while disability is an individual problem. For another example, the category of "learning disabled," used widely in U.S. schools, varies significantly in the measures used to define it. The term is not used in developing nations, where certain forms of technological literacy are not as important, nor is it used much in the corporate world to define categories of people (Cushner, McClelland, and Safford, 2000).

Much of the history of prejudice and discrimination against exceptional children has been based on a false sense of the meaning of "average," and on people's insecurities about their own abilities and talents. Those who differ often are labeled negatively to maintain the status of the favored. Although we often refer to an average, there may be no actual "average" person, in genetic traits, social characteristics, or preferred individual behavior. Who among us comes from a family of 2.3 children, are exactly average in height, weight, IQ, and shoe size, earn average grades or average test scores, and desires an average marriage when over 50 percent end in divorce? Each of us does many things far better or far worse than the average. Average also suggests dullness and conformity; richness comes from diversity. Average is suitable as a broad guide for making tentative comparative judgments about many conditions such as income tax deductions or sleep time needed each day, but should not be mindlessly used as a criterion to rank human qualities against. Exceptional children are exceptional when compared with certain measures of average, but every child differs from average in some respect.

Meeting Potential Problems in Full Inclusion

Full inclusion of all children into the lives of schools is not an easy task (*NEA Today,* 1999). As is clear from the history of special education, many problems are associated with implementing full inclusion. Schools must address the fears of some parents, teachers, administrators, and community members by developing strong programs of information, discussion, preparation, and positive interaction. Special education teachers may fear losing their expert status and, perhaps, their jobs; regular teachers are concerned about their lack of preparation and about no longer being able to send annoying students to special education classes. Beyond ignorance and fears is a history of slowness and resistance in most school reform efforts. Thousand and Villa (1995) identify frequently cited causes of school intractability as: "(1) inadequate teacher preparation; (2) inappropriate organizational structures, policies, and procedures; (3) lack of attention to the cultural aspects of schooling; and (4) poor leadership" (p. 53).

These factors have a detrimental impact on efforts to develop full inclusion programs in schools. Clearly, we need improved teacher education to better prepare teachers for educating diverse students and meeting individual student needs. Practicing regular education teachers also need assistance in changing their teaching practices and working with special education teachers and parents on well-designed and implemented plans for individual students. We need to shake the lockstep curriculum, tracking, and teacher isolation common in the current school structure. We need to recognize that school culture has been a long time in the making and change is difficult for many. We must seek involvement and support, provide high-quality assistance and incentives for improvement, and enlist school faculty and administrators in the process of full inclusion to implement the best forms. We must devote time, energy, and resources to help teachers become more collaborative and better oriented toward individual student needs, to help administrators become more supportive and visionary, and to help schools become more flexible.

We can learn from some of the mistakes made in trying to implement mainstreaming without thorough preparation. Mainstreaming has been a success in many schools and in the lives of many individual students who had previously been shunted to separate schools or classes. It also has been especially successful in alleviating the separation and isolation of special education students and in bringing their situation to light. The needs of these students, and previous inadequacies of schools in meeting their needs, now are part of the public discourse.

Mainstreaming failures in some schools usually occurred where students with special needs were dumped into existing classes without adequate support, without preparing school staff or community or considering students' individual needs. Some special needs students were unable to demonstrate "appropriate behavior and skills" under school guidelines, and these schools made little effort to change programs or personnel to ensure students' success (Lombardi and Ludlow, 1996). Mainstreaming became popular in the 1980s, but many schools and teachers were unprepared to handle special needs and faltered, or were unnecessarily limited in their vision and operation. The most severely disabled students still are mainstreamed in only a few classes each day, usually classes such as art and physical education (*Education Week on the Web,* 1998).

Partly in recognition of the problems involved in mainstreaming, Congress amended the IDEA in 1997 (Public Law 105-17) with substantial changes required in developing the Individualized Education Plan (IEP). The new requirements increase participation of general education teachers in planning for special needs students through membership on IEP teams and the development of a student's IEP. In addition, schools must consider how the student's disability affects involvement and performance in the school's general curriculum. These changes require general educators to become better informed and more actively involved in individualizing instruction for special needs children (*Teaching Exceptional Children,* 1998), which also can improve the quality of teaching for all students.

Inclusion, beyond mainstreaming, offers children with special needs the opportunity to be educated to "the maximum extent appropriate" (PL94-142) in "the school or classroom he or she would otherwise have attended if he or she did not have a disability" (Rogers, 1993). Inclusion offers a broad educational program even more consistent with a society based on democracy and ethics.

Global Needs for Inclusive Education

Full inclusion is not a topic limited to the United States. Moderate to severe disabilities affect about 5.2 percent of the world population. This figure includes 7.7 percent of populations of developed countries and 4.5 percent of populations of less developed regions (Mittler, Brouillette, and Harris, 1993); the total number of disabled persons is estimated to reach over 300 million in the early twenty-first century. Disparity between proportions of disabled persons in developed and less developed areas of the world reflects differences in the definitions of disabled, in health practices, and in governmental policies on reporting disabilities in different nations. Improvements in health practices throughout the world are expected to cause an increased proportion of disabled persons, since children who previously might have died at birth or in infancy will survive, but may have serious impairments (Mittler, Brouillette, and Harris, 1993).

In many nations, integration of children with special needs into regular schools is a contemporary movement. For example, Italy has developed national policies for integration, the United Kingdom has established legislative policies encouraging local schools to integrate, and Austria provides model experimental projects to demonstrate the value of integration (Wedell, 1993; Sefa Dei et al., 2000). The United Nations has a history of concern for children, including children with disabilities; the 1959 Declaration of the Rights of the Child recognized the right of every child to develop to his or her full capacity. The United Nations Convention on the Rights of the Child (1989) affirmed the right to an education and, for disabled children, services that "shall be designed to ensure that the disabled child has effective access to and receives education, training, health care services, rehabilitation services, preparation for employment, and recreational opportunities in a manner conducive to the child's achieving the fullest possible social integration and individual development . . ." (article 23,3, emphasis added). The United States has, over the past several decades, met or surpassed the legislative expectations of international human rights documents regarding disabled children. The United States now must extend its commitments and embrace the full inclusion approach to educating disabled youth.

Conclusion

Fully including disabled children into the lives of school and society has been a long time coming. From a period of exclusion, isolation, and separation, we moved to mainstreaming and limited inclusion. Now we should move forward to full inclusion. Strong arguments, from our basic principles as a free democracy to the positive effect inclusion would have on individuals and society, support the wisdom of pursuing full inclusion.

We all have needs and desires. We need food, clothing, and other necessities, want to be recognized for our individual merits and personalities, be respected as individuals, have our individual rights protected and the freedom to live without oppressive restriction. A democracy attempts to provide these by forging a generally understood social contract among its citizens. A sense of justice in such a society requires that all citizens have equal opportunity to build fulfilling lives in the society and the economy.

We also have social needs, such as the opportunity for full participation in the larger society and enjoyment of public resources and activities. With each of these sets of needs come both positive and negative features. Sometimes individual personalities are offensive to others, and sometimes social participation is frustrating and difficult. These are not good reasons to exclude people from participation; to do so is patently undemocratic. We don't need, as individuals or as a society, forced separation and the stigmatizing that results. It is ethically and practically inconsistent to continue separating children with special needs from other children in our schools.

POSITION 2: SPECIAL PROGRAMS FOR SPECIAL STUDENTS

> *. . . the problem with the inclusion debate is that, like the mainstreaming debate, it is a form of naïve pragmatism, . . . that reproduces problems of professional practice rather than resolving them. . . . Just as the mainstreaming debate reproduced the special education problems of the 1960s and 1980s, the danger today is that . . . the inclusion debate will reproduce them in the twenty-first century. . . . the inclusive education reform proposals require an adhocratic structure for schools.*
>
> —SKRTIC, 1995, P. 234.

Truly disabled youngsters have a particularly difficult situation, one that requires special treatment by special people. There was a time when disabled children were considered less than human, and were sacrificed, shunned, ignored, and institutionalized. Thankfully, that bleak period passed long ago. In the United States, recognition of the special educational and emotional needs of disabled children is one of our finest traditions over the last half-century. These children need more than what we provide in regular classrooms; they deserve special care. That special care does not include poor-quality education, improperly prepared teachers, misdiagnosis of disabilities, prejudiced classmates and school staff, unsuitable curriculums, or dumping in regular classrooms to satisfy the unthoughtful do-gooders. We need only read the papers and reports to recognize regular schools leave much to be desired in the education of regular students; how can they be expected to educate special students?

Humane and thinking people would not require a truly disabled child to undergo even more traumatic experiences to satisfy a stark , inflexible, and ill-informed interpretation of a law. But that is the apparent position of those who press for full inclusion of children into standard classroom settings. A central point of the Individuals with Disabilities Act (IDEA) is that "to the maximum extent appropriate," disabled children will be educated with those who are not. Claiming this requires schools to place virtually all disabled children in regular classrooms is faulty; they fail to note the significance of the term *"maximum extent appropriate"* in the law.

For many disabled children, placement into regular classrooms is a physical, mental, and emotional challenge that should not be mandated, and is certainly not "appropriate." For some "disabled" students, the label and interpretation of a law misleads regular teachers into inappropriate treatment of special students in regular classes. Because of misdiagnosis, inadequate preparation of regular teachers, and standardization of regular classes, special children are not treated specially. For these students, and many others hidden in the system, inclusion may not be the best treatment. Certainly, for some mildly disabled children, placement in regular classes, along with specially trained teachers, special programs, and appropriate instruction and standards, will help and should be provided. But full inclusion advocates seem to ignore significant distinctions among children and their needs. The mere fact that laws are passed does not make them wise or sound for every person; political power and educational wisdom are not necessarily collateral interests. Inflexible interpretation of laws adds further to potential damages to children and to schools.

For Careful Inclusion of Individuals

Full inclusion is not needed in schools. Thoughtfully involving certain children with special needs in regular school classes and activities, on an individual basis and in suitable situations, offers benefits to schools and to children. Careful inclusion of many students, offered by a well-prepared school district to parents of children whose academic work is likely to be enhanced and whose behavior is not likely to disrupt the education of others, is a positive step—but should be rare if we are to preserve the benefits of special education. But careful inclusion is not full inclusion.

Obviously, we already have careful inclusion in many good schools. Expert diagnosis, classification, parental involvement, individually developed special education programs, close evaluation of progress, and, for some, graduated access to regular classes have provided inclusion for individuals in many schools. These schools provide disabled children and their families with excellent resources, fine-tuned to the child's specific needs and carefully crafted to support the child's development. A focus on the child's highly individual needs and development is fundamental to this process.

Fads and schools go hand in hand. The best place to find the newest fads in young people's language, music, dress, and manners is in schools. Not only are fads in popular culture highly noticeable, but schools are the birthplace of many other types of fads, often as a response to calls for school or social reform. Unfortunately, many of these educational fads are poorly thought out and counterproductive.

Full inclusion appears to be one of the latest examples of education's susceptibility to fads and slogans. The damage that full inclusion policies and practices may create for the very children they claim to help can be significant. Full inclusion carries negative implications for schools, teachers, parents, children, and the community. Worse, the "pro-inclusionists" hide the inherent defects of inclusion behind noble-sounding slogans; they label opponents who speak against full inclusion as insensitive, inhumane, or undemocratic (Petch-Hogan and Haggard, 1999).

The mainstreaming movement, which thrust many disabled children into regular classrooms without adequate preparation for them and their new teachers, and with excessive expectations, elicited the same type of defensive rhetoric. Reasonable people who argued against large-scale mainstreaming have been chastised, pilloried, or ignored. Full inclusion has become another politically correct view, even though it would damage effective special assistance programs our schools have spent years to develop and improve. As many experts (Kauffman and Hallahan, 1995) suggest, full inclusion is an illusion because general classrooms and schools will never be capable of meeting the needs of all special or exceptional students. These children require separate assistance and facilities to meet their needs. Children with special needs suffer most from full inclusion. Kennedy and Fisher (2001) point out that "After almost 20 years of specific federal support through the Individuals with Disabilities Act (IDEA) of 1990, PL 101-476, [and other legislation], fewer than half of the students who receive special education services graduate with a diploma."

Regular classrooms and schools are designed to have nearly all students complete a diploma; they are not appropriate places to have the necessary interest, capabilities, and support for the special needs child. It will not be long before the early blush of full inclusion wears off for those teachers, students, and school staff—leaving the special needs child and family without proper attention and education. This is the fallout of the uncritical rush toward full inclusion.

Proponents of full inclusion advocate mandates, regardless of individual circumstances, school situations, or challenges to bureaucratic control. This limits children with special needs by requiring their attendance in regular classes without the high-quality help available in a separate program. Typical special education programs provide specially trained teachers and paraprofessionals, smaller class sizes, adjusted curricula, and fairer competition. Such programs allow parents and teachers to jointly fashion an individualized program that maximizes the child's strengths and remediates areas of need. They are also able to access experts outside the school to assist children with special needs in preparing for the transition from school to work life.

Full Inclusion and Common Classroom Limits

Inclusion limits regular classroom teachers by requiring them to allot extra time, materials, and energy to children who need extra support, as well as requiring them to prepare and monitor individual education plans for each of these children. Full inclusion also limits nondisabled children by diverting time and energy from teachers to meet the special needs of a few students and by sometimes disrupting their schoolwork when the behaviors of a child with special needs are inappropriate in a general classroom. Finally, full inclusion limits the school's ability to make educational decisions in the best interests of individual students. Full inclusion is a form of social engineering that cannot fulfill what it promises without serious repercussions for children and schools. Disruption and discipline problems can occur when some disabled students are mainstreamed or fully included in regular classes.

A study by the General Accounting Office ("Student Discipline: Individuals with Disabilities Act," 2001), noted that 81 percent of public middle and high schools surveyed responded that they had one or more incidents of "serious misconduct" during 1999–2000. Further, when the study accounted for the relatively small numbers of specially classified students in schools, the rate of serious misconduct for special education students in regular schooling was over three times as high as for regular students (15 per 1,000 regular students, and 50 per 1,000 of special students). Misconduct, of course, can be by regular or special students, but a situation of taunting or disrespect against the special student in regular classes offers good reason for a special student's misbehavior. Such situations are not always controllable by teachers and school staff, and clearly do not provide the proper setting and special treatment special youngsters deserve.

In addition, one in five principals reported that protective disciplinary procedures required for special students under the IDEA regulations are "burdensome and time-consuming." Many students with behavioral problems are mistakenly classified as special for a number of reasons, including the additional school income from state and federal sources. As Navarrette (2002) indicates, "Thus the mischievous and the misdiagnosed are mixed with those who really need special education, those with mental retardation and other disabilities" (p. B8). Full inclusion needs full examination before implementation.

Full Inclusion and School Reality

Theoretically, inclusion could provide all the good things special education now provides—special teachers, individualization, more self-esteem, but with the added benefit of allowing exceptional children to participate fully in the school program. Long-term experience with school reforms suggests that any immediate, positive effects of inclusion are likely to be overcome by long-standing conformist standardization, bureaucracy, and funding requirements that make most schools dull and ineffective even for many regular students. The special needs child will be overlooked in these schools.

With children of all abilities and disabilities mixed in a class and school, chances increase that special needs of select students will be missed. The focus will shift from giving special attention to individual children's strengths and disabilities toward conforming to group standards imposed by state officials, meeting community expectations in test scores, or facing other accountability measures of group success. Large class size will make it difficult for regular teachers to provide special assistance to exceptional children. Schools will not be able to fully control other students' disparaging or hurtful comments, and exceptional children again will suffer. School funds will decrease to a common standard, without special funds for special children. Exceptional students require exceptional effort, but schools will be stretched and unable to provide it.

In addition, advocates of full inclusion are wrong when they argue that interaction with regular students in a regular program will benefit those who are disabled. A sorry history of taunting, labeling, ridicule, and exclusion by regular students is not likely to disappear because of some legislated program of interaction. There is no evidence that nondisabled children will suddenly develop appropriate classroom behavior when full inclusion takes place. Lectures and admonitions by school officials, no matter how well intentioned, are not likely to make a dent in the problem. Even if the majority of children are well behaved and nonprejudiced, it takes only a few to spoil the school setting for children with disabilities who already have been subjected to frequent stares and slights. School is tough enough for many regular students who happen to be different from the group. Life in many schools is not pleasant for children from poor families, children who stutter, are noticeably shorter or taller or more plump, are slower in speed or intellect, are from certain cultural backgrounds, or are not as gregarious or athletic or pretty as others. School subcultures create cauldrons of despair for many students who are not accepted because of minor differences (Palonsky, 1975); consider the problem those with significant disabilities would face in regular schools.

Laudable But Unrealistic Goals

The goal of inclusion may be laudable under some conditions and for some individuals. However, full inclusion for all students represents an ideal that does not mesh with day-to-day reality for large numbers of students. Many children now are participating successfully in effective special education classes and schools. Full inclusion is a threat to these children; they will be thrown into regular classes, subject to the vagaries of standardized education and general school funding. Zigler and Hall (1986) noted this problem regarding excesses in the 1980s mainstreaming movement. This movement was based on the "normalization" principle, an idea that we should provide more "normal" school settings to socialize disabled children:

> Ironically, the very law that was designed to safeguard the options of handicapped children and their parents (the 1975 Education for all Handicapped Children Act) may, in the end, act to constrict their choices and result in disservice to the very children the legislators sought to help, by forcing schools to place them in programs that are not equipped to meet their needs. The normalization principle and the practice of mainstreaming may have deleterious effects on some children by denying them their right to be different. . . . Underlying the very idea of normalization is a push toward homogeneity, which is unfair to those children whose special needs may come to be viewed as unacceptable. (p. 2)

Full inclusion goes well beyond mainstreaming. As a result, it runs even greater risks of homogenizing our educational approach and causing a decline in special care and attention for children with exceptional needs. The political support for special programs and funds, support that took years to develop, will atrophy. Special education budgets will diminish. School administrators, with declining special education budgets, will be unlikely to champion the needs of this small and expensive proportion of their student populations. Regular class teachers, already overworked in large classes, will be unable to extend themselves even further for children who need more individualized help. Parents of nondisabled children may be sympathetic, but are unlikely to support the diversion of general education funds, resources, and teacher time from the education of their own children.

McKleskey and Waldron (2000), may advocate inclusive education, but they point out that studies have shown regular school staff continue to hold several unfortunate assumptions that undermine inclusion practices in schools.

These include the significant assumption that "inclusion" students should still be perceived as "irregular" even when they are in regular classes, and the assumption that inclusion students require specialized material and support that "could not be provided by the classroom teacher," depending instead on a special educator (p. 70). These assumptions are understandable, but they portend major problems in large-scale inclusion practices in school districts.

We want as many disabled children as possible to be self-reliant, equipped for successful and productive lives, participate constructively in the larger society, and develop feelings of personal worth. We want no less for any child, but the child who is disabled needs special attention and support to reach these goals. One of the primary purposes of special education programs is to provide the setting and individualized attention these children need to develop self-reliance, success, productivity, and feelings of personal worth. These programs are jeopardized by the steamroller tactics of the full inclusionists.

Well-Deserved Special Treatment

It is easy to fling out high-sounding phrases about full inclusion and democracy, but more difficult to critically examine potential consequences of a major change in the way we treat exceptional children in our schools. Inclusion of special needs children into regular schools and classes is an educational policy needing critical assessment. Waving the flag of democracy may stir the faddists in education, but will not hide the serious problems inherent in full inclusion.

Over history, children with disabilities have suffered; they have been reviled, ostracized, ridiculed, ignored, and destroyed. Some became members of circuses; some were hidden by their families; others were placed in ill-funded and ill-supervised institutions with no chance for improvement. The families of disabled children also suffered social maligning. And society lost the contributions it could have had from the many talents of people with disabilities.

Fortunately, society has made dramatic changes in the way it views the disabled. We now recognize that the special needs of these children require special treatment. Exceptional children can find success and develop on their own terms in school and life. Special programs offer a ray of hope to children who were ostracized and ignored in the past. Many special education schools and programs have been successful in preparing students to contribute to society. Extra funding for special education provides more individualistic education, better-prepared teachers, more appropriate teaching materials, superior facilities, and a setting better organized to help these children. Full inclusion could be used to control school budgets by decreasing current special funding for special education and gifted and talented programs. Of course, it is cheaper to educate children with special needs in regular classes. But that would be an unwise and, in the long run, economically foolish move. The actual proportion of exceptional children is very small, in the range of 5 percent nationally. That small number deserves special financing, special treatment, special teachers, and special programs to ensure they will become productive members of society, with the necessary self-respect.

Special education and exceptional programs offer important benefits to the child: a low student-teacher ratio for increased individualized instruction and attention; teachers especially trained to educate and develop the skills of exceptional students; experts organized into study teams to provide diagnosis, treatment, and evaluation of student development; homogeneous grouping to permit the teacher to concentrate on common needs and characteristics; more opportunity for student success among peers and more realistic competition in academics and/or athletics; funds for facilities, special equipment, and specially designed student learning materials; and increased student self-esteem from individual attention and by limiting negative interaction with nondisabled students. In addition, special education programs offer opportunity for remedial education that could return mildly disabled children to the regular program. These benefits continue to accrue to special education programs; they will be reduced with the advent of inclusion. Regular schools are unprepared to offer them in addition to their usual efforts, and initial extra funding will dry up or be absorbed into the ongoing operation of the schools.

Treating Other Exceptional Children: The Gifted

Another interesting, real-life issue arises when we discuss full inclusion. Presumably, full inclusion would require schools to eliminate separate, special programs, forcing all exceptional students into regular classes in regular schools. Presumably, the only deviation from this would occur when parents and school agree that a child cannot be educated in a regular class. But special school programs for exceptional children come in many varieties. Among them are programs for gifted and talented children, honors programs, and tracking.

Gifted and talented programs, for example, often are separately organized, taught, and evaluated. As Clark (1996) notes in a comprehensive analysis of such programs: "Gifted and talented students have more complex needs than average and below average learners . . . if these needs are not met we now know that ability cannot be maintained; indeed, brain research tells us that ability will be lost. . . . When no programs are available to this group of learners a disservice is done, not only to these students but to all of society, as our finest minds not only lack nurture, they are wasted" (p. 60). This is special education also, and these students ought to be fully included in regular classes and activities to meet the law as seen by inclusionists.

In addition, we must recognize the political realities involved in efforts to end special programs for gifted, honors, or high-achieving students. These programs usually include children from the more powerful families in a community, demonstrate how special treatment makes a difference in student achievement, and enhance the school's academic reputation. Under full inclusion, gifted and talented children presumably would be moved back into regular classes. Similarly, honors and remedial classes and tracking would be doomed. One-size-fits-all schooling, as full inclusion ideology proposes, is a prescription for mediocrity.

Classification and Myths

Many myths exist about the classification of children into separate special education programs. One myth is that classified students are unhappy or ill-served by programs and they drop out. In fact, the national dropout rate for all students over age 14 is about 25 percent, but for students with disabilities the rate is only about 4 percent (Carlson and Parshall, 1996). Another myth is that classification into special education is a one-way street, that those selected for special education never return to the regular program. In fact, the declassification rate of special education students is higher than their dropout rate; running from about 4 to 9 percent annually (Carlson and Parshall, 1996). A third, and most deleterious myth, is that classified children who are placed into separate special education programs are not challenged and are never able to make the school, social, and behavioral adjustments needed to fit into regular school or society. A significant study by Carlson and Parshall (1996) analyzed data about the approximately 7 percent of special education students who were declassified annually and placed into regular classes in Michigan over a five-year period. This study revealed two important bases against a one-size-fits-all full inclusion program:

1. Special education programs work, and students can achieve successful declassification; the vast majority of declassified children were well adjusted in academic, social, and behavioral categories.
2. There is a continuing need for special attention for a minority of declassified children; about 11 percent of the declassified students needed extra care, and about 4 percent returned to special education classes.

On the one hand, it is remarkable that a sizable proportion of students in special education programs are able to join regular classes and be successful in terms of school, social, and behavioral criteria. On the other hand, the very small proportion of those who still need special care suggests we should keep separate programs available for those who, for whatever reasons, are better served in classified programs or are unable to make necessary adjustments to the regular school. Carlson and Parshall's study noted the poorest results from declassification efforts occurred for students with emotional impairments. For those whose declassification was successful, Carlson and Parshall state: "Presumably, without special education services, these students would not have done as well in school as they did" (p. 98).

Slogans and Myths: Equal Education

There are many slogans in our society: save the whales, do unto others as you would have them do unto you, and keep a stiff upper lip. Each of these ideas is more complicated than putting a bumper sticker on a car, boycotting, or voting. Unfortunately, the simplicity and moral righteousness of such slogans can be deceptive. Life's problems are complex; slogans ignore the complexity and offer a tantalizingly singular answer. Simplistic answers may make problems worse.

Making education a cornerstone of democracy is an excellent idea, but to make it work requires more than unsubstantiated claims and moral posturing.

Free and open education, equally available to all with no differences in treatment or result, is an interesting utopian idea so far from reality it is painful. Yet this basic concept underlies the current interest in inclusion. We don't yet have free and equal education, equal treatment, or equal results for the wide variety of students who attend "regular" public schools. It is unrealistic to believe students shifted to meet inclusion goals actually will obtain equal access, treatment, or results. The "regular" classroom is a figment of ideological imagination; schools do not offer equality now.

Currently, even outside of separate special education classes, access to education differs along several dimensions. Tracking or ability-grouping students based on how they score on tests and how teachers evaluate them separates students for most of their school careers (Oakes, 1985; Urban and Waggoner, 1996; Spring, 1998). Schools in different communities offer differing advantages to their students as a result of funding differences citizens vote on (Kozol, 1991). High school athletes are more costly to a school district than humanities students, and only the best athletes are selected for team membership. Good readers are placed in one group and poor readers in another in elementary school classes. Not all students are admitted to college preparatory or honors classes. Advanced woodshop is limited to select students, as are advanced Latin and chemistry. Students who misbehave and disrupt others are separated in schools, and may be denied access by suspension or expulsion. Special education costs are about 2.3 times the cost of regular classrooms, most of which is covered outside of district funds. This funding, even with recent sizable increases in numbers of students classified as special, remains a relatively small proportion of school expenditures (Moe, 2002).

Where students live is related to how well they will do in school and in gaining access to further education; higher-income communities have schools where students obtain higher standardized test scores and higher rates of college admission. Female students have less access to higher-level math and science classes than males. Generally, minority students have less access to highly ranked colleges than majority students. When viewed on the basis of equality, these circumstances may not be ideal or even always supportable, but are the reality of schooling. Democracy does not require exact equality of condition. The economic ideas behind capitalism, which have made this nation so successful, are inconsistent with mandated egalitarianism; capitalism requires we reward competition and entrepreneurship.

On the Fairness of Life

Life, as we know, is unfair. We see unfairness in human relations of all kinds, including those in schools. We can't fix all unfairness, but need to limit inappropriate discrimination and prejudice. Discrimination is inappropriate if based on criteria that are illogical, unethical, or lack a scientific basis. Discrimination is appropriate if it means separating existing individual differences to treat, protect, or nurture them. We discriminate among people by granting academic awards, among people with certain illnesses by treating them and protecting the society, and among animals by determining which are endangered and therefore deserving special treatment. Prejudice means that we "prejudge" without knowledge; but making a judgment based on an understanding of available information is not prejudice. It is prejudice to claim, before ever tasting it, that broccoli tastes bad—but not to make the statement after tasting. Throughout life, we make judgments. Some may turn out to be wrong, but we can only try to use the best, most complete available information and reasoning to inform a judgment.

Fairness sometimes may mean providing different strokes for different folks if the criteria are sensible and consistent with social goals and individual interests. Putting all students into advanced Latin or into woodshop does not make sense; keeping disruptive or violent children in regular classes regardless of their behavior does not make sense; admitting all students to any college they desire does not make sense. We use criteria to limit those who can drive cars, handle food, practice medicine, cut and style hair, be convicted of a crime, or run for president. These limits are unfair only if they are abused, prejudicially applied, or not sensible.

One of the interesting ironies of the effort to establish full inclusion of exceptional children into regular schools is that many of its strongest advocates come from the special education network, and they do not want, themselves, to be integrated into "regular" departments or schools of teacher education. Surveys of leaders of schools of education across the United States in 1989 and 1994 found that almost three-fourths believed special education is best served by separating teacher education into general education and special education departments (Heller, 1996). One of the most frequent reasons given for the desirability of separation is the need to "identify with persons of equal interest, expertise, and common purpose" (p. 258). Another major reason was the increased status of or attention paid to special educators as a result of separation. Special education specialists do not want to be fully included in higher education for good reasons. Separate special education programs in the schools, when constructed properly, offer the same advantages to children with different needs.

People differ in a wide variety of characteristics. A system where all individuals are exactly the same is inconsistent with human nature. Our democratic society permits and encourages many practices of inequality. Sometimes these practices are designed to compensate for previous inequalities, such as racism or sexism. We develop programs to offer special treatment to those we think have been denied equal treatment in prior periods.

Affirmative action programs, when they use quota systems and remove merit considerations, have engendered strong criticism from all parts of the political spectrum. They are defended now mainly by a hard core of disciples. The main purpose of affirmative action, to assure equal opportunity under the Constitution, has been subverted by legislative zealotry and bureaucratic manipulation. Reasonable people from all sides decry prejudice, bias, hate crimes, and discrimination based on stereotypes—but they do not want government to mandate actions on matters best left to individual choice. That is a difficult line to draw, but is important to do so in a democracy.

Legislation, Courts, and Problems Caused by Full Inclusion

Full inclusion of children with disabilities into regular classes runs some of the same risks of arousing overzealous legislation and activist court interpretation. Legislated mainstreaming has created significant problems—for schools, teachers, communities, and for both disabled and nondisabled children. Court interpretations of laws threaten to leave mainstreaming in another social engineering predicament akin to those of affirmative action. Extending mainstreaming to full inclusion promises to cause even more complicated problems and more bureaucratic, bungling answers. A recent court case, *Oberti v. Board of Education of Clementon (NJ) School District* (1993), illustrates problems associated with mainstreaming, the laws governing it, and court interpretations.

The case involves an eight-year-old Down's syndrome child with impaired intellectual functioning and ability to communicate. The school district, after testing and review by specialists, determined his educational interests would best be served by placing him in a developmental kindergarten class in the morning to observe and socialize with peer children, but his academic work would be done in a separate special class in the afternoon. During the morning class, the child exhibited serious behavioral problems, including repeated toilet accidents, temper tantrums, crawling and hiding under furniture, and hitting and spitting on other children. Also, the child repeatedly hit the teacher and teacher's aide.

Obviously, he was disruptive and the frustrated teacher sought help from the district Child Study Team. The Individual Education Plan required under the IDEA law and used for the original placement did not cover ways to handle his behavioral problems. Interestingly, the child did not exhibit disruptive behavior in the separate afternoon special education class. After study, the district wanted to place the child in a completely separate program, but the parents refused. After a hearing, there was an agreement that he would be placed in a separate program for one year. In that year, his behavior improved and he made academic progress. When the parents found, however, that the district did not plan to place him back into "regular" classes the following year, they objected and another hearing occurred before an administrative law judge. The judge agreed with the district that the separate special education class was the "least restrictive environment" under the IDEA law, the child's misbehavior in the developmental kindergarten class was extensive, and there was no meaningful educational benefit from that class. Unsatisfied, the parents went to court, getting an expert witness professor from Wisconsin who claimed the child could be in regular classes, provided there were supplementary aids and special support, such as:

1. Modifying the existing regular curriculum for this student;
2. Modifying this child's program to provide for meeting a different set of criteria for performance;
3. Using "parallel" instruction—the child would be in the classroom, but would have separate activities; and
4. Removing the child for instruction in certain special areas.

The district's expert witness, a professor from a nearby college, claimed the child could not benefit from placement in a regular class, his behavior could not be managed, the teacher could not communicate with him because of his communication problems, and the curriculum could not be modified enough to meet this child's needs without compromising its integrity. Other witnesses, including people who had worked with the child in other public school and Catholic school settings, testified that he had very disruptive behavior, including hitting, throwing things, and running away.

This judge, citing the IDEA law, held that the district had the burden of proof and they had failed to meet the law's requirement for mainstreaming (*Oberti v. Board of Education*, 1993).

This case suggests a series of problems for schools, parents, communities, and children under mainstreaming. The court directed that a disruptive and misbehaving child is to attend regular classes, where his actions are likely to be detrimental to other students's academic work and to the teacher's ongoing work. The disabled child's schoolwork, apparently satisfactory in separate special education classes, suffered significantly in the regular placement, even on a part-time basis; yet under the court's order, he now would be in regular classes full time. The child's parents may feel better that their child is in regular classes, but how will he progress? Parents of the nondisabled children do not have the same right to refuse placement, require formal hearings on details they don't like, or protest in court when their children are subjected to a significantly modified curriculum or class disruption. School rules established for all children to provide order and safety are placed in jeopardy by a court order that makes the school ultrasensitive to the parents of a single student.

A number of classroom issues are raised by the suggestion of the expert witness from Wisconsin to mainstream with supplementary activities and support. Teachers work hard on a school curriculum and finding ways to teach it; how are they to modify that curriculum adequately for one severely disabled student without compromising the integrity of the curriculum as a whole? Is it equal and fair treatment if the teacher gives very special treatment to one disabled child, designing different activities and individual levels of performance, but does not do so for each of the other children? If the special needs child has "parallel" instruction provided in class and is removed from the class for certain special instruction, how does that differ in substance from a separate special education program? Although the child is in a regular class, he is to be separated for much of his work, and he may even become more of a target for other children because of his differential treatment.

Conclusion

The goal of inclusive school policies is to attempt to bring disabled children into the mainstream of American life. The ideal, however, is far removed from life's reality. Not only is inclusion unrealistic, given the obvious diversity among people and resources, but it is harmful to children now well served in separate special programs, hides an ideology of social engineering, debases individual initiative and freedom, and magnifies and enhances the value of conformity. This is not the ideal of equality of opportunity.

Excessive mainstreaming caught schools unprepared, frustrated good teachers, diminished special services provided to individual children, and created confusion in schools. Well-prepared schools, specially trained teachers, clear guidelines for diagnosis and education, smaller classes, special materials to enhance learning, and a setting conducive to the best education now exist in many places: special education and gifted and talented programs offer these advantages. Full inclusion would overturn these in favor of a mandate for standardization and chaos beyond what occurred in excessive mainstreaming programs.

Schools vary significantly: It is impossible to define a "regular" school or classroom. Is a one-room school in rural Nevada "regular"? What about an urban school in Manhattan, or a suburban school in Beverly Hills? Schools have some common patterns, but much schooling occurs with separate groups of students. The Bronx High School of Science, vocational-technical high schools, tracking programs, honors programs, remedial courses, basic and advanced courses, reading groups, and selection for music and athletic programs illustrate the common practice of educating certain students separately for particular reasons. Full inclusion threatens these efforts to provide the best individual education for different students.

For Discussion

1. Identify the best arguments for and against full inclusion. Analyze the evidence presented for each. What kinds of research would be needed to provide that evidence? Where would you go to find that kind of research? What research is currently available on these matters? What would be the most convincing evidence for you to change your mind on full inclusion?
2. How should gifted and talented programs be treated in terms of full inclusion policies? Should they be abolished, separated, enhanced, diminshed, or . . . ? On what grounds do you argue? Who should decide and on what criteria? Are separate programs appropriate in public schools in a democracy? How is this issue similar to and different from treatment of special education students under the IDEA?
3. Current U.S. Department of Education data show the annual growth rate in number of children ages 3 to 21 who receive special education (over 3 percent) continues to exceed the annual growth rate in the general population between ages 3 and 21 (about 1 percent). The proportion of children evaluated as gifted and talented is about 3 percent of the student population. What reasons would explain an increase in proportion of children needing special education? What difference should this increase mean for school decisions on full inclusion? To critically examine this topic, what evidence would you need, and where would you expect to find that evidence?
4. How should the movement toward mainstreaming and full inclusion influence teacher education programs? What should teachers know about and be able to do for special students included in general classrooms?

TABLE 18.1. Five-Year Trends in Disability Classification Under IDEA

	1990–1991	1994–1995	Percent Change
Speech/Language Disabilities	987,000	1,024,000	3.6
Specific Learning Disabilities	2,144,000	2,514,000	17.3
Mental Retardation	551,000	570,000	3.5
Serious Emotional Disturbances	391,000	428,000	9.6
Multiple Disabilities	97,000	90,000	–8.2
Hearing Impairment	59,000	65,000	10.7
Orthopedic Impairment	49,000	61,000	22.8
Other Health Impairment	56,000	106,000	89.0
Visual Impairment	24,000	25,000	.5
Autism	*	23,000	*
Deaf and Blind	1,500	1,300	–12.7
Traumatic Brain Injury	*	7,200	*
All Disabilities Total			12.7

*Data not available, categories added 1991–1992; autism cases in 1991–1992 were 5,000; traumatic brain injury cases in 1991–1992 were 2,500.
Source: U.S. Department of Education, Office of Special Education Program, numbers rounded.

5. Table 18.1 shows five-year trends in the number of children classified under federal categories to define disabled children under IDEA law.
   a. What does the table suggest about the definitions of disability?
   b. What would account for large changes in the numbers of classified children in different categories?
   c. What changes do you think schools would need to make to provide for full inclusion of these children?

References

ANDERSON, G. R., AND ANDERSON, S. K. (1983). "The Exceptional Native American." In L. Barton, ed., *The Politics of Special Education.* London: Falmer Press.

BARTON, L. (1988). *The Politics of Special Education Needs.* London: Falmer Press.

BATES, P., ET AL. (1984). "The Effect of Functional vs. Nonfunctional Activities on Attitude/Expectations of Non-handicapped College Students: What They See Is What We Get." *The Journal of the Association for Persons with Severe Handicaps* 9, 73–78.

BRANTLINGER, E. A., AND GUSKIN, S. L. (1987). "Ethnocultural and Social Psychological Effects on Learning Characteristics of Handicapped Children." In M. C. Wang et al., eds., *Handbook of Special Education,* Vol 1. Oxford: Pergamon.

Brown v. Board of Education of Topeka, Kansas. (1954). 347 U.S. 483.

BURRELLO, L. C., ET AL. (2001). *Educating All Students Together.* Thousand Oaks, CA: Corwin Press.

CARLBERG, C., AND KAVALE, K. (1980). "The Efficacy of Special Versus Regular Class Placement for Exceptional Children: A Meta-Analysis." *Journal of Special Education* 14, 295–309.

CARLSON, E., AND PARSHALL, L. (1996). "Academic, Social, and Behavioral Adjustment for Students Declassified from Special Education." *Exceptional Education* 63(1), 89–100.

CLARK, B. (1996). "The Need for a Range of Program Options for Gifted and Talented Students." In W. and S. Stainback, eds., *Controversial Issues Confronting Special Education.* 2nd Ed. Boston: Allyn & Bacon.

CUSHNER, K., MCCLELLAND, A., AND SAFFORD, P. (2000). *Human Diversity in Education.* 3rd Ed. New York: McGraw-Hill.

DICKMAN, I. (1985). *One Miracle at a Time.* New York: Simon & Schuster.

EDUCATION WEEK ON THE WEB. (1998). "Inclusion." Washington, DC: Editorial Projects in Education. (www.edweek.org)

EDUCATIONAL TESTING SERVICE. (1980). "New Vistas in Special Education." *Focus* 8, 1–20.

GROSSMAN, H. (1998). *Ending Discrimination in Special Education.* Springfield, IL: Charles C Thomas.

HELLER, H. W. (1996). "A Rationale for Departmentalization of Special Education." In W. and S. Stainback, eds., *Controversial Issues Confronting Special Education.* 2nd Ed. Boston: Allyn & Bacon.

HELLER, K. A., HOLTZMAN, W. H., AND MESSICK, S., eds. (1982). *Placing Children in Special Education: A Strategy for Equity.* Washington, DC: National Academy of Sciences Press.

HUXLEY, T. (1897). *Evolution and Ethics, and Other Essays.* New York: D. Appleton.

KAUFFMAN, J., AND HALLAHAN, D., eds. (1995). *The Illusion of Full Inclusion.* Austin, TX: Pro-Ed.

KENNEDY, C. H., AND FISHER, D. (2001). *Inclusive Middle Schools.* Baltimore: Paul H. Brookes.

KLEINFIELD, S. (1979). *The Hidden Minority: America's Handicapped.* Boston: Little, Brown.

KLUTH, P., ET AL. "'Our School Doesn't Offer Inclusion' and Other Legal Blunders." *Educational Leadership* 50(4), 24–27.

KOZOL, J. (1991). *Savage Inequalities.* New York: Crown Publishers.

LIPSKY, D. K., AND GARTNER, A. (1996). "Inclusion, School Restructuring, and the Remaking of American Society." *Harvard Education Review* 66(4), 762–796.

LOMBARDI, T. P. (1994). *Responsible Inclusion of Students with Disabilities. Fastback 373.* Bloomington, IN: Phi Delta Kappa Educational Foundation.

LOMBARDI, T. P., AND LUDLOW, B. L. (1996). *Trends Shaping the Future of Special Education.* Bloomington, IN: Phi Delta Kappa Educational Foundation.

MCKLESKEY, J., AND WALDRON, N. (2000). *Inclusive Schools in Action.* Alexandria, VA: ASCD.

MEISEL, C. J., ED. (1986). *Mainstreaming Handicapped Children.* Hillsdale, NJ: Lawrence Erlbaum.

MERRITT, S. (2001). "Clearing the Hurdles of Inclusion." *Educational Leadership* 59(3), 67–70.

Mills v. Board of Education of the District of Columbia. (1972). 348 F. Supp. 866.

MITTLER, P., BROUILLETTE, R., AND HARRIS D., EDS. (1993). *Special Needs Education. World Yearbook of Education.* London: Kogan Page.

MOE, T. M. (2002). *A Primer on America's Schools.* Stanford: Hoover Institution Press.

MURRAY-SEEGERT, C. (1989). *Nasty Girls, Thugs, and Humans Like Us: Social Relations Between Severely Disabled and Nondisabled Students in High School.* Baltimore: Paul H. Brookes.

NAVARRETTE, R. (2002). "The Special Ed Dumping Ground," *San Diego Union-Tribune.* April 17, B8.

NEA TODAY. (1999). "Inclusion Confusion." 17(8), 4.

OAKES, J. (1985). *Keeping Track: How Schools Structure Inequality.* New Haven: Yale University Press.

Oberti v. Board of Education of the Borough of Clementon (NJ) School District. (1993). 995 f.2d 1204 (3rd Cir. 1993).

PALONSKY, S. (1975). "Hempies and Squeaks, Truckers and Cruisers: A Participant-Observer Investigation in a City High School." *Educational Administration Quarterly* 2, 86–103.

PETCH-HOGAN, B., AND HAGGARD, D. (1999). "The Inclusion Debate Continues." *Educational Forum* 35(3), 128–140.

RISKO, V., AND BROMLEY, K. (2001). *Collaboration for Diverse Learners.* Newark, DE: International Reading Association.

ROGERS, J. (1993). "The Inclusion Revolution." *Phi Delta Kappa Research Bulletin* (no. 11) 1–6.

SAILOR, W., GERRY. M., AND WILSON, W. C. (1991). "Policy Implications of Emergent Full Inclusion Models." In M. C. Wang et al., eds., *Handbook of Special Education: Research and Practice,* Vol 4. Oxford: Pergamon.

SEFA DEI, G. ET AL. (2000). *Removing the Margins.* Toronto: Canadian Scholars' Press.

SEMMEL, M. I., GOTTLIEB, J., AND ROBINSON, N. M. (1979). "Mainstreaming." *Review of Research in Education* 7, 223–279.

SKRTIC, T. M. (1995). *Disability and Democracy.* New York: Teachers College Press.

"The Special Education Fiasco." (2001). Review of W. F. Horn, and D. Tynan, "Revamping Special Education," *The Public Interest.* Summer 2001. *Wilson Quarterly.* Autumn.

SPRING, J. (1998). *American Education.* 8th Ed. New York: McGraw-Hill.

STAINBACK, W., AND STAINBACK S. (1990). *Support Networks for Inclusive Schooling.* Baltimore: Paul H. Brookes.

STAINBACK, S., STAINBACK, W., AND JACKSON, H. J. (1992). "Toward Inclusive Classrooms." In S. and W. Stainback, eds., *Curriculum Considerations in Inclusive Classrooms.* Baltimore: Paul H. Brookes.

"Student Discipline: Individuals with Disabilities Act." (2001). *Report to Committees on Appropriations: House and Senate.* Washington, DC: General Accounting Office.

TEACHING EXCEPTIONAL CHILDREN. (1998). "Changes in IDEA Support." 30(6), 50+.

THOUSAND, J. S., AND VILLA, R. A. (1995). "Managing Complex Change Toward Inclusive Schooling." In R. A. Villa and J. S. Thousand, eds., *Creating an Inclusive School.* Alexandria, VA: Association for Supervision and Curriculum Development.

TURNBULL, H. R., AND TURNBULL, A. P. (1998). *Free Appropriate Public Education: The Law and Children with Disabilities.* 5th Ed. Denver: Love Publishing.

UNITED NATIONS CONVENTION ON THE RIGHTS OF THE CHILD. (1989). New York: United Nations.

URBAN, W., AND WAGGONER, J. (1996). *American Education: A History.* New York: McGraw-Hill.

VARGAS, S. R. L. (1999). "Democracy and Inclusion." *Maryland Law Review* 58(1), 150–179.

VILLA, R. A., THOUSAND, J. S., AND CHAPPLE, J. W. (1996). "Preparing Teachers to Support Inclusion." *Theory Into Practice* 35(1), Winter.

WANG, M. C. (1990). "Learning Characteristics of Students with Special Needs." In M. C. Wang et al., eds., *Special Education: Research and Practice.* Oxford: Pergamon.

WANG, M. C., REYNOLDS, M. C., AND WALBERG, H., eds. (1990). *Special Education: Research and Practice.* Oxford, Pergamon.

———, eds. (1991). *Handbook of Special Education: Research and Practice.* Oxford: Pergamon.

WEDELL, K. (1993). "Varieties of School Integration." In P. Mittler et al., eds., *Special Needs Education.* World Yearbook of Education. London: Kogan Page.

WINZER, M. A. (1993). *The History of Special Education: From Isolation to Integration.* Washington, DC: Gallaudet University Press.

ZIGLER, E., AND HALL, N. (1986). "Mainstreaming and the Philosophy of Normalization." In C. J. Meisel, ed., *Mainstreaming Handicapped Children.* Hillsdale, NJ: Lawrence Erlbaum.

CHAPTER 19

School Violence: School Treatable or Beyond School Control

POSITION 1: SCHOOLS CAN AND SHOULD CURB VIOLENCE

I believe that school is primarily a social institution. Education being a social process, the school is simply that form of community life in which all of those agencies are concentrated that will be most effective in bringing the child to share in the inherited resources of the race, and to use his own powers for social ends. . . . I believe that education, therefore, is a process of living and not a preparation for future living.

—DEWEY, 1897, "MY PEDAGOGIC CREED," REPRINTED IN DWORKIN, 1959, P. 22

John Dewey helped define the relationship between Americans and their public schools. Schools are extensions of the community in this country, he argued. Schools share in the burden of caring for the community's children and for equipping them with skills and habits necessary to survive and succeed. Schools take the community's highest ideals and translate them into academic and social programs for all children. As Dewey wrote, "What the best and wisest parent wants for his own child, that must the community want for all its children" (Dworkin, 1959, p. 54).

Dewey recognized social conditions constantly change and schools always have to adjust to new demands placed on communities. When social problems overwhelm community resources, schools are expected to lend strength and assistance. In a speech delivered in 1899, he said, "It is useless to bemoan the departure of the good old days of children's modesty, reverence, and implicit obedience, if we expect merely by bemoaning and by exhortation to bring them back. It is radical conditions which have changed, and only an equally radical change in education suffices" (Dworkin, 1959, p. 37).

In the late nineteenth century, the Industrial Revolution had upset the community's traditional structure and nature of work. Parents were working long hours, away from home, separated from their children. Many children also worked, at hard and often dangerous jobs. As a result, families had changed, and were not able to carry out the full range of their former functions. Schools were pressed to expand their role, to go beyond providing instruction in reading and arithmetic and help children adjust to the "radical conditions" of the day. Helping children adjust to the problems of a new industrial economy imposed a great burden on public education. Helping children understand and overcome the radical conditions of the twenty-first century may require even greater effort, but it is not a problem schools can shirk. The community's problems are always the school's problems. We are concerned with violence here, a social problem with a long history and many causes.

The Violent Community

Violence is among the most "radical conditions" now confronting the nation and its school-age children. Violence increasingly affects the daily lives of children, and violence-prevention and aggression-management programs have become part of the common curriculum in schools. Society has changed in the past decades, and students' lives are filled with problems never before the concern of schools. Testifying before Congress, the principal of a Miami high school notes:

> The primary differential between the high school environment we as adults recall and the present is the nature of the challenges the youth of today confront. Many of these issues, such as H.I.V., did not even exist when we were in school. Many students today face enormous pressures, isolation, and lack of support network mechanisms enjoyed by previous generations. . . . The primary concern of parents 20 years ago was academic progress; this has been replaced by a different concern—I want my child back in the same shape they left this morning. (School Crime Prevention Programs, 2001, p. 32)

In some ways school violence is a new American problem; in other ways, it is as old as the nation. American society is violent, and has been so for a long time. You may recall that Andrew Jackson shot and killed a man who made insulting comments about his wife,[1] and Aaron Burr killed political rival Alexander Hamilton in a New Jersey gun duel. The United States was born of revolution. It has made heroes of gunfighters and warriors. Americans have witnessed assassinations of national figures, racial lynchings, and riots by organized labor, farmers, and students. Until the 1930s it was not possible to quantify the rate of violence, but since that time, the FBI's *Uniform Crime Reports* document a dramatic increase in violent crime, including murder, forcible rape, robbery, and aggravated assault over time. The U.S. murder rate is the highest in the industrialized world, and we remain a leader in school violence.

[1]One scholar argues that retaliatory violence reflected in today's "street code" is simply a crude version of the "code of honor" that nineteenth-century gentlemen claimed as a right in protecting the reputation of their ladies (Spina, 2000, p. 12).

Violence and the Media

Violence currently presents unprecedented dangers to school-age children. U.S. films, music videos, and television are the most violent in the world (Derksen and Strasburger, 1996; Potter, 1999). Messages about aggressive behavior enter the world of children no matter how hard families work to screen them out. These messages flow not only from children's direct experiences, but also from news reports, film, music, and advertising. War toys line store shelves; cartoon heroes destroy villains on television and in films; music videos play darkly on themes of anger and destruction; and computer games encourage interactive simulations of murder and mayhem. Many children suffer nightmares stemming from the violence in their lives (Jordan, 2002).

Television brings a steady volume of vicarious violence into living rooms. Over 97 percent of U.S. households have at least one television set, and young children watch about four hours of television daily. They likely watch passively—typically without adults present—acts of violence at unprecedented levels. The typical child in the United States views an estimated 8,000 murders and 100,000 acts of televised violence before the end of elementary school (*TV Violence,* 1993) and another 100,000 hours before the end of high school. Among other things, researchers have found that viewing portrayals of violence leads to aggressive behavior. Regular watching of media violence can desensitize viewers to real violence as well as make them excessively fearful of the potential for violence in their own lives.

Violence is an increasingly familiar aspect of students' lives. Many students report that they do not feel safe in their schools. The executive director for the National Schools Safety Center, testifying before a congressional subcommittee, remarked, "Literally, our children are dying to come to school. . . . A lot of former fistfights are being replaced by gunfights; the former fire drills are being replaced by crisis drills, and even by the new drive-by shooting drills" (*Recess from Violence,* 1993, p. 37). It may be naive for us to think we are not vulnerable to violence. Although violence is more prevalent in urban areas and among the poor and minorities, no one in any neighborhood is immune. School violence affects the suburbs and rural areas as well as cities, white children as well as minority children.

> Violence is also increasing in suburban and rural schools, especially among white male students. Although not necessarily disadvantaged, white male students can be marginalized in other ways. Those who do not conform to accepted roles and expectations are often alienated from the dominant culture and at the bottom of the social hierarchy of schools (nerds, geeks, fags, etc.). These "minority" students are indoctrinated with almost the same message as inner-city students: pretty girls, strong boys, thin, rich, smart kids are the ones who matter.[2] (Spina, 2000, p. 13)

[2]If you think of violence only as the use of physical force that causes bodily harm, this example of psychological violence may come as a surprise. Violence is not limited to acts that cause bodily harm; violence includes actions that deny others the ability to be effective actors in their world. Bullies trade in threats and intimidations as often as they deliver physical blows. The victims of bullying suffer more embarrassment, rejection, and anxiety than bruises (MacNeil, 2002). One form of violence is the exercise of harmful physical power over another; it is also the exercise of social and psychological power over others that denies them their basic freedoms, an enjoyment of their lives, and a sense of their humanity (Henry, 2000).

FIGURE 19.1. Percentage of Students Ages 12–18 Who Reported Criminal Victimization at School During the Previous 6 Months, by Grade Level: 1995–1999.

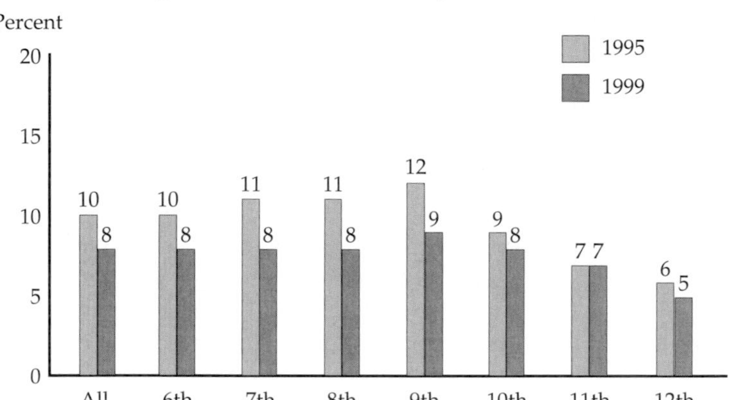

Note: *This figure presents the prevalence of total victimization, which is a combination of violent victimization and theft. "At school" means in the school building, on school property, or on the way to or from school.*
Source: *U.S. Department of Justice, Bureau of Justice Statistics, School Crime Supplement to the National Crime Victimization Survey, January–June 1995 and 1999.* Indicators of School Crime and Safety: 2001. *(October) Washington, DC: U.S. Department of Education, p. 8.*

Recent reports of school crime contain both bad news and good news. The bad news is that in 1999, students between ages 13 and 18 were victims of 2.5 million crimes at school, and of that number, 186,000 students fell victim to serious crimes—rape, sexual assault, and aggravated assault. The good news is that, as startling as these numbers are, they represent a decline in the nonfatal victimization rate, and students report feeling a greater degree of safety in school at the end of the 1990s than at the beginning of the decade. (*Indicators of School Crime and Safety*, 2001).

The bad news may not be getting worse, but it is disturbing nonetheless. From the standpoint of any victim of school violence or the parents whose children are victimized, there are no acceptable levels of violent behavior in schools (Astor et al., 2002). Overall, it appears more children are exposed to higher levels of violence than ever before, and more children are demonstrating more aggressive behaviors in school than earlier generations. Reports of increasing childhood aggression are especially troubling considering the research linking a child's inability to manage aggression with violent behavior in adulthood (Reiss and Roth, 1993; Caspi et al., 1994; Goldstein, Harootunian, and Conoley, 1994).

Violence-Prevention Curricula

The bad news is easy to tabulate. The statistics are alarming: Violence is common in schools; too many children feel unsafe in schools; many schools have to invest in metal detectors and guards instead of books and field trips. The good news is harder to quantify, but it should be reassuring: School programs can make a difference in preventing childhood aggressive behavior and future adult violence (*Recess from Violence*, 1993; Reiss and Roth, 1993; Bodine and Crawford, 1998; Astor et al., 2002; Bowen et al., 2002). While schools alone cannot overcome the problem of violence, they are central in the struggle to protect children from violence and teach them physical aggression is never the preferred solution to problems. The problem of violence is complex, and there are no simple solutions. It is not the sort of problem, however, likely to be solved by applying zero-tolerance policies and simple punitive measures. To solve the problem of school violence, children must learn how to understand and control their anger and practice using nonviolent problem-solving techniques. Schools can help students manage their aggression by teaching alternatives to violence through violence-prevention curricula.[3]

Consider a few violence-prevention strategies suggested by national organizations. We present them as illustrative examples rather than prescriptive remedies. Many schools now are using schooltime conflict-resolution approaches, teaching children to handle their own disputes and assume responsibility for helping other children find peaceful resolutions to their disagreements. These programs are disarmingly simple and effective. First, children are taught conflicts are inevitable, and in most disputes, both sides are apt to believe they and they alone are in the right. Conflict resolution approaches encourage students to listen to each other and take responsibility for ensuring they resolve conflicts by conversation and negotiation rather than by physical means. The process is similar for younger children and students in secondary schools. What varies is the nature and complexity of the problems. Consider this example for resolving a classroom conflict in elementary school: The teacher begins the activity by distributing an "activity card" to the class with a conflict that might be familiar to them.

> Mariah is riding the bus to school. Kateesha, another girl on the bus, is having a bad day, and she calls Mariah a bad name. Mariah is very upset and mad at Kateesha. When they get off the bus, they start yelling at each other and shoving each other until a teacher breaks up the fight. Both children are taken to the office for fighting, and both children are still mad at each other. What is the solution to their problem? (Osier and Fox, 2001, p. 10)

The teacher reads the card to the class and asks students to identify the problem. When the class agrees about the nature of the problem, the teacher asks students to recommend actions they could take to solve it. Younger children may draw a picture of the solution; older children write one. The teacher then asks the class to share their solutions and identifies those supported by students in the class. Students are asked to save the favored solutions and apply them when a new conflict arises in or outside of class.

[3]Schools across the country now are experimenting with hundreds of new curricular interventions designed to reduce violence. You may want to examine some examples in your community or check national sources. Information from the National Schools Safety Center (NSSC) is available on the Internet at www.nssc1.org. NSSC is a nonprofit organization, established by presidential directive in 1984, and is charged with promoting violence-free and crime-free schools. NSSC provides information about programs that support safe schools worldwide. Its website also contains current statistics about school crime and school violence.

Secondary school students are encouraged to use similar role-playing strategies to examine critical incidents in their lives. The goal is to have students see how simple, commonplace events can escalate into violence. In this example, taken from a videotape transcript written by eighth-grade students, one young woman taunts another:

> "I heard that she was at the movies with your boyfriend last night. All over him."
> "I wouldn't take it," adds another girl.
> "She doesn't need your boyfriend. What was she doing with him anyhow?"

The young women simulate pushing and shoving. They break off from the simulation with self-conscious laughter, recognizing, perhaps, that in real life the angry words they scripted all too often escalate into real acts of violence. On the videotape, the classroom teacher applauds the students' effort, and the class examines what has taken place. A rumor was spread; it led to an exchange of words; verbal accusations threatened to become physical. In real life, it could easily have resulted in injury. How could this have been avoided? the teacher asks. What did others do to make the situation worse? What could they have done to help? (*Violence in the Schools*, 1993).

Many schools have adopted school-wide violence-prevention programs that teach students a series of consistent, reasonable approaches to contend with conflict. In these schools, when a playground dispute occurs, an older child, trained by the teachers, asks both parties to tell their sides of the story. Certain ground rules are agreed to beforehand: no yelling, no cursing, no interrupting, no put-downs of the other person. The older student, acting as a conflict manager, seeks to guide the disputants to solutions of their problems. If they cannot, the conflict manager tries to help. A teacher or administrator always is available. The goal is to provide a caring community in which all children feel safe, where they can resolve their problems, and where everyone is responsible for others' well being. Caring communities teach children to handle problems without resorting to violence (Brendtro and Long, 1995; Bodine and Crawford, 1998). One student, trained in violence prevention, said the program "informed me on how to be a better listener and taught me how to help other people solve their problems." Another participant said, "I got a chance to understand people and the ethics of helping people solve problems" (Morse and Andrea, 1994, p. 82).

School programs can help students find alternatives to violence. Nonviolence can be an important curriculum strand running through social studies, language arts, and other subject areas. Violence is a learned response, and because it is learned, it can be unlearned (Noguera, 1995; Sautter, 1995). Schools, working with social service agencies and psychologists, can replace antisocial behaviors with prosocial behaviors and provide positive role models for children. Violence-prevention curricula are new and their successes have not been carefully evaluated or scientifically assessed. The evidence collected thus far, however, supports the effectiveness of conflict resolution programs and other violence-prevention interventions (such as anger management and anger-coping programs) in teaching students to manage conflicts through nonviolent means (Bodine and Crawford, 1998; Bowen et al., 2002). Even more convincing is the observable difference these curricula bring to schools. As one school administrator notes, "It makes a difference in my school, and I have a reduction of 10 percent in some problems. These materials are OK by me, and I don't need researchers to say it works" (Lawton, 1994, p. 10).

College and university students can help through mentorship programs. The absence of appropriate parental supervision is a strong predictor of trouble complying with school discipline. Once thought of as a problem confined to the poor, lack of supervision and absence of positive role models now are recognized as much broader problems. Students from all social classes need sources of support other than the family. Many undergraduate programs now match volunteer mentors with at-risk students. The mentors act as role models, older brothers or sisters, and surrogate parents. They help with homework and teach study skills. They are models of problem solvers who do not resort to violence and examples of success who have not succumbed to the temptations of crime. Above all, they offer at-risk children a caring, thoughtful person in their lives. Their presence cannot be underestimated. Children at risk for violence have had too few positive role models in their lives. Schools and teachers can help. Research indicates that "the involvement of just one caring adult can make all the difference in the life of an at-risk youth" (Sautter, 1995, p. K8).

Viewed simply, violence is irrational destruction, an explosion of spontaneous rage. But violence just doesn't happen. It is not an act without cause or one that defies understanding. To prevent violence, schools and society should examine how history, economics, and culture find an outlet in violent behavior. Violent acts cannot be prevented unless schools and communities attend to social and political forces producing them. Although schools can help to solve the problems of violence, in some ways schools may be responsible for causing violence (Spina, 2000; Yogan, 2000; Casella, 2001). For too many students, school itself is an alienating experience that promotes a violent response. Many students experience school only as a source of failure and exclusion. Distribution of school rewards falls to only a handful, and school success is defined very narrowly. The pleasures and recognition enjoyed by school athletes, the academically talented, and physically attractive are unavailable to most. For those at the top of the tracking system, school is rewarding. For those at the bottom, school is another barrier to self-esteem, a badge of lower status and shame, and a potential source of anger.

Violent behavior is one of the most frequently studied social phenomena of our day. The social and behavioral sciences have learned a lot about violence, and we have every reason to assume schools can successfully stem the tide of violent behavior and protect children and society from the violent among us. We are ultimately very optimistic about schools and the ability of school personnel to make schools more just and more satisfying places for all students. Teachers and principals can extend the power of schooling into students' daily lives. Schools can help to reduce social conflicts and individual violence. The process likely will be slow and expensive, but if not begun in schools, future social and personal costs will be more costly. Potentially violent children and their problems will not go away by themselves. To paraphrase John Dewey, what the best and wisest parents in the community want for their children should be made available to all children through the agency of the schools.

POSITION 2: THE PROBLEM OF SCHOOL VIOLENCE IS BEYOND SCHOOL CONTROL

> *Federal agencies are now making millions of dollars available for "conflict resolution" classes, for creating "safe haven" rooms in schools, and for "peer mediation" programs. Getting a federal grant has become simple: just start your own conflict resolution program . . . Statistics can be trotted out to "prove" that these violence-prevention classes and other cognitive approaches have culminated in a decrease in fighting and physical violence. . . . Older students, said to be peer mediators, "trained in conflict resolution" by conflict resolution teachers, ask younger bellicose students if they can agree not to bother one another, not to call one another's mother obscene names, not to insult one another. If they "feel comfortable" with such an agreement, they shake hands, congratulations are extended all around—and the fight resumes the next time they look at one another.*
>
> —DEVINE, 1996, PP. 161–166

U.S. schools began with modest academic goals: teach children to read and write. Over the years, schools enhanced their curricula to include academic instruction in content as well as skills, subject matter from art to social studies. The argument in this section is simple, direct, and straightforward: Schools should teach academic content in the most compelling and academically legitimate ways possible. This is the job schools are entrusted with, and is what teachers are trained to do. Without academic skills, students are at a disadvantage, will be unable to compete for places in the best colleges, earn scholarships, land good jobs, or launch satisfying careers. Schooling is primarily about teaching and learning academic subject matter and mastery of skills necessary for success in life. When society asks schools to engage in social engineering programs—such as preventing violence or solving the problems of crime and delinquency—it blurs the focus on cognitive learning, and spreads their efforts across too many areas (Finn, 1993). Schools must teach about our history and literature and instill in students a sense of civic responsibility, if we are to survive as a nation. School must equip students with intellectual skills necessary to understand science, math, the arts, and humanities, if they are to succeed individually. School focus should not be on social reform, but academic achievement. A school's success is measured by the rigor and quality of teaching, not by the extent to which it confronts social problems (Ravitch, 2001).

We will further argue that (1) violence in schools is an overstated problem; (2) violence-prevention curricula are of questionable value; and (3) schools should not try to do the job of welfare agencies, police, or social psychologists.

Decline of Family Values

To spend much energy arguing that these are not normal times is to belabor the obvious. Everyone knows that the family is in disarray, and family values are all but lost to many Americans. Thirty percent of all children are born to single mothers, and the problem is even greater in some minority populations. Too many youngsters have no one to teach them basic skills, socially appropriate behavior, and other family values. Too many children show up at the doors of the nation's schools with only a vague sense of right and wrong, no self-discipline, and a limited ability to get along with other children. Increasing numbers of today's youth claim that the counterculture or gang life offers the sense of belonging, worth, and purpose they fail to find within their families. Too many students refuse to accept responsibility for their actions, and teachers commonly report hearing excuses such as, "It's not my fault; other kids were doing it," and, "I wasn't late; the bell just rang before I got there" (Conrath, 2001, p. 586).

Children do not show up for the first day of kindergarten as blank slates: The experiences of their early lives have etched upon them many complex impressions, both good and bad. Most children are ready to begin school; their parents have invested tremendous amounts of time and energy in them. These children are self-controlled. They demonstrate mastery over their emotions, enthusiasm for learning, and respect for the teacher's authority. Others are not ready for school. Victims of poor parenting or no parenting at all, they come to school with insufficient preparation for the academic side of school and inadequate control over their own behavior to get along with classmates. Teachers spot these students quickly. They are overly impulsive, physically aggressive, and uncooperative. Psychologists have developed profiles of school bullies and other potentially violent youth. Among other things, they tend to be loners who lack empathy for others; frequently are victims of violence at home; have a great deal of pent-up anger, a low frustration tolerance, a record of involvement in substance abuse and other risky behavior, and a lack of moral conscience (MacNeil, 2002). They have been described as "youth with murdered souls" (Sandhu, Underwood, and Sandhu, 2000a, p. 27). These troubled youth likely have average or above-average intelligence, but are not likely to do well in school, and threaten the educational quality and physical well-being of other children and themselves.

Only a small fraction of students, however, exhibit aggressive behaviors or other traits that predict violence. In fact, school violence is an overstated problem. Potentially violent students represent only 1 percent of children who enter school, and the rate of violence in school has not changed significantly in twenty years. In 2002, the website of the National Center for Education Statistics (http://nces.ed.gov) reported data indicating a general decline in the victimization rate for violent crime between 1992 and 1999. According to self-reports, the percentage of students who were victims of crime in school decreased from 10 percent to 8 percent, and students indicate that they feel more secure in school than students have in the past. Furthermore, the data suggest students are safer in school than out of school. (See Figure 19.2.)

FIGURE 19.2. Number of Nonfatal Crimes Against Student Ages 12–18 per 1,000 Students, by Type of Crime and Location: 1992–1999.

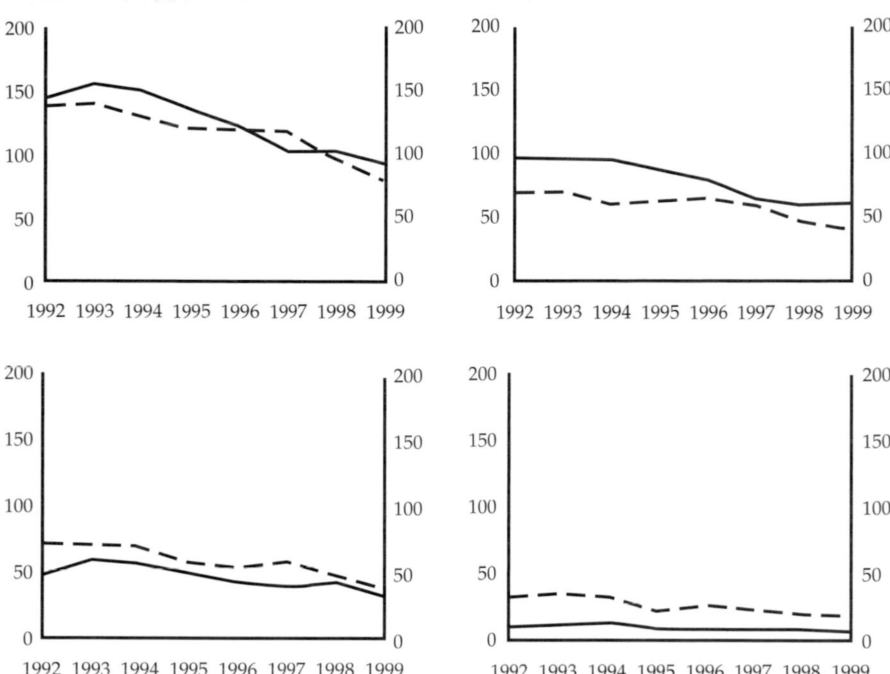

Note: *Serious violent crimes include rape, sexual assault, robbery, and aggravated assault. Violent crimes include serious violent crimes and simple assault. Total crimes include violent crimes and theft. "At school" includes inside the school building, on school property, or on the way to or from school.*
Source: Indicators of School Crime and Safety: 2001. *(October) Washington, DC: U.S. Department of Education, p. 5.*

Despite widespread publicity depicting schools as dangerous places, rife with crime and violence, the conclusion drawn from student reports of violence seems to say school violence may be more of a media creation than a serious school problem. After reviewing the research literature on school crime, Lawrence (1998) argues that "It is difficult to conclude that schools are violent places, when data indicate that on average 99 percent of students are free from attack in a month's time" (p. 29). For the moment, at least, it seems fair to argue that schools are probably less dangerous for students than they have been in the past two decades.

Teaching is among the nation's safest professions: According to statistics compiled by the Department of Justice, teaching remains one of the nation's safest occupations during the period studied, 1993 to 1999. By comparison, police officers hold the nation's riskiest job; 261 of every 1,000 officers were physically attacked or threatened during the period. The rate for junior high/middle school teachers was 54 per 1,000. Special education teachers were attacked or threatened with violence at a rate of 68.4 per 1,000, and preschool and elementary school teachers experienced these problems at a rate of 7.1 and 17 per 1,000, respectively, over the period (www.ojp.usdoj.gov/bjs/).

When teachers talk about problem students and classroom misbehavior, they usually are not talking about violent students or violent behaviors. The majority of students teachers identify as "problems" are described as such for reasons other than the potential to do physical harm to others or themselves.[4]

Schools are generally safe places, but disruptive students do exist. What responsibilities do schools have to teach the distracting handful of children who are unable to control their aggression? This is a difficult question. None of us wants to appear callous or indifferent to children, but schools are not social welfare agencies. Teachers are not social workers or psychiatrists. Educators are trained to teach children reading, math, social studies, and other important content and skills. We cannot reasonably expect schools and teachers to function as anger-management therapists or violence-control specialists. Violence-prevention curricula sound noble and high-minded, but they are a diversion from the schools' academic mission and are of doubtful benefit. After reviewing 70 federally funded programs with a total of $2.4 billion in funds aimed at reducing school violence and substance abuse, the General Accounting Office concluded these programs had not demonstrated their worth:

> Insufficient information exists on the programs' performance. Although we identified some promising approaches for preventing substance abuse and violence,

[4]Brophy and McCaslin list twelve types of "problem" elementary-school-age students examined in the research literature:

1. *Failure-syndrome exhibiting.* These children believe they cannot do schoolwork. They often avoid work or give up easily, expecting to fail and saying "I can't do it."
2. *Perfectionistic.* These children are unusually anxious about making mistakes. They have unrealistically high self-images, and they are never satisfied with their performance. They often hold back from class participation unless they are very sure of themselves.
3. *Underachieving/alienated.* These children do the minimum to get by. They do not value or enjoy schoolwork.
4. *Low achieving.* These students have difficulty with schoolwork even when they are willing to try. Their problem is low potential or lack of readiness.
5. *Hostile-aggressive.* These students express hostility through direct, intense behaviors. They intimidate and threaten other students, are easily angered, and may hit and push other students or destroy property.
6. *Passive-aggressive.* These students indirectly express their opposition and resistance to the teacher. They disrupt classrooms surreptitiously and exhibit subtle noncompliance.
7. *Defiant.* These children want to have their own way. They may resist the teacher verbally, saying, "You can't make me," or "You can't tell me what to do." They resist nonverbally, as well, by posturing, frowning, and sometimes by being physically violent toward the teacher.
8. *Hyperactive.* These children squirm, wiggle, jiggle, and show excessive and almost constant movement. They are often out of their seats and bothering other children.
9. *Distractable.* These children have very short attention spans. They are unable to sustain attention and concentration.
10. *Immature.* These children have poorly developed self-control, social skills, and emotional stability.
11. *Peer-rejected.* These children are often forced to work and play alone, although they seek acceptance by other students.
12. *Shy/withdrawn.* These children avoid personal interaction with other classmates. They are quiet and do not call attention to themselves. (Brophy and McCaslin, 1992, pp. 62–63)

> our work suggests that additional research is needed to further test these approaches' effectiveness and their applicability to different populations in varied settings. (U.S. General Accounting Office, 1997, p. 85)

In other words, a great deal of money is being spent on a small minority of children with little to show for the expenditure. Today a small group of problem students is attracting a disproportionate share of curriculum attention as well as federal and state dollars. The education of the majority of cooperative students is being held ransom by an unruly minority.

Who Are the Potentially Violent?

We know who is likely to commit crimes, early experiences that lead to violent behavior, and personal and family traits that tend to protect children from becoming violent adults. We know behaviors that alert teachers and administrators to the potentially troublesome. (See Table 19.1.) Unfortunately, beyond identifying troubled students, research has not yet developed a strong knowledge base about the causes of violent behavior or the ways it can be prevented (Reiss and Roth, 1993). No one knows how to prevent potentially violent children from becoming

TABLE 19.1. Characteristics of Troubled Students*

1. Has a history of tantrums and uncontrollable angry outbursts.
2. Characteristically resorts to name calling, cursing, or abusive language.
3. Habitually makes violent threats when angry.
4. Has previously brought a weapon to school.
5. Has a background of serious disciplinary problems at school and in the community.
6. Has a background of drug, alcohol, or substance abuse or dependency.
7. Is on the fringe of his or her peer group with few or no close friends.
8. Is preoccupied with weapons, explosives, or other incendiary devices.
9. Has previously been truant, suspended, or expelled from school.
10. Displays cruelty to animals.
11. Has little or no supervision and support from parents or a caring adult.
12. Has witnessed or been a victim of abuse or neglect in the home.
13. Has been bullied and/or bullies or intimidates peers or younger children.
14. Tends to blame others for difficulties and problems s/he causes her/himself.
15. Consistently prefers TV shows, movies, or music expressing violent themes or acts.
16. Prefers reading material dealing with violent themes, rituals, and abuse.
17. Reflects anger, frustration, and the dark side of life in school essays or writing projects.
18. Is involved with a gang or an antisocial group on the fringe of peer acceptance.
19. Is often depressed and/or has significant mood swings.
20. Has threatened or attempted suicide.

*Since 1992, the National School Safety Center has tracked school-associated violent deaths in the United States and has developed a checklist of behaviors to alert teachers and administrators to troubled students.
Source: http://www.nsscl.org/reporter/checklist.htm (2/1/02)

violent adults. Schools now embracing one violence-management curriculum or another are doing so without adequate evidence of its effectiveness. Many causes of violence are not within the schools' control (Weishew and Peng, 1993). Violent children become violent adults, and if children have not learned to control their aggression by the time they come to school, it may not be possible for them to disentangle the patterns of violence that took shape in their early years.

In a perfect world, all children would come to school with no violent inclinations. All children would be raised in loving, drug-free, nurturing homes. They would all bond with an adult who dispenses love freely and teaches them they belong to someone and someone belongs to them. Children's earliest experiences would have shown them that disagreements are part of life, but discord can be settled through calm discussions rather than rancor or violence. We would like all children to have high IQs, to have parents who are literate adults, free from alcohol and drug addiction, who study books about child rearing, read stories to their children, and place limits on television viewing. We would like all these things and more, but social policies cannot create them. Too many children are born to single mothers unprepared for the task or unable to give them what they need to be successful in life. Drug addiction, crime, and poverty are beyond school control. Schools cannot redistribute wealth or solve social problems. For better or worse, schools reflect society; they are not now nor have they ever been agents of social change. They have a mission to educate students and have little power and no authority to do anything else.

Although public schools must work with all students, they do not have to mix the disruptive and the potentially violent with the well behaved; nor do they have to encourage violent students to stay in school until graduation. Students who arrive at school ready to learn should be introduced to a rigorous, sound academic education. The academic side of school will matter to them in life. Children come to school to improve their academic skills and increase their store of intellectual capital—the knowledge needed for success in life. As Hirsch notes, "Sociologists have shown that intellectual capital (i.e., school knowledge) operates in almost every sphere of modern society to determine social class, success or failure in school, and even psychological and physical health" (1996, p. 19). Students are disadvantaged by too small a share of intellectual capital, and need to start early and move quickly in securing as much of it as they can. The vast majority of students do not need special curriculum treatments to teach them how to get along with others, settle disputes without violence, or manage aggression. They need academic content to succeed in life, and that's what schools should deliver.

Conflict-resolution curricula distract students from academic pursuits and send students an undesirable, if unintended, message: "We expect school to be violent, so let's talk about it" (Devine, 1996, p. 165). Violence is not a way of life for most children. Directing conflict-management programs to all students, rather than at the violent minority, sends a negative message that violence is a normal part of life and everyone must learn to manage it or otherwise cope with it.

Schools and Violence

Let's look at what we know about potentially violent children and what schools can reasonably do about them: Overly aggressive children should be identified in kindergarten and trained to work on anger management. Although a school cannot replace the family, it can provide some supports found in homes of self-controlled, high-achieving students. For example, school discipline policies should incorporate the reward-and-punishment systems successfully used by middle-class parents. Students should learn that appropriate behavior earns teacher praise and special privileges, while inappropriate behavior results in loss of praise and privilege. This would be reasonable, inexpensive, and not too intrusive on the privacy rights of students or their parents. Working individually with counselors—and not consuming instructional time—violent and potentially violent students should be the focus of appropriate intervention and prevention strategies (Bemak and Keys, 2000; Sandhu, Underwood, and Sandhu, 2000b).

Schools alone cannot solve problems of violence (Burstyn, 2001; Casella, 2001; Bowen et al., 2002). Influences of early family experiences and the greater society are pervasive (Caspi et al., 1994). Research provides little encouragement that school interventions successfully prevent violence, and the research may simply be confirming public knowledge. A Gallup Poll of the public's attitude toward public schools asked respondents to rate the importance of various factors as causes of school violence. Listed in order of frequency, the public rated these factors as "very important":

1. Increased use of drug and alcohol among school-age youth
2. Growth of youth gangs
3. Easy availability of weapons
4. Breakdown in the American family
5. Lack of school authority to discipline
6. Increased portrayal of violence in the media
7. Inability of school staff to resolve conflicts between students

Note that the first six responses are beyond the school's control. It is not until number five that schools are even mentioned. The public recognizes society has visited many of its problems on schools, including the vexing problem of school violence. The public, however, is not convinced solutions to the problem lie within the schools' power. Asked to rate various measures for their potential effectiveness in reducing violence, 88 percent of the respondents listed "stronger penalties for possession of weapons by students" first. At the bottom of the list, mentioned by 51 percent and 45 percent of respondents, respectively, were, "courses offered by the public schools in how to be a good parent," and "conflict education for students" (Elam, Rose, and Gallup, 1994, p. 44).

Of course, schools should try to help all students, but not impede the progress of the well behaved. Schools should try every measure to help young children adapt to school and school discipline. But some children never will adjust to academic demands and self-discipline required for success. According to one analysis of U.S. Justice Department statistics, about 6 percent of adolescents are responsible for two-thirds of violent crimes committed by juveniles (Bodine and Crawford, 1998, p. 6). This tiny percentage of students should not be a major focus of school attention and a constant drain on school budgets. If these students have not learned to control themselves by early adolescence, schools should waste no more time or money on them.

Alternative Schools

> A good but disaffected student who opts for the smaller, less formal environment [of an alternative school] may be told, "Only students who have messed up can go there," to which the student may reply, "How bad do I have to mess up?" (Gregory, 2001, p. 578)

Educators have long recognized that alternatives in public education are sometimes necessary to serve special populations of students—teenage mothers, for example, or the physically disabled. The one-size-fits-all model of the comprehensive public high school does not serve everyone equally well, and some students rebel against the competition, perceived conformity, and order of traditional education. Many educators now recognize the academic demands and social structure of traditional high schools may contribute to school violence. Students unaccustomed to impersonal rules governing school behavior and emphasis schools place on quiet compliance may lash out at teachers and other students (Epp and Watkinson, 1997; Lawrence, 1998). By the time they reach middle school, students learn the focus of schooling is on academic achievement, and unfortunately students who do not achieve well often develop indifferent or hostile attitudes. As one supporter of alternative schools notes, "Their behavior is not irrational. Just as it is rational to embrace the repetition of successful experiences, it is equally rational to avoid repetitions of unsuccessful experiences" (Conrath, 2001, p. 587)

Alternative schools can siphon off the troubled, disaffected, potentially violent, and others for whom traditional schooling is not a good fit. Alternative schools often are better able to serve nonacademic students while allowing traditional schools to focus on the majority's academic needs. Sometimes housed within the regular school building, and sometimes in separate facilities of their own, alternative schools are designed for students who, because of any number of problems—academic but more often behavioral, or social—are not able to learn well in a traditional academic environment.

Alternative schools are likely to be less formal than traditional schools, and typically offer a lower student-to-teacher ratio. The record indicates these schools can go a long way toward ameliorating the anonymity and isolation some students experience in traditional schools (Dunbar, 2001; McGee, 2001). Many formerly disruptive students behave better when they work in a small, supportive setting. They are able to find a niche that eluded them in traditional schools and teachers willing to focus on personal and social problems they bring with them to school (McPartland et al., 1997).

Alternative schools can be very effective, and should be viewed as appropriate educational options for disruptive students who have not responded to special curricular treatment and counseling in regular schools and classes. Unfortunately, although alternative schools try to accommodate students with a wide range of problems, they do not work for everyone. In fact, they may not work well for many of the most disruptive students (Lawrence, 1998). The same students that caused problems in traditional schools often continue to present problems when they transfer to alternative schools. For these students, more dramatic action is likely to be in order.

Schools should embrace all students equally when they first begin school. Special curriculum interventions—the so-called conflict- and dispute-resolution curricula—should be reserved exclusively for students who demonstrate behaviors associated with violence in adults (for example, physical aggression and lack of self-control). Schools should use every technique at their disposal to curb disruptive behavior and bring the unruly child back into the fold. However, by middle school, students who impede the learning process of their classmates or threaten the welfare of other children should be considered as candidates for alternative schools. Students who are not likely to succeed in one kind of school should be given another chance in a different kind of school. These alternative schools have amassed a sound, though not perfect, record for educating the disaffected. For the small handful of very disruptive students who are unable to cooperate in an alternative school, expulsion is a harsh but sensible last resort.

Will expelling problem students from the public school system be likely to increase their inclination toward further violence and criminality? Will these students inevitably wind up in the criminal justice system? It is hard to know. Research indicates future dropouts have high levels of criminal behavior while in school, but some evidence indicates that after these students drop out of school, they may have less trouble with the law (Herrnstein and Murray, 1994). Schools often add to the problems of young people. Many students who do not succeed academically feel frustrated. Others feel confined by school rules and the abrasiveness of school crowding (Noguera, 1995; Sautter, 1995; Lawrence, 1998). Some students may learn better in another environment, and schools should find places for such students. Schools are ultimately academic institutions designed to teach cognitive skills. Students who cannot learn to play by the rules of civilized behavior—to exercise self-discipline, order, and respect for others—ultimately have no place in school.

For Discussion

1. The media's role in causing violent behavior is subject to debate (Barker and Petley, 2001). One writer argues that it's not TV that causes violence among children. It is simply that society finds it easier to blame TV for promoting violence than to confront the real causes of crime: poverty, drug abuse, and other social conditions. He writes:

> Youths in different parts of the United States are exposed to the same media but display drastically different violence levels. TV violence does not account for the fact that the murder rate among black teens in Washington, D.C., is twenty-five times higher than that of white teens living a few Metro stops away. It doesn't explain why, nationally, murder doubled among nonwhite and Latino youth

> over the last decade, but declined among white Anglo teens. Furthermore, contrary to the TV brainwashing theory, Anglo 16-year-olds have lower violent-crime rates than black 60-year-olds, Latino 40-year-olds, and Anglo 30-year-olds. Men, women, whites, Latinos, blacks, Asians, teens, young adults, middle-agers, senior citizens in Fresno County—California's poorest urban areas—display murder and violent-crime rates double those of their counterparts in Ventura County—the state's richest. (Males, 1997, p. 2)

Do you find these arguments convincing? Can we excuse the media from responsibility? What role do the media play in promoting violence—or, at least, making it appear a normal and acceptable part of life?

2. Some social critics argue violence should be viewed as a legitimate protest against the injustices of a school system that include racial segregation, funding disparities among schools, a curriculum that avoids multicultural issues, and the wholesale discrimination against schools in African American and Hispanic neighborhoods (Casella, 2001, p. 11).

   Do you consider these arguments to offer insights into school violence? Should perspectives of the potentially violent be taken into consideration in the design of school violence-prevention strategies? How?

3. The National Association for the Education of Young Children (NAEYC) argues against the use of corporal punishment in schools. It argues that "use of corporal punishment in such situations teaches children that physical solutions to problems are acceptable for adults and that aggression is an appropriate way to control the behavior of other people. The institutional use of corporal punishment should never be condoned" (*NAEYC,* 1993, p. 83).

   What policies concerning corporal punishment exist in your state and in your local school district? What are your personal views about corporal punishment as a form of discipline? If some parents approve of the teacher's use of physical punishment and prefer that their children be disciplined in this manner, should the teacher accede to the parent's wishes?

References

ASTOR, R. A., ET AL. (2002). "Public Concern and Focus on School Violence." In L. A. Rapp-Paglicci et al., eds., *Handbook of Violence.* New York: John Wiley & Sons.

BARKER, M., AND PETLEY, J., EDS. (1997/2001). *Ill Effects: The Media/Violence Debate.* 2nd Ed. New York: Routledge.

BEMAK, F., AND KEYS, S. (2000). *Violent and Aggressive Youth: Intervention and Prevention Strategies for Changing Times.* Thousand Oaks, CA: Corwin Press.

BODINE, R. J., AND CRAWFORD, D. K. (1998). *The Handbook of Conflict Resolution Education: A Guide to Building Quality Programs in Schools.* San Francisco: Jossey-Bass.

BOWEN, G. L., ET AL. (2002). "Reducing School Violence: A Social Capacity Framework." In L. A. Rapp-Paglicci et al., eds., *Handbook of Violence.* New York: John Wiley & Sons.

BRENDTRO, L., AND LONG, N. (1995). "Breaking the Cycle of Conflict." *Educational Leadership* 52, 52–56.

BROPHY, J., AND MCCASLIN, M. (1992). "Teachers' Reports of How They Perceive and Cope with Problem Students." *The Elementary School Journal* 99(1), 3–68.

BURSTYN, J. N., ED. (2001). *Preventing Violence in Schools: A Challenge to American Democracy.* Mahwah, NJ: Erlbaum.

CASELLA, R. (2001)."*Being Down": Challenging Violence in Urban Schools.* New York: Teachers College Press.

CASPI, A., ET AL. (1994). "Are Some People Crime Prone?" *Criminology* 32, 163–196.

CONRATH, J. (2001). "Changing the Odds for Young People: Next Steps for Alternative Education." *Phi Delta Kappan* 82, 585–587.

DERKSEN, D. J., AND STRASBURGER, V. C. (1996). "Media and Television Violence: Effects on Violence, Aggression, and Anti-Social Behavior in Children." In A. M. Hoffman, ed., *Schools, Violence, and Society.* Westport, CT: Praeger.

DEVINE, J. (1996). *Maximum Security.* Chicago: University of Chicago Press.

DUNBAR, C. (2001). "Does Anyone Know We're Here?" *Alternative Schooling for African American Youth.* New York: Peter Lang.

DWORKIN, M. S. (1959). *Dewey On Education.* New York: Teachers College Press.

ELAM, S. M., ROSE, L. C., AND GALLUP, A. M. (1994). "The 26th Annual Phi Delta Kappa/Gallup Poll of the Public's Attitude Toward the Public Schools." *Phi Delta Kappan* 76, 41–64.

EPP, J. R., AND WATKINSON, A. M. (1997). *Systemic Violence in Education: Broken Promise.* Albany: State University of New York.

FINN, C. E., JR. (1993). "Whither Education Reform?" In C. L. Fagnano and K. N. Hughes, eds., *Making Schools Work.* Boulder, CO: Westview Press.

GOLDSTEIN, A. P., HAROOTUNIAN, B., AND CONOLEY, J. C. (1994). *Student Aggression: Prevention, Management, and Replacement Training.* New York: Guilford.

GREGORY, T. (2001). "Fear of Success: Ten Ways Alternative Schools Pull Their Punches." *Phi Delta Kappan* 82, 577–581.

HENRY, S. (2000). "What Is School Violence? An Integrated Definition." In A. W. Heston and N. A. Weiner, eds., *The Annals of the American Academy of Political and Social Science.* Special edition (Jan.), Vol. 567, 6–29.

HERRNSTEIN, R. J., AND MURRAY, C. (1994) . *The Bell Curve: Intelligence and Class Structure in American Life.* New York: Free Press.

HIRSCH, E. D., JR. (1996). *The Schools We Need and Why We Don't Have Them.* New York: Doubleday.

Indicators of School Crime and Safety. (2001). National Center for Education Statistics, Bureau of Justice Statistics (Oct.). Washington, DC: U.S. Department of Education.

JORDAN, K. (2002). "School Violence Among Culturally Diverse Populations." In L. A. Rapp-Paglicci et al., eds., *Handbook of Violence.* New York: John Wiley & Sons.

LAWRENCE, R. (1998). *School Crime and Juvenile Justice.* New York: Oxford University Press.

LAWTON, M. (1994). "Violence-Prevention Curricula: What Works Best?" *Education Week,* Nov. 9, pp. 1, 10–11.

MACNEIL, G. (2002). School Bullying: An Overview. In L. A. Rapp-Paglicci et al., eds., *Handbook of Violence.* New York: John Wiley & Sons.

MALES, M. (1997). "Who Us? Stop Blaming the Kids and TV for Crime and Substance Abuse." *The Progressive,* Oct., pp. 1–5.

MCGEE, J. (2001). "Reflections of an Alternative School Administrator." *Phi Delta Kappan* 82, 588–591.

MCPARTLAND, J., ET AL. (1997). "Finding Safety in Small Numbers." *Educational Leadership* 55, 14–17.

MORSE, P. A., AND ANDREA, R. (1994). "Peer Mediation in the Schools: Teaching Conflict Resolution Techniques to Students." *NASSP Bulletin* 78, 75–82.

NAEYC Position Statement on Violence in the Lives of Children. (1993). *Young Children* 48, 80–85.

NOGUERA, P. A. (1995). "Preventing and Producing Violence: A Critical Analysis of Responses to School Violence." *Harvard Educational Review* 65, 189–212.

OSIER, J., AND FOX, H. (2001). *Settle Conflicts Right Now! A Step-by-Step Guide for K–6 Classrooms.* Thousand Oaks, CA: Corwin Press.

POTTER, W. J. (1999). *On Media Violence.* Thousand Oaks, CA: Sage.

RAVITCH, D. (2001). "Education and Democracy." In D. Ravitch and J. P. Viteritti, eds., *Making Good Citizens: Education and Civil Society.* New Haven: Yale University Press.

Recess from Violence: Making Our Schools Safe. (1993). Hearings Before the Subcommittee on Education, Arts, and Humanities of the Committee on Labor and Human Resources. U.S. Senate, One Hundred Third Congress, First Session on S.1125 (Sept. 23). Washington, DC: U.S. Government Printing Office.

REISS, A. J., JR., AND ROTH, J. A. (1993). *Understanding and Preventing Violence.* Washington, DC: National Academy Press.

SAUTTER, C. R. (1995). "Standing Up to Violence." *Phi Delta Kappan* 76, K1–K12.

SANDHU, D. S., UNDERWOOD, J. R., AND SANDHU, V. S. (2000a). "Psychocultural Profiles of Violent Students: Prevention and Intervention Strategies." In D. S. Sandhu and C. B. Aspy, eds., *Violence in American Schools: A Practical Guide for Counselors.* Alexandria, VA: American Counseling Association.

School Crime Prevention Programs. (2001). Hearing of the Committee on the Judiciary, United States Senate, One Hundred Sixth Congress, Second Session (May 15). Washington, DC: U.S. Government Printing Office.

SPINA, S. U., ED. (2000). *Smoke and Mirrors: The Hidden Context of Violence in Schools and Society.* New York: Rowman and Littlefield.

TV Violence. (1993). *CQ Researcher* 3, 268–288, March 26. Washington, DC: Congressional Quarterly.

U.S. DEPARTMENT OF EDUCATION. (2001). *Indicators of School Crime and Safety.* Washington, DC: Author.

U.S. GENERAL ACCOUNTING OFFICE. (1997). "Substance Abuse and Violence Prevention." Testimony before the Subcommittee on Oversight and Investigations, Committee on Education and the Workforce House of Representatives. Washington, DC: Author.

Violence in the Schools. (1993). National Education Association Video, Teacher TV Episode #15. West Haven, CT: National Education Association.

WEISHEW, N. L., AND PENG, S. S. (1993). "Variables Predicting Students' Problem Behaviors." *Journal of Educational Research* 87, 5–17.

YOGAN, L. J. (2000). "School Tracking and Student Violence." In *The Annals of the American Academy of Political and Social Science.* Special edition (Jan.), Vol. 567.

Index

Note: page numbers in *italics* indicate illustrations; page numbers followed by *t* indicate tables; page numbers followed by *n* indicate material in footnotes.